THACKERAY

By the same author

Fiction

Great Eastern Land
Real Life
English Settlement
After Bathing at Baxter's: Stories
Trespass

Non-fiction

A Vain Conceit: British Fiction in the '80s
After the War: The Novel and England since 1945
Other People: Portraits from the '90s (with Marcus Berkmann)

THACKERAY

The Life of a Literary Man

D. J. TAYLOR

CARROLL & GRAF PUBLISHERS
NEW YORK

THACKERAY
The Life of a Literary Man

Copyright © 1999 by D. J. Taylor

Carroll & Graf Publishers
A Division of Avalon Publishing Group Incorporated
161 William Street, 16th Floor
New York, NY 10038

First Carroll & Graf edition 2001

Library of Congress Cataloging-in-Publication Data is available.

ISBN 0-7867-0910-3

9 8 7 6 5 4 3 2 1

Printed in the United States of America
Distributed by Publishers Group West

for Felix and Benjamin
who grew alongside

Contents

Contents

Illustrations

Illustrations in the Text

The decorated capitals introducing each chapter are Thackeray's own designs, from *Vanity Fair, Pendennis* and *The Book of Snobs.*

Illustrations

'I do not think we yet know how great that man was'

Anthony Trollope

Acknowledgments

It is a pleasure to acknowledge the many debts accumulated during the five years in which this book was written. Above all I should like to thank Mrs Belinda Norman-Butler, Thackeray's great-granddaughter, who not only allowed me to quote from family correspondence, both published and unpublished, but also allowed me to reproduce several portraits in her possession.

The 'Interlude' between chapters XIII and XIV is substantially my introduction to A Shabby Genteel Story and Other Writings, published as an Everyman paperback in 1993. I am grateful to Anthony Cheetham and the Orion Publishing Group for permission to reproduce this material. I should also like to thank Liberty Publishing Ltd for permission to quote from the record of Punch table talk kept by Henry Silver, and the National Library of Scotland for allowing me to make use of Thackeray's correspondence with Harriet, Lady Ashburton. In addition William Drummond has very kindly made available to me the numerous unpublished sketches and paintings in his possession. A description of his material, and a brief discussion of its significance, are included in the Appendix.

In the course of this work I have drawn on a wide range of scholarly expertise and advice. I should particularly like to thank Professor John Sutherland and Professor Michael Slater, both of whom were kind enough to read the book in typescript, Professor John Carey and Professor E.F. Harden. I owe a special debt to Professor K.J. Fielding, who kindly allowed me access to the fruits of his research among the Ashburton correspondence and was an invaluable source of help and information.

Among the various institutions and libraries, both public and private, that allowed me to work in their archives or answered enquiries, I should like to thank the University of London Library and its archivist Ruth Vyse; the Garrick Club and its librarian Mrs Enid Foster, MBE; the Public Record Office and Ann Morton of its reader services department; the Bodleian Library and Mrs Julie Anne Lambert, Supervisor of the John Johnson Collection; the Surrey County History Centre, Woking, and its principal archivist Mike Page; the *Punch* library and its consultant archivist Amanda-Jane Doran; and Eton College and its librarian Michael Meredith.

At Chatto & Windus Carmen Callil smiled on the early stages of the project, Jonathan Burnham commissioned it and Alison Samuel saw it through. As ever I owe a great debt of gratitude to my editor Jenny Uglow for her advice and support, and to my agent Gill Coleridge.

Throughout this time many literary editors happily kept me supplied with relevant books. They include Mick Imlah, Mark Amory, Harry Ritchie, Paula Johnson, Robert Winder, Natasha Walter, John Walsh, Lucasta Miller, Carolyn Hart, Boyd Tonkin, Peter Wilby, Terri Natale, Ian Hislop, Auberon Waugh, Nancy Sladek, Joanna Craven, Lisa Allardyce, Stephen Moss, Giles Foden and James Wood. Among a large number of friends and professional acquaintances who offered help and information, I should like to thank David Kynaston, Hilary Laurie, James Erskine, Margaret Forster, Gerald Gliddon, Karen Hope, Dr Richard Mullen and Professor Pierre Coustillas. The staff of the London Library, where much of my research was done, were, as ever, unfailingly efficient and courteous.

None of this could have been accomplished without the support of my wife, Rachel. I am profoundly grateful to her.

London, February 1999

The views of Thackeray attributed to 'Jacques', waiter at the Coq d'Or near Ivry, Alfred Bunn, theatrical manager, Mrs Bakewell, 'Samuel Jones', *Punch* engraver, and George Eliot, in a 'lost' fragment of her diary, are entirely imaginary.

A NOTE ON SPELLING: Thackeray's spelling and punctuation were erratic, even for the days before standardisation. In the majority of cases I have provided literal transcriptions from his letters, silently amending the original text only in cases where the absence of commas or transposed apostrophes (two of Thackeray's major failings) becomes confusing.

I

The Road to Kensal Green

riting many years after Thackeray's death, the Victorian man of letters George Hodder – who had known him towards the end of his life – sketched out some of the problems that awaited a future biographer. In effect, Hodder concluded, there was only one – the elusive, or even protean, nature of the subject: 'A hundred admirers of Thackeray might undertake to write a memoir of him, and yet the task of doing full justice to his career must necessarily await a chosen future historian, who shall zealously gather together all the bits and fragments to be found, scattered among books and men, and blend them into a substantial and permanent shape.' It had to be admitted, though, Hodder went on, that there was an exceptional difficulty in regard to Thackeray, 'in as much as there were few whom he allowed to *know* him, in the true sense of the phrase . . .'

Certainly the various compartments of Thackeray's comparatively short life – he was only fifty-two when he fell dead of a stroke on Christmas Eve 1863 – the range of personae that he adopted, or had adopted for him, and the way in which a multitude of relatives and friends regarded him, abets this view. To his mother he was an adoring infant whose delight at her return from India gave rise to one of the great nineteenth-century evocations of maternal love. To his school-fellows he was a lively, idle boy whose talents expressed themselves in scrawled caricatures rather than the antiquated Charterhouse curriculum. To his Cambridge contemporaries he was a genial, diffident companion who inspired great affection, and of whom 'much was made'. To the broken-down hacks and seedy financiers of 1830s' Grub Street he was a young man whose literary inclinations came backed by a substantial private fortune. To the magazine editors of the early

1840s he was a struggling freelance, ashamed of his recent poverty but not afraid to use it as a bargaining tool. To Isabella Shawe, who married him at eighteen, he was 'William', a prematurely grey-haired husband to be predominantly loved, occasionally feared and eventually (and tragically) forgotten. To his elder daughter Annie he was a doting and doted-upon father, whose death awakened in her masochistic recollections of past unworthiness. To his aristocratic admirers of the 1850s he was the best kind of literary man, gentlemanly, courteous and the ornament of dinner tables from Holland House to Berkeley Square. To Jane Brookfield, who has some claim to be regarded as the love of his life, he was 'my dear brother William', a soulmate and confidential friend forever held at arm's length. To the gossip-mongering society journalist Edmund Yates, who engaged him in one of the most famous literary rows of the Victorian age, he was a hypocrite who resented being judged by the standards that he applied to other people. To his cronies of the *Punch* table he was an avuncular drinking companion with a weakness for bad puns. He was much loved – Anthony Trollope kept a bust of Thackeray on his study desk until the day of his death – and, in his quarrels with Dickens, Forster and other Victorian notables, much disliked and misunderstood. When he died, the world of mid-Victorian London seemed diminished by his absence.

No doubt these varying perspectives are common to any life, Victorian, literary or otherwise. In Thackeray's case the contradictions are heightened by the way in which he regarded himself. Even by the standards of Victorian novelists, he was highly aware of his own temperamental shortcomings, and the vein of self-criticism in his writings frequently hardens into self-accusation. At the same time he was honest enough – sometimes laceratingly so – to try to separate out his emotions regarding the people and situations he came up against. Thus he loved his mother – their correspondence, begun in childhood, flared up whenever they happened to be apart – but disliked her notably severe version of Evangelical Christianity. He admired Dickens' writings, but thought the man himself deceitful and surrounded by flatterers. He relished 'good' society, and wrote many a respectful letter to a duke, but admitted that it often left him bored. It comes as something of a surprise to learn that a man who could muster half a dozen baronets on his side in the Garrick Club row with Dickens and Yates considered himself a Bohemian to the end.

Each of these finely judged positions lends something to the puzzle that surrounds Thackeray's life, and what was, in the last resort, his memorialists' inability to pin him down. As John Blackwood put it, when returning one of these manuscripts to an aspiring contributor to *Blackwood's Magazine*: 'None of the numerous sketches I have read give to me any real picture of the man with his fun and mixture of bitterness with warm good feeling ... I feel so truly about him I am frightened to give a wrong impression of him to one who did not know him.' These confusions were evident elsewhere. One obituarist praises him as a fluent and witty after-dinner speaker; another remembers only nerve-racked silences. Sir William Fraser thought that in no society where he saw Thackeray could he find 'anything to repay the interest which I took ...' Henry Silver's record of the *Punch* table talk shows Thackeray loquacious and mute by turns. Such lightning shifts of temperament, an ability to switch from cheery conviviality to remote self-possession almost between courses, were complicated by the ill health that afflicted the last decade of his life. Many an ambitious literary man, frostily received by the great novelist in some club smoking room – Trollope was a classic example – diagnosed haughtiness when the real culprit was physical discomfort.

Worse, perhaps, few of the conventional yardsticks used to measure early-Victorian lives are much help in Thackeray's case. Socially, he was born into a distinctive upper-middle-class stratum of Anglo-Indian administrators, and yet the loss of his patrimony forced him into a professional existence that, for all his Bohemian hankerings, was sometimes a little too low-class for his liking. Spiritually, he was a simple 'believer', as mistrustful of his mother's fanaticism as he was repelled by any kind of metaphysical speculation, whose religious pronouncements, such as they are, would have struck a late-Victorian free-thinker as laughable. Politically, he began life as a progressive Liberal and ended up a Whiggish conservative capable of commending a *Cornhill* article by James Fitzjames Stephen as 'a very moderate honest sensible plea for an aristocratic government, and shows the danger of a democracy quite fairly ... The politics of gentlemen are pretty much alike,' he concludes – a statement that even an amateur student of Victorian politics, with its spectacular faction fights and towering personal animosities, would have trouble in swallowing. Typically, when he stood for Parliament himself, at Oxford in 1857, it was as an independent. Rising above these imperfect attempts to make sense of the chaotic early Victorian landscape, and occasionally dominating them to the exclusion of all else, was a deep sense of insecurity: a lack of confidence not merely in his relationships with other people, but in his professional life. Even as a successful novelist he was forever on the lookout for a lucrative public appointment that would absolve him from having to work: as late as 1848 – the year he finished *Vanity Fair* – he contrived to get himself called to the Bar in the hope that it might improve his employability. There are times, in fact, particularly towards the end, when money worries began to press on him, when he seems to have been perfectly willing to sacrifice his career on the altar of the gentlemanly life.

No doubt these are false distinctions. To the hack-journalist of the early 1840s, with two children to bring up and doctors' bills to pay, money was money, whether it came from *The Times* or some government sinecure. Doubtless, too, the sinecure would have been preferable to the time-honoured journalist's obligation to ingratiate oneself with social inferiors. And yet somehow the professional insecurities are all of a piece with the other frailties and fractures of Thackeray's life. Even the portraits and photographs of him lack a prevailing pattern. Daniel Maclise's early sketch shows a burly and faintly arrogant young man with an eye-glass, sprawling over a chair; James B. Lambdin's 1855 painting depicts a rubicund but still slightly watchful middle-aged gentleman; the late-period photographs resemble a bad-tempered pug. Understandably, to set about penetrating this enigma was the delight of the mid-Victorian journalist. In the absence of any settled view of Thackeray, gossip-columnists and paragraph-mongers eagerly set about creating their own – often with bizarre results. As early as 1848, for example, he was being confidently proposed as the original of Mr Rochester. Posthumous speculation of this kind went on for as long as forty years, and there is a delightfully cross letter to Annie from Dickens' daughter Kate, written in 1905, complaining about Mrs Lynn Linton's memoirs ('How did she know who were our fathers' loves?' Kate wondered acidly. 'Of this I am certain, that neither of them ever loved *her* ...')

To the late-twentieth-century biographer, the challenge is that much more forbidding. Thackeray himself distrusted biography, famously instructing his daughters that none should be written. At the same time he believed very strongly that an author's personality is intimately revealed in the words he writes. 'All that I can remember of books generally is the impression I get of the author,' he wrote once. Here, perhaps, among the millions of words – the original Smith, Elder edition of his collected works runs to twenty-six volumes – words ground out on chop-house dining tables, in stage coaches, against deadlines with the printer's boy chafing in the hall, at leisure in the study at Palace Green, his true spirit resides.

One hundred and thirty-six years after Thackeray's death, George Hodder's 'bits and fragments' lie scattered about. In an age that encouraged solid memorials – it is hardly possible to lift the volumes of Moneypenny's and Buckle's life of Disraeli unaided – his is one of the better-documented Victorian lives. There are six fat volumes of letters. Philip Collins' selection of the reminiscences of Thackeray's friends runs to 400 pages. Annie spent the rest of her long life – she died in 1919 – refining the memories of her upbringing in the house at Young Street, where Charlotte Brontë once came to dinner. What impresses is not so much the volume of the material – after all, the collected edition of Carlyle's correspondence has just reached its twenty-sixth volume – as its sheer variety. There are tributes in verse, ranging from Tom Taylor's *Punch* memorial to some execrable lines contributed by Austin Dobson to the 1911 *Cornhill* centenary number. Half a dozen novelists, from celebrities like Disraeli to relative unknowns such as James Hannay, produced recognisable fictional portraits. Assimilating this tide of representations – some good-nature; others, like the embittered critic St Barbe in *Endymion*, transparently malign – can drag the biographer onto the wilder shores of Victorian literature: tracking down obscurities such as Hannay's *King Dobbs* (1849), which features a race called the 'Somniatics', inhabitants of an imaginary Pacific island, whose chief ornament is a 'philosophical novelist' strongly reminiscent of the author of *Vanity Fair*.

In the end, though, these are side-shows to the main event. Essentially the materials for Thackeray's life boil down to four main categories: correspondence, his daughter Annie's recollections, reminiscences of friends and his own works. Like many another Victorian novelist he was a prolific letter writer, whose correspondence formed an integral part of his routine. In mid-1852, hard at work on *Esmond*, he supplied a thumb-nail sketch of his daily life to a female friend: 'I write all day at my book – I go into the world then wh. is a part of my vocation, and takes up a woeful quantity of my time. Many a day I find my only resource is to stay up in my bed-room, in bed, and go on working there with an amanuensis – and when quite tired and fagged have commonly eight or ten letters to write many of them upon business not my own. Hence I correspond with scarce anybody ...'

Even given the Victorian tendency to insist that letters should be letters – George Gissing's communications to his intellectual friends almost demand separate volumes – this is a large understatement. Many of Thackeray's letters were narrowly reactive: business affairs, the inevitable invitations. At the same time, he kept up correspondences with a circle of close friends, which, in the case of confidantes such as Mrs Proctor or the *bonnes soeurs*, Jane Elliot and Kate Perry, could extend over decades. His friendship with Mrs Brookfield – the key relationship of his middle years – was largely conducted in ink; the Brookfield correspondence, in particular, shows Thackeray staking out a distinct environment in which he could address the woman he loved, untrammelled (up to a point) by drawing-room convention or, more important perhaps, by the presence of her husband. The 3,000 or so surviving letters of this non-correspondent must represent only a tiny fraction of the whole.

The tortuous publishing history of Thackeray's letters since his death is largely down to Thackeray. The ban on biographical speculation, dutifully extended by Annie to cover correspondence, held for nearly a quarter of a century. The first substantial breach came in 1887 when Mrs Brookfield, hard up and divining that she sat on a hot property, published a selection in *Scribner's Magazine*, and subsequently in book form. A decade later Annie unbent sufficiently to include many extracts (mostly from family letters) in her prefaces to a new edition of her father's works. Revised and enlarged, these later introduced the Century Edition of 1910–11. Meanwhile, the field was becoming crowded. General James Grant Wilson's two-volume *Thackeray in the United States* (1904), which printed over a hundred letters from American sources, emerged in the same year as Lucy Baxter's *Thackeray's Letters to an American Family*. Further extracts from the Brookfield correspondence, which had come the way of a private collector, caused a minor sensation on their press publication in 1914. Subsequently Clement Shorter's edition of the letters exchanged with Edward Fitzgerald (1916) and the posthumous *Letters of Anne Thackeray Ritchie* (1924) filled in certain gaps while hinting at the range of unseen material in the hands of libraries and private collections.

Eventually, three-quarters of a century after Thackeray's death, Gordon N. Ray – then a promising young American academic in search of a post-doctoral subject – started work on a definitive edition. But the visits to England that Ray anticipated after his initial trip in

1939 to receive the Thackeray family's benediction were postponed by the war. The six-year stint on his monumental *The Letters and Private Papers of William Makepeace Thackeray* (four volumes, 1945–6) consequently took place in America and was punctuated by war service, and apart from family correspondence and a few other letters from scattered sources, no English holdings are represented. Despite these omissions, Ray's edition is a landmark in Thackeray studies, not least for the series of biographical sketches that introduce the first volume. When the war ended, Ray returned to England – there is a wonderful account of him greeting the literary scholar Geoffrey Tillotson with a volley of questions about manuscript locations – to pick up the thread. Many of these discoveries were excerpted in his two-volume biography, *Thackeray: The Uses of Adversity* (1955) and *Thackeray: The Age of Wisdom* (1958), and in the earlier study *The Buried Life* (1952). Others have turned up in Ann Monsarrat's *Thackeray: Uneasy Victorian* (1980), and in numerous studies of the nineteenth-century publishing scene (a good recent example is Peter Shillingsburg's *Pegasus in Harness: Victorian Publishing and W.M. Thackeray*, 1992). All of this material, and a great deal more, appears in Edgar F. Harden's equally monumental *Supplement* to Ray, published at vast expense on the farther side of the Atlantic in 1994. If nothing else, Harden gives an idea of the huge volume of Thackeray material that has emerged in the past half-century: 1,400 new letters, nearly 250 re-edited from newly available texts printed in Ray from inaccurate sources; a number of diaries and account books, and the 'Firebrand correspondence', a political spoof from 1841. This is a genuine supplement, too, in that new and revised letters fit exactly into Ray's sequence, thereby simplifying comparisons of newly edited versions with Ray's originals. Given the conditions under which he worked, Ray's editing was little short of miraculous, but there are errors. Some of these are simply trivial slips in punctuation – an area in which Thackeray himself was notoriously erratic. Others are more significant. There is a revealing correction, for instance, to the letter of 5 July 1840 to Richard Monckton Milnes, planning a joint visit to the public execution of Courvoisier (the origin of one of his sharpest early sketches, 'Going to See a Man Hanged'). Ray's version runs: 'I must go to bed, that's the fact, or I never shall be able to attend to the work of to-morrow properly.' Harden has: 'I must go to bed that's the fact or I never shall be able to *enjoy the fun* of tomorrow properly' (my italics). The shift from sobriety to flippancy is marked, and the effect of 'Going to See a Man Hanged' and its stark conclusion – 'I fully confess that I came away down Snow Hill that morning with a disgust for murder, but it was for *the murder I saw done*' – that much more emphatic.

While the *Supplement* may not radically redefine our view of Thackeray and his position in the mid-Victorian ant-heap of scurrying literary journeymen, family connections and importunate hostesses, the effect of so much fresh material is to illuminate sharply most of the major areas of his life, in particular his ascent through the crowded literary world of the 1840s, the transformation of his social status brought about by the success of *Vanity Fair*, and the Indian summer of the early 1860s spent editing the *Cornhill Magazine* for George Smith. To it, and one or two other items – notably the thirty or so letters in the National Library of Scotland recently unearthed by Professor K.J. Fielding – can be added a second body of material, the vast weight of reminiscence brought together by Thackeray's daughter Annie, or 'Anne Thackeray Ritchie', as she styled herself after her marriage to her cousin Richmond Ritchie in 1878. After her father's death, Annie produced two unpublished memoirs, one written in 1864, a second composed some years later for the benefit of her niece, Laura Stephen (sadly, Laura's mental deficiencies meant that she would never read it). A later, formal autobiography, *Chapters from Some Memoirs* (1894), covers similar ground, while further variations turn up in Hester Fuller's and Violet Hammersley's *Thackeray and His Daughter* (1951). As well as contributing a series of introductions to what became known as the Biographical Edition of Thackeray's works, which are invaluable for their grasp of Thackeray family lore and first-hand observation of Thackeray's life, Annie spent much of her later years collecting remembrances of her father. Many of these can be found in the great mass of largely uncollected Ritchie papers kept in the Goldsmith Library of the University of London (Annie's manuscript letters, it should be said, are entertaining and infuriating in about equal parts – undated, written in a queer, jerky stream-of-consciousness, but full of interesting fragments).

Much more accessible – and decipherable – is a third block of material: the reminiscences of Thackeray's friends. Thackeray's involvement in the various compartments of London literary life covered a period of over thirty years. His spectrum of acquaintances was correspondingly wide, ranging from celebrities met on equal terms, such as Dickens and Carlyle, to younger acolytes such as Hodder and Hannay, who revered Thackeray and left admiring accounts of his patronage, or up-and-coming novelists such as Anthony Trollope, whose career Thackeray effectively made by serialising *Framley Parsonage* in the *Cornhill*. By the end of the century, as the generation of mid-Victorian literary journalists moved into garrulous old age, memoirs of Thackeray became a kind of growth industry, and there is scarcely a literary autobiography of the 1890s that does not contain its chapter or two of reminiscence. The late-Victorian magazine world, too, provided a ready market for memories of Thackeray's schooldays or clubland encounters. This well took many years to run dry, and Mrs Lynn Linton's memoirs, for example, to which Kate Dickens so strongly objected, were intended for the discerning reader of the Edwardian age.

Finally there are the works themselves. Whether or not, as he claimed, an author's shape hovers tantalisingly above his writings, hardly anything in Thackeray is directly autobiographical. Even the 'Oxbridge' chapters of *Pendennis*, which tend to be regarded as the closest Thackeray ever came to describing his own wayward youth, are a highly sanitised re-creation of his brief career at Trinity College, Cambridge. Pen may have failed his finals, first time around, but at least he sat them. None the less, most of Thackeray's fiction has at least a partial grounding in his own life – *The Newcomes*, for instance, feeds off his Anglo-Indian background, *Pendennis* gestures at his early literary career, while *Philip* contains some sharp glances at a young manhood lived out in the Parisian boarding houses of the 1830s. The mass of hack-journalism written in the decade before *Vanity Fair* made him famous – bibliographies of this period list nearly two dozen sources, ranging from *Punch* to forgotten ephemerals such as the *Torch* – can be even more revealing, notably in the account of his dealings with 'Mlle Pauline', who may have been the original of Becky Sharp, which appeared in an obscure publication called *Britannia* in 1841. Towards the end of his life this vein of nostalgia grew to dominate his writing, and the series of *Roundabout Papers* contributed to the *Cornhill* in the early 1860s, with their evocation of the Tunbridge Wells of his childhood and Mrs Porter's novels, are perhaps the nearest he ever got to conventional autobiography.

Trying to assimilate all these fragments of past life can be a sobering experience, and the temptation to agree with Noel Annan's comment, expressed in a letter to Leonard Woolf, that biographers 'should be warned that letters, and even diaries, do *not* necessarily reflect the inner man . . .' is rather too strong for comfort. Sooner or later, too, anyone who writes about Thackeray will be forced to acknowledge, and come to terms with, the vast gulf that separates the life he led from the experiences of the average late-twentieth-century novelist. More so perhaps than at any other time, the Victorian novelist was an *homme d'affaires*. It was a narrow world, and a novelist with good connections and an inquisitive eye could exist, if not at its centre, then at a sharp enough coign of vantage to make his (or increasingly her) observations worth having. The 'going into the world' that Thackeray imagined was 'part of his vocation' consequently takes in a range of experiences that would be wholly beyond those of a modern writer of equivalent status. The journey from the Cave of Harmony to Chatsworth and from the fourpenny brothels to hob-nobbing with Palmerston might not have seemed especially arduous to one of Thackeray's contemporaries; a century and a half later it would be unique. All this complicates the search for Thackeray, which as a result is less a quest of the kind occasionally devoted to the more *recherché* figures of modern literature than an endless series of discriminations. Wherever one looks amid the spreading compost of mid-Victorian life, Thackeray is there. For all his melancholy, and the tremendous sense of solitariness that pulses through this books, he was a worldly man, and the worlds in which he moved are not always detachable from one another. In the end one can only go back to George Hodder and his hundred aspirant memorialists, and admit that a definitive life is unachievable, if not undesirable; that one can interpret only according to one's own tastes, interests, literary perspectives, and in the last resort one's own cultural code. The point, one feels, would not have been lost on Thackeray himself.

Not long before he died, Thackeray summed up his life for the benefit of his younger friend George Augustus Sala: 'I have made my mark, and my money, and said my say, and the world smiles on me; and perhaps were I to die tomorrow the *Times* newspaper would give me just three-quarters of a column of obituary notice.' This is a characteristically rueful piece of late-period self-analysis, inaccurate only in its final detail. In fact *The Times* gave him nearly a whole column, ranking Dickens higher, but saying of his rival that 'no man of letters with anything like the same power of mind will be regarded as nobler, better, kinder than he'. Comparisons with Dickens had haunted Thackeray throughout his life, and would continue to dog his posthumous reputation. In the short term, though, the Dickens connection tended to work in his favour. A certain kind of late-Victorian middle-class home – its atmosphere is faithfully reproduced in Somerset Maugham's *Of Human Bondage* (1916) – found Dickens vulgar; a certain kind of late-Victorian intellectual found him incorrigibly sentimental. In both cases Thackeray was a highly acceptable substitute. The society poet Frederick Locker-Lampson considered that by the early 1880s Thackeray narrowly had the edge over his arch-rival.

Subsequently, though, his reputation pursued an erratic, but consistently downhill, path. The critics and status-brokers of the 1890s – a decade in which what late-Victorians thought about the Victorian age tends to come sharply into focus – were in two minds about Thackeray. He was a genius, one of the great prose stylists of his or any other age, no one was in any doubt about that. At the same time there were misgivings about his stamina, his 'cynicism', his whole commitment to the business of literature. Had he ever written a 'complete good story', Andrew Lang wondered? 'He is one of the greatest of novelists; he displays human nature and human conduct so that we forget ourselves in his persons, but we do not forget ourselves in their fortunes.' When it came down to it, was Thackeray really a novelist at all? Lang was prepared to allow that if he did not possess narrative gifts of the highest order, then at his best Thackeray achieved a kind of poetic quality that was beyond the range of any other English writer. W.E. Henley, writing at about the same time – the 1890s were a great age for books of reprinted literary criticism in which the same topics are repeatedly discussed – noted how opinions differed over Thackeray. Some people regarded him as the greatest artist of his age and country, and as one of the greatest of any country and any age; others could never manage to square his talent with a disregard for pure artistry that sometimes looked like simple philistinism: 'something artful in the man and insincere in the artist'. A club-man with a style, then, rather than a 'pure artist'? The distinction would have seemed odd to a critic of Thackeray's time, but this was the 1890s and the scent of modern aesthetic theory was in the air. None the less, Henley concluded, everyone agreed that this was 'one of the finest prose styles in literature'.

The problem, perhaps, was that Thackeray had spent so long in establishing himself; still more, that he wrote in such a variety of forms. George Saintsbury, one of his most ardent admirers, who edited the seventeen-volume Oxford Thackeray and kept an eye on

Thackeray studies for the best part of sixty years, was definite about this. What people said or thought about Thackeray, he proposed from the vantage point of 1895, could be divided into three or four stages: a slow arrival into public life as a man who wrote promisingly for the magazines; acclaim as a great novelist, balanced by a suspicion of 'dreadful cynicism'; a patch of unalloyed fame; followed by end-of-century decline, a time when 'his manners, his language, his atmosphere and society are getting a little antiquated for younger readers'. It took an arch-Thackerayan such as Saintsbury, whose A Consideration of Thackeray (1931) is worth reading even now, to acknowledge what Lang and Henley had only hinted at: that The Virginians, hailed in its day as one of the great masterpieces of the mid-Victorian age, is more or less unreadable.

Still, the editions kept coming: the Smith, Elder twenty-four-volume set of 1878–9, later extended by two further instalments of newly identified journalism; the Biographical Edition with Annie's prefaces; Saintsbury's seventeen-volume Oxford Thackeray of 1908; a Century Edition of 1910–11. The Cornhill marked the centenary of his birth with a special number containing Austen Dobson's execrable poem and some anodyne family reminiscences courtesy of his kinswoman, Mrs Warre-Cornish (to balance this there is a charming memoir by a woman who, as a small girl, had been befriended by him in Rome in the 1850s). No amount of editorial enthusiasm, though, can quite overcome the air of fustiness that hangs over this collection of superannuated Victorian memorialists. Twenty years later Desmond MacCarthy was wondering why people no longer read Thackeray. Gordon N. Ray's endeavours were respectfully received, without seeming to prod the public back into the path of the novels. The great mid-century revival in Trollope's fortunes, abetted by the availability of cheap Everyman editions during the book-hungry years of the Second World War, passed Thackeray by. One emerges from the fiction of the immediate post-war era with a feeling that this kind of quintessential mid-Victorianism had begun to grate. Gunning-Forbes, the caricature English master of John Wain's Hurry On Down (1953), who advises an aspiring novelist to take "'A course of Thackeray, that's my prescription – soon weed out these little faults'", is plainly exposing himself as a hopeless fogey. In some ways, perhaps, the difficulty lay in knowing where to start. As Orwell points out in his important Tribune essay of 1944 (its influence is acknowledged in John Carey's equally important Thackeray: Prodigal Genius, 1977), much of his best writing turns up in the early journalism, much of which, even today, is barely obtainable outside academic libraries.

Trying to estimate the extent of Thackeray's reputation in the late 1990s, one invariably runs up against the sheer vastness of his output, its variable quality and the different constituencies to which it appeals. *Vanity Fair* is an acknowledged classic, regularly filmed and televised, winner of the Cheltenham Literary Festival's 'Booker Prize of 1847', where it narrowly beat off the challenges of Dickens and Charlotte Brontë. *Pendennis* and *The Newcomes* are in print, and the *Irish Sketch Book* makes sporadic reappearances in the catalogues. *The Rose and the Ring* is still esteemed as a children's book, while fragments of the early journalism regularly turn up in collections of historical reportage. Meanwhile, transatlantic academic interest continues to produce specialist studies such as Deborah A. Thomas' *Thackeray and Slavery* (1993) or John Reed's prodigiously learned *Dickens and Thackeray: Punishment and Forgiveness* (1995). It would be fanciful to suggest that Thackeray is the forgotten man of the Victorian novel. At the same time not a tithe of the ink expended on – to take two representative examples – George Eliot and Anthony Trollope has been put to work in unravelling the career of the author of 'A Little Dinner at Timmins's', which has some claims to be regarded as the finest short story in the language. This is not a critical biography – critics criticise, biographers write biographies – but as well as providing an account of Thackeray's life, its aim is to demonstrate that he was the greatest English writer (writer, you note, not novelist) of the nineteenth century. And perhaps of all time.

Kensal Green, 10 December 1996: a freezing morning, the sky quite opaque. A threat of snow. Walking north through Ladbroke Grove, past parked cars with 'for sale' notices taped to the rear windscreens and down-at-heel West Indian takeaways, one picks one's way carefully through what seems like the litter of centuries. On the bridge spanning Regent's Canal, the stanchions are decorated with graffiti advertising a Peruvian Maoist guerrilla movement. On past the seedy shops and lock-ups, left into the Harrow Road.

The cemetery is set back from the pavement, administrative offices to the right. An obliging attendant: 'Mr Thackeray? Let's see if we can locate Mr Thackeray.' Armed with a green grid-map, I move off through wide, flung-back gates. No one about. In the distance, by the perimeter fence, mechanical diggers lock horns above the wet grass.

Skyline dominated by bare trees and, beyond, a towering gasometer. Graves themselves extraordinarily polyglot: Victorian family vaults, Russian mausoleums with inscriptions in Cyrillic, flaking Greek catafalques.

Thackeray's grave on the south side, where the tractors are out on the path, is difficult to find. Stumbling over the freshly dug turf, holding my coat against the rain – now sweeping in horizontally across the long ridge of stones – I finally discover the single weathered slab, its inscription barely decipherable, fenced off by rusting iron palings. To the left, and dwarfing its neighbour, a squat brick structure containing the family of someone named Charles Chell. In the foreground lie Richard Henry Harman (d. 1975) and his wife Doris Elizabeth (d. 1977). Thackeray's schoolfriend and *Punch* colleague John Leech is at hand. Shirley Brooks, another *Punch* staffer, lies a short way off.

More rain now, driving against the gravestones. Beyond, the grey expanse of north-west London stretches on into the distance beneath a blanket of mist. To stare at the ground that contains the bones of your foremost literary hero should be a solemn and inspiring moment. Somehow, water trickling down the back of my neck, balled hands feeling like blocks of ice, it is not. Back towards the main gate there are circling black cars, fresh roses on the verge. I wander off, past the mini-cab offices, the video shops and the burger dives, towards Paddington.

One hundred and thirty-three years before, it had all been very different. At about eleven on the morning of Wednesday, 30 December 1863 – a warm, crisp and clear day, George Hodder remembered – a hearse and a cortège of ten carriages set off from an imposing double-fronted residence at Palace Green, Kensington, through the drab back-streets of north-west London. Its destination may have surprised the more aristocratic of Thackeray's friends – even in those days Kensal Green cemetery had a reputation for being badly kept up – but it was known that the novelist had expressed a wish to be buried near his daughter Jane, who had died in infancy nearly a quarter of a century before. It took nearly an hour for the procession to wind through the empty, end-of-year streets, but by noon Thackeray's daughters, Annie and Minnie, pale-faced in sober mourning dresses, together with their escort Sir Henry Cole, were deposited at the mortuary chapel.

From the beginning, there was doubt as to who might attend. Thackeray had died on Christmas Eve, and fashionable society was out of town. In the event nearly 2,000 people crammed into the cemetery to witness his last rites. 'Such a scene! Such a gathering!' William Howard Russell remembered. If the aristocracy kept to their country estates, other parts of Thackeray's acquaintance were well represented. *Punch*, the magazine with which he had been associated for twenty years and whose dinners he had attended to within a week of his death, sent Shirley Brooks, Mark Lemon, Horace Mayhew, John Tenniel and Tom Taylor. Dickens and Browning were there, together with George Eliot's consort G.H. Lewes, the painter J.E. Millais and Anthony Trollope. The publishing world was represented by George Smith, who had persuaded Thackeray to edit the *Cornhill Magazine* three years before, and by *Punch*'s proprietors Bradbury and Evans. This much was recorded in the newspapers. What struck other onlookers, however, was the presence of a 'vast assembly of writers and painters clearly recognisable as such, although themselves and their works were unknown'. This was Bohemia, come to pay its respects. Yet by far the greater part of the crowd was made up of ordinary people. George Hodder, among others, noted 'the deep sympathy shown in the event by a very large majority who could have known nothing of Thackeray, except from his work'.

As the crowd gathered outside the chapel, the coffin was borne inside and the Reverend Charles Stuart of King's College, London, read the first part of the burial service before the procession moved on to the south side. Here they encountered an unlooked-for obstruction – a crowd of women in brightly coloured dresses whose 'scarlet and blue feathers', Millais' professional eye registered, struck an incongruous note against the surrounding blacks and greys. Who were these gaudy grave attendants? Where had they come from? In the end the women had to be moved away before the Reverend Stuart could proceed. He continued amid what the local paper described as 'occasional melancholy interruptions of weeping' and, in the distance, the sharp crack of rifle fire. There were sportsmen out shooting in the neighbouring fields, and the noise made the horses champ their bits with nervousness.

Eventually it was all over, the coffin was lowered into the brown earth and the dust sprinkled on its surface. Both the girls stepped forward to pay their final tribute. For Annie, in particular, the last farewell must have been unbearably poignant. 'His coffin was so long it was like him and I felt as if my head was on his breast.' It seemed to her 'as if he was with it' the whole time at Kensal Green. As Annie and Minnie moved back from the grave the crowds began to disperse, moving away in knots towards the cemetery gates. And yet, as the sextons began to pile earth on the coffin's upturned lid, one man remained at the scene. A sharp-eyed American journalist provided an exact description of this last mourner. Curiously, he was dressed not in black but in 'trousers of a check pattern, a waistcoat of some coloured plaid and an open frock-coat'. Stock-still at the graveside, the man 'had a look of bereavement in his face. When all the others had turned aside from the grave he still stood there, as if rooted to the spot, watching with haggardly eyes every spadeful of dust that was thrown upon it.' Finally the man began to walk away, at first with some friends, to whom he started to talk, but then finding the effort too much and despatching them with a rapid round of handshakes so that he could leave Kensal Green alone.

Dickens' distress at Thackeray's funeral was a matter of public remark. Alongside him, albeit with long faces, the polite colloquies of mid-Victorian society went on unchecked. Theodore Martin, recently appointed biographer of the Prince Consort, for example, went off to lunch with G.H. Lewes at the latter's home in order to be introduced to George Eliot. There was much comment on the results of the autopsy, at which the deceased's brain had weighed in at a stupendous $58\frac{1}{2}$ ounces: 'One of the greatest brains that England ever knew,' the *Kensal Green Handbook* proudly asserted. 'Its fiery fervour, its superb indignation against hypocrisy, pretension and deceit . . . is now hushed in the terrible serenity.' Imagining the scene, and the social context in which it took place, the immediate temptation is to visualise it as a painting by W.P. Frith (who, neatly enough, was present on the day) – ranks of grave, bewhiskered Victorian faces, sombre colourings given definition by the advent of Millais' *demi-mondaines*.

All this is true enough, and no doubt Thackeray's funeral *was* very like one of Frith's lavish panoramas. At the same time one gets a much more vivid sense of the world in which Thackeray moved merely by examining the Kensal Green burial lists. Here in death, curiously enough, is a microcosm of Thackeray's life. His mother followed him there a year later, and his daughter Minnie in 1875. There are close friends from every period of his existence – Leech the cartoonist, who had been at Charterhouse with him; Trollope; his Garrick Club crony

Robert Bell; Leigh Hunt, whom Dickens drew as Skimpole in *Bleak House*. Then follows a long list of people connected with him at some stage during his life: W.H. Ainsworth, whose novels he burlesqued; Dickens' friend Forster, with whom he had bitter quarrels; Wilkie Collins; Thomas Hood; Fitzjames Stephen, who contributed to the *Cornhill* and whose brother was to marry Thackeray's daughter; Alexis Soyer, the model for Mirobilant, the exotic French chef of *Pendennis*, who among other achievements revolutionised the diet of British troops in the Crimea. Finally, there is an even larger group of Victorians only tangentially connected to Thackeray, but whose imbrication in the patterns of his life and art is self-evident: Salter, the artist of 'Waterloo Banquet'; Sir John Goss, who composed Wellington's funeral anthem. Even the presence of Blondin, the celebrated tightrope walker, and Sir Julius Benedict, who wrote 'Lilly of Killarney', is somehow in keeping with Thackeray's interests and enthusiasms. Death found him united with the world that created him, and that he in his turn helped to create.

II

Eastern Child

'We are but young once. When we remember that time of youth, we are still young.'

The Adventures of Philip

'I am sure I must have been a most affected boy.'

Thackeray to his daughters, late in life

The Scottish man of letters James Hannay, who had an obsession with genealogy, was in no doubt about the comparative lustre of Thackeray's ancestry. 'Mr Thackeray is of Saxon descent,' he pronounced, 'and of a landed family settled from the earliest period in the county of Yorkshire.' The advantages of this location were obvious, Hannay thought. With Swift, Pope's mother and Bentley marked down as former residents, the county had produced its fair share of satirists. Thackeray would have been amused by this emphasis – as it appeared in his lifetime, he presumably read it – for in his novels the assumption of Saxon origins is usually a sign of overweening social ambition. The upwardly mobile Newcome family, for example, claim descent from Edward the Confessor's barber-surgeon and call their children Ethel, Alfred and Egbert. All the same, Thackeray would have welcomed Hannay's imputation of long-term gentility. 'Being a gentleman' was something by which he set great store, and rather in the manner of his younger contemporary Trollope, his writings and reported conversation come peppered with speculations about what it is that gentlemanliness implies. The Victorian man of letters John Cordy Jeaffreson, whose relations with Thackeray were at best ambivalent, records 'exhaustive conversations' with him on the nature of gentility. The novelist was heard to say that it took three generations to make a gentleman, and, as Jeaffreson somewhat acidly puts it, was 'not at all disposed to under-value his own rather slender title to be ranked with persons of ancestral dignity'.

If all this makes Thackeray sound like the worst type of bygone social climber, it can be said in his defence that the average Victorian bourgeois was prone to worry himself about this kind of thing, and that there were worse offenders than Thackeray. In fact the Thackerays were descended from a family of yeomen settled since about the time of James I at Hampsthwaite, a hamlet on the River Nidd in the West Riding of Yorkshire. Three hundred years before, the Thackwas, Thackwras or Thackreys were recorded as holding thirty acres and a dwelling house of the Abbot of St Mary of Fountains. These relatively modest origins were not transcended until the early eighteenth century, with the arrival of Thomas Thackeray (1693–1760), who won a scholarship to Eton, became scholar and fellow of King's College, Cambridge, and, after teaching for a time at his old school, crowned a distinguished career as headmaster of Harrow with appointments as chaplain to the Prince of Wales and archdeacon of Surrey. Even by the standards of the eighteenth century, the Thackerays were a philoprogenitive family. Of Thomas' sixteen children, several excelled themselves in the limited number of professions open to the sons of the aspiring middle class. Thomas junior (1736–1806) was a well-known Cambridge surgeon, while Frederick (1737–82) became a physician at Windsor.

All this was characteristic of the upper-middle-class family who had no land but numerous sons in search of a living. Typically, young male eighteenth-century Thackerays became surgeons, lawyers, academics (the Cambridge connection was so substantial that a large part of Thackeray's time as an undergraduate was taken up in calling on his relations). Above all, perhaps, they pursued careers in the colonial Civil Service, in particular the East India Company. Sir William Wilson Hunter, who examined the clan's pre-history in exhaustive detail, marked them down as 'a typical family of the Bengal Civil Service in the days of John Company', as the East India Company was popularly known.* The original William Makepeace Thackeray (1749–1813), Thomas' son and Thackeray's grandfather – the

---

* From the Dutch *Jan Kompanie* by which the Dutch India Company was known to natives in the East.

distinctive middle name came from a Protestant ancestor supposedly martyred by Mary Tudor – was sent out to the East in 1766. Four of his sons and at least fourteen descendants and collateral followed the same profession, and by establishing branches in the sister services – for example in the Indian army – and making prudent marriages they rapidly formed themselves into a poweful interest group both in India and in the company's Court of Directors in London.

Two centuries later it is difficult to appreciate the full extent of the power wielded by the East India Company – a private firm, which effectively ran most of what is now the modern sub-continent on the British government's behalf by means of 20,000 or so imported officials, traders and soldiers – or the opportunities offered to its servants in the transaction of private business. Nominally employed to collect taxes or administer blocks of territory, officials with the right connections at the company's upper levels and an entrepreneurial eye capable of spotting gaps in the local supply chains could make a large extra income by trading on their own account. Thackeray's grand-father is a pattern example of this kind of man. Taken up by Cartier, the governor of Bengal province, appointed factor at Dacca and later first director of Sylhet (he was subsequently known as 'Sylhet Thackeray'), he made a small fortune by supplying elephants to his own employers. Still only in his late thirties, he returned to England in 1776, bought a country estate at Hadley in Middlesex and set about raising a brood of twelve children. Their ramifications provided Thackeray with some of his own closer kin: his cousin Richmond Shakespear, the son of the third child, Emily, and her husband John Talbot Shakespear, and the family of his Aunt Charlotte, later Mrs John Ritchie.

By this stage the family's fortunes were firmly embedded in the East. Four of Thackeray's uncles were to serve in the Indian Civil Service. His father Richmond, born at Hadley on 1 September 1781, was despatched in 1798. Despite early attacks of malaria, he too began a rapid ascent through the company hierarchy, beginning as assistant to the collector of Midnapore – then a frontier tract of Lower Bengal – and then securing a post as assistant to the secretary of the Board of Revenue at Calcutta. By 1803 he was collector at another provincial district, Beerbohm – a considerable challenge, as this involved the reconstruction of an antiquated administrative system (the ruling Indian family was in decline: the 'assets' that supposedly greeted Richmond on his arrival were a mangy elephant chained to a tree and a single, rusting cannon). Again Richmond was a success. Four years later he was rewarded by the full secretaryship to the Board of Revenue, and an appointment as judge at Midnapore. Most of the clues to his personality are lost in the dust of official records, but there is evidence of a taste for social life. The *Calcutta Gazette* noted a 'masqued ball of peculiar splendour' given with the Hon. Mounstuart Elphinstone and two other civilians. Taste in general, if it comes to that. When he sold up his property in advance of a short-lived transfer in 1806, the sale notice offered 'valuable paintings, prints, and convex mirrors, in rich burnished gold frames'. There was also, in strict conformity with local custom, a native mistress, whose descendants were to cause his own heirs considerable embarrassment – both social and pecuniary – in the ensuing half-century. His granddaughter left a careful description of the single portrait that survives: '. . . a very young man in an old-fashioned dress and brass buttons, and white handkerchief round his neck, with brown hair falling loose, with bright soft hazel eyes and arched black eyebrows. The face is long and narrow, the nose is long, the complexion is clear, the mouth delicate and yet not without a certain determination and humour. The eyes have a peculiar depth of expression which I remember in my father. He looks simple and good and sensitive.'

An inventory of family callings in the early nineteenth century soon establishes the dynamic that drove its sons: two dozen soldiers and sailors; nearly twenty churchmen; barristers; medical men. Several displayed a literary turn, including Thackeray's Uncle Francis, who published his *Life of Lord Chatham* in 1827. This background, and the sense of solidarity it instilled, was important to Thackeray. On a practical level it meant that he could scarcely venture outside his front door without coming across one of his relatives: even traversing the wilds of Ulster, in the travels that produced the *Irish Sketch Book*, he managed to turn up his elderly cousin, the Rev. Elias Thackeray, Rector of Dundalk. The sense of clannishness, and recognisable patterns of career and ambition, was reinforced by the family into which Richmond married. Anne Becher, the seventeen-year-old local beauty who became his wife at Calcutta Old Cathedral on 13 October 1810, belonged to another old Bengal family: fifteen of her kinsmen were connected in some way with the sub-continent. If Richmond imagined that by marrying the flamboyant Miss Becher (her son would remember her in her early twenties 'splendidly dressed in a handsome carriage') he was selecting a female version of himself, he was to be proved dangerously wrong. As it turned out, Anne possessed an extraordinary recent history with grave implications for her married life.

The Bechers had a history of imprudent, and subsequently volatile, marriages. By 1808 Anne's mother had left her first husband and run off with a Captain Christie, whose death left her penniless. She then married a Major Butler, who happily frustrated the potential embarrassments of his insolvent death by taking out two insurance policies on his life. In keeping with the family background, most of these exploits took place in India; Anne and her two siblings being dumped in Fareham under the care of their grandmother, old Mrs Becher, and her unmarried daughter. The Fareham regime was strict, but it was liberal enough to allow the fifteen-year-old Anne to attend a ball at Bath, where she met a handsome officer named Lieutenant Henry Carmichael-Smyth. The lieutenant, currently on leave from his regiment, the Bengal Engineers, was a second son with no money and few prospects. His pursuit of his teenage inamorata, consequently, was carried out in the teeth of grandparental opposition. At first Carmichael-Smyth chartered a boat, and navigated the river that adjoined the Bechers' terrace. When these clandestine visits were discovered, Anne was confined to her room with the door locked, although a sympathetic maid smuggled in letters. Finally Mrs Becher tried a double line of attack, telling Anne that the lieutenant had died unexpectedly of a fever, and Carmichael-Smyth that her granddaughter no longer wished to see him. Neither having any means of authenticating their stories, both accepted the situation. Anne, dressed in a green riding habit that would prefigure a lifelong taste in eccentric clothes, was sent to India in the company of her mother, stepfather and older sister Harriet, to recover.

If this sounds like the opening chapter of a late-Victorian 'sensation' novel of the kind made popular by Elizabeth Braddon or Mrs Henry Wood, then the dénouement would be yet more startling. For the moment, though, the consequences of the Bechers' choice of India as a place from which to recover from a broken heart lay in the future. In the meantime Anne married Richmond Thackeray, and William Makepeace junior – his grandfather lived for another two years – was born prematurely on 18 July 1811. Anne was told that a full-term birth would have killed her (the trouble seems to have been caused by the baby's outsize head) and that she must never have another. Outwardly, this was the only cloud hanging over the Thackerays' early married life, as Richmond's career continued to flourish. At the end of the year he was appointed to the collectorship of a region known as the Twenty-Four Pergunnahs, one of the prizes of the Bengal Service, which customarily allowed its holders to lay up a fortune. It was a few months into this appointment, some time in 1812, that, apparently without warning, he brought a young officer met in the course of his travels home to dinner. Shortly after their arrival Anne looked up to find Carmichael-Smyth advancing into her drawing-room.

Detaching what really happened, and who said what to whom, from the accretions of family myth is scarcely possible at this remove, but it seems clear that the effect on Anne was seriously disturbing: not merely the return of an old flame, which could unsettle any relationship, but the reappearance of a man who had been represented to her as dead. Eventually, after matters had been explained between the two, they had to be explained to Richmond Thackeray, who listened studiously, made polite remarks, but was apparently never the same to his wife again. Within three years, in any case, he was dead of a fever. His son remembered only a tall man rising up out of a bath. Lived out in what must have been an atmosphere of considerable strain, the remainder of the Thackerays' married life together is beyond recall. A sketch by the celebrated 'Eastern' portraitist George Chinnery (who turns up in *The Newcomes*), highly stylised in the manner of the period, shows a diffident-looking Richmond seated in a chair, while a wild-eyed wife clutches at a monkeyish child with enormous eyes, who seems in grave danger of tumbling from the pile of books on which his mother has balanced him. But there are glimpses throughout Thackeray's writings of what Carmichael-Smyth's return must have meant to their lives. The novels are full of unheralded revenants – Amory, for instance, in *Pendennis*, whose wife has grown rich and married a baronet – and well-kept pre-marital secrets, like the brace of children unexpectedly presented to the newly married James Gann in *A Shabby Genteel Story*.

With Richmond in his grave – he lies in Calcutta's North Park Street cemetery, not far from one of his wife's Becher relatives – Anne and Carmichael-Smyth planned to marry as soon as the proprieties would allow. In the meantime, there were decisions to be taken about the four-year-old William. His father's fortune, to be left in trust until his son's twenty-first birthday, was found to amount to nearly £18,000. Peter Moore, a venerable John Company nabob who had known William Makepeace senior and also bought property at Hadley, was enlisted as the boy's guardian and administrator of this substantial estate,* together with a younger man named Robert Langslow, the husband of Richmond Thackeray's sister Sarah. Custom dictated that children whose parents lived in the East were sent home to school. While the five-year-old's despatch on board the *Prince Regent* late in 1816, together with his four-year-old cousin Richmond Shakespear and a native servant named Lawrence Barlow, seems barbaric to a modern eye (he was not to see his mother again for three years), it was standard practice for the time. None the less, the experience left an indelible mark on Thackeray's consciousness, and nearly half a century later he was still reliving the sensations of an enforced parting from someone he loved. 'Twang goes the trunk, down come the steps . . . I smart the cruel smart again; and, boy or man, have never been able to bear the sight of people parting from their children.' In his writings, farewells of this kind habitually take place off-camera. Yet the voyage, too, contained a significant formative event. The ship called in at St Helena, where William was taken to see a small, dumpy-looking man prowling the pathways of an enclosed garden. This, explained Barlow who accompanied him, as they examined Bonaparte's pacing figure, was an ogre who ate children.

The *Prince Regent* reached England in June 1817, and a phase of Thackeray's life came to an end. He never returned to the scene of his early childhood, and, apart from a vague scheme late in life to take his daughters there, never seems to have wanted to. India features in his novels as a place of mystery and excitement, the source of wealth and exotic gifts, like Miss Honeyman's embroidered shawls and ivory chessmen in *The Newcomes*, and of disaster. Bad news has a habit of coming from the East in Thackeray, either in human form (Amory, inevitably, is an old India hand) or in the shape of financial meltdown: the collapse of the Bundelcund Bank rubs out Colonel Newcome's patiently acquired fortune just as, twenty years before, the collapse of the Indian banking houses was to obliterate what remained of Thackeray's own. From somewhere – presumably his Anglo-Indian relatives – Thackeray acquired a considerable knowledge of late-eighteenth-century John Company history, and *The Newcomes*, a work

* Moore (1753–1828) is a good example of the way in which a man of relatively obscure origins could prosper in the East India Company's service – and also of some of the vicissitudes that might affect his later life. After serving on the Committee of Revenue, he retired to England at the age of thirty, set up as a local magnate in Hadley, began a long parliamentary career in the Whig interest and helped Sheridan to rebuild the Drury Lane Theatre. His bankruptcy in the financial panics of the mid-1820s, and eventual death in France at the age of seventy-five, probably contributed something to the latter part of *The Newcomes*.

steeped in Eastern allusions, is full of carefully arranged period detail. Old Lady Kew, for example, has attended Warren Hastings' trial, and there are references to Hastings' associate Richard Barwell, the fabulously wealthy 'Barwell of Stansted', who on his return to England in 1780 was said to have brought with him the largest fortune ever accumulated on the sub-continent. Barwell had been an ally of Thackeray's grandfather, and ruled in his favour in a controversial lawsuit. In a less blatant gesture to family heritage, 'Clavering', the name of the councillor sent to Bengal to investigate Hastings prior to his impeachment, turns up in *Pendennis*, where it is given to the conniving baronet. Again, by courtesy of his relatives, he seems to have gained some kind of entrée into the Anglo-Indian ghettos north of Oxford Street (an area of London known as 'Tyburnia' after the nearby Tyburn Tree), with their imported curries and queer Hindi slang. *The Newcomes* fairly bristles with references to *bahawders*, *mohurs*, *qui-his* and the like. India remains a signature mark in Thackeray's fiction: its appearance is generally the signal for a raising of the emotional temperature and the thought of danger. The moment the narrator of 'A Gambler's Death' in the *Paris Sketch Book* mentions that 'Jack was in India, with his regiment, shooting tigers and jackals', the reader knows exactly what to expect. For all this deliberate symbolism, it is possible to suspect that Thackeray's grasp on the realities of Indian life was fairly weak, and the accounts of Jos Sedley's career in *Vanity Fair* leave the reader largely in the dark over what he actually does in his capacity as collector of Boggleywallah.

Once arrived in England, Thackeray was first taken to the London home of his father's married sister, Charlotte Ritchie, in Southampton Row. Thackeray always had warm feelings for his aunt, wrote her many affectionate letters, kept up with her later when both were living in Paris, and in 1849 confided to her that his stays at the Ritchies' London house were the only 'decently cheerful' part of his childhood. Subsequently he was despatched to Fareham – presumably Anne had patched up her differences with her grandmother – and put in the charge of his great-aunt. If the Bechers noticed anything about their youthful lodger it was his talent for drawing. An early letter – the very first that he wrote – to his mother a fortnight before his sixth birthday, exclaiming over his Aunt Ritchie's kindness and the sights of London, is signed off with Aunt Becher's remark that 'William drew me your house in Calcutta not omitting his monkey looking out of the window

& Black Betty at the top drying her Towells. & told us of the number you collected on his Birth day in that large Room he pointed to us!' While being made much of by his relatives may have tempered some of the misery of his mother's absence, strange faces and a strange land, sterner realities lay close by. William was first sent to a school at Southampton run by a couple named the Arthurs, which had some reputation among Anglo-Indian parents. But not even the presence of his cousins Richmond and George Shakespear, who went there with him, could soften his ghastly first impressions of the Arthurs' establishment. Forty years later he could still experience a twinge of retrospective horror over 'that first night at school – hard bed, hard words, strange boys bullying, & laughing, and jarring you with their hateful merriment. And the first is not the *worst*, my boys, there's the rub.' Nothing very much compared to Dickens in his blacking factory, perhaps, but hugely traumatic to a six-year-old boy whose mother was a six-month sea voyage away. In later life Thackeray claimed to have knelt at the foot of his bed and implored God to allow him to dream of her. To these privations could be added 'cold, chilblains, bad dinners, not enough victuals, and caning awful!' A curious incident lodged in his mind. One night the boys were trooped into the hen-house and ordered, one by one, to place their hands in a bag of soot and show them to the master. Thackeray assumed that this Kafkaesque episode had something to do with a theft, and the Arthurs' efforts to track down the culprit. A couple of early letters to Aunt Ritchie are unrevealing of school routine (their formality suggests they were dictated by Mr Arthur), although Thackeray, prefiguring one of the great attachments of his adult life, declared himself 'much entertained' by a play to which they had been taken. An accompanying note from Mrs Arthur mentions the chilblains, but reassures that 'they are now quite gone, and with a little attention I hope he will have no more'. A note to his mother dated April 1818 and addressed to 'Mrs Carmichael-Smyth', which the widow Thackeray had recently become, regrets that he is not yet able to read her own letters, 'but hope I soon shall', and asserts – again the suspicion is that this was dictated by the Arthurs – that he has 'learned geography a long time an[d] have begun Latin and ciphering which I like very much'.

By the summer of 1818 it had become clear to his relatives that the Arthurs would no longer do. Thackeray welcomed the news in a letter to his mother from the Bechers' house on his seventh birthday. It is a charming, ebullient piece of writing, full of lively turns of phrase, in which, for the first time, the reader can detect an individual personality rather than the stilted conventions of the Arthurs' letters home:

> I am grown a great Boy. I am three feet 11 inches and a quarter high. I have got a nice boat. I learn some poems which you was very fond of such as the Ode on Music &c . . . I have lost my cough and am quite well, saucy, & hearty; & can eat Granmamas Goosberry pyes famously after which I drink yours and my Papa's Good health & a speedy return.

Presumably there was already some talk of the Carmichael-Smyths returning to England. For the moment, though, however much Mrs Carmichael-Smyth might grieve for her 'Billy Boy', they remained in India. Thackeray, meanwhile, was switched to a school in Chiswick run by a Dr Turner, who was related to the family by marriage. Dr Turner's establishment was a great deal superior to the Arthurs', as was Chiswick to Southampton – a small, residential town, then well beyond London, with a few thousand decidedly genteel inhabitants. A contemporary gazetteer lists ninety-one 'nobility, gentry and clergy' among the townsfolk, and there was an impressive senior member in the shape of the Duke of Devonshire. Chiswick was a popular place for schools – the *Middlesex Directory* of a few years later notes twenty-one 'Academies and schools', including seventeen boarding establishments – drawn by the semi-rural surroundings. Westall's lithograph of 1823 shows Chiswick Mall as a pleasant riverside walk. The town and 'Walpole House', where Dr Turner and his young gentlemen resided, undoubtedly had a lasting effect on Thackeray's imagination. Its appearance is faithfully reproduced in the description of Miss Pinkerton's Academy in *Vanity Fair*, where Becky Sharp and Amelia Sedley meet, and by an odd coincidence one of the more celebrated inhabitants of the town in Dr Turner's day, the engraver William Sharp, has Becky's surname.

Despite an attempt to run away – the trouble apparently arose out of a caricature he had drawn of one of the masters – Thackeray seems to have been reasonably happy at Dr Turner's. His lot was immeasurably improved in 1820 when his mother and her husband came back from the East. Mrs Carmichael-Smyth wrote an emotional account of their reunion, which also paints a striking portrait of the nine-year-old boy. Fetched from Chiswick by Robert Langslow, 'He had a perfect recollection of me; he could not speak, but kissed me and looked at me again and again.' To his doting parent, William was 'the living image of his father ... He is tall, stout and sturdy, his eyes are becoming darker, but there is still the same dear expression.' As with partings, so with reunions: intensely moved by the necessity of bidding farewell to the people he loved and then having to greet them again, Thackeray could never bring himself to put into words what these experiences meant to him. Even as a mature man, his return from foreign travels to his daughters' embrace rarely provoked him to comment. These were private raptures, not to be defiled by the penetrating gaze of the novelist.

Thackeray stayed at Chiswick until he was ten and a half. His mother and stepfather moved from Charlton, the home of Henry's elderly father Dr Carmichael-Smyth, to Addiscombe in Surrey when Major Carmichael-Smyth – he purchased his promotion in 1821 with money realised by the former's death – took up an appointment superintending the local military college. Though his wife enthused over what seemed to her to be admirable teaching standards ('I don't think there could be a better school for young boys', she remarked towards the end of her son's stay), and Thackeray managed a respectable class position of sixth out of twenty-four, his accomplishments at Dr Turner's were probably fairly limited. Certainly Dr Russell, on admitting him to Charterhouse, took a rather different view: 'The boy knows nothing, & will just do for the lower form.' Already Thackeray seems to have been shaping up as the kind of child whose talents find their fullest expression outside the classroom. His drawing continued to impress, and Mrs Carmichael-Smyth noted an idiosyncratic sense of humour. After a trip to Southampton, she informed a correspondent, 'He tells me he has seen the Prince Regent's yacht in Southampton Water, and the bed on which his Royal Highness breathes his *royal snore*.' There is a suspiciously comic gravity, too, in his account of a schoolfriend's serious illness. 'The weak state he is in and his soreness cause him a great deal of pain,' Thackeray suggested, 'but we still entertain some hopes of his recovery.'

The Prince Regent. Napoleon in his walled garden. The tantalising East. Loss. Plenty of the adult Thackeray can be seen in these early years. Rising to dominate them, an abiding image whose outlines were sharpened by her three-year absence, was his relationship with his mother. Thackeray adored Mrs Carmichael-Smyth, and their occasional conflicts in later life were all the more upsetting to him given the deep wells of emotion from which they sprang. Despite early misgivings – there was a queer moment when he heard his stepfather's snores coming from his mother's bedroom – he liked Major Carmichael-Smyth and was happy to welcome him into the family, but it was his mother who lit up his early life. As a young man he wrote to her on almost daily basis, and even in his twenties and thirties there are whole stretches of his life that can only be pieced together by way of these bulletins home. From an early stage his mother's imperious and certainly glamorous image – even in her sixties she remained a striking woman, whose granddaughter remembered her dressed in a red merino cloak trimmed with ermine, 'which gave her the air of a retired empress wearing out her robes' – was inextricably bound up with her religious beliefs. In his infancy, Thackeray later reminded Mrs Carmichael-Smyth, he had learned to associate Old Testament stories with her ministrations: 'When as a child I used to sit on my mother's knee & hear her tell the story of Joseph & his brethren, I received her ideas with her embraces. Heaven bless them & their sacred memory.' These nostalgic filial memories are genuinely meant, but they disguise the inflexibility that came to characterise an increasingly gloomy Evangelicalism. Other witnesses attest to this side of Mrs Carmichael-Smyth's nature, and the brand of early nineteenth-century religious fatalism that she espoused. When she talked of God, a family friend named Henriette Corkran remembered, 'she always made me think He was an angry, harsh, old gentleman, who saw every little act of mine, and would eventually punish me'. The temptation for her son to visualise God as the most exacting kind of schoolmaster was increased by the religious teaching on offer at Chiswick. Annie remembered it being said in the family circle that when Dr Turner used to read the Commandments to his boys, servants, wife and other members of his Sunday congregation, the effect of his resounding tones was to remind them of Sinai itself. Religious differences divided many a Victorian family: in the Thackerays' case the issues at stake were made that much more painful by the mutual love that underlay them.

For the rest of his days Thackeray had complex feelings about his childhood. In many ways his whole adult life was an endless journey back into the past, and an attempt to recover its sights, sounds and tastes. The series of 'Roundabout Papers', which he wrote for the *Cornhill Magazine* shortly before his death, contain some plangent re-creations of this lost youth. In 'Tunbridge Toys', for instance, he solemnly itemises the contents of his pockets *circa* 1823: 'pencil case, marbles, purse, top, string, knife, piece of cobbler's wax, two or three bullets'. Several essays wallow luxuriously in the memory of tarts and toffee (Thackeray had a notoriously sweet tooth and the 'tart woman' rattling her tray of hardbake makes regular appearances in his fiction) while ruefully acknowledging that such delights are beyond recall. 'I wish I *did* like them,' he writes sadly. 'What raptures of pleasure one could have now for five shillings, if we could but pick it off the pastry cook's tray.' Most lavish of all, perhaps, was Thackeray's affection for the books he read in childhood. His tastes ran to historical novels, such as Jane Porter's *Scottish Chiefs* and *Thaddeus of Warsaw*, along with Gothic shockers with titles like *Manfroni: or the One-handed Monk*. He liked illustrated books, too, and his enthusiasm for *Life in London, or the Adventures of Corinthian Tom, Jeremiah Hawthorne and their friend Bob Logic*, Pierce Egan's rackety account of Regency pleasure-seeking, which appeared at around this time, was enhanced by Cruikshank's drawings ('It had pictures – oh! Such funny pictures.'). The novels, in particular, gave Thackeray a deeply romanticised view of the past. '*There* was the old world,' he once gushed in a thumb-nail sketch of 2,000 years of English history. 'Stage-coaches, more or less swift, riding-horses, pack-horses, highwaymen, knights in armour, Norman invaders, Roman legions, Druids, Ancient Britons painted blue, and so forth – all these belong to the old period.'

Time did not dim these enthusiasms. Thirty years later he put the Cruikshank encomium into the mouth of a small boy in *The Newcomes*, while the occasional pictures that he drew of his boyhood invariably have reading materials well to the fore. He remembered first reading Mrs Porter in the Bechers' summer-house on the day George IV was crowned, while his great-grandmother looked on ('She was eighty years of age then. A most lovely and picturesque old lady, with a long tortoiseshell cane, with a little puff, or *toup* of snow-white (or was it powdered?) hair under her cap, with the prettiest little black-velvet slipper and high heel you ever saw.').

This carefully cultivated absorption in childhood bred an understandable sympathy for children themselves. Half a dozen memoirs of Thackeray dwell on his kindness to children, his unfeigned affection for them and interest in their point of view. Mindful of the 'tart woman', he was always ready with cash gifts ('Come here and be tipped!' he is once supposed to have instructed his friend Leech's son, to whom he stood godfather) and encouraged children placed in his care to stuff themselves with sweets. This is an attractive side to

Thackeray's character – who can resist the man who delights innocently in the company of children? – but it conceals, or fails to conceal, a determination, first, to recapture this lost time and, second, to compensate himself for something that was missing from it. In reading these accounts of his schooldays one often feels that something has slipped away out of them, that the recollections would be less intense had the reality itself been more fully realised. At the same time much of this early life seems to have been genuinely idyllic. Above all, perhaps, Thackeray remembered a superlative holiday spent in Tunbridge Wells, where his parents rented a cottage in the summer of 1823. The place stuck in his mind to the extent that, passing through the town twenty years later, he told his mother that he had examined his surroundings 'with a queer sort of feeling. That lovely cottage we used to inhabit has gone to heaven.' There we shall leave him, on a summer night in 1823, in a tableau redrawn many years later. 'The parents have gone to town for two days; the house is his own; his own and a grim old maidservant's, and a little boy is seated at night in the lonely drawing room, poring over "Manfroni: or the One-handed Monk", so frightened that he scarcely dares to turn round.'

III

The 370th Boy

'Men revisit the old school, though hateful to them, with ever so
much kindness and affection . . .'

'On a Joke I Once Heard from the Late Thomas Hood'
(Roundabout Papers)

ven though his father Richmond Thackeray – now dead
seven years – had been educated at Eton, it was the
memory of Major Carmichael-Smyth's schooldays that
decided the former Mrs Thackeray to send her son to
Charterhouse in January 1822. The omens were not
promising. In his first letter home Thackeray claimed
that his hands were so cold he could barely write. From
the outset he thoroughly disliked the place and the
people who taught him – making an exception of the boys, many of
whom became lasting friends – and chafed to be gone.

The ancient foundation of Charterhouse, still on its original site
near Smithfield in what is now London EC1, was currently undergoing
a galvanic transformation at the hands of a newish headmaster. Dr
Russell, still only in his mid-thirties, was one of those energetic but
irascible men – all too common in boys' public schools – who combine
immense industry with a complete lack of understanding of human
nature: juvenile human nature in particular. A youthful appointment
some years before (the statutes had had to be relaxed to allow him to
take the job) with excellent credentials – he was a former pupil, and a
fellow of Christ Church – Russell had immediately set about shaking a
sedate and old-fashioned institution into gear. His most spectacular
innovation was the arrival of the Bell-Lancaster system, by which most
of the teaching was done by the senior boys under the masters'
supervision. This had the additional advantage (at any rate in terms of

Russell's receipts) of allowing him rapidly to expand the number of pupils. In 1818 the school's population amounted to 238 boys and five staff, but by 1823, the year after Thackeray's arrival, the number of pupils had leapt to 438. There were administrative changes, too. Under the new regime the headmaster no longer took boarders in his own house (Russell preferred to live at Blackheath) and the old domestic arrangements were abolished. Farmed out among the houses of the teaching staff, the boys spent their leisure hours in a way that went largely unremarked. A witness testifying to the Public Schools Commission, which reported at about this time, deplored these alterations. 'No other system of maintaining order and discipline in the houses was substituted for that which had been destroyed: and the results of this change were not favourable to the comfort or morals of the boys.' Discipline, such as it was, consisted of Russell descending on the school with 'a forest of birch rods'.

Russell gets a bad press in the memoirs of early-nineteenth-century Carthusians. Leaving aside the school's exceptionally narrow curriculum – the boys did little except learn the Odes and Epodes of Horace by heart and go through a Greek play or two – the man himself was simply an oppressor. Martin Tupper, who left the school in 1826 aged sixteen and knew Thackeray slightly, left scarifying recollections of his old headmaster. 'For this man and the school he so despotically drilled into passive servility and pedantic scholarship, I have no reverence,' the author of *Proverbial Philosophy* complained in a memoir written a good half-century later. Russell's systematic harassment left Tupper with a nervous stammer that afflicted him well into middle age. As an old man, he wondered how he had managed to learn anything under the 'two ignorant old parsons' who ran the lower school. The senior staff – Lloyd, Dickens, Irvine and Perry – were better, and the upper school boasted a fine teacher and excellent clergyman named Churton. Unhappily, the entire teaching contingent was intimidated by Russell and his teaching methods. What would a modern onlooker think, Tupper speculated, of a schoolmaster smashing a child's head between two books until his nose bled?

But it was lack of supervision, rather than Russell's marathon caning sessions, that gave the school its bad character. What the boys did outside school hours was largely ignored. Extra-curricular activities consequently ranged from bringing in pornographic books and planning excursions to watch public hangings at nearby Newgate to wandering around Holywell Street, where the local prostitutes stood soliciting custom. Even the most innocent activities took place against a distant clamour of moaning animals – the beasts of Smithfield being herded up for slaughter. One does not want to exaggerate the deficiencies of Charterhouse under Russell – there were private schools in the north of the kind later investigated by Dickens, where the pupils simply vegetated. All the same, something of its atmosphere can be conveyed in the fact that day-boys were allowed two minutes' grace to escape the hostile mob of boarders that haunted the premises at the day's end. Both they and the elderly pensioners for whose benefit the place had been founded were 'utterly despised by the reverend brigade who kept all the loaves and fishes for themselves'.

The effect of all this on a diffident and sensitive boy like Thackeray must have been deeply shocking (many years later he told the *Punch* table that the first words spoken to him by an older boy were 'Come and frig me'). He survived, as schoolchildren generally do, by finding friends and establishing a routine that involved the minimum of work and the cultivation of his own interests. Beginning in the tenth form, where Russell's low opinion of his abilities had placed him, he was installed as a boarder in the Reverend Perry's house. Then, at thirteen, he switched to day-boy status. A day-boy at a modern public school normally lives with his parents. In Thackeray's case the change was more technical. In fact he merely went to lodge with a Mrs Boyes, whose son was one of his class-mates, a stone's throw away in Charterhouse Square. This was a great improvement. Mrs Boyes was a kindly woman who took care of her teenaged household. Hearing of her death in 1861, Thackeray reminded his friend Boyes of 'my illness at school and your mother's dear kind face staring over me'. As well as finding a congenial place in which to live, he began to find kindred spirits: John Leech, the youngest boy in the school, whom Thackeray remembered as a diminutive eight-year-old being put up by the bigger boys to sing 'Home Sweet Home'; Joseph Carne, who was his contemporary at Cambridge; William Stoddart, who later became a fellow of St John's College, Oxford; and Richard Gardner, who went on to become MP for Leicester. Other names in the Charterhouse list were to turn up in his writings: Timmins, for instance, and Clive. By 1825, when he had risen to the third form – the gateway to the senior school – the group of associates identified by his daughter included several more boys he would know in later life: James Reynolds Young; Henry Liddell, then in the fourth form, who became a distinguished clergyman; George Lock; Robert Curzon; and Henry Ray Freshfield.

Gradually a circle was establishing itself, in which his personality could begin to flourish. Several friends left memoirs of him at this time. Nearly all of them pay tribute to his charm and geniality. He was no scholar, everyone agreed, but he had a good memory and what John Boyes called the 'power of acquiring language'. At the same time Boyes was adamant that 'no one could in those early days have believed that there was much work in him, or that he would ever get to the top of any tree by hard activity'. Part of the trouble, hindsight suggests, was that he was intimidated by his contemporaries' better scholarship. Riding in Hyde Park many years later with Liddell and his wife, Thackeray suddenly demanded of Mrs Liddell: did she know that her husband had ruined his prospects by doing his verses for him at school and 'destroyed all my chances of self-improvement'? Liddell denied it, but the incident carries the whiff of an intellectual inferiority complex.

Physically, the fifteen-year-old was of medium height, 'a rosy-faced boy with dark curling hair, and a quick intelligent eye, ever twinkling with humour, and *good* humour'. There was a kind of insouciance in him, Boyes thought, a careless self-possession. He went on his friends' fishing trips to enjoy the talk, and hardly knew the difference between a roach and a gudgeon. Beneath this assurance ran a pronounced vein of diffidence. Pressed into service as Fusbos in a performance of William Barnes Rhodes' burlesque *Bombastes Furioso*, he 'did it very well', but could never be persuaded to repeat the experience. The same reluctance to obtrude characterised occasional appearances at a speaking club, where he would sometimes take part 'merely out of good nature', as Boyes puts it. But everybody liked him. He was notably kind to younger boys, rewarded them for running errands and hardly ever seemed to be in a bad temper. The unofficial routines of the place with which the boys beguiled their time appealed to him – Annie remembered him once opening an old schoolbook and finding a secret store of brown sugar, which he had hidden there thirty years before – along with the presence of London and its promise of entertainment. Without doubt he made his way around the stalls of Bartholomew Fair, which took place in the adjoining streets every September, stared at the lions and turned over the barrowloads of woodcut pamphlets at a halfpenny each. 'To get away from Smithfield, and show our best clothes in Bond Street was always a privilege,' the narrator of *Philip* recalls. More often than not this meant the theatre, which provoked some of Thackeray's most acute attacks of middle-aged nostalgia. The reminiscent fifty-year-old remembered stages 'covered with angels, who sang, acted, and danced'; Miss Chester and Miss Love of the Adelphi Theatre; Mrs Serle and her forty pupils at Sadler's Wells. Above all, there was the solace of scribbling pictures and caricatures. This never failed him, he once told a friend, as he could *always* do them. The other boys brought him requests: Don Quixote tilting at the windmills, for instance, or scenes from Shakespeare. Liddell remembered a burlesque of *Macbeth* with the thane of Cawdor as a butcher waving a bloody knife and Lady Macbeth, in the person of the butcher's wife, cheering him on.

As he reached his late teens, the question of a career began to exercise his parents' minds. For all the promptings of family history, the East seemed to have lost its allure. Mr and Mrs Carmichael-Smyth had cut their old ties. More to the point, perhaps, India had changed since the days of Thackeray's grandfather and Peter Moore. The government was whittling away the power of the East India Company, and the prospects for ambitious young men were less enticing. His father's fortune would assure him of a basic income – £18,000 invested in government stock would produce just over £500 a year – but not enough to make him a gentleman of leisure. Thackeray never had any hankering for the army (presumably money could have been found to buy him a commission) or the Church, and he seems to have settled on the idea of the Law, post-Cambridge, in a spirit of mild resignation. Meanwhile, there were the remaining terms at Charterhouse to be got through. Later letters to his mother combine lively reports of his amusements with an increasing contempt for Dr Russell. A note from June 1827 mentions a visit to the theatre to see the comedian Charles Matthews. In February 1828 he was at the Adelphi, admiring the celebrated actress Mrs Yates. 'She is so pretty, and so fascinating and so ladylike also – I need not go on with her good qualities' (what Mrs Carmichael-Smyth thought of this passion for actresses is not recorded, but she cannot have approved). But these last terms – it had been decided that he would leave the school in May – were dominated by the grisly spectacle of Dr Russell. In mid-February Thackeray told his mother that Russell was treating him with such flagrant unkindness that he could hardly stand it. It was so hard, Thackeray complained, when one tried to do one's best 'to find your attempts nipped in the bud – if I ever get a respectable place in my form, he is sure to bring me down ... He will have this to satisfy himself with, that he has thrown every possible object in my way to prevent my exerting myself.'

Thackeray seems to have guessed that Russell's temperamental failings were really a kind of displaced anger at the school's declining rolls. 'He has lost a hundred boys in two years, and is of course very angry . . .' Thackeray was anxious to be borne away on this retreating tide. 'There are but 370 in the school, I wish there were only 369.' It might have been an epitaph for his six-year stay at Charterhouse.

Holidays were a different matter. At first these were spent at the army school in Addiscombe. In 1824, however, Major Carmichael-Smyth decided to live on the half-pay pension allowed to retired officers, and removed himself and his wife to Devon, where they rented a house at Larkbeare near the village of Ottery St Mary. It was a relatively remote location – coming back from Charterhouse on top of the Exeter coach one winter, Thackeray was so frozen by the cold that he had to be handed down by the other passengers – but he relished his visits there. Becalmed in rural Devon, Major Carmichael-Smyth turned farmer, cultivated the soil and handed out flagons of cider to his reapers. After their peripatetic life in India and the Home Counties, the Carmichael-Smyths enjoyed the solidity of this placid West Country existence: to their last days, Annie recorded, they used to talk avidly about Devonshire people and places. A more settled life allowed them to expand their household to include Mrs Carmichael-Smyth's orphaned niece Mary Graham (sometimes known as 'Polly'), four years younger than Thackeray, who lived with them until her marriage in 1841 (although Thackeray wasn't above borrowing money from her in the hard-up 1840s, he eventually came to think her precious and 'spoiled' by her Devonshire friends).

The house, approached by way of an overhung beech avenue and a pond, 'pretty and lonely, with trees and shadows all about it', springs into life in a series of sketches that Thackeray later compiled for his friend Edward Fitzgerald. One drawing takes in the front of the house, with its porticos and straight windows. Another shows Thackeray on horseback, arms folded, looking up at the moon. There are further representations of armchairs, sparkling fires, singing kettles and the young artist in *déshabillé* lounging among this household inventory. The Fitzgerald drawings are of a slightly later date, but they confirm the attractions of Larkbeare, and also Thackeray's habit of using it for sketching practice. A visiting cousin remembered opening a drawer to find it crammed with drawings done on the backs of letters, bills and calling cards. Many years later Thackeray transferred much of the Larkbeare atmosphere to the Pendennis family home of 'Fairoaks':

Charterhouse sketches (including scrap of lottery ticket)

Pen's white duck trousers hung out on the currant bushes to dry, the servant bringing in the afternoon tea of bread and butter, and Mrs Pendennis' quiet, serious piety plainly derive from this source. As a young man on the verge of adulthood, Thackeray probably came to find this environment faintly constraining – *Pendennis* has a good picture of its *jeune premier* hero spending his last, restless days there before leaving for university – but as a boy he hated returning to school. His mother's present of a diary at about this time roused mixed emotions. He welcomed the gift, but had immediately to register in it 'that sad day when Doctor Birch's young friends were expected to reassemble'.

In the event, Thackeray left Charterhouse a month or two prematurely. On Good Friday 1828 he felt unwell on the way to chapel, and was soon lying ill in bed at Mrs Boyes' with a fever. He remained there for several weeks before being sent back to Larkbeare to recuperate. While it is impossible to diagnose the exact nature of his complaint, it was serious enough to delay his entry to Cambridge and compel him to spend several months recovering his strength. He endured the standard nineteenth-century remedy of having his head shaved and wore a wig until the hair grew back (this incident is faithfully reproduced in *Pendennis*, where the old Major's *coiffeur* is pressed into service). There was one lasting physical consequence, too: in the second half of 1828 he grew nine inches, to reach a height of six feet three. This was an enormous height for an early Victorian, when five feet nine was considered tall. Thackeray was proud of these extra inches. Meeting the willowy parson Samuel Hole later in life, he immediately suggested that they measure up (the result was a tie), while visiting a fairground freak's booth once with his even loftier friend the journalist Matthew Higgins, he was heard to whisper to the proprietor that they too were 'of the profession'. Now, at seventeen, taller, thinner and balder, he wrote a whimsical convalescent letter to Boyes, asking about the 'absurd' stories of the bankruptcy of their friend Carnes' father, and claiming that 'I have been quite rural since I came down here. I know turnips from potatoes and sheep from carrots, but my chief excellence lies in the strawberry.' Another schoolfriend, James Hill, received a variation on this theme. 'I lead a most Arcadian life . . . I wander around the fields with thick shoes on, I admire the beauties of creation, I smell thereof, I converse with the husbandmen, I store my mind with rustic perceptions &c.' Major Carmichael-Smyth, whose qualifications for the task were perhaps dubious, undertook to prepare his stepson for Cambridge. He later told Annie, a touch implausibly, that Euclid was 'like child's play' to Thackeray, who went through the first book at a gallop. His grasp of other subjects was less sure: he disliked algebra and for the rest of his life professed not to understand the difference between latitude and longitude.

Charterhouse, where he had remained for six years, left its imprint on Thackeray – literally in the case of his nose, which, broken in a fight with a boy named Venables, gave him his characteristic prize-fighter's profile. Though Annie claimed that he rarely spoke of the place within the family circle, much of his literary output – and his conversations with other men – shows an eagerness to establish both what he thought about his individual experiences and the overall nature of the public-school system. On one level, the mature Thackeray is the worst kind of educational pundit: the man whose early bitterness sometimes blinds him to the fact that not all schools are the same, and whose later nostalgia plays the trick in reverse. At the same time the depth of his feelings for Charterhouse, pro and anti, open a window into some of his most deeply felt anxieties: his desire to belong, to see children treated honestly and openly, and the power that tradition was capable of exercising over his mind.

Thackeray's early glances back at his schooldays are highly critical. A sharp letter addressed to his mother from Cambridge maintains that 'I have not that gratitude and affection for that respectable seminary near Smithfield which I am told good scholars always have for their place of education; I cannot think that school to be a good one, when as a child I was lulled into indolence & when I grew older & could think for myself was abus[ed] into sulkiness and bullied into despair.' His early writings strike the same caustic note: whisky-sodden old wrecks whose only distinction was that they won the prize for Sapphics; throwaway remarks to the effect that torture in an English public school is as licensed as the knout in Russia. His Christmas Book for 1848, *Dr Birch and His Young Friends*, in which a pretentious private school is seen from the vantage point of a timid assistant master, paints a devastating picture of brutality and neglect: Dr Birch is a shallow old snob who delights in fawning upon a mentally enfeebled nobleman's son placed in his care. In later life, though, the public school got irrevocably caught up in the general softening of Thackeray's attitudes to past time and his own past experience. Old Colonel Newcome ends up as a Charterhouse pensioner and actually dies murmuring the word 'Adsum' as the chapel bell peals in the distance. Heaven, as John Carey observes, was a public school. Given what we know of Thackeray's early life there is a huge irony in the *Examiner*'s complaint that he had been false to the realities of the Russell regime. Elsewhere, the *Punch* table talk, assiduously recast by Henry Silver during the last five years of Thackeray's life, finds him on the one hand displaying an acute awareness of how unhappy he had been, and on the other reaching out to rekindle the flame of bygone solidarity. How happy they had been forty years before, he remarked to Leech shortly before Christmas 1862, 'breaking up at Charterhouse'. Together they reminisced over a moral atmosphere symbolised by 'fresh young voices singing bawdy songs without knowing their intent' (one of these ran, 'Are your apples ripe, are they ready for plucking? How's your daughter Jane, is she ready for . . . etc.', which places it in direct ancestry to Max Miller) and the ghastly ritual of 'circumcision and gob', which apparently involved forcible buggery using the end of a candlestick. Silver himself had been at Charterhouse in the 1840s. 'Three *Carthusians* at table,' Thackeray commented excitedly when he found out. The pull of these old affiliations grew increasingly strong

towards the end of his life: not only did he talk incessantly about his
time there, and keep up with the careers of his old schoolmates, but he
began to revisit the place, and one of his last public appearances, so to
speak, was at a Founder's Day dinner in December 1863.

In a small way the atmosphere nurtured both his literary interests
and his artistic talent. Forty years later Boyes could still remember
Thackeray's parody of a poem by Laetitia Landon that began 'Violets,
dark blue violets' (Thackeray's version went 'Cabbages, bright green
cabbages'). It was at Charterhouse, too, that he became a diligent
reader of 'good English books' and part of an upper-school coterie that
took in magazines of the day, such as *Blackwood's*, the *New Monthly
Magazine*, the *Literary Gazette* and the *London Magazine*. In his memoir
Boyes notes the 'positive intellectual descent' that ran from this school
set to the circle that Thackeray gathered around himself at Cambridge.
He wrote poetry, too – 'devilish bad', as he later told a friend, 'but *then*
I didn't think so'. At the same time there is a less appealing side to this
literary legacy. Charterhouse undoubtedly nurtured the deeply ambiguous attitudes to physical violence and corporal punishment that
remained with Thackeray throughout his life. Catherine Peters has
noted the regularity with which the hero in his writing about schools
turns out to be a big quiet boy, who is reluctant to fight but then
distinguishes himself, and the queer absorption in Thackeray's
accounts of the battle. He was proud of his smashed nose and would
eagerly introduce Venables (with whom he kept up) to acquaintances
as 'my old schoolfellow – spoiled my profile, you know'. This ambiguity
– disliking violence, but secretly relishing its excitement – runs
through his work. A 'Roundabout Paper' of the early 1860s finds him
musing over a bygone boxing match and addressing 'Morality',
personified as a disapproving woman: 'Do, for goodness' sake, my dear

madam, keep your true, and pure, and womanly, and gentle remarks for another day. Have the kindness to stand a *leetle* aside, and let us see one or two more rounds between the men.'

The same ambiguities characterise his attitude to corporal punishment, which simultaneously fascinated and repelled him. Silver's *Punch* diaries are full of chatter about floggings and beatings. At one point Thackeray talks of a recent visit to Charterhouse, where he came across 'one little fellow with his hands behind his back, & a tear upon his cheek, and two little cronies with their arms around his neck, and I knew what had happened and how they'd take him to the bog and make him show his cuts'. There is something rather gloating in this, a kind of voyeurism that sits uncomfortably with Thackeray's genuine sympathy for children, and the tone is maintained in approving references to beating in the later novels. George Warrington laments of the disagreeable Barnes Newcome that '"he was my fag at Eton. I should have licked him more"', while little Rawdon in *Vanity Fair* receives only that amount of beating which is 'good for him'.

Undoubtedly, Thackeray was surreptitiously aware of the sexual element in beating, and there are some particularly nasty moments in the novels when non-violent punishments are described using the imagery of flogging. In *Philip*, for example, Thackeray begins a long passage in this style by remarking that the old Earl of Ringwood, when visiting the Twysden family (his niece, her husband and their children) 'always brought a cat o' nine-tails in his pocket and administered it to the whole household'. The conceit is developed when the French governess ('grinding her white teeth' as she does so) observes in heavily accented English: '"I like Milor to come. All day you vip me. When Milor comes, he vip you, and you kneel down and kiss the rod."' An even more sinister gloss comes in the figurative account of the earl upbraiding his relatives. 'Sometimes the lash fell on papa's back, sometimes on mamma's, now it stung Agnes, and now it lighted on Blanche's pretty shoulders.' Curiously, Thackeray liked to apply these metaphors to himself. In his letters, a bad review is nearly always 'a whipping'. He was coming down to breakfast one morning in New York, during one of his American lecture tours, when a lady blushed and tried to conceal under the table a copy of a newspaper containing an unfavourable criticism. 'I told her I had had my whipping in my private room,' Thackeray loftily observed, 'and begged her to continue her reading. I may have undergone agonies, you see, but every man who has been bred at an English public school comes away from a private interview with Doctor Birch with a calm, even a smiling, face.'

In memory, at any rate. For the moment he was merely glad to have escaped an oppressive regime. As the months passed in sequestered Devon and his health improved, he grew restless to be off. A letter to Boyes from January 1829, a month before his departure, describes a pre-emptive taste of the delights of university life by way of a visit to Stoddart at St John's College, Oxford. A drawing of one of the two wine and supper parties that Stoddart gave in his honour was enclosed: 'one man singing, another drinking – another smoking, a third talking obscenity, a fourth listening to him & so on'. A more sober prefiguration of what might await him at university came in a pair of letters from Carne, who provided 'a mathematical, critical and philosophical account of Cambridge'. Meanwhile, it seems more than likely that Thackeray was luxuriating in his first published work. The evidence for this lies in three slight poems published in an obscure Exeter newspaper called the *Western Luminary* – its full title was *Flindell's Western Luminary and Family Newspaper* – on 4 November, 21 November and 5 December 1828. The first, satirical verses on the recent meeting in support of Catholic emancipation on Penenden Heath, under the heading 'Irish Melody', is unsigned. The second, 'The Tear', is signed 'T'. The third, a twelve-line translation from Anacreon, is followed by the letters 'W.M.T.' Proof that Thackeray wrote these verses is no more than circumstantial. The 'Irish Melody' attribution comes from Dr Cornish, the vicar of Ottery St Mary, from whom Thackeray had borrowed books. The title 'The Tear' is all but identical to 'To A Tear', contributed by the young Arthur Pendennis to the 'County Chronicle', while Thackeray is definitely known to have produced a twelve-line translation 'From Anacreon' for a Cambridge undergraduate paper called the *Gownsman* in December 1829.

None of this is conclusive proof of Thackeray's authorship, although the vigorous description of Pen's career as an apprentice poet suggest that it had some grounding in reality. Better evidence, perhaps, can be produced by tracing a link between four 'Ramsbottom Papers', squibs in imitation of the popular humorist Theodore Hook, which Thackeray produced for Cambridge consumption in 1829 and signed with various forms of the name 'Dorothea Julia Ramsbottom', and five letters that the *Western Luminary* printed a short time later signed

'Dorothea'. Written in a whimsical pre-Victorian style, and featuring discussions between the author and her aged aunt on such subjects as unhappy marriages, the Dorothea letters are pattern exhibits of the kind of material sent in by correspondents to provincial newspapers in the 1820s. The first (published on 11 May 1830) seems connected to Thackeray by a reference to George Robins, the celebrated auctioneer. Robins, who died in 1847, turns up more than once in Thackeray's later writing. He is probably the model for Mr Hammerdown, who presides over the bankruptcy sale of John Sedley's effects in *Vanity Fair*, and his manner of doing business is roundly mocked in the *Fitz-Boodle Papers*. Dorothea's joke about 'the most desirable *freehold* estate ever offered to the public' – one of Robins' pet phrases – looks as if it may have been a first airing of this minor fixation.

What did Thackeray hope to find at Cambridge? Independence, perhaps, although there were shoals of his relatives installed in college combination rooms who could be guaranteed to keep an eye on his progress. No doubt the 'tolerably good fun' enjoyed in Stoddart's rooms at Oxford. Certainly a chance to sample some of the pleasures denied him in Devon: 'Tell him I long to hear about the theatre,' Thackeray had written avidly in one of his letters to Boyes apropos their mutual friend Hines. As the short February days began to lengthen, the Larkbeare preparations followed those that preceded Pen's departure for 'Oxbridge': Mrs Carmichael-Smyth and Polly labelling trunks and filling them with books and linen; his stepfather dispensing sound advice; until at last there came a night when the mail coach stopped at the Ottery St Mary halt, the major's and his stepson's luggage was hauled onto the roof, the two of them stepped inside, and the carriage clattered off along the London Road. The watching figures of Mrs Carmichael-Smyth and her niece receded into the gloom, the lights disappeared and the big house fell into darkness.

IV

Alma Mater

'Perhaps you would like to see how pert priggish & dogmatical
six weeks at Cambridge will have made me.'

Letter to his mother, 14 March 1829

'Even among those who go up to Cambridge under the strongest
necessity, and with the strictest determination to be economical,
very few I believe preserve their purpose entire.'

'Senior Wrangler', 'Struggles of a Poor Student Through Cambridge',
London Magazine, *April 1825*

 afely arrived in London, Thackeray and his
stepfather spent a couple of days paying visits.
Writing home from their lodgings at Slaughter's Coffee House in St Martin's Lane on 23
February, Thackeray reported that he had
been to see Dr Russell – no doubt both
parties found this a gratifying encounter –
Mrs Boyes in Charterhouse Square and Aunt
Ritchie in Southampton Row. The business of preparing Thackeray
for undergraduate life proceeded in tandem. Aunt Ritchie supplied a
letter of introduction to Dr George Thackeray, the provost of King's,
while Major Carmichael-Smyth forwarded his stepson's 'respectful
compliments' to William Whewell, his prospective tutor. Prefiguring
his later dislike of the chilly protocols of pre-Victorian Cambridge,
Thackeray pronounced this gesture 'quite gratuitous'. He had also, he
told his mother, agreed to meet his Uncle Francis the following day,
and, rising to the sartorial challenges of his new home, 'ordered a
bullish coat in blue black with a velvet collar'. He then travelled by
coach with the major to Cambridge to undergo the rituals described in

Pendennis. To matriculate at a Cambridge college in the late 1820s was not a difficult task. Candidates – Thackeray's name had been on the books since 1826 – were introduced to the place by their parent or guardian, presented to their tutor, allocated rooms and kitted out with gowns and mortar boards. There were no academic hurdles to clear: all that was required of an incoming undergraduate was a belief, or at any rate the profession of a belief, in the Thirty-Nine Articles of the Church of England. Subsequently Thackeray installed himself in his new premises (Pen takes up a morning 'with great satisfaction' making purchases to improve the look of his rooms); the boxes began to arrive from Devon – seeing his mother's handwriting on the labels gave him an unexpected jolt – and the major packed his bag and left.

'A *bullish coat*'

Cambridge was stuffed with Thackerays. There was an extensive King's connection that included the provost, vice-provost and two other fellows – so extensive that one wonders why Thackeray's parents settled on Trinity. A large and hospitable collection of relatives apart, what would Cambridge have offered to a boy of seventeen in the late 1820s? Compared to some of the great European universities, the place lay sunk in medieval torpor. With its outdated curriculum and its archaic administrative system, Cambridge was a promising target for a succession of early nineteenth-century reformers. Sir William Hamilton's attack on closed fellowships lay some years off, as did Charles Kingsley's strictures on the combination of social and religious exclusiveness. "'It is not merely because we are bad churchmen that you exclude us . . .'" the narrator of *Alton Locke* (1850) protests. "'The real reason for our exclusion, churchmen or not, is because we are poor.'" Yet critics of the 1820s had plenty of ammunition for their attacks. Leaving aside the curriculum, belatedly updated in 1824 with the arrival of a Classical tripos (although aspirants still had to pass the Mathematical tripos first), it was the social basis of academic life that enraged its detractors. The pseudonymous 'Senior Wrangler', a self-confessed 'poor student' who claimed to be the son of a Cumbrian farm labourer, produced an acid sketch of university life for the *London Magazine* in the year before Thackeray was entered for Trinity. The student population divided into three. On the one hand were 'fellow-commoners' ('the liveliest sons of ignorance'), often army officers or married men 'who sit on this gown merely to escape certain exercises and restrictions to which they would otherwise be liable'. On the other came a category of 'pensioner' – young men of independent means, usually with good allowances from their parents. Beneath them reposed a group of 'sizars', scholarship-winning students of humble origin with their eyes on curacies or teaching jobs.

These social demarcations were made worse by what critics diagnosed as institutional laziness and pretension. The supposed opulence of donnish life was a standing joke in the 1820s. J.G. Lockhart's novel *Reginald Dalton* (1823), for instance, describes an Oxford freshman's first encounter with his provost. Reginald is conducted into 'a very handsome house, furnished in every part in a style of profuse modern luxury, such as did not quite accord either with the character of the edifice to which it belonged, or with the form and structure of the different apartments themselves'. The provost's library, similarly, is dazzlingly well accoutred, with magazines and Maria Edgeworth's novels to hand, soft chairs in red morocco, a parrot-cage by the window and a poodle sprawling on the hearth-rug. High standards were not perhaps to be expected from this kind of academic sybarite. Lectures, according to 'Senior Wrangler', were little more than desultory conversation – 'meagre, unconnected and barren', a waste of time for the serious student, who tended to look elsewhere for his instruction. A consequence of these low standards, and the dons' eagerness to evade their teaching responsibilities, was the rise of the private tutor: young fellows of colleges, or recent graduates, to whom Thackeray and other 'reading men' would go for extra-curricular tuition. The disadvantages of this second tier in the teaching profession were obvious. If a man of genuine ability were awarded a fellowship, he was likely to expend most of his energies on his private pupils. There was one further snare awaiting the newly arrived undergraduate, 'Senior Wrangler' considered. 'The tradesmen of Cambridge will give credit to almost any amount, without any enquiry as to the means of the student. They are perfectly aware that his future situation will be such as to compel him, at whatever personal privation, to meet their exorbitant bills.'

Thackeray's destination was one of the largest and most prestigious colleges in this anachronistic seat of learning. At this point in its long history, Trinity was halfway through the mastership of Christopher Wordsworth, youngest brother of the poet: 'not a strong man', according to a later college historian, 'nor always judicious, but he had the good of the Society at heart, and was ever willing to spend himself in its service'. This sounds like a peculiarly genteel form of damning with faint praise, but in fact Trinity under Wordsworth harboured several notable scholars: Sidgwick the geologist, for example, or the distinguished mathematician George Peacock. All the same, a reputation for good living endured, and the cookship of Trinity was supposed to be worth as much as Wordsworth's mastership. Generalisations about undergraduate life in such a large establishment – there were several hundred students in residence – are probably unhelpful. Social groupings were heterodox: aristocratic dead-heads; hard-reading scholars; devout clergy in embryo; dissolute gambling men killing time before proceeding to their regiment or a life of dissipation in London. Intellect was not of course synonymous with hard work, and the narrowness of the curriculum encouraged many really clever men not to read for honours, but to sit for a pass degree while occupying their time with private study. Glimmerings of the social organisation that would characterise university life later in the century were also faintly in evidence: a Trinity boat club was founded at about this time to add to legions of impromptu debating societies and discussion groups. And from beneath a placid exterior rose the scent of religious agitation. The burning issue of Wordsworth's tenure was compulsory chapel, with the master grimly sticking pins into a list of names each morning to register attendance.

Knowing what we do about Thackeray's youthful habits and inclinations, it is easy enough to say that Cambridge was probably the worst place in England to which to send him. In the event, he spent little more than fifteen months there, idled away his time, despite countless resolutions to the contrary, fell into bad company and left without taking a degree. Undoubtedly, some of this was the fault of Cambridge and its strait-jacketed curriculum – the 1830s are littered with clever men who got no good from the place, including Thackeray's friend Edward Fitzgerald – but most of the blame lies with Thackeray himself. He was happy there, or so he claimed, in an environment full of familiar faces and beguiling newcomers, with the chance to organise his own affairs and distinguish himself in minor ways, but in the end lack of self-restraint pulled him down. Critics have often assumed that Pendennis' adventures at 'St Boniface College, Oxbridge' are a portrait of Thackeray's Cambridge career, but the picture of undergraduate life they supply is slightly misleading. On a very basic level, Pendennis, who cuts a considerable public dash, has his verses for the chancellor's poetry medal printed up in morocco bindings and enjoys cosy dinners with titled friends, is a much more conspicuous figure than Thackeray ever was. At the same time his debts are nothing like as great. Tracking Thackeray through the haze of wine parties, student conversazioni and pious resolutions to do better is not easy. His chief confidante, inevitably, was his mother, to whom he wrote on a weekly basis. A 'Roundabout Paper' from the last year of his life notes how Swift, in addressing his beloved Stella, would begin a fresh letter as soon as the last one was sent – 'never letting go the kind hand, as it were' – which is an exact description of his own Cambridge correspondence. For all the letters' vividness and (predominantly) high spirits, it is often necessary to read between the lines – the number of references to how hard Thackeray has been working is suspicious to say the least – to establish how he really spent his time, and the guilt that accompanied failings of which he was very much aware.

His rooms were on the ground floor of the front quadrangle, just to the right of the Great Gate – not a good place for study, as the location encouraged casual callers. One remembers Cousin Jasper's advice to Charles Ryder in *Brideshead Revisited* to change some similar accommodation: "'I've seen many a man ruined by having ground-floor rooms in the front quad ... Before you know where you are, you've opened a free bar for all the undesirables of the college.'" There were some distinguished former neighbours. Newton and more recently Macaulay had lived on the staircase, and Thackeray could not resist suggesting that posterity would add his name to the list. It was from here, in early March – in an age that was less scrupulous about such things, he had arrived in the middle of the Lent term – that he wrote his first letter home to his mother. He had returned to his rooms in rather low spirits after the major's departure, he recorded, and found himself just too late for lectures. It was an unhappy portent, but he consoled himself by going to tea at Mrs Thomas Thackeray's (then a very elderly lady – she had been born in 1737), the mother of his cousin Dr Frederick Thackeray, where the vice-provost of King's, Martin Thackeray, was present. The next few days brought a meeting with his private tutor, Henry Fawcett – Thackeray had reso-

'A decided reading character'

lutely chosen to read for an Honours degree – who looked 'a decided reading character', election to the Union and a wine party hosted by his old Charterhouse friend Carne. There were plenty of old Carthusians studying at Cambridge, and the majority of Thackeray's initial circle was drawn from this convenient reservoir. Trinity at this time was full of men who would go on to distinguish themselves in public life – Alfred Tennyson and his two brothers, Richard Monckton-Milnes, A.W. Kinglake, author of the Eastern travel book *Eothen*, and John Sterling – but it is difficult to insinuate Thackeray into this kindergarten of promise: his acquaintance with Tennyson, for example, seems not to have begun until his mid-twenties. Much of his free time at the start of his Cambridge life, naturally enough, was taken up in visits to his extensive collection of relatives. These included not only the King's connection, but Mrs Pryme, whose husband George was professor of political economy. These social calls had mixed results. Of the wine on offer at Martin Thackeray's, his cousin enthused, 'O such hock! never did I drink such hock', while regretting that only half a bottle made do for three people. Walking, either on his own or with Carne, was another relaxation. A trip to nearby Trumpington in early March supplied a vignette that could have come out of one of his novels. Strolling past a house, he and Carne heard the sound of a guitar and a woman's voice singing. The song was familiar and the two undergraduates joined in the chorus, until the rapid unlocking of the front door sent them on their way. A moonlit walk near Addenbrooke's Hospital brought a different kind of upset, when Thackeray fell into a ditch.

Already one can see a pattern emerging in these letters home: solemn resolutions to apply himself, coupled with mild disparagement of undergraduate diversions, which fail to conceal his enjoyment of them. Wine parties, he told his mother in early March, were 'miser[ably] stupid things . . . I shall keep clear of them'. A week later, though, he was bragging about his taste in wine and revealing that five men had come to his room uninvited, purposely to drink his Sauterne. None the less, he proposed to start 'a more regular course of reading than I have hitherto done'. The scheme of work that he outlined to his mother sounds horribly onerous: studying with Fawcett on alternate mornings from eight till nine, an hour's mathematical tuition from nine till ten, another hour with his classical tutor Hare, then an hour's reading with an undergraduate named Badger, followed by an hour and a half on Euclid or algebra. This impressive regimen was to be rounded off in the evening with an hour spent at 'one or other of the above or perhaps some of the collateral reading connected with the Thucydides or Aeschylus. This is my plan wh. I trust to be able to keep.'

Mrs Carmichael-Smyth's view of this ambitious study programme has not survived, but she seems already to have been sending back a certain amount of cautious advice: at one point, for example, Thackeray maintains that he finds no harm in Carne's idleness – on the contrary, 'for I am always rebuking him, & consider I ought to act up to the principles I profess'. One wonders whether his mother had already marked Carne down as an unsuitable acquaintance for her supposedly diligent son. Later letters from the Lent term show Thackeray apparently keeping up his studies, while sampling what to Mrs Carmichael-Smyth would have been more acceptable leisure pursuits. The Union debates, in which Carne was making a name for himself, seem both to have enticed and repelled Thackeray. Persuading himself to speak in a debate on the character of Napoleon, he was happy to confess that 'I have exposed myself'. Carne, who had gone on first, performed in 'a fluent and easy manner'. Attempting to emulate this casual mastery, however, Thackeray 'got up and stuck in the mud at the first footstep. Then in endeavouring to extract myself from my dilemma, I went deeper and deeper still.' Although he told his mother that this would be his only appearance in the debating chamber, it is clear that there were issues on which Thackeray had formed an opinion and hankered for a chance to talk about. Only the next day he informed Mrs Carmichael-Smyth that he might try to retrieve himself in a debate on the renewal of the East India Company's charter – a subject he knew something about, and on which he might have a better chance of distinguishing himself. It was at this time, too, that he signed the petition got up by the Trinity undergraduates against Catholic emancipation, after Lord Lansdowne's claim in the Lords that all 250 Trinity men were ready to approve a document in its favour. No doubt Mrs Carmichael-Smyth, a rabid anti-Catholic, approved.

The Easter vacation was now looming. This would normally have called for a visit home, but Thackeray, who had exams to sit in the summer, seems to have stayed at Trinity to work. Social life, though, continued to figure largely in his letters: watching a boat race with his Charterhouse friend Thomas Mazzinghi ('There are generally a thousand gownsmen on the banks who hie down to the place where the boats start; & accompany them on their return . . . I ran but it was very hot!'); eating a gargantuan breakfast with Badger, which gives a good idea of Thackeray's youthful appetite (two pigeon pies, two muffins, eggs, rolls, sausages, radishes); and, as he reassured his mother, getting the hang of wine parties. 'Yesterday I was at one, & drank a glass & a half of wine – Today I was at another and drank just the same quantity.' On 1 April he hosted his own gathering, at which, he informed his mother, 'the men were very sober. There were scarcely five bottles of wine drunk.' Fifteen years later, when he came to write 'University Snobs' for *Punch*, Thackeray was markedly less discreet. 'One looks back on what is called "a wine party" with a sort of horror,' he recalled. 'Thirty lads round a table covered with bad sweetmeats, drinking bad wine, telling bad stories, singing bad songs over and over again. Milk punch – smoking – ghastly headache – frightful spectacle of dessert-table and smell of tobacco – your guardian, the clergyman, dropping in in the midst of this – expecting to find you deep in Algebra, and discovering the gyp administering soda water.' Did Uncle Francis Thackeray, who seems to have succeeded Peter Moore in the role of guardian in the 1820s, call unexpectedly at Thackeray's rooms and witness such a scene? Whatever the reality, Thackeray had certainly spent money in the first few weeks of his Cambridge life. Whewell's bill for the term came in at £157. 'I am told that even this is moderate,' he explained to his mother.

Amid the distractions of his new life – planning an essay club with some fellow Carthusians, squatting in the absent Carne's rooms while his own were redecorated, exploring the countryside with a sketch-pad ('this country is of course ugly in the extreme but there are a number of quaint old buildings, and pretty bits scattered about') – the presence at Cambridge of so much of his old life, in particular the large number of old schoolfriends, encouraged him to take stock. Throughout his life Thackeray was prone to anniversary reflections, considering what he had been doing on a particular day in a particular year and analysing the change of circumstances. In later life the response was usually simple gratitude that he lived in such a comfortable house with a well-stocked cellar, and that his daughters were fed. As a man in his thirties, beset by care, he often tortured himself with the memory of past happiness. As a boy of seventeen, though, he was confident that the path ran upward. On the anniversary of his departure from Charterhouse he summed up his feelings to his mother. Now he was 'sitting at Cambridge writing a letter home with a mind perfectly contented with the change the year has wrought in my situation'. Material for these ruminations had been provided by the presence in his rooms of two old schoolfriends, talking about Charterhouse doings. Thackeray had not been impressed.

A year later Thackeray would be a great deal less contented. For the moment, with the summer exams in prospect, he was full of good intentions, intending to begin 'a course of ferocious reading', and, in a backhanded compliment to the excellence of the Trinity cuisine, resolving to put himself on a diet. There were other sides to his life, however, of which Mrs Carmichael-Smyth knew comparatively little, or indeed nothing at all. He had probably by this stage made the acquaintance of a man named Henry Matthew, a local celebrity – he was president of the Union in 1830 – who introduced Thackeray to the fast gambling set (Matthew is the original of the swindling Bloundell-Bloundell, who encourages Pen to dissipate his allowance in dice games). More innocently, he had launched himself into the world of the Cambridge undergraduate magazines. Thackeray seems to have come up to Cambridge with the aim of involving himself in this side of undergraduate life, and an early letter to his mother mentions an unrealised scheme for a paper to be called *The Chimaera*. *The Snob*, which ran for eleven numbers between 9 April and 18 June 1829, was a much more concrete proposition. Founded by a fellow Trinity undergraduate named W.G. Lettsom, and published by the prophetically named W.H. Smith of Rose Crescent, its full title was THE SNOB: A LITERARY AND SCIENTIFIC JOURNAL, NOT 'CONDUCTED BY MEMBERS OF THE UNIVERSITY' (presumably the addendum aimed to throw the university authorities off the scent). 'Snob', at this stage in its etymological development and prior to Thackeray's own expropriation of the word in the 1840s, meant 'townsman'. With columns devoted to 'Scientific Intelligence' and fanciful notes on 'Icthyology' and 'Nosology', the magazine was determinedly facetious in a style pursued by countless generations of undergraduates. Thackeray's first identifiable contribution, a spoof entry for the chancellor's Gold Medal for Poetry, whose subject that year was 'Timbuctoo', appeared in the number of 30 April. Given the title and the medium, the treatment is everything one might expect:

> In the vale of Cassowary
> By the plains of Timbuctoo,
> There I ate a missionary,
> Body, bones and hymn-book, too.

Curiously, 'Timbuctoo' has another footnote in literary history. The prize was eventually won by Tennyson, who adapted some existing verses on the theme of 'Armageddon'. Thackeray's effort takes its place as the first of many burlesques of the kind that he later submitted to *Punch*. Its target – awe-inspired accounts of 'mysterious' Africa – accurately prefigures much of his own travel writing. Faced with exotic climes and imposing scenery, whether actual or recorded by someone else, Thackeray was rarely impressed, and the Eastern traveller, with his book and his circle of admiring women, is a stock joke in much of his early work. The account of Clarence Bulbul in *Our Street* (1847), who smokes a Turkish pipe and likes to sit cross-legged on a pink satin sofa, is prefaced by some caustic remarks on the genre. Has not everybody written an Eastern book, the narrator wonders? 'I should like to meet anybody in society now who has not been up to the second cataract.' With its antistrophic descent into bathos ('There stalks the tiger – there the lion roars/Who sometimes eats the luckless blackamoors'), 'Timbuctoo' offers a ghostly preview of this kind of satire.

Undergraduate magazines are usually collaborative affairs, and it is difficult to establish Thackeray's authorship of particular pieces with any certainty. The 'Ramsbottom Papers' – Hook's Mrs Ramsbottom was an illiterate vulgarian who committed serial murder on the English language – are full of the clanging puns and cheerful malapropisms that later characterised the *Yellowplush Papers*, while a letter to his mother confirms that he was at least partly responsible for a 'tragic drama' entitled 'The Blood-Stained Murderer' that filled most of issue eight. Throughout the late spring and early summer, work on *The Snob* proceeded hand-in-hand with the serious business of preparing for the Tripos exams. At first the progress reports he provided for Mrs Carmichael-Smyth were mostly encouraging. At the end of April he claimed to be working hard at algebra, a Greek play and history: 'I am so steady & sober that I am quite a pattern . . .' A week later he reported that he had 'read very hard all week'. The prospect of college exams in the middle of May brought a note of caution: 'I am now certain of taking but a mediocre place . . .' He would show them a different game next year, though, he went on, perhaps even try for a scholarship. In the meantime he had walked to Newmarket with Carne.

The Tripos exam took up a week at the end of May and beginning of June. A fortnight beforehand Thackeray engaged the porter at six-pence a week to wake him up early. Despite his worries about algebra and Euclid – 'If I get a fifth class in the examination I shall be lucky' –

Thackeray was gratified by 'Timbuctoo''s warm reception among the undergraduates. 'I could not help finding out that I was very fond of this same praise,' he admitted. It was all the more satisfying in that no one knew the author's identity: 'how eagerly did I suck it in'. Reminders of boyhood continued to press upon him. He showed Trinity to a credulous undergraduate named Lamb who had been at Chiswick with him (Thackeray had a fine time with Lamb, representing busts of Caesar, Socrates and Demosthenes as former members, and directing him into a lavatory on the pretext that he needed to sign his name there before being allowed into the library – 'such a gaby I never in my life set eyes on'); he also met a gay young spark named Burton, a relic of the old Tunbridge Wells days. Writing to his mother, he was careful to distance himself from Burton's antics: 'a gay fellow commoner, cutting me of course, he had a supper for 30 last night, & the young heroes kept it up till five this morning'. And yet even Thackeray's formal account of his doings to his mother suggests that his exam preparations left much to be desired. A week beforehand he and Lettsom wrote the whole of 'The Blood-Stained Murderer' (a parody of *Bombastes Furioso*, in which he had acted at Charterhouse) in a five-hour stretch that ended at 2 a.m. Thackeray claimed to have been 'so afflicted with laughter' that it made him unwell, and he was ill on and off for the next few days. Fawcett, his private tutor, seemed more a hindrance than a help. At any rate his efforts to get his pupil up to scratch in trigonometry 'hath made that obscure, wh. I before thought that I pretty well understood'.

Exam week came. Thackeray professed himself tired by his exertions ('It is more fatiguing work than walking 20 miles'), so much so that one day he overslept and was half an hour late for the morning's paper. He took a fourth-class degree, and having engaged an acquaintance named Williams (who had recently graduated with a first) as his tutor, set off to spend the Long Vacation in Paris.

Whatever Mrs Carmichael-Smyth's private anxieties – and Thackeray's letters home look to have been carefully composed – the European, or in this case the Parisian, tour was a traditional vacation activity for a young undergraduate of means. Thackeray's three months in Paris with Williams were a formative experience. Though his dismissal of the local sights (Tivoli was 'nothing like our Vauxhall') prefigures nearly three decades' worth of refusing to be impressed by 'abroad', and there were some complaints about the food, he seems to have enjoyed his time there and begun a love-affair with France that, notwithstanding several fallings out, continued until the end of his life. It is significant, for example, that his first full-length publication, ten years later, was the *Paris Sketch Book*, and though his writings are studded with momentary outbursts of Gallophobia, his enjoyment of France and the amenities of French life stayed with him. The Paris trip was also important in another way – it brought what seems to have been his first major disagreement with his mother.

In the *Roundabout Paper* 'Notes of a Week's Holiday', Thackeray carefully re-created his seventeen-year-old self 'in a blue dress-coat and brass buttons, a sweet figured silk waistcoat . . . looking at beautiful beings with gigot sleeves and tea-tray hats under the golden chestnuts of the Tuileries, or round the Place Vendôme, where the *drapeau blanc* is falling from the statueless column'. The image of a teenaged *boulevardier* is a captivating one, and his letters home show him eagerly exploring the byways of Parisian life. Initially he and Williams took lodgings in the rue de Rivoli, before switching to a boarding house run by a Madame la Baronne de Vaude in the rue Louis le Grand near the boulevard. It was Thackeray's first experience of a Balzacian *milieu* that he was to make much of in his novels – polyglot expatriates 'of all Nations' and their servants brought together under one roof. Using this as base, he paid visits to the theatre and the opera, where he glimpsed a 'certain dancing damsel yclept Taglioni, who hath the most superb pair of pins, & maketh the most superb use of them that ever I saw dancer do before'. The description is carefully burlesqued to distance his mother from the very genuine emotional kick. It was his first sighting of the celebrated opera dancer Maria Taglioni (1804–84), later the Comtesse de Voisins. Though Thackeray was subsequently to poke fun at Taglioni and some of the absurdities of the Paris ballet, her name eventually became a kind of touchstone of his view of the past, and the late-period writings are full of nostalgic evocations of having seen her dance. Thackeray was also determined to introduce his own considerable frame (at six feet three, he probably weighed over thirteen stone at this time) onto the dance floor. To this end he took lessons from the renowned dancing master M. Coulon. This had unfortunate consequences, which Thackeray never forgot. Coulon, immensely proud of his personal dignity, was barely four feet six inches tall. Catching sight of a mirror reflection of the pair of them whirling round the room in a waltz, Thackeray could not help laughing. Gravely affronted, Coulon asked that the lessons should cease.

No doubt Mrs Carmichael-Smyth read these letters with considerable misgivings. A letter written on Thackeray's eighteenth birthday notes of the boarding house confraternity that 'They are most inordinate card players here, & I am told play rather high.' There was also a fascinating Mrs Twigg, separated from her husband on account of the latter's ill treatment of her, whose name recurs perhaps a little too obviously. But Thackeray seems to have been enjoying himself. He liked Williams, the hours of study he undertook with him each morning ('as different to that of my late worthy tutor as you may fill up the simile according to your imagination') and the saunters round Paris, even if Notre-Dame was not as fine as Exeter Cathedral ('the organ there only plays on particular days, & the whole place hath an appearance of dirt and decay wh. ill accord with an Englishman's idea of the great National temple'). If there was a drawback, it lay in the number of English people who frequented the house, which made it difficult to get on with his French. By early August the chatter of English voices prompted Thackeray and Williams to take lodgings at 54 rue Neuve, St Augustin, close to the boulevards. Thackeray assured his mother that the change was for the best – 'the boarding house was an idle, dissipated écarte-playing boarding house' as well as being Anglophone. More disquietingly, he records a visit to Frascati's, the great Paris gaming-house. Though he claimed neither to have won nor lost, Thackeray was honest enough to admit that he was powerfully gripped by the spectacle. In fact, unable to tear himself away from the sight of the baize tables, with their low-toned croupiers and eager clientele 'until I lost my last piece', he returned to the rue Neuve to dream about the experience all night, and to think of nothing else for the next few days. And yet, he hastened to assure his mother, he did not *return*.

All this, as Thackeray would have known very well, was storing up trouble. Given his mother's sensibilities, and the kind of sorrowfulness with which her love characteristically expressed itself, there is something almost premeditated in her son's little allusions to Frascati's and Mrs Twigg – the thought that he wished almost to challenge his mother over the style in which he led his life and his right to independence. To make this point is perhaps to unbundle a range of quite complex emotions, but we can see that while on the one hand, Thackeray wished to experience what Paris had to offer the tourist, on the other he knew that much of it would be distasteful to his parents. At the same time he wanted to be honest with the breakfast-table audience at Larkbeare. It would not have occurred to him to remain silent about his visit to Frascati's, but he knew that the revelation would anger Mrs Carmichael-Smyth. Lying beneath it, perhaps, was a desire to explain to her the kind of things that now interested him. The Paris letters are full of unselfconscious glances at his developing self: his absorption in the cult of Napoleon – M. Ori, who taught him French, had served under the emperor; a dissertation on Shelley that he intended to write for the still embryonic *Chimaera*; a realisation that the rigorous Cambridge curriculum bored him. 'My taste for Mathematics does not increase,' he told his mother early in August, 'my taste for old books and prints much.'

On 2 August 1829 a thunderbolt arrived from Larkbeare. Mrs Carmichael-Smyth's original has not survived, but it is clear that she reproached him for having gone to Frascati's. Thackeray's reply, written the instant he read it, such was his indignation, must have taken courage to write. The same motive that would have led him to the theatre had taken him to the gaming-house. Had he not done so, '*I should never have arrived at a piece of self knowledge which I can conscientiously thank God for giving me.*' By watching professional gambling he had 'discovered my temperament & inclination with regard to it, and the necessity wh. I did not then know of avoiding it'. Why should he be blamed, Thackeray quite reasonably wondered, for discovering through his own efforts information that would be useful to him? It is his peroration, though, that strikes the most resounding note. Mrs Carmichael-Smyth seems to have assumed that what took her son to the gaming-table was a desire for money. Thackeray denied it. 'May God grant that you never again call me avaricious and mean when I am but curious,' he sternly reproached his mother, 'that you never again think because I before was ignorant that therefore I was good; or that because I am now aware of my own weakness I must be wicked.'

This is powerful stuff for an eighteen-year-old of any era, let alone an only son fixated on his mother writing in the last year of the reign of George IV. Mrs Carmichael-Smyth's reply is not preserved, but Thackeray's next two letters home betray something of its contents and the tensions that now underlay their relationship. The first, written in early September, and containing 'best love to all at Larkbeare', is full of affectionate good humour, but it reveals that Mrs Carmichael-Smyth had ordered him to sever his connection with Mrs Twigg (among Thackeray's arguments in favour of a woman he thought ill used by her husband was that 'I never heard her speak a word wh. was not perfectly lady-like'). In a second letter, written a short time later, he proposes to return direct to Cambridge rather than visiting Larkbeare. The excuse offered is pressure of work ('I have read but not *got up* what I have read, I fear my acquirements would not tell in the Examination Room'), but it is difficult not to feel that Thackeray thought it better to avoid his parents, in the light of Frascati's, Mrs Twigg and who knows what quantity of maternal reproach.

In fact it seems clear that something had temporarily gone wrong between Thackeray and his mother. Only two letters from him survive between the autumn of 1829 and the summer of 1830 – this from a man who customarily wrote home on a weekly basis. Did he stop writing? Were the contents so painful to his mother that she did not care to preserve them? Whatever the explanation, the absence of letters makes the outlines of Thackeray's last year at Cambridge recede into a fog of guesswork. But these were significant months, if only from the vantage point of personal affection. It was at the rooms of his vacation tutor Williams, early on in the Michaelmas term, that he met a shy, diffident undergraduate named Edward Fitzgerald. Thackeray immediately took a liking to 'Fitz', went walking, sketching and singing with him, and addressed increasingly sentimental vacation letters either to his parents' house at Woodbridge in Suffolk or to the home of his married sister at Geldeston in nearby Norfolk. Fitzgerald was a wealthy young man with £300 a year, which later allowed him to lead what he fondly described as the life of a 'genteel gypsy' and produce his celebrated translation of the *Rubáiyát of Omar Khayyám* (1859). John Allen, another lifelong friend met at this time, was a much more sober proposition – a notably serious and devout undergraduate (he later became archdeacon of Shropshire), pious to the point of priggishness, but anxious for Thackeray's welfare and tolerant of his friend's habit of arriving at his own rooms to sit talking and sketching while Allen attempted to work.

Whatever the influence of Fitzgerald and Allen, the implication is that Thackeray's undergraduate career was running off the rails, and that wine parties and gambling began to take the place of algebra. In a note of 1 November he claims to be 'studying hard', while the final Cambridge letter to Mrs Carmichael-Smyth, written three weeks later amid bitter cold, again doubts the wisdom of a vacation visit home, 'for I fear I must read to take anything like a respectable degree'. Was

Thackeray studying, as he claimed? He certainly had time for extra-curricular activities that autumn, joining a seven-man debating society (the participants included Allen, Henry Alford and William Thompson, who left a record of its activities) whose members convened in each other's rooms to discuss topics such as the diffusion of knowledge and 'whether luxury is necessarily an attendant of Civilisation'. Thackeray spoke on 'Duelling'. Thompson, writing many years later, noted that 'we did not see in him even the germ of those literary powers which under the stern influence of necessity he afterwards developed'. *The Snob*, too, enjoyed a revival, or rather reincarnated itself as the *Gownsman*, appearing in seventeen numbers between the beginning of November 1829 and the end of February 1830. Though fragmentary, and mostly undetachable from a mass of jokes and puns, Thackeray's contributions seem to have been extensive. The issue of 12 November contains a Ramsbottom letter in which the authoress bids her readership 'a Jew' – the pun prefigures the wordplay of *Yellowplush* – and recommends purchase of the *Gownsman*, to which she is going to send some 'poetic diffusions'. Copies of the paper that may have belonged to Fitzgerald suggest that Thackeray also produced items such as 'I'd be a tadpole' (a parody of T.H. Bayly's enormously successful 'I'd be a Butterfly'), the translation from Anacreon previously mentioned and 'An Extract from the Diary of the late Thomas Timmins' – 'Timmins' being a stock comic name in Thackeray's work. Ephemeral as all this was, it is not fanciful to see the kernel of Thackeray's later involvement with *Punch* in these early bouts of undergraduate journalism, and *Punch*, with its cargoes of bad jokes, humorous sketches and piecemeal drawings, was produced in the same atmosphere of high-speed collaboration.

The Christmas vacation seems to have been spent in Cambridge, although Thackeray kept up a correspondence with Fitzgerald (a letter from Fitz to Allen, sent from Geldeston in January, asks that Thackeray send a drawing, 'as his are very much admired here'). But there was something nagging at him. The entries in Allen's diary for the early part of 1830, crammed with references to his friend, suggest a man scarcely at ease with himself, weighed down by religious doubts, full of remorse for unspecified past sins and resolving to do better. Early in February, for example, Allen writes that he and Thackeray had 'some serious conversation' in which Allen 'affected him to tears', after which he went away 'with a determination tomorrow to lead a new life'. Four days later Thackeray was back, expressing doubts as to whether Christ was equal to God. Allen hauled down a copy of St Matthew's Gospel, expounded the relevant verses '& he was convinced thank God for it'. There were further religious discussions in the following months, and a walk in which Thackeray is suddenly apostrophised as a 'poor dear fellow'. It is difficult to know which aspects of Thackeray's life Allen was concerned with – he was an excessively serious man, whose later comments on their mutual friend William Brookfield, whom Thackeray met at this time, are stuffy even by the standards of the 1840s – but clearly he was worried. It is clear, too, that Thackeray had taken to confiding his troubles to Allen, and that various aspects of his behaviour weighed heavily on his mind. What had he done that so alarmed him? For even the most mildly dissipated undergraduate, the Cambridge of the late 1820s offered every conceivable temptation. Leaving aside limitless credit, the town had a substantial population of prostitutes, whose activities were more or less tolerated by the authorities. Overseas visitors in the early Victorian period noted the corrosive effect of the place on a generation of young men mostly intended for the Church. Whether or not Thackeray patronised these 'Cyprians', as they were known, he would certainly have had friends who did, and while it is impossible to prove his authorship of an obscure drinking song in their honour, which is sometimes attributed to him, the flavour of the verses is highly reminiscent of some of the gentlemanly bawdy of the *Punch* table.

At the end of the Lent term he sat the Previous Examination, or 'Little Go', which at this time consisted of 'one of the Four Gospels, or the Acts of the Apostles, in the Original Greek; Paley's Evidences of Christianity; and one of the Greek, and one of the Latin Classics'. He took a second – not the relative distinction it sounds as over 200 undergraduates, including most of his friends, were given firsts. Practically speaking, it was the end of his undergraduate career. In any case his allies were slipping away. Fitzgerald had left and gone to Paris, which gave Thackeray the opportunity for a surreptitious vacation jaunt. Having got hold of twenty pounds from somewhere, and told Whewell he was staying with friends in Huntingdonshire – Mrs Carmichael-Smyth presumably received the usual excuse about hard work – he took ship for Calais. Thirty years later Thackeray could not quite get the thought of this duplicity out of his mind. 'Guilt, sir, guilt remains stamped on the memory,' he told the readers of the *Cornhill*, 'and I feel easier in my mind now that it is liberated of this old peccadillo.'

Other than that he stayed with Fitzgerald, we know of only one significant episode that occupied Thackeray's time in Paris at Easter 1830, but it is an intriguing one, which may well have had profound implications for his work. The circumstances were recounted eleven years later in an article that Thackeray, then in serious financial straits, wrote for the *Britannia* magazine. According to this account, it was Shrove Tuesday and he and some other 'great raw English lads' had turned up *en masse* at one of the vast pre-Lent public masked carnival balls (Thackeray's chronology is slightly suspect here – we know from Allen's diary that he was at Cambridge until as late as 31 March, but Lent that year began some weeks before). As he was staring at the throng, a woman whom he did not recognise tapped him on the arm and invited him to walk up and down the room. Flattered, Thackeray accepted. 'Mlle Pauline', as she styled herself, was about thirty-five, dressed like a man in dirty white trousers, a dirty white shirt, an oilskin hat with ribbons and a greasy wig. Thackeray's interest was redoubled when she enquired: Did he not remember her? The mask removed, he recognised a governess in an extremely sober English family whom he had met some time before. Mlle Pauline explained that, with her charges now outgrown the need for a governess, she could have returned to England – she had excellent references from her employers – but had opted for the Bohemian life of Paris. Subsequently Thackeray sought her out in the far from fastidious back-streets of the rue du Bac, where he found her 'eating garlic soup in a foul porter's lodge' and was conducted up six flights of stairs to a shabby apartment, where they discussed the half-dozen pairs of shirts that Mlle Pauline, by profession a seamstress, might make for him. No one need be in any doubt as to what went on in the seamstress's attic, amid the smell of garlic and the clacking of pigeons in the eaves, and the Thackeray who wrote the incident up for the *Britannia* would have expected his more sophisticated male readers to take the hint. A much later remark, made to the *Punch* table about having 'had a governess' in Paris thirty years before, can only refer to Mlle Pauline. It may even have been she who gave him the bout of gonorrhoea whose after-effects bedevilled his later years – though the infection healed, it left him with a urethral stricture that grew worse as he grew older. At any rate the reference, again to his *Punch* cronies, to his 'old complaint', which he had had 'thirty years', suggests an all too exact knowledge of its origins.

Who was Mlle Pauline? The mention of 'Sir John's family', in which she had worked, is deliberately vague, though Thackeray family tradition suggests that they came from Devonshire. The resemblances between the Parisian *grisette* and Becky Sharp – the latter's appearance at a masked ball, even her enticing Jos Sedley up the stairs to her shabby lodging-house chamber in Pumpernickel – have been endlessly picked over by critics. Whether or not Mlle Pauline is a model for the schemer of *Vanity Fair*, she is a good illustration of Thackeray's developing taste for resourceful, dashing and not necessarily particularly scrupulous young women who came his way. Mrs Twigg, with her marital difficulties and tales of injured innocence, was perhaps the first of these. No doubt the Parisian boarding houses in which Thackeray lodged, then and in later years, produced others. Theresa Reviss, the mistress of his friend Charles Buller, whom he met shortly after this, seems to have inspired similar feelings of cautious fascination. Undoubtedly the young Thackeray enjoyed puzzling out what seemed to him to be female ambiguities. There is an intriguing reference in one of his letters home from his first Paris trip where, amid a heap of fragmentary remarks, he tells his mother that 'I can not find Miss Sharp out by no means'. Who was Miss Sharp? Presumably her name occurs because Thackeray mentioned her in a previous letter that has not survived, or because he assumed (wrongly) that he had referred to her before and that his mother would know who he was talking about. But 'find out' carries the sense of 'get to the bottom of', and Miss Sharp, whoever she was – and whatever the later significance of her name – looks as if she falls into the category represented by Mrs Twigg and Mlle Pauline. Thackeray liked modesty and 'purity' in a woman – in Mrs Brookfield he was later to find the epitome of both – but he also liked a touch of Bohemian flamboyancy, something that the ex-governess who had pawned her gown to procure her 'disgusting old dress' for the carnival was well able to supply.

He went back to England in mid-April, not relishing the forty-hour coach trip from Paris to Calais. Money was in short supply. At Dover, having booked his seat to London, he had just twelve shillings left. Thirty years later Thackeray could remember the bill for his evening's entertainment – 'dinner 7s, glass of negus 2s, waiter 6d, and only half-a-crown left, as I was a sinner, for the guard and coachman on the way to London'. Notwithstanding the charms of Mlle Pauline, he seems to have been slightly subdued by his illicit holiday. Fitzgerald reported back to Allen that 'Thackeray came and turned away all my sorrow to joy; for I was really delighted to see him.' But in another letter, three days later, he describes his friend as 'a little gayer when I saw him last: but as kind as ever. He tells me he had not seen so much of you last term,' Fitzgerald innocuously concludes. In fact Allen's diary shows that he and Thackeray had met on nearly forty separate occasions between the end of January and the end of March 1830.

Whatever his private feelings, Thackeray seems already to have decided to leave Cambridge. There were various plans afoot. 'Has Thackeray got the commission in the Registrar's Office?' Fitzgerald enquired of Allen in May. Thackeray, meanwhile, was trying to persuade Allen to give up his own studies in favour of a schoolmastering job in Pimlico. Driving these schemes, perhaps, was lack of money. Whatever funds Thackeray was allowed by his parents seem to have been dissipated by this point. Presumably he was bailed out of the penury in which he found himself on the return trip from Paris, but he owed Fitzgerald five pounds, and Allen, who 'called on Thackeray about Fitzgerald's money' at the beginning of term, failed to secure it until 13 May. In any case, this was a drop in the ocean compared to the debts Thackeray had accumulated in other quarters. Exact details are sketchy, but by this stage in his undergraduate career he had been introduced – probably by the fast-living Henry Matthew – to a set of professional card-sharpers. These, sensing Thackeray's passion for play and susceptibility to flattery, took rooms opposite Trinity, invited him to dinner and, on a succession of evenings, playing at écarte, relieved him of promissory notes to the value of £1,500 – an enormous sum when the wage of the average governess (Mlle Pauline, perhaps, in 'Sir John's family') was forty pounds a year. Thackeray, still nearly two years short of his twenty-first birthday, had no control over his fortune: the debts would await his majority. Hard-up, and with the consciousness that he had failed to distinguish himself academically, he left Trinity in June 1830.

What had Thackeray got from Cambridge? First of all, some resentments. Fifteen years later he was still lampooning 'Doctor Why-ouwewyowhewell', by this stage Master of Trinity. Most obviously, it had awakened in him a profound distaste for social pretension and exclusiveness of any kind. *The Snobs of England*, written fifteen years later, contains some withering attacks on the dignitaries of 'St Boniface', 'Crump' and 'Hugby'. Crump, the college president, is characterised as a man of pedantic learning and colossal personal arrogance ('When the allied monarchs came down and were made

Doctors of the University, a breakfast was given at St Boniface; on which occasion Crump allowed the Emperor Alexander to walk before him but took the *pas* himself of the King of Prussia and Prince Blucher'). Crump is a former charity boy and brags about it. Hugby, on the other hand, the son of a Seven Dials haberdasher, has risen 'by kindness to the aristocracy'; a letter beginning 'My Lord Duke' lies unfinished in his lecture-room for a whole term. This is slightly unfair to Whewell, Crump's original, who was a considerable scholar – he has some claim to have pioneered the study of philosophy at Cambridge – but was handicapped by an unfortunate personal manner (as his biographer tactfully put it, 'though he was anxious to be hospitable, his sense of the dignity of his position led to a formality which made the drawing room anything but a place of easy sociability').* None the less, it is possible to locate much of Thackeray's later attitude to snobbery, if not the whole basis of his analysis of social hierarchies, in

Card-sharpers

* Stories of Whewell's legendary indifference to his students were still circulating in Cambridge as late as the 1880s. On one occasion he was informed by his servant that a list of invitees to a forthcoming wine party contained an undergraduate who had died the previous term. 'You ought to tell me when my pupils die,' Whewell is supposed to have remonstrated.

his period at Cambridge. At the same time Thackeray was honest enough to admit that by these standards he had been a snob himself, prone to look down on poor students who never missed chapel and carried off the college scholarships.

Above all, Cambridge gave Thackeray, through his own experiences, two characteristic figures in his writing: the callow, impressionable young man who is waylaid and fleeced by a more sophisticated predator. 'Captain Rook and Mr Pigeon', a savage early dramatisation of this theme, contains a devastating sketch of 'Young Rook of Trinity' who, while trying to excel academically, lives in 'the very best set', loses money gambling, fails at a fellowship, ruins his family and becomes a continental card-sharper with a set of duelling pistols in his valise.

What was he to do? The Carmichael-Smyths presumably sat in conclave, but there are no letters to hint at their deliberations. In the end Thackeray accepted that he would probably have to study Law. In the meantime, his cousin Martin Thackeray, who perhaps should have known better, had suggested that 'every young man shd go abroad after he had taken his degree'. Or given it up as a bad job. To his parents, Thackeray proposed a mini-version of the Grand Tour, which would take him to Germany. What the Carmichael-Smyths thought is not recorded, but they accepted the idea. His short-term future was mapped out, but his friends could not restrain their anxieties. 'What is to become of Thackeray?' Fitzgerald wondered to Allen in late July 1830, immediately before their friend set off. It was a good question.

V

Weimar Days

'I really think the Rhine is almost equal to the Thames.'

Letter to his mother, 31 July 1830

'In my reading & my pursuits here I have had a freedom which I never enjoyed in England – & I hope you will feel the benefit it has done me.'

Letter to his mother, 31 December 1830

Though the Continent lay enticingly before him, Thackeray's departure was delayed. He was trying to get away, he told his mother, but everywhere was closed, owing to the death of George IV. Eventually, in the week of his nineteenth birthday, he secured a passport, his passage and letters of introduction to Dresden, including one guaranteed to introduce him to 'the best literary society of the place'. His final days in England brought a characteristic tug of will with his mother. Mrs Carmichael-Smyth wanted him to stay with friends near the family's old haunts at Charlton. Thackeray pleaded the excuse of pre-booked German lessons, but his real interest seems to have lain in watching Edmund Kean's farewell appearance. He carried the day, and subsequently sat through a marathon performance by the great tragedian that included excerpts from *Richard III*, *The Merchant of Venice*, *Macbeth* and *Othello*. Then he was off on the Channel packet, presumably to Bruges, though a letter to his mother outlining progress seems to have got lost in transit. On the last day of July he wrote to report that he had arrived in Koblenz by way of Rotterdam: a thirty-six-hour trip in which the press of passengers obliged him to sleep on the open deck. 'I was out all the night, but managed to sleep snugly on the top of some coats . . .' Thoughtfully, he furnished his mother with sketches of the scenery and his fellow voyagers. For all his lively interest in his surroundings – the views of distant castles, ancient buildings crowding the shore – he was still the epitome of the cockney traveller, telling his mother that 'I really think the Rhine is almost equal to the Thames.' To complement the scenery there was a pretty girl to whom he talked 'the most delightful sentiment and quoted Shelley and Moore to her great edification and delight'. But she turned out to come from a Boulogne school, and he gave up the pursuit, consoling himself with dinner and a visit to the town of Bad Ems, nine miles from Koblenz, 'a beautiful place, magnificent old houses, old turrets old bridges & c'.

What was Thackeray like in the first weeks of his twentieth year? This is not such an idle question as it sounds. Nineteenth-century novelists had wildly differing upbringings and outlooks. Dickens' early trials are a biographer's staple. George Eliot spent her formative years in rural seclusion in Warwickshire. Trollope went to Harrow, but lived in the shadow of his father's debts. James Hannay, to take a representative minor specimen, was pitchforked into the navy at thirteen. These early experiences played an irrevocable part in the kind of people they were and the books they wrote. By the standards of the 1830s – there were early Victorian schoolboys who had never seen the sea – Thackeray was a fairly cosmopolitan young man: travelled, apparently sexually experienced, and the heir to what, despite the gambling debts, was still a substantial amount of money. His interests, too, were increasingly obvious to him. He liked the theatre, and the kind of people associated with it – an upper-Bohemian world of actors, singers, minor writers and librettists. He was also increasingly confident of his ability to move within it: quite capable, for instance, of asking the Jewish *improvisatore* Charles Sloman to dine with him in London and feeling disappointed when Sloman turned him down. There is an engaging kind of amateur worldliness in the letters to his mother from the immediate post-Cambridge months, an enthusiasm for the horizons opening up before him. However unenthusiastic Thackeray may have been about the prospect of a formal career, he was always searching for ways to satisfy his literary and artistic ambitions, and his letters are full of plans to translate German ballads, write a treatise on German manners or put together a German sketchbook. Doubtless there is something in the idea of an idle, pleasure-loving young man frittering away his time in continental watering holes, which occasionally surfaces in portraits of Thackeray. At the same time, his preparations for the German trip show that he regarded it as an experience from which he might bring back definite literary capital – capital, more to the point, that he was confident of his ability to make something of.

Slowly, and without having any clear idea of where he was going, Thackeray drifted down the Rhine to Godesberg. There was a plan to travel to Bonn, a few miles inland, but at Godesberg he fell in with an old Cambridge acquaintance, Franz Schulte, and changed his mind. If he were to join Schulte's party, he explained to his mother – the other members were a tutor from Jesus College, Oxford, and his pupil – Schulte would give him daily German tuition and, as one who knew the country, 'engage that I should live at as cheap a rate as at any place in Germany'. Together with Schulte he attended a student club ('The men are raw dirty rough looking cubs with little caps & long pipes,' he noted fastidiously) and watched their principal leisure activity – the provoking of duels. Six or seven of these were got up, but on going to inspect the fighting a day or so later Thackeray discovered that it was

largely ceremonial, and only one minor wound was actually inflicted. Ferocious amounts of wine were drunk, but after a year and a half of Cambridge port and punch, the effect on Thackeray was 'like so much milk & water' – or rather vinegar and water, he explained, in reference to an upset stomach. This observation of German undergraduate life imprinted itself on his memory, and the Pumpernickel chapters of *Vanity Fair* contain some closely reported student slang.

Three days later they were still at Godesberg. Thackeray read a German grammar, complained of fleas (one of his eternal laments about foreign travel), contemplated an 'Essay on Miracles', and wondered whether to attempt to translate Schlegel's *Lecture on the Fine Arts* (to which Schulte had introduced him) into English. Early September found them heading towards Dresden, via Cologne and Elberfeld, with the idea of staying with Schulte's parents. The effect of the July revolution in France had spread to northern Germany and the steam-boats on the river were bringing down troops in their thousands to deter potential agitators, but Cologne was 'comfortable & English-like' – so like England, in fact, that Thackeray was able to dine off roast beef and a glass of port. The destination changed again when news came that Schulte's sister had broken her leg and that his mother was unwell. Instead Thackeray set off for Kassell, reporting to his mother that the Schlegel book was 'spurious' and enclosing 'a new & pleasant ballad' of his own composition, entitled 'The Legend of Drachenfels'. The crags of the Drachenfels, passed on the way down to Koblenz, appear in Byron's *Childe Harold*. Thackeray's dozen sprightly stanzas turn on the depredations of a cannibal beast ('I could say he eat off fowl or fish/Alas – he eat *Maiden ladies!*'). In this way, reading,

idling and versifying – there was another, quite funny poem about the fleas – and after nearly two months' travel, he came at last to the tiny principality of Weimar.

In normal circumstances, perhaps, he might have stayed a week and then moved on. As chance would have it, he discovered Lettsom, his old *Snob* collaborator, staying with a German family and preparing for a career in the diplomatic service. Lettsom represented the place as 'exactly suited' to his friend's habits. Thackeray had made enquiries, he informed Larkbeare, '& found he was in the right, for without letters of introduction I have got into the best society of the place'. Weimar, at this point in its history, was an extraordinary little backwater of for the most part bygone European life. One of the thirty-two German principalities that had emerged from the break-up of the old Holy Roman Empire, its minute dimensions – ten miles in one direction to Jena, the same distance in the other to Erfurt – were balanced by a lofty, if by now pretty much antiquated, cultural status. Grand Duke Karl Augustus, who had lavishly patronised the local artistic life, was three years in his grave; most of the place's early-nineteenth-century luminaries (Schiller, the philosopher Johann Gottfried Herder and the playwright August von Kotzebue) were dead. Goethe, alone among this pantheon of German literary life, lived on into old age. But Weimar's genuine, if receding, cultural allure is hardly sufficient to mark out the place's oddity in the eyes of the average foreign traveller. Essentially the English visitor found there a kind of miniature version of the grand society he might expect at Dresden or Berlin, full of absurd ceremonies and formalities – there was a tiny army of a few hundred men – its social life dominated by the

Grand Duke's court and a magnificent *Hoftheater*, with a European reputation for classical German drama. Simultaneously, the area's quasi-rural character brought an odd air of seclusion to all this courtly bustle. There were only two hotels of any size in the place – the Erbprinz and the Elefant. One contemporary English visitor was moved to compare Weimar to the country residence of an English nobleman – a ducal seat, say, with a small town attached to the castle and park, the only difference being a collection of resident literati, bookshops and concert-rooms. At levels below that of the court, life was frugal, and in general Weimar had the feel of 'a remote country situation, where the people seem contented with little, where turf-fires are burned to save wood, and where, if there is no want, there is, at the same time, no luxury'. Amid the profusion of monuments to a past age there was a single living tourist attraction. Goethe was not always accessible to his countrymen, but he rarely refused to see an English visitor, and enjoyed airing his knowledge of Scott and Byron. Taken together these were faded glories, and Thackeray summed up something of the principality's sepia tint in a letter to his mother: 'It must have been a fine sight twenty years ago, this little court, with Goethe Schiller & Weiland and the old Grand Duke & Duchess to ornament it.'

But there were plenty of fine sights here in the diminished present. In particular, Thackeray was immediately seduced by what he called the 'charming polite societie of Weimar'. He took lodgings in the town with a Madame Melos – there were perhaps a score of Englishmen staying in Weimar at the time – and engaged an idiosyncratic German tutor named Dr Weissenborn, who, with his dog Waltina, pet chameleon, egg collection and what his pupil called 'numerous infirmities of mind and body', was one of the acknowledged characters of the place. Then he set about helping himself to the range of social opportunities on offer to a young and well-mannered visitor. Here again, in its round of winter balls and parties, Weimar life was substantially different from its English equivalent. By the standards of pre-Victorian London, morals were lax: several of the court's leading female lights were the product of irregular unions and enjoyed a degree of freedom that would have shocked the duennas of an average English drawing-room. For all this atmosphere of mild licence, prospective mothers-in-law abounded, and several of Thackeray's letters hint at his adventures among the Weimar husband-hunters. First, however, he had to make himself presentable. Mindful of court etiquette, he had a tailor convert a pair of his trousers into breeches and, thus glorified, was presented to the Grand Duke. He took dancing lessons and, impressed by the array of brightly coloured uniforms worn at court, wrote home asking his mother for 'a very absurd favour'. This turned out to be a cornetcy in Sir John Kennaway's regiment of Devon yeomanry (such commissions could be bought and sold in the days before the Victorian army reforms) – 'the men here are all in some yeomanry uniform', he meekly explained, reassuring Mrs Carmichael-Smyth that 'if hereafter I go to other courts in Germany or in any other part of Europe, something of this sort is necessary as a court dress'. His mother obliged, and Thackeray declared himself delighted by the results, 'Only I don't think the pink rosettes look well on the leather breeches.' Kitted out like an oversized morris dancer, Thackeray launched himself into local society – the court conversed in French, so at least he had no trouble in being understood – attending the theatres and concert performances and promptly falling in love, he informed his mother, with the Princess of Weimar, 'who is unluckily married to Prince Charles of Prussia'.

Although Thackeray appreciated the local theatre – he took a keen interest in the arrival of Ludwig Devrient, the celebrated German actor, and his wife Wilhelmina Schroeder – he seems to have been less immediately concerned with Weimar's intellectual attractions. In some ways this was to be expected. Carlyle's opinion, expressed in a letter to his brother Jack a year or two before, that 'Paris and London will stand throughout one's whole life and longer; but only one Goethe will be visible in this world, and that only for a short term of years', was not widely shared in England. Anglo-Saxons tended to distrust Goethe for what they saw as his dubious morals, in particular his liaisons with much younger women. The ambiguities of *Faust* and *Die Wahlverwandtschaften* (*Elective Affinities*) were no better, particularly in the primitive translations then circulating in England. *The Sorrows of Young Werther*, whose hero takes his own life as a consequence of his passion for a married woman, had been marked down as sentimental rubbish by English critics for the best part of half a century. Without doubt Thackeray shared – and continued to share – something of this prejudice, and his account of his first visit to the old man is given in a couple of non-committal but faintly self-congratulatory sentences (Thackeray implied that Goethe greeted him 'ver[y] kindly & rather in a more distingué manner than he used to the other Englishmen'). This relative indifference is odd, given that the author of *Wilhelm Meister* was, according to most contemporary accounts, a sight worth seeing: 'much like an apparition from another world' as one English observer put it, tall, grave and gaunt, but animated by a 'latent and subdued energy'. Thackeray was already a keen student of human quiddity, as can be seen from his relish of Dr Weissenborn's eccentricities, and yet the spectacle of one of the great monuments of recent European culture seems to have left him cold. Perhaps, on the other hand, he was simply steering clear of a subject of which his mother could be guaranteed to disapprove.

At the same time he was vigorously pursuing his other interests. He met Goethe in the third week of October, but an earlier letter already refers to the two women whose presence amid the round of parties and social events would absorb him for the next two months. A hundred and seventy years later, and given that most of what we know, or can guess, about them is refracted through the pages of Thackeray's fiction, the pair provide an odd study in contrasting personalities. Melanie von Spiegel, a maid of honour at the Weimar court and one of its acknowledged beauties, seems to have been an amiable and rather plump-looking girl. A surviving portrait of Jenny von Pappenheim – one of Weimar's several love-children, in this case the illegitimate daughter of Diana von Pappenheim and Prince Jerome Napoleon – shows a good-looking, if faintly intense young woman with dark eyes and hair. She was clever, and connected to the intellectual circle collected around Goethe's daughter-in-law Ottilie, which produced a literary magazine, *Das Chaos*. Presumably Thackeray's introduction to the *Chaos* set – contributions were anonymous and part of the fun for insiders was guessing their authors' identities – came from this source. Exactly what happened in Thackeray's relations with the two, sitting out dances and making small talk under the Grand Duke's chandeliers, is unclear. Writing many years later, Annie hints that he was more attracted to Melanie, but feared that he was the subject of a husband hunt. However, barely a week after their first meeting he was describing Jenny to his mother as 'the prettiest woman I ever saw in my life'. Towards the end of the year he could describe himself as falling in love 'once with a very pretty girl, & secundo with a very clever & amiable one'. Thackeray's frankness to his mother on the subject of these apprentice passions is one of his most engaging characteristics: assurances that these were merely innocent flirtations and that he was not to be taken seriously mask an occasional hint that his emotions were genuinely aroused. Presumably Larkbeare accepted the letters as Thackeray meant them to be read, for Mrs Carmichael-Smyth's replies, in so far as we can reconstruct them, seem more interested in the question of her son's church attendance.

Inevitably, the romantic undertones of these letters come mixed up with a great deal of mundane detail and evidence of Thackeray's continuing fascination with the odd routines of Weimar society. He approved of the *Hoftheater*, where the boxes were laid out gallery-fashion so that patrons could walk from one to another and pick out people to talk to. He suspected Madame Melos of swindling him, and threatened to go elsewhere unless he got cheaper terms. Amid the task of acclimatising himself to a range of new experiences and protocols, he was keeping up his literary interests. A letter to Miss Wilkie, the Charterhouse bookseller, dating from the end of October asks for copies of *Fraser's*, the *Literary Gazette* and a copy of *Bombastes Furioso* with Cruikshank's illustrations (in later life this would turn into a talismanic volume, trailing Thackeray around his work – as late as *The Newcomes*, the unpleasant Marquis of Farintosh is persuaded to appear in an amateur performance, taking Thackeray's old role of Fusbos and feebly breaking down). Meanwhile the flirtations of the ballroom continued and then, as far as we can judge, came to an end. Certainly by the close of the year Thackeray was telling his mother that 'Two months ago I was in love with two young ladies – but the day dream hath passed away, & I am left without a flame . . . & without a being who cares two pence whether I stay or go.' Again, it is impossible to establish exactly what took place. His estrangement from Jenny seems to have occurred when he was cut out by a wealthy young ex-guardee

'*Smitten by beauty*'

named Du Pré, but much of the trouble may have stemmed from the presumption, which Thackeray himself had encouraged, that he, too, was heir to a large fortune. Undeceived, the marriage-broking old ladies took their revenge, 'and as the respectable old dowagers find they can make nothing of me they almost cut me'.

In confessing this romantic disillusionment to his mother, Thackeray adopted a mock-solemn tone. He is not, you suspect, looking for sympathy, merely for an audience to whom he can represent himself as a man of the world, or at any rate an apprentice version by whom Mrs Carmichael-Smyth will be amused rather than alarmed. All the same, he felt strongly enough about Melanie and Jenny to make them the subject of two highly autobiographical sketches written ten years later as part of the series of Fitz-Boodle's Confessions contributed to Fraser's. The Honourable George Savage Fitz-Boodle, one of the many authorial personae in whose name Thackeray addressed magazine readers of the 1840s, is a languid, philistine, club-lounging swell ('To say I am a Fitz-Boodle is to say at once that I am a gentleman'); subsequently Thackeray revived the series to include his 'professions', in which this scion of ancient nobility sets up as an auctioneer and an organiser of dinner parties. The 'Confessions' find him arriving in the tiny German principality of 'Karlsbraten-Pumpernickel' (the town 'contains a population of a thousand inhabitants, and a palace which would accommodate about six times that number') and paying court, successively, to two young women named 'Dorothea' and 'Ottilia'. The sketch of Dorothea patently refers to Melanie von Spiegel's somewhat rotund charms. 'She was none of your heavenly creatures, I tell you. No, sir, she was of the earth earthy, and must have weighed ten stone four or five if she weighed an ounce.' Their association ends with a ballroom collision with another couple that sends both participants spilling onto the floor. We know that an accident of this kind actually took place, as Thackeray refers to it in a much later letter. Suitably reinvented, the incident reappears throughout his fiction (for example in Pen's misfortune with Blanche Amory) as a symbol for youthful pride unexpectedly brought low.

Subsequently Fitz-Boodle transfers his affections to 'Ottilia von Schlippenschlopp, the Muse of Karlsbraten-Pumpernickel'. Ottilia, transparently a play on Frau Goethe's Christian name, is of an intellectual cast: 'an historian, a poet, a blue [i.e. bluestocking] of the ultramarinest sort, in a word'. On one level the two girls are separated by their tastes in reading: 'What a difference there was, for instance, between poor simple Dorothea's love of novel-reading and the profound encyclopaedic learning of Ottilia!' In the end, though, the sketch reveals itself as an early attack on the elevated sensibilities and supposed affectations of the Goethe school, which turn up repeatedly in Thackeray's later work – the mockery of Blanche Amory, for example, with her sorrowful poems and secret tragedies. Ottilia, ominously enough, is 'pale and delicate. She wore her glistening black hair in bands, and dressed in vapoury white muslin. She sang her own words to her harp, and they commonly insinuated that she was alone in the world, that she suffered some inexpressible and mysterious heart-pangs . . . that she was of a consumptive tendency and might look for a premature interment.' This is hapless Blanche to the life, and one of the most regular themes in Thackeray's fiction – silly young women who get a kick out of thinking gloomy thoughts and fancying themselves heart-broken. Significantly, though piqued, Fitz-Boodle is much more sympathetic to the news of Dorothea/Melanie's marriage 'for the truth is, he has been a good, honest husband, and she has children, and makes puddings, and is happy'. The moral is the age-old one of making the best of the situation and talents allowed you, and Fitz-Boodle is especially caustic about Ottilia's literary magazine, again shamelessly modelled on *Chaos*, full of 'affected gloomy ballads' in which 'she never would willingly let off the heroine without a suicide or a consumption'. Repeatedly winged by accusations of pretentiousness and insincerity, Ottilia is finally brought to earth by a much more prosaic failing – gluttony. 'Marry a sarcophagus, a cannibal, a butcher's shop?' Fitz-Boodle wonders, having watched one of her performances at table. After seeing her wolf nine bad oysters at a sitting, he resolves to give the affair up.

Even at a decade's remove from the events that inspired them, the failings attributed to this brace of old flames are unremarkable. Dorothea/Melanie is too fat; Ottilia/Jenny writes affected poems and overeats. Similarly, Fitz-Boodle's mockery of Ottilia's poetic get-up simply mirrors the conventional English response to continental Romanticism – that it had no basis in ordinary life, and encouraged people to think and behave in ways that were at best silly and at worst morally corrosive. All the same, the imagery in which Thackeray expresses these dislikes marks the start of something central in his work. The siren, hunched over her harp far beneath the surface of the ocean, picking over the bones of dead mariners, is a characteristic figure in Thackeray. The idea of sinister, white-clad women, often with bare arms, who entice unwary men into their dens and consume them, obsessed him. While Ottilia's 'glistering black hair' and 'vapoury white muslin' are sinister enough, it is Fitz-Boodle's remark about marrying a butcher's shop that really strikes home – the image has somehow got out of hand, left the vantage point of recorded experience and gone to rest deep in the writer's subconscious. But it takes on an even more dramatic shape in a sketch-book Thackeray compiled for a young English girl named Caroline Vavasour during his time in Weimar. Even by the standards of the early Victorian age, when *The Fairchild Family*, whose grim paterfamilias takes his children to watch executed convicts hang in their chains, was thought 'improving' reading for the young, this contains some odd subject matter. Of the two stories, illustrated by vivid caricatures, the first recounts the marriage of 'Count Otto von Blumenbach' to 'Ottilia, Amelia, Melanie, Jenny von Rosenheim'. The bride turns out to be a corpse-chewing cannibal who pays nightly visits to the churchyard to satisfy her habit. The second features a mother who kills and eats her own son. Her husband, at first reluctant, is eventually persuaded to cast aside his scruples and join her in the feast. This was a queer gift for a small girl in the 1830s but imagery of this kind clearly excited Thackeray's imagination. A vividly executed sketch, which probably dates from this time, shows a grinning, necrophagous imp chewing on flesh from a grave whose tombstone reads 'WT OB 1802'.

'Minna Löwe', another of Fitz-Boodle's revelations, provides a further angle on Thackeray's time in Germany. Fitz-Boodle, at large in

the Cologne/Bonn region, lodges with Herr Löwe, a banker, and his family. The daughter, Minna, is powerfully described. 'I saw her for the first time at a window covered with golden vine-leaves, with grapes just turning to purple . . . The leaves cast a pretty chequered shadow over her sweet face, and the simple, thin, white muslin gown in which she was dressed. She had bare white arms, and a blue riband confined her little waist.' Any student of Thackeray's imagery would be yelling for Fitz-Boodle to leave by this stage, but understandably enraptured by her 'heavy blue eyes' and 'full red lips', he decides to stay. At first he engages a man named Hirsch to act as his go-between. When they fall out, Hirsch proposes a duel but is outmanoeuvred by Fitz-Boodle's flat refusal to demean himself by fighting a Jew. Eventually it transpires that Minna is a decoy, the lure by which Frau Löwe is inducing him to buy inferior goods at inflated prices. The story climaxes at a dance where Hirsch, supported by Minna, rounds on his rival. Many years later Fitz-Boodle catches sight of her in the front box of the Frankfurt theatre, married to Hirsch (who appears alongside her and has bought her a title), dripping with diamonds and weighing all of sixteen stone. Thackeray suppressed 'Minna Löwe' from later editions of his work – its anti-semitism had upset readers of *Fraser's* even in the Jew-baiting 1840s – but it is easy enough to recast it in autobiographical terms. The highly charged description of Minna sporting with a pipe – 'a pair of red lips kissing the amber mouthpiece with the sweetest smile ever mortal saw' – suggests that at some point in his travels down the Rhine Thackeray did encounter someone like Fräulein Löwe, and that something resembling the events of the story did indeed take place.

All this careful unpicking of old scars lay in the future. For the moment, despite the quenching of his romantic fires, Thackeray seemed happily immersed in Weimar's winter routine, noting Devrient's performances as Lear, Shylock and Falstaff, asking his mother for a warm winter coat, exclaiming – in sharp contrast to Fitz-Boodle – over the cheapness of the local tobacco. Towards the end of the year, though, a more thoughtful note creeps into his letters. These show that the fundamental disagreements between mother and son over choice of career, conduct, whole attitude to life if it came to that, persisted. Early December found Thackeray musing on whether he could fashion some kind of destiny in the diplomatic service. However, 'Most of the men are rich & idle', and Law it must be. The lack of enthusiasm ('As I have thought a great deal on the profession I *must* take; & the more I think of it the less I like it – However I believe it is the best among the positive professions & as such I must take it, for better or worse') is all too tangible. A letter written on the very last day of the year, one of the most interesting and powerfully expressed that Thackeray ever wrote to his mother, raises an even more nagging anxiety. Thackeray begins by confessing that his mother's letters always upset him, on account of 'some hidden causes of dissatisfaction', which Mrs Carmichael-Smyth neither admits to nor conceals. He suspects that his mother takes it to heart that he gave up Cambridge. Perhaps, Thackeray suggests, he was too young to form opinions, but form them he did '& these told me that there was little point in studying what could after a certain point be no earthly use to me'. It had been the same at school – he had not been stupid, but had achieved nothing. Yet his mother should not attribute this lack of achievement to simple idleness. Charterhouse had imposed a 'discipline of misery' whose aim was 'to improve & instruct me', and against which he deliberately rebelled.

This is a highly reasoned analysis of upbringing for a boy of nineteen, in which deficiencies of character are unfailingly located in environment (later the idea that people's behaviour is substantially formed by the circumstances in which they find themselves was to be one of his more controversial themes). Affectionate, but still determined, Thackeray goes on to reassure his mother that he does not blame her for the deficiencies of his schooling: any other choice might have had the same result. But now that he is old enough to think for himself he will do what he can to pursue a different course. He has tried to subdue these feelings, but cannot. As for his mother's letters, 'I have been almost afraid to open them knowing the reproaches & the misery which not the words but the tenor of them convey.'

Mrs Carmichael-Smyth's response to what, practically speaking, amounted to a declaration of independence has not been preserved. Whatever may have passed between them, his next surviving letter – from mid-January 1831 – returns to a more routine account of his doings. Having detected Madame Melos 'in one or two flagrant instances of cheating', he has changed his lodgings to the house of the court cooper in the Breiten Gasse; his reading is taking him 'through regions of wh. one has only heard, as of a Paradise to which only the elect are admitted'; his taste for backstage theatrical life has been whetted by a trip to Erfurt to see Schiller's *The Robbers* (banned from the Weimar stage) and by an introduction to Devrient. But another letter from the end of January returns to the earlier theme, apologises for the outburst of a month before ('an absurd & unkind effort on my part to put off the sense of my own unworthiness by laying it on *you*') and rather humbly enquires, 'Shall I then return to England and begin on my profession?' It is possible that Mrs Carmichael-Smyth had invoked the spectre of Richmond Thackeray, for his son notes that at the same age his father had spent five years in India. He ends by asking his mother not to despair of him: 'I will go to the bar not a good mathematician, but a good lawyer.'

But not quite yet. In the event Thackeray lingered in Weimar until mid-March – it was nearly eight months now since he had left London – working up an enthusiasm for Schiller, whom he thought second only to Shakespeare as a poet, and proposing to return to the principality at some point and undertake 'a survey of the woods and country of it wh. are little known'. In expressing his views of Goethe to his mother he was careful to separate the work from the life, or rather from the reputation. Goethe was, Thackeray concluded, 'a noble poet, & an interesting old man to speak to & look upon as I ever saw, but alas that I must say it – I believe he is little better than an old rogue'. This was the standard English drawing-room view, and would presumably have satisfied Mrs Carmichael-Smyth. Other aspects of her son's stay she probably found less satisfactory. Thackeray left Weimar conscious that he had been admitted, however temporarily and with however mixed an emotional result, to a world of substantially expanded horizons. As he put it to his mother in the grand remonstrance of 31 December, 'In my reading & my pursuits here I have had a freedom which I never enjoyed in England – & I hope you will feel the benefit it has done me.' The cultural atmosphere of the place, and the sense of the arts not being a rarefied preserve of the super-refined but a natural part of everyday life, stimulated his own literary ambitions. Back in England he kept up his connection with *Chaos*. Later in 1831 Ottilia von Goethe printed some verses entitled 'The Stars', though she seems to have turned down a translation from *Faust* and a drinking song. There is a notebook fragment, too, from the Weimar days, which sketches an imaginary argument between two footmen waiting at table and seems to contain the germ of the *Yellowplush Papers*. Above all, there is evidence that Thackeray seriously began to think of himself as a writer at this time. Though a German sketch-book never materialised, he was undoubtedly serious enough in his ambition to 'concoct a book wh. would pay me for my trouble, & wh. would be a novelty in England'. Manuscript drafts of

'The Stars' show the care that he was prepared to take with his compositions: a dilettante of the kind in which Weimar, and other places, abounded would have taken less trouble, one feels. If nothing else, literature was a field in which Thackeray was prepared to take pains, and consciously exert himself.

Along with this sharpened literary awareness, Thackeray brought back an abiding interest in German life and literature, which persisted throughout his career. The identification of Weimar with 'Pumpernickel' in *Vanity Fair* is a commonplace – if we are to believe the narrator, the evening on which Devrient and his wife appeared in *Fidelio* at the *Hoftheater* was the night he 'met' Dobbin and Amelia – but close inspection shows that Thackeray's work is peppered with German allusions that can only have had their origins here in this antiquated corner of *Mitteleuropa*. Some of these – dramatising the Newcome election with references to Schiller's play *William Tell* – are standard for the time; others rather less so. There is an odd moment in *Vanity Fair*, for example, when, discussing the incorrigible habit of domestics to sit in judgment on their masters' foibles, he refers to the '*Vehmgericht* of the servants' hall'. This turns out to be a reference to a judicial institution found in medieval Germany – a particularly neat allusion, as the original *Vehmgericht* was used to try crimes such as adultery, and the servants here are interested in Becky's affair with the Marquis of Steyne. Elsewhere, Thackeray's affection for German literature expresses itself in what were, for all the routine dismissals to his mother, some by no means straightforward feelings about Goethe. While he persisted in his view that *The Sorrows of Young Werther* was sentimental rubbish – there was a famous debunking ballad written in 1853 – the picture of his visit provided for G.H. Lewes' biography of 1864 is much more benign, and Thackeray even allows himself to remember (this was not a detail vouchsafed to his mother a quarter of a century before) that the poet's eyes were 'extraordinarily dark, piercing and brilliant'. His writings, too, are full of mostly approving references to Goethe. At one point in *The Newcomes*, for instance, Pendennis' wife Laura compares Ethel Newcome to a 'Bayadere' or Indian dancing girl, as in 'that poem of Goethe' of which Pen is so fond.

Less promisingly, Thackeray the diarist would also use German slang to record the debauchery of his first year in London. Above all, perhaps, there was the memory of his youthful romances, and the wider circle of friends of which they formed the centrepiece. To the

very end of his life he and his friend Dr Norman MacLeod, an old
Weimar compatriot, would wistfully refer to Melanie von Spiegel as
'Amalia' – once, on a lecture tour in Scotland, Thackeray recognised
MacLeod in the audience as he made his way to the platform, bent
down as he passed and murmured, 'Ich liebe Amalia doch.' There was
a sobering re-encounter in the flesh when Thackeray, coming down to
breakfast in a Venetian hotel in the 1850s and glancing at a stout
woman dressed in light green and eating an egg, discovered that it was
his old flame. What he felt about Weimar, and its effect on him, is
perhaps best conveyed in a letter written to Frau von Goethe some
months after his departure, in which he sends the copy of 'The Stars'.
In retrospect, given Fitz-Boodle's satire of 'Ottilia', this is a piece of
irony, but at the time it was undoubtedly sincere. Back in London,
immersed or otherwise in his legal studies, Thackeray gossips
desultorily about mutual Weimar acquaintances before combining a
plea for work with a wholly inaccurate prognosis of his future career:
'Whenever you want anything English, commission me, for now for
the next thirty years I shall be in London 8 months of the 12. At the
end of thirty years, I shall be most likely Lord Chancellor (at least my
mother believes so).' This is youthful self-mockery, perhaps, but there
is a plaintive little coda: 'Were I to ask you to remember me to
everybody who was kind to me at Weimar I must fill another sheet . . .'
At nineteen, despite the call of London, Law and filial duty,
Thackeray had at last glimpsed a prospect of the life he wished to lead.

VI
London and Paris 1831–5

'I was looking back yesterday, & I cannot find a single day in the course of my life which has been properly employed.'
Letter to Edward Fitzgerald, 18 July 1831

'The life I did not lead, the artist's life in Paris.'
Cyril Connolly

y the time he got home Thackeray was ill and had to go back to Larkbeare to recuperate. Whatever the nature of the complaint – and no details are specified – its effects lasted long enough to delay his return to London until June 1831, by which time the Law term was nearly over. It was the second time in three years that illness had postponed a supposedly important step in his career. While the chronic ill health that was to dog his later years was two decades away, there is a suspicion that Thackeray, despite his height and weight, was not a strong man. Certainly, he took little exercise – riding and dancing excepted – and the effect of his prodigious appetite could hardly have helped any underlying frailties in his system. But early summer found him safely installed in London, enrolled with a Mr Taprell, a special pleader of the Middle Temple, the proud possessor of chambers at 5 Essex Court – they cost only thirty pounds a year, which was thought cheap – and, so far as can be deduced from his letters, bored to distraction. 'Miserable and solitary' without the company of Fitzgerald, he saw out the few weeks that remained until the end of term and then headed west again, first to Larkbeare, then to Bridgewater. A letter to Fitz, written on his twentieth birthday, finds Thackeray renewing his acquaintance with some old friends. He had seen Schulte, he reported, and had a row with him over another figure lately resurfaced from his early life. This was Henry Matthew, who – whatever his part in Thackeray's Cambridge excesses – was now 'improved in mind & appearance for he does not look the rake he was'. In Bridgewater he read law books and kept up with his German before going off to stay with Matthew's family, who lived nearby, but he was out of sorts, prone to 'solemn and unpleasant feelings'. He had been looking back on his life to date, he told Fitzgerald, and could not find a single day on which he had been properly employed. It was not an auspicious start to this new phase of his life.

A pencil sketch by his friend James Spedding gives some idea of Thackeray's appearance at around this time. His expression – head set back, emphasising the distinctive profile – is faintly supercilious, with heavily accentuated eyebrows, chin emerging from the folds of a fashionably high stock, itself caught up in the outline of an equally fashionable waistcoat. Dainty spectacles – a characteristic of nearly every Thackeray portrait – cling to the bridge of his nose. He looks a meditative young dandy. This air of reflectiveness is typical of Thackeray's letters from the early 1830s, and their sense of setting out into a world which, for all its compensations, the writer does not much like and indeed rather suspects. World-weariness never loses its appeal to intelligent late-adolescents, of course, but there is a genuine sense of unease about some of the progress reports from Thackeray's early twenties, and the feeling that, quite apart from the money worries that were soon to oppress him, he found it all something of a struggle.

At any rate, as his letters tacitly admit, it was an exciting time to be a young man at large in London. Looking for an adjective to characterise the city in the early 1830s, one emerges, almost routinely, with 'pre-Victorian'. The first Reform Bill, which would symbolise the social basis of the Victorian age, was looming on the horizon. Metropolitan life was concentrated on a couple of square miles, and its inhabitants were highly visible. The Duke of Wellington could be observed walking in St James's, while the heirs to £10,000 a year looked on from the bay-windows of the nearby gentlemen's clubs. This is an exaggeration, but not much of one. There is a scene in *Pendennis*, for instance, in which Pen, out walking with his uncle, encounters the duke and is hugely gratified when Wellington gives the old man a pair of aristocratic fingers to press. It is difficult not to believe that something like this happened in life, and Thackeray greatly admired a friend who came to the duke's aid during a public altercation over Reform. By and large it was still an upper-class world – Wellington himself had been kept out of Almack's ballroom a few years before on the grounds that he was incorrectly dressed – into which the middle-class adventurers of the 1840s had yet to penetrate. Captain Gronow, a Regency buck who survived to ornament the salons of the mid-century, makes the point that Hyde Park, then a collection of semi-rural meadows where cows and sheep grazed under the trees, remained substantially an upper-class playground – 'regions which, with a sort of tacit understanding, were given up exclusively to persons of rank and fortune'.

Thackeray was not of this world – he was an Indian civil servant's son looking to become a barrister, and his imbrication in the *beau monde* came twenty years later. At the same time he was near enough to the kind of social milieu made up of aristocratic politicians, society hostesses and wealthy landowners, who lived in mansions in Belgravia and Mayfair, and whose doings were sycophantically reported in the *Morning Post*, to be able to roam some of its outer fringes and to know some of the people it included. His novels display a connoisseur's knowledge of fashionable life in the early 1830s, which could not all have been taken from the society novels of Mrs Gore. Philip Firmin, like Clive Newcome and above all Becky Sharp, is a survivor from a more expansive and simultaneously more enclosed metropolitan age where, as *Philip* puts it, 'The crack of a pistol-shot might still be heard in the suburbs of London in the very early morning.' In fact duelling was on the way out, along with prize-fighting and the efflorescent fashions of the 1820s, but Thackeray maintained a sneaking fondness for the raffish, aristocratic attitudes that it seemed to symbolise (two cabinet ministers, Canning and Castlereagh, had actually fought a duel twenty years before) and his books are full of haughty young men trying to call each other out. If nothing else, Lord Kew's near-demise at the end of a duelling pistol in *The Newcomes* is a sure sign of his noble qualities.

In a London made up of taverns and gaming-houses, theatres and print shops, pleasure boats to Richmond and Greenwich, study assumed a low priority, and Thackeray seems almost immediately to have written Law off as a bad job. His later work is stuffed with disparaging references to the legal life and its materials. *Philip*, in fact, presents the whole idea of being called to the Bar as a kind of pleasant pose: 'Like many a young gentleman who has no intention of pursuing

'The legal life'

legal studies seriously, Philip entered at an inn of court . . .' As for the tools of the trade, as the narrator of 'The Painter's Bargain', one of the short pieces collected in the *Paris Sketch Book*, puts it, 'It is useless and tedious to describe law documents: lawyers only love to read them . . .' Straight away alienated from his profession, though concealing the fact from the ever-admonitory Mrs Carmichael-Smyth, Thackeray spent his early days in London concentrating on his social life.

This had various compartments, mostly distinct but capable of unexpected intersections. Some of his Cambridge contemporaries had departed to curacies or schoolmasterships – or indeed were still at Cambridge – but friends like Charles Buller, the son of a well-to-do Cornish family, were already at large in public life (Buller had been elected to the Parliaments of 1830 and 1831 for his family's pocket borough of West Looe – another of his fascinations to Thackeray was that he kept a mistress, the enticing Theresa Reviss, who together with her equally raffish daughter may have contributed something to Becky Sharp). To eminently respectable associates such as Buller and his brother Arthur could be added more raffish figures, such as Matthew and a disreputable character named Savile Morton – a notorious womaniser who was eventually murdered by an outraged husband – whose failings Thackeray later transferred to the villain of A *Shabby Genteel Story*. Through his family he had an entrée into the Anglo-Indian society of Tyburnia, and a number of other upper-middle-class households dotted around central London. But he was also exploring the byways of contemporary Bohemia, to which the novels of his middle years so lovingly refer. The narrator of *Philip* reminds his readers that 'What is now called Bohemia had no name in Philip's young days, though many of us knew the country very well . . . a land over which hangs an endless fog, occasioned by much tobacco; a land of chambers, billiard-rooms, supper-rooms, oysters; a land of song; a land where soda water flows freely in the mornings; a land of tin-dish covers from taverns, and frothing porter.' *Philip*, his last completed novel, was begun in 1860, by which time the calcification of Thackeray's hold on past time was complete, but *Pendennis*, written a dozen years before, is quite as selective in its account of the delights on offer to young men in pre-Victorian London. Whatever else it may have encompassed, 'Bohemia' in Thackeray's time consisted principally of gambling, low company and sex. Thackeray's diaries from this period are not the most edifying documents he ever produced, or even the most complete (Annie went through them after his death censoring particularly indelicate material), but they paint a convincing picture of the kind of amiable, yet dissipated life on offer to relatively well-off twenty-year-olds neglecting their studies – a world crammed with drives, card games, idleness and whoring.

He began his London life with two main obsessions. One of these was the theatre, where he went twice a week, suffering immediate withdrawal symptoms when called out of London ('How I long for the sight of a dear green curtain again . . .' he wrote in the middle of one of these stretches, 'O the delight of seeing the baize slowly ascending'). The other was for the company of Fitzgerald, to whom in these first London days Thackeray became increasingly drawn. Though the two rarely met – 'Fitz' spent much of the summer staying with his sister's family at Geldeston before returning to Cambridge – their letters to each other, no doubt by way of compensation, have an intensity that is extravagant even by the standards of the 1830s. And while it is important not to read too much into the rhapsodising of 'Willy' and 'Teddibus', as they called one another – in an era where passionate male friendships were universally approved – nor to doubt their resolute heterosexuality, then and subsequently, the pitch of sentiment reached in their correspondence can still seem rather outlandish. By late September Thackeray was telling his friend, 'How happy you make me by telling me that you love me' (presumably the effect was slightly diminished by his speculating in almost the same breath that one could get married on £700 a year). Fitz's reply was full of gloomy foreboding: he feared that by meeting in the flesh they would destroy the cherished illusions built up on paper. 'Do not think I speak thus in a light-hearted way about the tenacity of our friendship,' he cautioned, 'but with a very serious heart anxious lest we should disappoint each other, and so lessen our love a little.' To slake this tumultuous flame, Fitzgerald included some ardent verses to 'My Willy', which pleaded 'Oh Willy be constant to me' while declaring that 'The thought of my Willy is always a cheerer.' There is a strong suspicion that Willy and Teddibus enjoyed dramatising their relationship in this way – 'Thackeray and I kept up a hot correspondence all the summer,' Fitzgerald told their mutual friend John Allen a month or two later – but the emotion of a letter written by Thackeray shortly after Fitzgerald's departure from one of their London trysts seems genuine enough: 'I don't think my room will ever appear comfortable again – here are your things lying in the exact place you left them – God bless you dear dear Fitzgerald.' Thackeray admitted that he had been reduced to tears by his desolation, and had not cried so much since he was at school.

Meanwhile, there were other siren voices calling. In December he had to sell out a hundred guineas' worth of stock to pay gambling debts – a transaction that involved his guardians, Francis Thackeray and Robert Langslow, as he was not yet of age. Settling the affair by letter with Major Carmichael-Smyth, he gave airy assurances about his routine at Mr Taprell's. 'I find this work really very pleasant – one's day is very agreeably occupied.' There were newspapers and a fire, he told his stepfather, and just enough to do. A letter to his mother, a week later, reporting four days spent 'feasting on my old friends' at Cambridge, strikes an ambiguous note – expressing vague hopes of returning to the university at some point, while sketching out, for maternal benefit, what seems an exemplary timetable. He goes 'pretty regularly' to chambers, remaining there until five or sometimes six, then returns home to read and dine, until nine o'clock comes, 'when I am glad to go out for an hour or so and look at the world'. As for the theatre, he claimed to be attending scarcely more than once a week. Whether or not this was true, he could not resist a typical shout of enthusiasm over an approaching seasonal treat – 'in a few days come the Pantomimes huzza –'. A sketch is appended, showing him seated at the top of an outsize desk, with a clerk ferrying volumes aloft by ladder: 'This wonderful Monster is to be seen every day between 12 & 5 at Mr Taprell's rooms in Hare Court Temple,' runs the caption. The realisation that once again he was embarked on the wrong course, together with the by now habitual reflection on his capabilities, turns up in another letter written early in the new year of 1832. Here, bright January sunshine prompted him to write to his mother 'before I go where I shall find no sun at all in Mr Taprell's smoky dingy back-shop'. As for reading for the Bar, 'this lawyers preparatory education is certainly one of the most cold blooded prejudicial pieces of invention that ever a man was slave to'. People were much wiser than he, he somewhat ruefully concluded, but he would back a young man's ideas, 'however absurd & rhapsodical', against 'old cold calculating codgers' – presumably an unflattering reference to such legal luminaries as he met at Mr Taprell's.

We get a much clearer idea of Thackeray's daily life at this time from a diary he began to keep in April 1832 and maintained until almost the end of the year. On one level it is simply a record of days not very constructively spent – extra-curricular reading, book-buying, the kind of spiritless lying around that he characterised as 'seediness' – but several sharper themes poke through. One of these is the continuing ferment over Reform, in which he took a keen interest. Thackeray's early manhood coincided with a sea-change in British politics. In 1830 the Tory party, which had governed uninterruptedly since 1812, fell from power and was replaced by a Liberal administration under Earl Grey. The Carmichael-Smyths were Liberals, that is to say Whigs, who, while supporting the aristocratic paternalism that was shaping up to push the Reform Bill through, felt that a wholesale extension of the franchise would be dangerous to the principles of Whig government – that it would produce 'delegates' rather than parliamentary representatives with minds of their own. At the same time, while disliking his politics, they venerated Wellington – Thackeray describes seeing him at this time, looking like 'an old hero' – and were disposed to view the passage of the bill as an attack on the hero of Waterloo as well as a necessary piece of constitutional tinkering. Outside the realm of public affairs, Thackeray was increasingly interested in the world of contemporary journalism, to the point where he wanted to use some of his money – prospectively, as no funds would be available until July – to buy or found a periodical of his own. And yet (ominously enough, as the one was largely dependent on the other) the first shadows were beginning to fall over his inheritance. Conscience, too, was troubling him, and the accounts of fast living, late nights and boozy dissipation are frequently trailed by pious resolutions to make amends, above all to make better use of his time. However much he may have rebelled against his mother's Evangelicalism, Thackeray undoubtedly shared her belief that time was precious, and that to squander it was a sin. As at Cambridge, though, he was rarely able to keep to his resolve.

One feature of this existence was its shifting levels – from drawingroom to gambling hell, from the respectable diversions of Astley's to the musical entertainment of tavern back-kitchen. On 3 April, for example, he spent the day with his mother but ended up at 'No. 60', a notorious hell at the bottom of Regent Street. He was back there the next day *'for the last time, so help me God'*. The next day he took a dancing lesson and sat up playing cards until 4 a.m., his losses amounting to £8 7s. His appearance at Mr Taprell's at some point the next morning was the first in ten days. And yet there was business of a kind being transacted, if not in the dingy purlieus of Hare Court Temple. Thackeray's ambition to own a magazine – in effect to make his fortune from newspaper proprietorship – lasted for many years. Even in the later 1830s, after the collapse of both the periodicals in which he is known to have had a stake, he could be found enquiring by letter whether the *Literary Gazette* were for sale. A week after his reappearance at Mr Taprell's he 'Walked in the park with Gunning [*sic*, probably Gunnell] & settled about the new paper'. There is also a reference to 'Goldshede', whom no Thackeray scholar has been able to identify, about money for the paper 'which he can't give me I think', and further mention of talks with Gunnell. Both seem to have been moneylenders who were prepared to discuss advancing funds in anticipation of his majority, a bare three months off. Thackeray continued to reproach himself for idleness. He had been absent from chambers for three days and confessed to having read not a syllable – 'I must mend, or else I shall be poor, idle & wicked most likely in a couple more years' – but he was at work at other schemes for selfadvancement, in particular a plan, apparently aborted, to share the profits in caricature drawings channelled through a Great Newport Street print-seller. And then, on 16 April – the second reading of the Reform Bill had been passed two days before with a slender majority of nine – comes a significant entry: 'Met Maginn at Somerset Coffee House'.

A hundred and sixty years after his death, William Maginn remains a potent symbol of the sheer liveliness, and also some of the worst excesses, of pre-Victorian journalism. Even today he is not quite forgotten, and any study of the mid-nineteenth-century magazine world, with its bitter quarrels and shady backstairs intrigues, has to start by acknowledging his influence. Like many another journalist of the 1830s – the folklorist Crofton Coker, for example, or the erudite ex-Jesuit F.S. Mahony, who wrote under the pseudonym of 'Father Prout' – Maginn (b. 1795) came originally from Cork. A former child prodigy – he is supposed to have been fluent in Greek, Latin and Hebrew by the time he arrived at Trinity College, Dublin, at the ripe age of eleven – he spent ten years as a schoolteacher in his native city before emigrating to London to try his hand as a freelance. Here he was enthusiastically taken up by John Blackwood, the proprietor of *Blackwood's Magazine*, and quickly became a fixture of what John Gross has called a 'stamping ground for riotous Tory Bohemianism'. The *Blackwood's* style – an idiosyncratic conservatism, in which serious scholarship, flippancy and wounding personal attacks were inextricably mixed up – was exactly the kind of thing that appealed to Maginn's sharp, rackety intelligence. He contributed political gossip, notes towards his projected editions of Homer and Shakespeare and slashing reviews, and features as 'Sir Morgan O'Doherty' in the magazine's celebrated *Noctes Ambrosianae*. Inevitably, a broad outline of his career does not quite convey the sheer scale of Maginn's interests, the intense feelings he aroused, and the genuine affection in which most (though not all) of his fellow journalists held him. He was, in addition, a ladies' man, whose association with the poetess Laetitia Landon, however innocent, probably helped cause her death, and a notorious drunk. Thackeray himself put him into *Pendennis* as 'Captain Shandon' (a predictably bowdlerised portrait), who indites the prospectus of the 'Pall Mall Gazette' from his room in a debtors' prison and then rushes out to get drunk on the proceeds.

With these gifts at his disposal, Maginn was well placed to dominate the feverish atmosphere of Tory journalism. In particular, he was a guiding light behind the emergence of *Fraser's Magazine*, founded in 1830 as a rival to *Blackwood's*, through his association with Sir Hugh Fraser (somewhat confusingly, it was Sir Hugh, rather than the proprietor, James Fraser, from whom the magazine took its name).

Boosted by Maginn's prodigious energy – he is supposed to have written the first few issues singlehanded – *Fraser's* offered a startling compound of *Blackwood's* borrowings, doggerel, Whig-bashing and high scholarship, in which the editor (again following the *Blackwood's* model) functioned as a 'Lord of misrule', gamely egging on his contributors to greater heights of invective and innuendo. Chronological fast-forwarding of this kind is not always helpful, but a fair comparison of *Fraser's* rancorous, collaborative spirit – many of the contributions were by several hands – would be with *Private Eye*. It was a volatile mixture – an abusive review of Grantley Berkeley's novel *Berkeley Castle* led to James Fraser being flogged at his shop in Regent Street and to Maginn, the abusive reviewer, fighting a duel with the author – but the magazine was an immediate success. Carlyle, who had spent an unhappy tavern-bound evening with the staff, described it as 'a chaotic, fermenting dung-hill heap of compost', but he was happy to let *Fraser's* serialise *Sartor Resartus*, the book that made his reputation.

Thackeray was receptive to the *Fraser's* ethos from the start. As we have seen, he was ordering up copies from Weimar, and a letter from him to James Fraser submitting a poem for publication – it never appeared – probably dates from 1831. One obvious question that hangs over his association with this kind of journal, and with these kinds of journalists, is why a Liberal should choose to ally himself with what were, in effect, his political opponents. In fact Thackeray's move towards the fringes of Bohemian Tory journalism has a social explanation. Journalism was still a far from respectable trade – the elder Pendennis has some shrewd words with his nephew on this subject. If there was one characteristic that separated the hard-drinking, classics-quoting *Fraser's* men from some of their Liberal rivals it was that they were, indisputably, gentlemen. Maginn undoubtedly fell into this category, and Thackeray took to him from the first. Even in Maginn's dog days – drink got the better of him and he died in his forties – the younger man could propose a toast to a writer who ornamented everything he touched, 'even Homer', and in the months before Maginn's death in 1842 Thackeray was instrumental in raising funds to keep him afloat. All this, though, lay in the future. The relationship inaugurated at the Somerset Coffee House in April 1832 rested on a single, and probably not fully articulated bargain: Thackeray would help the eternally improvident Maginn with money (he eventually lent him £500) while Maginn would give him introductions to the journalistic world where he plied his trade.

For the moment, however, literary schemes took second place to social life. Two days later Thackeray spotted Wellington in Hyde Park. A week later he and Charles Buller went to Greenwich and dined with another old Trinity friend. There are pages missing from the diary at the end of April, presumably torn out by Annie, but the entry for the 29th probably gives a good idea of Thackeray's pursuits at this time. Having 'Idled about all day', he dined at the Bedford, subsequently discovered his friend Kinderley 'tipsy with a common beast of the town, & took him away from her, & home to bed – much to the Lady's disgust & Kinderley's advantage'. Meanwhile, Maginn was fulfilling his side of the bargain. In early May he took Thackeray to the offices of the *Standard*, a Tory evening paper with which he was connected, and introduced him to the editor, also arranging for Thackeray to have dinner with F.W.N. Bayley, editor of *The National Omnibus*. There was more talk with Goldshede, interspersed with light reading. In particular, Thackeray went through Bulwer Lytton's *Eugene Aram*, which he much disliked, and the note of asperity in his comments was to resurface at the end of the decade in his contribution to the controversy surrounding the 'Newgate novel', of which Bulwer was a leading exponent. The book's hero (romantically represented) consents to a murder, done by his accomplice, under pressure of poverty. Affianced to the beautiful Madeleine, he finds his marriage cancelled and he himself is hanged when the accomplice reappears. Thackeray thought it 'a very forced & absurd tale to elevate a murderer for money into a hero – the sentiments are very eloquent clap-trap . . .' There were to be many similar assaults on Bulwer* over the next fifteen years. For the present, Thackeray consoled himself with the thought that 'when my novel is written it will be something better I trust'.

As the summer drew on, literary plans went hand-in-hand with a vigorous, if subsequently regretted, campaign of dissipation. On 8 May he dined with Maginn and one of his cronies, Buller and another friend named McDowell, lost ten pounds at the '64', two doors down from the 60 in Regent's Quadrant, and went back to the Piazza Coffee House in Covent Garden where he found his friends playing whist. Overcome with tiredness, Thackeray fell asleep on the sofa. Waking

---

* As the *Longman Companion to Victorian Fiction* points out, the correct name and title of Edward George Earle Lytton Bulwer (1803–73) presents a problem to the literary historian. Before 1843, the year in which he inherited the family estate at Knebworth, he is properly 'Bulwer', thereafter 'Bulwer Lytton', with optional hyphen.

up at first light he found the game still in progress. Agitation over Reform continued. Lord Grey, the Whig leader, had asked the king to create fifty new peers to push the bill through, but his request was refused, and in his extremity the king turned to Wellington. Like other commentators, Thackeray noted the prospect of rebellion, had Wellington taken office. Unhappy about the political situation (he visited the House of Commons on 9 May and speculated that 'It will be soon I suppose a house of delegates'), Thackeray was also in low spirits about his inability to do any work. His legal studies had by this stage been all but abandoned, and there is a note of genuine despair in the admission that he could no longer concentrate on his law books. 'I have tried it at all hours & it fails – I don't know so much now as when I came to town & that God knows was little enough.' He would make a vow to read fifty pages of law every day, Thackeray told his diary, but knew in advance that it would be useless.

There are more lines cut from the diary in mid-May. The momentous 18th, when William IV finally gave way and guaranteed the passage of the bill by allowing Grey authority to create as many new peers as he needed, was 'one of the most disgraceful I ever spent – playing from after breakfast till 4 o'clock at chicken hazard' (chicken hazard, then sweeping into popularity in London gambling circles, involved the participants playing against each other, with a settled profit going to the bank). Thackeray spent the weeks of late May and early June in similar fashion – reading French and Italian memoirs, driving in the park, eating and gambling. Simultaneously, his taste for fast metropolitan life came interspersed with oases of self-recrimination: 5 June, for example, was spent in 'seediness, repentance and novel-reading'. As ever, Thackeray seems to have been both attracted and repelled by the range of diversions on offer, and also by the figure in which they were personified. The attractiveness, and the danger, of Maginn as a companion is spelled out by the entries of the following week. The morning of 10 June, which they spent together, was 'one of the pleasantest I ever passed': Maginn read Homer to his young protégé and made him promise to read some himself every day. There was more talk about the magazine, as Thackeray mentions discussing 'Gunnell's roguery', although his companion was 'not angry enough at it'. Later, dining off turtle and cold beef at the Bedford, however, Thackeray was gripped by a fit of contrition. Recalling reproaches that had recently come from an aunt in India, to the effect that he was neglecting to pay the annuity due to his half-sister Mrs Blechynden,

Richmond Thackeray's natural child, under the terms of his father's will, he declared that he wished the turtle had choked him: 'There is poor Mrs Blechynden starving in India, while I am gorging in this unconscionable way here.' The following Sunday, 17 June, was at the very least a day of biting contrasts. After spending the morning 'reading novels & writing hymns', he called on Maginn, who later escorted him to a 'common brothel'. Thackeray's description of the facilities – and by 'common' he meant a house of the very lowest character, probably in the Lambeth area, where the charge would have been as little as fourpence – is worth quoting for the clarity of its reportage and the distaste of someone caught up in, and yet observant of, a spectacle of which he is fairly obviously a part. Whatever he may or may not have done, Thackeray eventually left:

> very much disgusted & sickened to see a clever & good man disgrace himself in that way. His money worries press upon him I suppose & make him reckless – Thank God that idle & vicious as I am, I have no taste for scenes such as that of last night – There was an old bawd & a young whore both of them with child. The old woman seemed au reste a good natured beast enough with a countenance almost amiable – The younger one was very repulsive in manner & face –

This is a revealing passage, not only for its self-disgust but for its attempt to find explanations for indefensible behaviour. Its conclusion – that there are 'clever & good' men capable of disgracing themselves, and that their actions are not simple acts of capriciousness but somehow rooted in their nature – would resonate through his later work.

Meanwhile, personal and political had begun to intersect in what promised to be an entertaining holiday. With the passage of the Reform Bill secured, there was a General Election pending. Charles Buller, needed in his new constituency of Liskeard, suggested that Thackeray come down and electioneer for him. Thackeray agreed, whereupon Buller fell ill and deputed his brother Arthur to go in his place. It was a 'dull, cold, hot, damp dusty uncomfortable ride' of twenty-four hours to Plymouth, but once arrived at the Buller family house at Polvellan near Liskeard, he began to enjoy himself. He and Buller looked vaguely alike – both were extremely tall, with crooked noses – and he was amused when the servants mistook him for his friend: 'this created a sentiment in my favour & I was very kindly received by Mr and Mrs Buller'. He stayed in the West Country for four weeks, finding plenty of time to sight-see in addition to the rigours of electioneering in a seat where the result was scarcely in doubt. In the evenings he read Goethe's *Wilhelm Meister*, in Carlyle's edition of 1824, 'and a wretched performance I thought it – without principle & certainly without interest – at least the last volume'. Thackeray's reading during the time he spent in Cornwall is perhaps more interesting than his accounts of helping to write Buller's election address or a comic song against Mr Jope, agent for Buller's Tory opponent Lord Eliot, as it shows a deliberate effort to extend his mental horizons. At one point, for example, reckoning up the day's reading (part of Thomas Moore's memoir of Sheridan, Charles Buller's pamphlet 'On the Necessity of a Radical Reform' and a magazine article, also by Buller) he comments that it is little enough, but more than he has read for a long time past. With luck this kind of 'half intellectual reading' might lead to deeper study. 'The last four years of my life have witnessed but very little improvement in it – at 17 I was well informed at my age, but at 21 I know less than most men, infinitely less than I ought to know.' Possibly the close analysis of Goethe had brought on this bout of introspection. Earlier Thackeray writes that he perceives, or thinks he perceives, a great change in his character, and that he has become much more worldly and far less susceptible to old enthusiasms like poetry. 'If I live to be 50 I dare say I shall be as cold-blooded & calculating as the rest of them,' he concluded, before slipping in a characteristic piece of deflation: 'but this is after the fashion of the German Prince so I will have done twaddling & go to bed –?'

His twenty-first birthday was looming. A letter to his mother, reporting a twelve-hour canvass of the West Looe electorate and a bad case of sunburn from sitting outside on the coach, announces some short-term plans for his majority. He wanted to keep up his chambers, owing to their modest price, and the sixty pounds per annum thereby saved would do 'excellently well for poor Mrs Blechynden'. He also proposed a French trip to be undertaken late in the summer when the Carmichael-Smyths were staying at Southampton. In the meantime he went visiting in Devon, to Newton Abbot, before returning to Liskeard for election day. His birthday, a week later, in the wake of a Liberal landslide (in a house of 658 members, Wellington's supporters were reduced to 185 seats) found him staying at Morval, the home of

'Morval'

Charles Buller's uncle, 'a nice old English house with an excellent specimen of a vieille cour gentleman for its master'. But he was not happy. 'Here is the day for wh. I have been panting for so long, wh. now that it has come has not brought with it any sensations particularly pleasant. But I am a man now,' Thackeray resolved, '& must deal with men –'

It is not unlikely that some of this gloom had to do with money, specifically the far from straightforward question of the estate that Richmond Thackeray had left him. The Thackeray money, so far as we can judge, had been laid out in two ways: several thousand pounds tied up in English stock under the trusteeship of Messrs Langslow and Francis Thackeray; the rest – a much larger sum – invested in Indian banking houses. Since Richmond's death, the English funds had been used to pay his widow an annuity of £225, and pay for Thackeray's education and upbringing. But not all the substantial sum allocated for this purpose (£200 per annum until Mrs Thackeray remarried, £425 thereafter) had been drawn on by the Carmichael-Smyths, and the capital, accumulating compound interest for a decade and a half, seems to have amounted to about £4,000 – at any rate, this was the sum Thackeray expected to receive shortly after his birthday. What happened to it? Six years later £700 was still outstanding – appropriated by Langslow, now several hundred miles away in his capacity as attorney-general of Malta and difficult to confront. Presumably, too, it was from this source that Thackeray sold out the £1,500 worth of stock needed to pay his old Cambridge gambling debts. Meanwhile the news from the East was bad – Palmer and Company, one of the great Indian houses, had failed for £5m two years before – and though Richmond Thackeray's Indian money, perhaps amounting to £15,000, seems to have been tied up in the still flourishing house of Cruttenden and Company, the non-payment of Mrs Blechynden's annuity looked like a bad sign. However uncertain the situation may have been, it was exacerbated by distance and the difficulty of establishing precise details. For all his professed misery over his half-sister's plight, Thackeray had opted to wait until he heard the news direct from her before sending any money.

The immediate prospect, though, was one of undiluted pleasure. A day after his birthday Thackeray left Cornwall '& all the kind friends there' and set off with Arthur Buller to Plymouth. The following day he took the steamer to Cowes and met his mother and Mary Graham. There followed a pleasant week's idling on the Isle of Wight visiting family friends. Three days later, having spent the intervening time with Aunt Becher, he travelled to Portsmouth and boarded the steam packet to Le Havre. Thackeray had wanted Fitzgerald to come with him, but they had failed to make contact – doubly annoying given that Fitz was actually staying a few miles away at Southampton. None the less, Thackeray proceeded in solitude to Le Havre, spent two or three days reading French novels and then took the boat to Rouen. A grim little sketch survives, presumably drawn at the city gaol, of a pipe-smoking man with hands plunged in his trouser pockets, captioned 'Man condemned to Die'.

Reaching Paris after a drive on top of the diligence 'among the boxes & carpet bags, wh. made a comfortable sofa enough' he found that Galignani's English bookshop was dunning him for books borrowed three years before. He celebrated his arrival in fine gustatory style, with a meal of steak and potatoes, dessert and half a bottle of white wine – 'there's a breakfast for you', he informed his mother.

He spent nearly four months in Paris and its environs. The bare account of his stay, as recorded in his diary, is one of idleness, dissipation, theatre-going and a certain amount of reading. In amongst the accounts of gambling and debauchery, however, we can see him pursuing several lines of enquiry into contemporary French culture that would later become important to him. It was on this trip, for example, that he read Victor Cousin's recently published *Cours de l'histoire de la philosophie*, which probably helped to form his mature view of crime and punishment. And he lost no opportunity to satisfy his curiosity about Napoleon and recent French history, exploring the Château de Gondy at St-Cloud, which had Napoleonic associations,

and paying an eager, if ultimately disappointing, visit to a melodramatic re-creation of the emperor's career at Franconis. The performance was inferior to a similar one staged at Covent Garden the year
before, he told his mother, mostly because the French seemed unable
to bring off fight scenes. 'Don't you love the combats when the fellows
come on with their fighting swords – they are not up to it here.'

What they were up to was the provision of a great many ways to lose
money. Mid-August brought a stark confession of his inability to keep
away from the gaming-tables. 'There is a vow recorded in this book &
God knows how it has been kept. Almighty God give me strength of
mind to resist the temptation of playing, & to keep my vow that from
this day I will never again enter a gaming-house –.' The resolution
lasted exactly twenty-four hours, although Thackeray tried to persuade
himself that he had learned something from the relapse. At first, on his
return to the table, he won back nearly all his losings and went away,
'but the money lay like fire in my pocket & I am thank heaven rid of
it –'. A fortnight later, presumably on grounds of expense, he
transferred himself to Choisy-le-Roi, a small village seven miles
outside Paris, engaging rooms for a month with a M. Au Roi, but for

all Choisy's attractions – he met his old French master Ori d'Hegenheim there and befriended a local school proprietor named Cook – the fleshpots of Paris were uncomfortably close at hand. Who did Thackeray spend time with in Paris? Aunt Ritchie and her family were there, along with his new acquaintance John Bowes and several Cambridge friends such as Harry Longueville Jones, who at one point lent him a welcome ten pounds, and a rather snobbish young man named Michael Le Mann, who introduced him to his fencing master. Thackeray had also struck up an acquaintance with an Indian army officer named Gerrard, in whose company he tried to visit the fortress at Vincennes, only to find there was no public admittance.

But he was keeping low company, and he knew it. 'Have been in Paris,' the diary records in late September, 'but dont feel inclined to mention the experiences or the occurrences of these days.' In early October he returned to the capital for good, attended the Opéra-Comique 'but found it dull, spielte und fegelte' [in other words 'gambled and fucked']. There was more theatre-going, idle days at Choisy and dining out and, with his friend Le Mann, a curious visit to an abattoir where the two 'assisted at the slaughter of certain sheep & oxen – The place is admirably managed & as clean as a drawing room,' Thackeray noted. 'At home all day – doing nothing'; 'For a minute to Frascati's where I lost all I had': the realisation that he was wasting his time and his money pressed home the advantages of marriage. A session with his friends spent talking 'of debauchery & its consequences' (by this Thackeray presumably means venereal disease) 'have made me long for a good wife, & a happy home', while on other occasions the diarist found himself 'growing loving on every pleasant woman I see'. The pleasures of the gaming-tables and their attendant delights – Frascati's, as Gronow and other observers point out, was a magnet for high-class prostitutes – were beginning to pall. On 23 November he determined on leaving Paris, 'took my place got my passport & paid my bills' and made a farewell visit to the theatre to see the celebrated Pauline Déjazet. The bills came to nearly £350, including £160 to his tailor and £66 on gloves. By 29 November he was back at Hare Court commissioning his cousin James Carmichael-Smyth, bound for Larkbeare, to tell the family that he was delayed by business and would be back in a fortnight, and supplying some amusing sketches of the household's reception of this news. The 170-mile journey from Paris to the coast had taken forty-four hours, he told James – 'such hours!' A drawing of a vomiting basin was appended.

'The news reaches Larkbeare!'

What were his plans? The reference to being delayed by business may have had something to do with his inheritance (two months before he had learned from his mother that 'the money was sold out – unluckily perhaps for me') or with magazine-owning schemes. Almost certainly he was extending his range of contacts. A letter from this period thanks George Cruikshank, whose engravings Thackeray had admired since his Charterhouse days, for sending one of his books and proposes dinner. But in many ways the next six months form one of the great gaps in Thackeray's life, unillumined by letters or diaries or even by accounts at second hand. Fitzgerald, formerly a mine of information on his friend's whereabouts, seems to have felt frozen out by glittering new acquaintances (this mild sense of exclusion was to become a feature of their later relationship). A letter to Allen from early December reports seeing Thackeray in London before the latter's departure to Devonshire. Fitz had enjoyed the meeting ('He came very opportunely to divert my Blue Devils'), while noting that the pair now saw little of each other, 'and he has now so many friends (especially the Bullers) that he has no such wish for my society'.

There were undoubtedly problems about money. This at any rate can be inferred from Thackeray's involvement, begun early in 1833, with a firm of bill-discounters in Birchin Lane. Although bill-discounting was beginning to assume a more respectable status in the contemporary money market – any visitor to Birchin Lane would have had to walk past the offices of the leading discount house, Overend Gurney & Co., which lay on the Lombard Street corner – anonymous minor firms of the kind with which he was connected lay at the seedier end of the pre-Victorian financial world. Thackeray, fastidious about the company he kept and the uses to which his name was put, would probably not have taken this step without very good reasons. More advantageously, and unlike more glamorous forms of city life, bill-discounting did not require any great ability or powers of judgment. Then, as now, it was merely a kind of transferred debt-collecting. To guarantee a debt, either of his own or someone else's, the signatory would put his name to a 'bill of exchange' – an IOU dated two or three months hence. The bill-discounter would then purchase this from the creditor at a discount, either with the aim of collecting the money himself or selling the bill on to someone else. In this way debts could be passed further and further along the financial chain, and the holder of the bill would have no personal connection with the debtor – hence the ominous remark of so many insolvent gentlemen in Victorian novels that 'X has paper of mine'. The transactions in which Thackeray was involved, cryptically enscribed in a notebook of the time, are impossible to reconstitute – though he seems to have pursued a strategy of keeping the bills going as interest-paying propositions rather than selling them on – but the knowledge he acquired gives bite to the many financial references in his fiction. Like Trollope, a little later on, the emissaries in his novels who come bearing pieces of stamped paper grow directly out of his personal experiences, and the spunging-house scenes in *Vanity Fair* and elsewhere have a very obvious grounding in contemporary circumstance. This was not a side to his life that Thackeray ever cared to be reminded of. Ten years later, when the journalist David Deady Keane wrote a lively account of the bill-discounting trade for *Fraser's*, in which Thackeray (immediately identified by his crooked nose) appears as 'Bill Cracka-way', he was hugely irritated and told the proprietor that either he or Keane had to go. He won the dispute, but one feels that Keane, who certainly knew Thackeray fairly well at this time – the two of them had Christmas dinner together a year later – had unwittingly strayed into an area of his ex-friend's life that was better forgotten.

Another scheme very obviously afoot in the early part of 1833 was the revival of Thackeray's plans to own a newspaper. At some point in the spring these focused on a newly founded periodical called – to give the magazine its full title – the *National Standard of Literature, Music, Theatre and The Fine Arts*. This periodical, whose first number had appeared on 5 January, was the brainchild of F.W.N. Bayley, to whom Thackeray had been introduced the previous year by Maginn. Bayley was a well-known journalist and literary entrepreneur – his long Fleet Street career reached its high point with a job as founding editor of the *Illustrated London News* in the 1840s – and his motive, in establishing a new periodical in what was already a crowded market, was strictly commercial. The first number, printed on sixteen quarto pages and costing twopence, advertised a three-point rationale. First and foremost, the *National Standard* was a budget-price literary paper (the rival *Literary Gazette* cost eightpence). Second, it would be a strictly literary concern, 'in which the books of the week will be reviewed, and the literary news of the week communicated'. Third, it was independent, with no inhibiting ties to publishers. Early issues stuck to this line, and the paper compared well with the *Gazette*, although its general air of sobriety was not calculated to appeal to the *Blackwood/Fraser* circle.

Thackeray's purchase of this far from established concern, whose circulation cannot have exceeded a few thousand copies, was negotiated in the spring, under the superintendence of Major Carmichael-Smyth. Annie, writing nearly seventy years later, maintains that the major was involved with the paper's affairs as early as January, and that his aim was partly to give his stepson a toe-hold on the literary ladder and partly to retrieve his financial losses. But Thackeray did not become editor until May 1833; nor, as far as we can gauge, was the remainder of his fortune irretrievably lost at this time. Undoubtedly he needed money – the 1833 account books show that he was trading in shares (in February, for example, he bought Belgian stock and sold consols) and on 1 February he records losing the unprecedented sum of £668 at 'play'. Whatever financial expectations he may still have had from the East, his personal finances must already have been in a precarious state: £700 of the £4,000 due on his majority had disappeared with Robert Langslow; £1,500 had gone on his Cambridge debts; the Paris trip had not been cheap. Presumably the Indian investments were still paying interest, but one can only speculate as to where the money came from to fund this first venture into newspaper proprietorship.

The deal was done, however, and Bayley bought out. Notoriously hard up, he was probably glad to escape while the going was good (according to his obituarist, 'like many other men of his class, Mr Bayley's habits were not so provident as his friends could have wished'). Thackeray seems to have been installed in the editorial chair by the beginning of May, as on 2 May he wrote to his mother explaining that the paper was now keeping him so busy that he had no time to see her. His first identifiable contribution – a drawing of Louis-Philippe and a review – dates from the issue of 4 May. A week later he composed an ebullient editorial address: 'We intend to be as free as the air. The world of books is all before us where to choose our course.' At the same time there was a minor change of format, from two columns per page to three, and a new publisher in the shape of Thomas Hunt of 65 St Paul's Churchyard (previous numbers had appeared under the name of J. Omwhyn of Catherine Street). These facts apart, details of how the *National Standard* was conducted – who wrote for it, and what they were paid – are sketchy to the point of non-existence. Maginn may have helped out with the occasional sanguinary review, while in the four months until the beginning of September Thackeray probably wrote most of the material himself. He may, for example, have reviewed Sarah Austin's *Characteristics of Goethe* on 25 May – he had met the book's compiler at the Bullers', and the piece betrays personal knowledge of Weimar, in particular the comment that the fountain outside Goethe's house, beloved of the poet, was 'a most ordinary waterspout'. And he was definitely responsible for the extraordinary attack in verse on Lionel Rothschild the week before, complete with a venomous caricature and the concluding couplet 'Hath a pig monies? Is't possible/An ass can have three thousand ducats?' The Rothschild squib is interesting on two counts: the financial terminology picked up in Birchin Lane, which Thackeray contrived to work into the text, and its virulent anti-semitism (Thackeray, who later came to know various members of the great banking family socially, would never allow it to be reprinted). Throughout his life Thackeray maintained mixed feelings towards the Jews. Many of his later jibes at Disraeli, for example, were aimed at his racial origins as much as his politics or his novels. As a bill-discounter he would have been in regular contact with Jewish businessmen (the account book notes such names as 'Goldsmid' and 'Meyer'). Equally, he would have been encouraged to regard such people as untrustworthy. Mistrust of Jews, especially those who ventured into commerce, is an unpleasant but routine mark of contemporary chroniclers. Gronow summed up the feelings of many a Victorian businessman when he declared that 'The characteristics of the Jew are never more perceptible than when he comes in contact with gentlemen to ruin them. On such occasions, the Jew is humble, supercilious, blunderingly flattering: and if he can become the agent of any dirty work, is only too happy to be so, in preference to a straightforward and honest transaction.'

Much of what Thackeray contributed to the *National Standard* is understandably lightweight, but several of the pieces that can be attributed to him are sharply prefigurative. In particular, a withering account of the ballet *Flore et Zephyr*, performed at the King's Theatre in early May, contains the germ of what was, three years later, to be his first published book. The piece was a vehicle for Taglioni, of whom Thackeray, as ever, approved. But he disliked the ballet itself, and above all the spectacle of the aged male dancers who appeared in supporting roles:

> M. Albert followed, in a glossy black wig with a blue fillet. It is needless to speak of him; the world for sixty years past at least, having had a full opportunity of judging of his merits. We should be glad to know what can be the pleasure of seeing persons of most unprepossessing physiognomies and unclassical figures tricked out in such extraordinary costumes as those worn by Messieurs Albert and Daumont [another dancer]; it is a shame to shorten the days of a poor old man like M. Albert, by making him take such violent exercise, and wear such light clothing; particularly at a late hour of the night, when he ought to be in his own quiet home, with his grandchildren.

One can also detect Thackeray's hand in the lampooning of Alfred Bunn, the unctuous manager of the Drury Lane Theatre – Bunn was to become a perennial victim of his satire – and in a killing review of Robert Montgomery's sententious *Woman: The Angel of Life, A Poem*. There was a single deserving line, the reviewer concluded, and that was the name and address of the publisher on the final page.

For all Thackeray's enthusiasm at conducting his own literary magazine at the age of twenty-one, one wonders if his heart was really in it. Early July found him in Paris again, in the guise of French correspondent. Writing from 'my old quarters' in the rue de Rivoli, he

did not relish the prospect of returning to London, he told his mother, 'but I must try & make this paper worth something'. Yet although it went on 'very flourishing as I hear' (the second volume, beginning on 6 July, claimed an 'extraordinary success'), he was already meditating on a new scheme: 'I have been thinking very seriously of turning artist.' Having shot this arrow of disquiet into the maternal bosom, Thackeray immediately went on to reassure his mother that 'an artist in this town is by far a more distinguished person than a lawyer & a great deal more so than a clergyman'. A visit to the Scots painter John Brine in his princely atelier proved the point. He was 'a second-rate man, a little better than a drawing master', Thackeray concluded, 'but I envy him his charm and cabinets'. Seven years later Thackeray would put Brine into A Shabby Genteel Story as the ludicrous Andrea Fitch, who writes risible poetry and fancies himself as a ladykiller, but for the moment he was impressed.

The trip produced four Paris letters for the paper. One of them, a short story entitled 'The Devil's Wager', about a struggling painter who gets the better of a Faustian bargain, would eventually reappear several years later in the Paris Sketch Book. Back in London at the beginning of September, and writing from the Garrick Club, where he had recently become a member, Thackeray was displaying further signs of irresolution. He would go back to Paris, he suggested, and marry someone. Moreover, the National Standard was ruining him for any other kind of writing. Leaving the production duties in other hands – there are no references to the day-to-day conduct of the paper, other than that in September he sacked his clerk for 'drunkenness & lying' – he crossed the Channel once again, and by late October was back in Paris, already trying his hand at his new vocation. He spent all day at his atelier, he told his mother, and was very well satisfied at his progress: 'I think that in a year were I to work hard I might paint something worth looking at, but it requires at least that time before one can gain any readiness with the brush.' The accounts of his hard-up companions were not calculated to impress Mrs Carmichael-Smyth with the sanctity of the artist's calling. 'The artists, with their wild ways & their poverty are the happiest fellows in the world,' he breezily consoled her, before describing a breakfast for five persons consisting of bread, sausage and wine, to which all those present had contributed threepence.

Whatever Thackeray's precise knowledge of his financial prospects, he could not have failed to be aware that the storm clouds were gathering. All that autumn news of the frailty of the Indian banks trickled west. Piecing together the exact sequence of events from the stray references in letters and diaries, by those who were presumably so well acquainted with the situation that they did not need to recapitulate it, is not easy, but it seems clear that by November 1833 Thackeray's money was gone. The dissolution of the Indian banking houses, which had begun as far back as 1830 with the bankruptcy of Palmer and Company, ended in January 1834 with the failure of Cruttenden and Company for £1.3m. Major Carmichael-Smyth and his stepson were definitely interested in this firm, and also anxious to obtain precise intelligence of its affairs, as one of Thackeray's letters home from Paris in October 1833 talks of 'excellent accounts of Crittenden' (presumably a mis-transcription) and mentions that 'a gentleman here has just got letters from the Partners who write in excellent spirits and have been joined by Mr Mackellop with £130000 in specie'. The reference to Mr Mackellop, with his £130,000 of fresh capital, prefigures the gentleman in *Vanity Fair* who invests his life savings in the Calcutta House of 'Fogle, Fake & Cracksman' immediately before its demise. But when did Thackeray know he was ruined? A remark about the pretty Theodosia Pattle, whom he professed himself delighted to marry if only she had £11,325 in the 3 per cents, is often taken as a reference to the amount of money he had lost. Yet the mention of her occurs in the same letter as the reassurance about Cruttenden and Company, and it seems more likely that Thackeray was simply advertising the amount he needed (£11,325 would have yielded about £340 a year) to bring his own income up to the £700 below which he thought it imprudent to marry. Moreover, the general air of this letter, written in late October, is not that of a man in urgent need of money. References to the *National*

'The artists'

Standard make it appear more in the nature of a hobby (should the paper eventually form a 'property', as Thackeray puts it, 'it would be pleasant as an occupation and an income') while even a piece of whimsy about marrying someone with money and coming to live in the London house that the Carmichael-Smyths were on the point of renting is prefaced by a hankering for more continental travel.

But some time between early November and the year-end the true scale of his losses became clear. He returned to London on 12 November to damp chambers and rusty keys. He intended to give up both rooms and paper, he told his mother, 'by wh. I shall have the pleasure of losing £200'. The *National Standard*'s sales, he revealed, had increased by only twenty copies a month. It is a gloomy letter – the sight of his 'horrible chambers' was so dispiriting that he wanted to cry – and reflects a time at which Thackeray was obviously pondering his options (there is also talk of an offer from a newspaper to go to Madrid at £300 a year). A second letter, though, written just before Christmas, while thanking heaven 'for making me poor' (an obvious reference to the news from the East – in fact the final embarrassment of Cruttenden and Company was made public a fortnight later) goes on to talk about the *National Standard*'s prospects in tones of comparative optimism. He was anxious to make the first number of the new year a particularly good one, he told Mrs Carmichael-Smyth, and proposed both a change in name and an increase in the cover price. The issue of 28 December advertised these alterations in a two-column editorial address promising improvements, including 'a series of Original Tales, by the most popular English authors, and translations from the best French and German stories'. A week later the name was altered to the *National Standard and Literary Representative*, with a further inducement in the shape of a facsimile of a poem by Lord Byron. But there was no money left and after a final number, published on 1 February 1834, the paper closed after an existence of little more than a year.

What did Thackeray do? What proved to be the death-throes of the *National Standard* kept him in London for Christmas, and he seems to have installed himself at 18 Albion Street while awaiting the rest of the family's arrival from Larkbeare. The immediate problem was to sort out his shattered finances, and in particular find the money necessary to pay the various annuities for which he was responsible under the terms of his father's will. In the end, by selling out the remainder of his UK property, accepting a cash gift from his grandmother, Mrs Butler, and loans from his stepfather, and remitting family property left in

India, he seems to have amassed a sum of around £7,000. However, Mrs Carmichael-Smyth's annuity stood at £225, while Mrs Blechynden took up a further £52 (in fact Richmond Thackeray's will specified £100): even supposing an interest rate of 4 per cent, there would be very little left for Thackeray himself. At some time early in 1834 he was forced to appeal to his Uncle Francis about Langslow and the vanished £700. Appalled by his fellow trustee's 'infamous conduct', Uncle Frank took upon himself the responsibility of making good the sum, offering his nephew £150 in July and the same amount a year later, and further sums until the debt was paid off. Thackeray never forgot 'saintly Francis' and his efforts, and was presumably embarrassed by them – neither the old man nor his wife was in good health, and he was compelled to take pupils to raise the money – but by this stage the £700 was vital to him. By mid-1835 Uncle Frank's quarterly remittance of £25 seems to have been his only reliable source of income, although there is a reference to 'the poor little capital', possibly either the money that Francis Thackeray still owed him or the larger sum whose interest paid his mother's and Mrs Blechynden's allowances.

He was twenty-one and a half, and had squandered or had removed the best part of £20,000. Thackeray was sensitive about the loss of his fortune, a sensitivity that gave rise to various rumours about the circumstances of its disappearance. Henry Vizetelly, who met him at a slightly later date and left some entertaining glimpses of his early days as a hack-journalist, maintains that three explanations were current among Thackeray's friends: that he had been swindled while in Rome (a city Thackeray had not yet visited); that he had lost it at the tables at Frascati's (undoubtedly a contributory factor); or that he had distributed it with too generous a hand to deserving colleagues. The source of the last rumour is obviously Maginn's £500. As far as we know this loan was never repaid, but although Thackeray may never have recovered his capital, he certainly regarded it as a *bona fide* business transaction, as the interest payments due are recorded in his 1833 account book. However they may have explained it, Thackeray's friends were all too aware that his money was gone – a reference in the actor William Macready's diary in 1836 suggests that it was more or less common knowledge in the circles he frequented – even if, as Vizetelly puts it, Thackeray stayed silent about his lost patrimony 'whenever any faint allusion happened to be made to it in his presence'.

There are no letters to his mother from the first nine months of 1834 – unsurprisingly, perhaps, as the two were quartered in the same premises. Lodged in Albion Street, off the Bayswater Road and a stone's throw from Hyde Park, Thackeray applied himself to art. The detailed account of 'Gandishes' in *The Newcomes* is probably based on the art school run by the academician Henry Sass, which he may have attended at this time. He was also making valuable contacts in the art world. Maginn had introduced him to the young prodigy Daniel Maclise; he was also friendly with George Cruikshank, and seems already to have come across George Cattermole and Frank Stone. Certainly his sketch 'The Artists', which appeared in *Heads of the People* in 1840, with its glimpses into the Soho garrets, suggests a more than passing acquaintance with the world of struggling portraitists and down-at-heel engravers. For all his status as the ex-proprietor of a literary magazine, his journalistic connections were still not strong. He appears in Maclise's drawing of 'The Fraserians' from 1835, but his lack of importance can be gauged from the fact that Maclise left him out of the preliminary sketch. The first *Fraser's* contribution that can be assigned to Thackeray with any certainty is a translation of Pierre Jean du Berenger's verses *Il était un Roi d'Yvetot* in May 1834, and even that is part of a larger miscellany produced by various hands. Fitzgerald, anxiously watching from Suffolk, was doing his best to help – suggesting that he underwrite an edition of the Sir Roger de Coverley papers from Addison and Steele's *Spectator*, illustrated by Thackeray, or a translation of Friedrich Fouque's fairy romance *Undine*, with 'about fourteen little coloured drawings' from the same pen. But the schemes came to nothing, and Thackeray, presumably feeling the constraints of life in the family home, began to plot a return to the kind of Bohemian artistic life of which he possessed such a fond recollection. A rather sad letter in French, dating from March 1834, to a friend named Cazati whom he had met in Paris the previous autumn, wonders if his fellow artist has forgotten 'that unfortunate young Englishman who was with you in the atelier for a month, and who left Paris, to find ruin, and boredom, at home in England'. After soliciting Cazati's hospitality for his Cambridge friend William Brookfield, who took the document with him as an introduction, Thackeray signed off with a wish 'to return soon to Paris to study the arts, as an artist and not an amateur'.

By early October he was in Paris once again – not, alas, on his own but in a boarding house in rue Louis de Grand under the supervision, and at the expense, of his venerable grandmother Mrs Butler. This was a different, but no less exacting, kind of tension. While acknowledging to his mother how 'kind and good she is', Thackeray admitted that at the moment of writing (5 October) he was 'writhing under the stripes of her satire & the public expression of her wrath –'. There was also the question of Mrs Butler's companion, Miss Langford. Thackeray was not impressed: 'this girl is very rich,' he informed Fitz, '– she wears rouge & sticks little bits of sticking plaster about her face by way of ornament, and drops all her h's – the people of the boarding house have settled that I am going to marry her –'. He fled from his grandmother's fond tyranny to the Louvre to copy portraits: 'They are all of them very bad, but I don't despair.' Within a fortnight the ménage composed of himself, Mrs Butler and Miss Langford had relocated to an apartment in the rue de Provence, and he was attending Lafond's art school to draw from life. For all his relish of Bohemia, the goings on at Lafond's awakened his fastidious, censorious side. He noted in his diary that 'The conduct of the model, a pretty little woman, the men & the master of the establishment was about as disgusting as possible – the girl wd. not pose but instead sung songs & cut capers; the men from sixty to sixteen seemed to be in habits of perfect familiarity with the model.' There is something revealing about the images this conjures up: the lines of desks and palettes; a naked girl dancing wantonly between the rows; smirking, hard-eyed onlookers; the tall Englishman not troubling to hide his contempt. Significantly, Thackeray – detached, and yet obviously caught up in a situation of which he is a part – ends by placing a nationalist gloss on his disapproval: 'It is no wonder that the French are such poor painters with all this –'. Much of his life was taken up in treading this fine line between liberty and licence, often with faintly incongruous results. A print-seller whose shop was directly opposite the Garrick Club in King Street once sold him a book of comparatively racy French engravings illustrating les liaisons dangereuses, only to have his client return them the following day on the grounds that closer inspection had assured him that he 'could not keep such things in the house'.

Thackeray's social life in Paris took its usual varied form. He was constant at Aunt Ritchie's drawing-room, saw a certain amount of his friend Bowes and was a regular visitor at the house of the Morning Chronicle's Paris correspondent Eyre Evans Crowe, where he arrived on Saturday afternoons well before the dinner hour in order to draw caricatures for the children. But the majority of his days were probably spent on a much lower social plane. According to *Philip*, Philip Firmin's bachelor existence in Paris was 'the happiest of his life. He liked to tell in after days of the choice acquaintance of Bohemians which he had formed ... he knew some admirable medical students, some artists who only wanted talent and industry to be at the height of their profession ...' Presumably the last remark is a rueful look back at his own efforts. Tracing his progress through the ateliers of the artists' quarter, one encounters the usual catalogue of pious intentions undermined by lack of application and, above all, self-belief. Even the faithful Fitzgerald had his doubts. He believed that Thackeray was still in Paris, he told Allen in December, 'but his last letter to me did not give much hope of his having set seriously to work. I wish he would with all my heart.'

For all Fitz's misgivings, the evidence of the countless sketches and miniature paintings stuck into a contemporary scrapbook shows the seriousness with which Thackeray took his studies. Many of them are the kind of productions that would have been expected from an 1830s art student – historical scenes, fashionable actors, reproductions of old masters, Parisian architecture – but they are interspersed with tantalising glances at Thackeray's day-to-day life: a graceful sketch of a young woman student sitting at an easel, a half-finished drawing from the life class depicting a human leg. However disillusioned Thackeray may have been by his failure to make formal headway as an artist, the vein of inventiveness and amusement that runs beneath these fragments suggests that the foundation stones of his imagination were already in place: a painting of an enormously fat man, dressed in a military uniform belonging to no known British regiment, which probably dates from this time, looks extraordinarily like an early version of Jos Sedley.

The greater part of Thackeray's life at this stage can only be guessed at, with hints in letters and diary entries pointing to experiences made use of in later published work. Henry Reeve, who had come to know him during his early days in London – the two had mutual Cambridge friends – was in Paris taking the first steps in his own literary career. He reported going to the opera with Thackeray in mid-January (there was later a dinner *à trois* with Mrs Butler) and afterwards discussing the doings of French artists. In line with his accounts of Lafond's salon, Thackeray complained of the impurity of their ideas and 'the jargon of a corrupt life which they so unwisely admit into their painting-rooms'. Judging by his notebook, Reeve thought, Thackeray's drawing was 'as

pure and accurate as any I have seen'. A fragmentary mention of the suicide of a schoolfellow, in a letter to Fitz from early 1835, looks as if it refers to the material of 'A Gambler's Death', one of Thackeray's sharpest early pieces, which eventually found its way into the *Paris Sketch Book* of 1840. Here, in the guise of Michael Angelo Titmarsh, Thackeray re-encounters 'Jack Attwood', an old schoolfriend, who having served in the Indian army sets up as a professional gambler. When his winning streak comes to an end Attwood kills himself. Everything in the piece, from the language of the protagonists to the mass of Parisian detail, suggests that the story is a minimally embellished record of actual events, in particular an extraordinary scene in which Titmarsh, visiting his gambling chums at breakfast, hears the news of Attwood's death. Has he 'cut his stick'? (i.e. absconded) the narrator asks. Not exactly, his friend replies. What then? '"*Why, his.throat.*"' With dramatic symbolism, the man's mouth is 'full of bleeding beef as he utters this gentlemanly witticism'. Subsequently Titmarsh assures his readers that the sketch of the dead man, along with a pathetic letter from Attwood's mistress, is taken from nature.

In retrospect it is easy to see Thackeray storing up experiences that could be put to good artistic use. At the time, as so often in the preceding six years, he was uneasily conscious of wasting his life. A diary entry from mid-April notes that 'In these last five months I am puzzled to think what good I have done except a small, very small progress made in my profession – having read nothing but a few dull novels & painted nothing worth looking at for a moment.' His friendships of the time – the diary exults over letters from fellow artists such as Maclise, Cattermole and Stone – suggest a commitment to art that was not borne out by parallel attempts to earn a living. Late April found him writing to John Payne Collier, a member of the staff of the *Morning Chronicle*, asking if he could exert his influence with regard to a job as the paper's Constantinople correspondent. Eyre Evans Crowe was also enlisted in the pursuit and for a time Thackeray seemed confident that he would get the post, even speculating on the opportunities for extra-curricular work (it would give him 'a handsome income for a year and fill my sketch book into the bargain' he suggested to Fitz) but the scheme eventually collapsed. Its prospect undoubtedly gave a sense of anticipation to his life for a month or so, for as late as the end of July Fitzgerald was asking him what had become of his Eastern plans.

Constantinople aside, it was a melancholy period in his life. His diary records dinner at Aunt Ritchie's, visits to the opera, re-encounters with his kinsman Martin Thackeray, the vice-provost of King's, and his vulgar wife: 'what an ass must a man be to espouse such a little piece of insignificance merely for the money she carries with her', Thackeray commented acidly, conveniently forgetting his own thoughts on the advantages of marrying for money. In mid-May he was ruefully concluding that 'for the last 10 days I have seen or done nothing worth looking at –'. After two months his silence was broken by a gloomy letter to his mother containing the news that he had moved from his grandmother's apartment to his own rooms in the rue des Beaux-Arts. While this involved giving up the small sums of money that Mrs Butler allowed him, Thackeray thought that he was right to enforce the separation: 'I believe we are better friends now than when we were together,' he told his mother. 'She comes to see me very often – and I walk stoutly up there three times a week to be scolded.' He had been ill again, with a sore throat and fever, and came close to injuring himself seriously in a fall from a horse. This took place at a *déjeuner sur l'herbe* organised by Mrs Trollope, the mother of Anthony, who had recently taken the literary world by storm, outside Rousseau's house at Montmorency. Here, according to the hostess, the 'wounded cavalier' – at the time Mrs Trollope seems not to have known her guest's identity – was 'taken up for dead'. He recovered, although as Mrs Trollope's elder son Thomas later recalled, the fall was really a severe one 'and at first it was feared that our picnic would have a truly tragic conclusion'.

Meanwhile, the financial situation was becoming bleaker by the day. Uncle Francis had sent him twenty-five pounds, but he needed a further ten pounds to survive until the next remittance – 'I must begin on the poor little capital that's flat.' The devil was in it, he thought, 'if I can't make my own livelihood in a couple of years'. A publisher had asked him for some views of cities, but having made five drawings of a single Parisian location he had destroyed them as being too bad to submit.

Repeated disappointments made him 'ready to hang myself: in fact I am as thoroughly disheartened as a man need be . . .' The Carmichael-Smyths were preparing to set out for Paris, and Thackeray asked his parents to 'set out on your journey, & bring a little consolation to your uncomfortable & affectionate son'. Fitzgerald must have noticed his friend's melancholia, for a letter of the following week asks what has been ailing him ('You, who defied all these weaknesses'). Thackeray was twenty-four, an age when young middle-class gentlemen were expected to have begun their careers. Gladstone, for example, was already in Parliament, while within months Charles Dickens would publish the book that would establish his reputation. To set against these stirrings of promise Thackeray could show only a failed career as a newspaper proprietor, a folder full of indifferent sketches and some stray pieces of journalism. The sum total of his literary output for 1835 was a few short pieces for the *Paris Literary Gazette* on such subjects as 'England' and 'German Songs'. And yet, here and there in his diary, significant names, books and experiences were beginning to shine through. Napoleon. Waterloo. Mrs Gore's novel *Fair of Mayfair*. The bloody beef mimicking the gambler's slashed throat. Amid the complaints about his health, doctors' bills and straitened finances there was another fact that he did not reveal to his mother: he was falling in love.

VII

'The Gal of My Art'

'I have nothing to tell you, except that I am grown strangely fat, and am the happiest man in this neighbourhood: I have a good wife, good dinners, plenty of work and good pay – Can a man want more?'

Letter to John Kemble, 13 December 1836

er name was Isabella Gethin Shawe, she was seventeen years old and lived with her mother and sisters at a boarding house in the rue Ponthieu, Faubourg-St-Honoré; it was either there or at the house of some mutual acquaintance (possibly chance had brought her to the Ritchies) that Thackeray first set eyes on her. Ardently attracted from the outset, he immediately set about pressing his suit and advertising the fact to his friends. The crucial preliminaries seem to have taken place in the late summer and early autumn of 1835, as a letter to his cousin William Ritchie in September declines to accompany him on holiday on the grounds that he was going away with his mother (the Carmichael-Smyths had now arrived from England) and that, simultaneously, he had reached 'such a pitch of sentimentality (for a girl without a penny in the world) that my whole seyn, être, or being, is bouleversé or capsized – I sleep not neither do I eat, only smoke a little and build castles in the clouds, thinking all the time of the propriety of a sixième, boiled beef and soup for dinner, and the possession of the gal of my art'. Kept up to date with bulletins of the affair's progress, his friends were approving. Henry Reeve, reporting back from a dinner, thought Isabella 'a nice, simple, girlish girl'. Fitzgerald, forwarding the news to Allen, was thoroughly agog: 'What do you think! Thackeray has engaged himself to be married to a young lady at Paris – a Miss Shawe,' Fitz wrote in late October, by which time he had already received two 'rapturous' letters on the subject. More were to follow.

In fact no engagement had yet taken place, and the course of the relationship was by no means smooth. Reading the letters exchanged prior to the marriage, it becomes clear that a less tenacious man would not have got what he wanted. But the announcement to Fitzgerald was typical of Thackeray's enthusiasm. Like the teenaged Arthur Pendennis, enamoured of an actress eight years older than himself, he could see no reason why something he had set his heart on could not immediately be achieved. The whimsy with which Thackeray dresses up the idea of marriage – the vision of sixth-floor apartments and solid dinners – has the same characteristic touch, conveying the idea of different kinds of sensual pleasure run seamlessly together. It is significant, perhaps, that the dinner menu takes precedence over the 'possession' of the chosen woman. At the same time the desire to possess Isabella has a strictly sexual connotation. As the evidence of the letters of his early adulthood shows, Thackeray had had marriage on his mind for several years. While his dealings with the Weimar marriage brokers seem to have been approached in the spirit of an amusing game, albeit with occasionally wounding emotional consequences, they also show that the idea of marriage had been present well before his twentieth birthday. Throughout his life Thackeray remained matter-of-fact about his sexual impulses – he is notably candid with his mother on this point. As a twenty-four-year-old, who had already contracted gonorrhoea, he was anxious to provide himself with a respectable outlet.

He was also, quite transparently, deeply in love with what appears to have been little more than a schoolgirl. Thackeray drew several portraits of Isabella in the early days of their courtship: slim, red-haired, with delicate features. In one she stands posed before a vaguely rural backdrop, wearing an amount of drapery that seems excessive for her skimpy figure. Another, dating from late 1835, showing her hair bound up in an elaborate chignon, emphasizes her dark eyebrows and graceful neck. She was a thin, underdeveloped girl, prone to minor health worries, including constipation, in which Thackeray took a benevolent interest (one early letter enquires about the efficacy of salts in 'healthifying herself'). Her accomplishments seem to have been limited to singing, and although there is an early reference or two to her 'drawing', no trace of this hobby survives. As a seventeen-year-old of scant formal education and child-like demeanour – a half-formed quality that Thackeray obviously found attractive – Isabella came much under the influence, if not the outright control, of her redoubtable mother. The Shawes came from Ireland; there was a family house in Cork. Mrs Shawe herself was an Anglo-Indian widow whose five children and modest pension steered her towards the genteel economy practised by the Parisian boarding houses. Thackeray, who regarded her warily from the start, left an unflattering caricature of a sour-looking woman wearing a headdress, with a bizarre, fantastical glint in her eye. The suggestion – no more than a joke when it was first made – that Mrs Shawe was, in however modest a degree, not entirely sane is strangely prophetic, as there was a pronounced streak of eccentricity in the family. Jane, Isabella's younger sister, was notoriously flighty and prone to take offence (an odd exchange between the two in 1838 seems to have been sparked off by Jane's jealousy at Isabella's friendship with Mary Graham) and a brother eventually became an alcoholic, while Mrs Shawe herself displayed an emotional range not out of keeping with a manic-depressive. A prudent man might have investigated more thoroughly these tendencies, whose cumulative effect suggested at the very least some kind of hereditary flaw, but Thackeray was enraptured and cared only for the consummation of his love.

Achieving this was not as easy as it seemed, and the progress of their courtship during late 1835 and early 1836 can often seem like a long-drawn-out war of attrition, in which successive obstacles – ranging from Isabella's general timidity to her obvious fear of the physical consequences of marriage, with maternal disapproval lurking all the while in the background – are blown aside by a persistent and single-minded swain. Undoubtedly something of the atmosphere of this nine-month period is conveyed by the chapters of *Philip* set in Madame de Smolensk's seedy boarding house, where Philip Firmin and Clara communicate through notes smuggled back and forth by the servants, and Philip spends hours outside in the moonlight staring up at the darkening windows and imagining that he sees the extinguishing of his beloved's lamp. The series of long, regular letters that Thackeray addressed to Isabella before their marriage – staying in London in spring 1836, he was capable of writing to her three times a week – are important not only for the window they open up into Thackeray's heart, so to speak, but for the light they shed on his view of women and their position in marriage. From the beginning, he and Isabella appear to have contrived distinct roles for each other. She was 'puss' or 'little woman' – lazy, irresponsible, yet affectionate and adored. He was a 'sulky grey-haired old fellow' (later on Isabella would refer to him as 'the old man'), gloomy but warming himself at the flame of her love, anxious to improve her habits and way of life both for her benefit and – it has to be acknowledged – his own. Without doubt Thackeray was deeply affected by the prospect of marriage to Isabella: a letter to Fitzgerald from this time describes rising early with the aim of working, but able only to 'open his heart' either to his mother, 'my Isabinda' or Fitz himself. The letters written during the London visit are hugely affectionate, full of wistful imaginings and 'sweet thoughts about my little woman'. Writing from Calais on 10 April, en route for the Channel, Thackeray notes that he 'can hardly fancy yet that we have parted, for I had you with me always in my sleep . . . I saw the moon shining in the night, and do you know it made me happy to think that it was shining on the dear little house in the Pelouse.' He had found a packet of letters relating to his ruin three years back. These were cheerless mementoes, but Thackeray found he could not regret the experience: '. . . I never could have found my little woman had it not been for the loss of my money, so I think I have reason to be thankful.' He enjoined his 'dear little wife' to 'write directly, and four or five times a week'.

Several schemes had taken to him to London that spring. One was the publication of his first book, although this is probably too grandiloquent a description for a slim pamphlet containing only eight lithographic caricatures. The idea for Flore et Zephyr, underwritten by Bowes, ascribed to 'Theophile Wagstaff' and printed by the Bond Street publisher John Mitchell, seems to have grown out of the ballet that Thackeray had reported on for the National Standard back in 1833. Certainly the frontispiece sketch of 'Flore' owes something to A.E. Charlot's earlier representation of Taglioni, while the drawings of 'Zephyr' – an aged male dancer launched uncomfortably in mid-air – seem to refer back to the venerable Albert. There are also two lithographs captioned 'backstage', each crammed with the kind of shabby but vivid detail that would crop up in Thackeray's early journalism. In the first 'Flore' is being saluted by two male admirers under the gaze of an elderly duenna. In the second a resigned-looking 'Zephyr' is contemplating a pot of porter and a pinch of snuff. Both pictures are shot through with an ironic, melancholy realism. Matched against the hard faces of the old roués who congratulate her, 'Flore' is ingratiating but cautious; the old woman's stare mingles indifference and complacency. The final effect is of compromised glamour, illusions irrevocably spent.

Flore et Zephyr seems to have been published at about the time Thackeray returned to England in April 1836, as a note to Mitchell of the previous month mentions a final drawing wanted to complete the set, while a letter of 22 April, written during his stay, begs a favourable review from William Jerdan, the editor of the *Literary Gazette* (Jerdan duly obliged with a half-column encomium). Thackeray probably regarded the pamphlet as a useful advertisement for his artistic skills, and certainly tried hard to promote it: he supplied 'three puff-provokers' to Mitchell, as well as asking for a copy to be sent to Maginn. Meanwhile, a second scheme was under way under the aegis of Major Carmichael-Smyth, its aim simultaneously to shore up the waning family fortunes and secure Thackeray a paying job. This was nothing less than the marshalling of a set of investors prepared to fund a new daily newspaper. Given his experience of the *National Standard* three years before, Major Carmichael-Smyth's enthusiasm looks optimistic to the point of imprudence, but in fact the major and his fellow investors had done a certain amount of market research. Here, at the fag-end of William IV's short reign, there was considerable sympathy for the cause of constitutional reform, which it was intended that the paper should espouse. At the same time the forthcoming reduction in Stamp Duty would enable any new publication to be sold at a relatively cheap price. As such it ought to be attractive to the great mass of the unenfranchised populace.

The complexities of post-Reform Bill politics, and Thackeray's involvement with them, are not easily disentangled. After Welling-ton's cataclysmic defeat in the General Election of 1832, the Tory party, reeling from its rejection by a previously supine electorate, promptly split into factions of die-hard 'ultras' and liberal conserva-tives, influenced by 1820s leaders such as Lord Liverpool, Canning and above all the party's rising star Sir Robert Peel. Most of the political developments of the next thirty years – on which Thackeray kept a keen eye – can be traced back to this source, and there are fascinating parallels with contemporary arrangements. For much of the 1830s the policies of the two main political groupings were hard to differentiate, and the problem for the shattered Tory rump under the *de facto* control of Peel (although Wellington was still active in politics) was to distinguish itself from a government with popular support and a huge parliamentary majority. There, however, the resemblance ends. Party allegiances were infinitely more fluid and the 'Liberal' administrations of the period were grand coalitions of aristocratic Whigs and their middle-class supporters, radicals and Irish MPs, always liable to be split apart by ecclesiastical questions. The collapse of Grey's government in 1834, which allowed Peel to form a brief '100 day' ministry, was caused by a row over Irish church revenues. The Whigs, under Melbourne, were soon back in Downing Street, but powerful interest groups remained at work within their ranks. The *Constitutional* was aimed at the party's advanced wing, both inside and outside the House of Commons (signatories to a prefatory statement of aims that appeared in later editions included the parliamentarians Sir William Molesworth, whom Thackeray had met some years before while canvassing for Charles Buller; George Grote, the historian of Greece; and John Gully, the former prize-fighter – the pre-Victorian Commons had a wider catchment area than is sometimes imagined). Thackeray was promised the post of Paris correspondent, a fact he lost no time in communicating to Isabella. As spring progressed, plans for the new radical daily grew more concrete. An existing – and more or less moribund – paper called the *Public Ledger* was to be purchased, renamed the *Constitutional (and Public Ledger)* and launched on a platform of press freedom, extension of popular suffrage, voting by ballot, shorter Parliaments, equality of civil rights and religious tolerance, and anti-monopoly legislation – the whole advanced Liberal package, in fact, intended to head off the popular agitation that would a few years later find expression in Chartism by preaching reform via constitutional means. Encouragingly, from Thackeray's point of view, there was even talk of salaries. By 14 April he was writing to tell Isabella that the job would definitely be worth £300 or £400 a year – 'think up on this, dear Puss'.

Isabella thought. Thackeray's ensuing letters are all too revealing of her state of mind, and the difficulties that their relationship was experiencing. Backed up by the prospect of a job (by the standards of the Parisian boarding houses, £400 a year was a very reasonable sum) and the approval of his parents, Thackeray was all for pressing ahead. 'So, dearest,' he enjoins, 'make the little shirts ready, and the pretty night caps, and we will in a few months, go & hear Bishop Luscombe read, and be married, and have children, & be happy ever after, as they are in the story books. Does this please you as it does me?' The thought that this glutinous vision of domestic harmony might not have appealed to his teenaged fiancée seems to have occurred to Thackeray, for the same letter goes on to urge Isabella to think hard about whether she really wants to marry him. Suddenly, having invoked a sugary prospect of little shirts and pretty night caps, the enraptured swain is suggesting that 'you have avoided any thoughts as to the change of your condition, & the change of sentiments & of duties, wh. your marriage with me must entail – '. This strikes a faintly accusing note, and it confirms Thackeray's role as the impresario of the relationship – organising, solicitous, hastening on towards the altar. Caught between a man she liked but was chary of committing herself to and a dominating mother, Isabella was understandably confused and upset.

In the meantime Thackeray's London trip had brought him an important professional connection. It seems to have been at about this time that he made the acquaintance of Charles Dickens. This encounter should not surprise us – London literary society in the 1830s was small-scale and tightly knit, and Dickens was additionally a member of the Garrick Club – but Thackeray's ability to strike up a connection with the rising literary star of the day is a tribute to the network of contacts he had developed in the previous three or four years. A cartoon which he produced at around this time shows the two of them lounging in a tavern at St James's Square together with Maclise and Mahony: Dickens, slim and dandified with the longish hair of the Maclise portrait, smokes a cigar; Thackeray, eyeglass drooping, stands over him like a burly waiter. Shortly afterwards a chance emerged to hitch himself to Dickens' burgeoning career when Seymour, the melancholic illustrator of the *Pickwick Papers*, killed himself after the appearance of the second number. According to a speech he made many years later at a public banquet, Thackeray immediately hurried round to Dickens' chambers at Furnival's Inn with two or three hastily executed drawings and offered himself as a replacement. Dickens was unimpressed, but the two men remained friendly and a year later, as editor of *Bentley's Miscellany*, Dickens was responsible for putting Thackeray's first published story into print.

More letters, meanwhile, were speeding across the Channel. Something of Thackeray's and Isabella's attitudes to their relationship and its destiny can perhaps be gauged from the regularity with which each wrote to the other: Thackeray as much as three times a week; Isabella a great deal less often. Thackeray's letter of 18 April strikes a robustly didactic note – trusting that Isabella is 'healthifying' herself

Dickens, Thackeray, Maclise and Mahony in 1836

against a coming event (four days before he had conveyed Mrs Carmichael-Smyth's urgings that she should go to a homoeopathic doctor in Paris) before turning to various reservations that she seems to have expressed about married life. So far as they can be reconstructed from Thackeray's replies, these concentrated on her forthcoming detachment from her family. 'The separation to wh. I alluded,' Thackeray told her rather frostily, 'did not go further than the bedroom.' The hint about Mrs Shawe and her influence on Isabella's life and opinions was clear enough, and Thackeray obligingly spelt it out: 'If you are my wife you must sleep in my bed and live in my house – voilà tout.' Subsequently he nagged her about not writing enough: 'I won't say I am content with a half sheet once a week, but you will write more easily as you grow more used to it, & before long I shall have a couple of half sheets a week I hope.' There is something schoolmasterish about this exhortation – the sense that in choosing Isabella he had deliberately selected an immature intelligence he could form to his own design is sometimes rather too strong for comfort – confirmed by Thackeray's reminder that regular letter writing plays an important part in keeping him happy. Later, he instructed her to 'follow my example in letter writing – And give me a few lines every day, and you will see a half sheet grow speedily into a sheet, & what is more you will give me no cause to grumble.'

Rereading these letters over a century and a half after they were written, one notes what to a modern sensibility is a paradox – deeply felt affection contrasting with relentless patronage – but to an early Victorian would have seemed an appropriate tone for a young man to address the woman he intended to marry. A potential husband was expected to stamp his personality on a relationship, to make clear what he wanted in advance so that he could expect to receive it. Running through Thackeray's exhortations, however lumpenly expressed they may seem, is a feeling that Isabella needs to be kept up to the mark, is prone to a kind of congenital laziness that can only be kept at bay by constant stimulation. This produces a curious view of their relationship – a kind of *grande passion* hedged about with sentimental whimsy, in which the desired object is regarded as a wayward schoolgirl.

Thackeray's letters from this period in his life are strewn with references to his dislike of female cleverness – the bluestocking with her pamphlet and her severe expression was an eternal butt for his humour – yet he seems to have been equally dismissive of conven-tional female 'accomplishments' (each of these dislikes burns through his most sustained discussion of 'the woman question' in *The Newcomes*). Where did this leave Isabella? Presumably restricted to attributes such as humility and loyalty, and, so far as one can make out, forbidden to take the steps that would have enabled her to grow up. A final letter from the London trip supplies a further lecture. Mimicking what he presumed were Isabella's own thought processes with regard to her future husband, Thackeray asks, 'Could I not manage to sacrifice a little of my idleness to devote to him ten minutes a day, and to favour him with a whole sheet of paper?' Surely, he goes on, a woman who has 'mastered the mysteries of stocking mending' and 'arrived at the perfectibility of pie crust' has another conjugal duty to perform, and this is 'the duty of affection'. Isabella must take these scoldings as compliments, he subsequently – but not at all apologeti-cally – assures her, 'for I should not scold if I did not care for you'. There is something fantastically insensitive about these strictures – doubly so in the reference to Isabella's stockings and her pie crusts, which point her in the direction of a married woman's 'proper' activities while simultaneously mocking their triviality. Yet, to do him justice, Thackeray is capable of following them up with the most heartfelt laments about his separation from the woman he loved, characterising Isabella as a 'little red-polled ghost' pursuing him through the day and complaining that in the morning 'I wake very early and toss about in my bed & think of you.' He couldn't live without her, he concluded, 'that's flat –'.

Back in Paris, Thackeray looked forward eagerly to his approaching marriage, and it seems that by now he and Isabella regarded themselves as formally engaged. However, the plans to launch the *Constitutional*, on which their income depended, were subject to delay – in particular, the reduction in Stamp Duty, on which the paper's popularity was predicated, would not now take place until the autumn. At this point Mrs Shawe, who had not approved of the relationship from the beginning, seems to have done her best to effect a separation. Some letters from early July give the impression that she began by suggesting that, given the uncertainties of Thackeray's position, it would be as well if he and Isabella did not meet quite so regularly. At any rate on 2 July he tells her that 'I don't mean to give up seeing you altogether, but will call with your Mother's permission once or twice a week', while a day later he muses that time apart may have a good effect – making Isabella love him better by virtue of his absence, improving his relationship with Mrs Shawe ('for I think that when we are not too intimate or familiar we shall be much better friends') and curing Isabella of 'two lazinesses that beset her, not writing letters, and lying abed'. It seems plain that by this time a war was being waged over Isabella's head between fiancé and mother. Certainly this would explain Thackeray's injunction to Isabella to think for herself and break free from maternal bonds. With feelings 'scarcely permitted to show themselves' it was hardly surprising that 'a certain habit of coldness & indecision should have sprung up'. For Thackeray it was all or nothing: 'you must love me with a most awful affection, confide in me all your hopes and your wishes your thoughts and your feelings; for I want you to be not a thoughtless and frivolous girl, but a wise and affectionate woman, as you will be, dearest Puss, if you will but *love* enough'.

It was hardly the way to address an emotionally distraught girl of eighteen who hardly knew which way to turn. In particular Isabella resented the accusation of frivolousness and expressed this resentment in a letter. Thackeray replied that he had meant no harm, that all women were so as a result of their education, and that he wanted his wife to be better than all women. The letter is further evidence of the unravelling of Thackeray's views on the proper occupation of women. It divides womankind into three categories: those who occupy themselves with their houses and servants; a second class who devote themselves to marginal activities such as painting and music; and finally the woman who 'piddles about prayer-meetings and teaches Sunday school'. Thackeray wanted his wife to be 'a little paragon, and so it is that I am always belabouring her with advice'.

There are already signs of an estrangement. This letter, written on 5 July, was sent via the lodging-house porter 'in order to save appearances', but the writer 'must and will' write to her and hear from her every day. Matters reached a head shortly afterwards when Isabella – prompted, or perhaps ordered by her mother – attempted to withdraw from the engagement. Thackeray responded ardently and furiously. 'My love for you is greater than I thought, for it has withstood this terrible three days trial. I have tried to leave you, & you will hardly credit me that I felt obliged to return – for I do not believe in spite of all this heartlessness on your part, that you can ever be other than my wife.' Despite the accusation of heartlessness, he clearly suspected that more experienced hands had been at work – at one point he demands that if she is tired of him she should '*tell me so with your own lips*' – but most of the letter is written in tones of angry perplexity, an attempt to uncover the roots of the estrangement in his own behaviour. Had he pressed his suit too urgently? He had prayed to God 'to give me aid in quelling any improper desires wh. might create your disgust or lessen me in yr. esteem'. Was it that Isabella fancied his love not *pure* enough? Well, 'it was a love of wh. any woman in the world should have been proud, & wh. I never can give to any other – but still dearest, I love you; forgive me my trespasses as I have remit you yours, and you will restore happiness to your family, & to one whose misery you never can feel or know, please God –'.

Evidently this did the trick. Torn between filial obedience and her fiancé's commands, Isabella decided to break free. It is impossible to piece together an exact chronology of the remaining weeks of their courtship. All that is known is that the couple were married on 20 August by Bishop Luscombe at the British Embassy. Presumably Mrs Shawe was reconciled, as Isabella was still only eighteen and parental consent would have been required. Subsequently they left for a honeymoon at the Ritchies' country house 'les Thermes' on the outskirts of Paris, where the only memory that anyone preserves is that

Mrs Thackeray's 'carefully trained voice and charm in singing were long remembered by all who heard her ...' No doubt Thackeray, admiring her from his armchair as the long summer evenings faded into twilight, the Ritchies' servants arrived to light the lamps and the shadows fell over the lawn, was content.

By mid-September they were back from their wedding tour and living in an apartment in rue Neuve St-Augustin. A rapturous letter to his mother reported that they were 'the laziest people in Paris' and spent eleven out of each twenty-four hours in bed. As for his bride, 'my little Puss bating [possibly a mis-transcription of 'barring'] the laziness is the best little wife in the world; I never knew a purer mind or a better temper, or a warmer heart ...' There was an ominous reference to Mrs Shawe, however, whom her son-in-law described as a 'singular old devil', although 'quite civil of late'. He could not establish why it was that he disliked her so much, he told his mother. Another letter to Fitzgerald paints an even more roseate picture of the married state. Marriage, Thackeray philosophised, did not change one in the least: it was simply a new quality that one discovered in oneself. The unmarried could not imagine the delight of sitting at home in the evening and spending 'pleasant long nights' on the sofa smoking and generally enjoying oneself. 'Dear Edward' should come and see him, Thackeray instructed, as it would do him good to see the extent of his friend's happiness.

Isabella was pregnant almost immediately. Meanwhile the *Constitutional* had begun with a flourish of trumpets. Conducted from offices at 162 Fleet Street, the first number appeared on 15 September – the day on which Stamp Duty was reduced from fourpence to a penny – at a price of fourpence-halfpenny. A long address to the readership, probably the work of the editor Samuel Laman Blanchard, began by complaining that the tax had not been abolished altogether before widening out into a discussion of the paper's rationale. Those who wrote for the *Constitutional* were, he declared, 'REFORMERS in the strictest sense of the word'. In this way the paper would always distance itself from extra-parliamentary radicalism. 'The political reforms, the social remedies, it will urge upon the Legislature, will contain nothing dangerous or visionary – for they will be purely "Constitutional".' The true spirit of 'that mystery the Constitution' would be the true spirit of legislation for all. Notwithstanding the gravity of references to the paper's noble and lofty aims, and some stern reflections on the nation's current state, the tone is upbeat. When the writing is dull, the prospectus concludes, 'it will not be design, but because we cannot help it. Instead of wearing a visage ever rueful, in season and out of season, we shall be cheerful while we can – in the conviction . . . that although there is much to mourn over there is infinitely more to hope for and rejoice in.'

A glance through the early numbers reveals the *Constitutional* to be a fairly typical London daily newspaper of the 1830s. Four pages in length, it carried columns of 'Foreign Intelligence' and 'City Intelligence', notes on 'The Court and Fashion' and police news. Douglas Jerrold wrote a lively theatre column covering performances such as Charles Kemble's *Hamlet* and Macready in *King John*. Various attempts were made to bump up the subscription, and by the end of the year a testimonial was appearing before the editorial, in which distinguished supporters, including a score of Liberal MPs, recommended the paper as the organ of UNCOMPROMISING LIBERAL PRINCIPLES and urged it on their friends. Thackeray's contributions, mostly straight topical reporting on the issues of the day, pro-British if occasionally severe on English diplomacy, are not remarkable, and George Saintsbury, culling his early writings for the Oxford Thackeray seventy years later, ignored them altogether. For all that, there are occasional hints of what was to come, and some stern reflections on Louis-Philippe ('You boast in France and England that you are the most civilised people in the world, among whom freedom is best understood, and justice most enlightened, and yet the axe and the gallows are always at work') foreshadow the theme of 'Going to See a Man Hanged'.

With much of Thackeray's time taken up in newspaper work – although many of his contributions were lifted from or suggested by French periodicals – the young couple spent most of the winter in their apartment. Thackeray seems to have been eager to extend his range and increase his receipts, for he wrote to his friend John Kemble in December mentioning a rumour that Beaumont, the MP for Northumberland, was starting a new newspaper – the Stamp Duty reduction was launching a flood of new publications onto the market – and wondering if it, too, would need a Paris correspondent. To his mother he reported that he and Mrs Shawe were on the most civil terms: they never saw one another. More seriously, he gave an interesting glimpse of how the experience of living in Paris and monitoring the French political scene was beginning to affect his own political views. In fact this correspondent of an advanced Liberal newspaper feared that France was turning him into a Conservative. The French Republican party was 'the most despicable I ever knew'. He identified an increasing tendency in English politics towards 'the gentleman radical' (presumably the kind of person who could be expected to support the aims of the *Constitutional*). But it seemed to him that in their agitation over public matters people forgot 'the greatest good of all, social good. I mean fine arts, and civilisation, dandyism as you call it: we owe this to the aristocracy, and we must keep an aristocracy (purged & modified as you will) in order to retain it'. This is a less hidebound version of a comment on an essay submitted by Fitzjames Stephen to the *Cornhill* a quarter of a century later, and if nothing else it shows that the seeds of the aristocratic Whiggism into which he ultimately lapsed were present in his political thinking from a very early stage.

One or two letters survive from this period from Isabella to Mrs Carmichael-Smyth. They are brief, hastily composed scraps, but taken together they offer some fleeting glimpses of a personality that does not always completely emerge from Thackeray's own bulletins. There is a fetching little note written towards the end of 1836 in which she recounts their entertainment of Ismael Mohammed Khan, ambassador of the King of Oude, who had arrived in Paris to visit the Ritchies, whose relatives he had known at Lucknow. Usually the ambassador dressed himself in 'a turban, gold tissue robe and fine cashmere shawl'. One day, however, he walked in dressed as an Englishman, 'which I did not think at all becoming and William declared he looked like a *Snob*'. Isabella wondered archly whether her mother-in-law was 'acquainted with that elegant expression'. She reported that she was mildly unwell – she must then have been about three months pregnant – 'but for so pleasing a cause that I do not mind it', and signed herself 'Goodbye dearest Mrs Smyth'. They were soon on much more intimate terms as a second, later letter ends 'Goodbye dear Mother I may call you now'. The warm feelings that existed between Isabella and her mother-in-law were to be potent ammunition in Mrs Shawe's subsequent quarrels with the Thackeray family.

If there was a cloud hanging over this Parisian idyll it was the poor state of the *Constitutional*. Crowded out by a tide of new publications, and insufficiently distinctive to separate itself from its rivals, it was not prospering. As the stepson of one of the directors, Thackeray was presumably aware of the feeble sales – no figures survive, but it is unlikely that the paper ever sold more than 3–4,000 copies a day – and of its uncertain future. The letter to Kemble may simply refer to an attempt to increase his receipts by using materials that were already to hand, but the early part of 1837 saw him making serious efforts to find additional sources of income as a hedge against the *Constitutional*'s likely failure. In particular there was a scheme for him to illustrate William Ainsworth's novel *Crichton* for its publisher Macrone. This came to nothing, although at one point Thackeray wrote to Macrone promising to send half a dozen drawings, putting the delay down to dissatisfaction with his efforts – 'what I did was so bad, that I felt mortified at my failure, and did not care to write to you about it'. Another plan advertised to Macrone was for a series of 'Rambles and Sketches' in Paris. This, too, had no immediate result – Thackeray admitted that hardly any of it was yet written and Macrone was soon dead, prematurely, of influenza – but the scheme for what became the *Paris Sketch Book* was clearly turning in his mind.

But February 1837 brought an end to the Paris letters signed 'T.T.' The *Constitutional*'s affairs were by this time so precarious that he was summoned home. As far as we can make out, the plan was for him to swap his correspondent's duties (although the paper's interest in France seems, if anything, to have increased after his return) for an involvement in day-to-day administration. The Thackerays packed into Albion Street, where Isabella settled down to await the arrival of her baby – now only three months distant – and her husband and his stepfather made anxious visits to Fleet Street. Throughout the early months of 1837 considerable efforts were made to revive this ailing organ of parliamentary radicalism. The number of columns per page was increased from six to seven and then reduced again. The price rose to fivepence. Come March there was an additional call of one pound per share on the company's 6,000 shares. By this stage in the paper's brief history it seems clear that Thackeray and Major Carmichael-Smyth were deeply involved in its financial affairs – perhaps exclusively so. This seems the only explanation for Thackeray's appointment late in April as the company's managing director. In this role he grimly informed the directors that 'our funds are totally inadequate to meet the present expenses'. In fact closure would already have been enforced, had it not been for the devoted (and by this stage wholly quixotic) efforts of the major. According to Thackeray's calculation the paper needed an immediate cash infusion of £1,000. But though he himself promised £100 (where from, one wonders?) and canvassed several people for loans, including his uncle John Ritchie, who was briskly informed that 'our paper is well-nigh ruined for want of a few pounds', it was plain that the end was not far off.

Isabella's baby was born on 9 June into an atmosphere of debt and threatened livelihoods. It was a 'bad business', Thackeray later told the child, a girl christened Anne: the homoeopathic doctor favoured by Mrs Carmichael-Smyth turned out to be incompetent. Thackeray, fearing that his wife and daughter's lives were in danger, eventually ran out and fetched a replacement. Three weeks later, its funds exhausted, the *Constitutional* finally expired. Ironically, the last number appeared over a black border in tribute to the simultaneous death of William IV. A long valedictory editorial attributed its demise to bad luck (in particular the delay in Stamp Duty's reduction was supposed to have 'operated disadvantageously in the minds of many who were originally parties to the enterprise'), inexperience, lack of resources and general misgivings about the project's chances of success. 'Much advice was subscribed, and little money.' The paper closed with a warning to both Whig and Tory that their joy over a Radical failure was in danger of being quickly followed by 'a lamentation over Radical triumphs'. But there was a new era in prospect. The *Constitutional*'s obituarist signed off with two cordial wishes – a long and merry reign to the young Queen Victoria, and to the people the extension of the franchise and the elevation of Lord Durham. Meanwhile, in a cramped house north of Hyde Park, together with a sick wife and a month-old baby girl, an unsuccessful journalist within sight of his twenty-sixth birthday was looking out for ways of earning a living.

VIII

The Drowning Woman

'You must not go for to alarm yourself about my infinite struggle hardships & labours every one of them do good –'

Letter to his mother, 19 November 1839

'O Titmarsh Titmarsh why did you marry?'

Letter to his mother, 10 September 1840

The Thackerays stayed at Albion Street until early 1838. Not much survives from this period in their life, although there is an encouraging but mock-solemn letter from Fitzgerald suggesting that 'now you are married, I dare not write nonsense, and what Mrs Butler calls "patter" to you'. When would they go to Rome together, Fitz wondered, reminding his friend of an old scheme to witness the life of the Bohemian artist at first hand. It was a good question. The Albion Street household was breaking up. With debts from the *Constitutional* still piled around his head, Major Carmichael-Smyth decided that he could drag out what remained of his meagre income more satisfactorily on the Continent. In early spring he and his wife gave up their lease and departed for Paris, leaving the Thackerays with the problem of finding somewhere to live. They seem to have house-hunted around the Bloomsbury area for some time – Thackeray later remembered turning down a house in Brunswick Square on the grounds that eighty pounds a year was beyond his means – before settling on a smallish terraced property in Great Coram Street.

Money was tight. Guilt-ridden by his stepfather's tribulations over the *Constitutional*, Thackeray voluntarily turned over a tiny income that remained from his annuities. He was still in pursuit of Langslow and what amounted to six years' unpaid dividends. A letter of early 1838 talks sternly of 'being compelled to pay an annuity wh. your debt to me would as nearly as possible cover'. Presumably this was Mrs Blechynden's money. Pressures of this kind placed significant strain on a family income that, a year or so on, when Thackeray had begun to make a name for himself as a literary freelance, never amounted to more than £600–700.

Poverty, especially of the shabby genteel kind that Thackeray became so expert in depicting, is relative of course and by contemporary standards the Great Coram Street establishment was resolutely *bourgeois*. Two maids and a cook were indispensable to any kind of decent middle-class life at this time. These ranks were swelled by the presence of a *bona fide* manservant, an old gentleman named John Goldsworthy, formerly the Larkbeare footman, who wore faded knee-breeches in the family livery (there were frequent embarrassments over Goldsworthy's wages, which were supposed to be remitted by Mrs Butler). Cramped, genteel households where harassed married couples spend their time making ends meet and quarrelling with their servants are a feature of Thackeray's early fiction – the packed Bloomsbury tenement of 'Miss Shum's Husband' in the *Yellowplush Papers* probably owes something to Great Coram Street – but a year and a half into his marriage Thackeray considered himself to be blissfully happy. Writing home from a Parisian trip early in 1838 he told Isabella that he felt as if he had left one of his legs in Great Coram Street, 'and get on very lamely without it'.

The French trip was a pointer to the course of the next three years. His primary need was to earn money, even if that meant drudging for a few francs a day on papers such as *Galignani's English Messenger*, which consisted simply of extracts robbed from other periodicals. The experience made him an *habitué* of the odd world in which the light literature and bread-and-butter journalism of the late 1830s came together, and which is modestly outlined in the first half of *Pendennis*. To adapt a remark of John Gross', the reason why a satisfactory history of the early-Victorian literary scene will never be written – any literary scene if it comes to that – is that 'literary scene' itself is such an elastic term. In the 1830s it could have been stretched to cover the editor of the *Edinburgh Review* and the editor of the *Eatanswill Gazette*, the writings of a Maginn and a John Stuart Mill, *Oliver Twist* and the chocolate-box 'keepsakes' of the kind in which Arthur Pendennis makes his first showing in print. One does not have to go as far as exacting late-nineteenth-century critics such as Charles Whibley, who simply writes the period off as 'marked by bad taste and lack of restraint', to wonder at some of the constitutional oddities produced by this early-Victorian combination of taste and prejudice. At its upper levels 'literature' was still the preserve of fashionable patrons – one remembers the Honourable Percy Popjoy in *Pendennis*, whose three-volume novel is actually put together for him by a ghost-writer, or, from the same source, aristocratically edited 'Books of Beauty' in which portraits of society hostesses marched hand-in-hand with sycophantic versifying. Slightly further down the scale the 'silver-fork' novel, with its gossipy revelations of high life – George IV described Mrs Gore's *Women As They Are, or The Manners of the Day* as 'the best and most amusing novel published in my remembrance' – was giving way to a craze for 'low life' fiction of the kind made popular by Bulwer and Ainsworth's highwaymen. The critical climate, meanwhile, remained uniformly partisan, characterised by vicious personal attacks (Crofton Croker once referred to Lady Morgan as 'a female Methuselah', going on to accuse her of licentiousness, profligacy, irreverence, blasphemy, libertinism, disloyalty and atheism) and political infighting. Thackeray himself was not immune to this atmosphere of backstage intriguing, and one feels that his partiality for Miss Landon's poetry owed at least something to her friendship with Maginn. Inevitably, perhaps, given the catchment area from which early-Victorian journalists were drawn – daily papers tended to be staffed by tribes of expatriate Irishmen – this volatile and shifting landscape had a social dimension. Other than at the highest level – Wordsworth, say, or the aristocratic Bulwer – literature was hardly respectable (the elder Pendennis offers some sage advice to his nephew on this subject), and the gulf between a nobleman's son who wrote sonnets published at his own expense and a magazine hack was one of which any fashionable drawing-room would have been sharply aware. As a 'gentleman' who had lost his money and as a result was forced to associate with some distinctly non-gentlemanly colleagues, Thackeray appreciated this division. All his early works are credited to aliases, and it was not until the early 1840s that he felt confident enough to publish a book under his own name.

The six months preceding the Carmichael-Smyths' departure for Paris were taken up by a desperate search for work, in which the pay was quite as important as the respectability of the paymaster. A list of all the journals for which Thackeray wrote over the next three years would fill a good-sized index card. They range from forgotten literary magazines such as the *Parthenon* and the *Torch* to up-market items like Mill's *Westminster Review*, owned by his old acquaintance Sir William Molesworth. His principal outlets in these early years, though, were *Fraser's*, where an increasingly battered Maginn hung on as editor (eventually Thackeray dealt direct with James Fraser) and *The Times*. *The Times* connection, curiously enough, came through Isabella. Through her great-uncle Merrick, the Shawes were friends of the paper's leader-writer Edward Sterling and his wife, and as a child Isabella had spent a good deal of time at their house in South Place. In later life Annie would recall that her mother liked laughingly to boast that she had made her husband's fortune by introducing him to *The Times*. His first contribution, a long review of Carlyle's *French Revolution*, appeared in early August ('One is obliged to men in these circumstances who say even with blunder and platitude greater than Thackeray's, Behold this man is not an ass,' Carlyle commented – an ambiguous remark that prefigures some of the strains of their later relationship). At an early stage Thackeray seems to have tried to ingratiate himself with the editor ('My game as I see it is to stick to the *Times*,' he told his mother); by November 1838 he was invoicing the paper for five articles in the space of a single month. There were more book reviews, but also a certain amount of theatre criticism. In that November, for example, he reviewed Macready's performance in *Macbeth* (the actor, who had a low opinion of *The Times*, recorded that many of his friend's encomia had been cut out 'by that scoundrel paper'). The tricks of the trade came easily, and by an early stage Thackeray was resorting to the time-honoured journalist's standby of reusing material. A review of Lady Charlotte Bury's *Diary of George IV and Queen Caroline* in early January 1838 provided material for a March *Fraser's* paper, and a batch of Christmas novels reviewed in December 1837 underwent similar recycling.

In amongst the hack-work lurked the germ of an idea that would have long-term implications for his progress as a writer. Conning over a pile of new publications for *Fraser's* in the autumn of 1837, Thackeray came upon an etiquette manual entitled *My Book, or, The Anatomy of Conduct*. John Henry Skelton's contribution to an enormously popular contemporary genre was without merit, but Thackeray was amused by its pretentious tone. He determined to send up its hints for the living of a civilised life by reviewing it in the persona of a footman. Having written the piece in the character of Charles James de la Pluche – ('Yellowplush') in honour of Goldsworthy's faded knee-breeches – Thackeray knew that he was on to a good thing. 'I think I could make half-a-dozen stories by the same author, if you incline,' he told Fraser. The formula worked, and Yellowplush's memoirs, full of cockney malapropisms and comic mis-spellings, ran through much of 1838 in *Fraser's* and were revived a couple of years later for an attack on one of Thackeray's regular targets, Bulwer Lytton. It was the young journalist's first hit – Fitzgerald reported that both his sister and brother-in-law had praised the piece without knowing the author's identity – and Thackeray was now confident enough of his selling power to strike for better wages when he found that he was getting less than some of the other *Fraser's* contributors. Looking to explain the appeal of 'James de la Pluche', as the *alter ego* formally styled himself, a gentleman's gentleman who trains his worm's eye view on the society in which his various employers operate, one turns inevitably to the social context which these despatches from below stairs reflect. To a middle-class magazine reader, obsessed by the idea of class distinctions, domestic servants were figures of absorbing interest. Dickens caught something of this fixation in his account of the footmen's 'swarry' in the *Pickwick Papers. Punch*, too, subsequently produced a long-running series of 'servant gal-isms'. Such humour was invariably snobbish – the Bath footmen, as Dickens sees them, are merely aping their betters – but Thackeray's attitude to Yellowplush is relatively complex. On the one hand he sympathises with him (sympathy with servants is always a marked feature of Thackeray's writings); on the other he is happy to mock him for a snobbery that Thackeray himself shares, as at the end of 'Miss Shum's Husband', when Yellowplush quits his post in disgust having discovered that his employer is actually a crossing sweeper. Yellowplush's shrewdness, considerable when helping to manouevre Altamont into the arms of Miss Shum against her stepmother's wishes, is deployed to even greater effect in the later *Yellowplush* episodes featuring the Honourable Mr Deuceace. This fashionably conducted son of the Earl of Crabs, an archetypal card-sharp and exploiter of naïve young men, wanders through much of Thackeray's fiction. Throughout, his adventures have a kind of circumstantial detail – even down to his minutely itemised bills – that tether them to some of the experiences of his creator's own early life.

Yellowplush's frenetic wordplay is very much of its time – though there is the odd Joycean moment, as when Altamont is described as 'anchoring' after Miss Shum – but the liveliness of the observation is something new in Thackeray's work. 'The great slattnly doddling girls was always on the stairs,' Jeames writes at one point about Mrs Buckmaster's establishment, 'poking about with nasty flower-pots, cooking something, or sprawling in the window seats with greasy curl-papers, reading greasy novels.' However, life in Great Coram Street could not be indefinitely sustained on the three guineas a sheet (sixteen magazine pages) that Thackeray eventually succeeded in winkling out of Fraser. Isabella was pregnant again, and in March 1838, with the idea of working up some of the material that would later appear in the *Paris Sketch Book*, he left to spend a month in France. His letters home are a mixture of updates on his social life, apparently heartily enjoyed, and wistfulness for what he has left behind. A note of 11 March records attending an evening party at the Crowes', and then proceeding to the Café Anglais where he discovered two old Charterhouse men and stayed up until three in the morning. The Shawes were still in Paris: accepting an invitation to dinner, Thackeray found his mother-in-law 'very gracious' and spent the whole evening talking about Isabella. The experience produced a heartfelt expression of love for his wife: 'Here have we been nearly 2 years married & not a single unhappy day. Oh I do bless God for this great happiness wh. he has given us. It is so great that I almost fear for the future . . .' He wrote another rapturous paragraph and then sat staring at it, so great was his emotion.

Meanwhile the financial situation was becoming alarming. Thackeray reported that he had done too little work and spent too much money. 'We must work like tigers when we get home & no mistake,' he decided – 'breakfast at 8 walk at 2 with Mrs Thack: no club, and a light dinner.' Subsequently he reported doing 'a little towards the book', 'some very splendid articles for *Galignani*' (Isabella would have realised the joke) and taking on the duties of Battier, the *Morning Advertiser*'s Paris correspondent, 'who is now lying at the point of death, with a wife & 4 children and not a penny in the world'. There were other, closer anxieties. In particular, Thackeray was worried that Major Carmichael-Smyth (presumably Thackeray's parents were in Paris, but there is no record of his having visited them) intended to return to India in an attempt to recoup his fortune. Surely he could live at Boulogne on £200 a year, Thackeray wondered, and his income must surely be that. At the same time he had begun to comprehend some of the Shawe family's intrinsic oddity, in particular the variety manifested in his sister-in-law Jane. Talking about Isabella, she 'burst out crying in a kind of agony'. Thackeray suspected that the problem might be simple loneliness, and wondered whether it would be a good idea to bring her to England. 'She has no one to love or to speak to: and your mother's solicitude only makes matters worse,' he told his wife. As for Mrs Shawe, Thackeray confidently reported, 'Your Ma & I are on the best terms possible, & have not had the shadow of a row.'

Without doubt the domestic life in Great Coram Street to which Thackeray now returned had its tensions. Some of these were caused by lack of money – in one of the Paris letters Thackeray warns that they may have to let part of the house and cut down on servants; others seem more integral to the respective characters of husband and wife. Isabella had not conquered the idleness of her girlhood, and had difficulty in managing the household. Mrs Carmichael-Smyth and Mrs Butler, exigent housewives both of them, were shocked by the general air of dereliction. To make matters worse, the house was cramped and flea-ridden (Thackeray reported that his brother-in-law Arthur Shawe squashed fifteen in the course of a single night) and frequently stank of the turpentine used as a preventative. Driven out by the noise made by children and domestics, not to mention Isabella's frequent appearances at his study door, Thackeray cultivated what became one of his most settled working habits – the ability to write in inns, clubs or even on the tops of omnibuses – and consented to be put up for the Reform (which cost twenty pounds a year) on the grounds that it had a pleasant and well-stocked library. There was a second reason, too, he explained to his mother – he wanted to extend his acquaintance with Liberal journalists and thereby avoid having to work for Conservative papers. Often these working days away from home telescoped into bachelor supper parties or Bohemian evenings at the Cyder Cellar in Maiden Lane. Isabella seems to have resigned herself to these absences, excusing them as a necessary consequence of hard work. 'We see nothing of William,' she explained at one point in a letter to Mrs Carmichael-Smyth, 'but it is for the best I suppose.' As he got up so early in the morning she was prepared to let him 'gad of an evening'. But she resented Thackeray's bachelor entourage, 'Fitz and his tail' as she called them, who seemed 'as if they could not breathe' without her husband's presence. Such company was all very well, she tartly informed her mother-in-law, 'but they forget they have 300 or 400 a year to take life easy on, and though we may have *double* that yet it must be earned'. All the same Isabella liked Fitzgerald, who would, she thought, give Thackeray his last shilling if it were needed 'and often thinks of what he can do that is obliging to me'.

Thackeray's absences from home were not merely selfish. Like any young professional man he was hard at work forging the alliances that would be useful to him and immersing himself in a way of life at which he now desperately wanted to succeed. More perhaps than many other professions, literature has always depended to a disproportionately large degree on the personal touch. Certainly the marketplace of the late 1830s was an increasingly complex one, where personal connections counted for quite as much as innate talent. The rising, indeed risen, star of these coteries was Charles Dickens. Even in his mid-twenties, with *Sketches by Boz* and the *Pickwick Papers* behind him and *Oliver Twist* appearing in *Bentley's Miscellany* (in fact the opening numbers of *Twist* overlapped with the closing numbers of *Pickwick*), Dickens was a man of enormous influence, and Thackeray was careful to keep up his acquaintance. Though Dickens was probably not directly involved in the appearance of 'The Professor' in *Bentley's* in September 1837, the two met at the Garrick, and Thackeray seems to have visited the cottage that Dickens rented at Twickenham in the summer of 1838. Many of Dickens' guests here, including his friend John Forster, turned up at Kensal Lodge, home of the novelist William Harrison Ainsworth, then at the height of his popularity, where Thackeray was also present. A slightly different kind of literary companionship was provided by Alfred Tennyson, whom Thackeray probably encountered through Fitzgerald: the young poet was a frequent caller at Great Coram Street, and both men were members of a group that met at the Cock Tavern in Fleet Street, immortalised in Tennyson's 'Will Waterproof's Lyrical Monologues' ('And softly, through a vinous mist/My college friendships glimmer').

In many ways, though, the most significant alliance that Thackeray made at this time was with the veteran comic illustrator George Cruikshank. Thackeray had known Cruikshank for some years, and had admired his work since his schoolboy days. On his return from Paris in early 1837 he became a regular visitor to Cruikshank's studio. Simply in terms of published work, the Cruikshank connection was vital to Thackeray: he collaborated with him several times, notably on Cruikshank's *Comic Almanack* for 1839 and 1840 (these sold 20,000 copies apiece, although Thackeray's fee for supplying the text was modest), and contributed pieces to *George Cruikshank's Table Book* as late as 1845. By haunting the studio at Amwell Street, Thackeray was drawn further into a loose-knit circle that included Dickens and Ainsworth, both of whose works Cruikshank illustrated. Undoubtedly Thackeray existed on the fringes of these collaborations: both he and Dickens, for example, may have worked at different times on a book called *More Hints on Etiquette*, which appeared with Cruikshank's illustrations in March 1838. More important even than this, though, was what Cruikshank represented – a direct link back to the satirical pamphleteers of the Regency and a tradition of comic draughtsmanship from which Thackeray felt himself to be in linear descent. Dividing nineteenth-century literature into family trees of 'influence' is not always helpful either to the artists involved or our perception of them, but the long and admiring essay on Cruikshank that Thackeray supplied to the *Westminster Review* in 1840 reads like an appraisal of his own mature techniques. 'Remark, too, the conscientiousness of the artist,' he advises, in a discussion of Cruikshank's illustrations to Ainsworth's *Jack Sheppard*, 'and that shrewd pervading idea of *form* which is one of his principal characteristics.' As Cruikshank's biographers point out, Thackeray's praise of his mentor is intimately related to his own development as a writer. Yellowplush's mockery of the pretensions of contemporary urban life; later attacks on the Newgate school of crime fiction; the pervasive Regency nostalgia – all these were given focus and validation by Cruikshank's pictures.

There was also the fact – something that would have meant a great deal to Thackeray at this time – that Cruikshank was an *artist*. Thackeray's artistic ambitions died hard, and he undoubtedly obtained a vicarious satisfaction from watching Cruikshank at work. The older man took a sympathetic interest, while suspecting that Thackeray's real bent lay elsewhere. As he put it to a friend many years later, 'I used to tell him that to be an artist was to burrow along like a mole, heaving up a little mound here and there for a long distance. He said he thought he would presently break out into another element and stay there.' As it turned out this was an accurate forecast, but much of the evidence from this period of Thackeray's life suggests that he regarded the commitment to journalism as a rather obvious settling for second best. There are several wistful little glances at the life that might have been, and as late as 1839 Isabella reported to Mrs Carmichael-Smyth that 'the painters get round him & tell him it is ten thousand pities he does not follow that vocation and W says let us sell all and go to Rome'. He contented himself with art criticism for

Fraser's, beginning with an account of the Royal Academy Summer Exhibition of 1838 entitled 'Strictures on Pictures'. The piece foreshadows Thackeray's general stance as an art critic – lively but middle-brow. His suggestion as to the correct attitude for an amateur art-lover to display towards paintings – 'look to have your heart touched by them' – was, as Charles Whibley pointed out, not terribly good advice even by the standards of 1838, while an appreciation of Charles Eastlake ('as pure as a Sabbath hymn sung by the voices of young children') prefigures some of the *Boy's Own Paper* art criticism attributed fifteen years later to Clive Newcome.

Thackeray's first significant collaboration with Cruikshank came in mid-1838, when he was invited to provide the letterpress for the *Comic Almanack* of 1839. An early letter outlining his plans ('I am going to write a kind of rambling biography of a Mr Dobbs, dividing his life into 12 periods, & making them correspond with the year') gives only a vague idea of the swingeing piece of satire into which *Stubbs's Calendar, or The Fatal Boots* would eventually metamorphose. A later note written as the work progressed shows the full extent of the collaboration, with Thackeray giving detailed instructions on the scope of Cruikshank's design ('The parlour door may be opened, and some people observed coming in –'; '– Make Tims a very military man in an immense braided frock coat'). Work on *Stubbs's Calendar* and a host of other projects was, however, interrupted by pressing domestic matters. On 12 July, a week before his twenty-seventh birthday, Isabella gave birth to another daughter. The child was named Jane. Announcing her arrival to Mrs Shawe, Thackeray pronounced that Isabella 'produces children with a remarkable facility. She is as happy and as comfortable as any woman can be.' Mary Graham came to supervise the nursing and the ever-attentive Fitzgerald presented the convalescent mother with a copy of the *Pickwick Papers*. Thackeray reported that Annie, on seeing her sister, 'wanted to poke one of her eyes out and said teedle deedle, wh. is considered very clever'.

It was a crowded, hand-to-mouth existence, with little time for reflection: the reckoning up would come after it had ended, and the hindsight with which Thackeray came to regard the Great Coram Street days can sometimes seem chilling in its clarity. In the meantime the winter of 1838 passed in a strew of journalism, work with Cruikshank and a stream of ideas, some realised and some aborted. It was at about this time, for example, that Thackeray sat down with a tableful of acquaintances – they included his old *Constitutional* colleagues Laman Blanchard and Jerrold – and sketched out a plan for what looks suspiciously like an early version of *Punch*. Unfortunately Thackeray got it into his head that each co-partner in the proposed new venture would be liable not only for the debts of the publication but also for any private debts of the co-partners. As no one possessed sufficient legal knowledge to point out the absurdity of this suggestion, the project foundered and was not revived for another three years. In amongst a round of low-key socialising with friends such as the Kembles (John Kemble, whom Thackeray had known since Cambridge days, edited the *British and Foreign Review*, his brother Henry and sister Fanny followed their father Charles onto the stage), the Bullers and the Proctors (Bryan Proctor held a lucrative appointment as a Commissioner of Lunacy, while his wife had some reputation as a

literary hostess) and money worries – several of Thackeray's surviving letters from the period are angry notes to editors complaining about poor rates of pay – an alternative view of Great Coram Street emerges from Annie's childhood memories. Annie's reminiscences of infancy are full of sharp, affectionate glimpses of her parents' home life – Isabella carrying her on her back into a small room on the ground floor where someone, found bent over a desk, seemed 'pleased, smiled at us, but remonstrated'; a place somewhere near Russell Square with children playing and the sound of music, where she succeeded in escaping from her nurse only to be picked up by a tall person who carried her home on his shoulders; John Goldsworthy (who used to let her sip porter from his tankard and always took her part in disagreements); Isabella again with 'pretty shining hair' playing the piano in the upstairs drawing-room that opened out onto the balcony.

If Annie is a constant presence in her parents' brief married life – both through frequent appearances in Thackeray's letters and in her own copious memoirs – Jane is a small, shadowy figure who exists only in a drawing of Isabella breast-feeding her and the memory of her precocity in crying 'Pa, pa' whenever Thackeray came near her. She survived for just over eight months before dying of a chest infection in March 1839. Writing to his mother, Thackeray wondered sadly what

Richmond Thackeray
as a young man

'The Thackeray
Family', by George
Chinnery, c.1814

15 Jermyn Street. Sunday November 13. 1831.

Possible self portrait in
Jermyn Street, 1831

Thackeray
by Maclise, 1833

Possible sketch of Isabella
in France, early 1840s

Thackeray's
watercolour of
Isabella, 1836

Thackeray's miniature
of Annie as a baby

Brodie in old age

Thackeray's drawing
of Edward Fitzgerald

Douglas Jerrold,
from an etching by
Kenny Meadows, 1845

Jane Brookfield,
aged 30, from the painting
by George Richmond

William Brookfield
in later life

Thackeray's letters
to Lady Ashburton

D'Orsay's sketch of Thackeray, 1848

he could say 'about our little darling who is gone'. The experience stirred a characteristic fatalism in him: he did not feel sorry for Jane, he told Mrs Carmichael-Smyth, but thought of her 'only as something charming that for a season we were allowed to enjoy'. Just as when Annie had been seriously ill in infancy, it had seemed wrong to pray for her life, 'For specific requests to God are impertinencies I think, and all we should ask from him is to learn how to acquiesce . . .' He would not ask to have his daughter back 'and subject her to the degradation of life and pain'. Isabella wrote to reassure Mrs Carmichael-Smyth, who had reproached herself for a lack of interest in her granddaughter, reminding her that she had provided nightdresses and Jane's little white frock. 'As long as she was spared me,' Isabella declared, 'she was attended to with all the care I had *learnt* from *you* in watching Annie . . .' Both parents found consolation in their surviving daughter. 'Young as she is she chases away sorrow,' Isabella decided. Thackeray's letters are full of references to Annie's beguiling precocity. At twenty months 'Totty' or 'Missy', as she was nicknamed, knew not only the names of farmyard animals but the noises they made. Thackeray was anxious that the creative spirit he detected in his daughter, and for that matter in other children, should be appropriately stimulated. 'There is a grand power of imagination about the little creatures and a creative fancy and belief that is very curious to watch,' he told his mother; 'it falls away in the light of common day.' He determined that Annie's reading should consist of Tom Thumb and Jack the Giant Killer rather than the 'twopenny-halfpenny realities' offered by popular children's writers such as Maria Edgeworth.

His own career was slowly advancing. The opening instalment of *Catherine*, his first novel, had appeared in *Fraser's* in May 1838, alongside the continuing exploits of Yellowplush, while *The Tremendous Adventures of Major Gahagan* – a skit on the Indian reminiscences narrated to him by his stepfather – ran simultaneously in the *New Monthly Magazine*. Many doors remained firmly shut, however, and a series of letters from late 1839 to John Kemble show some of the difficulties Thackeray had in placing his work, even with people who might legitimately be regarded as personal friends. There is a plaintive note to a letter of July 1839 in which he asks Kemble not to 'turn away better pens for mine: but my dear fellow try and give me all the work you can'. October found him proposing a scheme of work that Kemble failed to back, while a letter from December mentions a piece on Napoleon. This ended up in the *Paris Sketch Book*, however, without having previously been published. Yet another communication proposes 'a sweet article of twenty pages on French fashionable novelists . . . This you must make room for: and have in a fortnight, poz.' Again, this only appeared in the *Paris Sketch Book*. Other openings could turn out to be less attractive than they seemed. An unlooked-for visitor in the summer of 1839 was the buccaneering American magazine editor Nathaniel Parker Willis, who claimed that his mission was to identify the authors of *Yellowplush* and *Major Gahagan*, 'the two best periodical series of papers that have appeared for twenty years'. Flattered, Thackeray agreed to send contributions to Willis' New York magazine, the *Corsair*, only to find that Willis, one of the great copyright pirates of his day, was a bad payer and that the *Corsair* lived up to its name: having struck up the acquaintance, Willis immediately began to pilfer old *Fraser's* articles. While regretting that he had been sold short, Thackeray seems to have been as much amused as exasperated by Willis, used his journalistic approach (the visiting American writing up his English hosts with near-anthropological mock-naïvety) in several pieces of his own, and later wrote a humorous review of Willis' autobiographical *Dashes at Life*.

Willis' compliments – he described Thackeray as 'the very best periodical writer alive. He is a royal, daring, fine creature, too' – were no substitute for ready money. And yet amid the round of routine hack-work and humiliating applications for employment, his interests and concerns as a writer were beginning to declare themselves. Thackeray's early writings – the *Yellowplush Papers*, *Major Gahagan*, *The Fatal Boots*, which appeared late in 1838 – are largely about semblance, duplicity, calculated misrepresentation. Even *Catherine*, which ends up as a much darker piece of work, began life as a burlesque of the Newgate fiction then being popularised by Dickens and Ainsworth. These apprentice writings frequently have their roots in the burgeoning middle-class world of social advancement. Typically their focus is the person attempting to move upwards through a social landscape whose rules and barriers he barely comprehends – Barber Cox, for example, the hapless hero of *Cox's Diary*, which surfaced in Cruikshank's *Comic Almanack* for 1840, who inherits a fortune and sets out to live like a gentleman. The series of assumed voices that Thackeray created in order to relate these adventures – even *Catherine*, perhaps the least characteristic, is narrated by 'Ikey Solomons jr' – gave him an important degree of artistic elbow-room. Their function, in fact, was to supply a kind of inner disturbance that gives the work its tensions, and the result is a pervading irony that inevitably fractures the harmonising elements of his style. Yellowplush, Michael Angelo Titmarsh and Goliah Gahagan are not quite Thackeray, and at the same time not quite independent of Thackeray, for there is always a rasp of ulterior design that drags the reader back to the impresario behind them. Yellowplush's occasional bouts of moralising are a good example of this. When the sentinel of the back kitchen pronounces that when you vex him a rogue is no longer a rogue, that you find a villain out in his passion, for he displays his cloven hoof etc., the reader is conscious that the voice hashe story or

its comic effects, and in some ways Yellowplush is more rather than less real to us as a result of these interventions. Their ultimate effect, too, is to entice the reader even further into the narrative game that Thackeray plays, to strain his or her credulity and demonstrate its extravagance – you put down each chapter of *The Fatal Boots*, for example, wondering how Bob Stubbs could be such an idiot – and finally overcome his resistance through sheer comic high spirits.

Cox's Diary, or to revive the original title *Barber Cox and the Cutting of His Comb*, is a vivid snapshot of how Thackeray's writing had developed by this time. While Thackeray's own sense of class-consciousness is sometimes a little too unmediated for comfort, the occasional sourness of the tone is redeemed by its painstaking inventory of social advancement and the duplicity with which it is invariably attended. Inheriting a fortune from a relative, the Coxes set out to better themselves, are patronised, hoodwinked and gulled by the new acquaintances they meet in the course of this ascent, and end up no better off than when they started. As ever, the money comes from India: Mrs Cox's uncle is 'a mighty rich East India merchant, who, having left this country sixty years ago as a cabin-boy, had arrived to be the head of a great house in India, and was worth millions, we were told'. Almost at once the Coxe-Coxes, as they swiftly rechristen themselves, are plunged into a world of desperate snobbery and showy excess. Prudently deciding to keep the dead uncle's servants 'to show us how to be gentlefolk', the ex-hairdresser and his wife are soon rubbing shoulders with seedy continental noblemen, such as Count Mace and his Excellency Baron von Punter from Baden, and enduring a series of exquisite social humiliations (a duchess condescends to grace their first entertainment, provided she does not have to speak to her hosts). Much of this can seem

unnecessarily cruel to a modern eye – there is no harm in Cox, and the
fun poked at his ignorance betrays Thackeray's own innate snobbishness – but there are some sharply written scenes in which the barber's
shattered illusions hint at the wider corruption of the society in which
he is trying (and failing) to make his way. 'If you *could* but have seen
Munseer Anatole!' Cox muses, backstage at the theatre. 'Instead of
looking twenty he looked a thousand. The old man's wig was off, and a
barber was giving it a touch with the tongs; Munseer was taking snuff
himself, and a boy was standing by with a pint of beer from the public-
house at the end of Charles Street.' This virtually re-creates the *Flore
et Zephyr* caricature, as Thackeray, with his keen eye for continuity in
his work, no doubt intended that it should.

Money worries continued to press on both generations of the family.
The Carmichael-Smyths were still thinking of going back to India.
Isabella hastened to assure them, with an emphasis reminiscent of
Queen Victoria's journals, that 'we see *no* necessity *under* the *sun* why
you should tear your dear hearts and make us unhappy . . .' In any case,
she went on, there was a strong chance that Charles Buller would be
made a Cabinet minister, thereby opening up a lucrative avenue of
patronage and public appointments. In the event these dreams went
unrealised, and Thackeray continued to juggle their finances, borrowing money from the major and returning it on the proceeds of a piece
that he had finally managed to place with Kemble, and contemplating
the arrival of Bryan Proctor's younger brother as a lodger. As he put it
succinctly in a letter to James Fraser in early July, 'I am hard up and
want money.' There were further trips to Paris. Thackeray went on his
own in the summer, presumably in search of material, returning with
his family in November to stay with the Carmichael-Smyths. Husband
and wife each provided accounts of the journey back. Thackeray
reported 'a dismal coach trip, a pleasant passage and nobody sick',
although Annie kept many of the passengers awake with her cries.
Isabella remembered Thackeray going to sleep beneath a table on deck
after gravely asking the man who slept on top to be careful which side
he chose if he were taken ill in the night.

'You must not go for to alarm yourself about my infinite struggle
hardships & labours everyone of them do good –' Thackeray wrote
telegraphically to his mother in November. To his financial worries
could be added the first signs that something was wrong with Isabella.
An odd hint of dreaminess steals into several of her letters to Mrs
Carmichael-Smyth from this time. A letter of March 1839, written in

the aftermath of Jane's death, complains of sluggishness. Two months later she was still fatigued, confiding that 'My life of late has slipped by so quietly reading or *sleeping* or musing that I find myself quickly done up.' She put it down to the rather vague cause of novel sensations: 'I suppose the sight of anything new about creates a restlessness and unsettled feeling that subsides when things become familiar to one.' For all this inanition, Isabella retained her imaginative grasp of language. Worrying that her mother and sister – then on a visit to London – might lose themselves, she decided that 'Jane has a large bump of locality.' Almost certainly Thackeray did not notice this change in his wife's temperament – with hindsight he was to reproach himself bitterly for this failure. Busy, pressed for money and habituated to what he had come to regard as simple idleness, he did not suspect that his wife's languor might have a more sinister cause. Christmas 1839 found him enmired in work and discussions on how to reduce the household expenses. He was disappointed of 'my great fifty pound article', he told his mother – there had been no time to write it. Meanwhile he disparaged Mrs Carmichael-Smyth's plans to sack their nurse, a kindly and devoted woman named Brodie, whose wages were fourteen pounds a year, and replace her with a less experienced country girl at six pounds. It was a poor economy, he told her. Besides, Isabella was pregnant again and Brodie would have plenty to do come June. Ill and out of sorts with what Isabella described as influenza, a severe cough and a kind of low fever, he cannot have been cheered by one of his mother's melancholy epistles on religious topics that arrived just before Christmas. This sparked a characteristic rebuttal of Mrs Carmichael-Smyth's Old Testament notions of everlasting hell. Good was 'of necessity Eternal', Thackeray told his mother. After death 'our souls if they live cannot but be happy'. By the same token, the idea of divine retribution was false. Punishment, terror and revenge did not prove themselves, and 'One act of violence is not right because it has been preceded by another.'

The New Year brought a quickening in the pace of his professional life. The firm of Hugh Cunningham had agreed to bring out the collection of miscellaneous pieces on French subjects that he had been contemplating for the past three years (he did not build any great hopes on it, Isabella reported to her mother-in-law, as Cunningham was such a very obscure publisher); the final chapter of *Catherine* had been despatched to Fraser ('thank Heaven it's over', the author remarked); while a note from mid-January 1840 to an anonymous politician mentions a letter for a continental newspaper, 'the most influential perhaps of any published abroad', on which he is engaged, and ventures 'to ask permission again to wait on you sometimes'. Neither the politician nor the continental paper has ever been identified, but it seems clear that Thackeray (who mentions a previous connection through the *Globe*) is in search of confidential communications that will add spice to his report.

At the same time he was playing a significant role in one of the period's major literary controversies, the continuing row about the so-called 'Newgate school' of crime fiction. Thackeray's dislike of what he regarded as the sentimentalising of base emotions went back as far as his first encounter with Bulwer's *Eugene Aram* in 1832; the *Fraser's* tradition of bitter personal attacks had given him ample scope for sniping at Bulwer's pretensions. The Newgate row, though, was part of a wider public backlash against the growing volume of low-life and delinquency novels, whose respectable end was represented by *Oliver Twist* and Ainsworth's *Jack Sheppard*. There are interesting parallels with late-twentieth-century agitation over violent films – opponents of the highwayman novel, for example, pointed out that at one stage street vendors were selling 'Sheppardbags' containing housebreaking tools, while a notorious contemporary murderer was supposed to have got the idea from seeing a theatrical adaptation of Ainsworth's novel. In addition to *Catherine*, whose account of Catherine Hayes, burned in 1726 for the murder of her husband, parodied the whole genre, Thackeray's contribution to the dispute began with a *Fraser's* essay of April 1839. He objected to the Newgate novel on two grounds. One was simple realism: 'The present popular descriptions of low life are shams.' The other was taste. The public was sick of heroic griefs, passions and tragedies, Thackeray declared, 'but take them out of the palace, and place them in the thief's boozing den . . . and tragedy becomes interesting once more'. Like many a later contributor to this kind of debate, Thackeray was convinced that people who should know better were allowing themselves to be led by public taste into areas it would do better not to colonise. As he put it, 'Gentlemen and men of genius may amuse themselves with such rascals, but not live with them altogether. The public taste, to be sure, lies that way, but these men should lead the public.' February 1840 brought the high-water mark of the *Fraser* assault on the Newgate school, with a number containing an essay by J. Hamilton Reynolds on 'William Ainsworth and *Jack Sheppard*' and the final part of *Catherine*, together with a supplementary chapter unfavourably comparing Dickens and Ainsworth to Gay and Fielding and concluding: 'in the name of common sense, let us not expend our sympathies on cut throats, and other such prodigies of evil.'

Thackeray was depressed in the early months of 1840, worried about the political situation – there had been a Chartist attack on Newport the previous November and further trouble was stirring – and, close to home, with the problem of John Goldsworthy's wages, still unpaid by Mrs Butler. The tensions of his personal life were capable of spilling out in unexpected ways. There is an odd letter to James Fraser, for instance, in which he airs a 'confused notion' of 'having made myself disagreeable at dinner'. In fact, presumably inflamed by drink, he had grievously insulted the publisher John Murray: Fraser urged him to write and apologise. Perhaps divining something of the effect that her remarks had on Isabella's lowered morale, he instructed Mrs Carmichael-Smyth to stop her criticisms of the running of the Great Coram Street household. He was particularly upset by the suggestion – it had come from Pauline, his mother's French maid – that Brodie ill-treated Annie. His mother was too hard on Isabella, he deposed, who now rose at eight '& if she leaves the washment of the child to the nurse, at any rate the child is healthy, and as clean as can be, and the nurse treats her with the utmost care and tenderness'. The pleasures of married life, such as going out with Isabella to watch the celebrations following Queen Victoria's marriage in early February, had to be squeezed into a punishing work schedule. Thackeray reported that he had a dozen irons in the fire – a plan for a weekly paper written entirely by himself (eventually aborted on the grounds of inadequate salary), plus an introduction to John Blackwood, the proprietor of *Blackwood's*. There was no lack of work, 'but the deuce is the wear & tear of it'. *Catherine* was 'not generally liked', he concluded, although Carlyle and others had praised it highly. Thackeray could not help wondering whether popular opinion was right, for he had chosen 'a disgusting subject & no mistake'.

Late February found him in a furious temper, enraged by noise in the house that stopped him working. He spent a week away with his old friend Lettsom, reflected dispassionately on his prospects, and cheered up. He was not at all afraid, he told his mother, 'for I owe scarcely twenty pounds, am rising in the world, and don't see any cause to be uneasy'. There was plenty of cause to be uneasy, had he but known it, and yet Isabella's letters to Mrs Carmichael-Smyth in the weeks before her confinement give little hint of the trouble in store. The only thing she suffered from, she explained, was violent cramp 'that makes me dance out of my sleep' and convinced Thackeray that he ought to run for the doctor. A similar vein of humour runs through a letter to her sister Jane, recounting the entertainment offered to their brother Arthur, then staying at Great Coram Street. With the vacationing India officer in tow, the Thackerays had 'called on everybody we knew, *except* the Duke of Wellington, the Queen, Prince Albert and a few of that "clique" whom *we* thought *we might* dispense with'. Thackeray reported his wife 'fat, rosy and healthy' and getting up early. He was behind with the *Paris Sketch Book*, he admitted, 'but I am in a ceaseless whirl and whizz from morning to night, now with the book, now with the drawings, now with articles for Times, Fraser, here and there . . .' Mrs Carmichael-Smyth, who mistrusted Shawe ramifications, was quickly reassured about Arthur's presence: the 'poor lad' hardly cost them ten shillings a week, Thackeray promised, and the impending arrival of Mrs Butler would in any case be a good excuse to send him about his business.

In fact this ten shillings a week was money that the family could have done with. According to Thackeray's calculations, they had spent nearly £200 in the four months since Christmas. Further maternal criticism of Isabella, now within weeks of her confinement, was brushed aside. 'I think you are inclined to be hard upon – but never mind that.' The birth of the baby, a girl christened Harriet Marian on 28 May, coincided with a financial emergency. With exactly seven shillings and sixpence in his pocket, Thackeray discovered that the fifty pounds he had expected from Cunningham on completing the *Paris Sketch Book* would only be paid after the book was published. He would now be 'obliged to make a dreadful scuffle of work all next month instead of idling', he told his mother. Fortunately the 'two small patients' were getting on well, and the baby 'flourished beautifully'. Annie remembered being shown a small bundle wrapped in flannel lying on the nurse's knee, and Brodie instructing her to watch as Minnie, as the baby was soon known, kicked her feet.

Undoubtedly the volume of work that Thackeray was forced to undertake in the months after Minnie's birth was the principal reason for his neglect of Isabella – something he would regretfully acknowledge in the succeeding months – and at a time when she badly needed his support. Surviving letters from mid-1840 are full of unrealised plans: for a scheme called 'The Foolscap Library', or a series of papers for Blackwood (Thackeray suggested 'No politics, as much fun and satire as I can muster, literary lath[er] and criticism of a spicy nature, and general gossip' – he belonged to a couple of clubs, he added, and could 'get together plenty of rambling stuff'). Blackwood declined, but one of the ideas that Thackeray offered him, eventually submitted to *Fraser's*, turned out to have an unlooked-for significance. Along with half of London, his eye had fallen on the figure of Francis Courvoisier, a Swiss valet who had recently been convicted of the murder of his employer, Lord William Russell, at the latter's house in Norfolk Street. The trial had excited tremendous public interest, and Courvoisier's execution – due to take place at Snow Hill, not far from Thackeray's old Charterhouse haunts – was set to become a public spectacle. Thackeray arranged to go with his friend Richard Monckton-Milnes, now Liberal MP for Pontefract. The tone of his letter to Milnes suggested that he envisaged it as simply another journalistic assignment, albeit one with a greater degree of human interest. In the event Courvoisier's death in front of an audience of nearly 20,000 Londoners had a profound effect on him, and his account of the proceedings, the starkly titled 'Going to See a Man Hanged', is one of his sharpest early pieces. The accuracy of his reporting is confirmed by contemporary press accounts. *The Times*, too, noted Courvoisier's 'extraordinary appearance of firmness' and how the victim's clasping together of his hands two or three times 'was the only visible symptom of emotion or mental anguish which the wretched man exhibited'. The experience made Thackeray miserable for weeks afterwards, with the doomed man's face continually appearing before his eyes and the scene, as he told Mrs Proctor, mixing itself 'with all my occupations'.

Dickens was another interested spectator at Snow Hill, watching from a rented room in a nearby house with Maclise and his brother-in-law Henry Burnett. Like Thackeray, whose distinctive figure he spotted in the crowd, he was appalled by the atmosphere ('nothing but ribaldry, debauchery, levity, drunkenness and flaunting vice in fifty other shapes') and came to see the experience as a conclusive argument against capital punishment. Courvoisier's execution, in fact, is an early example of the odd, shadowing process by which Dickens and Thackeray often seem to have conducted their working lives – a parallel track that would lead to them writing similar books, making similar changes in professional direction and, in Thackeray's case at least, treading a delicate path between emulation and resentment.

For the moment their differing status was symbolised by the

respective vantage points that each took up before the gallows – Thackeray in the crowd; Dickens watching from above. Yet, however slowly, Thackeray's reputation was on the rise. The *Paris Sketch Book*, published almost simultaneously under the signature of M.A. Titmarsh, was well received. Cunningham disposed of upwards of 400 copies, and Thackeray reported favourable notices in *The Times* and *Athenaeum* (Dickens' friend Forster did his best in the *Examiner*, but Thackeray suspected that he did not much care for the book). By the standards of the 1840s, the *Paris Sketch Book* is a fairly miscellaneous affair, with extended literary pieces such as 'On Some French Fashionable Novels' walking side-by-side with art criticism, the straightforward reportage of 'A Gambler's Death' and fabular fiction like 'The Painter's Bargain', but the general effect is surprisingly prophetic of Thackeray's later concerns and styles. 'The Painter's Bargain', for example, in which a man makes a seven-year pact with the Devil on the understanding that he will ultimately become his property, then gets out of it by demanding that the Devil take his termagant wife, uses food/sex imagery of a quite lurid kind. According to her father, the butcher's daughter whom the painter marries is 'as lovely a bit of mutton as ever a man would wish to stick a knife into'. The same piece gives an early outing to one of Thackeray's most consistent moral beliefs – the idea that money encourages you to behave better. Just as, some years later, Becky Sharp would declare that she could be a good woman on £5,000 a year, so Simon Gambouge, once in receipt of the Devil's bounty, becomes a model father and friend of the poor.

The modest success of this first book encouraged Thackeray to press ahead with his next scheme. Irish travel books were much in vogue, and 'Titmarsh in Ireland', he suggested to his mother, might be the stepping stone to prosperity. Having opened negotiations with Longman and with Dickens' publishers Chapman and Hall, he sketched out the exponential rise in his earnings that might ensue. With a £150 advance, he reasoned, he could write a book worth £300, pay the £150 off, have another £150 to go on with, and then write a book worth £400. Amid this airy castle building, the reference to Isabella – 'all but well thank God, & the baby a dear little fat flourishing podge of flesh' – is all but parenthetic. In the meantime he planned a trip to Belgium in search of material for a guidebook that Chapman and Hall might publish. But Isabella was far from well. In a letter of 4 August to Mrs Carmichael-Smyth she apologises for the long delay in writing, on the grounds that 'my body has been unhealthy and *consequently* my spirits low'. Although she felt herself 'excited', she was still not strong, 'and my head flies away with me as if it were a balloon'. It is a sad, confused letter, full of reproach and apology. 'This is *mere* weakness and a walk should set me right but in case there should be incoherence . . . you will know what to attribute it to.' She had begged Thackeray not to go to Belgium, she confided, 'but it seems as if I was always to damp him . . .' Still not thinking her depressed state of particular account, Thackeray duly went. When he bade her goodbye, he later confessed to his mother, Isabella burst into uncontrollable peals of laughter.

There is no record of what happened in Great Coram Street during Thackeray's absence in early August, but he was alarmed by what he found on his return. The 'extraordinary state of languour and depression' into which Isabella had lapsed led him to seek urgent medical advice. Armed with a prescription for sea air, he took the family for a three-week holiday to Margate. The change of scene and the sunshine seemed to do Isabella good, he told his mother; at any rate she was 'better in health, but very low'. Did Thackeray appreciate the seriousness of what was happening – the letter to his mother announcing the Margate trip is full of gossip about sales of the *Paris Sketch Book* and a particularly pleasing review in the *Spectator*, which praised his illustrations – or did he merely shut his eyes in the hope that the situation would improve? Early September brought a gloomy communication to his mother. Daily life in their lodgings, with Isabella's 'pitiful look always fixed on me', and the consequent difficulty in working, had become insupportable. Thackeray thought his wife was slowly improving, although in the mornings she was 'so absent that I don't like to trust her'. Trust her to do what? Remain alone in the room? Not to injure herself? It is difficult not to think that the insanity into which Isabella's post-natal depression steadily transformed itself was by now fairly well advanced. It was at this time that a ghastly incident took place on the beach, when Isabella, walking on the shore with three-year-old Annie, suddenly tried to drag the little girl into the sea. She relented a few seconds later and Annie was unharmed, but the memory imprinted itself on the child's mind and it was years before she could bring herself to tell her father.

With his wife in this odd state of mute self-absorption, and negotiations for the Irish tour progressing, Thackeray was more than ever concerned about money. He borrowed £100 from Mary Graham as security to finance the trip, telling his mother that as soon as he was decently in the way of making money and had had his stricture cured – he was still a bad risk in medical terms – he would insure his life. Happily there was an immediate improvement in his finances on 8 September when he signed a deal with Chapman and Hall. The terms – an advance of £120, with the prospect of total earnings of £385 if the book sold 1,250 copies – were highly favourable, even if the publishers insisted that he leave the family plate with them as security before his departure. None of this, though, could mitigate his growing alarm about Isabella. Back in London, without the benefit of the Margate ozone, she was 'just as bad as ever she has been'. Thackeray decided that the only solution was to leave immediately for Ireland in the hope that Isabella could recuperate at her mother's house in Cork while he set about fulfilling Chapman and Hall's commission. A spate of letters was despatched on 10 September to arrange all this. To his mother Thackeray confided some of the exasperation that the business had provoked in him, confessing that to continue looking after Isabella in her current state would drive him mad, that he and the children were well, but 'only my rogue of a wife makes me melancholy'. Illness was expensive. Margate had cost thirty-two pounds – 'O Titmarsh Titmarsh,' he demanded of himself, 'why did you marry?'

It would be easy to use these passages as proof that Thackeray was indifferent, or at least unsympathetic, to his wife's condition, but all the evidence suggests that they betray only a momentary exasperation. Essentially his annoyance stemmed from ignorance of the situation's gravity. Isabella was tired and listless: she should, could and would eventually recover. In the meantime, though he devoted himself to looking after her, he was angry at the disruption to his routine, and in particular to the all-consuming need to earn money. The steamer trip from London to Cork, which can be pieced together from letters to Mrs Carmichael-Smyth, finally demonstrated to him the enormity of what had happened. At some point on the evening of Sunday, 13 September Isabella's condition worsened from a kind of alarmed nervousness to 'absolute insanity'. Shutting herself in the ship's lavatory, as Thackeray and Brodie amused the children, she threw herself out of the window in an attempt at suicide. Twenty minutes later a passenger looking out over the rail at the ship's wake noticed an object splashing in the water. It was Isabella, kept afloat by the air trapped in the flounces of her crinoline and now paddling feebly with her hands.

Fished out and returned to her husband's care, Isabella was brought to the harbour at Cork 'quite demented'. She seems to have made a second attempt to kill herself on the evening of the 14th. In the end Thackeray spent the night stretched out beside her, chaining her to him with a ribbon so that he would be woken if she stirred. The significance of the events of the past two months immediately became apparent. 'I can see what I never did until now that she has been deranged for several weeks past,' he decided, recounting these events to his mother. The rest of the voyage, amid high seas, would have been unendurable had it not been for Brodie's solicitude. Thackeray was lost in admiration for the nurse's sense of duty. At one stage she was being sick every quarter of an hour, but soon afterwards could be seen 'staggering after the little ones feeding one & fondling another'.

Once settled in a boarding house next to the Shawes' domicile at Grattan Hill, he could do nothing but wait and see. At first Isabella seemed better, made what the local doctor thought was extraordinary progress and sat up in bed repeating the psalms, which her sister Jane read to her. 'She could no more have done this three days ago than fly,' Thackeray assured his mother. He was already mildly annoyed by Mrs Shawe, who though ready enough to bring Isabella meals at the lodging house, declined to admit her to her own spare room on the grounds of 'nerves'. But she meant well, he thought, and one should not judge too hardly 'a woman who is really & truly demented'. And yet in the midst of their troubles it pained him that Mrs Shawe could not keep her 'monstrous tongue' quiet. Meanwhile he noted grimly that Isabella cared not the least for him or the children and, if not carefully watched, would certainly try to kill herself again.

And there they stayed as September wore on: spending money on lodging-house fees, doctors' bills – a kindly local practitioner eventually offered his services *gratis* – watching Isabella turn now a little better, now a little worse, and listening to the prattle of Mrs Shawe who, as her son-in-law put it, 'brags bustles bothers prates incessantly of her great merits & sacrifices'. Left largely to her own devices, Annie played with the lodging-house children and acquired a villainous local brogue. She remembered Minnie as a tiny child with a long green veil – a preventative against sore eyes – sloping fields leading to a river full of ships, and buttercups. Isabella's condition fluctuated. In a bulletin of 21–3 September, Thackeray could talk of her 'wonderful progress towards convalescence', record her laughing and talking affectionately and simply, and at last taking an interest in the children. A day or two later, however, the reports were not so good, although Thackeray, somewhat bizarrely, took comfort in the fact that Isabella's melancholy seemed to have a *moral* basis. She spent her lucid moments consumed with guilt over what she regarded as her 'unworthiness'.

His careful tolerance of Mrs Shawe, meanwhile, was beginning to disintegrate. He scarcely liked to tell Mrs Carmichael-Smyth of her conduct, he reported, 'so unmotherly has it been'. Mrs Shawe had compounded her neglect of Isabella by abusing Thackeray for taking his wife away from London, and trying to persuade Brodie to admit that he had ill-treated her. It was hardly surprising that in this tense and unhappy atmosphere of mutual suspicion Isabella should be 'devoured by gloom' and lament that 'she was never fit to be a wife' – an old story that her husband suspected was partly true. Her madness took odd forms, and at one point she feared that if the people who stood talking to her left the room they would never come back. By the end of September, a fortnight after their arrival, she was well enough to take part in family rambles, and Thackeray, itching to take up his sketching book, seems still to have thought that his original plan – leaving Isabella and the children in Cork while he went off travelling – was practicable. However, 4 October found her 'cloudy & rambling again', although Thackeray thought that progress had been made (it was at this stage that he disclosed the full details of the suicide bid lest his mother should hear an account from Mrs Shawe's friends in Paris). He wished his mother could see Annie in the bath, while Minnie was 'the sweetest tempered little thing God ever made'. The mother 'notices them but seldom', he noted sadly.

The situation might have lasted for months, although by this time Thackeray was down to his last twenty pounds. The most serious question in his mind was how to convey Isabella back to London without worsening her condition. At first he conceived a plan to practise for their return by taking her out in a little boat, then working up by degrees to a voyage home via Dublin, during which time she could be drugged with opium. In the end, with his wife 'really worse than she had been for some time', and infuriated beyond endurance by Mrs Shawe, he took a spontaneous decision to leave, packed the family onto the Cork steamer and left for Bristol. From Clifton on 11 October, with Isabella 'better for the change', he wrote coolly to Mrs Shawe informing her that he had composed a nine-page letter to her, which he was debating whether or not to send. 'It is a very free one, but I shall be able to know at the week's end whether you are as much in fault as I think you, or whether I have been in a passion, or whether I have any business to lecture you.' A second letter, to his mother, begged the Carmichael-Smyths to come to them. When Mrs Carmichael-Smyth telegraphed to say that this was not feasible, Thackeray took what seemed to be the only course open to him – to reunite wife, children and nurse with his parents in Paris. This was a fearsome journey, even by the standards of the mid-nineteenth century, involving a coach-trip across England, a Channel crossing and forty hours in the diligence. The memory of the final leg lodged itself in Annie's mind: travelling all night in the great coach, with Thackeray trying to amuse her by striking a match and lighting a little lamp; a Frenchman in the corner with his face pressed up against the window complaining of her cries. If she went on crying, Thackeray told her, she would wake the baby and he would put out the lamp. But she continued to yell, Minnie woke up and the flame was extinguished. 'Light it! Light it!' Annie cried, as the carriage jolted and the man by the window moaned. Eventually she fell asleep on her father's knee (there is no record of how Isabella passed the journey). Waking in the morning, however, an air of cheerfulness had supervened. The sky was light and the great buildings of Paris were visible on either side. Finally they came to a halt and the Thackerays clambered out to greet the spectacle of 'my grandmother and grandfather coming down the curling stairs to meet us in the early morning and opening their arms to us all'.

'Jacques', waiter at 'Le Coq d'Or', near Ivry

Monsieur and *Madame* had desired a private room. I was
pleased to gratify their wish ... One could not fail to have
remarked them – a great tall Englishman, like a giant almost,
a grenadier, the lady on his arm barely reaching his shoulder.
They were confidential to one another, indeed we suspected
that they might be *en voyage de noces*. Certainly *Monsieur* was
insistent about the private room. I do not recall *Madame*
speaking ... *Monsieur* ate prodigiously of his dinner – *entrées,*
bifteck aux pommes, dessert – it did one's heart good to see
such appetite. I brought coffee in the usual way. Great was
my embarrassment when I discovered *Madame* embracing
Monsieur on the cheek. *Madame s'amuse naturellement,* and I
must confess I laughed too, whereupon *Monsieur* observed,
comme un vrai gentilhomme, 'Garcon! You are a good fellow,
and here is something to remember us by' and gave me a
Napoleon ... They left soon after, hand-in-hand through the
fields, and though we wondered if we should see them again,
they never came ...

IX

The Uncleared Table

'Well, I have not the courage to clear the table, nor indeed to do anything else, for I have had ten months of wretchedness, and truth to tell am quite beaten down.'

Letter to Mrs Proctor, 28 May 1841

aving arrived in Paris, the four Thackerays and Brodie crammed into Major and Mrs Carmichael-Smyth's apartment in an old courtyarded mansion on the avenue de Sainte-Marie near the Arc de Triomphe. Here, in a tiny room overlooking bleak gardens white with winter snow, the cold air full of the noise of the nuns at a nearby convent going about their devotions, Thackeray took stock of his shattered life. Few records exist of this dismal winter, but it seems that at first some attempt was made to keep Isabella in the apartment with the idea of re-integrating her into the family circle. This delicate operation cannot have been helped by the cramped living conditions – old Mrs Butler and Mary Graham were also quartered in the avenue de Sainte-Marie at this point – and the lack of money. In a famous passage from her memoirs, Annie remembered Thackeray telling her of a day on which Brodie came and asked him for money, causing him to change his last five-pound note and hand it to her, 'and we children were in one room crying and mamma was raving in the other'. This may sound melodramatic – the daughter recalling past traumas from the comfort of middle life – but the chances are that it reflects a distinct and ultimately unsustainable reality. Thackeray needed to work to support his family; Isabella's presence would have disrupted the entire household's routine. By early December he had decided to install her in M. Esquirol's highly regarded 'Maison de Santé' at Ivry, slightly beyond the Paris suburbs. By the standards of the time Esquirol's methods were thought to be enlightened: he had made his reputation at the hospice of La Salpêtrière, where he took a particular interest in mental illness among the local prostitute population. The fees were high, though – twenty pounds a month – and Thackeray, who had left England six weeks before with exactly that sum in his pocket, wondered how to pay them. He spent Christmas and the New Year of 1841 in a state of profound gloom, solemnly analysing his predicament in a letter to Fitz. 'This blow that has come upon me has played the deuce with me that is the fact, and I don't care to write to my friends and pour out lamentations wh. are all the news I have to tell.' His mood was scarcely improved by seeing Isabella for the first time since her sequestration. 'She bemoans her condition and that is a great step to cure'; she knew everyone and remembered things, but remained 'stunned' and confused. She had kissed him warmly at first, Thackeray reported, but then went away 'as if she felt she was unworthy of having such a God of a husband. God help her'.

What was wrong with Isabella? No formal medical records of her condition exist, but it seems clear that the Shawes' congenital oddity had manifested itself in an extreme form and that the post-natal depression brought on by Minnie's birth had gradually hardened into a form of autism. Equally clearly, the origins of Isabella's madness extended back beyond the summer of 1840. In his continual musings on the source of her affliction and the part he himself may have played in it, Thackeray tended to parcel out the blame for his marital tensions equally: reproaching himself for his frequent absences, and his wife for her inability to cope. Undoubtedly her lassitude infuriated him, and he seems never to have realised that it was an underlying symptom of her condition rather than a kind of moral weakness. Almost certainly this disapproval placed Isabella under enormous mental strain, in which her chief feeling was one of guilt. The reports of her conversation, which Thackeray occasionally refers to in letters to his mother, are usually about her 'unworthiness', her maternal failings and unfittedness to marry. Looking back at the three-way relationship that existed between Thackeray, Isabella and Mrs Carmichael-Smyth, one can detect a long-term atmosphere of minor fault-finding and repeated exhortations to 'improve'. By the time Thackeray realised that this pressure might be too much for Isabella to bear it was too late: heredity, strain and guilt had combined to push her over the brink. Or so we can assume. One wants always to know more about Isabella, certainly more than is provided by the fragmentary remains of her letters and accounts of her life – the bashful seventeen-year-old being fought over by two formidable adults, the young woman imitating the cries of the street hawkers with Annie (Thackeray commented that the two-year-old probably knew more about the price of potatoes than her mother) – but it is almost impossible to re-create her from the materials that survive.

A certain amount of light is shed on her mental state, at any rate from the vantage point of half a century, by the case notes relating to her grandchild, Minnie's daughter Laura, who was placed in a mental asylum in the 1890s. Laura was born prematurely, which undoubtedly affected her development, but her medical records identify 'heredity' as a contributory factor. Laura's memory is described as good, in contrast to her powers of concentration. Like her grandmother, she suffered from dental trouble. More important, she seems to have displayed the same degree of confusion and volatility, became 'silly, talkative and excitable when upset' and had a tendency to ramble in her speech. It would be overstating these similarities to say that Laura was fashioned in her grandmother's image – the one was 'backward', the other a lively adolescent flipped into insanity by pressures she had no way of resisting; equally, one cannot ignore the twitch on the genetic thread.

Even if her case had been correctly diagnosed – in a medical landscape that had barely begun to consider the question of mental illness – there was very little that could have been done. One suspects that if anything could have restored Isabella to sanity, it would have been some extremely gentle form of therapy. As it was, her treatment consisted of rest and removal from the only environment that, however much it may have contributed to her collapse, was capable of providing her with reassurance; in some ways it is difficult not to feel that Isabella was lost from the moment she flung herself into the sea from the stern of the Cork steamer.

Thackeray's encounter with his deranged wife at Ivry set the pattern for the next five years of his life. Until deep into the 1840s he was constantly on the move, struggling to make ends meet, pay Isabella's bills (Fitz loyally settled at least one of M. Esquirol's monthly accounts) and search for the panacea that would make her well. The friendships that he had begun fairly sedulously to cultivate in the literary London of the late 1830s were allowed to lapse, or kept up at arm's length. It hardly needs saying that Thackeray was ashamed of

Isabella's condition – mental illness was all but unmentionable to the early Victorian – but he was also disgusted by the desperate straits into which he had fallen and the regularity with which he had to solicit work. This continual promotion of himself to magazine editors and proprietors wounded his sense of delicacy, and his professional correspondence from this part of his life is shot through with a queer kind of self-abasement, which is perfectly aware – even humorously aware at times – of the predicament in which the writer finds himself. There is a nicely judged letter of 1842 to Chapman and Hall, for example, enquiring about the vacant editorship of the *Foreign Quarterly Review*: 'If you have a new Editor, as you will no doubt, and when you have a great man like Mr Carlyle at the head of your undertaking: please to think of your humble Servant, who is very anxious to have a calling & regular occupation of some kind and who could really I think, do your duty very well.' The mock-jauntiness, the embarrassment, the joke about Carlyle, the underlying confidence in his own abilities – each is somehow characteristic of the pre-*Vanity Fair* writer for whom journeywork of this kind (he did not get the job) was a financial necessity.

Many letters of this sort got written during the bitter winter of 1841. Part of the problem was that Thackeray had burned some of his bridges with the magazine world the previous autumn. In particular there was a coolness with one of his regular employers, James Fraser, which he attempted to overcome in a painfully honest letter written in late February. When he left London in September, he explained, he had been so puffed up by the success of Titmarsh and the agreement with Chapman and Hall that he aimed to 'scorn all minor pay'. In any case three months spent caring for Isabella had largely prevented him from setting pen to paper. Whatever Fraser might think of his inconstancy, surely he could not resist an appeal on humanitarian grounds: 'If you have no fancy for me, think of my dear little wife so wretched yonder and I am sure you will lend a hand to save her.' Who can know what effort it cost Thackeray, a man who was at times immoderately conscious of his social background and Richmond Thackeray's vanished *lakhs* of rupees, to write what was in effect a begging letter. But he was obviously worried by Fraser's likely reaction, to the point that he wrote separately to Jane Carlyle urging her to get her husband to intervene and persuade Fraser to accept the two submitted articles – 'Memorials of Gourmandising' and a piece on Gisquet's memoirs.

Happily Fraser approved, and the magazine remained one of Thackeray's most reliable outlets – a relationship that survived Fraser's death later that year and the elevation of his former subordinate G.W. Nickisson. Thackeray was less lucky with Bentley, who despite being sent a bundle of material published nothing of his in 1841.

Throughout the first six months of the year the demon work had him by the shoulder – 'When Monsieur Titmarsh works in this way, be sure there is a reason for it,' he told Mrs Carlyle. As well as magazine work, he had also embarked on a more substantial enterprise. Nearly eight chapters of a novel set in the time of Henry V, entitled 'The Knights of Borsellen', got written in the Carmichael-Smyths' back bedroom, and in the nearby lodgings to which Thackeray eventually transferred himself, together with the opening section of what was to become *The Great Hoggarty Diamond*. There may even have been work on a mysterious play, the fourth act of which Thackeray mentions completing in Ireland, but which subsequently fell off the literary map. Simultaneously he was pursuing other financial avenues – chasing debts and debtors that went back as far as his bachelor days (they included Maginn, now nearly destitute, who is unlikely to have paid him a shilling) and accepting Mary Graham's offer of a loan of £500 in instalments. For all his mixed emotions about his cousin, in particular his feeling that her Devonshire friends had contrived to 'spoil' her (presumably this meant giving her ideas above her station), Thackeray was grateful for what he regarded as an act of great generosity. 'My dearest Poll,' he wrote in accepting the first twenty-five pounds, 'you have done well in offering it – done well in helping a man who is not such a great and good personage as his Mamma fancies him – but a fellow with some brains & a good heart, and who now almost for the first time in his life is about to have fair play.'

What does Thackeray mean by this? Presumably the old resentments going back to his undergraduate and law-student days had combined with a new awareness of what his marriage was costing him to produce the conviction that he was wasting his talents and that the great novel he believed he had within him – references to which start to crop up regularly in his letters – might stay permanently unwritten. Yet amidst these indignities and morale-sapping spurts of hack-work, his trajectory as a writer was firmly in the ascent. In particular, he had already taken advantage of the experience – the event took place a few weeks after his arrival in France – of watching a piece of contemporary pageantry on a par with the marriage of Queen Victoria: the return of the body of the Emperor Napoleon to Paris from Elba. The significance and symbolism of this spectacle for French nationhood were not lost on the inhabitants of the apartment in avenue de Sainte-Marie, who attended *en famille* and, wintry weather notwithstanding, made a picnic of the day. Napoleon's second interment made a profound impression on three-year-old Annie, who later remembered the procession 'sweeping up the great roadway of the Champs-Elysées'. There was snow on the ground. To the child, who had never seen snow in her life before, this 'mighty pall' fused effortlessly with the procession itself – the black, glittering carriages that sailed noiselessly along the silent street 'like ships' and which frightened her, 'for I thought there was a dead emperor in each'. Thackeray elaborated his own impressions in three long descriptive letters to an imaginary 'Miss Smith' which, bulked out by an anti-militaristic ballad, 'The Chronicle of the Drum', made a single slim volume. Cunningham published it in January 1841 at a price of half a crown, of which Thackeray's royalty per copy was a magnificent sevenpence-halfpenny. Fitzgerald wrote urgently to his friends advising them of the fact.

Though continually absorbed by the incidentals of scene and pageantry, *The Second Funeral of Napoleon* is a transparent attack on Gallic pretensions, swagger and bumptiousness. 'Real feelings they have,' Thackeray apostrophised the people amongst whom he had found a home, 'but they distort them by exaggeration; real courage which they render ludicrous by intolerable braggadocio.' Thackeray's inherent nationalism is at its most pronounced in his treatment of the French. As a member of what might be called the non-military middle classes – the distinction is an important one, as a high percentage of Victorian male middle-class employment was provided by the armed forces – some of the rampant Gallophobia that characterised Tory newspapers of the day, such as *John Bull*, is rather beyond him. All the same, it is impossible to browse for very long in his writings of the early 1840s without coming across a passage like:

I say to you that you are better than a Frenchman. I would lay even money that you who are reading this are more than five feet seven in height, and weigh eleven stone; while a Frenchman is five feet four and does not weigh nine. The Frenchman has after his soup a dish of vegetables, while you have one of meat. You are a different and superior animal – a French beating animal (the history of hundreds of years has shown you to be so) . . .

'England versus France'

There is a faint tremor of irony in this – it comes from 'Memorials of Gourmandising', which just happens to be a paean in praise of French cookery – but it is very faint. Other, similar, passages contain none at all. The *Paris Sketch Book*, for example, is full of hulking slabs of xenophobia, as when Thackeray attends a French dramatisation of *Nicholas Nickleby* and is appalled by the characterisation of 'Prospectus' (in fact Wackford Squeers jr., a plump, healthy child and supposedly an advertisement for the Squeers regime): 'Such a poor shrivelled creature I never saw; it is like a French pig, as lanky as a greyhound. Both animals give one a thorough contempt for the nation.' Thackeray cannot have been unaware of this paradox: that his liking for French books, French theatre and many individual Frenchmen (the *Paris Sketch Book* is dedicated to his tailor, M. Aretz, who had generously declined to press him for a debt), his habit of referring to Paris as 'home', should be cancelled out by routine disparagements of 'the French' as a collective entity. All that one can say in his defence is that such habits were deeply engrained – there is far worse in Trollope, for instance – and a crucial element in his family's mental outlook. Major Carmichael-Smyth, for example, lived most of his later life in France but christened his dog 'Waterloo', so that he could have the pleasure of annoying passers-by when calling for it in the street. Significantly, Thackeray's later treatment is more circumspect, and although French characters in his fiction are frequently ludicrous, they are often used to teach Englishmen unwelcome lessons about themselves. Mirobolant, the lady-killing chef of *Pendennis*, is a figure of fun, but Arthur's mockery of him shows the boy in an unpleasant light in which he momentarily forfeits the reader's sympathy.

As well as rushing out *The Second Funeral*, which was well received – although it failed to sell – Cunningham also agreed to subsidise a project that had long been dear to Thackeray's heart: the issuing of a selection from the best of Yellowplush and Major Gahagan. *Comic Tales and Sketches* (again credited to Michael Angelo Titmarsh) was published in April 1841. Although he was now detached from the drawing-rooms of literary London, Thackeray tried hard to promote it, asking Jane Carlyle to help interest *The Times* and the *Examiner*: 'Think of nothing but puffing the book,' he instructed her. 'Incite everyone: and then my dear little woman will have her pension secure.'

Domestically, some kind of routine had begun to impose itself on the life of avenue de Sainte-Marie and Thackeray's lodgings, between which there was a regular commerce. In the spring the Carmichael-Smyths left for Italy to meet the major's younger brother Charles, then on his way back from military service in India. They took with them Mary Graham, who though barely half the age of the fifty-year-old colonel had corresponded with him since infancy and – affection having blossomed by letter – was now preparing to marry him. In their absence, Annie and Minnie were looked after, or notionally supervised, by Mrs Butler, who 'certainly thought us inconveniently young'. As a treat Brodie would sometimes take the girls to Thackeray's lodgings early in the morning. Here they delighted in watching him shave – mixing soap with a little old silver brush and wiping it off the razor onto his shirt sleeve – or draw, or tear little processions of pigs with curly tails out of paper. At other times, though, they arrived to find him already hard at work, and to Annie's surprise and annoyance there was no time to tear out pigs. She remembered him in these days as 'a tall young man with black hair and eyeglass' (in fact Thackeray's hair had already begun to grey) who used to hold her forefinger as they walked and speak to her as if she were already grown up.

Before long he became habituated to this new life. 'As for us we are going on in the old way,' he wrote to his mother early in March (the Carmichael-Smyths were in Naples, where a marriage between Mary and her Indian colonel would shortly take place). 'I seem to work very hard but don't get much done.' He could see no improvement to speak of in Isabella – a little more active and talkative, perhaps, and on his last visit to Ivry apparently anxious for him to stay with her. And yet, taking her for a long walk in the country, he noted that 'Her remarks were those of a child.' With his mother absent – the Carmichael-Smyths remained in Italy for some months – Thackeray was in need of a confidante. He seems to have found one in Mrs Proctor, to whom he could relay information about Isabella while exchanging items of literary gossip (there was the added advantage that Bryan Proctor was a Commissioner of Lunacy, whose professional advice Thackeray was glad to take when the need arose). It was to Mrs Proctor, for instance, that he communicated the rumour that people believed him to be the author of Mrs Gore's anonymously published *Cecil*. 'How I wish I had written it,' he declared bitterly, ' – not for the book's sake but for the filthy money's, which I love better than fame.' Mrs Proctor, too, became an audience for one of the most affecting accounts of his relationship with Isabella in the days of her madness. Visiting her at Ivry, he decided to take her for a walk to an inn, where, in a private room, they dined and drank champagne. 'It did her a great deal of good and made her eyes sparkle, and actually for the first time these six months, the poor little woman flung herself into my arms and gave me a kiss . . .' At this point, inevitably, the waiter burst in, setting Isabella off into skirls of laughter. 'The first these six months again, and since that time I have had her at home not well, nor nearly well, but a hundred times better than she was this day week . . .'

There were several reasons for Thackeray's decision to bring Isabella back from Ivry. One was that the doctors there had admitted they could do nothing for her. But visiting the place, Thackeray had been alarmed to see 'wild fierce women rambling in the gardens' and, conscious that Isabella's derangement was of a much less dramatic nature, he became convinced that it was wrong 'to keep her in such company'. With his wife back in the apartment, and apparently all the better for her removal, he wrote a relatively optimistic letter to his mother in mid-April. His plan was for Isabella to spend each day in the care of a Mrs Spencer who lived nearby, but her behaviour made him wonder whether this was the right thing to do. He reported that on hearing talk of her being sent away again, she 'put on such a pitiful look' that this, together with her apparent cheerfulness, convinced him that 'leave her I will not, it wd. be a sin to throw away the chance of good I may do her'. It was an unenviable dilemma. His own close care and supervision might make Isabella better, but this cut into his working arrangements and made him less able to support his family. In the end Isabella went to Mrs Spencer's for five days out of seven, with Thackeray going to fetch her in the evenings. Some days later he reported to his mother that she continued to get on. 'I don't mean to say she is much better today than yesterday, but she is evidently happy . . .' She was also better disposed to her children, and took Annie on her knees to tell her a story. In the end memory failed her, 'but it was a satisfaction to me to see this weakness and that she felt she was at fault'.

His optimism continued throughout April. In particular, he had plans to install the family under a single roof back in England. When the Great Coram Street lease was up they should take a bigger house with a garden for the children, he told his mother, 'and there is no reason why we should not be all decently happy'. With a substantial quota of work out with the magazines, and Isabella's health apparently improving, Thackeray felt he could now look to the future. 'Here I am in clover, happier than I have been for many months, back with the poor little woman mending, perfectly quiet, & every now & then affectionate . . .' If he could find time to get on with his 'novel' (presumably 'The Knights of Borsellen') he could get back to Ireland and fulfil his commitments to Chapman and Hall, whose £120 was still, metaphorically at any rate – it had long been spent – burning a hole in his pocket. With this more confident mood came a sharper awareness of the inequalities of gender that prevailed in this society in which he moved. Writing once more to Mrs Proctor, he marvelled at the two elderly Miss Hamertons, friends of his mother, toiling up to visit him in eighty-five degrees of summer heat out of sheer good nature. The 'sacrifice' of the average female life contrasted sharply with his own lack of resilience. The six weeks in which he had been Isabella's sole attendant had left him almost broken with fatigue, whereas womankind 'does it with the utmost cheerfulness for ten francs a week, and never thinks about being miserable at all'. But however cheerfully Mrs Spencer went about her work, by mid-1841 his attitude towards Isabella was more resigned. His wife would eventually get well, he told Mrs Proctor, maybe in a month, maybe in a year. Even now he does not yet seem to have comprehended that Isabella's languor was a symptom of her inner distress. 'There is nothing the matter with her except perfect indifference, silence and sluggishness,' he concluded: when she chose to wake from her lethargy, her ideas were 'quite distinct'. It was Minnie's first birthday. When told of this Isabella kissed the child but otherwise took no interest in her. The letter to Mrs Proctor ends with a sad sketch of his tiny room and its cramped working conditions – a little table covered with manuscript, ink, paint box and cigars, 'the whole of my ménage'. He had not the courage to clear the table, Thackeray confessed, 'nor intend to do anything else, for I have had ten months of wretchedness, and truth to tell am quite broken down'.

Matters improved slightly in the course of a short summer holiday in England. There was a General Election in progress, which kept his hosts – Monckton-Milnes and Bowes, the latter now Liberal candidate for South Durham – occupied, and Thackeray threw himself into Bowes' electioneering with the same enthusiasm he had shown for Charles Buller's campaign nine years before. The stay at Streatham Castle in late June and early July provided an abundance of literary material, put to both short- and long-term use. An N.P. Willis-style spoof, *Notes on the North What-d'ye-Callem Election. Being the Personal Narrative of Napoleon Putnam Wiggins of Passimaquoddy*, appeared over two issues of *Fraser's* in the autumn (supposedly addressed to a wealthy aunt living in Kentucky, and developing a fantasy of temporary ownership, the descriptions of life at the castle are done in meticulous dead-pan: 'On the right of the plate, letters and newspapers. On the side table grilled ham, a silver mustard pot, a cold chicken, and a sort of pig's head jelly – very good indeed.'). Simultaneously, talking family history with his host, Thackeray turned up the story of Bowes' rackety step-grandfather, Andrew Robinson Bowes. The details of these ancestral wanderings through the early eighteenth century had an immediate effect and he wrote to Fraser with the root of what was to become *Barry Lyndon* in his head ('I have in my trip to the country found materials (rather a character) for a story that I'm sure will be amusing'). For all the uncertainty of his domestic life, his confidence in his creative powers was increasing sharply. The letter to Fraser tried to persuade him of the merits of issuing the as yet unwritten novel in shilling numbers, following the example of Charles Lever's enormously successful *Harry Lorrequer*. From Thackeray's point of view, this method of publishing had several advantages: as well as public attention, he could expect twenty guineas per monthly number, and the chance of more when the novel was eventually published in book form. 'Think over this please,' he begged Fraser. 'It certainly seems to me between you & me that there is as much stuff in Mr Titmarsh as in almost the best of the people writing comicalities, and why shouldn't he turn out successful? – I mean, pecuniarily so.' As it turned out this enthusiasm was premature and *Barry Lyndon*, not begun for another two years, appeared as a conventional *Fraser's* serial.

The approaching return to Paris and the awareness of what he might find there produced a reflective mood. A sad little diary, kept over a two-week period in late July and early August, contains a poignant and guilt-ridden prayer:

Oh Lord God – there is not one of the sorrows or disappointments of my life that I fancy I cannot trace to some error crime or weakness in my disposition. Strengthen me then with your help, to maintain my good resolutions – not to yield to lust or sloth that beset me: or at least to combat with them and overcome them sometimes.

The rest of the prayer, or at least a part of it, acknowledges his own selfishness – asking God to have mercy upon the people whose well-being depends on him; to empower him to set them a good example; to keep them from misfortunes 'wh. result from my fault'; and to enable him to 'discharge the private duties of life – to be interested in their ways & amusements, to be cheerful & content at home ...' Above all, Thackeray asks that he be given 'your help strenuously to work out the vices of character wh. have borne such bitter fruit already'. He returned late in July via Boulogne to find Isabella 'very glad to see me, and the dear little ones very well and happy'. There was also a letter from his mother pressing the potential benefit to Isabella of a hydrotherapic sanatorium in Silesia, which Mrs Carmichael-Smyth was in the process of investigating. The presence of wife and children, and the reminder of his mother's constant interest in her son and his dependants' well-being stirred more pious exhortation. 'My heart felt very humble & thankful for God's kindness towards these beautiful children, and I do humbly pray that I may be kept in a mood for seriously considering & trying to act up to my duty.'

Clearly a major part of his duty was to investigate some of the treatments available to Isabella. A year on from the first signs of her collapse, her condition fluctuated between occasional periods of lucidity and consuming inertia. A day after his return to France, Thackeray judged her 'certainly better – very little feeling, but a little memory and justness of speech'. Mrs Carmichael-Smyth's letters had continued to supply details of the supposed advantages of hydrotherapy (the 'water cure', then much in vogue), and Thackeray was sufficiently impressed to enrol Isabella with a local practitioner, Dr Weincke, 'a clever personable man but whose system is frightfully complicated'. The Weincke regime consisted of an intricate arrangement of sweat-baths, cold-water immersion and walks. Isabella's introduction to this system took the form of a four-hour sauna. Subsequent sessions went 'pretty well', but by Wednesday, 4 August she became 'exceedingly violent', so much so that Thackeray was forced to remain with her for two days. The sense of a fortnight spent in limbo while decisions were made about Isabella is reflected in the diary entries, which talk of days spent 'working or idling in the morning' and evening carouses with a journalist chum named Stevens. On 6 August the news of Mrs Blechynden's death was in the papers: Thackeray forbore to comment on the financial implications, remarking only that the sorriest point he had on his conscience was 'never to have taken any notice of her'. He was now in no doubt about the gravity of Isabella's condition, and his eventual decision to take her to the Silesian clinic recommended by his mother looks like a panic response to an increasingly untenable situation. His stark summary, in a letter of 7 August to Nickisson at *Fraser's* was that 'My wife is in a shocking state of health, and I am going in a sort of desperation to a German Quack on the Rhine, who says he thinks he can help her.'

Isabella's condition had improved sufficiently for them to set off at the end of the second week in August. A letter to Aunt Ritchie written a few days later from the sanatorium – lodged in a former convent near the Rhine town of Boppard – enthuses about the nature of the treatment and the chances of a cure. 'Gout & rheumatism & other inflammatory ills go off here as if by magic. People begin at four o'clock in the morning to be wrapped up in blankets, where they lie & melt for four hours, then come shower-baths, hip-baths, all sorts of waters taken within & without, and at the end of a certain number of months: they rise up and walk. I have a strong hope that under this strange regimen my dear little patient will recover her reason.' Whatever its ultimate effect on Isabella, Thackeray retained a favourable impression of hydrotherapy. Reviewing a book called *Life at the Water Cure* some years later for the *Morning Chronicle*, he praised 'the noble science of water healing' and suggested that 'the great merit of the system seems that the mind is constantly occupied while the body is being healed'. Isabella's needs seem to have been precisely the reverse of this, but she was well enough to ask to be remembered to Aunt Ritchie and 'sends her love to Charlotte & Jane', the Ritchie daughters. Was Thackeray putting words into her mouth? We shall never know. In between accompanying his wife to her treatment sessions – he joined her in the sluice at first as she was nervous of going in alone – and spending time with his mother, Charles Carmichael-Smyth and Mary, who had made their way there from Italy, he had time to reckon up a much less dismal financial state. Mary had just bestowed on him the balance of the £500, which together with the capital that had formerly provided the late Mrs Blechynden's annuity 'puts me out of the reach of fortune for some years to come . . .' In fact he may have continued to support his father's natural family: when his uncle, Charles Thackeray, wrote from India begging that Mrs Blechynden's pension should be kept up for the benefit of her daughter, Thackeray replied that he would make arrangements, but did not believe that the daughter should now receive as much as she and her mother had jointly been allotted. Whatever settlement may have been made, he continued to feel guilty about this 'black niece', had her to stay with him later in the 1840s and may even have allowed her to fraternise with Annie and Minnie.

These new sources of income were a necessary compensation for his inability to work. A letter to Cruikshank of mid-September apologises for his inattention to a 'long story' that the two had discussed, but explained that his time had been wholly occupied in tending Isabella. Another letter to Fitzgerald, begun around this time but not completed and sent until October, reflects Isabella's erratic progress during these weeks, in which Thackeray's hopes of an improvement in her condition were first raised and then cruelly dashed. The first part is almost jaunty in tone – '. . . I do begin to think we are at last to have her well. She *is* in fact all but well, and at last, Thank God for it, laughs and is happy' – and includes a jovial picture of husband and wife beneath the sluice. It would have made a fine picture, he decided: 'Mrs Thack in the condition of our first parins, before they took to eating apples, and the great Titmarsh with nothing on but a petticoat lent him by his mother, and far too scanty to cover that immense posterior protuberance with wh. nature has furnished him.' The second half, addressed from Heidelberg a month later, is inexpressibly gloomy. He had not finished the letter, Thackeray confided, because he had not been fit to write. Isabella was not so well: reasonable 'but excessively violent & passionate'. Although the local sanatorium doctor maintained that this was a good sign, Isabella's behaviour had depressed him so much that he had set off on a tour of nearby German towns, thinking that the change of scene might do him good. However, the trip had made him 'as miserable as the deuce'. If he wrote to Fitzgerald, he explained, it was because he wished to 'take refuge from cursed loneliness & low spirits . . . My God, how I wish I had you to be with,' he despairingly concludes.

The late autumn of 1841 and the early part of 1842 represent another barely documented stretch in Thackeray's life, taken up in worry about Isabella and his own future course of life. Apparently more weeks were spent at Boppard, until there could be no further doubt that the treatment had failed, before a final return to Paris. Thackeray's dilemma was an unenviable one. He could make no long-term arrangements until he knew if or when Isabella would recover, and no doctor could tell him that. His professional appearances, meanwhile, were kept up by *The Great Hoggarty Diamond*, whose serialisation began in the September number of *Fraser's*. Though it attracted little attention at the time, Thackeray always had a soft spot for *Hoggarty* ('If it does not make you cry I shall have a mean opinion of you,' he once told Mrs Brookfield). Written in the months after Isabella's collapse, it is full of sad little touches of melancholy drawn from his own recent life. Ultimately, though, this connection to his private experience is the book's aesthetic undoing, and the liveliness of the opening scenes relating the career of 'Samuel Titmarsh' (Michael Angelo's cousin) at the West Diddlesex Bank and his impoverished married life (the death of Sam's infant daughter is clearly based on little Jane) is a bit too marked for comfort. Significantly, Thackeray's precise eye for financial arrangements is well in evidence, and no sooner has the idea of Sam's engagement been broached than the reader learns that his beloved possesses £2,333 6s 8d in the 3 per cent consols – that is, an income of seventy pounds a year.

Back in Paris early in the new year of 1842, he resolved to place Isabella in Dr Puzin's private asylum at Chaillot. The decision seems to have followed a protracted wrangle with Mrs Shawe – then living in Paris – the roots of which look as if they lay in a request by Thackeray that his wife's relatives should take charge of her. Certainly a letter of 10 February to Isabella's companion-cum-minder Mrs Spencer, the day after the former's departure, carries some sarcastic remarks about Mrs Shawe, in particular the suggestion that Mrs Spencer convey the news of Isabella's new home 'lest her mother should suffer by an abrupt announcement & the sight of my handwriting'. There had been a ghastly visit to Mrs Shawe a couple of days before, in the course of which Isabella – who had gone against Thackeray's advice – became greatly agitated, causing her mother to wonder aloud that she should have been allowed out. The note to Mrs Spencer was accompanied by a letter outlining Mrs Shawe's various delinquencies and abrogations of duty, with the aim of convincing Isabella's relatives in Ireland how barbarous her mother's conduct had been. This letter has not survived, but the nature of its contents seems all too evident from these remarks to a third party. There was no love lost between Thackeray and Mrs Shawe, and the tribe of despotic and ill-favoured mothers-in-law that tramps through his fiction – Mrs Gashleigh in 'A Little Dinner at Timmins's', Mrs Hobson Budge, Mrs Mackenzie in *The Newcomes* – awaited its marching orders.

He saw Isabella at Chaillot late in February, where she seemed 'very comfortable . . . and much better'. A sketch of the interior of the local church, pasted into Thackeray's scrapbook, above the portrait of a woman bearing a clear resemblance to Isabella, may date from this time. Less ambitious than the hydrotherapy sanatoria, Dr Puzin's establishment seems to have offered only basic care, rest and, when necessary, restraint. Again, writing in early March to Fitz, Thackeray reported her 'perfectly happy, obedient and reasonable'. Although he saw Isabella frequently, he confessed that it made him sick to be parted from her. And yet he was clearly planning other schemes. Ireland beckoned, and the literary world in which he desired to shine lay across the Channel. Moreover, his decision to leave Isabella with Dr Puzin carries the hint that he had concluded that her condition could only be contained, not ameliorated. Chaillot, in effect, freed Thackeray for a return to a kind of bastard bachelordom. By May 1842 he was back at Great Coram Street, currently inhabited by Charles Carmichael-Smyth (soon to truncate his name to 'Carmichael'), Mary and their four-month-old son. The house also sheltered Mrs Butler for a time, and the atmosphere was not conducive to work or peace of mind. Thackeray decided to go to Ireland if he could put together enough money to pay his expenses. In the note to his mother announcing his plans he mentions a letter from Isabella, apparently written without dictation, which 'comforted me hugely'. Lonely and irritated, he was homesick for France. The domestic arrangements of Great Coram Street – all too reminiscent of his own early married days – irked him. Mary annoyed him both by the 'exaggerated terror and hatred' she appeared to have conceived for old Mrs Butler, and for being 'excessively fond of domination and first-fiddle-playing'. This catalogue of bad temper, which also took in Mary's doctor, was mitigated only by the pity he felt for the child, whose persistent eye trouble would eventually require surgery.

In the midst of his Irish plans, he continued to solicit work, proposing the idea of a piece on 'Modern English Comedies' to the *Westminster Review* (the editor was keen but failed to offer enough money) and trying to get Bentley to let him translate an unidentified French novel. Writing to his mother at St-Germain, in advance of a visit by the Carmichaels, he assured her that freelance work was easy to come by: 'There seems so much of it here that I have only to pick & choose, and make in a certain way, a decent income.' Ireland still hung in the balance – impediments included not only Chapman and Hall's spent advance but the prospect of a law suit by various of the *Constitutional*'s disgruntled creditors. As negotiations continued, Thackeray left for a working holiday at Southborough near Tunbridge

Wells, 'the pleasantest greenest place in the world'. Here he went about breathing life into his childhood memories. Although Tunbridge Wells was greatly changed, he told his mother, it was better than Great Coram Street 'and that unhappy little room where I can never remain for five minutes without someone rattling at the door, wh. I've vainly locked'.

No lock, however, could prevent Isabella's ghost from gliding in to haunt him. Musing over the wreckage of his married life he came up with a judgment on Isabella that functioned simultaneously as a reproach to Mrs Carmichael-Smyth and her mother. 'Ah! There was more nobleness and simplicity in that little woman than neither of you knew, than I've seen in most people in this world. God help her, and if he ever please to restore her to me help both of us.' His work done, he walked in the fields, thought of Annie and enjoyed some rare moments of leisure. Ireland was fixed, Chapman and Hall appeased, and he looked forward to his departure from 'the tea-parties . . . and endless racket of this place'. In the meantime, his work continued to appear in any publication that would print and pay for it. The first of the 'Confessions' attributed to the pen of 'George Savage Fitz-Boodle' had appeared in *Fraser's* and was 'a sort of a hit', he told his mother. At the same time he had written another piece, 'The Legend of Jawbrahim-Heraudee' – an orientalised spoof of the biblical epics of a now forgotten writer named J. Abraham Heraud, author of *Descent into Hell* (1830) and *The Judgment of the Flood* (1834). This appeared in the 18 June number of a comparatively new magazine, 'a very low paper', Thackeray informed Mrs Carmichael-Smyth, enjoining her to secrecy about the affair, 'only it's good pay and a great opportunity for unrestrained laughing sneering kicking and gambadoing'. The title of the new magazine, under whose auspices Thackeray would eventually go on to make his name, was *Punch*.

Thackeray: The Pursuit

The 'I knew a man who knew a man . . .' routine is usually a failsafe pathway back into past time. Not that long ago I remember being enraptured by a newspaper obituary of a nonagenarian lawyer who as a tiny baby had been given Mr Gladstone's finger to touch. Suddenly the Grand Old Man, stooping gamely over the cradle, was vividly alive in one's mind. The best version of this formula I can offer is to say that I knew a man who knew a man who had met Dr Routh, president of Magdalen College, Oxford, who died in 1854 at the age of one hundred (in his late nineties some of his junior fellows heard him muttering gloomily about 'these late disturbances' and it was thought at first that he was lamenting the Chartist Riots – in fact the old man was referring to the Duke of Orange's arrival in 1688). In his youth Routh, who wore a periwig until his dying day, had seen Samuel Johnson walking up St Giles. And there you have it. Three baton changes in the relay race of memory and we are back with the Great Cham himself, as remembered by a man born a quarter of a millennium ago.

It is easy to play this trick with Thackeray. The last person to have known him – that is, to have talked to him and remembered what he said and looked like – would have died at about the time of the Second World War, so there must be any number of late seventy-somethings still alive whose grandfathers nodded at him at one of his clubs, or whose grandmothers offered him cups of tea at some drawing-room bunfight. If it comes to that, I have met Thackeray's great-granddaughter, Mrs Belinda Norman-Butler (born 1908), who retains vivid memories of her grandmother, Anne Thackeray Ritchie, who wore black even in summer and beat her parasol on the ground if crossed by her four-year-old grandson. Again, two nudges and one is back in the cramped apartment in avenue de Sainte-Marie with her father changing his last five-pound note, the children squalling in one room and their mamma 'raving in the next'.

Although I have never 'pursued' Thackeray in the way of some 'in the footsteps of . . .' biographers, I have taken up various opportunities to visit some of the places he went and to inspect some of the scenes that attracted his attention. In London this is a simple business. Palace Green, his final home, is long pulled down, but Onslow Square survives, and Kensington Square Gardens – often visited on the way back from the *Mail on Sunday* – which abuts the blue-plaqued and renumbered premises in Young Street (now opposite a car park) cannot have changed much since the young Miss Thackerays played there in the 1840s. Most of the coffee-houses where Thackeray dined and drank are gone, but the Cock Tavern in Fleet Street where he went with Tennyson survives, along with half a dozen other ports of call, from the Garrick to Charterhouse Square. As for some of the out-of-town sites, the cottage in Tunbridge Wells where he first pored over *Manfroni: or the One-handed Monk* is a chintzy restaurant much featured in the Sunday supplements (you feel that Thackeray would probably have approved this transformation). Once, coming back from a family holiday in Cornwall on the A303, I saw the sign to Ottery St Mary. A true biographical bloodhound would have followed it, but time was pressing and the children were turning fractious, so we never went in search of Larkbeare.

I have always been suspicious of the idea of writerly 'presences' that supposedly hang about in the ether long after their originals have disappeared. None the less, I felt surprisingly close to Thackeray once in a car out on the coast road between Galway City and Clifden in the west of Ireland (they had just begun to build the road when he went there in 1842), mostly because the landscape at which he marvelled – flattened bars of rock pushing up out of the thin grass – was instantly recognisable from the *Irish Sketch Book*. Walking up the main staircase of the Garrick Club, too, it is possible to imagine turning into a room and coming upon him chatting to Andrew Arcedeckne or lobbying some sympathetic baronet about the miscreant Edmund Yates.

And then there are the representations of him. Orwell always maintained that he carried an image of his favourite writers in his head. These were not exactly facsimiles of well-known portraits, he decided, but interesting variations on them. My inward projections of Thackeray conform to this pattern. The genial old-buffer pictures of his maturity I can do without, but I have always been fascinated by the

Maclise sketch, done in his twenties, in which he sprawls open-legged across a chair. Outwardly he looks a typical pre-Victorian buck – lounging, eye-glassed, haughty – but there is an uncertainty, too, and perhaps a kind of defiance. Above all rises a sense of amusement, a way in which the bulky young man in the pince-nez knows that he is striking a pose and is rather tickled by the ambiguities of the relationship struck up between subject, artist and audience. As am I.

X

A Cockney in Ireland

'There is that poor fellow Thackeray gone off to Ireland: and what a lazy beast I am for not going with him.'
Edward Fitzgerald, 24 June 1842

'Poverty and misery have, it seems, their *sublime*, and that sublime is to be found in Ireland.'
Review of J. Venedey's Ireland, Morning Chronicle,
16 March 1844

 e left London for Bristol on 24 June 1842, having failed to persuade Fitzgerald to go with him. Fitz, although merely 'idle & moping in the country', could not be shifted from his inertia: it was some consolation, perhaps, that in the course of his Irish travels Thackeray turned up two of his friend's relatives. Tempting social invitations had to be declined, and one of his last acts was to write to Forster lamenting the fact that he could not be present among the homecoming committee got up to welcome Dickens back from America.

At first he had planned to travel via Wales – which explains his leisurely progress to Liverpool via Chepstow, Hereford and Tintern Abbey – subsidising this detour by way of journalism, but as he explained to his mother, 'sight-seeing and writing too occupy a deal of time for a man of my lazy habits, and very seldom can I do either'. The things he had left behind weighed on him. Above all he had had a letter from Isabella – the contents are unknown – which at first had greatly upset him. A careful re-reading, however, convinced him that he could understand it and follow the train of thought, 'if a train you can call it'. He could not help but think that she had improved, he told his mother, and was glad above all that she wanted to see him and hear of him. At Liverpool, where Dickens' ship had recently docked, he noted that Boz and Titmarsh had both arrived in the city on the same day, 'but the journals have not taken notice of the arrival of the latter. Gross jealousy!' This is another early example of his and Dickens' careers running in parallel – the one returning from an overseas trip as the other embarked on one – and even at this stage one can see the way in which Dickens' spectre nagged Thackeray and spurred him into action. Not long afterwards, for example, he wrote to Chapman and Hall to reassure them of his commitment to the task in hand. 'Let us pray that you may publish *two* decent books of travels this year.' The other would be Dickens' immensely successful and controversial *American Notes*. With his name unrecorded in the Liverpool newspapers, Thackeray boarded the boat for Dublin.

Even at this stage, Ireland was an early-Victorian obsession. The ground that Thackeray now proposed to tread had already been extensively covered by travellers such as Crofton Croker, Barrow and Hall. The books that these journeys produced, elegant topographies, 'romantic' in the sub-Wordsworthian sense, gave little idea of the state of the country and the divisions that lay at its core. Dominating them was the iconic figurehead of Irish nationalism, 'The Leader', Daniel O'Connell, who almost singlehandedly had managed to polarise the Unionist and Nationalist communities. These contrasting attitudes to the cause of Emancipation easily transcended the ancient barriers of class or geography – on the one hand uniting Protestant aristocrats, minor gentry and Ulster farmers into a single point of focus; on the other bringing middle-class Catholics and the rural poor together under the Nationalist flag (one curious by-product of this unification was the gradual emergence of a stereotyped 'Irishman' for English consumption – an intriguing and collusive process reflected in many a later book of Victorian 'Irish Travels'). In many parts of the country Nationalist agitation had already transformed itself into direct action, with the rise of rural protest movements of 'banditti' or 'Whiteboys', and the issue of Irish law and order was high on the Westminster agenda.

To do them justice, observant English politicians had taken note of the complexities of current Irish political feeling. Sir Robert Peel might talk about 'the Irishman's natural predilection for outrage and a

lawless life' (which he believed 'nothing can control'); more perceptive onlookers suggested that the rural secret societies could better be
interpreted as peasant trade unions. Yet it was Peel, fresh from his
success in reforming the Metropolitan Police, who had the most
influence on issues of Irish security. In fact Peel's creation of a
centralised, paramilitary police force, whose officers doubled up as
magistrates, was a blueprint for policing systems throughout the British
Empire. Its effect was to cement yet further the town/county alliances
of liberal Catholics and produce some significant shifts in Irish
political alignment and influence. The good result that O'Connell's
Nationalists achieved in the 1832–3 elections allowed them to
intervene in Westminster power-broking. Subsequently, from 1835 to
1841, they existed in an uneasy alliance with the Whigs, who
suspected their ultimate aims. The arrival of Peel's Tory administration in 1841, a year before Thackeray's visit, had led to renewed calls
for Emancipation. Ireland, then, presented a queer spectacle to the
early-Victorian traveller – a place hymned for its natural beauties, but
seething with political, religious and (though the famine lay four years
away) economic tensions. Many of them are reflected in the *Irish
Sketch Book*, which, for all Thackeray's occasional inability to come to
terms with what he saw, provides some vivid snapshots of a country in
a state of mounting crisis.

Reaching Dublin, Thackeray put up at the Shelburne Hotel ('such
filth, ruin and liberality', he told Fitzgerald, adopting a tone that would
characterise his Irish reportage) before moving on to stay with the
novelist Charles Lever, whose rollicking tales of national life he much
admired, at the latter's house at Temple Logue. Here he made himself
an agreeable guest and became a favourite with Lever's children: the
Irish Sketch Book was eventually dedicated to his host, who reviewed it
favourably, but their relationship subsequently cooled after Thackeray
included an affectionate parody of him in *Punch's Prize Novelists*.
Twenty years later, in a letter offering the then impoverished Irishman
a loan, Thackeray reminded Lever of his free-handedness one night at
Temple Logue in July 1842. By the end of the month he was properly
embarked on his travels: a two-stage process that took him first to
Cork and along the west coast via Killarney, Tralee, Limerick, Galway
and Westport, before returning to Dublin by way of the midland city
of Athlone; followed by a second excursion to Ulster and Donegal.

Inevitably the visit to Cork, with its painful memories of bygone
distress, greatly upset him. But he was astonished, and pleased, by the

long memories of the local people. The carman who drove him to his hotel recollected him perfectly and asked after the family. Moved by a spirit that was half nostalgia and half reminiscent terror, he walked up Grattan's Hill (Mrs Shawe had since moved) looking for the children Annie had befriended two summers before, only to find them out with their mother – 'what a sickness the place gave me!' he reported bitterly to his own parent, '& this opposite door where the mother used to live!' News of Thackeray's recreations in London seems to have got back to Mrs Carmichael-Smyth, presumably through the Carmichaels, for he assured her: 'make yourself easy about the drink. I am very moderate, drinking sherry and water after dinner and can't-abiding whiskey. I don't know what the young people have frightened you about with my London doings – It's the soda-water and the not eating breakfast.'

It would be easy to present the Thackeray who racketed around Ireland in a succession of jolting 'cyars' in the summer and early autumn of 1842 as a solitary and embittered man, drinking away his evenings in a series of shabby hotels and pining for company, but this was not the case. For all its discomforts and annoyances – the swarms of beggars, the infernal dirt and the omnipresent Catholicism – Ireland intrigued him, and his efforts to make sense of it, to reconcile his prejudices with a deeper awareness that they were prejudices, are an underlying current in everything he wrote about the place. At the same time, in his letters, and in the *Sketch Book* itself, he is constantly looking over his shoulder at the people and the predicaments he had left behind him. Much of the complex psychological feeling that lies behind the *Irish Sketch Book* has roots beyond the Irish Sea: Isabella, Annie and Minnie are irrevocably mixed up with the pinched roadside faces and the crowded coaches, sometimes to devastating effect. In Dublin in the autumn, for instance, a child in its nurse's arms caught sight of him and began to shout 'Papa, Papa'. Thackeray reported that the misidentification 'gave me such a turn of the stomach as never was'.

Stuck in Killarney amid driving August rain, he brooded about Minnie, whom – he was ashamed to confess to his mother – 'I don't love as I ought.' He was always thinking of Annie, he declared, 'but not of the little one God bless her; though for the first 3 months of her life I was immensely fond of her; but the mother makes half the children that's the fact'. The image of Isabella as a dreadful weed wrapping herself around his honest affections is a disquieting one, but

it shows the extent to which Thackeray thought his life had been systematically warped by the events of the past two years. Predictably solitude played a part in these musings. In Killarney he found the loneliness 'by no means bearable'. He was disgusted with Fitzgerald for not coming with him, but wondered whether being on his own might not work in his favour in the end 'as it forces one to push on ...' A letter to his mother from Dublin is full of small and large matters crowded together: Maginn's premature death ('He died of sheer drink I fear'); a pleasant moment the previous day when a man on the coach quoted '*by heart* passages out of Titmarsh!'; stern instructions about Annie's 'wilfulness', news of which had come back from Paris. Thackeray's enthusiasm for corporal punishment as a cure for juvenile obstreperousness can seem odd coming from such an otherwise gentle and indulgent parent, but these were strict times for childcare. At the same time he was beset by aesthetic anxiety: how to do justice to a country of several million inhabitants in which he was quartered for little more than a season. A man ought to be forty years in a place instead of three months, he complained to his mother, and '*then* he wouldn't be able to write about it'. Who did understand Ireland, he wondered? Where, in the midst of 'all the lies that all tell', was a stranger to seek the truth? O'Connell was the biggest liar of all, he decided. Anyone coming to the country prepared to sympathise with oppressed Catholic nationalism would only end up repelled by the 'slavish brute superstition' of the Roman faith. Gloomily, Thackeray predicted that whatever he might produce would be shot at by both sides – the Catholic press would attack him for abusing priests, while the Tory papers would criticise his Liberal sympathies. Meanwhile the problem of Isabella continued to rise above the comparatively minor dilemma of how to write a book. Ideally he would prefer her to come

and live in London, but he knew of no establishment where she would be as comfortable as she was at Chaillot. All of a sudden one gets a dreadful, hard-eyed glimpse of what the early-Victorian treatment of the insane actually involved. Before his departure for Ireland Proctor had given him a tour of his 'favourite place'. However, this had made Thackeray 'quite sick to think of even now'. Worse, perhaps, was that Proctor 'shook his head about other places'.

Ireland was full of connections – people to whom he had been recommended, chance encounters pleasant and unpleasant. He spent some happy days staying with Fitzgerald's uncle Peter Purcell and his family ('such people are not to be met with more than a few times in a man's life') and visited his friend's kindly brother in County Meath (Mrs Fitzgerald, 'a hard bigot of an Irishwoman', made a less favourable impression). The guard on the Dublin mail turned out to be a cousin of Mrs Crowe's. Less happily, the country harboured many members of the Shawe family. Coming across one of Isabella's cousins on the Killarney race-track, Thackeray reported to his mother that 'He evidently from his behaviour thinks me a dreadful reprobate, but what then?' Thackeray knew that Mrs Shawe had circularised her relatives with disparaging accounts of his conduct, but at this stage in the proceedings he scarcely cared. Mrs Carmichael-Smyth might wax indignant about these slanders: her son questioned whether it was worth while trying to set the record straight. At one time, he revealed, he had composed 'a thundering letter for the family'. In the end, though, it had never been sent. He was much happier in the company of good-humoured Colonel Merrick Shawe, Isabella's great-uncle, with whom he dined in Dublin, and happiest of all visiting his elderly cousin, the Rev. Elias Thackeray, at his vicarage in Dundalk. The sight of Rev. Thackeray's model infant school, with its fresh-faced children singing hymns, was too much for Thackeray's paternal feelings and he was reduced to tears.

There are several independent accounts of Thackeray's progress around Ireland. Lever seems to have liked him, while not particularly valuing his encouragement: he told a friend that the young Englishman was 'the most good-natured man alive', but help from him would be worse than no help at all. Thackeray was 'like a man struggling to keep his head above water, and who offers to teach his friend to swim'. Lever also believed that he wrote too promiscuously and was losing his identity as a writer because of it. To balance Lever's relative coolness and his apparent disavowal of Thackeray's suggestion that the best place for an Irish writer of ability was London is the fact that in three years' time he would take exactly this step. A much sharper perspective comes from Lever's friend Major Frank Dwyer, who met Thackeray at Temple Logue and seems to have accompanied him on several of his excursions. All the more revealing for its lack of preconceptions – the major had never heard of the tall young Englishman to whom Lever introduced him – Dwyer's memoir not only supplies shrewd glimpses of Thackeray at large, but also shows him taking a detailed interest in some of the subjects that were to become an integral part of *Vanity Fair*. Their introduction came at a dinner convened by Lever at which the third guest was Captain William Siborne, a Waterloo veteran and the author of A *History of the War in France and Belgium in 1815*. At the dining table Thackeray's manner was at first 'reserved, earnest and quiet; rather a disappointment, perhaps, to those who may have expected some external manifestation of his supposed humouristic proclivities' (Lever had represented Thackeray to Dwyer merely as a 'comic writer'). Dwyer sensed that the younger man was 'carefully observing and desirous of not being drawn out, at least, not prematurely . . .' Dwyer assumed, not unreasonably given English interest in Irish affairs, that Thackeray was a political partisan who had come to Ireland to work up something that would be useful to his party. Subsequently the conversation turned to Waterloo. Again Thackeray said little, but in a later conversation he told Dwyer of the great interest in the battle that still prevailed in England. Since the dinner, he confessed, he had been thinking of writing something about it, without yet seeing a way in which it could be adequately dealt with in prose. Lever's own attempt, in his novel *O'Malley*, was much too imaginative and high-flown, he thought. Clearly he was fascinated by the deep-rooted national feeling that Waterloo had stirred, and also by its survival: how intense it must have been at the time, he told Dwyer, and how utterly spread through society. But from what Siborne had said, and his own experience of attending a military review, he seemed, Dwyer thought, to have concluded that it would be useless to attempt anything in the way of military description. And yet the thought prevailed that 'something might be made of Waterloo' – Dwyer had a distinct recollection of him saying these words – without necessarily supplying a blow-by-blow account of the battle. Later, when he read *Vanity Fair*, Dwyer became aware of what he termed 'the great thoughtfulness and foresight with which Thackeray planned out his work, and how careful he was to attempt nothing doubtful or beyond his powers'.

There were other pointers to the world that was to spring into existence, apparently fully formed, five years later. On the second leg of his travels he visited Ulster and spent several days in the company of officers from the British regiment stationed at Newry. Dwyer noted that on his return he had 'got up a considerable stock of military characteristic and anecdote'. Dwyer was also able to observe Thackeray as he went about getting his material. At the review, which helped to convince the novelist that he should not write directly about military life, he noted Thackeray's extreme nervousness, which Dwyer thought strange in 'such a great powerful man'. Another time at the Catholic college of Maynooth, he watched Thackeray looking on with 'a sardonic smile of utter derision and contempt'. Dwyer was taken aback by the expression, which seemed to him to display a rather unwholesome satisfaction in finally tracking down something that confirmed his worst suspicions of Ireland and the Irish.

In the end one is left with the impression that Dwyer esteemed Thackeray as a companion while rather doubting his motives. Having read the *Irish Sketch Book*, he criticised the author on the grounds that his abhorrence of boasting and exaggeration was such that he was often tempted to disbelieve what was self-evidently true, and to substitute something that, if not exactly false, was 'a clipped and shorn distortion of reality'. This tendency to call every positive statement into question was particularly blatant in his judgment of Irish people and Irish affairs, Dwyer thought: 'he distrusted everything he heard, and a great deal of what he saw in Ireland'. Was this true? The fleeting, impressionistic quality of the *Irish Sketch Book* comes from its being written on the hoof – writing to Mrs Carmichael-Smyth from Dublin in late October, Thackeray could tell her that it was 'very near done' – and some, though not all, the judgments are sharper for being instantaneous. It was an important book for Thackeray, the first that appeared under his clear authorship (the name M.A. Titmarsh is on the title-page, but the dedication to Lever gives the game away). The first, too, perhaps, in which his personality plays off the material, instead of the one alternately swamping the other. All the same, Dwyer is right about Thackeray's refusal to be impressed and his readiness to judge, although he misses the profound pyschological struggle that eventually dominates and often undermines the judging process.

There are several recognisable varieties of travel book, of course. There is the book by the writer effortlessly at home in his milieu, who plainly regards the experience of travelling there as a terrific privilege (Gissing's *By the Ionian Sea* is a good example of this type of work). There is the writer who uses a journey as a way of imparting some piece of propaganda about an essentially alien culture (for instance Robert Byron's *The Road to Oxiana*). There is the writer who travels out of sheer curiosity and accepts the dangers and discomforts as an incidental benefit (Chatwin, Theroux). But there is also the writer who knows that he or she has come late to the feast, who suspects that other people may already have dealt more efficiently with whatever it is that seems worth writing about, and whose every utterance, consequently, is shot through with a combination of wariness and mild resentment. On the evidence of the *Irish Sketch Book*, Thackeray falls into the final category. Although he spent four months collecting material, visited every major town and, for all his haste, seems to have composed the resulting narrative with a certain amount of care, the consciousness that other people had been there before hangs over nearly everything he writes. Being Thackeray, he is naturally able to pass the presence of these ghostly exemplars off as a kind of running joke – there are any number of satirical references to the 'guidebooks' of Crofton Coker and Barrow – but the attempt to distinguish himself from this collection of earlier literary travellers does not always convince. Even in his bravura passages one gets a sense of a writer continually looking over his shoulder, baffled by half a dozen existing vade-mecums and a mass of received opinion.

As Dwyer had suspected, Thackeray came to Ireland as a progressive Liberal unsympathetic to the cause of Irish Nationalism – a stance that enabled him to sneer equally at O'Connell and the Catholic Church – but he also came as a writer determined to pick a quarrel with the prevailing romantic orthodoxy. He distrusted very deeply the nineteenth-century obsession with the picturesque, that characteristic Wordsworthian 'sublime': almost all his descriptions of scenery are defiantly low-key. What can you say about a mountain, he wonders at one point, other than to advise other people to see it for themselves? Halfway through an account of a visit to a spectacular waterfall he simply stops in his tracks to enquire: What is the use of putting this down? Much of this is sharply prefigurative of the later Victorian reaction against Romanticism. Macaulay's review of *The Prelude* in 1850 – 'the old raptures about mountains and cataracts; the old flimsy philosophy about the effect of scenery on the mind; the old crazy, mystical metaphysics' – strikes an intensely Thackerayan note. The effect of this anxiety is all the more marked in that the reader suspects that something in Thackeray's own nature is pulling him firmly in the opposite direction. Time and again, caught two or three sentences into a purple passage, he will pull up sharply and deliberately let the prosaic side to his character get the better of him. The Thackeray who reminds us – this in the middle of a description of the Giant's Causeway – that he is a cockney and would rather be in Pall Mall is not being true to himself, and at the same time rather redeems himself by being half aware of his dishonesty.

This uncertainty, the uncertainty of a man who does not quite know how to respond, is all the more striking in his account of the 'Irish question' – the problem of how nearly eight million people, sat upon alternately by English landlords and Catholic bishops, were to support themselves in conditions of mounting economic distress. The great famine of the late 1840s was still some years off, but even at this stage the crop failures and hordes of semi-starved children were a subject of remark to English visitors. Thackeray's instinctive response to this sink of human indignity is simply a tremendous explosion of temperament, initially aimed at the Catholic Church. A Trappist monastery is 'a grovelling place'. The religious rites practised at Croagh Patrick reduce him to silent fury. Taken to an Ursuline convent near Cork, he feels 'quite sick' and can only thank God for 'honest Martin Luther' (to do Thackeray justice he is equally unimpressed by the fashionable Protestant congregations at Dublin). Practically the only Catholic whom Thackeray mentions favourably is the famous temperance campaigner Father Matthew – he recognises Matthew's desire to keep out of politics and help people lead better lives. He sees details – the ruined houses, the great gates that lead nowhere, the unfinished churches (which, typically, he converts into a grand metaphor of Irish life), the dirt and the flocks of idlers – without ever addressing their cause. A revealing instance of this failure to connect comes after he visits a country house in Wicklow and marvels at the number of hangers-on, the half-dozen parlour maids and the hordes of 'scoundrelly grooms'. The fact that this overstaffing might be a humane response to chronic local unemployment seems scarcely to occur to him.

In his calmer moments Thackeray is honest enough to admit that this kind of contempt, the sour complaints about idleness, the jokes about 'the finest peasantry in Europe', will not do. Something of this uneasiness manifests itself in his treatment of the most visible sign of Irish poverty: the crowds of beggars who accosted him whenever he set foot outside his carriage. At first he merely despises the 'hideous leering flattery', wonders why the poor-houses lie empty – presumably the people prefer begging, etc., etc. – and works himself up into a fine lather about 'servility' and 'hypocrisy', but later on there are some queer passages in which he catches himself in the act of spurning some request for charity and tries to satirise his immediate reaction: 'The unconscionable rogues!' he exclaims at one stage, an attempt at sight-seeing having been met by the usual demand for sixpence – 'How dare they, for the sake of a little starvation or so, interrupt gentlefolk in their pleasure?' It strikes a curious note and the result, for all the good intentions, is oddly disagreeable.

Like nearly everything Thackeray wrote, the *Irish Sketch Book* is a series of departures, a continual accumulation of superfluous material, and it is these rather than the fulminations over native shiftlessness or the self-satirising guilt that give the book its edge. Thackeray digresses incorrigibly. At the drop of a hat he will give you his opinion of low-church sermons or how to cook a dinner. He spends eighteenpence on a collection of old Irish story books and immediately launches into a résumé of the career of the eighteenth-century highwayman Captain Feeny (who turns up some years later in *Barry Lyndon*) and the battle of Aughrim. He reads a Dublin newspaper and at once sets off on a trawl through the court cases, notionally for what they can tell him about Ireland, but in reality because they allow him to ride what has become one of his favourite hobby horses, the question of the death penalty.

On the surface this might seem nothing more than a display of traditional early-Victorian *longueurs* – there is nothing quite so tedious as a Victorian travel book if you don't happen to be a Victorian – but it is actually a profound part of Thackeray's appeal as a writer in his mature work. His skill, in fact, lies partly in incidentals, in straying away from the main point, using some tiny scrap of detail (a fragment of conversation, say, or an item of clothing) to emphasise a wider truth. And despite the reflex contempt for begging, despite the crowing Englishness that declares itself at every turn – whenever he eats a meal or steps into an inn – none of his assumed superiority survives the personal encounters of the journey. Talking to a sad, penurious fellow traveller on the road to Westport, taken to visit a self-absorbed hermit of a priest in the wilds of Galway, taking down the conversation of a Ballinasloe squire who might have jumped straight out of his friend Lever's novels, the writing transforms itself into something sharp, generous and sympathetic. Typically it is the *detail* he notes – the starving man's occupation, the names of the squire's racehorses. Towards the end of the book he sits in Dublin Bay watching a crowd of pleasure boats and suddenly lights upon the hulk of a convict ship lying ready for sail 'with a black mass of poor

'Gambling at the races'

wretches who too were eager for pleasure'. Again, it is a typical Thackeray observation – something he *would* see – and it conveys perfectly the odd mixture of barbarism, decency and pity that separates his age from our own.

Finishing the second half of his tour late in October, Thackeray returned to Dublin. Writing to his mother after three days at work on the manuscript, he reported steady progress. He was optimistic about the *Irish Sketch Book*'s chances: it was 'a clever book', he thought. Moreover, the forthcoming appearance of Dickens' *American Notes* would materially assist its prospects 'as people who have read that & liked it will like more reading of the same sort'. He delivered a final verdict on Ireland that reflected many of the irritations of the previous four months: 'the country, Protestant & Catholic, is priest-ridden beyond all bearing; it is well to see, but as for living in it I would sooner live in a garret in dear old smoky London than a 50 windowed house. The parties never cease quarrelling – the society is under-educated – the priests as ignorant as boors –.' In the end there was nothing quite as acceptable as Pall Mall cockneydom. He spent the last four days in Dublin visiting Lever and taking a fond farewell of the novelist's children, dining out and party going, and watching the installation of the city's lord mayor and the 1 November's opening of the Law Courts, in the hope that these spectacles might provide him with further copy. Finally he took his place on the Dun Laoghaire boat. It would be wrong to say that he returned to the troubles of his

London life, for in reality he had carried them with him around Ireland throughout the summer and early autumn. By the time he set sail Isabella's white face, the children's voices and the clattering doors of Great Coram Street had become inextricably linked to the experiences of his trip: Captain Feeny's adventures read by the light of a tavern's rush lamp, or the great bare fields with granite poking through the grass on the road to Clifden. Many years later Anthony Trollope's Irish groom, who had divined something of the *Irish Sketch Book*'s tone, reproached Thackeray for not caring about Ireland or its inhabitants. Thackeray denied it. On the contrary, he replied: it was from there that had come the thing he loved most.

Alfred Bunn, theatrical manager

That *Punch*, sir, played the very devil with me. Never a
month went by without I'd find myself in there – 'My kyind
friends', 'The poet Bunn', that kind of thing. It got, sir, so
that people would *remark* it. Why, I'd have young sports up
in their boxes laughing when they set eyes on me. And all
over what sir? Can't a man address the folks as pays his
salary? Is he always to be lampooned in this way? It was
cruel, sir, cruel what they did to me – an advertisement, in a
manner of speaking, but at my expense you know . . .

I met Mr Thackeray only the once – in America it was –
and he was civil, I'll give you that: 'How do, Bunn' or some
such. But many's the time I've had him pointed out to me.
He used to come to the theatre with his friends. A tall
gentleman, and haughty-like, I gather. But I'll say this much
for him, he used to enjoy himself regular. I've heard it said
the smell of the greasepaint was like nectar to him, and I've
known him send his card backstage to an actor or two. He
mocked me though, sir, he exposed me to ridicule in my
profession, and it's laughter I could have done without.

XI

The Vagrant Heart

'Had it not been for *Punch*, I wonder where I should be.'
Quoted in M.H. *Spielman*, A History of 'Punch'

'To the Pyramids, and 3 cheers for Punch on the top'
Diary, 19 October 1844

hackeray returned from Ireland to find what he had left when he set out four months before: his family in France, a house in London where he could live if he wanted, and an obligation to work. It was a bachelor life devoid of the bachelor life's usual attractions: as he once explained to a friend, he was a widower with a wife alive. The last days of 1842, spent back in Paris putting the *Irish Sketch Book* into final shape, must have shown him how precarious his situation was. Petty irritations, such as Mrs Butler's decision to stop paying old John Goldsworthy's wages, mingled with more serious threats to his solvency. The matter of the *Constitutional*'s debts still burned on, and a creditor named Hickman was threatening to bring a law suit. Effortlessly surmounting them all was the larger question of the Thackeray family's future existence. 'Something afterwards must be done that is clear,' Thackeray wrote to his mother in the spring of 1843, 'and we must determine whether the little ones are to stay abroad with their granny or at home with their father.' In the event this dilemma hung over Thackeray's life for another three years. Would Isabella ever recover her wits? Nobody knew. In the meantime her condition fluctuated back and forth. Undecided over his future plans, Thackeray chafed at his daughters' absence and its consequences, in particular the girls' exposure to Mrs Carmichael-Smyth's gloomy and exacting brand of Evangelicalism. Before long Annie would be using some of her natural intelligence to question various of her grandmother's ordinances. Thackeray, to whom application was eventually made, could only vacillate between diplomacy and honest expressions of annoyance.

Meantime there were delays over the *Irish Sketch Book*, which Chapman and Hall sat on until May 1843. Writing to his mother on New Year's Day, stuck at Le Havre on the way back to England, Thackeray turned inevitably to domestic matters. Mrs Butler had suggested that the Great Coram Street lease, up for renewal in May, should be continued in her name, and had also offered to accommodate her friend Bess Hamerton there. If this invitation extended to Isabella – with whom, he told his mother, he intended to try and live in the spring – Thackeray was all for it. However, he suspected Mrs Butler also wanted to house the Carmichaels, in which case another property in Eaton Square would probably be more convenient. There were several injunctions for his absence. In particular, Mrs Carmichael-Smyth should 'Mind the little ones go often to their mother' (this was followed: in later life Annie remembered roaming with Isabella in the gardens at Chaillot). On his last visit, he confided, he had taken his wife a writing book that she had asked for and appeared to want to use. 'Try & put her in mind of her promise,' Thackeray asked his mother, adding rather wistfully, 'but I don't care much for long letters from her – only a word or two.' Two and a half years into Isabella's madness, he seems to have been determined not to let her slip away from him, and to create the conditions in which 'Mr and Mrs Thack' and their children could live together according to the pencil sketches of the mid-1830s.

Work, too, continued to haunt him: a vast freelance output, which is even now partly beyond the grasp of the bibliographers. *Fraser's*, now edited by G.W. Nickisson, was still his mainstay, but he was also associated with papers as diverse as the newly founded *Pictorial Times* (a forerunner of the *Illustrated London News*), the *Calcutta Star*, where his old India connections procured a commission to write a monthly London letter, and, from early 1844, the *Morning Chronicle*. But by far the most important link forged in these locust years was with *Punch*, a publication that despite unpromising beginnings had already begun to change the face of English comic journalism.

If the early-Victorian era was a boom time for print journalism – over 800 periodicals were floated in London alone during the 1840s –

then these were, by contemporary standards, fairly modest explosions. *The Times'* circulation hovered at around 40,000 copies a day; other daily papers struggled to reach even one-tenth of this. Among weekly publications, Dickens' *Household Words* averaged 38,000 ten years later. To sell nearly 50,000 copies an issue within the first five years of your existence, to achieve – in an age of mass illiteracy – a *readership* conservatively put at four times that number, was little short of miraculous, and yet this was what *Punch*, founded on a shoestring and nearly stifled six months after its birth, managed to do. The achievement was all the more impressive in the light of its antecedents. Its closest ancestral ties were with scurrilous gutter-papers of the 1830s, like *The Squib*, the *Penny Satirist* and *Figaro in London*, and its leading lights – Douglas Jerrold, Gilbert à Beckett and the editor Mark Lemon – had no conspicuous political or cultural agenda to pursue. They were simply working journalists – Jerrold's Fleet Street credentials went back to the 1820s – with a living to make. Somehow, treading gingerly between their own moderate radicalism and a gentility frankly designed to appeal to the sensibilities of their middle-class readership, they stumbled on a formula that worked.

Trying to explain their appeal to the average early-Victorian bourgeois, one runs up against a complex mixture of comedy and conscience, erudition and whimsy, gelling itself into an instantly recognisable whole. At threepence a number, this kind of thing undoubtedly had the edge over lighter aspects of the half-crown magazine. And yet, from the outset, *Punch's* status was always faintly ambiguous. Technically not a newspaper (it paid no tax, which kept the price down), it enjoyed a two-way relationship with the rest of Fleet Street, plundering from it and being plundered in its turn. Above all, perhaps, *Punch* humour was participative – topical, allusive, intended in the last resort to keep the reader in the know. One of its earliest roles, significantly enough, was as a recycler of catchphrases, and many an early-Victorian signature remark – most famously 'Does your mother know you're out?' – owed its popularity to the *Punch* seal of approval.

Unprecedentedly, despite early setbacks, it worked. Although an early historian claimed that '*Punch* was *not* born in a tavern parlour. He came into the world in rather a businesslike way than otherwise', the first few months of the magazine's existence were a struggle. In particular, the road to solvency was not smoothed by a four-way split between the principals – a printer named J.V. Last; Horace Mayhew, to whom Last had proposed the idea of a comic and satirical weekly; Mark Lemon; and an engraver called Ebenezer Landells. Bankruptcy threatened, but, bought up by the publisher Bradbury & Evans, the concern rallied. Within a year of its first appearance in July 1841 it had been endorsed by *The Times* and the *Quarterly Review*. More important, perhaps, in terms of its wider cultural impact was a fifty-page imprimatur from the ultra-highbrow *Westminster Review* (the modern equivalent would be a *Private Eye* symposium in the *Times Literary Supplement*). What had at first been not much more than a collection of hack-journalism quickly broadened out to include more up-market contributions.

Thackeray's arrival on the paper coincided with a process that began with the appearance of 'The Song of the Shirt', Thomas Hood's famous attack on sweated labour (a sensation in the Christmas number of 1843) and continued with Jerrold's series of marital dialogues, *Mrs Caudle's Curtain Lectures*, which ran for most of 1845. All this had the welcome effect of keeping the paper in the public eye. Its political jibes were quoted in the House; the Queen – presumably gritting her teeth against the jokes about Prince Albert and the royal household – was known to see a copy; and it brought an enviable whiff of urban sophistication to many a provincial middle-class home (the inhabitants of the Brontë parsonage at Haworth were subscribers, for example). By the end of the decade this self-perpetuating image was helped by a series of ingenious publicity stunts, to which Thackeray himself was not above contributing.

Punch, famously, made Thackeray's name. His pseudonyms were known to the literary-minded public, and his appearances there urged on the steady growth of his reputation throughout the 1840s. For all that, Thackeray's association with a weekly periodical of this type could still have mixed consequences. The social status of journalists remained low, and their presence in the kind of social circles in which Thackeray aspired to move was more often tolerated than encouraged. One of his cartoons for the paper shows a footman at an evening party surveying a file of guests, one of whom is obviously the cartoonist, and murmuring to a colleague, 'That's him, that's *Poonch*!' Some years later, leaving the Whig salon at Holland House with a fellow guest, Thackeray remarked on the free-and-easy atmosphere that prevailed. Yes indeed, the man replied: he had heard they even received Mr Thackeray of *Punch* celebrity. Thackeray laughed it off as a joke, but the imputation of social inferiority rankled. For these and other reasons, a faint ambiguity always characterised his dealings with *Punch*. As we have seen, he began by regarding it as a 'low' paper and swore his mother to secrecy over his involvement. Fitzgerald, hearing a rumour of his friend's intentions, counselled caution – advice that Thackeray ignored. When his first series for the magazine, *Miss Tickletoby's Lectures on English History*, proved unsuccessful and was discontinued, he wrote to Bradbury & Evans from Ireland with what looks very like disdain. 'I wish that my writings had the good fortune to please everyone,' he loftily observed, 'but all I can do, however, is my best, which has been done in this case, just as much as if I had been writing for any more dignified periodical.' The inference is clear: *Punch* is a low paper. Whether, despite his assurances to the contrary, Thackeray thought he could get away with slightly inferior goods in such poor company is not clear, but *Miss Tickletoby* – a series of historical disquisitions delivered by a faintly sinister schoolmistress who is always threatening to cane her inattentive audience – is a laboured performance. There is a bizarre sub-text to its title, too. 'Toby' is early-Victorian slang for 'buttocks'. 'Tickletoby', consequently, is a joke about flagellation. But 'Toby' was also one of Thackeray's pet-names for Isabella. Despite this rebuff Thackeray persevered, contributing parodies and other comic pieces throughout 1843 and eventually joining the magazine's staff in December on the departure of Albert Smith. This was a gradual process, and for a time his contributions appeared simultaneously in *Fraser's* – *Barry Lyndon* was serialised there throughout 1844 – but by the mid-1840s Thackeray's principal loyalty was to Lemon and Co., who paid well and gave him greater scope for the exercise of his comic powers.

And yet in some ways one senses that Thackeray found the *Punch* atmosphere less congenial to him than his socialising with the *Fraser's* set. He enjoyed the weekly dinners convened to discuss the main illustration or 'large cut' (these were held at Bradbury & Evans' offices, successively in Wellington Street, the Strand, Fleet Street and Bouverie Street) and attended them to within a week of his death, long after he had ceased to write for the paper. But he was irked both by the amount of time that the connection extracted from him and by a brand of radicalism which, for all his well-advertised liberal sympathies, Thackeray thought occasionally went too far. This disquiet invariably focused on the irascible figure of Douglas Jerrold, with whom Thackeray was on uneasy terms throughout an association of nearly twenty years. Undoubtedly some of this had to do with

Jerrold's prickly manner (he once characterised some of the magazine's plagiarists as 'biped vermin which . . . are generated in the dregs of an ink-bottle, and sting, in so far as they can sting, at so much the column'). A little more, perhaps, had to do with professional jealousy, as when *Mrs Caudle's Curtain Lectures*, Jerrold's great hit of 1845, was overtaken by Thackeray's *The Snobs of England*. Social origins, too, played a part. Thackeray preferred public-school men like his old schoolfriend Leech for his companions among the *Punch* staff, and Mark Lemon was heard to comment wryly that he feared his contributor was too good for ordinary conversation (this aloofness went down badly with the engravers who converted the paper's illustrations into woodblocks, at least one of whom complained that Thackeray was the only journalist who never spoke to them). At the same time Thackeray sincerely admired *Mrs Caudle* and reviewed it warmly in the *Morning Chronicle*, and many years later he lobbied hard to get its author elected to the Reform Club ('I think we have got the little man in,' he is supposed to have remarked when the desired result was achieved). The mixture of apprehension and wary esteem that Jerrold inspired in him is captured in Henry Vizetelly's memory of Thackeray 'nervously' picking up the week's edition with a cry of 'Now let us see what young Douglas has to say this week.' But he could be vicious over Jerrold's supposed lapses of principle. Vizetelly, again, remembers him finding a copy of one of Jerrold's books on the shelves of the Earl of Carlisle, and opening it to discover a respectful inscription. 'Ah,' Thackeray remarked. 'This is the sort of style in which your rigid, uncompromising radical always toadies the great.' For his own part, Jerrold was happy to poke semi-public fun at his colleague. Once Thackeray arrived late at the *Punch* supper, having been detained at a christening at which he had stood godfather (presumably this was his friend Leech's son). 'Good Lord Thackeray!' Jerrold is supposed to have exclaimed, 'I hope you didn't present the child with your own mug!'

In the end, though, it was some of the satirical targets favoured by 'that savage little Robespierre', as Thackeray once characterised him in a fit of passion, that did the damage: in particular the clergy and the royal family. Thackeray was happier in the field of middle-class manners – a *Punch* speciality, and in some ways the compost in which *Vanity Fair* took root and grew. But if *Punch* provided him with an increased scope and irritated his touchy side in about equal parts, it was at least work. Early 1843 found him as eagerly in pursuit of this as ever, writing to Chapman and Hall to propose a 'Fairy Ballet' on the French model and an article for the *Foreign Quarterly Review* (nothing came of either scheme). 'You will I'm sure be glad to hear my wife is extremely better,' he concluded – Chapman and Hall knew all about Mrs Thackeray's sojourn at Chaillot – 'all but herself again.'

Fitzgerald paid the first of several visits that year, which Thackeray told his mother was 'a great comfort . . . We only talk nonsense: but that is the best kind of talk.' Amid a round of dinner parties – he reported five invitations one March Saturday – and 'cozy smokes' late at night over the fire at Great Coram Street with Fitz, the familiar questions were beginning to reassert themselves. Isabella had written a 'very comfortable' letter, though it contained an odd passage about somnambulism; he was still wondering where to live, and to this end had looked at a house in Brunswick Square. Lurking in the background, meanwhile, was the figure of Mr Hickman and his writ. Writing to his mother in March, as the *Constitutional* business dragged on, Thackeray announced a decision: 'as I think over the various businesses I really see no end to them: but if end there is to be it is clear to me that I must live in London and not lose my place and my chance and be always on the move from one country to another'. Maintaining his present lifestyle was an expensive business. Not counting his private expenses, but including the ninety pounds taken up by Isabella's care, he had spent £370 in the past eight months, an outlay that had forced him to break into the sum of money he had begun to set aside for Annie and Minnie. 'What was to be done else?' he wondered. The children's absence haunted him, and the letters to his mother contain frequent enclosures. A charming note to Annie from around this time describes coming upon two little girls singing in the street. When questioned, they explained that their mother and three more children were at home without food. Thackeray gave them money and sent them on their way with a loaf of bread.

It would have been more bearable had the blows fallen singly. In his melancholy state, Thackeray was furious to open the April issue of *Fraser's* and find Deady Keane's exposure of his bill-discounting days. Why Keane should have taken against an old friend in this way remains a mystery, but it was a notably savage portrait of 'Bill Crackaway', a 'bird of ill omen' whose mouth is 'physically incapable of the candour of the honest laugh', and Thackeray quickly informed Nickisson that if Keane continued his contributions in 'any shape, mine must cease'. Nickisson took the hint. The by-product of these tribulations was a gloomy letter to his mother in early May. Nothing was settled about the house, and he had had to pay for forty-five pounds' worth of dilapidation under the terms of the Great Coram Street lease. Worse, Hickman had announced his intention of carrying on with his suit, which if successful would cost Thackeray £400 'or else a bankruptcy'. His stricture was bothering him (Thackeray was always candid with his mother about the legacy of his old venereal complaint). 'Ye Gods assist an unfortunate literary man,' he implored. Writing to Isabella on the same day he managed to strike a more relaxed note, telling her of another visit by Fitzgerald ('It is delightful to have him in the house but I'm afraid his society makes me idle, we sit and talk too much about books & pictures and smoke too many cigars') and of his attendance at Mrs Proctor's grand ball, which featured Catherine Dickens in a dress of pink satin and 'Mr Dickens in geranium & ringlets'. '. . . Write me a line ever so short,' he ended plaintively, 'it will always be worth a guinea to me.'

Fitz's letters to friends from Great Coram Street give a lively picture of Thackeray's ersatz bachelor life in London. In one he records the last proof sheets of the *Irish Sketch Book* being brought in as they sat over breakfast, the traditional attacks of the establishment's fleas ('Thackeray said he was bit last night') and the sound of John Goldsworthy taking down the curtains from his host's bed in the room above. Another notes a dinner with Tennyson and Dickens. Shortly after Fitz's departure, still troubled by his stricture, which had now developed a painful abcess, Thackeray took himself off for a restorative trip to Brighton. Here he was able to read the first reviews of the *Irish Sketch Book*. These, and their successors, were almost uniformly favourable. English critics liked the book, which became the first of Thackeray's works to go into a second edition. There was some hostility from Catholic papers – in fact Chapman and Hall had already toned down the anti-Catholic slant – but even the *Tablet* went out of its way to distinguish between the author and his material: 'At bottom, the man is as good-natured, cant-hating, humanity-loving a creature, as any cockney that ever got smoke-drenched by the atmosphere of Bow-bells.' This was gratifying, but as Thackeray told his mother towards the end of May, the 'perplexities' of his life had not decreased since he last wrote. Fortunately the abcess, having lingered for six weeks, 'has disappeared in the usual way and I'm now quite a different man'. This letter suggests that the urethral trouble was now periodic, but that Thackeray had refused – as he was to do for the rest of his life

– the offer of surgical intervention. 'The complaint itself does not annoy me. I have gone a good way towards curing it, and see no reason to regret having refused the aid of the Doctors.' Meanwhile there were the usual money worries. In particular, a mix-up over Isabella's removal from Chaillot (presumably following some prior arrangement: Thackeray seems to have thought that his parents had taken her away from Dr Puzin) meant that he had failed to remit her fees. Financially, he declared himself £100 ahead of the world, and hoped to make another £100 out of the book, which continued to attract good reviews. 'The literary people like it generally very much', and Dickens himself had written a complimentary letter.

One of the dilemmas hanging over him he did manage finally to resolve. The lease on Great Coram Street was given up, and he removed his belongings to a hotel in Covent Garden. The remainder of 1843 was spent living out of suitcases – staying with his parents, travelling in the Low Countries, taking temporary quarters off St James's Square, before coming to rest in December in Jermyn Street. Throughout this peripatetic existence, work stayed at the top of his agenda. The trip to the Low Countries, undertaken with his friend Stevens early in August, was a deliberate attempt to add to the material he had brought back from the ill-fated visit of summer 1840 in the hope of producing some saleable articles. This excursion, which realised 'Little Travels and Roadside Sketches', a conflation of the two separate journeys eventually unloaded on Nickisson, was uneventful. Leaving Paris on 4 August, he and Stevens travelled via Brussels to Antwerp, only to discover on their arrival that Thackeray had lost his pocketbook *en route*. This necessitated a return to Brussels, after which they pressed on to Rotterdam and The Hague. Mid-August found them about to leave Ostend and they were back in Paris by the end of the month, having spent much of the intervening time at Lille. Thackeray admitted to his mother that the trip had been a mistake: 'Of all the failures in the world this expedition has been the greatest ... I think I have not gained twopence worth of ideas in the course of the journey –.' Admitted to the royal picture gallery at The Hague, where the king himself could be seen supervising the papering of a new apartment, he was unmoved. 'The palace is a poor little place, and the gallery is a tawdry, though comfortable & handsome affair.' He was short of money – the ten days in Lille were spent waiting for his mother to send ten pounds to finance the rest of the journey – and Stevens was a bit of a bore, making him wish he had brought Fitz or

Savile Morton instead. Nevertheless he went steadfastly about the task in hand, telling his mother that he was 'determined to see these towns alone once more' (Stevens left him shortly after the middle of the month) 'and make something saleable about them'.

He was becoming increasingly gloomy about Isabella. Writing to Aunt Ritchie from the Carmichael-Smyths' Paris address, while the rest of the family was at Montmorency, and hard at work on what was to become *Barry Lyndon*, he described her as 'provokingly well – so well I mean, that I can't understand why she should not be quite well'. The tone is markedly different from the letters of earlier in the year when he had assured correspondents of her improving health and his plans to live with her once more. Three years on since the voyage to Cork, he began to worry 'that the poor little soul will never be entirely restored to us'.

By late autumn he was back in London, complaining to Chapman and Hall about the poor rate of pay offered by the *Foreign Quarterly Review* ('It is *too* low; and for the sake of human nature & your property, I would recommend you to put a couple of guineas more upon the value of the article'), and reassuring his mother both about his eyesight, currently requiring 'doctoring', and the state of his affairs in general. The world wagged pleasantly enough with him, he told Mrs Carmichael-Smyth – breakfast with Fitz, a day spent writing at one of his clubs, dinner with friends. 'It is quite curious to see how work falls in London wh. would be quite out of one's way at Paris . . .' Beyond his immediate concerns, he was following the current agitation over the Corn Laws with great interest. 'It will be a magnificent peaceful Revolution,' he told his mother, '– the government of the country will fall naturally into the hands of the middle classes as it should do: and the Lords and country gentlemen will – only have their due share.' This is a revealing comment in the light of the hidebound Whiggish conservatism of his declining years, for it shows him, effectively, approving the general tendency of mid-century *embourgeoisement* then enveloping early-Victorian society – a process of which the young Queen was very much a symbol and middle-class publications such as *Punch* an obvious outgrowth.

Thackeray kept up his rooms at 27 Jermyn Street for nearly eighteen months. Vizetelly, who visited him there in the winter of 1843–4 to negotiate freelance work, was struck by the sparseness of the premises and the evident frugality of the lodger's lifestyle. Admitted by a maid, he was escorted to the very top of the house. Here, his card having been sent in, he was led into the presence of 'a tall, slim individual between thirty and thirty-five years of age, with a pleasant smiling countenance and bridgeless nose, and clad in a dressing-gown of a decided Parisian cut'. The room's ceiling was low, Vizetelly noted, exaggerating Thackeray's height when he stood up. Subsequently his eye roved over 'an exceedingly plainly furnished bedroom, with common rush seated chairs and painted French bedstead, and with neither looking-glass nor prints on the bare, cold, cheerless-looking walls'. At one end of a small table lay the remains of Thackeray's modest breakfast – a cup that had contained chocolate and some pieces of dry toast – at the other end two or three recent numbers of *Fraser's* and some slips of manuscript. Vizetelly's business was to induce Thackeray to contribute a couple of columns a week (book reviews, art and opera criticism) to the recently founded *Pictorial Times*. He needed little prompting to accept the three-guinea fee on offer: the paper's emissary remembered him being 'so satisfied' that he jokingly proposed to sign an agreement for life. Vizetelly, who would later help Thackeray in negotiations with publishers, wondered at the tall young dandy with the frank face in his shabby lodgings: 'The humble quarters in which he was installed seemed at any rate to indicate that for some reason or other strict economy was just then the order of the day with him.'

Vizetelly, of course, knew little of Thackeray's circumstances. In fact the £160 a year that came to him as a result of this encounter (although the *Pictorial Times* was often a laggardly payer) made a welcome difference. Writing to his family a week before Christmas 1843, and blaming pressure of work for his inability to return before New Year's Day, he noted that 'it is a comfort to think there is a decent income arranged for 1844 (please God my health hold good) and actually a prospect of saving money at the year's end'. His life, he maintained, 'is a very jolly one – plenty of work that is and plenty of fun'. The dramatic changes of tone in Thackeray's letters from this period are one of their most marked features. At one moment he seems filled with optimism over his prospects, at another cast down by the thought of the prisoner at Chaillot. The explanation lies both in the volatile life he was leading, where a couple of magazine commissions could work a miraculous effect on his short-term finances, and in the nature of his audience. The letters meant for wholesale family consumption are invariably more cheerful than the bouts of melancholy occasionally unleashed on Mrs Carmichael-Smyth, whose own low spirits may have had an equally depressing effect on her son when he wrote back. Certainly her morbid imagination and general puritanism were getting worse. Thackeray had promised to bring a copy of Dickens' Christmas book *A Christmas Carol* with him, but knew that his mother disliked its author's emphasis on festive good cheer. 'I have made friends with him,' he warned, 'and think your tirade against good dinners a monstrous piece of superstition. Why not be happy when one can?'

Why not indeed? At any rate it cannot have been a lonely Christmas, as, sending his 'respectful wishes' to Fitzgerald's uncle Peter Purcell, he revealed that he had 'on this sacred day ELEVEN invitations to Dinner which I can't help thinking of with a sort of pride . . .' The social career that was to dominate certain aspects of his life over the next decade was already well advanced. So, too, was a growing status as a circumspect literary operator whose opinions on the state of the marketplace were eagerly canvassed. Thackeray's comments on the manuscripts offered to him by hopeful novices (a category that eventually included Mrs Carmichael-Smyth) are interesting for their grasp of the way in which London literary life worked in the 1840s, and the mechanisms by which it could be exploited. A letter to his cousin Richard Bedingfield, whose novel *The Miser's Son* Thackeray had tried and failed to puff in Jerdan's *Literary Gazette*, carries a neat conspectus of the prevailing literary climate. Had Bedingfield's publishers advertised in Jerdan's paper or elsewhere? 'A laudatory paragraph here and there will do you no earthly good, unless the name of your book is permanently before the public . . .' Thackeray advised his friend. 'Shakespeare himself would not get a hearing in Gray's Inn Lane.' Bedingfield should steer clear of publishers who failed to offer him money – *The Miser's Son* seems to have appeared at its author's own expense – should write short stories and make a dash at the magazines. These might not accept his articles, but they would at least give him a fair hearing. 'It is, however, a bad trade at the best,' Thackeray warned.

New Year's Day found him back in Paris. The early days of 1844 were spent working on reviews and other freelance commissions. Isabella, at home on a visit, seemed wonderfully better. 'Pray God to keep her so and restore her love for me,' Thackeray entreated. All kinds of things were flowing back and forth across his desk: there were more articles for *Fraser's*, while a connection struck up with the Liberal *Morning Chronicle* looked as if it would provide a welcome boost to his finances (by June Thackeray was able to tell Major Carmichael-Smyth that he was making twenty pounds a month from this source). His forte continued to be light articles, book reviews and opera criticism. He made occasional forays into weightier political journalism, but confessed that 'I am a very weak & poor politician'. Elsewhere, he sometimes tried to procure translation work, undertaking at one point to render Eugène Sue's *Mystères de Paris* into English, but soon gave it up. Unwell, both from his stricture and a sore throat, his consistent challenge was to finish the monthly instalment of *Barry Lyndon*, which had begun in the January number of *Fraser's* and was to continue throughout the year. He found the going hard, reaching the end of chapter four on 20 January 'with a great deal of dullness unwillingness and labour'. His lack of interest in this faked memoir of a rackety eighteenth-century Irish adventurer continued during the rest of the book's composition and throughout its subsequent publishing history: he told Annie not to bother to read it when the novel was finally reprinted in volume form a dozen years later.

On one level this dismissiveness is understandable, for there is a brutality about Barry's adventures – supposedly edited for public consumption by George Savage Fitz-Boodle – that the original early-Victorian audience must have found hard to stomach. Unlike some of Thackeray's earlier comic villains, Barry is a rogue through and through, and the relish with which he kills men in battle or double-crosses his adversaries is sometimes a little too unmediated for comfort. By the standards of conventional fiction there is a peculiar purposelessness about his career, which taken in the round is simply a series of failures. Barry merely drifts through life, grasping at whatever opportunity presents itself. Running away from home after falling in love with his cousin and, he is led to believe, killing her fiancé in a duel, he deserts from the Allied army in the Seven Years War, re-emerges as a gambler in the salons of Europe and marries a rich woman, only to end up as a worn-out bankrupt in the Fleet Prison, from which these memoirs are supposedly indited.

Thackeray's achievement, in this worm's eye view of the debt-bilking, heiress-chasing side of eighteenth-century life, is the assumed voice in which Barry addresses his audience: as Trollope once put it, the marvel of the book is not that the hero should think well of himself but that the author should appear to be on his side. In fact this narrowing of the gap between voice and ventriloquist allows Thackeray to achieve a profound truthfulness about his creation's inner life.

Though he is happy enough to stamp on anyone who gets in his way, Barry still possesses a queer kind of inverted moral code. Asked by a Prussian police-chief to spy on an Austrian diplomat, for example, he cheerfully enters into the plot until he realises that the man is his uncle, whereupon family loyalty supervenes and he absconds for a career as the Chevalier de Balibari's gambling accomplice. Predictably the scenes at the gaming-tables are some of the best in the book. If *Barry Lyndon* owes a rather obvious debt to Fielding's *Jonathan Wild*, then it also bears a passing resemblance to another eighteenth-century classic, Smollett's *Roderick Random*. This kinship is most marked in the sharp, hard glimpses into bygone codes of behaviour. Just as Roderick thinks it the most natural thing in the world that he can get satisfaction from a government office only by paying a bribe, so Barry is a stickler for what he calls the 'chivalry' of the card table: while he is prepared to back an obvious cheat, he would not care to mix with him socially. There is an intent, brooding realism about these attitudes – one can see, for example, why Stanley Kubrick seized upon the book for his 1975 film, and *Barry Lyndon*, consequently, has survived as one of those odd but rewarding novels valued more by posterity than by its original audience.

He stayed for just over two months in Paris, labouring over his novel and articles for *Punch*, going to the theatre, dining with friends such as the Ritchies, the Stevenses and the Corkrans (John Frazer Corkran was Paris correspondent of the *Morning Herald*) and spending time with Isabella – either at home, where she made daily visits, or at Chaillot. Professionally, he was growing more confident of his ability to command space and fees to match, and full of sound schemes to promote public awareness of his work. A letter to Chapman and Hall, late in February, proposes three pieces for the *Foreign Quarterly Review* and further advertising for what remained of the print-run of the *Irish Sketch Book*. 'Would not now be a good time to gather together in one vast broad sheet all the puffs concerning Titmarsh's Ireland and see whether the public will not take off the few remaining copies of the work?' A letter to Bradbury & Evans, three days later, has a similar tone. Noting that 'I have got a public now', Thackeray would be glad to bring out 'a good stout book full of tales, reprints from Fraser – literary articles &c ...' Alternatively, perhaps the firm might care to 'bring me to London and put me at the head of a slashing brilliant, gentlemanlike, sixpenny, aristocratic, literary paper ...' He knew of no man in Europe, the prospective editor added vaingloriously, who would handle it better. These letters are revealing for the way in which they show that even now, moving towards his middle thirties – he would be thirty-three in July – Thackeray still had no fixed plans. He wanted to write – he believed he was capable of – a great novel that might encapsulate much of recent English history, but in the meantime a post on a newspaper (he seems to have been applying for two jobs of this kind in early March) would be preferable to hard work.

By the second week in March he was back in his old haunts of London clubland, and exchanged nods with Daniel O'Connell at the Reform ('the old rogue gave me a fierce look at wh. I felt as if my heart was coming into my mouth'). He passed through Great Coram Street on some errand, he told Isabella, and 'slunk through it with a heartache'. The letter found him voicing a familiar lament: when he was in one place he invariably hankered after another, 'and I think now about the little room in the Champs Elysées as the most delightful little retreat in the world'. He was still pondering how best to bring his family together, telling Bedingfield that he proposed to ferry his wife and children to London as soon as he could get a house and the money for its upkeep. That this resolve had hardened in his mind seems clear from a letter to his mother of 1 June in which he tells her that he has 'written to my wife to say I should have her over and mean to keep my plan'. The scheme was confirmed in a second letter, ten days later, in which he announced his intention to stay with his parents at their country retreat until the end of June, then go to Paris for Isabella and bring her back to Twickenham – Thackeray had stayed at Richmond the summer before and explored the area – to lodge in the house of 'an honest half-pay captain named Alexander, his wife and family'. It was a big house, he reported, where Isabella could have three rooms of her own and a maid to attend her. He would live there for two days during the week. All this would cost £150 a year, 'and the people seem so honest, well-bred and kind that I don't think I can do better than give the poor little woman into their charge'. A day later he wrote to his cousin Charlotte Ritchie confirming these arrangements, asking her to notify Dr Puzin that he intended to remove Isabella at the start of July, and to give his love to the Hamertons 'for their kindness to my poor little invalid'.

All this had the makings of a decisive step. Clearly Thackeray intended to place his wife in a house where she would be well looked after by respectable English people, with himself in constant attendance and the prospect of her children's return. What went wrong?

Naturally the scheme would have cost money, but Thackeray's friends at least were in no doubt of his improving situation. Fitzgerald, reading his May 'Academy Exhibition' spoof in *Punch*, noted that 'He is full vigour and play and pay in London, writing in a dozen reviews, and a score of newspapers, and while health lasts he sails before the wind.' Few letters remain from this period in Thackeray's life, and the diary he had begun to keep at the start of the year is mostly silent. He was with the Carmichael-Smyths near Liège in late July and the beginning of August, working on a one-volume life of Talleyrand that he had persuaded Chapman and Hall to commission (it was never delivered), but the talk was all of the children's precocity: Annie was 'not improved in looks but wonderfully intelligent and affectionate. Harriet too amazingly advanced.' At one point Annie, seeing the passengers in a passing coach smoking cigars, cried, 'Papa those men have glowworms in their mouths.' Annie herself remembered 'an Arcadian sort of country with pleasant trees ... In front of the house with its many green shutters was a courtyard, enclosed by green gates, where we used to breakfast, and outside the gate a long terraced road along the dried-up river where I used to walk with my father, holding his hand.' There is no reference to Isabella, who presumably remained at Chaillot. One can only assume that a deterioration in her health caused him to abandon, or at any rate postpone, the scheme (certainly a letter to his mother a fortnight later mentions that Charlotte Ritchie had just forwarded an 'odd *hopeless* letter of her's').

Whatever the cause of this postponement, it was rendered indefinite by a sudden change of plan. Thackeray spent a fortnight in France. By 6 August he was back in England to pursue a week of hard work and socialising – *Punch* articles, dining with the rising Tory politician-cum-novelist Benjamin Disraeli, the publisher Henry Colburn, Mark Lemon and Frederick Evans, *Punch*'s joint proprietor; 17 August, however, found him closeted with Evans 'about the foreign trip'. This excursion took on a sharper focus at a dinner at the Reform Club two days later given by an acquaintance of Thackeray's named William Bevan for his friend James Emerson Tennent, a well-known politician – he was MP for Belfast and secretary to the India Board – and writer who was on the point of setting out on a tour of the Near East. Given the fact that his meeting with Evans took place two days before, Thackeray's interest in the trip prefigured the dinner, but it may have been here that Tennent produced the clinching argument in its favour – the apparent willingness of the directors of the shipping company, the Peninsular & Oriental, to give Thackeray a free passage in the hope of favourable publicity. Several other factors must have influenced Thackeray's decision to accept. Presumably Isabella's condition was such that it scarcely mattered to her whether he stayed or went: in some ways the Eastern trip, taken at short notice only three weeks after the date at which his new domestic arrangements were to have begun, marks the first faint ruling of a line under their relationship. Though he would miss his family, the chance to travel again – something he always enjoyed – through exotic locales and at someone else's expense, with the chance to recount his exploits both in *Punch* and subsequently in book form, was too good to turn down.

A slight drawback was that the P&O vessel, the *Lady Mary Wood*, was due to leave Southampton on 22 August. As a result Thackeray spent the next three days in a fever of anxiety – dashing to the City to make further arrangements, going to an evening party with Fitz (he was too overwhelmed by the approaching departure to enjoy himself) and dining again with Bevan at the Garrick, where he 'took leave of the good fellows there'. In between trying to complete as much as possible of the still unfinished *Barry Lyndon*, he wrote hastily to friends and family to inform them of his future whereabouts. 'I hope it will be a tender haunch,' he wrote to Stephen Spring Rice, characteristically equating the trip with another of his favourite sensual pleasures. 'My heart is too full to say more. Write to Fitz with my love and tell him the wonderful news. THE PYRAMIDS – Mong Jew!' A more sober letter to his mother, begun on 21 August, played down much of this emotion. Conscious that she would bemoan the notional ten-week absence (in fact he was away for nearly six months), he predicted that he would be miserable, 'But it offers such a chance as I may never get again.' His mother would have crossed the Channel enough times to raise a smile at his vision of the opening leg of the voyage: 'Think of tossing in the Bay of Biscay, and the steward and the basin!' 22 August dawned with a Punch deadline still unmet: he carried the piece about with him and finished it just as the coach swept into Southampton. The last glimpse he had of London was of his friend the architect Joseph Gwilt's grey head bending over *The Times* in Abingdon Street. Inducted onto the *Lady Mary Wood* and introduced to his fellow passengers, he noted 'the first evening very pleasant and beautifully calm'. He finished off the letter to his mother with a rousing flourish: 'a fine ship, comfortable cabin – and quiet weather. God bless all behind and give us a merry meeting at Xmas.'

*

The P&O trip was essentially an elliptical tour of the Mediterranean: to Gibraltar via Vigo and Cadiz; a change of vessel (the *Tagus*) and on via Malta, Athens and Smyrna to Constantinople; a further change of vessel (the *Iberia*, to whose captain, Samuel Lewis, Thackeray's record of his adventures would be dedicated) and round to Jaffa, Jerusalem, Alexandria and Cairo, before heading homewards by way of earlier ports of call (in the event Thackeray left the *Iberia* at Malta on the return leg and headed for Rome on the pretext that he wanted to 'take one peep at Italy' – there was an added stimulus in the possible presence of the Carmichael-Smyths at Nice). His exploits on the trip are well documented. He kept a travel diary, which formed the basis both of his *Punch* articles – initially 'Wanderings of our Fat Contributor', subsequently 'Travelling Notes. By our Fat Contributor' – written *en route*, and of *Notes of A Journey from Cornhill to Grand Cairo*, thereafter *Cornhill to Cairo*, published in 1846; he also despatched his usual budget of letters. From Gibraltar, for example, at the end of August he complained to Chapman and Hall that he could find no material to make an article for the *Foreign Quarterly Review*. Unfortunately 'All my news is about mosquitoes and the 1000 inconveniences of this filthy place ... Tell those who would travel that they may go farther and fare much worse than in the blessed neighbourhood of The Strand,' he concluded. By the same post Mrs Carmichael-Smyth was asked to write to Isabella (Thackeray enclosed his own ten-line note for forwarding) explaining the reasons for his hasty departure. 'I enjoy myself very much all things considering,' he ended ('viz bugs mosquitoes &c').

Thackeray's tone in these despatches from the Near and Middle East is a variant on his *Irish Sketch Book* voice: less irritated, for he had no political axe to grind, but blasé and concerned to emphasise the superiority of English ways of doing things to local arrangements. The Spanish town of Vigo, typically, was 'a little show got up to amuse us' before returning to the 'great stalwart roast-beef world' of the *Lady Mary Wood*. Lisbon contained 'no smoke, as in honest London, only dust'. Thackeray's trademark disinclination to be moved by the picturesque – of which, to do him justice, he was highly aware and often inspired to mock – declares itself in a number of half-ironic passages about the tedium of sight-seeing. 'You must go through the ceremony, however much you may sigh to avoid it; and however much you know that the lions in one capital roar very much like the lions in another; that the churches are more or less large and splendid, the palaces pretty spacious, all the world over; and that there is scarcely a capital city in this Europe but has its pompous bronze statue or two of some periwigged, hook-nosed emperor, in a Roman habit, waving his bronze baton on his broad-flanked brazen charger.' As for the mosaic work in Lisbon's Church of St Roch, 'it is a famous work of art, and was bought by I don't know what king for I don't know how much money'. Every so often, though, something catches his imagination or his painterly eye (Catherine Peters has observed that these moments tend to appear more often in the *Punch* despatches than in the smoother-flowing *Cornhill to Cairo*) and he becomes unselfconsciously absorbed in the scene. A street leading down from the quayside in Cadiz drew comparisons with the artist's palette ('The tall white houses with their balconies and galleries shining round about, and the sky above so blue that the best cobalt in the paint-box looks muddy and dim in comparison to it. There were pictures for a year in that marketplace!'), while the voyage along the Algerian coast inspired an eerie vision of 'gloomy purple lines of African shore, with fires smoking in the mountains, and lonely settlements here and there'.

As in Ireland, by the time something genuinely worth seeing arose Thackeray was conscious of his deficiencies as a registrar and uncertain how to react. From Constantinople, in mid-September, with *Punch* and *Barry Lyndon* pressing (there were to be endless worries over meeting *Fraser's* copy deadlines), never mind the scenery, he confessed his bewilderment to his mother. 'For the first fortnight there was scarce anything to see; then comes such a heap of sights all at once as should take a man 2 months to visit properly, and I don't know how long to describe.' He had been to buy the children slippers in the bazaar, which he characterised as 'the Arabian Nights come to life'. Even before he went East, Thackeray, like many another early Victorian, had been fascinated by the idea of the 'Orient'. Trying to work out the most startling incident of 'this little cockney voyage' for his mother's benefit, he came up with his first sight of a camel, a month's seasickness, women's voices behind the lattices at the Sultan's palace, and a slave market 'where you can buy a tolerably ugly and healthy negress for 20£'. But he began to worry 'whether I shall be able to make anything like a book of it'. An accompanying letter to Isabella supplies brief descriptions of Algiers, Malta and Smyrna, encloses a sketch of the slave market and a prospect of the gardens of the seraglio across the Bosphorus, and recounts his experience of a Turkish bath –

'sweated and shampooed and kneaded by a great grinning Turk, as bad as you used to be at Château Boppard'.

He left Constantinople with some regret, telling Bradbury & Evans that he wished he could have stayed a few months, such was his desire to sketch 'a few hundred of the astonishing figures to be seen every day'. Above all, though, he wanted to be back in 'poor dear old England'. Then it was on via Syria and Jerusalem to Egypt. Here, having taken himself off to the pyramids, he perpetrated what must have been the most audacious piece of advertising in *Punch's* three-year history:

> The 19th of October was *Punch's Coronation*; I officiated at the august ceremony . . . ON THE 19TH OF OCTOBER 1844, I PASTED THE GREAT PLACARD OF PUNCH ON THE PYRAMID OF CHEOPS. I did it, the Fat Contributor did it. If I die, it could not be undone. If I perish, I have not lived in vain . . .

With the help of bemused Arab factotums – Thackeray's own illustration shows three native assistants manhandling an enormously fat, moustachioed man in a sun-hat – the placard was pushed into place as the clock of the great Cairo minaret reached nineteen minutes past seven. 'My heart throbbed when the deed was done . . .' Thackeray told his readers. 'There was *Punch* – familiar old *Punch* – his back to the desert, his beaming face turned to watch the Nile.' It is impossible not to read something symbolic into this episode: the shimmering sands, the Cairo minaret visible in the distance, the puzzled onlookers, the burly Englishman come 2,000 miles, whose idea of a joke is to deck a pyramid with a poster advertising a comic magazine.

From Alexandria he wrote to Charlotte Ritchie exulting over a letter received from Isabella, 'far the best and most reasonable she has written yet: and it is almost equally gratifying to find that she continues to be happy and pleased with her home away from us all –'. From Malta, a few days later, he sent a progress report to Chapman and Hall: he had communed with forty centuries on the summit of the pyramids, he advised them, but he could not stand the infernal sea-sickness any longer. Once the fifteen-day Malta quarantine period was up, and believing that his family was in Italy, he thought that the temptation to see Rome, Naples and Florence was too much to resist. He asked both Chapman and Hall and Bradbury & Evans to forward money – fifty and twenty-five pounds respectively – to cover the expenses of his stay. In fact neither family nor money was in evidence in Italy, and the second discovery in particular was to cause Thackeray serious inconvenience. 'My letters *must* have miscarried,' he told Bradbury & Evans from Rome early in December (the continental posts were notoriously erratic, and four *Punch* contributions sent from Constantinople disappeared without trace). 'Do let me hear from you – with a little whatdeyecallem inclosed.' He was aggrieved, too, about the Carmichael-Smyths' absence. 'My parents too have bilked me – After writing to me to come to Nice at the end of 15 days quarantine the news that they were in France. – but for them I might have dined in Bouverie St a month ago.'

Each day for seven weeks Thackeray traipsed from his hotel in the via Carlotti to the post office to be told that nothing had arrived for him. He spent a penurious but none the less enjoyable Christmas 'hand in glove with the jolly artists with broad hats & long beards & we commit huge twopenny debauches at the Lepre' (a trattoria). A portion of *Cornhill to Cairo* was complete by this stage. He told George Bell, physician to the British Embassy in Teheran, whom he had met earlier on the voyage, that it seemed 'devilish clever, impertinent & feeble'. But for all his delight in Rome's artistic colony, to which he had been introduced by William Bevan's brother Samuel, he pined for home, longing in particular for 'dear old Pall Mall and the fog and the men of all sorts and conditions'. Bevan remembered him rummaging through the artists' dusty portfolios and critically scanning their pictures on the walls, sitting down once after dinner at Bertini's to improvise one of his best-known ballads, 'Little Billee'.

In the end the money turned up, having arrived weeks before but

'*A negro holiday at Alexandria*'

217

been kept under the name of 'Jackeray'. There were further annoyances in store, however, for the credits were at Torlonia's bank: this establishment declined to cash bills on Thackeray's London bankers without a covering letter. Finally he found another banker ('a sweet Xtian of a banker') prepared to help, but the experience of Roman inefficiency disgusted him: he would not be happy, he told Chapman and Hall, until he was gone. Time had slipped away – it was now the second week of January 1845 – and there was work outstanding: not only the Eastern book but the life of Talleyrand. As he explained, 'For the last 3 weeks my annoyance has been so great at receiving no letters that I've done nothing – and it's only now the letters *are* come that I feel what a rage I have been in really.' Dickens was expected in the city, but Thackeray, now on the point of departure, feared that he would not see him. He spent a fortnight in Florence enjoying the pictures under the supervision of Lady D'Oyley, wife of the Indian civil servant Sir Charles D'Oyley, and then made his way back to Paris. Half a century later Annie would recall the consternation caused among the children by his newly grown moustache. Minnie burst into tears and could not be persuaded that it was her father. Thackeray found a newspaper and kissed her through it: Minnie was not appeased. Next morning, when he came down to breakfast, the moustache was gone.

XII

Duty Kept

'My life is passed in monotonous quill-driving in joke-spinning, in overeating myself in the season, in family duty now.'

Letter to Sir James Tennent, 1 October 1846

'Vanity Fair may make me – The thought thereof makes me very humble & frightened: not elated. God Almighty keep me to my duty.'

Letter to his mother, 25 December 1846

utwardly the world to which Thackeray returned in spring 1845 was the same as that which had greeted him thirty months before at the end of his Irish tour: work, bills, a restless and ultimately unsatisfactory social life mitigated by occasional visits to his family in France, and forever hanging over it the thought of the woman in the room at Chaillot. There were differences, though, between the Thackeray of the *Irish Sketch Book* days and the thirty-three-year-old who now resumed his work on *Punch* and the *Morning Chronicle*. For one thing his prospects were improving: within twelve months, in February 1846, he would begin the *Punch* series that would definitively establish his name, and gear himself up to publish the big novel that had haunted his imagination for years. His annual earnings were moving towards the £1,000 mark in the mid-1840s, and although there were foolish dabblings in railway shares and other speculative investments, not to mention the £450 still owed to his cousin Mary Carmichael, the residue made a substantial sum. Certainly his annual income at this point was enough to start thinking seriously about a decent establishment for his family, in a London where you could rent a large residential property for under £100 a year. Finally, and in some ways most important of all, after four and a half years of constant anxiety, in which his hopes had been raised and dashed from one week to the next, he was nerving himself to solve the problem of Isabella.

His letters from the week after his return show him picking up the threads he had left behind: dunning Vizetelly for money owed him by the *Pictorial Times*, writing to tell his mother of a part-time job on the *Examiner* (this seems to have been in a fairly humble, probably sub-editorial capacity – certainly the editor, John Forster, kept the book-reviewing for himself). *Cornhill to Cairo*, meanwhile, was 'just going into hand'. The note to Mrs Carmichael-Smyth, in particular, betrays an almost tangible sense of restlessness. He had been inspecting rooms in St James's Street, he recorded (in the end he moved from his Jermyn Street lodgings in April) 'and I have been looking at scores of houses and longing to take one . . . But until you settle I can't settle.' If he had his wife with him, would she have 'a pennyworth more of happiness', he wondered sadly? He negotiated with Thomas Longman for work on the prestigious *Edinburgh Review*, but despite editorial encouragement and the promise of good pay (the *Review* paid as much as twenty guineas a piece) managed only a single contribution. He was becoming – and this was important for the novel taking shape in his head, whose first fragments were already upon the small table in Jermyn Street – a sharp literary operator, with an eye for what magazine editors and publishers, and their readers, wanted to buy. This awareness is evident in another letter to his cousin Bedingfield from around this time. Bedingfield, still nurturing his own literary aspirations, had sent him a couple of short stories for comment. Thackeray knew they were too old-fashioned to be saleable. Topicality, he explained to Bedingfield, was at least as important as merit. 'It is not because a story is bad or an author a fool that either should not be popular nowadays . . . Quiet, sentimental novelets won't do nowadays, I'm sure.' It was not a mistake that Thackeray himself, with his superior knowledge, was prepared to risk.

Thackeray's first sustained attempt to move forward what was eventually to become *Vanity Fair* belongs to these early months of his return. His ideas about the novel's conceits and materials had been taking shape for years: the fascination with Regency high-life; the memories of old Chiswick and Soho where the book takes root; the meeting with Lever's friend Sibthorpe, the Waterloo veteran. The

vanitatis vanitatum theme had probably been in his head since the late 1830s, when as an apprentice journalist running in and out of Cruikshank's studio in Amwell Street he would have seen his mentor's illustrations for a new edition of *The Pilgrim's Progress*. There is a rather sinister sketch of an expostulating cleric in his 1830s scrapbook captioned 'All is vanity saith the Preacher'. As for assembling the contents of this mental lumber room into some kind of order, he may well have made a start while stranded in Rome at the end of 1844. Certainly by February 1845, in between resuming his routine journalism and renewing his social life with friends like the Proctors and the Prymes, he was hard at work on what was to become chapters I to IV, which describe Becky's arrival in London and her attempts to get Jos Sedley to propose to her, and on an early version of chapter VI (chapter V, which introduces Dobbin, came later). It is more than likely that at this stage Thackeray had no set idea of what he might do with the manuscript: whether it might become the basis of a three-volume novel, a magazine serial or a work sold in monthly parts (he had suggested this idea, without success, when trying to place *Barry Lyndon* two years before). Similarly, its provisional titles, 'Novel without a Hero' and 'Pen & Pencil Sketches of English Society', give little idea of the novel's ultimate shape: in fact they sound much more like the kind of society fiction that Mrs Gore, whom Thackeray admired, had been unloading on her readers for the best part of twenty years, or the outline for a *Punch* series. One makes this point to emphasise the fact that Thackeray was not a natural novelist (only *Catherine* and *Barry Lyndon* among his books to date could be classified as novels) and that *Vanity Fair* did not spring fully formed from his pen. Rather, it began life almost as a series of sketches designed to whet the appetite of editors and publishers, and it was in this spirit that the manuscript was submitted to the veteran publisher Henry Colburn in May 1845.

At first sight Colburn looks an odd choice as the sponsor of what was to turn out to be one of the greatest novels of the century. The *Longman Companion to Victorian Fiction* correctly describes him as 'the most notorious publisher of nineteenth century fiction', and it was a notoriety that by no means confined itself to literature: among other accomplishments, he was rumoured to be the bastard son of the Duke of York. None the less he was an innovator in his way. The 'silver fork' novel of the 1820s and 1830s was practically his invention; beneath his touch 'puffing' reached a new level of flamboyance; while the list of novelists he boosted into celebrity includes Disraeli, Bulwer Lytton, Mrs Gore, Charles Marryat and G.P.R. James. He was a magazine proprietor, too (such periodicals were a useful venue for reviews of his books), founding the *New Monthly Magazine* as far back as 1814, and the *Literary Gazette* (to which Thackeray's *National Standard* had fancied itself a rival) three years later; he had even been in at the birth of the *Athenaeum* – a much more serious and long-lasting proposition. To posterity Colburn may look like the ultimate publishing brigand, but to Thackeray, whose connection with the *New Monthly Magazine* went back to Major Gahagan in the 1830s, he would have seemed a natural ally for a work that could at best have been described as embryonic. There was a small problem, however, in that Thackeray's offer of his twenty or thirty pages of manuscript to Colburn coincided almost exactly with the publisher's decision to sell the *New Monthly* to Ainsworth. One of the new proprietor's first acts was to return 'Pen & Pencil Sketches of English Society' to its author. Accustomed as he was to editorial slights and asperities, Thackeray – probably because he had regarded Colburn as a long-term supporter – took this rejection very hard, and much of his writing over the next few years betrays a spectacular animosity to both old and new owner. A pretentious advertisement in which Ainsworth proclaimed the 'eminence' of his contributors was the target of a *Punch* squib within days of its appearance, and may have lent something to the later series of parodies, 'Novels by Eminent Hands', while Colburn himself is immortalised as the vulgar opportunist 'Bungay' of *Pendennis*.

Although his resentment was real enough, Thackeray cannot have been unduly discouraged by this early rejection. His immediate reaction was to approach other potential publishers. According to a much later letter to his mother there were three or four of these, and the process seems to have occupied most of the rest of 1845. Meanwhile, another part of his life had begun to concentrate itself with ultimately significant consequences. This was his relationship with his old Cambridge friend William Brookfield and the latter's wife Jane. Since leaving university Brookfield (who had begun his undergraduate life as a sizar before being taken up by a circle of well-connected friends) had not prospered in his career. At first he had stayed in Cambridge and taken pupils, until his old tutor's recommendation found him a temporary job instructing Lord Lyttelton's teenage son. By September 1834, heavily influenced by his employer's pious wife, he had decided to take orders and, having been ordained by the Bishop of Lincoln, was given the curacy of Maltby. This decision has been plausibly represented as the worst mistake of Brookfield's career. Not noticeably devout – though he was remembered as an effective clergyman – or interested in the ever-raging doctrinal controversies, his laggardly progress through the hierarchy of the Anglican Church seems to have been impeded by a suspicion of irresponsibility on the part of his superiors, and for many years the efforts of well-placed friends (Thackeray was one) to get him a better job were cancelled out by a feeling among clerical patrons that Brookfield, in the last resort, was somehow unreliable. Even his preaching, though eloquent, was criticised for its melodrama; and behind the flamboyance of the pulpit lurked a bleak interior. A memorialist once remarked of Brookfield the undergraduate that 'when he left his party and retired within himself, he found himself in very grave company', which is less a put-down than an acknowledgment of inner fires steeply banked; and at the very least there is something odd about a man whose sense of humour was tickled by having himself introduced at parties in the name of the defendant of the latest sensational murder trial.

Nevertheless, Brookfield's personal charms – surviving portraits show a cool and ironical-looking customer with an abundance of wavy hair – were sufficient to win him the affections of the highly eligible Jane Octavia Elton soon after his move to the curacy of All Saints, Southampton, in early 1838 (he had spent a short intervening period at nearby Holyrood). Jane, born in 1821 and twelve years his junior, was the youngest of the eight daughters of Charles Elton of Cleveland Court, later sixth baronet of that name on the death of his father, Sir Abraham. Well established in the Bristol area – Mrs Elton was the daughter of a prosperous local merchant – the Eltons were also decidedly literary. Sir Charles was the friend of Lamb and Coleridge and the author of a much-admired poem 'The Brothers', written after his two eldest sons drowned while swimming in the Bristol Channel. Jane herself remembered seeing Landor and Southey walking along the Crescent at Bath, and the knot of black ribbon that restrained Southey's hair. In 1837 the Eltons removed to Southampton. Five feet nine inches tall – an immense height for a Victorian woman (Laura Bell in *Pendennis* is considered a 'maypole' at five feet four) and nicknamed 'Glumdalclitch' by her father, after the giantess in *Gulliver's Travels*, the seventeen-year-old girl whom Brookfield encountered at his church was of striking appearance. A family memoir recalled her as 'fair and rosy, with large and lustrous eyes neither blue nor grey, a sweet and beautiful voice, a graceful carriage, and an irresistible, intangible charm', which even the servants were apparently unable to resist. She was clever, too, and when detached from the family circle sent back letters that were received with 'great applause and pleasure'. Courted by the enraptured young curate, she became engaged at the end of 1838. The wedding was delayed for some time, in the face of mild opposition from the Eltons, while attempts were made to get Brookfield a better job. Eventually he was appointed to another curacy at the highly fashionable St James's, Piccadilly, and the couple, their income still far below the £800 a year thought to be necessary, were married in November 1841.

The nature of the Brookfields' marriage is open to debate. Twelve years older than his wife and the son of a Sheffield solicitor, Brookfield was no catch. While Jane's letters to him are lively and agreeably complicit (he addressed her as 'My dearest Glum' or 'My dearest Jenny', the bride-to-be settling for the more discreet 'Dearest Mr Brookfield'), their early years were characterised by genteel poverty – at one point Brookfield was reduced to sleeping in the church crypt – and Jane spent much of the time billeted on relatives. Although he eventually managed to carve out a moderately successful career for himself, including a much-coveted schools inspectorship, Brookfield was already conscious that he had failed to live up to the promise of his undergraduate days. The effect of these disappointments on his queer, self-absorbed personality, together with his wife's self-confessed 'foolish blind fondness of being admired', undoubtedly contributed something to their later difficulties and to Thackeray's own inextricable entanglement.

It is always assumed that Thackeray first met Jane in 1842, at what was subsequently immortalised as 'the dear old twopenny tart dinner' (a reference to the young and flustered hostess's despatch of her maid to a confectioner's shop for the dessert). The intimacy between Thackeray, his old friend and his old friend's wife was sporadically kept up during the early 1840s, but it seems to have reached a higher pitch in the months immediately after Thackeray's return from the Middle East, when he became a regular visitor at the Brookfields' house in Great Pulteney Street, among a group of literary notables who included Tennyson, Samuel Rogers and Jane's idiosyncratic historian uncle Henry Hallam. Something of Thackeray's growing attachment to his young married friends is conveyed by Brookfield's diary for these months. On 25 March, Jane's twenty-fourth birthday, he recorded Thackeray coming to dinner with another friend and presenting Jane with a Turkish shawl brought back from the Levant. Four days later he turned up at Henry Hallam's house, where the Brookfields were dining, with the aim of smoking an after-dinner cigar. It is important not to read more into the relationship – or rather relationships, for in fact there were three (husband and wife, Thackeray and husband, Thackeray and wife) – at this stage. Judged by the rigid demarcations of early-Victorian society, Thackeray was an old family friend, part of a closely knit circle of acquaintances that included the *habitués* of Mrs Brookfield's Great Pulteney Street salon and others from further afield – for example, both Thackeray and the Brookfields had mutual friends in the Southampton area. As Brookfield's sincerely attached friend (he features in a shortish list of persons confided to Annie whom Thackeray believed that he had truly cared for), it was with the husband that Thackeray spent most of his time. Students of the Brookfield marriage have noted that from about mid-1845 the relationship began to undergo a change, with Jane spending more time away and Brookfield, left in London, thrown upon his own resources. In fact the clergyman seems to have relished the mock-bachelor 'debauches' of late-night smoking. For Thackeray, consequently, to tell his mother, as he did a year later, that Mrs Brookfield was his 'beau ideal' and that he had been in love with her for the past four years is merely a piece of half-wistful, half-humorous sentiment. One of the agreeable things about the Brookfields' correspondence, at any rate at this early stage, is its complicity. There is never a feeling that one is concealing anything from the other. Mrs Brookfield was a pretty woman who expected her husband's friends to admire her. Brookfield, for his part, was flattered by his wife's distinction as a literary hostess. That is about as far, at this point, as it went.

But bachelor nights with Brookfield were no substitute for the regulated domestic life, preferably in the company of his children, that Thackeray craved. By the summer of 1845 Annie was eight and Minnie nearly five, and their father was conscious that the Carmichael-Smyths' apartment in the Champs-Elysées was not an ideal environment in which to raise two small girls. While the children adored their grandparents, Annie's recollections of her early Paris life tend to dwell on the inflexibility of the routine. One day was much like another, with the major and his wife sitting on either side of the hearth. The flat was on the fourth floor, with windows facing east and west: when the windows were opened in summer the noise of the traffic resounded in their ears. In winter they dined at five and then retired to the drawing-room, where Mrs Carmichael-Smyth read aloud from the evening paper while the girls drowsed over story books until 'company' arrived and they were sent to bed. Brodie, returned to England to take up another job, had not been replaced, and one senses from Thackeray's efforts to feed their imaginations from afar – he sent them books of fairy tales, in particular the 'Felix Summerly' books written by his friend Henry Cole – that he felt he was neglecting their upbringing. In the last resort neither his parents nor old Mrs Butler (still living in Paris and with whom the girls were regularly at loggerheads) were effective substitutes. His letters to his mother from this period have a single theme: the necessity of reuniting the family. Yet this was not as straightforward as it sounds. Apart from the difficulties of procuring a suitable house in London – at one point Thackeray even toyed with the idea of renting a farm – the Carmichael-Smyths, long resident in France and still worried about the major's creditors, were reluctant to return to England. It was clear to Thackeray that the only person capable of taking a decision was himself.

He made a preliminary move in the early summer of 1845, joining his family at Calvados in Normandy and taking them back for a short holiday in England. To please his mother they went first to stay with the Bechers at Fareham: the visit was a disaster, ruined by rain, and Thackeray consoled himself by escaping to Southampton for the day, where the Brookfields were staying with friends. Subsequently he left the old people in the country and had the girls to stay with him in St James's Street. The experience of sight-seeing in London with her father left a vivid impression on Annie. Arriving to meet them at the station, he 'immediately gave us each 2 wax dolls, and at breakfast he gave us bigger helps of jam than we had ever had in our lives and after breakfast he took us to feed the ducks in St James's Park'. There were gifts of picture books – the *Arabian Nights* and Grimms' fairy tales – and expeditions to the 'Diorama', the zoological gardens, Westminster Abbey and the Colosseum. 'I thought he would spend all the money he had in the world when I saw how much he had to pay for us,' Annie recalled. There was also a visit to Mrs Brookfield, whom the children remembered as 'quite a young lady with curls . . . who gave us a book'. Enjoyable as this experiment in family life may have been, it brought an inevitable cargo of anxieties. In particular, Thackeray was worried at what Isabella might think when she heard that the children had been staying with him. He feared that she might be offended 'at hearing they were come without her', he told Charlotte Ritchie. As for Isabella's mental state, he managed a rueful smile over a 'crazy letter' he had received, 'wh. is consoling at any rate in as much as it shows she's happy'. Was she happy? It was impossible to tell. As for his own sorrows, in the wake of the children's return to Paris, Thackeray was shrewd enough to draw a distinction between real and artificially stimulated feeling. He reassured his mother that it was the 'abstract pathos' of the situation that moved him. 'I never could bear to think of children parted from their parents somehow without a tendency to blubbering: and am as weak to this day upon the point, as I used to be at school.'

But he was reaching a stage in his life where decisions – about Isabella's welfare, the children's upbringing, his professional future – had to be made. 'There are 100 things for and against all plans at present,' he told his mother in early July. Somehow a way had to be found through the labyrinth. Meanwhile work pressed. *Cornhill to Cairo* was still unfinished, and his *Punch* and *Morning Chronicle*

commitments continued. The pressure became so great that he gave up his *Examiner* connection on the grounds that it took up more time than he could afford. He may not have performed his duties on Forster's paper particularly satisfactorily, telling his mother that 'I was much too clever a fellow to do it well.' There were other ways of increasing his income, however, and an injunction to Mrs Carmichael-Smyth not to be 'alarmed about the stockbroker' suggests that he had begun to make minor speculations on the stock market. The news from Chaillot was bad: another crazy letter, and reports that Isabella had been suffering from headaches.

It was at this point, unhappily – characteristically heedless of the effect it might have – that Mrs Carmichael-Smyth, worried by her son's hints about what he intended to write on the subject of religious tolerance in the Jerusalem chapter of *Cornhill to Cairo*, decided to weigh in with another of her stringent letters about religious belief, or rather the duties of the believer. It has not survived, but Thackeray's reply, harking back to the remonstrances of his undergraduate days, suggests that this was another flurry in their continuing argument over the merits of the Old Testament and the unassailability of the Protestant view. It was presumptuous, Thackeray told his mother, for anyone ('Bishop, Priest, layman or laywoman') to say that they had the true faith. 'What did the Saviour mean by searching the Scriptures? – that a man was to read them to the best of his own reason – or to take his neighbours'?' It seemed to Thackeray, who took the opportunity to point out to his mother what a good Catholic she would have made if raised in the old faith, 'almost blasphemous' that any 'blind prejudiced sinful mortal being' should dare to be unhappy about another person's belief.

Recasting the incident for the benefit of Charlotte Ritchie, to whom he wrote sending Isabella's fees for the coming two months, Thackeray tried to make light of his mother's complaints, but it is clear that the episode brought his work on the chapter to a temporary halt. As he put it, 'my dear old Mother has written me a letter so full of terror and expostulation, and dread of future consequence for my own heresy that I have to cancel it and begin afresh'. It was August now, and the London season was over ('Scribble scribble in the morning, hob and nob in the evening' was Thackeray's account of his routine during the preceding three months). A letter to Isabella from about this time strikes a jaded note. 'Go on,' he abjured her. 'Get well and strong' (Isabella had recently been 'magnetized', which was thought to have done her good), 'and come and live in a pretty cottage I have my eye on.' He had been momentarily cheered by another precocious letter from Annie and the return of Arthur Shawe ('greatly improved ... altogether as manly good-natured and honest a fellow as I have seen for a long time'), but even the sight of his brother-in-law's friendly face was capable of stirring unwelcome memories. Did Isabella remember Arthur coming to see her as she lay in bed just after Minnie's birth, he wondered, 'and my dear little woman looking so happy and pretty? O for those days. I'm getting weary of being alone, and want some other companions beside those of the bottle.'

With Jane off staying with relatives, Thackeray spent much of his free time in Brookfield's company. Brookfield's diary for 5 August records him calling at Great Pulteney Street and the two of them visiting Mrs Proctor. 'Then he dined with me but seemed quite out of sorts.' The evening concluded with a bachelor party in Thackeray's rooms, from which Brookfield returned at half-past one in the morning. Another three-hour 'serious debauch' of smoking followed shortly afterwards, and over the next week they dined together two nights out of three. Jane, to whom news of these dissipations had obviously been communicated, wrote back from Bristol to suggest that 'You seem very hand in glove with Thackeray: don't become a second Father Prout.' This warning was not as light-hearted as perhaps it sounds, and Thackeray himself was later to worry that Brookfield's association with *Punch* journalists had hindered his chances of preferment.

At the end of the month, nursing a sprained ankle acquired by turning his heel as he walked along the Haymarket, and taking a bag of books and a young manservant named William (the veteran John Goldsworthy having died earlier in the year), Thackeray left for Brighton. Here Brookfield joined him, arriving at the lodgings in Grand Parade to find his friend drawing on a woodblock amid the remains of an enormous breakfast. The two companions spent their time lounging on the beach while Thackeray sketched, and dining at the Star and Garter inn. To his mother, a fortnight later, Thackeray reported that as ever Brighton 'agrees with me excellently', and that William in his dark pepper-and-salt livery was proving an admirable servant. He was trying to finish *Cornhill to Cairo*, but 'that remonstrance of yours' was still impeding him. Above all, his mind was occupied by the usual family problems – he missed his daughters (whose faces he continued to see in other children) and was turning over once again the question of Isabella. As ever, it was difficult to know how to interpret the conflicting reports of her condition. His old friend Lettsom, who had been to visit her at Chaillot, represented her as perfectly collected and reasonable, capable of asking him about his experiences in America and suggesting topics of conversation, and yet the letters that came back across the Channel were rambling and foolish. Similar cases that came to Thackeray's notice were not encouraging, and he noted the condition of Ainsworth's daughter who, after some kind of breakdown, had re-emerged into the world with her faculties clearly impaired. 'The poor girl's intellect is evidently gone,' he reported.

But amongst his usual negotiations with editors, and his struggle to finish the book, he was edging towards that decisive step. In the early autumn he made up his mind that, as a first move in reuniting his family in England, he would bring Isabella back and place her in the care of a private keeper. In fact certain elements of this scheme had been proposed some years before, and the woman whom Thackeray selected for the job, a Mrs Bakewell, was an old connection of his mother's. In a letter addressed to his mother from the Bakewell residence in Camberwell New Road, Thackeray set out his plan. Mrs Gloyne, an associate of Mrs Bakewell's, would travel to Paris, fetch Isabella and take her to Boulogne, where Thackeray would be waiting to bring them back (simultaneously he made another attempt to entice the major home, assuring his mother that given the current railway mania, his stepfather's experience as a military surveyor would guarantee him an income). With the arrangements for Isabella's reception in hand, he resolved not to waste any further time. A week later Mrs Gloyne set off, and by 29 October Isabella was lodged in south-east London. Thackeray dined that night with Brookfield, who reported to Jane that 'He brought back his poor little wife yesterday – she is at Camberwell and he seems well pleased with the people.'

It was a symbolic journey. Paradoxically, by bringing Isabella nearer to him – Camberwell was a bare three miles from his lodgings in St James's – Thackeray found that he had pushed her further away. Once returned to London and installed in the quiet side-street of Foxley Place, Isabella effectively disappears from public history. Though at first he went regularly to see her, and set aside evenings when they could dine together, within two years Thackeray no longer cared to visit, on the grounds that Isabella's indifference made these expeditions pointless. In the absence of any documentary evidence –

Thackeray rarely spoke or wrote about his wife – the domestic arrangements at Camberwell, and Isabella's part in them, are simply a mystery. And if Isabella begins to fade from view, Mrs Bakewell, in whose charge she remained for several decades, is an even more elusive figure, whose activities and responsibilities are beyond all means of calling back (by an odd coincidence a Lunacy Act regulating mental health care was passed in the year of Isabella's return to England, but its stipulations applied only to asylums). Something of Thackeray's subsequent attitude to his wife may be gauged from a letter he wrote to an unidentified 'Mr Sterling' in the early years of her confinement: 'if you have not troubles enough of your own – I wish you would look at her some day & report that she is comfortable – for me, I keep away because I think it is best not to see her'. There is no getting away from the wording: Thackeray does not want to know how his wife is, but he wishes to be reassured that she is comfortable.

The idea of Isabella as a kind of spectacle that prurient visitors can go to 'look at' – there is another letter in which he proposes to inspect her from the window of a cab – raises the whole question of Thackeray's feelings towards his wife in these later days. In an essay that considers the Thackerays in the context of Bulwer Lytton's and Dickens' attempts to repudiate their wives (Lady Lytton was at one point abducted by her husband's bullies and dumped in a private asylum until a public outcry secured her release), John Sutherland suggests that by installing Isabella with Mrs Bakewell, whose modest charges apparently betokened 'basic' care, Thackeray merely 'erased' her from his life and effectively ruined her chances of recovery. One can accept Sutherland's point about Thackeray's reluctance to talk about his wife – few of the records of his conversation make any mention of her – while wondering if this doesn't overstate the case. Modern medical opinion suggests that Isabella's condition was degenerative: Thackeray's visits tailed off during 1847–8, not so much because of literary commitments and the pressures of an increasingly glamorous social life, but because Isabella became steadily less interested in seeing him. Moreover, he did continue to make them: had he ceased to care, he would have effected a more decisive break. Then there is the question of Mrs Bakewell and her satellites, who, if not expensive (though Thackeray calculated that he had spent £3,000 on Isabella's care during his lifetime) were hardly cheap – even half a century later the two pounds a week that Thackeray allowed her would have maintained four women in a London lodging house. More important, perhaps, Isabella seems to have liked her chatelaine. To talk about 'erasing', too, hardly explains the years of touting for work, which came from an endlessly reiterated need to provide for his wife and daughters, the former often explicitly invoked.

Thackeray was scarcely an ideal husband, and his neglect of Isabella in the summer of 1840 probably contributed to her decline (as Sutherland points out, there is a rather ghastly symbolism in the venue for her suicide attempt – a watery gulf halfway between the homes of the two people who dominated her life). Nor can one honestly deny the profound irritation that Isabella caused him both before and after her collapse – his declaration that she was driving him 'mad' or his regret that he had ever married (which, to do Thackeray justice, is more of a general lamentation than a specific hit at his wife). To set against this are persistent outbreaks of emotion over Isabella. The letter written some time later to his sister-in-law, which recalls the young girl singing, is clearly not the product of a literary careerist who cast his wife aside because she was an impediment to his ambitions. Nor does it seem to be written with the aim of conciliating its reader. But in the end Sutherland's insinuation of Thackeray into a clandestine network of mid-Victorian asylum keepers and facilitators such as the sinister-sounding John Connolly and Robert Bell (who was certainly one of Thackeray's closer friends) just doesn't work. To suggest that Bryan Proctor 'probably arranged the business of the medical certificates which would have been required for long-term confinement', as if this were some kind of dubious undercover transaction, ignores the fact that Proctor was a Commissioner of Lunacy and an obvious source of advice (as we know, Thackeray had already consulted Proctor about English asylums before entrusting Isabella to Dr Puzin). Similarly, to suggest that in removing her from his own and his daughters' lives he 'lessened the chance of her recovery to zero' begs at least as many questions as it solves. Ultimately one can only conclude that Thackeray had reached a point where he believed he could go no further with Isabella, and that no significant improvement in her condition could now be expected. Having made this decision, he placed her in the care of people she seems to have liked, in a comfortable environment on which he kept a close and eternally regretful eye. Little attempt was made to disguise from the girls what had happened to their mother. Sutherland has an emotive line about Thackeray's daughters being brought up 'with an idealised picture of their absent mother who was, during the whole of their girlhood, never more than five miles away'. Annie, at least, seems to have been under no illusions about the lodger at Camberwell, and judging from the tone of her later reminiscences (notably the picture of Isabella 'raving' in the next room) she treated her mother's insanity with a certain matter-of-factness. Thackeray's friends, too, were conscious of the efforts he had made on his wife's behalf: lamenting his death to the American pastor Moncure Daniel Conway as they stood at the graveside at Kensal Green, George Cruikshank made a point of stressing his devotion to Isabella in her insanity.

Inevitably, too, Isabella's spectre – whether deliberately introduced or only tacitly admitted – hangs over the rest of Thackeray's life and work. The madwoman in *Denis Duval* who throws her baby into the sea has an obvious connection to the pale-faced girl dragging her little daughter along the sands at Margate in 1840. It cannot be coincidence that in devising Becky Sharp, whose prototype was already beginning to stalk the pages of his notebooks, Thackeray gave her several of Isabella's physical characteristics – her red hair, slender figure and pale complexion. On a much wider scale, the fear of madness and the apparent arbitrariness with which fate could deprive a previously sentient human being of reason is a consistent theme of Thackeray's later work. The noble house of Gaunt in *Vanity Fair* has an insane heir, who lives in a secluded cottage with his keeper and cries if there is too much water in his wine. Think what the gods can do to you on a whim, Thackeray reminds his readers; they can tap you on the head in an instant and leave you senseless, beyond the power of friends, fortune and influence to bring back. *Dr Birch and his Young Friends* has another drivelling noble idiot – a mentally deficient young man kept forever out of harm's way at a private school. In later life Thackeray allowed himself a certain amount of black humour about insanity, even to the extent of making jokes that were closely connected to his own circumstances, and there is a whole series of rather odd letters sent back from his second American trip to Mrs Proctor (wife of the Lunacy Commissioner) in which he talks exasperatedly about 'going mad', being put in a strait-jacket and getting Proctor to have him committed.

The immediate results of transferring Isabella to Camberwell seemed to be positive. Late November found her 'wonderfully well'. One of the chief benefits of Mrs Bakewell's regime was the change in Isabella's personal appearance: 'the difference . . . is remarkable now that she has someone to look after her and keep her clean'. At first Thackeray visited nearly every other day – his arrival seemed to 'please her', he noted – dining with her and taking her on small excursions in a hired fly. Meanwhile his 'railroad matters', he told his mother, were 'very bad' (few investors emerged unscathed from the railway mania of 1845–6), mitigated only by the excellence of his credit with the publishers – 'I have only to ask and have.' This is an exaggeration, but Thackeray's stock in the world of publishing continued to improve. A measure of his rising status was that he contemplated writing a Christmas Book – a newly fashionable genre, popularised by Dickens – in the autumn of 1845. In the event *Mrs Perkins' Ball* had to wait until Christmas 1846, put aside in the rush to finish *Cornhill to Cairo*, whose final garnishes were not delivered to Chapman and Hall until 22 December, but its conception shows how far Thackeray had come in the five years since he had been thrown upon the literary market and forced to fend for himself.

He ate his Christmas dinner at Camberwell, finding Isabella 'very well and happy' but reduced to tears by mention of the children. Having spent Boxing Day dining at the Prymes' and going on to an evening party, he had intended to prolong the festive season with a trip to Paris, but work and other plans delayed him. In particular, a likely-looking property slipped through his fingers when Lubbock, his bankers, declined to provide a reference. The scheme must have been fairly far advanced, as he had already engaged servants for the house. Though Thackeray was irritated by Lubbock's lack of confidence in his finances, he conceded that the setback was probably a blessing in disguise and that a better plan would be to search for a bigger house in a cheaper part of London (the original scheme seems to have involved living somewhere in the West End). 'A place however I will have & I'll have it big enough for every one of you so there,' he assured his mother. Money worries still pressed on him, although again he volunteered to pay his stepfather's old debts if necessary. The major was now involved in a dispute with his brother Charles that threatened to embroil Thackeray himself, on account of the £450 still owed in settlement of Mary's loan. And yet, reckoning up his projected receipts for 1846, Thackeray was entitled to feel optimistic: he did not like to startle her by revealing just how big an income he would have, he told his mother in an end-of-year letter explaining his delay in visiting her. There was also a charming note to Annie, thanking her for a letter of her own ('they cannot be too long for me'), praising her proficiency and concluding that 'I would sooner have you gentle and humble-minded than ever so clever.'

With one part of his family plan accomplished, he began 1846 in a ferment of activity. *Cornhill to Cairo* was at the printers. Having been shown to three or four publishers, the opening chapters of *Vanity Fair* (although it was not yet called that) had been accepted by Bradbury & Evans, the proprietors of *Punch*. Vitezelly remembered his friend settling the business one afternoon, arriving to see him after an initial meeting with the publishers and then departing to conclude the transaction: 'a monthly story at £60 a number' was Thackeray's description of the bargain in a letter to his stepfather, although a commencement date had still to be fixed. At the same time he was at work on the opening numbers of what was to become perhaps his most famous *Punch* series, *The Snobs of England*, which began in February and lasted right through to 1847. All this, he calculated, added to his other earnings from *Punch* and the *Morning Chronicle*, would bring his income for the year up to £1,200. Such comparative riches lent an air of authority to the advice to his stepfather, which he continued to offer through the early part of 1846. Urging the major to pay his brother Charles the dividend that was at the root of their quarrel, Thackeray instructed him to 'shut up the Paris house, and come over and live with me'. It would take him three years to pay off Mary's money, he supposed, after which the prospects looked bright.

Early in February, with some 'mighty polite' reviews of *Cornhill to Cairo* appearing in the press, he left London for a short holiday in Brighton. His satisfaction at seeing another book enthusiastically received by the critics was tempered by what seems to have been a substantial falling out with Carlyle. A staunch upholder of the dignity of literature and its practitioners, Carlyle had let slip some tart remarks comparing Thackeray's sponsorship by the P&O to a blind fiddler working the Highland ferry boats; these had been thoughtfully conveyed to Thackeray by their mutual friend Charles Buller. Shortly after this, presumably with some idea of making amends, Carlyle called twice (Thackeray told Fitz that he returned the compliment once 'in a rather haughty and patronising way') but, although the two continued to meet, and Mrs Carlyle was to be a notably kind friend to Annie and Minnie, this breach was never really healed. Five years later, for example, Carlyle was woundingly sarcastic on the subject of Thackeray's first American lecture tour. And something of Thackeray's mixed feelings about a man he had once revered can be seen in a letter written later in the year to a correspondent who had asked for more information about Carlyle. Thackeray referred him direct to the object of his enquiries, 'for I think there is a coolness between him & me'. In the same letter he describes Carlyle, not unaptly perhaps, as 'this old rugged brave prejudiced but great man'.

If such proceedings sometimes seem to invest Thackeray with a kind of hauteur, an exaggerated reaction to minor slights that is a mark of his early career, then it should also be pointed out that this period in his life, characterised as it was by a sharp improvement in his finances, brought a first flowering of the sustained philanthropy that was to be a feature of his declining years. His letters from this time are full of stealthy acts of charity and schemes to set lame ducks back on their feet – a plan concocted with Fitz to help one of Savile Morton's discarded mistresses (Thackeray stumped up £3 6s 8d to keep 'Elizabeth' for a month – nearly half his wife's monthly keep, it must be pointed out); help for the young poet Coventry Patmore, whose parents had left the country in a hurry over railway shares; even a letter in support of his creditor and erstwhile guardian Robert Langslow, now a judge in Ceylon and, Thackeray concluded, unfairly oppressed by the colonial administration. Generous, tactful, ever ready to petition the Royal Literary Fund in support of a penniless author, he was none the less very far from being a soft touch, and the surviving correspondence from his involvement in the Edward Marlborough Fitzgerald affair (so called to distinguish him from Fitz) of spring 1846 shows Thackeray's determination to do what he conceived to be his moral duty while offering help where it was most needed. Fitzgerald, a minor writer of the period, had scandalised his friends by throwing over his wife and installing his mistress in the family home (Alexander Kinglake had been so infuriated by an introduction to this woman, without being informed of her status, that he challenged Fitzgerald to a duel: the two got as far as Calais, but in the end Fitzgerald cried off). Thackeray volunteered some stark advice: 'Go away in God's name & work & humble [yourself] and amend.' He offered Fitzgerald one pound a week to go to a cheap foreign town and write, and in addition help to dispose of any articles he might produce. Significantly, though, his chief concern was for the miscreant's wife and children. 'Depend on it that tender & affectionate creature who has pardoned you so much without repentance on your part, will not be hard-hearted on your return. But prove it. You are bound to do this as clearly as any other criminal.'

Thackeray arrived at Brighton in 'a most restless & misanthropic state' but the resort quickly worked its usual restorative effect. One thing that irked him, he told his mother, was the suspicion that he was making a failure of his *Morning Chronicle* pieces covering non-literary topics. This is an interesting admission, for there is little doubt that in the mid-1840s Thackeray considered himself an aspiring political journalist, keen to solicit dinner invitations from leading politicians of the day and prosecute their affairs in print. Dwyer, who met Thackeray again at around this time, recalls him offering to use his influence with Palmerston if it could assist Dwyer's prospects in any way, and he certainly dined with the veteran Whig statesman Lord Melbourne early in 1846. Doubtless Thackeray did possess an entrée to the tables of various Liberal magnates (if nothing else, he was a member of the Reform Club), including Lord John Russell, prime minister from 1846 to 1851, connections that proved their worth a decade and a half later when he was editing the *Cornhill*, but they can have been of little value to him at this time. A genuine ministerial confidant would have been able to fix himself a soft administrative job in a way that the Thackeray of a few years later, desperate to find something that would absolve him from the necessity of having to write, conspicuously could not. Whatever the degree of political influence he exerted, or imagined that he exerted – and the offer to Dwyer looks suspiciously like bravado – the mid-1840s seem to have marked a conscious decision not to aspire to the kind of journalistic high ground subsequently occupied by a Bagehot or an R.H. Hutton.

All the same Thackeray's status as a well-regarded journalist who hovered on the fringes of high politics cannot be discounted. Working out precisely where he stood in the political debates of the late 1840s is less easy. Fifteen years after Wellington's electoral disaster, the consequences of the Tory annihilation were still working themselves out. Peel had formed a government in 1841 but had fallen from power five years later after an internal schism involving protectionist 'ultras' opposed to the repeal of the Corn Laws (this led to a highly confused General Election a year later, fought by Peelites, protectionists and the increasingly rainbow-hued Liberals). Although he remained sympathetic to Liberal policy, with occasional mistrust of what he regarded as aristocratic jobbery, Thackeray tended to take politicians as he found them. Peel, who had attempted to flatter him, he greatly disliked, but he certainly socialised with Disraeli, who succeeded to a somewhat ambiguous leadership of the Tory party in 1849, until literary differences drove them apart. Significantly, perhaps, the politician he admired above all, once doffing his hat to him at the Reform Club, was the radical MP John Bright.

Lodged in Brighton, and recruiting himself amongst its many diversions, he was still scheming about the house, asking his mother what she thought of the idea of 'a beautiful house and farm of seven acres at 3 miles from London'. Back in town, Isabella's behaviour seemed customarily erratic: she was 'tolerably sensible' and one of her letters to Annie began 'very well indeed' before rambling off at the end 'to the Queen of Spain and the King of Hanover in unintelligible inanity'. Isabella in print, in fact, looked much the same as Isabella (at her best) in conversation – an initial semblance of normality swiftly undermined by confusion and then stark derangement. Uncertainties about Isabella and the house sparked a mood of restlessness and reflection. His 'gaieties', he told his mother, had been in abeyance. He did not like or trust the new acquaintances he made, the female representatives of whom in particular were 'intolerably free and easy'. Mrs Brookfield, then out of the country on a continental tour, remained his 'beau ideal – she always seems to me to speak and do and think as a woman should'. As for the other woman in the Camberwell lodgings – and one makes this comparison because Thackeray unconsciously made it himself by his juxtaposition of the remarks – her role could be glimpsed in the vignette of 'the three Camberwell ladies' provided for his mother: Isabella, Mrs Gloyne and Mrs Bakewell sewing up holes in Thackeray's coat-tails and trouser-pockets. It is a pleasant piece of scene-sketching, but the contrast between the mad seamstress and the 'beau ideal' is too obvious to escape the reader's eye. It can hardly have failed to escape Thackeray's.

In the meantime 'The Novel without a hero' was due to begin publication on 1 May. The casual way in which Thackeray threw out this remark to his mother sometime in March, and the novel's subsequent postponement, confirm that at this stage no one – publisher or author – was sanguine of its prospects. There are a number of plausible explanations for *Vanity Fair*'s delayed appearance. Dickens' new novel *Dombey and Son* was known to be beginning in monthly numbers in the autumn, against which any competition could expect to be blown out of the water. Then again, monthly publication was a notoriously risky business – mid-nineteenth-century publishing history is littered with the bones of unsuccessful serial novels, and Bradbury & Evans may already have got cold feet, or have decided to see more of the novel with which Mr Thackeray – a decided hit with magazine readers, certainly, but with no real track record as a writer of fiction – proposed to entertain the reading public. In the end, though, the problem may have lain with Thackeray himself, with other commitments and uncertainty over the novel's ultimate design causing him to fall in with whatever schemes Bradbury & Evans came up with for deferral.

Thackeray's creative energies, too, were firmly concentrated on *The Snobs of England*, which began in *Punch* on 28 February and eventually developed into a work of nearly 80,000 words. Thackeray took pains over the 'Snob' papers, which contain some of his sharpest observations on social advancement, often at his own expense (significantly, the series' full title was *The Snobs of England by one of themselves*) and anticipate many of the themes and situations of *Vanity Fair*. In its title alone the series harks back to Thackeray's undergraduate days (he proposed to dedicate the collected volume to his old collaborator Lettsom, who for some reason – probably the cautious diplomat's fear of being associated with a gang of radical journalists – declined the honour) but its etymology had undergone considerable development in the intervening fifteen years. To Cambridge undergraduates 'snob' meant 'townsman', but there was another, more specialised, usage. As Thackeray remarks in chapter 15, 'On University Snobs', 'We *then* used to consider Snobs raw-looking lads, who never missed chapel; who wore highlows and no straps; who walked two hours on the Trumpington road every day of their lives; who carried off the college scholarships, and who overrated themselves in hall.' Although Thackeray goes on to confess that 'we were premature in pronouncing our verdict of youthful Snobbishness' and that these humbly born students fulfilled their 'destiny and duty', this is slightly disingenuous, for 'highlows' (footwear so called because they were too high to be a shoe and too low to be a boot) are a kind of litmus paper for the detection of vulgarity in his work: in *Pendennis*, for example, Fanny Bolton cannot help but compare Pen's feet with those of Sam Huxter and note that the former's 'shining boot' is 'so, so unlike Sam's highlow'. Subsequently Thackeray defined a snob as 'he who meanly admires mean things', but the snobbishness outlined in the case-book studies of *The Snobs of England* might better be described as the assumption of a false superiority. This had been a favourite *Punch* theme since the magazine's inception, buoyed up by items such as Albert Smith's 'The Side-Scenes of Every-Day Society', which described the social insecurities of the upwardly mobile Spangle-Lacquer family. Thackeray's exemplars are those who allow themselves distinction by means of quite valueless criteria – the ability to dress well or scrape acquaintance with people of higher social standing. Significantly for Thackeray's fiction, the most effective sections are those in which he provides extended pieces of reportage on particular social groups. Chapters 24–32 of the collected volume, for example, are an altogether deathless anatomy of a visit to 'some country Snobs' – the Pontos, who hastily fling themselves into their best clothes at the unexpected arrival of their neighbours, Lord and Lady Hawbuck, sit happily over the shrivelled corpse of a fieldfare on the pretext that they are dining off 'game', and starve themselves in order that their tuft-hunting son can allow himself the airs that befit an officer in a fashionable regiment. As ever, it is Thackeray's eye for detail that gives these acid little sketches their bite: Lieutenant Wellesley Ponto's extravagance, for instance, is scrutinised by way of his bills ('Three hundred and forty pounds for a young chap's saddle and breeches! Before George, I would rather be a Hottentot or a Highlander.').

The success of the Snob papers among *Punch*'s burgeoning middle-class readership was accentuated by clever internal publicity – such as Jerrold's letter (signed 'Slaverly Fitztoady') urging Mr Punch, on behalf of 'the truly patriotic and respectable', to discharge immediately the person who defiled *Punch* with these slanders – and by linking the series to the magazine's continuing attacks on the exceedingly snobbish *Morning Post* and its sycophantic résumés of 'the fashionable intelligence'. Written throughout the rest of 1846, as Thackeray simultaneously tinkered with and extended the ground-plan of *Vanity Fair*, they are effectively a series of rehearsals. Certainly the famous chapter 'How to Live Well On Nothing A Year', with its item-by-item recapitulation of the Rawdon Crawleys' debt-bilking, has exactly the kind of remorseless attention to detail previously unveiled in *The Snobs of England*. At the same time it would be misleading to suggest that the novel grew exclusively from the *Punch* seed-bed: several of Thackeray's reviews and articles from the early part of 1846 give an idea of the way in which his mind was working and the kind of materials that attracted his interest. A respectful *Morning Chronicle* review of Mrs Gore's *Sketches of English Character*, for example, published in May 1846, displays both his fascination for the novel of society and something of the moral stance that eventually underlay *Vanity Fair*. Thackeray's predominant reaction to the book is simple wonder. How is it that the author came by her knowledge? 'She knows things which were supposed hitherto to be as much out of the reach of female experience as shaving, duelling or the bass violin.' Significantly, he admires the sketches' apparent familiarity with clubland and the servants' hall: 'They are not a little curious as pictures of the present world, and of the author's mind. They are clear, sprightly (too sprightly), coarse and utterly worldly.' He doubts whether anyone's mind will be refined or exalted by reading the book, owing to the nature of the subject matter. However, if one wanted a faithful picture of Pall Mall in the 1840s, 'of the dandies who frequented Crockford's, the dowager virgins who resorted to Willis's, their . . . intrigues, amusements, and ways of life, their lady's maids, doctors and flunkies both in and out of livery', all these could be obtained in Mrs Gore's microcosm. Expertise; specificity; realism; the painterly eye for detail; the sense of a world brought into being by a hard, sharp intelligence – these are intensely Thackerayan characteristics. And curiously the sentence that Thackeray singles out as an example of Mrs Gore's powers of observation – 'You see the same people waiting, fiddling and serving the refreshments, and hear the same phrases exchanged among them, at every fête given at the West End of the town between May and August' – has a highly Thackerayan air.

Domestic responsibility joined forces with creative work to keep him busy. A slight note of patronage begins to creep into his accounts of Isabella. Taken to the theatre and installed in a private box, she enjoyed herself 'in her little way', he observed loftily. He dined at Camberwell when he could, he told his mother, but it was a poor recreation after a hard day's work. He was house-hunting, too, with a renewed sense of purpose brought about by his increasing income, and with a set of requirements that undoubtedly prolonged his search. Ideally, he needed a spacious property not too far from central London (the idea of a farm had been given up) and relatively inexpensive – certainly under £100 a year to lease. Eventually, towards midsummer, and presumably with the approval now of his bankers, he found what he was looking for: a substantial house at 13 Young Street, between Kensington Square and the High Street. Writing to his mother from this address – he seems to have moved there almost immediately with the object of getting the place in order – he anatomised its advantages: two 'capital' bedrooms for Major and Mrs Carmichael-Smyth, a room for the ever more venerable Mrs Butler on the first floor, two rooms for the children on the second, servants' quarters, a further two small rooms for himself, study, dining-room and drawing-room. To these amenities could be added 'Kensington Gardens at the gate, and omnibuses every 2 minutes. What can mortal want more?' He took a seven-year lease at sixty-five pounds a year, well within budget, and by 2 July – the date at which his mother was informed of the arrangements – was hard at work opening trunks, many of which had been in storage for decades. These 'woful relics of old days', he told Mrs Carmichael-Smyth, included a whole chest full of ancient shirts from India.

Initially he had hoped to have everything ready in a fortnight, yet the question of who exactly would be living in Young Street had not been settled. Isabella was never mentioned as a potential inhabitant. Thackeray made another offer to pay off the major's creditors, to no avail. All this threatened to postpone any kind of family reunion: in particular, without their grandparents, the children would need a governess. This meant more delay. 'So I lose my mother and my children for some time at least,' he grumbled to his sister-in-law Jane Shawe. A letter to Paris on his thirty-fifth birthday found him in the reflective mood habitually produced by anniversaries. Sackcloth and ashes would be the best wear for this kind of holiday, he told his mother, 'and all sorts of sorrow and humiliations for sins follies shortcoming – money and talent wasted and long chapters of faults and error ...' But he was thankful for his mother's affection, and the ability of Major and Mrs Carmichael-Smyth to act as surrogate parents to his children. And he was pleased with his new situation. 'My house is very comfortable and I like the quiet and the walk into town and the homely air it has.' He held his first dinner parties (Brookfield, coming in late to a gathering that included Kinglake, Arthur Shawe and Leech thought the evening 'pleasant' but that it 'lacked fire'). Far bigger than any of his previous London dwellings, and quasi-rural in setting – Kensington was still virtually a village in the 1840s – Young Street was every inch the gentleman's residence that had long been denied him.

But there was still a great deal to do. Between working on his *Punch* contributions, fulfilling his *Morning Chronicle* engagements and presumably trying to agree a commencement date for his novel with Bradbury & Evans, setting the house to rights took longer than he had anticipated. There were servants to hire, and a deluge of 'governidges' to assess ('For God's sake stop Mme Bölte!' he instructed Jane Carlyle, when one aspirant too many threatened to arrive on his doorstep). The Carmichael-Smyths, alert to their responsibilities despite – or perhaps because of – their absence ('William should have a very respectable female to look after the children when he cannot be with them,' the major pronounced, 'and he should also devote as much time as he can spare to their instruction') recommended Bess Hamerton. These pressures took their toll. Feeling the strain, Thackeray began to wonder whether he had been overconfident. He was 'full of business and racket' he told his mother early in August, 'working every day, and yet not advancing somehow, and poor too – although everybody gives me credit for making a fortune'. There was little scope for saving money out of the £800 a year he could guarantee himself until the novel began. Meanwhile the news from Camberwell was bad, Isabella being no better and playing 'the nastiest pranks' (some commentators have suggested that these had a sexual element, but there is no corroborating evidence) and 'domestic storms' provoked by Mr Bakewell, of a nature sufficient to make Mrs Gloyne think of leaving. In the end Thackeray bribed her to stay. The contrasting sides of Thackeray's life at this time – *Punch* socialising, the solitary study, the Camberwell connection – can be glimpsed in a short diary that he kept for a week in mid-August: reading Hume and Montaigne; dinner with Isabella followed by an uproarious water-party with his *Punch* colleagues, which could have made a chapter in a novel by the racy French writer Paul de Kock; and a walk on Wimbledon Common with Proctor, Forster and the veteran man of letters Leigh Hunt. He took Isabella to Camberwell Fair, after which they chartered a cab and drove up Norwood Hill to Beulah Spa. The excursion produced a melancholy vignette: 'There wasn't a soul in those charming gardens. Tents down, ponds seedy, roses moulting, troubadors fled.'

The summer was nearly over, with no sign of a governess or indeed any children for her to supervise. Brookfield, still awaiting his wife's return from her continental tour, took the opportunity to slot in a few more bachelor dissipations – calling again at Young Street, and on the following day going to a Garrick Club party at Thackeray's invitation. Writing to his old travelling companion Sir James Tennent in Ceylon a few weeks later, Thackeray claimed to be bogged down in routine. 'My life is passed in monotonous quill-driving in joke-spinning, in overeating myself in the season, in family duty now.' He was also growing tired of his association with the *Morning Chronicle*, complaining that 'they don't bring me into their confidence'. Amid this tumult of activity, one old friendship was starting to wither. 'Do you ever see Thackeray?' Fitzgerald wondered to his friend Fred Pollock that autumn, adding that he had seen some of the former's verses (the poem 'Piscator and Piscatrix') in a fashionable album. Elsewhere, though, there were signs of movement. Bradbury & Evans, reassured by the success of *Snobs* and the manuscript of *Mrs Perkins' Ball*, due for publication in early December, had fixed a date for the commencement of his novel – New Year's Day 1847. And although the 'Pen & Pencil Sketches' heading was not discarded, he had a title. Staying at the Ship Inn at Brighton, doing more work on the early chapters, he had found himself repeating the words 'Vanity Fair, Vanity Fair, Vanity Fair' over and over again. Best of all, the question of the governess finally having been resolved by the appointment of Miss Hamerton, was the arrival of the children. This took place towards the end of a dark afternoon in late November. Owing to a mix-up Thackeray was not there to receive them, but the servants he had engaged were in attendance – Mrs Gray the cook and housekeeper, Eliza the housemaid, and a handyman. Recalling the scene nearly half a century later, Annie remembered the fires that had been lit in readiness, and Eliza conducting them on a tour of the house. Her father's touch was everywhere – in familiar prints on the wall, and a picture of himself as a child which, Eliza said, he had hung up with his own hand. Early next morning, when they were half dressed, he tapped at the door and came in and took them in his arms. Everything seemed so strange and delightful, Annie remembered – bound volumes of *Punch* and keepsake books on the drawing-room table, the old schoolroom with the bookcase and the cupboard, and their father's room with the sun pouring in through the window.

Thackeray relished his daughters' presence. He told his mother that thoughts of them chased 'I don't know how many wickednesses out of my mind. Their society makes many of my old amusements seem trivial and shameful.' All the same, he could be frighteningly, even masochistically, down-to-earth about his daughters. Shortly after their arrival, as Annie read a letter from Mrs Carmichael-Smyth aloud, he burst into tears at the memories it stirred. Annie, though astonished at seeing her father cry, remained dry-eyed. 'They don't care: not even for you,' Thackeray briskly informed his mother. 'They'll have to complain some day of the same indifference in your Grand-grandchildren.' He used the letter, written a few days after the girls' arrival, as an opportunity tactfully to explain that the separation was for the best: 'there can't be two first principals in a house'. As Christmas approached he was struggling to complete the first numbers of a novel whose title still hung in the balance. Returning the title-page to Bradbury & Evans, he remarked that he did not care which was used, 'only I should like some mention to be made of the novel without a hero'. In the end all three suggestions were incorporated into a title-page that read *Vanity Fair: Pen and Pencil Sketches of English Society –* 'A Novel without a Hero'. Thackeray's pre-publication letter to his publishers betrays his excitement: 'I have corrected the last corrections: and say now Amen & good luck to Vanity Fair – May the public relish it may the publishers profit may the author always be honest & kind-hearted.' He took up the theme again in a Christmas letter to his mother. *Mrs Perkins' Ball* had been 'a great success – the greatest I have had – very nearly as great as Dickens' (this can only have been ironic: sales of Dickens' Christmas book, *The Battle of Life*, had exceeded Thackeray's 1,500 copies by nearly fifteen to one). Solvency still seemed some way off, but 'my prospects are very much improved and Vanity Fair may make me – the thought thereof makes me very humble & frightened: not elated. God Almighty keep me to my duty.' He was right. *Vanity Fair* was to make him one of the most successful novelists of the Victorian age.

Mrs Bakewell's report

At the start he used to come here regular. Two or three times a week to dine or take a glass of negus. Sometimes he'd hire a fly and take her driving. To Camberwell Fair he took her once, though I'm sure I don't know what they did there. But then he came less often. Half an hour, say, of an evening, and always eager to get away. Sometimes he'd have the cab waiting in the street, with the children playing cock-shies at the wheel. A very queer look he used to give her, as if he was angry and puzzled and unhappy all at the same time. But he was patient with her, I'll allow him that, and never a cross word did I hear, which is not always the case.

As for her, poor lady, who could say what was in her head? Many's the time she'd start off on some notion that troubled her and a team of horses couldn't have dragged her back to reason. Other times when he was here and talked about the children, about Miss Annie's cleverness or Miss Minnie's cats, she'd be that upset it was hurtful to see her. And yet an hour later, perhaps, she wouldn't know he'd been there. But I liked her and was glad to have her in the house. She could be violent now and again – she blacked my husband's eye once in a temper – but it was only her fancies getting the better of her. Most of the while she was peaceable, though, sitting there in our front room with some sewing or looking over a picture book. She said reading always made her thoughts run away with her . . .

But in the end he stopped coming. The money arrived as regular as clockwork, but not him. I've heard say as he had other fish to fry, and who can blame him perhaps. Though it was a pity she took on so. He used to ask friends to step in to see her sometimes – gentlemen mostly, who looked very shy of her now and again . . .

The last time he came he said nothing at all. I remember it above all, not the month or the year, but him standing there in the little hall with his hat in his hand, not speaking a word, and her sitting by the fire combing out her hair in that way she had. Beautiful hair it was, that a princess would have been proud of. You'd think it a sad life, I daresay, but who's to say where sadness lies, and she was always happy enough with us, I believe.

XIII

'All but at the Top of the Tree'

'You must know I am become quite a Lion now, and live with all sorts of great people: but their flattery has not turned my head as yet, please God, and my reign as a fashionable literary man will very soon be over: and somebody else will be favourite in my stead.'

Letter to Aunt Ritchie, 5 February 1848

 ith the publication of the first number of *Vanity Fair* Thackeray seems to have realised that the path to literary success lay open to him. His letters from the early part of 1847 show a sharp awareness of the need to promote himself, and of the vagaries of a marketplace in which he was determined to shine. It seemed that he had never had any ambition before or cared what the world thought about him, he told his friend William Aytoun. Now, though, the truth forced itself upon him, and 'if the world will once take to admiring Titmarsh, all his guineas will be multiplied by 10'. By coincidence those of his readers *au fait* with the literary world had a chance to admire his physiognomy in *Punch* a week later, when the magazine caricatured its staff as the orchestra accompanying the dancers – themselves caricatures of contemporary celebrities – at 'Mr Punch's Fancy Ball'. Mark Lemon, as befitted his editorial role, conducts an assortment of musicians including Gilbert à Beckett (violin), Percival Leigh (double bass), Richard Doyle and John Leech (clarinets), Tom Taylor (piano) and Horace Mayhew (cornet). Thackeray broods seriously over a flute, while the tiny yet pugnacious figure of Douglas Jerrold assaults a drum with two sticks. At the same time Thackeray was conscious that he

had moved a rung up the ladder, had arrived so to speak at the condition of proper authorship. The decision to give up his *Morning Chronicle* work, taken at the end of the year, looks like a symbolic piece of bridge-burning. A note to Caroline Norton, who had requested a puff for her newly published book of children's ballads, emphasises the seriousness of this attempt to distance himself from some of the hurly-burly of the freelance life. '. . . I have no place left either for praising or railing,' he explained. 'I am no longer a writer in the Chronicle but author on my own account . . . and if I admired Aunt Carry's ballads ever so (and I dont until tomorrow, for I've not had the time to read them yet) I dont know where I could proclaim my feelings –.' But he was nervous about *Vanity Fair's* reception, telling Aytoun a week later that women seemed to like it and that 'the publishers are quite in good spirits regarding that venture'.

It is fair to say that Thackeray's life between January 1847 and July 1848 was altogether dominated by the writing and reception of his novel. 'You see I am always thinking about Vanity Fair,' he told his mother. The book's characters marched through his subconscious at all hours; at least once his anxiety to meet Bradbury & Evans' monthly deadlines sent him scurrying down to the study in his night-shirt to scribble through the small hours. As well as advancing his literary career, the book's eventual success had profound social consequences for its author. By mid-1847, taken up by 'grand people' and invited to make his bow in some of the most fashionable drawing-rooms in London, he had entered on a phase of his social life that was substantially different from the modest middle-class entertainments of a few years before. Early-Victorian social divisions and their accompanying class consciousness are thrown into sharp relief by Thackeray's ascent from Mrs Proctor's soirées and the *Punch* entertainments to the evening parties of Belgravia: gratifying as it was, his new-found celebrity attracted suspicion both from the newer circles in which he moved and from the older compatriots who imagined (in one or two cases correctly) that they had been left behind. From this point onwards, in fact, Thackeray's social life increasingly resembles a kind of high-wire act, across a tight-rope stretched from Kensington to the great houses of the West End.

Other aspects of his existence were quite as demanding of his time. Settling into Young Street brought all manner of domestic problems associated with the care of two small girls. The Brookfield intimacy continued apace. These commitments left him permanently harassed,

ever frustrated at the want of time. Even his resolve to make space for his daughters could sometimes reduce itself to a single day in the week spent in their company, he confessed. In this atmosphere of haste, deadlines and social glamour, it is hardly surprising that Isabella begins to disappear from the formal record of his life. Such mentions of her that do occur in his letters – usually in notes to her brother Arthur – are perfunctory in the extreme. In June 1847, for example, he records a visit by Mrs Bakewell 'with good accounts of the poor little woman. She doesn't want to see me or the children . . . She is quite happy & perfectly quiet.' A letter from that November is uncharacteristically flippant: 'The poor little woman is as usual having had a smart fit of cholera or something from wh. however she rallied speedily.' Early in January 1848 he notes without comment that Isabella is 'gradually sinking lower I think'.

But it was *Vanity Fair* that claimed him; his real life was always subordinate to the imaginary world issuing forth each month in Bradbury & Evans' thirty-two yellow-bound pages. Retrospect imparts a kind of teleology to the emergence of great books, in which the seeds of success can be detected almost from the moment the writer first sets pen to paper, but the development of *Vanity Fair* was almost startlingly *ad hoc*. Thackeray had three numbers written before the first was published, which meant that there was no room for complacency about deadlines. Worse, perhaps, was the air of precariousness that hung over the whole enterprise. Serial publication could make a publisher's fortune if the public bit, but it could also send him – and the unfortunate author – on the road to ruin. Charles Lever's *The Knight of Gwynne*, for instance, was one of the great publishing disasters of 1847. Ominously, the Bradbury & Evans contract failed to specify how many instalments Thackeray was expected to deliver.

However high their estimation of Thackeray's ability, they had provided themselves with a fail-safe insurance policy, which could quickly be invoked if sales became economically unsustainable.

It was in this tense and uncertain atmosphere that Thackeray sat down each month during the early part of 1847 to begin his work. From an early stage the manner of *Vanity Fair*'s composition became a staple of Victorian literary legend. Henry Vizetelly, to name only one memorialist, left an engaging picture of an essentially slapdash and deadline-haunted writer completing his monthly number with the printer's boy waiting in the hall below. In fact, as Peter Shillingsburg has demonstrated, the popular concept of a harried Thackeray dashing off the last line of the monthly number for the printer just in the nick of time is a romantic misunderstanding of the nature of serial publication. So how did *Vanity Fair* get written? And what procedures did Thackeray have to follow in order to ensure that each number came out in time? As we have seen, the first five chapters were completed by spring 1846 when Bradbury & Evans had them set up in type. Here, however, a problem presented itself. Traditionally, the monthly number of a serially published novel ran to thirty-two pages. Four of Thackeray's chapters made twenty-eight pages; five, though, extended to thirty-five. In the event, the need to find a solution to this drawback was set aside by the novel's postponement. The type was knocked out and redistributed, ready for another attempt on a revised manuscript in December. Thackeray's contract for *Vanity Fair* specified a submission date of the fifteenth of each month, yet Thackeray's letters from the period of the novel's composition often refer to finishing the number on around the twenty-fifth, barely a week before the publication date. Outwardly this seems to support the Vizetelly portrait of an eternally harassed improviser racking his brains for inspiration as the compositors work to arrange their type. In fact the progress of *Vanity Fair*'s monthly number seems to have followed a much smoother and more regular routine, based not on the formal demands of the contract but on an awareness of the needs of serial publication. As publishing historians have shown, submission of a finished manuscript on the fifteenth of the month preceding publication was at best impractical: frequently the author would have over- or underestimated the extent of his material and be forced to make later repair work. Thackeray's method seems to have been to submit around three-quarters of his instalment by the end of the third week in the month. With the comparatively high-speed methods of Victorian type-setting – often using five or six compositors – this could be turned round in a day or so, leaving Thackeray several days in which to tamper, amend and revise, while knowing exactly how much space remained to be filled. Spirited away from Young Street by the printer's boy, this material would be returned in the shape of final proofs on the twenty-fifth or -sixth of the month, leaving Bradbury & Evans a further five or six days to print and distribute it.

It was a rigorous schedule with little room for manoeuvre – either artistic or technical – but Thackeray seems to have found it invigorating. The pressures of serial publication undoubtedly concentrated his mind; the tiny window between final proof and finished copy allowed him to add topical allusions that pleased both his readers and his own taste for immediacy. Moreover the knowledge that he was writing to impress both purchaser and publisher was a constant stimulus to his creative powers. As a commercial proposition, *Vanity Fair* 'hung fire', to use Annie's expression, until the fourth number, and as late as October 1847 Thackeray was complaining to his mother that it did everything except sell. The threat of discontinuation that hung over the early numbers produced a determined effort to entice the public – notably the mystery of Becky's husband that bridges parts four and five. Written more or less on the hoof, the novel draws its strength from the balance that Thackeray managed to maintain between forward planning and spontaneity. Surviving notes for the monthly instalments include sheets of pencilled sketches in which he can be seen developing his ideas in advance. Simultaneously, much of the considerable research and the marshalling of historical detail that went into the book's composition was done at break-neck speed. A letter written late in December 1847 to an Indian army major shows both the pains that Thackeray was prepared to take and the haste in which the final garnish to individual numbers was applied. Describing himself as so late with his month's work as to be almost distracted, Thackeray declares that 'I want awfully to see you – and tonight if poss – I have a chapter about Madras in VF and dont want to make any blunders.' This was chapter XLIII, the first part of the thirteenth instalment, then only three or four days away from publication.

Subjected to the cold light of late-twentieth-century academic scrutiny, *Vanity Fair* betrays some of the haste in which it was composed, and it is easy to show how the strain of monthly publication occasionally led Thackeray to misremember pieces of minor detail. But for the most part the tensions of the form give it a singular vividness. In this context, it is possible to acknowledge the depth of Thackeray's artistic vision and the way in which wayside episodes and vignettes adhere to the wider pattern, while wondering if some of the grander claims occasionally made about the novel's aesthetic underpinning do not somehow ignore the conditions under which it was written. Such claims tend to focus on the undeniable change in direction that the novel underwent between initial conception and actual appearance. It seems reasonable to suppose on the strength of the early material – what later became chapters I–IV and part of chapter VI – that Thackeray envisaged *Vanity Fair* as a continuation or extrapolation of *The Snobs of England*. Subsequently, at some point in the autumn of 1846, a much more ambitious project began to take shape in his mind, incorporating significant changes of characterisation and emphasis. Chapter V, which introduces Dobbin to the reader, must have been written at about this time, and it would have been then that Thackeray decided to turn George Osborne into a wholly bad man. These developments, along with the existence of some rather odd passages of quasi-moralising in the early chapters, have led one or two critics to suppose that the change in Thackeray's domestic circumstances in late 1846 induced a 'change of heart', that – to reduce Gordon N. Ray's argument to a bland sentence or two – new-found domesticity and direct parental responsibility encouraged Thackeray to take a more mature view of the world and to practise his profession with a greater degree of seriousness. But while a fair amount of sermonising does occupy parts of chapters VIII and IX, it co-exists with a high degree of authorial ambiguity towards characters whom convention would require Thackeray to condemn. *Vanity Fair* is not merely a 'novel without a hero'; it is also, at any rate covertly, a novel *with* a heroine, and that heroine is Becky Sharp, Thackeray's partiality to whom is almost undisguised (he is on record as saying that the Bohemian element of the book, which Becky personifies, was his favourite).

Then again, certain bits of Ray's evidence have a habit of not performing the role that he assigns to them. Chapter VIII, for example, has a curious six-paragraph section appended to it, which at first sight looks like an exemplary piece of moral comment. Moving on from a mischievous (and observant) letter from Becky – by this stage lodged at Queen's Crawley – to Amelia in Russell Square, Thackeray begins by remarking that it is 'quite as well' that the two girls are parted. He then reminds his readers of the novel's title, professes an obligation to 'speak the truth as far as one knows it', and suggests that 'a deal of disagreeable matter must come out in the course of such an undertaking'. There follows a second paragraph outlining the techniques of an itinerant Neapolitan storyteller whose audience would join him in abusing the villainies of his characters, and a third describing how in French theatre the actors positively refuse to play wicked parts. The two stories are set off against one another, Thackeray explains, so that the reader may understand that 'it is not from mere mercenary motives that the present performer is desirous to show up and trounce his villains; but because he has a sincere hatred of them, which he cannot keep down, and which must find a vent in suitable abuse and bad language'. He then warns his readers that he is going to tell a story of harrowing villainy and complicated vice, whose rascals are 'no milk-and-water rascals, I promise you', and that he intends occasionally to 'step down from the platform and talk about them'. Otherwise the reader might fancy that it was the author who 'sneered at the practice of devotion, which Miss Sharp finds so ridiculous' or who laughs at old Sir Pitt Crawley, 'whereas the laughter comes from one who has no reverence except for prosperity, and no eye for anything beyond success'.

At the very least, this is deeply ambiguous. Outwardly Thackeray is advising his readers not to confuse an author's judgments with those of his characters, emphasising this point by stating his intention to 'step down from his platform' and pitch into them himself. But the ulterior knowledge we possess about his attitude to Becky – his mixed feelings about the novel's supposedly 'good' characters, too, if it comes to that – makes this difficult to accept. Then there are the topical allusions – a reference to 'kyind friends' (another in the long series of hits at Alfred Bunn, manager of the Drury Lane Theatre), a satirical nod towards the abolitionist slogan 'a man and a brother' – whose cumulative effect is to leave the reader mildly confused. Satire? A statement of moral intent? Whatever the answer (and the probability is that it lies somewhere between the two), the thought that the paragraphs also function as last-minute embroidery to a chapter that ended up a page and a half short can hardly be discounted.

This sense of something that grew, changed shape and redefined itself almost day by day, susceptible at all times to a range of visual and imaginative impulses, is confirmed by what we know of the host of other factors that impinged on the book's composition. Most obviously, throughout *Vanity Fair*'s development, Thackeray can be seen pursuing parallels in the life he was living as he wrote it. If Becky's physical appearance owed something to Isabella, and Miss Crawley was transparently modelled on old Mrs Butler – to name only two borrowings from the family circle – then Amelia bore an obvious similarity to Mrs Brookfield (Jane seems to have detected this resemblance quite early on and played up to it: there is a jokey exchange of letters from mid-1848 about 'Payne', Jane's maid, whose name Thackeray gave to Amelia's domestic). Simultaneously, he took pains to locate the novel in a recognisable social and topographical milieu. Late in 1847, for example, he purchased a horse and throughout the autumn and early spring, often with Leech as a companion, took long rides from Kensington to the area north of Oxford Street. Even the heart of the fashionable West End glimpsed from the saddle of his cob had a tendency to 'fructify', he told his mother, 'and I see a great deal of sights from his Punchy back' (these excursions were noted by his *Punch* colleagues, and one of Doyle's illustrations to *Punch's Almanac* for 1848, published at the end of December 1847, contains a fat, bespectacled figure astride a tiny horse). Many of the thoroughfares he traversed, or amalgams of them, provided a stage for the cast of *Vanity Fair*. 'Great Gaunt Street', where the Crawley family has its London house, is modelled on Harley Street, while 'Gaunt Square', site of the Marquis of Steyne's mansion, looks as if it was drawn from Cavendish Square, with other material and historical associations supplied by Manchester Square and Berkeley Square. Touches of this kind were important. By tethering the novel to recognisable locales and atmospheres, Thackeray gives it an almost documentary solidity and specificity – a quality that endures despite the book's grounding in a period twenty or thirty years before the time of writing. The historical detail of *Vanity Fair* is, as several modern explorers have shown, a cunning mixture of chronological precision and deliberate anachronism. Drawn into what, strictly speaking, was an historical novel, the reader of 1847 found himself immediately reassured by a riot of contemporary allusions and up-to-the-minute jokes.

The miracle of this sustained exercise in improvisation – in volume form *Vanity Fair* would eventually run to over a quarter of a million words – was its imbrication in a wider framework of routine journalism and other literary commitments. *The Snobs of England* came to an end in February 1847, but even before this date Thackeray had begun to plan another *Punch* series. The extended parodies of *Punch's Prize*

Novelists, later retitled *Novels by Eminent Hands* (which may have been another dig at Colburn) did not begin until April, but Thackeray seems to have been aware of the tensions that the series would uncover much earlier in the year. In late January, for instance, he declined a dinner invitation from his old literary friend Albany Fonblanque on the grounds that Bulwer would be there (as 'George de Barnwell', Bulwer was the first of Thackeray's victims). 'I can't afford to give up my plan,' he explained, somewhat anxiously, to his host. 'It is my bread indeed for the next year.' It was not only Bulwer who took offence when the series was published. Of Thackeray's six other targets – Disraeli, Lever, G.P.R. James, Mrs Gore, James Fennimore Cooper and, somewhat surprisingly, Thackeray himself – Lever was unexpectedly hurt by the fairly genial satire of 'Phil Fogarty – A Tale of the Fighting Onety-Oneth', while Disraeli ('B. De Shrewsbury') never forgave him for 'Codlingsby'. Thackeray had reviewed *Coningsby*, on which the spoof was based, for the *Morning Chronicle* in May 1844, enjoying its 'superb coxcombry' even as he lambasted an example of 'the fashionable novel, pushed . . . to its extremest verge'. Introduced by a mutual friend, the two subsequently struck up an acquaintance that survived a great deal of *Punch* lampooning: a diary entry from the mid-1840s records 'a pleasant dinner at Disraeli's'. 'Codlingsby', however, was a different matter from the routine anti-semitism of the *Punch* jokes. The theatrical producer John Hollingshead remembered the two of them coming abreast at the sequel to the Great Exhibition a decade and a half later and cutting each other dead, while as late as 1880, seventeen years after Thackeray's death, Disraeli caricatured him in *Endymion* as the envious critic St Barbe.

There were tensions, too, in one of his closer relationships. A letter to Brookfield in early February apologises for some 'uncouth raptures' pronounced over the latter's wife while on a visit to Southampton. Thackeray's excuse for what he called his 'insanity' was that he was under the influence of ether – administered by a local physician, Dr Buller, who experimented in anaesthetics; clearly, though, this had brought some strongly felt emotions to the surface. Even in the act of apologising, Thackeray goes on to remark that 'her innocence, looks, angelical sweetness and kindness charm and ravish me to the highest degree . . . They are not in the least dangerous – it is a sort of artistical delight,' he reassured his friend. Brookfield cannot have been alarmed by this enthusiasm – the very expression of it robs it of any sinister implications – for his diary entry of ten days later shows him calling at

Young Street and talking until the small hours. But these were difficult times for Brookfield, which may have made him even touchier than usual. Something of this unease may be gauged from a letter that Thackeray wrote a few days later to their mutual friend John Allen on the subject of Brookfield's candidature for a vacant schools inspectorship. Allen, who never allowed personal associations to interfere with moral rectitude and, as one of the original inspectors – a national educational bureaucracy had only recently begun to take shape – had been consulted by the appointing body, had written to his friend suggesting that he was simply not a fit man for the job. Understandably humiliated by this rebuff, Brookfield had wondered whether Allen was judging him from the observations of their college days. Thackeray eagerly developed this theme: 'I wonder whether you *are* judging of him from fifteen years ago? my dear fellow: if you are I think you do him a great wrong ... If he had not been a just and generous heart, I dont think he would have taken your letter as he did –.' Allen's original letter has not survived, but its strictures seem to have been levelled at the kind of company Brookfield kept, in particular his association with a gang of radical journalists, and indeed Thackeray himself: 'smoking pipes at midnight with a caricaturist, a writer in Punch &c &c'. Invoking his own row with Jerrold over the paper 'On Clerical Snobs' (whose reproofs on the subject of journalistic anti-clericalism Jerrold took personally), Thackeray claimed that 'it is not Punch that has perverted Brookfield; but Brookfield has converted Punch! & that's something to have done in these days'. He went on to characterise Brookfield's contribution to the magazine's raised moral tone in grandiloquent tones: 'It is something to stop half a million of people from jeering at the Church every week ... It's William Brookfield who stopped it, & you may tell the Board so and I wish you would – by his kindness, his tenderness, his honest pious life.' In fact Brookfield had done nothing of the sort, but Thackeray knew how much the post meant to his friend (and his friend's wife) and the effect that rumours of this sort would have on Brookfield's chance of future preferment.

A flurry of letters from Southampton and back in the latter part of February testifies to Thackeray's efforts to help his friend in the matter of the schools job. Mrs Brookfield wrote to assure him that on his departure 'You left a great blank behind you – not to be filled up at all'; Thackeray wrote again to Allen telling him that he had 'cruelly wronged' Brookfield by imputing to him 'levity & looseness of talk', and also to his friend Henry Reeve, who worked at the Privy Council office and knew Dr Kay Shuttleworth, with whom Allen had been conferring; Mrs Brookfield wrote again suggesting that William should collect testimonials in support of his suit. But it was all to no avail, and the position went elsewhere. As ever, Brookfield's superiors thought him suspect. Meanwhile, Thackeray had other tasks to complete. The final instalment of *Snobs* was delivered to Mark Lemon, along with a note trusting that the concluding paragraph (which hopes that Mr Punch may 'laugh honestly, hit no foul blow, and tell the truth when at his very broadest grin –') would not be misinterpreted by his colleagues, and in particular by Jerrold ('I think his opinions are wrong on many points, but I'm sure he believes them honestly,' Thackeray reassured his chief). In celebration of the forthcoming third number Annie had knitted him a pin-cushion, she told her grandmother. Her excitement over the latest instalment of *Dombey and Son*, which had just reached the death of little Paul, combined with a tacit assumption of Dickens' superiority, was shared by her father: there was no writing like it, he told George Hodder when the two of them met in the *Punch* office.

The letter of mid-February to John Allen carries a postscript that has nothing to do with Brookfield's suitability for the post of inspector of schools. In it Thackeray wonders whether his friend knows of 'a very good governess & perfect lady to command my house and children?' Establishing a set of routines for the house at Young Street was another of his challenges for the early part of 1847, and Annie's memoirs give a good idea of the ways in which Thackeray set about trying to organise the lives of his two small daughters. Annie characterised the house as 'more or less a bachelor establishment', noting that the arrangements varied between 'a certain fastidiousness and the roughest simplicity'. This collision of styles was most apparent at meal times, when a shabby tablecloth lay beneath their great-grandmother's fine linen, and cracked cups and saucers received tea poured from a silver Flaxman teapot. The house's focal point, as Annie's recollections make clear, was Thackeray's study. This lay at the back of the premises, looking out through vine-slanted windows onto a garden dominated by a medlar tree and an ancient brick wall. Thackeray's bedroom was directly above, and above that was the schoolroom with its sloping floor and a mysterious trap-door between the windows. Annie remembered the evening bells from the nearby Kensington churches clanging across the garden at sunset. The paternal sanctum two floors below was officially sacrosanct, but this rule was always being broken, especially on Sunday morning when friends came to call. Nearly twenty years later Annie still recalled a splendidly dressed person who 'seemed to fill the bow-window with radiance as if he were Apollo'. This was the superannuated Regency dandy Count d'Orsay, who on his departure was found to have left a tiny pencil sketch behind. The nine-year-old Annie was a severe critic: it was a very feeble sketch, she remembered, and 'scarcely possible that so grand a being should not be a better draughtsman'.

Much as he loved having the girls to live with him, Thackeray worried about their upbringing. This anxiety was shared by his mother, who became ever more alarmed by reports of good-looking governesses and eventually persuaded old Mrs Butler to cross the Channel to keep a notional eye on her grandson's behaviour (in the event the old lady spent most of her time in her room and her influence on the household was negligible). Fortunately Annie and Minnie quickly began to acquire a life of their own: there were invitations to spend time at the Proctors or the Crowes in Hampstead, or to visit Mrs Carlyle in Chelsea (Annie always remembered walking there on a bitter winter's day and being served steaming mugs of chocolate). Home life, meanwhile, was enlivened by pets. There had been a diminutive black cat waiting to greet them on their arrival. Subsequently Minnie built up a collection from the vagrant population of Kensington, naming them after her favourite fictional characters: a huge grey tabby called Nicholas Nickleby; a half-starved bag of bones christened Barnaby Rudge. Under the benign superintendence of their father, who the girls supposed liked animals ('at least he always liked *our* animals'), saucers of milk were laid out on a little terrace at the back of Thackeray's study, under the vine where sour green grapes grew, at the far end of an empty greenhouse.

Annie's memoirs paint a cheery picture of the early days in Young Street and the social life that accompanied them: Alfred Tennyson glimpsed through a cloud of pipe smoke; the ritual excursion on the day that the monthly number was finished, to Hampstead, Richmond, Greenwich or the theatre (*King Lear*, which the Thackerays attended *en famille*, was not a success – Annie was so upset by the king's curses on his wicked daughters that she put her hands over her ears). The only problem – one that was to afflict Thackeray for several years – was the question of the girls' day-to-day supervision. By March Thackeray had decided that Bess Hamerton, despite her status as a family friend and the kindness she had shown to Isabella, would not do: 'She's not an English lady – that's the fact,' he told his mother, having penned a tactful letter of dismissal. A series of successors followed: Miss Drury, who lasted until October; Miss Alexander (daughter of the Richmond family with whom he had originally decided to install Isabella), dismissed in June 1848. Each of these appointments tended to be accompanied by long-distance interference from Mrs Carmichael-Smyth, whose wariness of the most marginally eligible female extended even to Mrs Bakewell's satellite Mrs Gloyne. After the arrival of Mrs Butler – now in an extremely decrepit state – in early April, Thackeray had encouraged Mrs Gloyne to visit the house regularly to nurse and be a companion to the old lady, but Mrs Carmichael-Smyth distrusted her motives. 'As for me and poor Gloyne fiddledeedee,' Thackeray told his mother. In the end, though, he took the hint. Mrs Gloyne was banished, with her ex-employer acknowledging that she was indeed 'a very awkward customer in my house – being neither a servant or a lady'. Thackeray feared he had treated her badly, and regretted his 'haughtiness'.

With the help of Annie's memoirs it is possible to build up a fair-sized inventory of Young Street's paraphernalia: the cracked cups and saucers on the ancient tablecloth; Thackeray's coat in the hall dwarfing the children's tiny ulsters. But one of the most characteristic sights to a visitor would have been the rows of woodblocks lying about the rooms, some untouched, others with drawings chalked on their surfaces. Thackeray was contracted to provide his own illustrations to *Vanity Fair*. These – both full-page drawings and smaller designs for chapter-heading capital letters – show another side of the inventiveness that underpinned the book's composition. In fact the drawings can be seen as a kind of running commentary on the text, embellishing or confirming what is sometimes only suggested within, and occasionally encouraging new interpretations of the incidents they represent. Chapter IV, for example, shows a girl, not unlike Becky Sharp, sitting in the circle formed by the letter P and dangling a net into a river occupied by an enormously fat fish: the fish, transparently, is Jos Sedley and the illustration a gloss on Becky's efforts to hook herself a husband. This is perhaps only a corroboration of what the reader has already guessed. Other drawings encourage trains of thought not always prompted by the text. The chapter introducing Miss Swartz, the West Indian heiress whom George scornfully declines to marry, opens with a drawing of a white girl playing with a black doll:

the effect is to a create a degree of sympathy for Miss Swartz that is not evident in the letterpress.

The presence of these lumps of wood – literally cross-sections of trees – with their chalked surfaces was a nod to Thackeray's limitations as a draughtsman. By the 1840s wood engravings had come to be used almost exclusively for satirical illustrations of the kind that appeared in *Punch* or monthly serials. Their advantage, in contrast to the more expensive lithographic process, was that illustration and text could be combined on the same page. More than any other of the *Punch* artists, Thackeray relied heavily on the services of Bradbury & Evans' professional engravers. He never found it easy to put his original sketches onto wood, a process that involved drawing with an extremely fine pencil on a surface prepared with moistened bath brick and the subsequent application of Chinese white, and usually subcontracted the work to a more skilled hand. The poor quality of many of the *Vanity Fair* drawings stems from the fact that a fair proportion of them were actually drawn onto the blocks by other people, using Thackeray's sketches. The best are those that Thackeray himself managed to chalk onto the wood for subsequent engraving by a professional, who could bring out the effect he was trying to achieve without robbing the sketch of its individuality. For all his enthusiasm for drawing, Thackeray never really progressed beyond the stage of competent amateur, and the explanation of this failing lies squarely in his inability to master engraving techniques. The chalk drawings that lay around the house at Young Street frequently needed two or three attempts, and Annie, who helped her father by washing off unsuccessful try-outs, once got into terrible trouble for erasing what was actually a finished drawing waiting to go off to the engraver's shop.

As the spring wore on and *Vanity Fair* lurched towards its sixth number, the strain of these varied commitments began to tell. 'What has happened since I wrote a year ago?' Thackeray wondered to his mother late in May. 'The same story of everyday work work gobble gobble scuffling through the day with business and a sort of pleasure wh. becomes a business, till bed-time – and no prospect of more than temporary quiet.' But he enjoyed himself on 28 May, Minnie's seventh birthday, 'a day of heat and idleness at Hampstead Court'. Miss Drury, the new governess, seemed sensible, and Annie continued to blossom. 'She'll be a young woman directly,' he predicted, 'and please God a she-friend to me.' Meanwhile another source of stress had begun to boil steadily away in the background. Tom Taylor, his *Punch* colleague, had been on his way to dinner with Forster when the latter had angrily remarked that Thackeray was 'as false as hell'. Taylor, assuming that the notoriously thin-skinned Forster was enslaved by some momentary grievance, 'laughed excessively'. A day or so later, not imagining that his friend would be especially put out, he repeated this outburst to its subject, 'remarking on its vehemence laughingly'. Unfortunately Taylor's idea of a joke was not Thackeray's. Early in June, meeting Forster at one of Mrs Proctor's evenings, in a small room where discreet avoidance was impossible, Thackeray refused to shake the hand that Forster held out to him.

Forster was not the man to take this kind of insult lying down. In addition, he had powerful friends. The next morning, consequently, brought Dickens to the doorstep at Young Street with a note from Forster demanding an explanation. All at once a classic Victorian literary row moved effortlessly into view – collaborative, conducted by letter, and attended by much cautious skulduggery and insinuation. Thackeray wrote immediately to Forster stating what Taylor had told him. Forster wrote back defending himself: he had no recollection of using the words quoted. Had he done so, then in 'conveying to you any portion of a very private conversation which passed in my own chambers', Taylor had committed 'a gross breach of confidence'. This was all very well, but Forster could not resist a second paragraph suggesting that the 'private pleasantries of your pencil and pen with me for your theme' had given him several previous opportunities, not taken up, to act 'with just discourtesy towards you'. This elegant form of words referred to caricatures of Forster which Thackeray certainly had produced in the past, but Forster's defence is highly disingenuous: he believes he did not say the words, but if he did they are justified by Thackeray's previous conduct towards him.

Arguments of this kind in early-Victorian society had a habit of mimicking the protocols of the duels by which, in a not so distant age, they would regularly have been settled: representatives were appointed and negotiations conducted while the protagonists stood loftily to one side. Within hours of discovering Dickens on his doorstep, Thackeray had appointed his friend Sir Alexander Duff Gordon to handle his side of the dispute. Writing to Forster later the same day, Dickens reported that he had seen Sir Alexander, handed over Forster's letter and supposed that the matter was closed. The rest of Dickens' letter is interesting, though, in that it reveals his own reservations about Thackeray's seriousness, and his nervousness at the prospect of becoming an object of Thackeray's satire. 'I said that as far as Thackeray was concerned, and separating my remarks from you, or your affair, I should tell him, if he were there, that I thought these things arose in his jesting much too lightly between what was true and what was false, and what he owed to both, and not being sufficiently steady to the former.' Dickens then brings in the 'Imitations in Punch' (a reference to *Punch's Prize Novelists*) – the Forster/Taylor conversation had apparently arisen out of these – remarking that 'I had a strong opinion of my own: and that it was they did no honour to literature or literary men, and should be left to very inferior and miserable hands . . .' As regards 'that paragraph of retort on Thackeray', he had reason to know its force 'better than you did even'. Clearly Dickens himself had fallen victim to Thackeray's talent for caricature. Clearly, too, he was anxious not to appear in the series of *Punch* parodies. But the evidence points to a wider division between the two men, based on Dickens' suspicion that, in the last resort, Thackeray did not take his profession with sufficient gravity. Producing parodies for a weekly magazine was a hack's job, not a calling for a serious literary man.

Given what he must have known, or suspected, about the temperaments of the contending parties, it seems odd that Dickens should assume Forster's letter would settle the quarrel. In fact it still had some way to run. On the next day, 10 June, Forster wrote an immensely pompous letter to Taylor breaking off their relationship ('Few things could have given me greater pain, or could have been more unexpected by me, than such an interruption of that familiar intimacy with you in which I have always had sincere pleasure'). Thackeray, realising that he had got his friend 'into a scrape', as he put it, composed an emollient letter to Dickens confessing that he could understand 'how a man of Forster's emphatic way of talking . . . chafed by ridicule, should have uttered the words wh. formed the subject of my difference with him'. He also provided a painfully accurate summary of the quarrel to date ('Forster ought not to have used the words: Taylor ought not to have told them: and I ought not to have taken them up'). Sir Alexander Duff-Gordon added his own ironic gloss to the proceedings ('It would be absurd that Tom Taylor and Forster should no longer be friends because Thackeray, for once in his life, took things too seriously') and the whole business was eventually patched up with a grand reconciliation dinner at Greenwich. On the Richter scale of Victorian literary rows this one does not perhaps rate very highly; at the same time it does demonstrate one or two of the alliances that underlay the literary world of the late 1840s, the essential touchiness of both Dickens and Thackeray, and the existence of a deeper argument that went beyond the exchange of injurious gossip. As such the Taylor/Forster row is a revealing dry run for the much more serious disagreements of the 1850s. It had an immediate consequence, too: Thackeray, who had been toying with the idea of putting Dickens into *Punch's Prize Novelists*, almost certainly thought better of it as a result of this disagreement.

The Forster quarrel probably held up work on the July number of *Vanity Fair*. In its wake Thackeray explained to his mother that he got so nervous in his efforts to complete his monthly task 'that I don't speak to anybody scarcely'. Miss Drury, meanwhile, continued to be 'a very jolly honest lady I think and the children are still tolerable'. Annie, now following her father's novel with the same avidity as *Dombey and Son*, had seen the woodblocks for the next number. 'I think it will be in next V Fair that George Osborne is killed and Amelia will have a little boy,' she confided to her grandmother. 'Do not tell this to any bodie because it is a secret and if any bodie knew they would not buy V Fair.' There were further Brookfield schemes in prospect and Thackeray enquired of Mrs Proctor if she knew the Duke of Bedford, in whose gift lay the vacant living of St Paul's, Covent Garden. The season was coming to an end and the exit of the fashionable classes from London was about to begin, but Thackeray, mindful of his deadlines, had to forgo a long holiday. He managed a small excursion to the Rhineland and Belgium (the children went to Boulogne with their grandparents) and returned to the dead streets of late-August London, enlivened only by the company of Brookfield. There was the usual rush to finish the September number, with Brookfield writing to Jane – again on one of her provincial visits – that 'T sits beside me – brewing Vanity – in a dreadful fright'. The Brookfields were by now assiduous critics of *Vanity Fair*, with Jane's interest in particular awakened by some chance remarks let slip by the author. However, seeing oneself represented in print could work both ways. The October number was a disappointment, she told her cousin Harry Hallam. 'Mr Thackeray has now got a 2nd Amelia, Lady Jane Sheepshanks. I wish he had made Amelia more exciting, as the remark is he had thought of me in her character ... You know he told William that though Amelia was not a copy of me he should not have conceived the character if he had not known me.' Although Amelia had 'the right amount of antiphlegm and affectionateness', she was really uncommonly dull, Jane concluded. This was not an opinion shared by many contemporary critics, who tended to seize on Amelia as the epitome of pure Victorian womanhood. Coming back from a jaunt to Brighton in October, Thackeray appraised the momentum of his by now half-finished work. The novel did everything but sell, he told his mother, 'and appears immensely to increase my reputation, if not my income'.

This was an accurate perception of his growing status. No doubt it had been encouraged by some of the social experiences of the previous few months. In a comparatively short space of time *Vanity Fair* had made Thackeray's name, or rather it had made it among what might loosely be called 'fashionable society'. As we have seen, even as a young man Thackeray had hovered on the fringes of the world represented by the grand houses of Belgravia and Mayfair, but he had never penetrated it: even in the 1840s 'society's' protocols were quite as freezing as they were earlier in the century, when Wellington himself was turned away from Almack's ballroom. By birth Thackeray was a well-bred upper-middle-class gentleman, but this was no means sufficient to procure an entrée to a Whig salon such as Holland House. Still less was his professional calling. But Thackeray had good connections in the political world about which much of this upper-class social life tended to revolve; at six feet three he cut an imposing and dignified presence; he had written, or was writing, 'a clever book'; and by mid-1847 a strew of invitations altogether beyond the range of the average literary man had begun to fill the mantelpiece at Young Street. At the same time this new world of fashionable hostesses and grand dinners represented only a small part of the social orbit in which he moved, and to arrive at a fuller understanding of the life he led at this time it is worth trying to separate out (in so far as some of them are separable) the various circles to which he had access.

First came a group of old friends, many of them with young families, to whose houses he could take his daughters. These included the Proctors, then living in Harley Street; the Kembles – in particular the younger daughter Adelaide, a professional singer now known under her married name of Mrs Sartoris; the Coles and the Crowes, who resided in Hampstead. Then there were old university friends – Brookfield fell into this category – such as Fitzgerald, Lettsom and Allen, with whom he continued to keep up. A third cluster takes in the *Punch* circle of journalists and illustrators (with a preference for gentlemanly ex-public-school men such as Leech) and other scattered literary connections picked up over the past ten years – Matthew Higgins, for example, met during Thackeray's time on the *New Monthly Magazine*, who wrote under the pseudonym 'Jacob Omnium' and, at six feet eight, dwarfed even his towering friend. One feature of Thackeray's literary friendships from about this time was his ability to command the loyalties of a group of younger acolytes – men who were just beginning to make their mark in journalism and looked to Thackeray as a source of guidance and inspiration. George Hodder was one of these, but the most fervent of Thackeray's younger admirers was James Hannay, at this point in his mid-twenties and newly arrived in London after being thrown out of the navy. As a contributor to small-circulation magazines like *Pasquin*, founded in 1847, and its successor the *Puppet-Show*, Hannay became a consistent supporter, frequently comparing the author of *Vanity Fair* to Dickens and using insider knowledge picked up through his *Punch* connections to promote his mentor at the expense of lesser rivals such as Jerrold (the preface to Hannay's first book, *Biscuits and Grog* (1848), pays tribute to Thackeray, together with Carlyle, as the most serious and estimable writer of his day). For his part, Thackeray liked Hannay – Annie maintained that, sketching in the bow-window of Young Street as the younger man walked up the steps, he took his face as the model for Arthur Pendennis' features – and went out of his way to find him work, probably helping him to become a *Punch* contributor a year or so later.

A fourth social hub was provided by the Garrick Club, 'the G', 'the little G' or 'the dearest place in the world', as Thackeray was fond of calling it. In the fifteen years that he had paid his subscription Thackeray had moved on from the figure that one member recalled as 'a slim young man, rather taciturn and not displaying particular love or

'Blessing Mrs Proctor's daughters'

talent for literature who could be seen covering scraps of paper with drawings' to become one of the Garrick's principal ornaments. His cronies tended to belong to the staider element of the club's *habitués* – Robert Bell, for instance, who spent much of his later years working on an annotated twenty-four-volume edition of the English poets, or Francis Fladgate, who had inherited £60,000 from his attorney father – but they also included more Bohemian types such as Andrew Arcedeckne. This 'indescribably grotesque personage' – to borrow a phrase from a late-Victorian memoir – though born into a respectable county family, fancied himself as a comic actor and in pursuit of this calling spent much of his time staying at inns, where he entertained captive audiences of tradesmen and travelling salesmen with ludicrous monologues. Thackeray used many of his affectations for the none the less highly sanitised portrait of Foker in *Pendennis*, but the amused patronage that characterised their relationship can sometimes disguise the fact that Arcedeckne was more than capable of getting his own back – once yelling out his trademark 'Hello Thack!' at Derby Day on Epsom Downs when he saw his friend walking sedately with a lord.

A fifth element in this ever-expanding tableau consisted of more recently acquired friends drawn from more or less the same social background as himself. Pre-eminent among these, perhaps, were Jane and Kate Perry, two inseparable daughters of a former editor of the *Morning Chronicle*. Thackeray had first met Kate at Brighton in 1846, and was swiftly inducted into the family circle at Belgrave Square where she had gone to live after her sister's marriage to Thomas Elliot, a Colonial Office civil servant. The society offered by the Elliots was not grand in the accepted sense, but Thackeray liked it, and felt that he received a more genuine welcome there than at some of the big houses where he was now regularly invited. The latter form another aspect of his social universe. He retained some status as a party man, and his chief patrons in the early days of his social ascent tended to be Whig aristocrats. Vouched for by parliamentary friends such as Monckton-Milnes and Charles Buller, he came to know Palmerston and the Russells, was seen at Holland House, and struck up a considerable intimacy with the Ashburtons – William Bingham Baring, 2nd Baron Ashburton, and his wife Lady Harriet – whom even Carlyle marked down as 'the greatest lady of rank I ever saw'. Though gratifying to Thackeray's own sense of himself and his merits, these were not easy relationships. The staider element among his new acquaintances wondered – sometimes publicly – why they should be encouraged to entertain middle-class satirists, and old Lady Stanley, whose family Thackeray came to know a year or so later, professed herself scandalised by *Vanity Fair*. Really, she declared, he should be banished from the society he had so 'wonderfully found his way into only to hold it up to ridicule'.

For his own part Thackeray was acutely sensitive to accusations of tuft-hunting. Many of his letters from this period contain oddly proleptic defences of a position that had not yet been challenged. All this about being a lion was nonsense, he told Fitz. 'I cant eat more dinners than I used to last year and dine at home with my dear little women three times a week: but 2 or 3 great people ask me to their houses.' An earlier letter to Aunt Ritchie is more honest about his changed circumstances – 'You must know I am become quite a Lion now, and live with all sorts of great people' – but equally defensive: 'Their flattery has not turned my head as yet, please God, and my reign as a fashionable literary man will very soon be over: and somebody else will be flourishing in my stead.' This faint note of paranoia grows louder in a revealing diary entry from March 1848, recounting a trip to the Drury Lane Theatre with some *Punch* colleagues to view an 'Equestrian Performance'. Halfway through, an invitation arrived for Thackeray to join the occupants of the stage box – a select pantheon including D'Orsay and Lords Chesterfield and Granville. 'All these great persons were perfectly good humoured & unaffected – enjoying the sport before them with the utmost simplicity & childish good humour,' Thackeray noted; but, returning to his seat, he detected an air of sulkiness and surmised that Leech and Lemon had used his absence to talk about 'that d—— lickspittle Thackeray &c'. This rebuke, real or imagined, bred an understandable caution in Thackeray's dealings with his exalted acquaintance. Candid about his liking for the society of great people, and ever ready to write deferential letters to literary-minded aristocrats such as the Duke of Devonshire (who had enquired about the further adventures of Becky, Dobbin and Co.), he was also capable of taking profound offence. A quarrel with Lady Ashburton, for example, over some of the raillery for which Lady Harriet was famous, blew on for several weeks until he was persuaded to write a conciliatory note.

But amid these grand engagements, Thackeray's liking for the humbler diversions that he had first discovered in the 1830s persisted. He was as happy spending an evening listening to vulgar songs in a Bohemian resort like the Cyder Cellar as he was rubbing shoulders with the Whig grandees. This ability simultaneously to live his life on several different levels can sometimes seem confusing: distinguishing between the *habitué* of the Back Kitchen and the Duke's punctilious correspondent is not always as easy as it sounds. In the last resort, perhaps, these distinctions do not need to be made. One of the strengths of *Vanity Fair*, after all, is the way in which it contrives to integrate Becky's Bohemianism with the protocols of pre-Victorian upper society.

There were other distractions, quite apart from the pressures of social life. A day that should have been spent on the November number was taken up in reading an intriguing new novel called *Jane Eyre*, sent to him by its publishers Smith, Elder: Thackeray declared himself 'exceedingly moved & pleased' and also showed a shrewd interest in the identity of the pseudonymous author (it was a woman's writing, he noted, but whose?). In the meantime the traffic to and from Young Street had not diminished. Old Mrs Butler, now exceedingly frail, had gone back to Paris and was not expected to survive the year. Miss Drury had been succeeded by Miss Alexander, 'a very nice plain kind-looking governess – about 28' (the 'plain' was for Mrs Carmichael-Smyth's benefit). At the same time Thackeray reported a proposal received from Brookfield – still hard-up and unable to afford a proper London establishment – that the two families should combine their resources and go halves on the housekeeping. However much the idea may have appealed to Thackeray, he was conscious that it would not do, and offered a characteristically frank assessment to his mother. 'Mrs B managing the children – loving her as I do – Mong Dieu what a temptation it was! but you see the upshot. That *would* be dangerous, and so I keep off –.' Here, as elsewhere, the distinguishing mark of Thackeray's regard for his friend's wife was its transparency. By late 1847 his affection for Jane had reached something like the level of a family joke – earlier in the year, for instance, he had told Arthur Shawe that she still kept possession of his heart, 'but this romantic passion doesn't disturb my sleep or my appetite for vittles'. This seems an odd admission to make to the brother of the woman to whom you happen to be married, even if she has lost her reason, but one suspects that Arthur was fully aware of the situation and able to react in appropriately knowing terms.

Mrs Butler died in Paris on the first day of November. Back in London, Thackeray had begun work on a second Christmas book, a series of character sketches of the inhabitants of 'Our Street', set in a

London suburb that bore a clear resemblance to Kensington. He was hard pressed financially, complaining to Arthur about Mrs Shawe's continued refusal to acknowledge 'poor Isabella's claim upon her'. It was always the same, he lamented – earning, always paying, never having. Literary celebrity was taking its toll, too, in the number of requests from aspiring authors. He apologised to Bedingfield for not having reviewed his book on the grounds that 'By Jove, I have not time to do $\frac{1}{2}$ what I ought to do . . .' Mrs Carmichael-Smyth, who was incubating her own literary ambitions and had sent a manuscript for consideration, needed more careful treatment. He would send her 'wonderful story' to Chapman and Hall and to Smith, Elder, Thackeray promised, but he knew it would come back. The only recourse, he feared, was for her to pay for publication. Pressure of work and the consciousness of his changing position produced another taking-stock letter early in 1848. Here money worries and the prospect of a law suit over the wretched railway shares contended with an appreciation of his new-found status: '– o what a turmoil it is – under wh. I live laugh and grow fat however'. There was no use denying the matter, he concluded, 'I am become a sort of great man in my way – all but at the top of the tree: indeed there if the truth were known and having a great fight there with Dickens.' It was a precarious state, however, in which even well-intended criticism could drive him to fury, and he was particularly annoyed by an enthusiastic piece in the *Edinburgh Review* (written by Abraham Hayward with help from Mrs Proctor, who selected useful passages from *Vanity Fair*) that ventured to connect his literary and social triumphs. As a puff, the review was famous, he assured Mrs Carmichael-Smyth. As a criticism, on the other hand, it was 'utterly drivelling: the man who wrote it has no more idea of humour than I have of Algebra'. Hayward's comment that after 'great pains' Thackeray had worked his way into a number of great houses, that his manners were brusque but they liked him, brought a withering riposte. Critics and society hostesses were 'too surprised' to discover that this upstart journalist was a gentleman, ignorant of the fact that there were two old people living in Paris on £200 a year who were 'as grand folks as they ever were'.

The early part of 1848 went in a whirl of work and social life. 'My life is passed in dining and penny a lining,' Thackeray explained to one correspondent: he had only one day free in the week, and that must be given up to the children. Mrs Carmichael-Smyth, who continued to write sorrowful letters about the children's health, which revealed her distress at being separated from them, needed constant reassurance ('always tormenting herself about the children, and their illnesses . . .' Thackeray noted in a perceptive account of his mother's innate melancholy). The unpleasantness with Dickens was over, and the two exchanged respectful letters ('You have given me a new reason (if I wanted any) for interest in all you do . . .' Dickens assured him) and a day's work was lost to the after-effects of attending Dickens' ball on 26 January. The receipt of the second edition of *Jane Eyre*, which turned out to be dedicated to Thackeray – he was now aware of the author's identity – stirred more ambivalent emotions. Pleased by the compliment, he was all too aware that his own circumstances were in some way similar to those of Mr Rochester. Sure enough, a rumour went the rounds of literary London that the novel had been written by Thackeray's governess.

Some revealing snapshots of the life he was leading at this time are provided by a diary that chronicles a week in the early part of March. It began with an elegiac visit to Addiscombe, where his stepfather had been superintendent a quarter of a century before, at the invitation of his friend Frederick Goldsmith, now an orderly officer at the college. Goldsmith, who later wrote an account of the visit, noted that Thackeray examined his parents' old bedroom with particular interest: 'he was much affected and made a hurried movement to the door'. Thackeray confessed to feeling 'very queer' at the sight of what he was sure was his mother's bed. His own bedroom had metamorphosed into a general's dressing-room. Back in London he wrote for *Punch*, went to a play staged at a saloon in Hoxton, rode with Leech and dined among distinguished company at Lady Blessington's. But the ambiguous position he occupied amid these high-toned drawing-rooms shines through the account of his presence at a soirée given by Mrs Foxe, one of the hostesses of the day. Here he became involved in an earnest discussion of the consequences of the prevailing social unrest. Thackeray's suggestion that 'we were wicked in our scorn of the people' (he had recently reported on a Chartist meeting at Kennington Common for the *Morning Chronicle*) was greeted with apparent incredulity. 'They all thought there was poverty & discomfort to be sure,' he recorded, 'but that they were pretty good in themselves; that powder & liveries were very decent & proper though certainly absurd' – the footmen themselves would not give up these badges of office, declared one lordly contributor to the debate. Yet if Thackeray was happy to play Devil's advocate when the rights of the people came up as a conversational topic in polite society, then he was also showing the first signs of a willingness to tailor his opinions to the expectations of his audience that was to characterise much of his later work. The widespread praise for *Vanity Fair* had been tempered by complaints about authorial cynicism, and the evidence of a letter to Lady Holland suggests that these criticisms had been echoed by one or two of his high-born friends. 'I am beginning daily to see the folly of my ways and that people are a hundred times more frank kind & good natured than a certain author chooses to paint them,' he explained. He would not wear yellow any more, he maintained, in a reference to the wrappings of the monthly number: it was he who was jaundiced and not the world that was bitter. 'I will have my next book in rose colour and try and amend,' he gamely concluded.

A similar anxiety to please, or at the the a willingness to forgive old slights, seems to have coloured his attitude to the Dickens/Forster set. He was invited to the party Dickens gave at his Devonshire Terrace house to celebrate the conclusion of *Dombey and Son* on 11 April, and a few days later could be found writing to thank Forster for the latter's 'delightful' life of Goldsmith. It could hardly be said, though, that his own final stint on the concluding numbers of *Vanity Fair* took place in a congenial atmosphere. The railway shares were still costing him money, and he continued to negotiate with his stepfather's creditors. More important than either of these obligations, perhaps, he had decided that Miss Alexander, like her predecessors, was simply not up to the job of coping with Annie's precocious intellect. Still, he enjoyed bragging to his mother about his new-found acquaintance with the Duke of Devonshire, which had culminated in the duke's request that Mrs Norton should escort him to a party at the ducal mansion. The duke had called at Young Street and Thackeray had now been invited back. 'I don't care a straw for the great people I find,' he declared, having anatomised these transactions for his mother's benefit. 'Only knowing them makes me a little more impatient of the airs of the [s]mall great.' Ingratiating though the subsequent letter may be, it contains some amusing projections of the cast of *Vanity Fair*'s future careers. Becky, for example, 'now lives in a small but very pretty little house in Belgravia: and is conspicuous for her numerous charities wh. always get into the newspaper, and her unaffected piety'.

He was a success. Or was he? *Vanity Fair* had sold well, if not outstandingly (a 5,000 print-run for the first number, rising to 6,000, then falling to 4,000 for numbers seven to eleven, before settling again at 5,000 – not spectacular by early-Victorian standards). The plaudits arrived together with the bills; the pleasures came mixed with the eternal money worries. The signs of his new-won fame were everywhere apparent – in Bradbury & Evans' willingness to reprint his old favourite, *The Great Hoggarty Diamond*; in some rhapsodical compliments paid by the speaker at the annual dinner of the Royal Literary Fund – but he spent much of early May in pursuit of his stepfather's old creditors. Thirty pounds would settle the major's long-standing obligations to the gas company, he told his mother. At the same time '£300 of debts of one sort or another have been paid out of my earnings of the last 6 months Thank God'. There was another £100 owing as a result of his recent decision to have himself called to the Bar. Financially the future looked bright – Bradbury & Evans were suggesting £1,000 a year for Vanity Fair's successor, and *Punch* looked good for £700 or £750 more – but it was still difficult to predict when he might 'turn the corner', as he put it. This inbred caution, combined with the themes of *Vanity Fair*'s dénouement, produced some sober reflections on the perils of worldly success. 'But God –' he declared in a letter to his mother, 'I mean that I have many serious thoughts and will try & not be vain of praise, and humbly to say & remember the truth.'

Fending off a host of early season invitations – he apologised to Mrs Proctor on the grounds that he had been asked to three entertainments on the same evening – he pressed on with the last number. The novel's final metaphorical touch emerged in a typically spontaneous way. Dining at the Crowes' house at Hampstead, the Irish MP Torrens McCullagh leaned across to remark, 'Well, I see you are going to shut up your puppets in their box.' Thackeray beamed at the comparison, and asked permission to 'work it up'. The final paragraph, which contains these words, was written on 28 June. Dashing off a note to his mother – currently an alarmed spectator of the 1848 Paris revolution – he acknowledged a mixture of emotions: 'I have been worked so hard that I can hardly hold a pen.' He was very pleased to have done, he explained, 'very melancholy at heart, and humble in mind', trying not to feel elated 'for I get so much praise that I want keeping down'. To Mrs Proctor he declared that he had spent the previous evening 'in such a state of work and excitement as have put me in a fever'. But the task was done. The weeks leading up to his thirty-seventh birthday, which Bradbury & Evans marked by bringing out the book in volume form, brought a series of celebratory parties and dinners. The record of

18 July supplies a series of snapshots of the various things that pressed upon him – petty obligations, public success, deep emotion gathering pace behind it. In the morning he wrote to Edward Chapman asking for a fifty-pound advance on *The Kickleburys on the Rhine*, intended as his Christmas Book for 1848, to pay off his outstanding debts, and finally settled the major's account with the gas company. Later on he scribbled his mother a note 'in the midst of a tea and dinner party – apropos of the finale of VF'. Lady Pollock presided, fifty people sat down to tea, but there were 'no lords' he assured his mother, adding for good measure, 'May God Almighty keep me honest and keep pride and vanity down.' Then, returning to Young Street, he found an unexpected gift. The study was full of flowers, sent by Mrs Brookfield 'to ornament your room This Evening, with best wishes for very happy returns on your birthday'. He must believe her, Jane signed off, 'Your affectionate friend Jane O. Brookfield'. Five miles away in Camberwell, Isabella ate her dinner in Mrs Bakewell's parlour.

Why Thackeray Matters

Thackeray's collected works extend to twenty-six hardback volumes. Apart from the obvious exceptions, it is a bold hand that disturbs them on the second-hand bookseller's shelves, and for everyone who has ever ploughed through *Philip* or *The Virginians* – novels that now retain only a faint curiosity value – there must be a dozen readers of *North and South* or *The Mill on the Floss*. It is Thackeray's misfortune that, with two or three exceptions, the books on which he made his reputation should almost have disappeared from view. *Vanity Fair* remains an early-Victorian classic, with *Pendennis* not far behind, *The Book of Snobs* (as *The Snobs of England* was eventually retitled) has its admirers, and no study of nineteenth-century children's literature can quite ignore *The Rose and the Ring*, but the great works of his maturity – *Esmond* and *The Newcomes* – lie in the Victorian remainder-bin along with obscurities like *Mrs Caudle's Curtain Lectures* and *A Gallery of Literary Portraits*. For all Thackeray's status as a late-Victorian literary figurehead, this process of diminishment has been going on for over a century. Carlyle may have thought *The Newcomes* one of the grandest novels in the language, yet, as we have seen, by the 1880s critics of the Lang and Henley stamp were busying themselves with questions such as 'Is Thackeray a Cynic?' (a question that had in any case been levelled long before Thackeray's death). And when Henry James wrote his famous attack on the 'loose baggy monsters' of the Victorian novel, the author of *The Virginians* was one of his principal targets. The response of a bustling proto-modernist like James is understandable, for there is a peculiar woodenness about some of Thackeray's later work, a sad slackening of interest and design, and it is this – rather than the eternal complaints about cynicism – that led to the reaction against him. With the exception of a few things written at the very end of his life – *Lovel the Widower*, for example, or one or two of the less clotted *Roundabout Papers*, produced during his time as editor of the *Cornhill* – his post-*Vanity Fair* career is, as John Carey once put it, the history of a capitulation.

That Thackeray's genius should have fallen apart in this depressing way is a measure of his complex relation to his time. There is a rather obvious irony in the process by which the cutting young satirist of *Fraser's* and *Punch* transformed himself into the sedate and sentimental fogey of *The Newcomes*, and the irony lies in Thackeray's inability to prevent himself falling victim to the attitudes he had burlesqued in his early work. Elevated to the status of a grand literary panjandrum after the success of *Vanity Fair*, he was never quite sure of his stance towards the society he had once poked fun at but simultaneously wanted to become a part of. Like Evelyn Waugh, perhaps, a century later, Thackeray was prepared to sneer at fashionable newspapers that toadied to aristocrats, while complaining that lords no longer asked him to dinner. Throughout the second half of his career he was largely writing against the grain of his own nature, and it shows. The result is a series of intermittently dull and unhappy books, in which the sharp opinions of the early days are progressively watered down, youthful hard-headedness is coated over with sentiment, and – as Thackeray was perfectly well aware of this slide into mediocrity – the reader is presented with the spectacle of an author falling asleep over his work and then recovering himself almost from paragraph to paragraph. Nearly any chapter of *The Newcomes* picked at random will give a good idea of its curiously erratic motivation. Nothing could be flatter than the prose that discusses female constancy, the virtues of old Colonel Newcome (universally held up by Victorian critics as one of his greatest achievements) or the merits of a public-school education, and the flatness is compounded by a suspicion that the writer knows he is being false to himself. But then, almost by accident, Thackeray touches on something that really interests him – the exact shade an artist would need to use in painting Ethel Newcome's hair, say – and suddenly the style is back to its old, racy, colloquial exactness. The value of *The Newcomes* lies almost entirely in these digressions, and the sense of an older voice reasserting itself every so often amid a great deal of studied gentility. The scene in which the Reverend Honeyman gets imprisoned for debt, for example, is more or less irrelevant from the point of view of the plot, but somehow it is worth half a dozen encomia of the old colonel, simply because Thackeray is genuinely absorbed in the exposure of human folly. As a result his descriptions of the debtor's lodging house in Cursitor Street has a kind of conviction that the sham sentiment and the nods to his middle-class readers never manage to bring off. Much the same thing happens about halfway through *Philip*, when Thackeray suddenly starts interesting himself in the question of how Philip Firmin supports himself as a journalist in Paris, and for a chapter or so the novel's suety quality – its grotesques re-invented as comic villains, its odd *dutifulness* – is forgotten.

This is an exaggeration, perhaps, but not much of one, and it would be idle to pretend that Thackeray's creative decline began overnight. Nonetheless, to turn from the self-conscious 'fine writing' of Thackeray's later novels to his early work as a reporter and magazine essayist can be a bracing experience. His great period as a journalist and sketch-writer lasted from about 1840 to 1848, an apprenticeship that produced sharp-eyed pieces of reportage such as 'Going to See a Man Hanged' and 'The Second Funeral of Napoleon', a mass of burlesques and comic fragments, and longer stories that we would probably now call novellas, like *A Little Dinner at Timmins's*, *The Fatal Boots* and *A Shabby Genteel Story*. As literary journalism it has a restless, rackety quality that reflects the circumstances of its composition – written in haste, against deadlines, begun and abandoned to satisfy fleeting private or commercial whims: *A Shabby Genteel Story*, for instance, stops abruptly after a hundred pages, presumably because its author lost interest (*Philip*, written twenty years later, is an unsatisfactory sequel). But the chopped-up, fragmentary form of Thackeray's early work is an important part of its charm. *Vanity Fair*, which grew alongside it, has the same sprawling air – a jumble of queer, impressionist glimpses, scraps of detail, pieces of wayside moralising, almost any one of which can be detached from the plot without the reader noticing. Orwell thought that one of the great advantages of *Vanity Fair* was that you could pick up the book at almost any stage and still have a reasonable idea of what was going on. In saying this he was making an important point about Thackeray's attraction as a writer, his ability to saturate narrative with detail and create a world that, though bristling with intrigue, has a curiously lived-in feeling, simultaneously exotic and familiar. At the same time there is a way in which all that is memorable in *Vanity Fair* grows out of the sketches that precede it. Thackeray's minor characters, the shabby procession of cashiered officers and card-sharpers, such as Captain Rook and the Honourable Mr Deuceace, are as much at home in Becky's entourage as in an early piece like 'Captain Rook and Mr Pigeon'. Even a very early sketch like

'The Artists', which describes the painters' colonies of Soho, turns out to be a dry-run for the scenes describing Becky's home life with her profligate, portrait-painting father, and from here it is only a short step to Gandish's academy and the microscopic account of the 1830s' art world that occupies the first half of *The Newcomes*.

The range of these early pieces also reflects their grounding in Thackeray's own life. For a man born into the affluence of early-nineteenth-century Anglo-Indian society, the late 1830s brought a series of humiliations: the loss of his money, Isabella's insanity and dreary hack-work – something he found doubly disagreeable as it meant being polite to people he considered his social inferiors. All this played its part in defining the character of his locust years. Even the gradual confirmation of his abilities carried its own fatal quota of distress, and the constant reminders of his poverty were guaranteed to take the bloom off relatively exalted commissions. When Chapman and Hall made him deposit the family plate with them as security for the *Irish Sketch Book*, he characterised it as 'a kind of genteel pawn'. As it was, success hung in the balance for several years. *Vanity Fair* was very nearly a failure and never matched the sales of *Dombey and Son*, which ran concurrently. The embarrassments and indignities of these early years created a reservoir of personal experience that filtered through into his published work. The fleecing of impressionable young men by the seedy sharks of 'Captain Rook and Mr Pigeon' mirrors his own embarrassments at the card tables – travelling on the Continent in middle life, Thackeray once startled an acquaintance by claiming to have spotted Mr Deuceace's original – and the succession of rebarbative mothers-in-law harks back to his dealings with the redoubtable Mrs Shawe.

This immersion in his own experience gives Thackeray's early work an oddly personal quality. It is a cliché, of course, to say that a writer resembles a character from his own novels, but Thackeray is present in his writing in a way that many Victorian novelists are not. Whether disguised as 'Michael Angelo Titmarsh', 'Mr Spec', 'Our Fat Contributor' or any other pseudonym from his extensive list of authorial personae, he pops up continually, inserting himself into *A Shabby Genteel Story*'s list of wedding guests and even turning up at the Timminses' pretentious dinner party. In much the same way, even his more straightforward pieces of reportage are rarely detached, for the reader is always conscious of Thackeray at his elbow, so to speak, simultaneously presiding over and criticising a spectacle that consequently becomes a matter of joint appreciation. The sight of the author – or rather someone who is both more and less than the author – at large in his own text has a double function. Most obviously, it imparts a nice ambiguity to some of the moral judgments – after all, the Thackeray who discourses so wittily on the collective gluttony of 'A Dinner in the City' had presumably worked his way through the multitude of courses on offer himself – but at the same time it gives the subjects on which he touches a tangible authenticity, the feeling that the world of Fitzroy Timmins, Mrs Gashleigh and the Lough Corrib railway dispute is the author's own.

And, curiously enough, it *is* a world. The early nineteenth century comes alive under Thackeray's hand in a way quite unlike that of any other writer. A *Shabby Genteel Story* is barely a chapter old before the reader is plunged into a tremendous sub-universe made up of the melancholy history of the firm of Gann, Blubbery and Gann, small-town snobbery and tip-top fashionable swells. For a social chronicler, Thackeray's range is surprisingly narrow. He could rarely be got to see the working classes as anything other than servants – though he was capable of sympathising both with his own servants and with the servant class as a whole – and he tends to notice the effects of social phenomena rather than their causes. However, this narrowness can work to Thackeray's advantage. In particular, his interest in the club-lounging, prize-fighting, rat-catching side of early-Victorian life, with its faded bucks in padded stays and decadent young men, enabled him to create characters that were beyond the range of a Dickens or a Trollope. Major Pendennis seems rather a subtle creation compared to the pantomime aristocrats of *Nicholas Nickleby*. Lord Cinqbars in *A Shabby Genteel Story* belongs to a distinctive early-Victorian fictional genre – the lisping young sprig of nobility with his dandified airs and his passion for 'intrigues' – but the sharpness of the portrait stops him from degenerating into a simple type.

This eye for human quiddity is especially important when it comes to determining what it is that Thackeray writes about, and the way in which he approaches his task. Broadly speaking, he wrote at a time when social barriers were markedly more fluid than they had once been or were subsequently to become. To read any novel of the 1840s is to enter a world of clamorous social upheaval in which new money, founded on industrial and business expertise, is trying to infiltrate the old *rentier* class. A characteristic symbol of this social battle is the alliance between blue blood and commercial know-how. Mr Dombey, whose social origins are obscure but whose financial cachet is sufficient to allow him to marry the quasi-aristocratic Edith Granger, is a man of his time. Sir Brian Newcome, the son of a self-made manufacturer, who becomes a Tory MP, acquires a baronetcy and carries off the niece of the Marquis of Steyne, belongs to the same category of upwardly mobile entrepreneurs. Understandably, the knock-on effects of this process of assimilation were felt further along the social ladder. Whereas in a late-period novel like *The Newcomes* Thackeray takes a keen interest in the ability of an older, aristocratic class to sustain and reinvent itself through infusions of mercantile money, his earlier work is pitched rather lower down the social scale, at about the level of the professional middle classes, with occasional variations upward (Fitzroy Timmins is a barrister on nodding terms with the local MP) and downward (the Ganns, say, in *A Shabby Genteel Story*). Whatever the precise gradations of status, nearly all of Thackeray's early work is concerned with social advancement: the Timminses, who *would* give their little dinner; Stubbs in *The Fatal Boots* and his preposterous 'marriage in high life'. The early sketches are full of this kind of vainglory, and the satire is nearly always directed at the type of mind that regards an invitation to dine with a peer as the absolute guarantee of moral excellence. As a writer, Thackeray is at his best when observing social distinctions – his high-flown passages are invariably failures – and their corollary, the dreadful sham of 'keeping up appearances'. The exposure of the debt-bilking, fly-by-night side of Victorian life, in which the possession of a house in Mayfair is pretty sure to be balanced by a grocer's bill a yard long, is a kind of obsession with him. In the Ganns' attempt to eke out a spurious gentility with the proceeds of a lodging house may perhaps be detected the origins of the famous chapter in *Vanity Fair* describing the lavish lifestyle of Colonel and Mrs Rawdon Crawley, 'How to live well on nothing a year'.

Typically Thackeray achieves these effects by way of an intense comic specificity, an attention to detail that can sometimes become rather stifling. Any modern reader of his work must be struck by its practicality. He is one of the few Victorian novelists from whom you could find out how to order a dinner or discount a bill, and in 'Memorials of Gourmandising' he produced an extended version of the modern restaurant column. One result of this absorption in milieu is a chronic digressiveness, a continual shifting away from the main progress of the story in search of fragments of detail that fascinate Thackeray simply because they are detail. When Fitch, the painter based on John Brine, whom Thackeray had met in the Paris ateliers, falls in love with Caroline Gann we get three stanzas of his sententious poetry. Similarly, Rosa Timmins' social crusade is prefaced by all kinds of information about her previous triumphs, how she outdanced Mrs Rowdy in the Scythe Mazurka at the Polish ball, headed by Mrs Hugh Slasher, thereby revenging herself for Mrs Rowdy's success at the bazaar in aid of the Daughters of Decayed Muffin Men, etc., etc. It is worth pointing out that these digressions are not simply incidental: they are also there to make an artistic point. One can acknowledge Walter Bagehot's complaint that Thackeray had a compulsion to 'amass petty detail to prove that tenth-rate people were ever striving to be ninth-rate people' while wondering if this does not miss an important part of Thackeray's acuteness, for nearly every scrap of outwardly superfluous material that he intrudes into his character sketches turns out to have some bearing on the finished portrait. The details about Mrs Timmins' married life, for example, and Mrs Rowdy's allegations that she threw over Captain Higgs on her mother's instructions, are not just an optional garnish but the first hint of the underlying tension that exists between Rosa and Mrs Gashleigh. The description of Mrs Topham Sawyer sitting down to breakfast in a Madonna front, a kind of hairpiece fashionable at the time, has a similar effect in harnessing people to their environment by way of specifics. Another writer would have said merely that she wore a wig. By going into detail, and hinting at the absurdity of a haughty old woman got up in the style of a biblical painting, Thackeray manages to burlesque Mrs Sawyer out of existence.

Amid all these accretions of detail, the moral point is usually a very simple one. The 'message' of a piece like A Little Dinner at Timmins's is straightforward – don't live above your income; don't nurture foolish ambitions – balanced by the hint that by and large such injunctions are futile, that the average human will always nurture foolish dreams, and it is of this that the fundamental comedy of life consists. It is impossible to read Thackeray for very long without being pulled up sharply by his matter-of-factness, his casual acceptance of rogues and rascals, his delight in establishing that even the most outwardly scrupulous people are still motivated by selfishness and vanity. The idealism that animates a contemporary like Dickens is, to Thackeray, a flying in the face of human nature. In the context of Victorian notions of improvement and self-help, this can make some of his judgments look highly subversive. One of his favourite themes, for instance, is that to come down in the world is not necessarily a bad thing. The Ganns in A Shabby Genteel Story are, if they did but know it, far happier in fly-blown middle-class Margate than they would have been in the polite society they regard as their due – the husband a figure of consuming interest at his club, his wife able to brag endlessly about her noble forebears to a circle of draggled acquaintances who treat her with unfeigned respect. Thackeray takes up this idea again in The Newcomes, going so far as to suggest that one of the principal pleasures of human existence lies not in living with your equals but with your inferiors. Society is naturally competitive, and only a fool would try to pretend otherwise. Only a fool, too, would shuffle people unhesitatingly into packs marked 'good' and 'bad'. For all the contempt levelled at the Captain Rooks of this world, a sketch like 'Captain Rook and Mr Pigeon' is surprisingly even-handed. Rook may be a heartless villain, but he lives a wretched life – and knows he lives it – while Pigeon is a fool for allowing himself to be duped. These attitudes might make Thackeray an imperfect moralist by the lofty standards of the mid-nineteenth century, but they give his best work a kind of sharp-eyed common sense, a refusal to settle for easy sentiment when hard experience suggests otherwise. The episode in Vanity Fair in which the bankrupted Sedleys end up in lodgings in Fulham run by an old retainer who protests undying loyalty is a typical example of this. Dickens would have painted the scene up in a rosy glow of faithful servitude. Thackeray, being Thackeray, treats the ensuing quarrels between Mrs Clapp and her former employers as the most natural thing in the world.

The Sedleys are a good example of what might be called the regressive tendency in Thackeray. His characters have a habit of returning to the point in life where they began, cancelling out the achievements of their interim careers by over-reach or foolishness. Colonel Newcome ends up a pensioner in the almshouse attached to the school of his boyhood – Charterhouse, of course, which his creator had so disliked. By transferring himself from the grandeur of Russell Square to the faded gentility of the Fulham Road, old Mr Sedley is returning – figuratively at least – to the circumstances of his early life. In one sense this is what Thackeray himself did throughout his own career. As a general rule, his gaze is wholly backward-looking, and even the very early pieces of reportage are shot through with an aching nostalgia. In preferring the past to the present, Thackeray was doing no more than follow the general tendency of the Victorian novel – *Middlemarch*, after all, is set at around the time of the Reform Bill, and Dickens' novels typically lag twenty or thirty years behind the date of their composition – but there is a peculiar intensity about this evocation of bygone experience. George Eliot's abiding interest may lie in the repercussions of 1832, but Thackeray's gaze extends even further back to the Regency world of his boyhood. In the end there is a way in which this vanished paradise of Miss Decamp's dance and footmen in floury wigs – a sort of fairy-tale world ablaze with light and colour – is more real to him than his adult life. The great inventions and scientific discoveries of the 1840s are at best noisy inconveniences, and if he mentions the existence of the steam train it is generally the prelude to a lament about the decline of the stage coach. Usually Thackeray's nostalgia emerges through his obsession with artefacts – books, kinds of food, styles of dress. Bob Stubbs' desire for a pair of top-boots in *The Fatal Boots* reflects Thackeray's own boyhood yearnings, and it is rare for two or three chapters of his occasional writings to pass without some mention of confectionery, rout-cakes, the tart-woman and so on. As we have seen, the literature of Thackeray's childhood supplies an enduring theme to his work. It is significant, perhaps, that *Manfroni: or the One-handed Monk* and Mrs Porter's novels, which Caroline Gann pores over in *A Shabby Genteel Story*, should turn up again in 'Tunbridge Toys', a piece written at the very end of his life. There are differences of emphasis, certainly, and the reminiscences of Thackeray's later years can sometimes seem quite wooden in their sorrowings over lost time, but the elegiac note is a constant. One of the most attractive features of his writing, even as a very young man, is his apparent ability to measure experience and sensation by yardsticks that frequently predate his own birth.

Looking for the moment when this immense, teeming world – dominated by the figure of the writer moving within it – first moves into focus, one returns inexorably to 'Going to See a Man Hanged', first published in *Fraser's* in 1840. At first it seems to be not much more than a series of digressions: the recent debates in the House of Commons; notorious executions of the past; the composition of the crowd; Rabelais, Fielding and Dickens. Courvoisier's despatch, when it comes, is done in a few swift brush-strokes – the death bell making 'a dreadful quick, feverish kind of jingling noise', the victim himself, who 'opened his hands in a helpless kind of way and clasped them once or twice together' – but you are suddenly conscious that it is the centrepiece in a panorama of early-Victorian England, and that in assembling all his incidental remarks about Lord John, the crowd shouting 'butter fingers' after the clumsy execution of the Cato Street conspirators, and the comments of the onlookers, Thackeray is saying something important not only about the shape of contemporary society but about human psychology in general. When he writes about his disgust for murder, 'but it was for *the murder I saw done*', the reader emerges with the queer sense not only of history having come alive but of something else, something at once awful and universal, walking side by side with him down Snow Hall past the murmuring crowds into the silent dawn.

XIV
The Angel at the Hearth

'V.F. being over it is as if the back bone of your stays were out.'
Letter to his mother, July 1848

'If you were only in some way related to me, I might say what I chose.'
Mrs Brookfield, 2 January 1849

I n 1848 Thackeray was thirty-seven, an age at which most champion novelists are merely getting the bit between their teeth. But the success of the previous year had been won at a price. He was tired, over-stretched – Mrs Brookfield's letters frequently lament the pace at which this new hothouse life got lived – aware of the pressures he was placing himself under but constitutionally unable to ease off. No sooner had he finished *Vanity Fair* than *Pendennis* was beginning to take shape in his mind, another huge Victorian doorstopper that would not be finished until the end of 1850. To add to the family worries that continued to press upon him was the question of his own health. For all his burly physique – his weight went up to sixteen stone in his late thirties – he was not a strong man. In the autumn of 1849 he was seriously ill, forced to endure a long convalescence and put off work on *Pendennis* for several months. It took another serious illness at Rome in the winter of 1853–4 to establish an irrevocable pattern of physical decline – it is true to say that in the last ten years of his life he was never really well – but already in the late 1840s one can see the advancing spectre of illness rising up to claim him. He was also oppressed by the fundamental necessity to earn a living. This anxiety over the need to provide for Annie and Minnie in the event of his death, not to mention the recluse at Camberwell, eventually became a kind of mania: the letters back from his second American trip of 1855–6 – undertaken solely for financial reasons – are quite monotonous in their obsession with money: life seen simply as a profit-and-loss account.

None of this, inevitably, was calculated to inflame his muse; but there was also a suspicion that the muse would turn out to be inconstant. In the late twentieth century we tend to take writers' 'commitment' to their profession for granted. Compared to a Borges or a Mahfouz, Thackeray's attachment to his trade – and for all his gentlemanliness he rarely baulked at calling it a trade – looks shaky in the extreme. Significantly, he marked the final leg of *Vanity Fair* by having himself called to the Bar – his name-plate remained on the wall outside his *Punch* colleague Tom Taylor's chambers for several years – on the grounds that it would help land him a job that would absolve him from the need to write for a living, and he spent much of his later life angling for a public appointment, preferably one with minimal duties. September 1848, for instance, brought the enticing news that the job of assistant secretary at the Post Office would shortly be falling vacant. 'What a place for a man of letters!' he exclaimed jocosely to Lady Blessington, his confidante in these and other matters. 'I think if Lord Clanricarde [the postmaster general] would give it to me I would satisfy my employers, and that my profession would be pleased by hearing of the appointment of one of us.' Would it? In fact many of Thackeray's fellow authors, particularly at the lower end of the scale, resented this hob-nobbing with lords and his apparently effortless transformation into a creature of what would now infallibly be stigmatised as the 'Establishment'. These were the kind of people who took the side of his adversary, Edmund Yates, in the Garrick Club row of a decade later. Lady Blessington promised to put in a word, Lord Clanricarde was sympathetic, but as Anthony Trollope later pointed out, 'The services were wanted of a man who had experience in the Post Office; and, moreover, it was necessary that the feelings of other gentlemen should be consulted.' The age of aristocratic jobbery in public appointments was coming to an end. There was a nervousness about some of these attempts on the mid-Victorian upper labour market, a profound anxiety over his professional stamina. Why could one not be like Dickens, a fount of seemingly inexhaustible application and imagination (one of the reasons that Thackeray admired *David Copperfield*, which began serial publication early in 1849, was that it put him on his 'mettle')? And yet there were other reasons for Thackeray's decline as a writer that had nothing to do with fatigue, money worries or doubts about professional commitment. They were artistic, or perhaps social, in origin and arose out of his efforts to adjust his temperament to the sensibilities of the people for whom he wrote.

Pendennis, which occupied him for nearly two years, exemplifies the beginning of this process of retreat. Without labouring the point, it is a novel whose ultimate aesthetic effect is compromised by a reliance on what its audience expected from the fiction they read. *Vanity Fair* had been quite impartial in its attacks on human folly and selfishness – this was what attracted discerning early critics such as G.H. Lewes. Its motivating force, perhaps, was an attempt to see people in the round; its irony the fact that the villain of the piece has ten times the vitality of the 'good' characters who supplant her and whose virtue is, in consequence, equally flat. Though it contains some subtle portraits – Major Pendennis, for instance, with his far from straightforward moral code – *Pendennis* is much more a matter of 'good people' and 'bad people'. Simultaneously, the novel is hamstrung by its subservience to one of the chief conventions of the early-Victorian novel. One of the features that gives *Vanity Fair* its dynamism is its status as 'a novel without a hero'. *Pendennis*, on the other hand, concerns itself almost exclusively with the doings of Arthur Pendennis – a conventional enough premise for a Victorian novel, but one that presents its creator with at least two insoluble problems. The first was of his own making. 'Since the author of Tom Jones was buried, no writer of fiction among us has been permitted to depict to his utmost power A MAN,' he declared in the preface to the first hardbound edition, before going on to suggest that 'a little more frankness than is customary has been attempted in this story'. For all this, the novel virtually falls over itself in its haste to call a spade a large blunt instrument used for shovelling earth. The early scenes, in which the teenaged Pen falls in love with a travelling actress eight years older than himself and has to be rescued by his worldly old uncle, are brilliantly done, but the Cambridge section is a highly misleading portrait of the kind of life that Thackeray himself led at Trinity in the late 1820s. Later on, in his London career, Pen's real-life equivalent would almost certainly have seduced Fanny Bolton, the lodging-house keeper's daughter whose virtue becomes one of the novel's great moral issues, and Thackeray knew it. The consequence is a sort of eternal half-heartedness, a pulling of punches that leaves Pen's character stranded halfway between an acute psychological study of early-Victorian young manhood and sheer wish-fulfilment. This kind of geniality penetrates deep into the novel's core. The collection of shabby literary hangers-on who cluster round the tables of the publishers Bacon and Bungay are the objects of some very mild satire indeed, while the portrait of 'Captain Shandon', clearly based on Maginn, who writes the *Pall Mall Gazette*'s prospectus from his den in the Fleet Prison, carefully omits all reference to Maginn's womanising: his *alter ego* is presented merely as an uxurious literary gentleman in reduced circumstances with a weakness for drink.

The other problem that Thackeray faced in his creation of Arthur Pendennis was the one confronting virtually every Victorian novelist. Having produced your hero, what do you do with him? Essentially the plot of *Pendennis* consists of Pen undergoing a few vicissitudes of a not very exacting kind, experiencing a slightly ambiguous moral transformation, marrying the infinitely dreary Laura Bell – the agent of this change in character – and going off to a life of dignified domestic bliss. Orwell made the point of Dickens' heroes that they tend to combine a tremendous vitality with utter purposelessness, and to a degree – even given his calling as a literary man – this is true of Pen. In fact old Major Pendennis' snobbish vision of the ideal gentlemanly life – an exacting round of carriage drives, pompous dinners and 'seeing your friends' – is one to which Pen, with a few slight reservations, would probably subscribe himself. The resultant impasse between on the one hand psychological realism and on the other period convention turns up once more in the major's all too docile old age, when he is reconciled to Laura (previously seen as an impediment to his schemes) and succumbs to her pious blandishments. A shallow old snob of the major's type would, one feels, have gone on being a shallow old snob. To do him justice, Thackeray was aware of these compromises, and there is a kind of fatalism in the way he knuckles down to some of the contemporary proprieties and accepts some of the rewards on offer. His letter of May 1849 to Lady Blessington suggesting that the world is a great deal better than some satirists have painted it goes on to remark that 'I believe the world goes on being very gay. I reel from dinner-party to dinner-party. I wallow in turtle and swim in claret and Shampang.'

A similar fatalism, one imagines, informed his relationship with Mrs Brookfield, here entering its most intimate phase. The Thackeray/Brookfield correspondence extends to several hundred pages, bulked out yet further by the letters exchanged between the two men and between husband and wife. The prevailing tone is confidential, fond, unquestionably sincere, and yet, for all Jane's subsequent overscorings and excisions, painfully innocuous. Both parties, for the most part, seem to know exactly what they are doing and the limits that constrained them, to the extent that they sometimes appear to be consciously living up to the roles that the situation had assigned to them. At the same time, if this was an archetypal 'passionate friendship' of the kind enjoyed by muscular young undergraduates, then, like even the feeblest of Thackeray's novels, it was always capable of flaring up in unexpected ways.

As a famous novelist, at a time when literary celebrity possessed a glamour since transferred to the cinema, Thackeray was subject to the most intense public scrutiny. He dined out, was seen everywhere; half of London wrote accounts of his appearance and demeanour. What remains, a century and a half later, is a bewildering mixture of opinion. Even among the literary world – especially among the literary world – there were wildly differing views of his achievement, and what he might be thought to represent. To an aspiring literary man like the young James Hannay, Thackeray seemed the epitome of principled authorship. Such was Hannay's devotion that he dedicated his 1849 novel *King Dobbs* to his hero 'with the respect and affection due to his genius and character'. Charlotte Brontë, who was introduced to Thackeray in 1849 by her publisher George Smith, had much more mixed feelings. These were largely to do with his inability to live up to the Olympian ideals she had credited him with, but also to do with his colossal lack of tact. To read her remarks about him from the early 1850s, mostly conveyed in letters to Smith, is to chart a long process of disillusionment. 'He is a very tall man', she wrote after meeting him for the first time, '– above six feet high, with a peculiar face – not handsome, very ugly indeed, generally somewhat stern & satirical in expression, but capable of a kind look.' Subsequently a succession of minor awkwardnesses began to mar the idealised portrait she had built up of him. When she came to dine at Young Street with Smith, Thackeray grew so bored with the post-prandial atmosphere of the drawing-room that he left the house for his club, compounding this failing by blowing his guest's incognito ('Boys,' he is supposed to have exclaimed to the circle of heads that greeted him at the Garrick, 'I have been dining with Jane Eyre'). By early 1851 Charlotte was writing to Jane Taylor to confirm that 'All you say of Mr T is most graphic & characteristic. He stirs in me both sorrow & anger. Why should he lead so harassing a life? Why should his mocking tongue so perversely deny the better feelings of his better moods?' And she assured Smith that Thackeray's dilatoriness over finishing *The Kickleburys on the Rhine* – his Christmas book for 1850 – made her hair stand on end. Though her first estimate was that Thackeray was a 'great and strange man', she left a tart little portrait of his social aspirations – dancing attendance on a collection of society ladies as they prepared to attend a fancy-dress ball given by the queen. 'Their pet & darling, Mr T, of course sympathises with them,' she wrote. 'He was here yesterday to dinner, & left very early in the evening – in order that he might visit respectively the Duchess of Norfolk, the Marchioness of Londonderry, Ladies Chesterfield and Clanricarde, and see them all in their fancy costumes of the reign of Charles II before they set out for the Palace!' Charlotte concluded that her former idol was 'a good deal spoiled by this', which is not so much a display of sour grapes as an expression of genuine moral unease.

There was to be a good deal of spoiling in the second half of 1848. Late July found him staying at Canterbury, where Arthur Shawe was quartered with his regiment. There was a plan to accompany Arthur on his forthcoming march to London, but in the end Thackeray cried off. 'I thought it sounded like very good fun,' he explained to Mrs Proctor, 'and so it would be if I had the courage to go through with it. But I'm too old.' Reviews of the bound edition of *Vanity Fair* were coming in – a good one from Forster in the *Examiner* cancelled out by R.S. Rintoul's suggestion in the *Spectator* that Thackeray's interest in Bohemia implied 'a want of imagination and large comprehension of life'. From Canterbury he moved on via the Channel ports to Brussels and the beginnings of a solitary continental holiday. The emotional release of finishing his novel had left him exhausted and depressed. *En route* he reported himself 'utterly cast down and more under the influence of blue devils than I ever remember before', until the dawn sky and the feeling of the boat cutting through the water beneath him restored his good humour. From Brussels he sent back a brilliantly funny and observant letter to Jane, in which memories of life and art came mingled together: a French lady at the table d'hôte briskly sending away dishes ('Experience told me it was a little Grisette giving herself airs'); going to the Hôtel de la Terrasse where Becky had stayed and on the way passing George Osborne's lodging. In the aftermath of his sustained feat of creative imagination it was difficult to distinguish between illusion and reality. 'How curious it is!' he exclaimed at one point. 'I believe perfectly in all those people & feel quite an interest in the Inn in wh. they lived.' The journey from Brussels to Spa and the first few days spent at this fashionable summer watering hole sparked an equally vivid and sharp-eyed letter. Installed at the Hôtel des Pays Bas, he worked on *Pendennis* and spent hours at the gaming-tables, fascinated by the attitudes of the players. The intensity of a woman player particularly intrigued him. 'She has her whole soul in the pastime, pulls out her five franc pieces in the most timid way, and watches them disappear under the croupier's rake with eyes so uncommonly sad and tender.'

Such is the sparkle of these letters that one wonders, for all the evidence of the superscription, to whom they were actually addressed. Jane certainly had her doubts, forwarding one to her husband with instructions to take care of it, as it might be intended for publication for all they knew. In making this point Jane was also demonstrating a certain shrewdness about the nature of her relationship with Thackeray, and in particular its semi-public character. One may admire a lady, with the full if occasionally rather haughty consent of her husband, and one may send her effervescent letters from abroad, but the reader is entitled to wonder – seeing that each letter was immediately passed on to a third party and that the thought of eventual publication was already in the air – just how intimate they were intended to be. The answer, perhaps, is that it reflected a certain kind of intimacy with which an early Victorian would have been much more familiar, and infinitely more capable of assimilating, than the audience of a century and a half later. Confronted by Thackeray's feelings for Jane, and vice versa, the late-twentieth-century observer immediately looks for subterfuge, concealment and guilt. Had such materials been available to them, the contemporary audience would have looked for (and found) brotherly and sisterly affection, transparency, a mature acceptance of known feelings. All the same the nature of these relationships – between Thackeray and a woman he was clearly moving closer towards, between Jane and her husband, and between Thackeray and his old college friend – was beginning to change, and the tensions that eventually overcame them have their roots in the events of late 1848.

Ironically, it was an improvement in Brookfield's fortunes that brought Thackeray and Jane closer together. Earlier in the year he had finally obtained his schools inspectorship and a consequent rise in salary. But if poverty had enforced one kind of marital separation, then relative affluence tended to promote another. By April, and with the aid of family subsidies, Jane and her maid were installed at 15 Portman Street, joined soon afterwards by her young cousin Harry Hallam, then in his early twenties. From both parties' point of view there was something unsatisfactory about the situation. Brookfield's new duties frequently took him out of London for weeks at a stretch. Meanwhile, Jane's health remained poor – Thackeray diagnosed hypochondria – and she spent much of her time languishing on the drawing-room sofa. Although this sequestration gave Thackeray a welcome excuse to visit, it would be wrong to read too much into his continual calls at Portman Street in the early part of 1848. Jane's reputation as a minor literary hostess endured: 'around that sofa gathered all that was best and brightest then in London', one of her descendants proudly asserted. This is an exaggeration, but she had her admirers, notably Aubrey de Vere, who sent her his poems, and Thackeray's friend Stephen Spring Rice. In this context, Thackeray's attentions were only those that could have been expected of a devoted family friend. Even when professional obligations kept them apart, he sent books and magazines that he thought might raise an invalid's spirits, and at one point asked his friend Mrs Sartoris to go and sing to 'a sick lady of his acquaintance' (overcome by the beauty of Mrs Sartoris' voice, and finding words inadequate to express her thanks, Jane kissed her entertainer's hand, only to suffer agonies of embarrassment over whether this was the correct thing to do). Simultaneously he kept up his usual stream of letters to Brookfield, whose attitude to the salon regularly convened in his drawing-room was one of mild satisfaction: in fact he seems rather to have relished the attentions paid to his wife on the not implausible grounds that they reflected well on himself.

All the same he was capable of complaining, and one or two of his rejoinders to his wife on the subject of their mutual friend in the summer of 1848 betray a streak of tartness. Thackeray's letters were becoming more personal, more exclusively devoted to Jane's interests rather than those of the husband to whom they were forwarded or who read them over her shoulder, and Brookfield did not like it. 'Thank you for the Thackeray note,' he wrote to his wife on receiving one of the Brussels letters. 'I think him a very much over-rated person.' This may just be one of Brookfield's little jokes to his wife – and their letters abound in complicitous private amusements – but it may also denote unease, not so much at the depth of feeling being expressed towards Jane but at his own exclusion from it. Undoubtedly Thackeray's presence on the edge (or rather in the centre) of the Brookfields' marriage exacerbated some of the fractures that existed within it. Aloof and outwardly unemotional – he is on record as expressing his 'detestation' of sentiment – Brookfield was a difficult man to get on with. The couple's childless state had lasted for nearly eight years and there were times when Brookfield seems to have shied away from the conventional intimacies of married life. Staying with Jane in Southampton at around this time, he decamped to a neighbour's house on the grounds that their original hosts could not provide him with a separate dressing-room. This does not mean that Brookfield did not love his wife, merely that there were fissures in their marriage, which Thackeray's presence could only enlarge. Almost certainly Thackeray was unaware of this. For all his subtlety in analysing emotion in print, he could be highly imperceptive of the real emotional life going on around him, and the realisation that a young married man with his own relationship to lead may not have wanted his constant presence on the drawing-room carpet came comparatively late. His tactlessness occasionally reached elephantine proportions, as when Brookfield discovered that Thackeray had snipped the valedictory 'Yours affly JOB' off one of Jane's letters and carried it about in a purse as a kind of talisman. This led Brookfield to remonstrate with his wife. 'I do think at near 30, one may take up a line of one's own,' Jane replied, kindly but firmly, 'and when one feels affectionately, one may venture to say so . . . It is not as if Mr Thack. were some young Adonis in the guards.' It was not – he was grey-haired and nearly forty – but the increasingly intimate tone of the correspondence that autumn must have given Brookfield considerable grounds for disquiet.

Meanwhile, Thackeray was still at Spa enjoying his leisure and sending long letters back to friends and relatives. Writing to his mother he acknowledged that his financial worries would be diminished if he could learn to live frugally. A careful appraisal of the Young Street establishment suggested that this was impossible. He needed somebody to run his messages; there had to be a cook and someone to look after the children; the horse – he persisted with his afternoon rides – 'is the best doctor I get in London'. In short, he concluded, 'there are 100 good reasons for a lazy liberal not extravagant but costly way of life'. But the blue devils had gone and he was enjoying himself – writing the first chapter of *Pendennis* and taking walks and rides. The countryside around Spa appealed to him: 'a sweet peaceful friendly look, that I'm sure I shall remember with pleasure a long time hence'. From Twickenham, where the children were quartered with Miss Alexander, came a 'stunning' letter from Annie, which seemed quite wonderful for its cleverness and humour. He prolonged his holiday until the end of the third week in August. Literary London was deserted (the *Punch* Authors book for 12 August runs 'Douglas [Jerrold] at Guernsey, Taylor on the Circuit, Thackeray at Brussels, Horace Mayhew at Margate' – somehow a skeleton staff managed to keep the paper in production). Thackeray returned to find that 1,500 copies of *Vanity Fair* had been sold in volume form, and to recommend the advantages of Spa to Brookfield, who was prone to worry about his lungs. 'Y not take Madam there: go drink, bathe, and be cured.'

Early September, however, found him returned to his former melancholy. The Post Office job was slipping between his fingers. He went to Brighton for two days intending that the rest of Young Street should follow him, but then cancelled the excursion owing to lack of funds. 'I have got a pile of bills before me now that by heaven are perfectly ludicrous,' he informed Mrs Proctor. 'I can't think of transporting this extravagant household out of the parish.' An old flame, Virginia Pattle, sister of the equally attractive Theodosia, had been at Brighton, 'lovely, interesting and unwell', but the re-encounter left him unmoved. 'I did not care two pence,' he decided: in any case he knew that she had never cared for him. Still, it was painful to recall how 'we used to admire the Scottish Chiefs once and cry over Thaddeus of Warsaw. Fond follies of youth.' But it was another youthful memory that lay at the heart of his depression. Exactly eight years had passed since Isabella threw herself into the sea off the Isle of Wight, 'and she has been dead or worse ever since'. All he could remember of the time, Thackeray concluded in testimony to the Proctors' help, was that 'some people were very kind to me'. He took up the theme again a few days later in a farewell letter to Jane Shawe, who was about to leave for India. This is worth quoting at length, not simply for its genuine sense of affection and loss, but for the shrewd appraisal of an imaginary Isabella who had kept her sanity long enough to see him triumph:

What a whirl of life I've seen since then, but never better I think . . . – don't you recollect her singing and her sweet voice? She goes to Epsom tomorrow when you sail for India. Go, stay, die, prosper, she doesn't care. Amen. Her anxious little soul would have been alarmed at my prosperities such as they are. She was always afraid of people flattering me: and I get a great deal of that sort of meat nowadays –

Simultaneously his affection for Jane Brookfield – at any rate that part of it expressed in his frequent letters – grew ever more intense. Off to stay with Sir Thomas and Lady Cullum at Bury St Edmunds early in October (Jane was visiting the Elton family seat at Clevedon near Bristol), he reported a bachelor dinner with Brookfield and a forlorn excursion along Portman Street shortly after her departure: 'the usual boy started forward to take the horse – I laughed a sad laugh – I didn't want nobody to take the horse. It is a long time since you were away.' This strikes a plaintive note, but one can speculate over the degree of self-consciousness that may have invested it. If Jane sometimes wondered whether his letters to her were ultimately intended for publication, then clearly the same thought had occurred to Thackeray. A month or so earlier he had lamented his inability to write natural letters any more. On the point of making some joke about his money worries, he signs off: 'I was just going to say something, but think I in future ages when this letter comes to be seen, they will say he was in embarrassed circumstances, he was heedless and laughed at his prodigality, he was etc.' This desire not to be misrepresented in any future reckoning up of his life emerges in a second letter to Jane, sent a few days after the fruitless visit to Portman Street. Writing from Brighton, where he had retreated once more, he reports re-reading *The Great Hoggarty Diamond* on the occasion of its reissue, 'and after all I see on reading over my book, that the woman I have been perpetually describing is not you nor my mother but that poor little wife of mine, who now does not care 2d. for anything but her dinner and her glass of porter'.

Was Jane cast down or reassured by this revelation? It is impossible to say. Back from Brighton, Thackeray found the usual distractions rising to waylay him. Major and Mrs Carmichael-Smyth had arrived on a visit ('It was quite a sight to see the poor old mother with her children,' he reported to Brookfield): he was writing for the *Morning Chronicle* again, seduced by an offer of five guineas a piece; and wishing that the first number of *Pendennis*, out in a fortnight, was 'better'. His projected Christmas book, a satirical account of a continental journey entitled *The Kickleburys on the Rhine*, looked as if it would have to be postponed: there was a revolution taking place in Germany, which made it all 'much too serious', he told Edward Chapman. In its place he set to work on a tale of unrequited love set in a public school, *Dr Birch and His Young Friends*. Then, in the fourth week of October, he set off to visit the Elton family house at Clevedon Court.

What took place at Clevedon at the end of October 1848 is beyond the range of forensic analysis. Both the Brookfields had been staying in the house, but William had left before Thackeray's arrival. In his absence, late one evening, something happened between Thackeray and Jane that took their relationship into a new orbit. Thackeray's recapitulation of the incident, written in French – which he tended to adopt at moments of high emotion – talks about 'that clear voice which called me at night at Clevedon'. The same letter represents him as one of the damned and Jane as an 'angel full of pity', adding, 'You will come to me in that way, I am sure – You will give me one of your sweet smiles.' What seems to have happened is that Jane, alone and bemoaning her solitary condition, confided some of her unhappiness. Whatever was said, and whatever chaste hand-clasps may have been exchanged, the letters they subsequently sent one another during the remainder of 1848 show a sharp rise in the emotional temperature. Jane's sign-off now becomes 'Always your faithful sister Jane' and 'Ever your friend Jane Brookfield'. 'I must say to someone that I love you,' Thackeray wrote in the letter recalling their time together at Clevedon. 'Why not? To you, to William, to anyone who will listen to me.' The last six weeks of 1848 brought a continual exchange of notes in which Thackeray, at least, grows steadily more confidential: discussing Lever's lampooning of him in *Roland Cashel*, published that autumn (where he appears as 'Elias Howle'); musing over the unexpected death of Charles Buller ('If I were to die I cant bear to think of my mother living beyond me, as I daresay she will,' he wrote prophetically, 'but isn't it awful awful sudden? There go wit fame friendship high repute'). Perhaps most significantly – for it shows once more his deep, elegiac yearning for lost time – he turned up a copy of the essay on Fielding written for *The Times* in summer 1840. Immediately a series of painful recollections came surging back: of writing the piece at Margate, where he walked each day to a bowling green three miles away and sat scribbling in an arbour before returning to his lodgings 'and wondering what was the melancholy oppressing the poor little woman'.

As Christmas approached and he struggled to complete *Dr Birch and*

His Young Friends (working 'day & night' he told Fitz) along with the next number of *Pendennis*, the stream of letters grew to a torrent. Jane was staying at Southampton, prompting Thackeray to write in a highly sentimental vein: 'When I am alone I come back to you & think of you o so kindly. It is just $10\frac{1}{2}$ o'clock. I wonder what you are doing . . .?' (Here Jane cut out twenty words beyond recall.) There is also an odd, tentative postscript, much overscored by Jane, which shows Thackeray momentarily losing his nerve and hesitating before taking the letter to the post office. Even without the excisions it has a peculiar, fragmentary quality, intimating that 'Wm. does not like too much writing', that 'I am only to write occasionally to you', plus a reference to 'dignified and quite proper'. Eventually the letter got posted. Three letters from Jane followed in the space of as many days. One skirts around the question of how her husband might be receiving these tender notes: 'I can't help adding from a sudden impulse how *very* kind Wm. has been to me all the time we have been here & he is now much fonder of you than of anyone . . .' All the same, she thought that he sometimes wished 'less said', only 'you are a poetical kind of writer & recalling *that*, I believe after all he wd. not wish it otherwise – so write as you like & please to forgive this rambling letter & will you *burn it*?' The letter stayed unburnt. On Christmas Eve came the report of William's response to Thackeray's previous letter. 'I wonder how you mean to answer it,' Brookfield is supposed to have said. Jane asked what he meant, upon which her husband laughed '& said he was not going to dictate my letters, but that I was rather peculiar in my views & he was not sure that we should all be agreed as to what was suitable to be written however great an intimacy might be'. It was all very well to write, but she had better keep to the commonplace. Another letter was despatched on Boxing Day, in which Jane confessed to 'brooding', 'fatigue' and 'a painful state of sensitiveness', suggesting that 'sometimes kindness *crushes* instead of raising one's cheerfulness'. She added that William had told her some time ago that she ought never to write anything she would not care to see put on public display at Charing Cross.

Each of these, of course, is a love letter. But what, collectively, do they amount to? Occasionally one emerges from them with the feeling that the person Jane is really addressing is her husband, that in returning these solicitous replies she is talking to Brookfield by default. Certainly his shadow hangs over the correspondence with sufficient regularity to draw him irrevocably into it. The catchpenny question about Thackeray's intimacy with Jane – how far did it go? – is scarcely worth asking. Thackeray was a married man, or as he once tellingly put it 'a widower with a wife alive'. Jane was a clergyman's wife, whose sense of propriety occasionally seemed rather alarming even to her friends ('I defy any man to take a liberty with you,' one of them once told her). A chaste embrace or two at Clevedon was probably as far as it went physically. There is a poem entitled 'What Might Have Been' – no copy exists in Thackeray's handwriting – which may or may not have been written by him and may or may not refer to an actual event, containing the lines 'You drew my arm against your heart/So close I could feel it beating near' and with references to 'chestnut hair' touching the author's cheek. To counter the deeply felt emotion of Thackeray's letters, though, is a sense that he was consciously pursuing an illusion, deliberately misreading the Brookfields' relationship and his own connection to it. He wrote once to his mother that he knew the secret of Jane's 'malady': a husband 'whom she has loved with the most fanatical fondness and who – and who is my friend too – a good fellow upright generous kind to all the world except her'. This was very far from the truth, and one suspects that Thackeray knew it to be so. There is something about the Brookfields' letters to one another that, in the last resort, excludes third parties. Thackeray suspected that the two of them sometimes laughed over his sentimental protestations. Elsewhere, in an odd flash of self-knowledge, he wrote that Jane did not love him but pitied him. Each, one feels, used the relationship – and the medium by which it was conducted – as a kind of emotional safety-valve: Thackeray ardent, resigned, self-pitying; Jane nervous, flattered, indulgent, in the end entirely capable of looking after herself.

Whatever the precise feelings involved, this kind of correspondence was not indefinitely sustainable. The eventual remonstrance appears to have come not from Brookfield but from Harry Hallam, who, early in the New Year, seems to have told Thackeray that he was making a fool of himself. Thackeray was indignant, walked out of the house in Portman Street where the rebuke was administered, but was later calmed down by a conciliatory letter. Jane's note of 2 January 1849, with its talk of the pain that a lapsing of their friendship would cause her, is delicately written and transparently sincere. 'It has made so great a part of my happiness ever since I felt you were so exceedingly kind as to care about me – that I have a sort of superstitious dread of its coming to an end some day,' she went on. 'This is not a right feeling to have – but when I find you so little trusting in my affection which I *know* to be so entirely secure for you & this only because I do not say much of it, & on the other hand when I am desired to feel as much as I like but not to express it – what can I do to convince you more than I do – if you were only in some way related to me I might say what I chose ...' Brookfield seems to have accepted that the feelings being expressed were those of fraternal affection, and the relationship continued in more or less the same way. If Thackeray called less frequently at Portman Street, then he had sympathetic allies such as Mrs Elliot and Kate Perry, who were prepared to provide a neutral ground on which the two could meet (in acknowledgment of this role the sisters became his chief confidantes in the affair). At the same time Hallam's remonstrance did not solve the problems that existed between Thackeray, Brookfield and the latter's wife; it merely postponed their resolution.

In the meantime all the other sides to his life continued to boil away. The list of addresses for the complimentary copies of *Dr Birch* sent out on Christmas Eve was brimful of social and literary éclat: Lady Cullum, Viscountess Castlereagh (in fact Thackeray subsequently took her off the list), Lady Ashburton, Mrs Dickens, Mrs Carlyle. Towards the end of January he left for a five-week stay in Paris, dining and theatre-going with gusto, and sending back his usual detailed letters to Jane. These alternate high spirits – bragging about 'my friend Jim Rothschild' who secured him a box at the opera – with more sober reflections on past life. A letter from early February, for example, reports a visit to the old haunts of his painting days. 'It was a very jolly time,' he recalled. 'I was as poor as Job: and sketched away most abominably, but pretty contented: and we used to meet in each other's little rooms and talk about Art and smoke pipes and drink bad brandy & water.' What had happened to Art, he wondered, 'that dear Mistress whom I loved though in a very indolent capricious manner but with a real sincerity'. He saw her, Thackeray concluded, but very far off; fate had ordained that the marriage should never take place. No doubt these slightly coy metaphorical musings about love, mistresses and marriage served to maintain the emotional temperature of his relationship with Jane. In his wilder moments he did perhaps speculate that at some point, in the unlikely event of Isabella and Brookfield both dying, they might become man and wife. For the moment there was consolation in hints, oblique references to words that lay beyond recall. A particularly allusive letter preceded his departure on the French trip. 'I wish to be calm, and jocular when my feelings are perhaps outrageous and melancholy,' Thackeray had written from Dover. 'I wont say a word to you of reproaches piling up I mean about that note of Saturday wh. I *dont* forget . . .'

Many of the details of Thackeray's life at this time come courtesy of his appearances in the Brookfield family correspondence. Back in England in the early spring, he and Brookfield took off for a nostalgic visit to Cambridge. The letter that Brookfield wrote home to his wife has a portrait of his friend on the envelope, suggesting that Thackeray stood over him while it was written (these ghostly intrusions can also be glimpsed in his habit of standing by Jane as she wrote to her husband, then either signing the letter or adding the pair of spectacles that authenticated his *Punch* drawings as a hint that he had been present). The visit took in breakfast with college dignitaries and a trip to Norwich to hear Jenny Lind, having encountered the singer's agent at an inn, but although he enjoyed the time spent with his friend and the chance to talk about his friend's wife, he wondered whether the journey had been a success. In his new-found role as a public man, he discovered that he was treated with a mixture of awe and suspicion. 'The young men wouldn't talk to me, the Dons thought I had come to put them in a book,' he complained to his cousin Dr Frederick Thackeray, 'everybody suspected me: and I felt myself so miserable, that I thought the best course was to fly.' A slightly plaintive but enticing note from Jane welcomed him home. 'I cannot help writing to you to say how much I wish you to be happy & that I always love you & pray for you & would do anything that I could to make you easy . . .' she confided. 'I often feel in a kind of dream when you are talking to me & quite unable to say anything to the purpose –'.

The extent of Thackeray's imbrication in the Brookfields' lives was, as perhaps all three parties began to speculate, a little too large for comfort. He presided over their correspondence. In Jane's absence, William, as Brookfield's descendants put it, 'seems to have lived in the constant society of Mr Thackeray'. Thackeray even attempted to draw them into his own social circles, notably by trying to get them better acquainted with his new friends, the Ashburtons. Something was welling up to disturb this idyll, but as yet Thackeray had no inkling of its approach. The start of the London season restricted his opportunities ('Mr Thackeray steps in more rarely now,' Jane reported to Harry Hallam in April, 'but he is as cordial and kindly as ever') and there were other writing commitments beyond *Pendennis*, in particular a series of *Punch* letters in which Thackeray featured as a worldly, club-lounging 'Mr Brown' dispensing sage advice to his nephew. But he grasped at any chance that became available, incorporating into a West Country tour a visit to Mrs Parr, another of Sir Charles Elton's daughters. 'A very pleasing person was staying at her house,' he reported archly back to Mrs Elliot, 'a Mrs Bloomfield or some such name: her husband a clergyman & Schools Inspector very pleasant too.' There is a great sense of immediacy in the letters of the post-*Vanity Fair* period, a sense of Thackeray reaching out to grasp pleasures that had long been denied him. But the past continued to exert its stranglehold. Mid-May, for example, found him paying a visit to his old college chum Henry Matthew, 'that friend of mine whom I used to think 20 years ago the most fascinating accomplished witty and delightful of men'. Arriving at Islington late in the afternoon, he found an old man in a room smelling of brandy and water. What struck Thackeray about his friend, and appears to have alarmed him, was that he seemed the same, only somehow grown coarser and stale, like a piece of goods that had hung too long in a shop window. The image is typical of Thackeray's fiction, with its interest in buying and selling, life as a kind of commodity that could lose its freshness, and you sense that Thackeray found the re-encounter depressing not merely for the sight of Matthew's seedy decrepitude but in its implications for the broader human landscape. Another of his letters to Arthur Shawe, written shortly afterwards, contrasts his present good fortune with a reminder of what lay behind it. Here Thackeray represents himself as being 'at the top of the tree in my business' – he estimated his earnings at £2,000 a year – but only just out of the wood. As for Isabella, 'she is at Epsom very well' (some arrangement had been concluded whereby the Camberwell contingent regularly transported itself to Surrey). He had received a letter from Mrs Bakewell saying that she was quite happy 'and very much pleased to see the folks pass by to the Derby'.

In June a thunderbolt struck. After nearly nine years of marriage, Jane was pregnant. The news, passed on to Thackeray by Harry Hallam, was supposed to have been kept within the family circle, and Brookfield was furious when he discovered it had got out. Thackeray himself seems to have been disagreeably shaken, if only because it shattered so many of his illusions about a ministering angel unhappily, and presumably sexlessly, married to another man. There could be no more confidences about William declining to stay in houses where he was denied a separate dressing-room. Worse, perhaps, than the shutter falling across a crucial if illusory part of his social life were the implications for the casual intimacy that Thackeray had previously enjoyed with his friends. Yet more deadly than either of these considerations would have been an awareness that he had no real grounds for complaint. By July, on holiday once more at Brighton, he had cheered up sufficiently to send a prophetic sketch of Jane and baby recumbent on a sofa, as Brookfield looks proudly on. He describes himself as 'tranquil' and 'pleased that he [Brookfield] should have this happen' but one senses the unhappiness behind the company manners. As ever Brighton raised his spirits. 'Why is a day's Brighton the best of Doctors?' he wondered to Jane, a few days before his thirty-eighth birthday. '. . . I got up hungry and have been yawning in the sun like a fat lazzarone with great happiness all day.' Doubtless by arrangement, Brookfield arrived in Brighton on his way back from a professional tour of the West Country, and Thackeray accompanied him to a National School, where he sat and wrote a letter to his mother while the children were put through their paces. The Dickens family, also staying on the coast, were seen walking on the pier and Brookfield reported his usual pleasure at sampling a kind of bachelor life not always allowed him, in this case a dinner party with two dragoon officers of Thackeray's acquaintance accompanied by 'the wickedest weed and wickeder distillations'.

Back in London, Thackeray spent a quiet August working on his novel and the weekly 'Mr Brown' letters for *Punch*, finishing *Pendennis'* eleventh number on the day that a letter came from Charlotte Ritchie telling him that his father's sister Mrs Halliday was dying in Paris. Thackeray had fond memories of the old lady, who had nursed Richmond Thackeray in his final illness, and resolved to give her 'a parting shake of the hand'. He arrived in France to find his aunt *in extremis* ('in her bed, asleep and groaning an old old woman – it was rather an awful sight') but patently not yet dead. He whiled away the time dining, visiting the Tuileries, beginning his next number and sending immense bulletins back to Jane, in which the sincerity of his feelings for his dying relative was coupled with the happy thought that there might be a legacy. In the end Mrs Halliday died in her sleep, and having attended the funeral Thackeray proposed 'a week's touring' through France. Duty got the better of him, however, and he ventured only as far as Chambourcy, where Count D'Orsay now lived in continental exile, spending the rest of the time seeing his bereaved uncle and Aunt Ritchie.

He was home by the middle of the month, but unwell. Dining at Lady Rodd's on 17 September, his ankle gave way beneath him again and his doctor confined him to bed with what Thackeray described as bilious or liver trouble, but what looks – given the fact that an epidemic was currently raging in Paris – like cholera. At first little fuss was made, and Mrs Carmichael-Smyth, then holidaying in Wales with the children, was not even informed. The subsequent course of his illness was remorselessly tracked by the Brookfields. A week later Brookfield wrote to Harry Hallam that 'our friend Thackeray has quite turned the corner', but calling on him three days later – she sent word from her cab that she would be writing to his mother if he wanted to send a message, and he begged her to come up – Jane was shocked by how 'terribly pulled down' he looked. He was anxious to have Brookfield back, she reported, confessing that she did not feel easy about him. Certainly by this stage Thackeray's recovery seemed to be taking longer than his doctors had predicted. The October number of *Pendennis* was postponed (as it turned out, there would not be another until the New Year). Thackeray's distinctive role in the Brookfield circle by this stage can be measured by the concern that was expressed on all sides. Hallam, for example, called daily, sent back bulletins and even lent one of his domestics to help Thackeray's in any case highly competent servant John.

A week later, however, his condition worsened and Jane reported in some alarm to her husband that he had had a very bad night: 'his room is darkened, and he is ordered to be perfectly quiet and not to talk at all'. Apparently the doctors had become anxious about 'some former complaint' (presumably Jane means the stricture, though even allowing for the depth of their intimacy she can hardly have known what it was). Without doubt, and with some justification, Thackeray thought he was dying. He confessed as much at a *Punch* dinner a decade later, and Jane recorded a morbid conversation later that day: 'he talked of the end, as possibly near at hand, and said he could look forward without dread to it, that he felt a great love and charity for all mankind, and tho' there were many things he would wish undone in his life, he yet felt a great trust and hope in God's love and mercy . . .' Initially Jane tried to turn the conversation, but seeing how serious he was later reproached herself for what she thought might be construed as making light of his fears.

Help came from a slightly unexpected quarter in the shape of Forster, who, alarmed at Thackeray's condition, despatched his extremely competent medical man Dr Elliotson* (Thackeray always remained grateful to Elliotson, dedicated the volume edition of *Pendennis* to him and wrote to him each Christmas). Under his care the patient rallied, and by mid-October was out of danger. Major and Mrs Carmichael-Smyth, finally apprised of their son's illness, came tearing back across Wales in a carriage – ironically through crowds of black-clad church-goers marking a day of prayer against precisely the illness from which Thackeray was suffering. Annie remembered his 'great wan eyes' looking up at her from the bed when they reached Young Street and were allowed to see him. A week later he was in Brighton recuperating, 'greatly invigorated and pleasantly tired', but the illness had shaken him and he took a long time to recover. Meanwhile the next number of *Pendennis* took root and grew within him, as, sixty miles or so distant from him, did Jane's child. Both were to have an unforeseen impact on the smooth course of his life in the year that lay ahead.

---

* Elliotson (1791–1868) is best remembered as an early exponent of 'Mesmerism', advocacy of which had him dismissed from his post of professor of medicine at University College, London. See Alison Winters, *Mesmerized: Powers of Mind in Victorian Britain*, University of Chicago Press, 1998.

XV
Edged Tools

'And I write because I'm unhappy – if I write my book in this
frame of mind it will be diabolical.'
Letter to Mrs Elliot and Kate Perry, 26 September 1851

 e recovered slowly. Invited to stay with the Ashbur-
tons at the Grange, he cried off on the grounds that
he was 'still very tired and weak and a great deal too
much of an invalid ...' Confined to a sofa by Dr
Elliotson, he declared himself longing to resume
work on *Pendennis*, which was 'coming to the
interesting part now'. The only drawback was that
people had been so kind to him during his illness
that he felt he had no bad temper left in him.
The second half of the novel would show him as a 'maudlin
philanthropist' beloving all the world. *Pendennis* was booked to resume
publication in January 1850, but there was other work in hand. A
Christmas book had begun to take shape on the sofa of his Brighton
lodgings and at Young Street – a sequel to his childhood favourite
Ivanhoe. The germ of this continuation had been in his head for years.
Now, with the young *Punch* artist Richard 'Dicky' Doyle commissioned to do the illustrations – Thackeray felt that both text and
engravings would be beyond his enfeebled state – he set to work.
Rebecca and Rowena was published a few days before Christmas 1849,
its comic conceits – Rowena is a mixture of jealousy and piety, Robin
Hood has metamorphosed into the fat Earl of Huntingdon – balanced
by some darker moments more appropriate to Thackeray's mental state
when he began it. He had thought he was going to die. Wolfing
mutton chops at his lodgings, where Harry Hallam found him one
morning, he was grateful to have survived, yet conscious of the

precariousness of the average man's hold on life. At the same time he busied himself to complete a task promised for an old friend. His connection with Louis Marvy went back to the Paris days of the early 1840s, when Isabella had been lodged at the *Maison de Santé*. Now a refugee from the political upheavals that had put Louis-Napoleon into power, Marvy had found a publisher prepared to bring out his *Sketches after English Landscape Painters*, if Thackeray would supply the letterpress. As with his Christmas book, the whole job was beyond him. He commissioned Eyre Crowe, the son of his old friend Eyre Evans Crowe, the *Morning Chronicle*'s Paris correspondent, to act as his secretary, making notes in libraries and museums. Thackeray dictated the final text from the sofa in Young Street – a valediction, as it turned out, for Marvy was dead within the year.

The early December weather was mild and bright, and he went back to Brighton to think about *Pendennis*. The note informing Jane was delivered by hand to Portman Street: he had been riding in the park, Thackeray confessed, but had not the time to call. From Kensington, hard at work on his February number, he wrote her a Christmas Day letter that turned into a statement of his religious beliefs. What emerges from these criticisms of Evangelicals who assumed that God could be called up 'to interfere about the 1000 trivialities of a man's life' is a great straightforwardness and simplicity. It was sufficient to 'Bow down, Confess, Adore, Admire and reverence infinitely Make your act of faith and trust Acknowledge with constant awe the Idea of the Infinite Presence over all.' To agonise over whether one loved God enough was simple effrontery. 'Wretched little blindlings What do we know about him?' In middle life Thackeray's spiritual position was still that of humble acquiescence, sharpened by scepticism of orthodoxy's more grandiloquent claims. The writings of his late thirties and early forties are strewn with illustrations of these views. Chapter 60 of *Pendennis* finds Arthur Pendennis questioning what 'the truth' is, whether in fact there are not two sides to any question, as in the contrast between two brothers (in reality the Roman Catholic convert John Henry Newman and his rationalist brother Francis William), the one driven to transfer himself to 'the enemy', the other 'whose logic drives him to quite a different conclusion, and who, having passed a life in vain endeavour to reconcile an irreconcilable book, flings it at last down in despair and declares, with tearful eye, & hands up to heaven, his revolt and recantation'. A recently identified review of Carlyle's *Life of John Sterling*, contributed to the rationalist

Leader in November 1851, restates this position. Here Thackeray observes that when Carlyle had previously written on religious subjects 'he had always seemed *to have a Bishop in tow*'. Now 'he has fairly left cables, and leaves the Bishop to tow himself as he best may'. This did not mean that anyone could determine what Carlyle's religious opinions were, Thackeray goes on to assert, merely that Carlyle is denouncing *make-believe*. 'For it is in the want of recognition of free thought that so much hypocrisy lies; men pretend to believe what they do not believe, because that belief is called respectable.'

Undoubtedly Thackeray did believe what he believed. He believed it profoundly. Paid-up rationalists of the period tended to treat these views with a certain amount of scepticism. John Chapman, editor of the *Westminster Review*, recalled a conversation of June 1851 in which he diagnosed that Thackeray's religious views were 'perfectly *free*, but he does not mean to lessen his popularity by fully accounting them'. Charles Bray, on the other hand, author of *Philosophy of Necessity* (1841) and, coincidentally, another of George Eliot's early mentors, witnessed an outpouring of 'beautifully simple faith', at the end of which Thackeray remarked, half apologetically, 'But I have a dear old Gospel mother who is a good Christian and who has always chapter and verse to prove everything.' One Newman brother was a saint. The other was a brave and admirable man. Personal faith was exactly that – private, and not to be colonised by fanatics. Thackeray continued to dislike low-church enthusiasm in much the same way as he later deplored Anglo-Catholicism, on the grounds that it was presumptuous and sought a relationship with God that could not possibly exist. To put it another way, indigestion came from eating too much supper; it was not some kind of spiritual hurdle to be briskly cleared with the help of divine grace. Though he was not above airing his support for free-thinking bishops, an unwillingness to place intensely felt private views under a relentless public scrutiny was to remain his position until the end of his life. To make this point, in a religious landscape characterised by schism and secession, is not to say that Thackeray cared too little about his beliefs, rather that they were so central to his outlook that they did not trouble him in the way that – to use an obvious point of reference – religious questions reduced Mrs Carmichael-Smyth to a state of spiritual turmoil. 'Goodbye dear lady & my dear generous old Wm.' he signed off to the Brookfields before leaving for Oxford and a New Year's Day at the home of Jane's uncle Henry Hallam.

*

To talk about a writer's life being 'in transition' is a rather suspect biographer's commonplace. Nearly any life, inspected at a fixed point in time, has a tendency to turn into a series of interconnecting paths, some of which are coming to an end as others begin to open up. Nevertheless, it is hard not to fix this label to Thackeray in the early 1850s. The success of *Vanity Fair* and his transformation into a public figure were only a couple of years behind him. The new world of the successful mid-Victorian novelist was still taking shape. This consciousness of changing status affected what might be called Thackeray's sense of himself in several ways. For all the good company he kept, he was still slightly unsure of himself in society, prone to make neurotic little jokes, worried that his motives might be misunderstood. The letters that he wrote to the exceedingly grand Lady Ashburton at around this time are not those of a man addressing a friend who is also his equal: Thackeray is too conscious of the social divide that exists between a novelist and a baronet's wife. A part of him, too, was happy that this social divide should exist. Leaving aside his appearances at great country houses and in grand Belgravia drawing-rooms, he was aware that his new-found position, and the stanchions on which it had been built, was likely to draw him into controversy. The succession of small quarrels with Forster and his satellites – a continuing argument about what came to be known as the 'Dignity of Literature' – which simmered on throughout the next two years arose directly out of the subject matter of his novels and his own professional status. It is also true to say – although Thackeray would never have thought of it so reductively – that he was determined that success should not spoil him. While he was capable of standing on his dignity with almost ducal frostiness, he continued to do his best for less exalted connections and tried hard not to patronise or ignore those whose relationship with him stopped at the drawing-room door.

But he was not the same man. His illness, which had left him weak and spiritless, was probably as much a reaction to the strain of the past three years as an actual physical disease. Creatively, the fire had died down. There are good things in the last dozen numbers of *Pendennis*, but the note of fatigue is clear. In some ways this quietened tone was as much an aesthetic decision as anything else. More sedate, less consciously attacking, the *Punch* essays of early 1850 mark a determination to write in a different way. Thackeray admitted as much in a letter to Lady Ashburton in the summer. After he had made his fortune in America and had the time, he hoped 'to write a book containing not the portraits of my friends, but the results of experience and true description of society such as it appears to a middle-aged calm person, whom personal conceit or prejudice or foolish passions and preferences for individuals of your sex, have ceased pretty much to disturb'. Heartfelt as it may have been, there is something faintly disturbing about this quietism. Granted, the satirist's tragedy is that he grows old, but need he do so quite so self-consciously and with such a deliberate casting aside of the materials and the world-view that made him a satirist in the first place? Even in a *Punch* that had tempered some of its original sharpness, the kind of softening that these ambitions represented was liable to cause strain, and Thackeray's relationship with Lemon and Co. was subject to several upsets, culminating in outright resignation late in 1851.

Thackeray's professional life, too, was changing course. On the one hand, as a man in his late thirties with the rest of his career before him, he can be seen consciously framing some of the alliances and career paths that would help him in the future – letting George Smith publish *The Kickleburys on the Rhine*, his Christmas book for 1850, after Chapman and Hall had jibbed at his terms, deciding to set himself up as a lecturer (this in spite of a public diffidence that often extended to simple stagefright). On the other hand, the comparative eagerness with which he embraced the world of public meetings and wandering around like a 'literary harlot', as he put it, shows his anxiety that the books alone might not be enough. Above all this – the *Punch* manoeuvrings, the search for what he told Mark Lemon was 'a higher tone', the emergence of the *English Humourists* lecture series – rose the greatest transition of all, his relationship with Jane. 'I am an extinct crater and my volcano is poked out,' he maintained, but this was clearly not true. Despite the impending birth of the Brookfields' first child, he was still intimately concerned by the news from Portman Street, keen to know where he stood and yet not keen, for he knew that any unravelling of the complicated mixture of evasions and refusals to face facts that characterised his relationship with the Brookfields would leave him cruelly exposed.

Uncertain about the direction that his work and his emotional life were taking, he could make bad errors of judgment, not realising that he had given offence or shutting his mind to the possibility that it could have been taken. The stupendous lack of tact that typified some of his previous dealings with the Brookfields – the puzzlement that a recently married man could find his perpetual presence in his house in any way irritating – re-emerges in a row brought about by one of his *Punch* 'Proser' papers, 'On a Good-looking Young Lady', which appeared in June 1850. This was an allegorical reworking of the admiration of the elderly poet Henry Taylor for Virginia Pattle, sister of the Theodosia whom Thackeray had considered marrying a decade and a half before. Taylor's infatuation, expressed in some cloying verses, was something of a public joke – had his wife not behaved with exceptional sensitivity there might have been serious trouble – and the *roman-à-clef* element of the piece, which appeared shortly before Miss Pattle's marriage to Viscount Eastnor, would have been obvious to anyone in the two families' immediate circle. Not unnaturally, friends and relatives of 'Erminia' and 'Timotheus', as Thackeray coyly renamed them, were furious, and Lady Ashburton at one point suggested that he put off a visit on the grounds that Taylor would be present. In the end Thackeray was persuaded to apologise, but one leaves the episode with the sense that he thought he was being got at and could not see what he had done to offend, as well as a hint of the inflexibility that was to characterise some of the literary jousting-matches of the last ten years of his life.

The year 1850 began with a literary row of sorts, although Thackeray's response to it was essentially good-humoured. The *Morning Chronicle* and Forster's *Examiner* were currently conducting an argument about the propriety of giving public honours to writers. Although opposed to one another, neither approved of the literary party in *Pendennis*, and its mild guying of the collection of deadbeats gathered around the fustian table of Bungay, the Paternoster Row publisher – the lugubrious Captain Sumph, for example, with his time-worn anecdotes about Byron, or the superannuated poetess Bunion, author of 'Heartstrings' and 'Deadly Nightshade'. Thackeray's reply, in the form of a long letter to the *Chronicle*, can be read in the same light as Orwell's later attack on what he called 'Benefit of Clergy' – the idea that writers are exempt from ordinary standards of behaviour simply by virtue of their professional calling. He agreed with Forster that if literary people deserved honours then they should have them, but if they were foolish or venal they should expect to have these faults pointed out to the world at large. Thackeray took pains with the letter, which addressed a subject he felt strongly about, taking the manuscript round to Portman Street to try it out on Jane. The consistency of his attendance can be judged from the fact that at least one of his letters from early January – to his old schoolfriend J.R. Young – was sent from the Brookfields' address. As in many another account of his doings from this time, Thackeray is conscious of advancing years ('You I know are still a young fellow,' he told Young. 'I am grown quite an old one.'). He then left London to pay a New Year visit to the Ashburtons.

How did Thackeray view the prospect of Jane becoming the mother of another man's child? Undoubtedly he was preparing himself to play a benevolent, avuncular role: given his intimacy with the family, he probably expected to be asked to stand godfather. At the same time he cannot but have realised that the child was not his and that his continuing presence in the household would be superfluous, if not downright embarrassing. As it was, he continued to haunt Portman Street like a ghoul. On 26 February he contrived to remain in the house until a mere fifteen minutes before the child was born ('It's a wench & came at 12.30 P.M. this day,' Brookfield reported telegraphically). The baby was named Magdalene – Brookfield's appropriation of the 'fallen woman' of scripture seems somehow typical of his temperament – and Thackeray wrote a delicate and rather wistful note to her in which a great deal of his own feeling is laid bare ('What he would like you to remember is that he was very fond of your dear mother, and that he and your Papa were very good friends to one another, helping each other as occasion served in life'). But he was not allowed to see the child – there was a brief audience with Brookfield and the family's friend Mrs Fanshawe, who had come up from Southampton to superintend the nursing – and had to content himself with a letter, including a thumbnail sketch of mother and baby walking in the park.

A few days later Thackeray left for Paris with his daughters – much of the previous months had been spent away from Annie and Minnie – staying once again at the Hôtel Bristol, where he wrote to inform the *bonnes soeurs*, Mrs Elliot and Kate Perry, that he was 'not near so miserable as I try and make myself out to be, and intend to be jolly for 10 days or so here'. Jane wrote on the same day, explaining that she had nothing to say 'but what you know quite well, that I am always loving you, & that you are *never* really away from me'. His reply mixed tourist's reportage – accounts of various entertainments and a trip to the Bibliothèque Nationale – with an admission of heavy-heartedness. He had no right to indulge in sentimental miseries, he told her, only there came 'moments of depression and a sense of loneliness, about wh. I talk frankly to you as about everything else'. To Kate Perry and

Mrs Elliot he was more emphatic: he was in Paris 'trying to get his wounds healed', trying hard to distract himself with pleasure 'and very unhappy'. His unhappiness presumably increased when he got home a fortnight later. There was still no sign of the baby, and no invitation to the christening. Worse, Jane was soon placed well out of his reach. As soon as she had recovered her health she was sent off to Clevedon and subsequently to Southampton. Thackeray moped about this sequestration, which can be interpreted as Brookfield trying to assert himself – it was also perfectly natural that Jane should take the baby to her family home and to her old friends in Southampton – but, again, one wonders what he really wanted out of the episode. To hover over the cradle? To dance attendance on Jane's sofa, thereby damaging his own and other people's feelings? The Brookfields returned to London in the late spring and were at Portman Street during the summer, but Thackeray saw little of them (they appear to have come to dinner early in June with Henry Hallam and the Duff Gordons). He felt – and the evidence suggests that he was right – that the Brookfields' marriage was still unhappy, the husband distant, the wife delighting in her child but conscious of a wider dissatisfaction.

Meanwhile the 'Proser' papers were taking shape in his head – a series of essays which, he told Mark Lemon, he intended to be 'better and in a higher tone if I may be so permitted to speak of humour and morals than anything I have done'. The series, conducted by 'Dr Solomon Pacifico', ran from late April to early August, taking in such subjects as 'On a Lady in an Opera Box', 'On the Pleasures of Being a Fogey' and 'On an American Traveller'. They are bland and unexceptionable pieces, full of fragments of semi-comic moralising – one of the pleasures of being a fogey, Dr Pacifico assures us, is that one can 'enjoy and appreciate duly the society of women' – and pursue the line taken by the earlier 'Mr Brown's Letters to his Nephew'. And yet the difference between the two is considerable. For all Mr Brown's easy bourgeois maxims – don't live beyond your means, don't give dinners you can't afford – the sting in his observations remained. In the midst of the smoking-room chatter the narrator would suddenly remark, 'I don't see why one shouldn't meditate upon Death in Pall Mall as well as in a howling wilderness', and the backdrop of the club dinner and the lurking card-sharps strengthens rather than dissipates the moral point. Undoubtedly Thackeray thought he could bring off the same effect with Dr Pacifico, but the majority of the essays ended up being uncomfortably sedate.

Early in July, 'so sick and ill this morning that I determined on instant flight', he escaped to Dieppe for a week. He would have done so, however, in the knowledge that a good time lay ahead. With Magdalene now nearly five months old, Brookfield unbent sufficiently to nod at a suggestion that the two families should spend part of August together keeping house in Southampton (Brookfield himself was mostly absent on a cruise). Thackeray, who put up at a nearby inn but paid daily visits, remembered the two-week holiday as one of the happiest times of his life. 'I wonder whether ever again I shall have such a happy peaceful fortnight as that last?' he wondered to Jane a day or so after it was over, adding, 'I can hardly see as I write for the eye water.' As well as gazing fondly backwards, he was busy planning his autumn schedule, telling his Scottish friend Alexander Christie that it was more than likely he would travel north. He had a whole pocket of invitations, he declared, 'to Yorkshire Squires, to Lowland Lairds, to gentlemen in the Highlands, to Dukes and Duchesses by the immortal gods, and the only thing wh. makes me think I shan't go is the fear of encountering these great folks . . .'

In some ways this passage is an example of Thackeray's wanting to have his cake and eat it too with regard to society – bragging about his fine acquaintances ('Dukes and Duchesses' is presumably a reference to Chatsworth) while simultaneously throwing out broad hints that he can take it or leave it. Above all, it raises the question of his relationship with the *beau monde* when he was invited into its drawing-rooms, what he really thought of the great people who offered him hospitality and what they in return thought about him. Perhaps his most important 'upper society' friendship of this time was with Harriet, Lady Ashburton and, to a lesser extent, her husband (to whom *Esmond* is dedicated), both of whom came to know the Brookfields – largely at Thackeray's instigation – and were to play a sympathetic part in smoothing his final break with Jane. Thackeray's early letters to Lady Ashburton (they had been introduced by Charles Buller in the *Vanity Fair* days) are marked by a determination to establish the ordinariness of his life and the pettiness of his obligations. 'I have 3 different books to launch and all the engraving for all the three to do' runs an explanation of his inability to accept an invitation, 'I have a sprained ankle, and my parents come to stay.' The sub-text is rather obvious: *I am not like you, my life is not like yours, it is as well for you to realise this.* Their early dealings were characterised by a slight off-handedness on Thackeray's side and a tendency to make his excuses. When he did accept a dinner invitation for the first time he returned the card with a sketch on the back showing him kneeling at his hostess's feet, his head in flames from the hot coals she is pouring from an ornamental brazier. By December 1848, though, writing to condole with her on Buller's death, he strikes a note of genuine intimacy: 'What does one care about honours and successes, and that Lord John thought he was a clever man? Psha – why are we always to be gauging men by success or failure?'

At the same time this reminder of the essential equality of the human lot would have been noted by a woman whose husband had made a fortune out of Baring's bank. But whatever Thackeray's intentions in memorialising Charles Buller, he was also capable of the most lavish flattery. A note about a grand fancy-dress ball that Lady Ashburton proposed to attend in summer 1851 has him offering to lend a scarlet Turkish dress and asking, 'Is your Ladyship going to appear as a Marquise, that you speak of brocade waistcoats & powder?' Elsewhere, one can detect genuine amity undercut by occasional bouts of self-consciousness, the latter nearly always turned into a joke. Writing in the summer of 1850, for example, while the 'Proser' papers were coming out, he notes that Dr Pacifico 'remarks in his No. upon the absurd quasi dignity and suspicion wh. distinguishes some folks at the commencement of their intercourse with persons of condition who only mean kindness to them and of course never think about their silly pretensions'. Thackeray brings in this apropos of Brookfield being 'greatly pleased' by a letter from Lady Ashburton and a visit from her husband, but he could just as well have been writing about himself. The next sentence – 'It is good when persons of condition pardon these errors' – is double-edged, too. 'Persons of condition' is a phrase that the younger Thackeray loved to mock, and it is difficult not to imagine that its use here is more than half ironic.

He spent a solitary four weeks on the Continent, visiting Cologne, Frankfurt and Hamburg, returning via Brussels and not much liking the English company he found along the route: Hamburg was full of acquaintances from whom he was glad to get away, he maintained in a letter to Annie and Minnie. An early autumn visit to the Grange looked as if it might be jeopardised by the presence of Henry Taylor among the guests, but Thackeray was induced to send a graceful letter of apology and subsequently arrived to amuse the company with bad puns over the breakfast table and nod his way through what he told Jane was a five-hour stint of shooting. The rift caused by the 'Erminia' essay must have been healed, as he attended Virginia Pattle's wedding shortly afterwards. Other tempting social invitations beckoned, but he was uneasily conscious that money had to be earned. Putting off Lady Cullum, he complained that he had to write 'a Christmas Book & 3 numbers of Pendennis in the course of the next six weeks. How can I do so much work? Perhaps not at all, certainly not by going to take my pleasure at friends' houses.' The Christmas book was *The Kickleburys on the Rhine*, a return to earlier themes and preoccupations, which finds M.A. Titmarsh travelling through Germany in the company of a snobbish band of aristocrats with whose daughter he is unrequitedly in love.

Pendennis was finished in late November: the resolution of its love triangle, in which Pen is allowed to marry Laura while Warrington (hamstrung by a foolish early marriage) nobly consents to remain their attached friend, was presumably noted in Portman Street. Already, though, Thackeray's mind was examining another scheme. Exhausted by his literary labours – in the last four years his output had gone well beyond a million words – he determined to try his hand at one of the most popular and lucrative of early-Victorian entertainments: the public lecture. The lecturer, with his handkerchief, his glass of water and his learned address on bimetallism or Eastern travels, is a stock figure in Victorian comic journalism. All the same this was an environment in which fortunes could be made, even if the serious-minded (Carlyle, for example, who having tried it denounced it as a 'mountebank's trade') tended to look down on lecturing as a kind of intellectual slumming. To his friends, Thackeray's plan to put himself on public display in this way must have seemed an odd one: he was an erratic speaker (two years later at the opening of the Manchester Free Library, flanked by Dickens and Bulwer, he broke down after a few minutes and had to resume his seat) and hated the publicity that necessarily accompanied these events. There is a rather plaintive letter, written in advance of an engagement in Oxford, where he asks if placards and posters can be kept to a minimum. But he knew that his new-found celebrity would bring people to see him, and the financial rewards – a good lecturer could make £100 from a week's work – were unignorable. Careful thought produced a subject – humorous writers of the eighteenth century – after which, early in January 1851, he left for Paris with Annie and Minnie and a bundle of books. The previous week had been overshadowed by Brookfield family tragedy. In November, while on a journey through Italy, the twenty-six-year-old Harry Hallam had contracted malaria and died at Siena. Brought back to England, his body was interred at Bristol immediately before Christmas. Thackeray went to pay his respects, reminded of Hallam's kindness to him during his own illness. 'He did the very same thing for me when I was ill,' he told Lady Ashburton in a letter written on Christmas Eve, 'and came, did I tell you? 120 miles to see if he could be of any service to me.'

Thackeray was unwell again early in the New Year, 'so beat that I feel as if I had no pluck to go to Paris'. There was another row brewing, too, with *The Times*, which had printed an abusive review of *The Kickleburys* (the anonymous reviewer, Samuel Philips, was rapidly to become one of Thackeray's *bêtes noires*), but he rallied himself to produce a bristling rejoinder, 'On Thunder and Small Beer', which prefixed the book's second edition: 'a very pretty controversy for any body who likes mischief', he concluded. From Paris long letters winged back to Portman Street containing accounts of his leisure pursuits. At the president's ball, he reported to Jane with his archly ironic eye for social detail, 'The company was not so select as you like – When I tell you Ma'am that there were TRADESMEN and their wives present! I saw one woman pull off a pair of list slippers and take a ticket for them at the great-coat repository: and I rather liked her for being so bold.' Jane's letters back were unusually subdued, much italicised (she apologised for a *downcast* tone and for *moroseness*); her listlessness cannot have been improved by her current recreation: helping her school-inspector husband to compile the index to his annual report. The Portman Street ménage – March 1851 saw them remove to Cadogan Square – was plunged into gloom, the tensions between husband and wife compounded by intimations of mortality. Hallam's funeral was followed early in the New Year by the death of Brookfield's brother. The double blow seems to have persuaded Brookfield to take his own bad health, manifested in a series of chest complaints, more seriously than in the past.

Back in London, Thackeray seems to have been denied as much access as he would have liked. A wistful note from some time in February runs: 'I daresay you are having tea now. How I should like to have a cup! There are many things one wd. like.' The death in March of Brookfield's father further restricted Thackeray's social opportunities, although he put Jane's non-attendance at Young Street down to illness. 'What have I been doing these many days?' he asked himself for her benefit. 'I hardly know. Thinking about you chiefly I think; and wanting you back, as a peevish baby wants back his nurse –.' Meanwhile he was working hard to complete the six lectures needed for the May unveiling. As the spring approached, his nervousness grew. He was satisfied by his appreciations of Swift, Congreve, Hogarth, Goldsmith and Co., but fearful of the ordeal of delivering them. There was a dry-run to a friendly audience in the Brookfields' drawing-room. Three weeks before the commencement date he went down to Willis's Rooms in St James's and recited part of the multiplication table to a waiter to test his voice. The waiter approved, as did his Garrick Club cronies when he spoke at the annual Shakespeare dinner a few days beforehand. His speaking style was judged 'conspicuous for consummate ease and impudence' he reported to his mother, adding that he was in such a state of panic that he scarcely knew what he was saying.

The choice of Willis's Rooms for the lectures was a mark of how seriously Thackeray took the business once he had begun on it, how desperately he wanted to succeed and, it must be said, how embarrassing would be any suggestion of failure. The premises in King Street, where the Almack's balls were held, were the acme of *ton*: a venue of this kind increased the likelihood of aristocratic patronage. As it turned out, the fashionable world flocked to Thackeray's six-week stint in the great ballroom, and the streets outside were clogged with carriages. To the lecturer and his family – Mrs Carmichael-Smyth had come over specially from Paris – the build-up to the first lecture passed in a frenzy of nerves and apprehension. Annie, writing forty years later, had 'no very pleasant recollection of that particular half-hour of my life'. She remembered the unoccupied chairs and people coming in 'rather subdued, as if into a church'. Backstage Thackeray was taking some last-minute professional advice from Fanny Kemble until an accidental collision caused him to drop his script on the floor. Mrs Kemble was aghast, but the lecturer reassured her that the time it would take him to reassemble the pages would set his mind perfectly in order. As the lecture began Annie thought that her father sounded strained for an instant before dropping into his usual vocal range. Mrs Carmichael-Smyth looked on proudly, and with considerable relief. A small lady sitting nearby in a Quaker cap was identified as the Duchess of Sutherland – proof, if it were needed, of the undertaking's success.

Good-humoured and gentlemanly, the lectures went down well with the fashionable, unliterary London audience. Serious historians of the period were less enthusiastic. Macaulay commented acidly that

Thackeray knew little of those times and his audience even less. Other critics regretted the cosy characterisations of 'old Noll Goldsmith' and 'sad loose' Richard Steele. 'I wish I could persuade Thackeray that the test of a great man is not whether he would like to meet him at a tea-party,' Carlyle observed. Charlotte Brontë's irritation was straightfor-wardly personal. Greeting her in the throng after the first lecture, Thackeray again blew her incognito by blithely saluting her as 'Jane Eyre'. Returning to his house the next day, George Smith was startled to find her diminutive figure berating the lecturer as he stood abashed before her in the drawing-room. Thackeray's friends looked on the lectures approvingly. In particular, there was great excitement at Cadogan Place. Brookfield was at Southampton, consulting his friends the Bullars, two of whom were doctors, about his chest. Jane's letter of 31 May contains only a sentence about 'my dearest William's cough' before launching into a report of the second lecture: 'much more popular than the one before. Mr Thackeray was much less nervous, indeed quite cool and collected, and gave out his voice, so as to be well heard, and having a higher desk this time, had his papers on the desk instead of in his hand, which gave a freer look to the thing'. Other friends tried good-humouredly to puncture the relative solem-nity of the proceedings. What Thackeray really needed, Arcedeckne told him, was a *pianner*.

Gradually the lectures became a part of the family's everyday life – just as much, Annie considered, as the books and the articles, or the printers' boys waiting and swinging their legs in the hall. The early summer brought another flare-up in the continuing 'Dignity of Literature' row. With a scheme now afoot spearheaded by Dickens and Forster to establish a professional guild of some kind, Thackeray feared that some remarks of his let fall at a dinner of the Royal Literary Fund might be misconstrued, and wrote to the *Morning Chronicle* to reassure its readers that 'the public was most generously & kindly disposed towards men of letters'. Forster, however, had already ventured some niggling criticisms of the Swift lecture in the *Examiner*, which Thackeray suspected had their roots in simple personal distaste. 'He's angry with me for succeeding, it personally chafes him,' he explained to Mrs Proctor; 'he's hurt at my getting on in Society, & knowing fine people.' The lectures ended in early July, whereupon he packed up his daughters and headed for the Continent ('the Rhine Switzerland Como Milan Venice Trieste Vienna Prag Dresden &c.'). Jane reported to Brookfield, currently amusing himself in France, that the three of them had called at Cadogan Place on their way down to London Bridge *en route* for Antwerp. It was an eventful trip. Charles Kingsley and his brother, who joined the boat at Antwerp wearing poetical brown felt hats with pointed crowns and wide brims, were thrown in prison by the Cologne police on suspicion of being Italian revolutionaries. The girls, too – Annie was now fourteen, Minnie eleven – found their tastes in headgear called summarily into question. Sporting their new bonnets, decked out with flowing streamers, they were surprised to be told by their father to put them back in the box. They would be mobbed, he told them, if they went out in 'such ribbons'.

Despite this temporary sharpness, Thackeray was delighted to be abroad and to have both his daughters with him (Mrs Carmichael-Smyth had tried to take Minnie back to Paris with her after the London lectures and been stoutly repulsed). Heading eastward via Heidelberg, they stayed for a while at Weimar, encountered Thackeray's old tutor Dr Weissenborn and took tea with Madame von Goethe. From Vienna early in August Thackeray reported 'a capital journey', while informing his mother that 'I'm longing to be at work again'. Minnie had been sick in the Adriatic, he disclosed, but it was 'a most splendid night to be sick in, and a sunrise as if it had been done on purpose for us'. They returned later in the month with Thackeray, as he had told Mrs Carmichael-Smyth, anxious to get on with his next project. Some time previously George Smith had offered him £1,200 for a novel, to be published in volume form rather than in serial parts, with the lure of £600 on account. Thackeray had eagerly accepted – the late seventeenth- and early eighteenth-century background of *Esmond* was already in his mind from the lectures – and agreed a delivery date of January 1852, which now seemed uncomfortably close. Ill on his return from the Continent, and with the first chapters of his new work down on paper, he retired to Brighton, 'hiding from mankind and trying to work and get well'. A fortnight later an explosion in his emotional life threw all these plans into turmoil.

The exact circumstances of Thackeray's break with the Brookfields can never be definitively recast. Jane's descendants were understandably reticent. All that remains are some impassioned and largely undated letters from Thackeray to the *bonnes soeurs*. But he seems to have taken the crucial step himself. Husband and wife, when he saw them again in September, seemed desperately unhappy: the one cold and haughty, the other faded and cast-down. Thackeray's own feelings towards Jane were revolted by what he saw as her husband's high-handedness. Knowing that she would never be his, he seems to have decided to try and reunite her with Brookfield by way of his own behaviour. Either that or he had concluded that the existing situation between Jane and himself, notwithstanding four years of soft words, simply mocked him – this is certainly the implication of one or two of his letters. Again, the exact chronology is beyond recall, but on or about 23 September Thackeray reproached Brookfield for his treatment of Jane in what he admitted were quite unjustifiable terms, 'high words' were exchanged and the doors of Cadogan Place shut firmly behind him. The angry, expostulatory letters to Kate Perry and her sister that seem both to have preceded and followed this confrontation are remarkably candid, and full of reproach. In one he claims that he could not see 'how any woman should not love a man who had loved her as I did J'. But then, he added, he was 'safe' – impropriety was out of the question, on the children's account. It would have been easier had he broken off at an earlier stage, 'but a part of poor Brookfield's pride of possession was that we should envy him and admire her; and of all this weakness goodness love generosity vanity *playing with edged tools*, we are all paying the penalty'. Gradually the suspicion rose in his mind that he had been 'played with'. Reading over Jane's letters, he had not been reduced to tears – on the contrary, they had made him laugh. 'The thought that I have been made a fool of, is the bitterest of all perhaps – and a lucky thing for all it is perhaps that it should be so.' In his agony he prowled around the streets near Cadogan Place hoping to catch sight of her. She still loved him, he decided, but it was the love of an angel, 'with a soft pity, a holy tenderness and modesty'.

Finally he informed the sisters that 'the affair is at an end and the rupture complete'. Furious at himself, at Brookfield, at Jane, not sure if he was a victim or a transgressor, he fled London: 'I am going out of town and I dont know where.' For the next few days his doings can only be guessed at. Moping in alien hotel rooms? Solitary train rides over the Midland plain? We shall never know. His life slips back into focus once more at the end of September, when he came to rest in Derbyshire, was plucked from his lodging by the Duke of Devonshire and conveyed to Chatsworth by the latter's celebrated gardener Joseph Paxton. From the ducal seat he wrote to Kate Perry and Mrs Elliot. He had toured the great house, he reported, 'and oh but the Devil is with me still gnawing away and making me miserable'. In his frenzy he had picked up his manuscript, but what he wrote rather scared him. 'If I write my book in this frame of mind it will be diabolical.' Letters from

Brookfield, whom he referred to as 'Tomkins', showed that lines of communication were still open. 'He clings to the fancy that nobody knows anything about his interior,' he noted. The best news he could hope for, he maintained, was 'B continues to be good and gentle: that the reconciliation is complete: that, with all their might, he is striving to win her back, and she to return to her first affection.' Subsequently news arrived that Brookfield, ostensibly for the sake of his lungs, was taking his wife to Madeira for the winter. There was a single meeting at the end of October, convened at the Grange by a sympathetic Lady Ashburton, where a morning's 'parleying' produced 'not a reconciliation but a conciliation', after which the Brookfields quitted England, leaving Thackeray alone with his misery and his notebooks.

Inevitably one looks to fiction to discover what the parties thought of the inalienable fact of their separation. *Esmond*, on which Thackeray soon resumed work, together with his preparations to take *English Humourists* out into the provinces, is full of tantalising glimpses of his predicament. At its heart is not so much an emotional triangle as a quartet. Lady Castlewood, who guiltily loves the young Henry Esmond, is trapped in a once-happy marriage that has turned to wretchedness. Henry, meanwhile, is pursuing her daughter Beatrix. In the end, in a wish-fulfilling conclusion that shocked some Victorian critics, the mother wins out. Along the way, though, are many passages that look as if they have some kind of grounding in real arguments, notably the scene in which Lady Castlewood visits Esmond in prison and reproaches him for his interference. '"Why did you come among us?"' she demands, claiming that '". . . you pretended to love us – and we believed you"'.

Yet Thackeray was not the only creative writer involved in this emotional impasse. After his death Jane herself wrote several novels, at least two of which seem to have some bearing on her earlier life. The love-triangle of *Only George* (1866) is standard for the time – a young girl is tricked and effectively morally blackmailed into marrying a chilly old earl – but a number of its situations bristle with ulterior design. 'Ah! If we look back, how much the happiness or misery of our lives may depend on a few minutes – a chance visit, or, perhaps, a single word!' the narrator enigmatically pronounces. There is a revealing description of a young man named Basil Maitland, who dies – almost literally – of unrequited love. Worn out by illness, his eyes, 'which were the most remarkable feature of his face, appeared now unnaturally bright and large, and turned upon her with a melancholy

wistfulness'. This is couched in much the same tones as Jane's letter of
1849, which followed the visit to Young Street during Thackeray's
own serious illness. *Influence* (1871) is outwardly less promising, the
story of a girl named Alice Fenwick who is drawn into the circle of a
wealthy do-gooder named Miss Bickersteth. All the same, something
of the Brookfields' situation can perhaps be glimpsed in the portrait of
Alice's father: 'Mr Fenwick was sincerely attached to his wife. He
never forgot that he had taken her from a luxurious home when she
was young and handsome, and with the probability of a more brilliant
marriage before her, to share his fortune at the small vicarage on her
father's estate.' There is also the dashing young Frank Shirley, an
undergraduate at Trinity College, Cambridge, whose inflexible guardian complains that '"he is wasting his time over his drawings, one half
of them being foolish caricatures of his betters . . ."' and who
eventually loses his money in the collapse of the Indian banking
houses.

The emotion that Thackeray put into *Esmond* was all the more
impressive given the circumstances of its composition. Much of it was
written in hotel bedrooms or in vehicles of various kinds as he roamed
around the country on an autumn lecture tour. Three weeks' shuttling
between Oxford and Cambridge netted between £100 and £150 for
each engagement. Early in December he headed north by train to
Scotland, 'losing the romantic scenery along the line and only waking
up at the border to demm the railway man who asked for his ticket', he
told his daughters. Among the local dignitaries introduced to him was
Dr John Brown, a Scots physician with pronounced literary interests,
who wrote for *The Scotsman* and the *North British Review*. Thackeray
was delighted to meet the originator of his first public tribute – a silver
statuette of Mr Punch sent to him by his Edinburgh admirers during
the *Vanity Fair* boom – and haunted the latter's house. Brown, for his
part, left some shrewd impressions of his guest. In particular, he noted
his restlessness and his absorption in politics. 'He has much in him
which cannot find expression in mere authorship.' Surviving business
correspondence from this period shows how quickly Thackeray
acclimatised himself to the lecture circuit, enquiring after new
engagements and fixing up terms. These were generally advantageous –
he made £300 from his first Scottish trip. He was helped in these
arrangements by a resourceful new confidential servant, an appealing
and intelligent character named Samuel James, who proved adept at
smoothing over the thousand-and-one difficulties thrown up by this

kind of work. James, who had read his employer's books, was a man of parts, writing letters to *The Times* signed 'James de la Pluche' (Thackeray played up to this by addressing him as 'My dear de la P.') and before his eventual departure to Australia presenting the family with a set of china. Thackeray mourned his passing and presented him with an engraved silver watch.

The political interests that Brown had noted played their part in another storm that blew up over Christmas. Russell's Whig government was fading fast, not helped by criticism of Palmerston's Foreign Office approval of Louis Napoleon's bloody *coup d'état*. *Punch*, hugely critical of Palmerston, marked the latter event with a Leech cartoon of Louis Napoleon riding towards hell brandishing a bloody sword. To Thackeray, who had shaken his head about previous attacks on the Crystal Palace Exhibition and guyings of the Prince Consort – there had also been disagreements about money – this was the final straw. The assault on Palmerston was unfair, he thought; and the attack on Louis Napoleon unwise. He resigned, without apparent ill will on either side, continuing to make occasional contributions and enjoying the hospitality of the *Punch* dinners. He was sure it was best for both his own reputation and the paper's that he should go, he later told Frederick Evans. 'I fancied myself too big to pull in the boat; and it wasn't in the nature of things that Lemon & Jerrold should like me.' A by-product of the wider political crisis was that Eyre Evans Crowe and his son Joseph lost their jobs on the *Daily News*, and Thackeray applied himself strenuously on their behalf in the search for new employment.

There was no Christmas book for 1851: *Esmond* and the lectures claimed all his time. By now, too, enticed by the promise of high fees, he was contemplating an American tour some time in the next year. Boxing Day found him back from Scotland – he was 'immensely better' he told Smith, and had brought back a hatful of money – in advance of visits to the Grange and Lord Broughton. It was difficult to work in these circumstances, he complained, as he began to feel that he was a gentleman of leisure on £5,000 a year. He was less concerned by the Ashburtons' habit of spoiling Annie and Minnie. Meanwhile there was news of the Brookfields. While the invalid seemed to be recovering, 'the climate disagrees with his wife, who suffers ill health and prostration'. The flat tone of Jane's journal from this period confirms her listlessness in the aftermath of her severance from 'dear brother William'. Early in the New Year Thackeray gave his lectures again in London before settling down to a burst of work that saw him complete the second volume of *Esmond* at the end of March 1852. Something of his emotional state – his susceptibility and sudden impulses – may be divined from the interest he took in Mary Holmes, a relic of the old Devon days who wrote to him from Yorkshire asking for help in regard to a book she had published and in getting a post as a governess. Interested and sympathetic, Thackeray wrote her several kindly and confidential letters (one, about Jane, destroyed at his request), had her briefly to stay at Young Street, where she taught music to Annie and Minnie, and then began to regret the intimacy: in addition to being unattractive, Miss Holmes was a fanatical Catholic. Nevertheless, though the letters became less frequent he continued to interest himself in her efforts to find a job.

There was another Scottish tour in prospect, but Thackeray seems to have regarded it with mixed feelings. He arrived in Glasgow on 13 April with, he told Brown, 'a strong belief that it will turn out by no means a brilliant expedition'. The city, with its large Irish population, reminded him of Dublin – a 'queer sight'. He disliked its commercial air, too, which seemed disagreeably detached from Edinburgh's calm gentility. A day later he was asking William Stirling, 'For God's sake come North or I shall commit suicide. What a place it is! What a hatmosphere!' Worse, he felt that America would be the same, 'in which case I shall die'.

A civil letter from Bradbury & Evans shortly afterwards brought further indications of his success: since *Vanity Fair* he had brought the firm profits of £3,000. Gratified, Thackeray went so far as to ask for a testimonial – nothing excessive, perhaps 'a couple of plain cups or something of that sort, that the children might have after me'. One of them might be called the Dobbin and the other the Warrington, he joked. He was still struggling to finish *Esmond* – 'The book seems as if it would never end,' he complained – and taking a detailed interest in its production (ultimately an antique typeface was pressed into service to enhance the period flavour at which he aimed). The Brookfields were back from Madeira, but he refused the invitation that came and fled to the Continent. It was an uneventful excursion, taken on his own (his mother had the children staying with her), marked by the loss of his pocketbook with £100 inside and the prospective forfeiture of the £200 George Smith had promised for an unwritten travel book. Back in London, he was conscious that a hard autumn lay before him – more trips to north-west England followed by his American tour.

Fearful of the volume of work that awaited him, he had already engaged Eyre Crowe once more as secretary, telling him that 'six months tumbling about the world will do you no harm'. Crowe spent the late summer correcting the proofs of *Esmond* as they came in, while Thackeray went on jaunts to Fitzgerald's mother's home at Richmond and to Holland House. Writing to the girls, still staying in Paris with their grandmother, he explained the saga of Miss Holmes, now gone abroad as a governess on twenty pounds a year ('She is friendless alone but courageous & highminded and I've done no harm in doing what good I could'), spoke of Mrs Bakewell's favourable reports of Isabella and mused over the proofs of his novel. 'It reads better in print, it is clever but it is also stupid and no mistake.' A sentence or two of hints dropped about his next book suggests that *The Newcomes* was already brewing in his mind.

Early in September he went north to deliver the abortive address to the Manchester Free Library Association, feeling 'very foolish', he told Minnie, before recovering sufficiently to speak without upset later in the day. For the seventeen-day stint at Manchester and Liverpool he shuttled back and forth on a daily basis, speaking on the Tuesday and the Thursday in one city and on the Wednesday and the Friday in the other. Crowe, monitoring the attendances, noted the contrast between the well-filled room at the Manchester Athenaeum and the poor turnout at Liverpool. The *Liverpool Mercury*'s report of 1 October lamented that 'a more heart-depressing sight than that which presented itself to Mr Thackeray I have never witnessed . . .' Subsequently, however, the numbers picked up. It was while staying in Liverpool, early in October – he took lodgings in Renshaw Street – that he heard of the death of his old friend Savile Morton, murdered by a compromised husband. Thackeray reminisced mournfully to Crowe about his friend's life: 'one scrape', he concluded. To Richard Monckton-Milnes he acknowledged that there was no excuse for Morton or his end, however badly the woman had been treated by Morton's assassin. He had been 'the maddest wildest & gentlest of creatures – scarce answerable for his actions or his passions'. Liverpool brought other jolts. Looking into the window of a print shop, he found the likeness of another dead friend, the city's former chief magistrate Edward Rushton, whom he had known at the Reform Club. Then in the library of the Manchester Athenaeum he discovered an article in the *New York Herald*, an American newspaper known for its hostility to visiting English celebrities, denouncing his forthcoming visit.

The days were slipping away. From Liverpool on 13 October he wrote to Jane, regretting that he would miss seeing 'my dear sister' when he returned to London. The lecture series ended two days later and he sped home. His departure to America was barely a fortnight distant, but there were still arrangements to make. In particular, he wanted someone to work up additional notes for *English Humourists*, due to be published during his absence, and, he felt, too insubstantial to be issued without some kind of critical apparatus. A letter was sent to James Hannay, then in his home-town of Dumfries, offering him the job. Always attentive where Thackeray's interests were concerned, Hannay wrote immediately to accept and rushed south in a mail coach. Thackeray was staying at the Grange, and contact was not established until 28 October, when Hannay 'Breakfasted and spent the morning', and received instructions about the lectures and a parcel containing Thackeray's manuscript. Although his employer had suggested that the work might prove 'a pleasant occupation', Hannay spent several weeks chained to a desk at the British Museum, made himself ill in the process and ended up producing a volume of material that practically exceeded Thackeray's text. With Hannay set gratefully to work, nothing else remained to be done. Farewells were exchanged and bags packed. The New World beckoned.

The engraver's tale: Samuel Jones, Punch *engraver*

Well, no, I never did like him above half, and I don't mind who knows it. He was a trifle haughty, a high feller (as we used to say of swells in those days) and I don't recall him taking much interest in chaps of our kind. Oh, he was pally enough with Mr Lemon, and there were one or two of the younger sort – that Hannay was one – who looked up to him, but with me it was always 'Day to you, Jones', sometimes not even that. Which was gammon, if you like, when you think that we were doing for him something he couldn't do himself. He could draw, you see, after a fashion, but he couldn't do it *professional*-like, and some of the blocks as he set to work on himself, well you could have wept over the botch he made of them – dust all smeared up, great ugly lines hacked into the wood . . .

A haughty kind of a cove, then, looking at you over his eye-glass. A great one for the nobs, too, I heard say, always ready to tip his tile to Lord John or a bishop. But he was affable with his daughters, I'll allow him that – I was collecting a block once at Kensington when one of them bounced up to him, and it was a sight that would do your heart good. And I did hear that when Jackie Forrester, who was one of our set – used to work for Mr Swain – and a sad one for the drink, died unexpected, it was he that looked to his family and subbed two guineas for the funeral fund. So perhaps there was good in him that I didn't see . . .

XVI

Stepping Westward

'Life passes in such a whirl here that I have scarcely even time to write to my own children. But I think about 'em a great deal and talk about 'em so as to bore people.'

Letter to Annie and Minnie, 7 December 1852

e left London on 29 October 1852 and, together with Crowe, took the train to Liverpool. The two of them dined at the house of a local iron-merchant, which looked out over the Mersey and its forest of ship's masts. In addition to the host, Mr Ratcliffe, other local grandees including the mayor of Liverpool were assembled to say farewell to a man who had been a fixture of the city's cultural life for the past month. Ten o'clock the next morning found them on the landing-stage, where a messenger narrowly managed to deliver some early copies of *Esmond*, before embarking on the Royal Mail ship *Canada* under Captain Lang.

Thackeray's letters from around this time betray some of the anxiety he felt about this extended working holiday. Part of this had to do with the journey itself, and its 3,000-mile sea voyage. Rather more concerned Annie and Minnie and the restrictions that would undoubtedly be imposed on them by Mrs Carmichael-Smyth. A third element lay in what he might find in America itself. Transatlantic interest in English novelists – Thackeray had been widely pirated by US firms – was balanced by a widespread resentment of the kind of book that Englishmen and -women wrote about their travels. Dickens' *American Notes*, now a decade old, had gone down just as badly as Mrs Trollope's earlier *Domestic Manners of the Americans*. To some

American newspapers the news that Thackeray was arriving for a lecture tour could only have one consequence, and the *New York Herald* in particular had already unleashed several proleptic brickbats. Then there was the burning social issue currently dividing American society, on which nearly every overseas visitor found himself asked for an opinion. Well before he left England, Thackeray seems to have decided to keep quiet, at any rate publicly, on the question of slavery – as Crowe put it, 'judicious friends had dinned well into his ears the propriety of his not committing himself to either side . . . if he wished his career as a lecturer not to become a burthen on him'. But he knew that it would be all around him and that his attitude towards it would be closely monitored. All this bred an understandable caution and nervousness. Three days before his departure he wrote a highly emotional letter to Fitz, commending the girls to his care should anything happen to their father. In thinking about his 'dear old boy', his great comfort was 'that recollection of our youth when we loved each other as I do now while I write farewell'. Once having arrived in America, he found it 'absurd' that he should have been so gloomy. Crowe had witnessed a road accident in which a boy was flung out of a cart and killed, and Thackeray realised that a calamity of this kind set some of his fears in perspective. For the moment, though, he was fretful and morose, not relishing his departure from England or what he might find on the farther shore.

Many years after his travelling companion's death, Crowe wrote an account of their trip entitled *With Thackeray in America*. It is not a particularly informative book – the Thackeray who wanders through it is a queerly anonymous figure – nor does it leave much of an impression of Crowe, who features as a rather inefficient and accident-prone companion, always liable to forget the luggage or, on one occasion, himself. Crowe's oddest characteristic, perhaps, is his unwillingness to engage in any meaningful way with the events he was recounting, or to do so in a way that seems faintly gauche. Much of this stems from the distance imposed by time, but something of Crowe's naïvety perhaps emerges in his account of an odd and, given their destination, symbolic incident that took place in the ship's bar late one night a few days into the voyage. Here, inflamed by drink, several of the passengers got up a mock slave auction in which the Negro bar steward was eventually knocked down at a tremendous price. 'The free man probably took it as a great compliment' is Crowe's only comment, 'and an acknowledgment of his efficiency in the serving line', which seems criminally patronising even by the standards of the nineteenth century. None the less, Thackeray liked his companion, not so much for what he was as for what he represented: the memories of an earlier life when the Crowes' house in Paris had been one of his regular ports of call. Crowe's account of the voyage out and their subsequent travels up and down the north-eastern seaboard does convey a certain amount of camaraderie. Plenty of this was in evidence on the *Canada*, which offered several other distinguished travellers – in particular the American man of letters James Russell Lowell and the poet A.H. Clough – and a fund of conviviality. Six days out, Thackeray confessed himself already 'weary of guzzling and gorging and bumping in bed all night and being sick all day'. In this hermetic atmosphere the immediate past telescoped away into the distance. As for Esmond, Thackeray told Annie and Minnie that he had already forgotten about him 'and seems like everything else to have happened 100 years ago'. But he appears to have enjoyed this sea-bound interregnum in his life: it had been a very kindly, companionable voyage, he told his mother, with 'plenty of good fellows, merry dinners and pleasant cigars'.

They arrived in Boston on 9 November to a muted welcome. *American Notes* had dampened Yankee ardour for publicly greeting distinguished foreign visitors, and Crowe noted the absence of reporters at the quayside. Proceeding to the Tremont House hotel, they were met by James T. Fields, the trip's principal sponsor, in the banqueting room: 'a very snug room in a very good hotel', Thackeray informed his daughter, even if the people had not been out with 'flag and drum' to receive him with the enthusiasm that had attended Dickens. Still, there were substantial compensations. Clough turned out to be staying on the same premises, and after a session at the dinner table even the Garrick Club gourmand was prepared to speak of native oysters with respect. The experience had been like eating a baby, he told Fields.

Thackeray was impressed by his first glimpses of America. He liked the people, relished the hospitality they offered him and appreciated the financial results. Within a fortnight of his arrival he was writing to tell the girls that he felt certain he had taken the correct decision in coming: 'barring accidents and ill health we shall all profit by this venture . . .' The fêting that accompanied Dickens' travels may have eluded him, but there were plenty of local celebrities eager to shake his hand and watch him perform. In this way he was introduced to

Emerson, Longfellow, the elderly Washington Irvine, Charles Eliot Norton and Oliver Wendell Holmes. An incoming president and his retiring predecessor came to hear Thackeray lecture. Occasionally these encounters had implications for his future work: it was in the study of the blind historian William Prescott that he saw the crossed swords belonging to two brothers who had fought on opposing sides in the American War of Independence, which gave him the idea for *The Virginians*. If the American newspapers' obsession with personal detail rather bewildered him (he wrote and despatched a parody self-portrait on these lines to *Fraser's*), he liked what he diagnosed as honesty and openness and the relentless bustle. More important, this frank enjoyment of the teeming American streets was not compromised by the obligation to collect 'impressions' for later use. At an early stage he made a firm decision not to use his experiences as material for a travel book. There were aesthetic reasons for this – what could Dickens mean by writing 'that book of *American Notes*', he wondered later on in the trip. 'No man should write about the country under 5 years of experience, and as many of previous reading' – but they combined with a shrewd idea of the practical consequences. With the example of Dickens and Mrs Trollope before him, Thackeray was convinced that anything he wrote would be damned.

His lecture tour was due to begin a week later in New York. Thackeray filled in the time with sight-seeing and visiting itinerant notabilities. Alfred Bunn, of all people, turned out to be staying at a nearby hotel, along with the celebrated prima donna Madame Sontag. Thackeray took the opportunity to hear her sing at the Melodeon Hall, where he was due to lecture a month later, so that he could get an idea of the acoustics, but the occasion was marked by an odd party trick. Sitting with Crowe and Fields, Thackeray began to amuse himself by devising imaginary character sketches of the people sitting around them. Crowe's mild interest turned to astonishment when Fields, who knew many of the subjects, pointed out that in most cases the sketches were uncannily accurate. They left Boston by train for New York early on the morning of 16 November. A further fillip to Thackeray's esteem came when he discovered that the young bookseller making his way down the carriage was offering pirated copies of his own works. He bought a copy of *A Shabby Genteel Story* and drowsed over it as the train sped through Massachusetts. Crowe, meanwhile, had laid out twenty-five cents on *Uncle Tom's Cabin*. Moved by the contents, he tried to press it on his employer. Thackeray declined. Such painful themes, he told Crowe, were 'scarcely within the legitimate purview of storytelling'.

Thackeray arrived in New York alone. Crowe, stepping out onto the platform for lunch *en route*, got left behind and had to follow in a later train. By the time he arrived, Thackeray had extricated their baggage, conveyed it to their hotel, the Clarendon, and dealt with a clutch of waiting interviewers. Callers included the historian and politician George Bancroft, with whom he struck up a friendship during his stay, but more immediately productive was a visit from the newspaper magnate Horace Greeley, founder of the *New York Tribune* and the *New Yorker*. Identifying a useful pawn in his circulation war with the *Herald*, Greeley instructed one of his senior staff writers to compose a puff in the *Tribune*. Henry James senior, whose nine-year-old son Henry junior Thackeray met at this time, laid it on with a trowel. 'He comes on the invitation of the Mercantile Library Association,' the *Tribune* grandly informed its readers. This organisation and its supporters 'aspire to the culture of scholars and gentlemen, and import from abroad – not the latest teacher of double entry, but the most thoughtful critic of manners and society, the subtlest humorist, and the most effective, because the most genial, satirist the age has known . . .' However much Thackeray may have disliked the relentless publicising of the American papers, such encomia undoubtedly brought people to see him. A first series of lectures, staged in a Unitarian chapel in Manhattan (the lecturer mounted a rostrum erected in front of the pulpit) had been planned to run from 19 November to 6 December, but demand prompted Fields and his colleague Willard Felt of the Mercantile Library Association to advertise a second, extended series running to the week before Christmas. Thackeray gladly acceded. Irrespective of the warm reception, it upped his profit on the first six weeks of his stay to £500 (the money went into US railway shares, which paid 7–8 per cent interest, twice the rate of English consols). Comment was largely favourable. R.H. Dana junior thought that 'His enunciation is perfect. Every word he uttered might be heard in the remotest quarters of the room, yet he scarcely lifted his voice above a colloquial tone.' Meanwhile, the first of Thackeray's enthusiastic letters home had reached Annie and Minnie in Paris. Annie reported to her friend Laetitia Cole that 'Papa had got there quite safely though with rather a bad passage & says he lived upon champagne all the way out . . .' Even at a distance of 3,000 miles, Thackeray was concerned that his daughters should not think that he had forgotten them. One treat, fixed up by Mrs Proctor, was the despatch of a lavishly decorated cake. Minnie wrote excitedly to thank him – 'It is so big and such beautiful gentlemen and grapes and above all an English cake from an English papa.'

The English papa was still enjoying himself. At the end of November he wrote to Mrs Elliot and Kate Perry enthusing over what he imagined to be an absence of American social demarcations. 'Everybody seems his neighbour's equal. They begin without a dollar and make fortunes in 5 years –' Simultaneously the success of the first lecture series had made Thackeray an object of consuming interest to local panjandrums. In particular, among the notes from autograph-hunters and the hatter who wanted to acknowledge the pleasure he got from his work by presenting him with a hat (Thackeray declined and sent Crowe in his stead) came an invitation to meet P.T. Barnum at his famous museum. Ostensibly the great impresario and freak-collector wanted Thackeray to collaborate in a newspaper venture in imitation of the *Illustrated London News*. His real interest, however, seems to have been in acquiring some kind of financial stake in what promised to be a lucrative tour. Thackeray, who knew something about Barnum's promotional methods, and in any case wanted to keep control of both his itinerary and the bulk of the profits, declined. He also turned down the invitation to appear in Barnum's newspaper.

But New York offered both professional and personal comforts. His attitude to Harper Brothers, who had shamelessly flouted his copyright to produce unlicensed (and unpaid-for) editions of his books, characteristically became more benign when, on a visit to their offices, he was introduced to a young Miss Harper. Shaking her hand, Thackeray could not resist remarking, 'So this is a pirate's daughter, is it?' James Harper subsequently redeemed himself by offering $1,000 for a book based on the lectures. Meanwhile Thackeray's first lecture in Manhattan had brought an even more significant introduction. Curiously, the entrée to the Baxter household on Second Avenue came courtesy of one his recent aristocratic connections, Lady Ashburton's nephew Henry Brigham Mildmay, who was attempting to court the elder daughter Sarah, commonly known as Sally. There were male Baxters – George, the head of the household, and his two young sons – but it was the ladies who stirred his interest: Mrs Baxter, then in her early fifties, Sally and her sixteen-year-old sister Lucy. The Baxters were middle-class New Yorkers (one of Thackeray's grander local friends asked him not to reveal the fact that he had brought him to their door) and it was the liveliness of their household rather than any social advantages that explained Thackeray's continual visits. Letters back to Mrs Proctor and the *bonnes soeurs* made clear how entirely – if self-consciously – besotted he was: Sally featured as 'Beatrix', her mother as 'Lady Castlewood'. Later, as he headed south towards Virginia, a lavish correspondence kept these new relationships aflame. There was even a plan that the Baxters should visit London the following summer. What seems a classic case of middle-aged infatuation is always tempered by Thackeray's awareness of what he was doing. He knew very well that in writing tender notes to a girl less than half his age – among her many beaux, he once deposed, there was 'not one who regards her so *very* truly as this present one' – he was laying himself open to ridicule, and his response was merely to acknowledge his own absurdity. As with Jane, there is a sense in which this is a paper relationship, fashioned out of absence, and attended by an absolute fatalism. Sally would get married, Thackeray knew, to some New York buck next to whom his own masculine pretensions – at forty-one he was already feeling the weight of advancing age – would seem ludicrous. To delude himself would be futile, and yet more painful.

His New York schedule was packed – four lectures at the Female Academy, Brooklyn, in the space of eight days – but he kept up with the news from home. Early reviews of *Esmond* were favourable, and the *Spectator* notice, which suggested that he 'could not have painted Vanity Fair as he has, unless Eden had been shining in his inner eye', reduced him to tears. George Smith had already reported that the first edition of 3,000 copies had been disposed of. The end of the first week in December found him analysing the experience of America for the benefit of Mrs Elliot and Kate Perry. It was 'the most curious varnish of civilisation', he thought. 'The girls are dressed like the most stunning French actresses – the houses furnished like the most splendid gambling houses . . .' – so new, in many cases, that the walls were not yet papered. In time the novelty of American life, the lack of tradition or even settled habit, would begin to pall, but for the moment Thackeray exulted in it, detecting what he later diagnosed as a sense of 'citizenship and general freedom'. He wrote a long letter to Lady Ashburton analysing the habits of New York's 'Upper Ten' and concluding that 'It's just like London, only the laws of fashion are different . . . In order to be able to be quite at the head of fashion you needn't be able to speak or write English or any other language, you may sell coals or bones or drugs, but your wife must build a wonderful house must dress in a wonderful way a new gown every night . . .' He was amused, at a house 'not *quite* Upper Ten', to see two ladies of the most matchless social reputation arrive. 'They came quite late – they looked round quite blandly just for all the world like London – only instead of being introduced to Lady Jasey or the Marchioness of Heydownderry – you are presented to Mrs. Jones & Mrs. Haight.' However delighted by the novelty of these social arrangements, Thackeray was also keen to offer up some distinctly hierarchical oblations back in England. A letter to Smith of 7 December accompanied two dozen canvas-backed ducks – Christmas presents for, among others, Lord Stanley of Alderney and the Ladies Molesworth and Talfourd.

He stayed in New York until a few days short of Christmas, then returned for more engagements in Boston and the surrounding area; 22 December took him to Providence, Rhode Island. For relaxation he went to the Museum of Pictures in Boston (Crowe noted that he was particularly struck by the portrait of General Washington and his wife by Gilbert Stuart) and conducted a by now customary round of celebrity visits and tea-parties. There was time, however, on Christmas Eve to write his usual letter to Dr Elliotson. He was laying up a good bit of money on his daughters' behalf, Thackeray reported. 'But for you I should have died most likely and left them without a penny, and I like to think of you at Xmas time in their name & mine.' On Old Year's Night, lecturing on Prior, Gay and Pope, he attracted a 'prodigious audience' of a thousand people. The following week would have brought him a rather sad little letter from Jane – it was written three days before Christmas – then at Clifton nursing her sick father. Brookfield was seriously depressed, she confided, so much so that had she not trusted her judgment of him 'I should dread his taking poison or doing something desperate.' Two-year-old Magdalene, meanwhile, maintained that she could remember Thackeray's face. Jane's comments on Brookfield are perhaps her strongest acknowledgment of the aloof, deliberative side of his character. He grew more sad and silent as time went by, she revealed, and was 'evidently dissatisfied in that last parting with you'. She disclosed that afterwards Brookfield had called on the Elliots to ask if he had been *especially* cold: had the answer been 'yes', she thought he would have taken steps to ensure that they parted in a more friendly way. But the Elliots were non-committal, and nothing had been done.

What did Thackeray make of this letter, with its plaintive tone, its odd gratuitousness over Magdalene – Jane's exact report of her words were that 'You look like *somebody* – I don't remember the name, but your face looks like – oh, Mr Thackeray, that we met at the Grange', which seems faintly implausible – and the vision of Brookfield brooding on in solitary desperation? His only comment on Jane at this time came a month or so later in a letter to the *bonnes soeurs*, where he noted the value of the American trip in 'consummating' their separation, as he put it, and hoped that she would be away when he returned in the summer. It was 'decent' that they should not meet, he concluded, before ending with a lacerating piece of ironic self-disparagement: 'However much I may love her & bless her and admire her, I can't forgive her for doing her duty.' But if Jane's voice continued to speak to him, there were also pressing daily concerns to deal with. Early January 1853 brought a series of engagements in Philadelphia and Baltimore, as well as a return to New York. It was on the way to Baltimore – he had gone in advance to arrange the lecture – that Crowe had his first taste of racial segregation, when a Negro passenger on the train whom he had begun to sketch was ordered into another carriage by the conductor. At Baltimore Thackeray lectured from a pulpit at the Universalist Church. Back in New York he wrote to Smith enthusing over the 'capital time' he had enjoyed at Boston and the money put away, casting a rueful eye over the latest reviews (the notices by Forster in the *Examiner* and Samuel Phillips in *The Times* were clearly intended as counterweights to the earlier enthusiasm) and asking for some engraved notepaper and envelopes as a present for Sally Baxter. There had been no reports of Isabella, and Smith, who seems to have been happy to carry out commissions of this kind, was also requested to write to Mrs Bakewell, then residing in Essex, in search of news.

As the whistle-stop tour around the north-east continued, Thackeray found himself increasingly absorbed in recent American history, largely because its trail lay all around him. On 18 January, prior to leaving Philadelphia, Crowe had sat and sketched the portico in front of which the Declaration of Independence had been pronounced, while much of Thackeray's hospitality in the city was provided by its district attorney William Bradford Reed, a future American minister to China, with whom he pursued several conversations about colonial

Statuette of Thackeray by Sir Edgar Boehm

Annie

Minnie

The Thackeray family's *carte de visite* in the late 1850s

A later portrait of Minnie with Laura Stephen

Major and Mrs Carmichael-Smyth in 1855

Brecquerecque, near Boulogne, the Carmichael-Smyth's holiday home in 1854

Aunt Ritchie

Edith Story as a young woman

(*Below left*)
James Hannay

(*Below right*)
Edmund Yates

Dr Elliotson

(*Below left*) Charles Collins

(*Below right*) Kate Collins
(*née* Dickens, later Perugini)

Chalk drawing of Thackeray by Samuel Lawrence, 1862

Thackeray's newly dedicated gravestone at Kensal Green, with wrong date of death

history. Thackeray liked Philadelphia, went down well among the resident English community and was even urged to apply for the job of British consul (he declined, but there was an odd coda to the episode a year later when the secretaryship to the Washington legation fell vacant – this time he allowed his name to go forward, but was turned down). He was similarly appreciative of Washington, where the tour now moved on, enjoying the expatriate hospitality, and what Crowe calls the 'high jinks' of balls, concerts and parties. It was here that the two presidents – Fillmore and Pierce – turned up to hear him (Thackeray had earlier dined with Fillmore, the outgoing head of state, at the White House). To their amusement the lecturer compared them to 'the two Kings of Brentford smelling at one rose'. Not all of his expeditions were being undertaken for personal profit, and Crowe records how a spare day at the end of January produced the lecture 'Charity and Humour'. Having briefly returned to New York, he was approached by some supporters of a 'Ladies' Society for the Employment and Relief of the Poor', and volunteered to produce something for them. With the luxury of a day off before him, he spent it in bed smoking and scribbling. When the dinner gong sounded he discovered, to his surprise, that the manuscript was complete. 'I don't know where it's all coming from,' he told Crowe. The lecture, which eventually became one of his staples on the charity circuit, was publicly aired a day or so later at the Church of the Messiah on Broadway, where 1,200 people paid a dollar each for admission.

In the ten weeks he had so far spent in America, Thackeray had tried not to attract any personal publicity to himself or to become involved in any of the controversies of the day. Hitherto his defence had held, but there was trouble in Washington, where he was invited to inspect the recently unveiled statue of President Jackson. Privately Thackeray sympathised with some of the criticism that had been aimed at this not very distinguished piece of art, but he was determined not to make a public comment. Eventually, prompted by a mischief-making congressman, he ventured a mild remonstrance, only to be rebuked for arrogance and impertinence by a Washington paper that had got hold of the story. Thackeray seems to have ignored the incident in his letters home, but one wonders whether his love affair with America had already begun to lose something of its bloom by this stage. Certainly he was bored with lecturing – 'that dreary business' he called it in a letter to Mrs Elliot and Kate Perry, begun in a spare half-hour one evening in early February before he was called to the rostrum. At the same time his comments on the society laid out for his inspection were becoming more discriminating. He liked New York, Boston and Philadelphia, he told the *bonnes soeurs*: they were not as civilised as London, perhaps, but better than Manchester and Liverpool. But always in the journeying to and fro, in snatched half-hours between engagements, dull mornings in distant hotel rooms, he had the Baxters to keep him company. A letter from Philadelphia early in January asks for 'a little word of SSB'. The ensuing fortnight brought a reply from 'your little Lucy', standing in for her sister on the grounds of the latter's ill health, and a letter from Sally herself acknowledging some verses. 'I have found Miss Beatrix in New York,' Thackeray wrote to Jane not long afterwards. 'I have basked in her

bright eye: but ah me, I don't care for her – and shall hear of her marrying a New York buck with a feeling of perfect pleasure.' A large part of this is the habitual ironic self-deflation; a little more is the beckoning of Mrs Brookfield into an alliance of middle-aged persons looking fondly down on the doings of young people; but there is also the faint sense of Thackeray enjoying himself by advertising to an old love his new-found susceptibility to female charms that are emphatically not hers. His relationship with Jane would never regain its former height, and his sentimental yearnings over a New York teenager marked out the distance between them.

His stay in Washington lasted three weeks. A letter from Sally Baxter towards the end of February brought the news that Lucy had seriously injured herself in a gymnasium accident, thanked him for his *thoughtfulness*, but put an end to his hopes of welcoming the family to England ('. . . even had Lu been well I should have hesitated about the expediency of such a pleasure just at this time'). He wrote to Minnie enclosing a picture of the Negro servant who cleaned his hotel chamber. 'Isn't she a pretty dear?' Thackeray wondered. 'She goes about with that pipe in her mouth and leaves it sometimes about in our room.' At this point he was still intending to stay in America until July, following up a tour of the South with an excursion westward to St Louis and possibly even an assault on Canada. For the moment, though, the trail led down the Potomac River by steamship to

Virginia. Delays *en route* meant that they were late arriving in Richmond, the state capital, and the first of Thackeray's initial three lectures waited until the last day of February. He was amused to find his arrival announced in the local paper together with that of a travelling conjuror and his retinue: 'Mr Thackeray, the celebrated author; Mr Anderson, Wizard of the North'.

Thackeray enjoyed the hospitality that was offered to him in the South. Undoubtedly, along with the juleps and the local cuisine, he imbibed a certain amount of propaganda about the merits of slavery, but the evidence of his letters suggests that his scepticism towards the abolitionist cause was already engrained. He knew that slavery was wrong – his moral sense could never allow him to think otherwise – but he thought that the majority of slaves were well treated. 'The happiness of the nigger is quite a curiosity to witness,' he wrote in a letter to Albany Fonblanque, which remains an odd blend of complacency and shrewdness. Significantly, he felt that the English abolitionists who fêted Mrs Stowe were blind to some of the miseries endured by the population of their own country: if you wanted to 'move your bowels with compassion for human unhappiness', as he put it, plenty of that aperient was to be found at home. Moreover, it was 'the most costly domestic machinery ever devised' – at least a dozen slaves to do the work that would be performed by four English servants, and to a worse standard. And it was all too clear to him what freedom, and the obligation to compete with whites in the labour market, would mean to the average black inhabitant of Virginia: 'The most awful curse & ruin . . . which fate ever yet sent him'.

At a distance of almost 150 years there is not much point in belittling Thackeray for attitudes that a modern eye would immediately mark down as racist. Scrupulously polite and kindly disposed to the slaves he encountered, he nevertheless did not regard them as his equals and thought English agitation on their behalf misplaced. 'They are not suffering as you are impassioning yourself for their wrongs as you read Mrs Stowe,' he told the fervently abolitionist Mrs Carmichael-Smyth, 'they are grinning & joking in the sun.' He admitted that he found the physical appearance of the negro distasteful. 'Sambo is not my man & my brother; the very aspect of his face is grotesque and inferior.' All that can be said in his defence is that such attitudes were shared by large numbers of early-Victorian men and women, and that the kind of emotional displacement that allowed Victorian philanthropists to talk of their 'duty to the poor black' while ignoring their duty to the crossing sweeper twenty yards away (think of the Jellabys in Bleak House) was commonplace. This is not to excuse or defend anything that Thackeray wrote or said about the slave question, merely to place his remarks in a context that is not and can never be our own. Also, as even the most cursory trawl through The Newcomes makes plain, the experience of viewing the slave plantations, if only from the verandahs of his wealthy hosts, had profound consequences for his work.

Thackeray was careful not to go public with his opinions, which he knew were liable to be expropriated (and misrepresented) by both sides. However, this careful attempt to distance himself from the issue came close to destruction on 3 March. Leafing through the local paper, Crowe saw an advertisement for a slave auction in a street near the hotel ('Fifteen likely negroes to be disposed of between half-past nine and twelve – five men, six women, two boys and two girls') and decided to attend. Having watched the Negroes being inspected, he took out his sketching pad and began making drawings of the scene. Assuming that they were being spied on by some northern propagandist, the dealers and buyers suspended operations and drew the auctioneer's attention to Crowe's presence in the crowd. According to his own account – one of the livelier episodes in his book – Crowe's parting words to the angry onlookers were 'You may turn me away, but I can recollect all I have seen.' Thackeray's judgment in a letter to a friend was that 'Crowe has been very imprudent.' His immediate fear was that it would be picked up by one of the newspapers – as it happened, the New York Tribune did subsequently refer to it in a letter written by a New Yorker on a tour of the South who had also been present at the auction. Crowe thought that only a well-connected friend's intervention stopped details of the incident from gaining wider circulation.

Audiences in Richmond had been good. As they went deeper into the South, the enthusiasm became less marked. At Petersburg, 'a somewhat somnolent-looking town' where Crowe went in advance to make arrangements, the hall was so destitute of furniture that he ended up buying a desk at a local drugstore. Hardly anyone came, even the customary crowd of post-lecture hangers-on failing to present themselves, and Crowe remembered the sight of his employer 'philosophical over this queer breach in the hitherto continuous spell of successes, as he afterwards whiffed his cigar, without anyone joining us, in the hotel parlour'. The most interesting parts of Crowe's reminiscences can be found in these descriptions of the South. The Richmond slave auction seems to have brought home to him some of the implications of slavery in a way that the mocked-up version of the ship had not, and his account of the remainder of the tour contains several examples of secretary and lecturer taking the opportunity to examine local conditions. Crowe, for example, button-holed a young Negro whom he saw digging in a small field: the man turned out to be working an allotment, and reported that many of his fellow labourers had been allowed these smallholdings by a liberal-minded landlord. Investigations of this kind presumably spurred Thackeray to write a later letter to Dr John Brown – one of several in this vein – claiming that 'It's all exaggeration about this country: barbarism, eccentricities, nigger-cruelties and all.'

From Petersburg they headed back towards Richmond, taking tickets on a steamer that plied between Wilmington and Charleston. Their arrival in Charleston was announced in the local paper of 8 March with Thackeray's name misspelt, but the series of lectures given at the town's Hibernian Institute attracted enthusiastic audiences. Despite the approbation of the Charleston élite, Thackeray was fast becoming jaded. Writing to Lucy Baxter, he declared himself 'brown-house-sick' (a reference to the Baxters' brownstone house), homesick, 'and as for lecture-sick, O Steward! bring me a basin!' Lucy had been reading *Villette*, and Thackeray's estimate of the novel's points – he commended its 'fine style' and the author's ability to carry a metaphor through to its logical conclusion – combined with a shrewd idea of its connection to Charlotte Brontë's own life. He could read a great deal of her in her book, he reported, 'and see that rather than have fame or rather than any other earthly good or mayhap heavenly one she wants some Tomkins or another to love her and be in love with. But you see she is a little bit of a creature without a penny worth of good looks, thirty years old I should think buried in the country, and eating up her own heart there, and no Tomkins will come.'

There were still a few more stops to be made on the southern tour, and their observation of Negro society continued. Crowe sketched a young Negro girl who confided her great grievance to him: she was not allowed by her master to go and see a play. Back at Charleston they paid another visit to a slave auction, this time without controversy. Again Crowe's account is oddly disengaged, and the men and women put up on the block by the auctioneer seem little more than exotic curiosities. Even in the American South, Thackeray kept up his habit of falling in with the ramifications of his family. A young English army officer named Rankin whom they picked up at this time, penniless after the ransacking of his luggage, turned out to be a distant relative. Thackeray obligingly bailed him out. The final leg of the tour took them even further south, to Savannah, Georgia, where wayside accommodation left much to be desired. Coming into Thackeray's hotel bedroom on the morning after their arrival, Crowe discovered that his employer's face and limbs were blotched with flea bites, while the floor and chairs were covered with the spent matches Thackeray had used in an attempt to drive the beasts away. They were rescued by the English consul, who carried them off to stay in his private residence, but such indignities increased Thackeray's disillusion with his working holiday.

April found them heading northwards, for more engagements in Albany and New York, but although Thackeray still appeared to have his sights set on Canada, his private doubts were mounting. He had been away nearly half a year and missed his family, worrying especially over his stepfather who had recently suffered a minor stroke. While he tried to make his mind up there was an altogether more pleasant commission to fulfil: a poem for Lucy Baxter's seventeenth birthday. The scheme was advertised in a letter to Mrs Baxter written on the morning of the day in question – 15 April ('Is anyone going to give Miss Lucy a bokay wth 17 rosebuds?' he wondered. 'I have been making some verses under that idea: but it won't be worth while to purchase *two* bouquets. So if you have ordered one, I will only contribute the rhymes, wh. are not completed yet by . . .') Some elegant stanzas followed later in the day:

Seventeen rose-buds in a ring
Thick with sister-flowers beset
In a fragrant coronet
Lucy's servants this day bring . . .

Still he was trying to make up his mind. The temptation to add to his substantial receipts was strong. A letter to George Smith of 16 April, lamenting mistakes in a recently received printed copy of the lectures, suspected that 'my lecturing is pretty well over', although at this point the Canadian trip still seemed to be on. In the end the departure signal came with what Crowe called 'the suddenness of a thunder clap'. On 19 April Thackeray told his mother that 'my conscience revolts against reading these old sermons over and over: and I have given up St Louis & the West, and declined Montreal'. Coming into Thackeray's room early on the morning of the next day, Crowe found his employer bent over a newspaper. There was a Cunarder leaving that morning, he explained, and he was off to Wall Street to book a passage. Some hasty farewells – there was only time for a brief handshake with the Baxters – were followed by a breakneck cab-ride down to the East River, where the boat, the *Europa*, lay ready to depart. Thackeray wrote his final goodbyes – to friends he had expected to meet in the next few days – on board ship, apologising for his haste. 'It was all thought of and done in a couple of hours,' he explained to Mrs Bancroft. The ship, with its mixed cargo of travellers ('we have Spaniards and Frenchmen and a Bishop (apparently) and a Negro clergyman on board') set off towards the open water, and Thackeray became aware, yet again, of one of the queer coincidences that seemed to haunt his life. One of the *Europa*'s officers turned out to have been on board the boat that Dickens had sailed out in a decade and half before. Interested, Thackeray asked if the weather conditions had been as terrific as Dickens had painted them in *American Notes*, and was assured that they had. Fortunately his own return trip was uneventful. By 2 May, after a fortnight's voyage eastward via Cork, he was deposited once more at the Adelphi Hotel. He had been away exactly six months.

XVII
The Newcomes

'You are quite right that I might have done my work just as well at Brompton as at Rome. I haven't seen Rome, and don't know a single Roman except the housemaid, and my landlord speaks English. But the girls are as happy as young women need be.'

Letter to Mrs Proctor, January 1854

 hackeray lost no time in leaving Liverpool. By the evening of the next day he was back in London, making a surprise entry at one of Lady Stanley's Dover Street balls. The sensation of this unexpected arrival was enhanced by the fact that his watch was still set to New York time. There was a great deal to do, not least six months' correspondence to catch up on. He spent a week at Young Street declining all but the most tempting dinner invitations, before hurrying off to Paris for a long-awaited reunion with his family. America was not easily forgotten; nor did it easily forget him. Mrs Baxter wrote almost immediately after his departure to assure him that they talked of him very often, 'and we have not got over the missing you every day'. He replied with similar enthusiasm: 'Some day, please God, I will walk in as suddenly as I ran away.' Whatever the tedium of its latter stages, he was conscious that the American trip had been a success, rounded off by some gratifying plaudits from US commentators. 'We welcomed a friendly, genial man . . .' as one put it, adding for good measure that 'there is no man more humble, nor more simple'. Not every Victorian novelist, perhaps, would have welcomed the sight of his humility and simplicity being held up to public acclaim: Thackeray seems to have accepted the remarks in the spirit in which they were intended. For his own part, he still maintained that it was his mission

to din it into the ears of the English public that the United States contained 'folks as good as they'. Meanwhile there were other compartments of his life to turn out and re-examine. In particular, an evening party shortly before his departure for Paris turned up the spectacle of Brookfield, 'guarded ... and most polite'. At a loss to know how to deal with a man he had not seen for so long, Thackeray adopted a tone of desperate joviality, which he later suspected had 'scared' his old friend. There were to be several more encounters of this kind over the next few months.

He would be forty-two in two months' time. He felt and acted a great deal older. He had enjoyed America, but the visit had taken its toll, if only by giving him a glimpse of the kind of treadmill his life might become in the quest for financial security. A dejected note creeps into some of his letters from this period, which no amount of socialising or domesticity can entirely subdue. The pattern of his life from 1853 to 1855 was hardly calculated to help. He spent a peripatetic couple of years in the mid-1850s, taking in frequent continental jaunts, an Italian trip and numberless visits to Paris. Illness, too, became a regular feature of his existence, exacerbated by a bout of malaria at Rome in the winter of 1853–4. Strain, bad health and the usual hard work brought an uncharacteristically morbid tone to some of his confidences to friends: as early as 1854 he could be found musing about death and hoping to live '2 or 3 more years'. In an age when the average well-nourished professional man could expect to reach sixty, this strikes an unusually despondent note. Family cares, too, pressed down on him. He fretted about his daughters' education, finding the governess question no less intractable now that Annie and Minnie were in their teens than it had been six years before. At the same time Mrs Carmichael-Smyth's fond, solicitous gloom was still capable of driving him to distraction. 'The dear old Soul made me pass thirty miserable hours ...' he noted in the course of one French trip, adding with an acuteness altogether typical of his dealings with his mother, 'It is a sort of fury of balked fondness because I won't like her enough.' Even moving house – the Young Street lease expired in the spring of 1854 – proved unexpectedly traumatic, involving a deluge of workmen and tradespeople.

All this – the foreign holidays, governess-hunting, the new premises in Onslow Square – cost money. By the standards of the mid-nineteenth century Thackeray was a highly successful writer – *The Newcomes*, which he began as soon as he returned from America, brought in £3,600 for the English rights alone – but he was never secure, at least not in the terms in which he envisaged financial security. Establishing exactly how successful an operator he was, even in Victorian terms, is not a straightforward business. Sales of his major novels were good but not spectacular: 10,500 copies of the first edition of *Vanity Fair* had been sold by the time of his death, for example, along with over 20,000 copies of a cheap edition. *The Newcomes* went on to sell 14,000 copies in his lifetime, while 700 of the 13,000-copy first edition of *The Virginians* remained unsold in 1865. At the same time he did well out of his copyrights. A four-volume edition of his early writings had brought in over £2,600 by 1866. Fearing an early death, he grew steadily more neurotic about the need to provide for the girls and the recluse at Camberwell. Just as in his calculations about prospective wives twenty years before, he was precise about the amount of money he wanted – £10,000 apiece would give Annie and Minnie £400 a year and a handsome marriage settlement. The same figure, he later decided, would provide for Isabella. Despite the lavish sums that his novels and his personal appearances could now command, Thackeray realised that £30,000 would take some earning, and the letters of his early forties are awash with money-making schemes. A return visit to America moved quickly into focus, along with the usual interest in public appointments – 1854 found him trying for a magistracy – and an unrealised plan for a literary magazine, to be called *Fair Play* and subsidised by George Smith, in which can be detected the origins of the *Cornhill*. Given all the contending financial pressures that beset him, he was often desperate for ready money, and there are several letters to Bradbury & Evans asking for cash by return in order to pay a tradesman or his landlord. Life was full of obligations: to write a book, to think about his next series of lectures, to eat a dinner or make his bow in somebody's drawing-room, to write or dictate the letters by which his social and professional life was transacted. His correspondence became prodigious at this point. On the day he moved into Onslow Square in May 1854 he wrote at least fifteen letters – Lucy Baxter, to whom this secret was revealed, got the fifteenth – thirteen of them on business.

Emotional life might have provided a safety-valve, but setting aside his love for his daughters it is hard to say of what Thackeray's emotional life at this time actually consisted. Mr and Mrs Brookfield were reconciled; Thackeray got back from America to find that a second child, a boy named Arthur, had been born in his absence. He looked on, for the most part from afar, and muttered. Meanwhile the Baxter correspondence forged on, its habitual jokiness on the subject of Sally's male admirers and life in New York altogether failing to disguise the note of genuine feeling. There is a revealing letter written from Paris in which he tells Sally of seeing a young American girl stepping into a cab and being so moved at the apparent resemblance that it was all he could do to stop himself rushing forward to talk to her. The Baxter letters are a good example of Thackeray giving himself some emotional elbow-room by acknowledging that any greater emotional space is denied him. Deeply attracted to a girl over twenty years his junior, and aware that there was not the slightest chance of a serious relationship, he made a joke of his infatuation: simultaneously the joke allowed him to express his feelings in ways that might otherwise have been denied him. Coated over as it is in middle-aged sentiment, the relationship with Sally Baxter is actually an example of Thackeray's emotional realism, his readiness to accept that half a loaf was better than no bread.

The symbolism of Thackeray's attachment to a young American girl living 3,000 miles away whom he knew he would never possess – and almost certainly preferred not to possess – is rather obvious. He was growing away from his past, becoming middle-aged; the breaks he made with aspects of his earlier life could sometimes be uncomfortably clear-cut. There was a famous row with some of his old *Punch* colleagues early in 1855 after an incautious remark in an essay written for the *Quarterly Review*. Thackeray declared – with evident sincerity – that he had not meant to offend, while offering various well-intentioned bromides about his inability to read proofs. He was forgiven, but the air of loftiness, of distance from the scurrying world of journalists that he was glad to have left behind, is symptomatic of his later years. The sense of mild persecution mania that the episode aroused is all the more marked in that it co-exists with a creeping emollience. Looking back at some of the things he had said and written a decade before he was often deeply embarrassed, and a skim through reprints of his early work left him shocked at bygone asperities. On one of these occasions he went so far as to write to Bulwer Lytton to apologise. 'I own to a feeling of anything but pleasure in reviewing some of these juvenile misshapen creatures wh. the publisher has disinterred and resuscitated,' he assured the man whom he had spent much of the 1840s roundly abusing.

*

At Paris he was rapturously reunited with Annie and Minnie. There was no governess waiting in Young Street, however, so he decided not to take them back to London but to commute between the two cities while he arranged his affairs in preparation for a continental holiday. One of his first acts, back in London in the summer of 1853, was to engage a new manservant, Charles Pearman, previously a footman at a London club. Thackeray liked Pearman, frequently regretting the social distance between them, and their association only ended when Pearman seduced Eliza, the long-standing family housemaid. A potentially lucrative auction was brewing over who should publish the new novel, but Thackeray decided that loyalty to Bradbury & Evans compelled him to reject George Smith's offer of more money. To sweeten the pill Thackeray dropped broad hints about Smith's chances of being involved with the book he intended to write after *The Newcomes* and his next set of lectures, concluding that 'I see a tolerable amount of work before both of us.' Early July found him in Paris about to depart for a tour of Germany and Switzerland. Here, he told Sally Baxter, he hoped to begin on the new work. Already he was doubtful of its prospects, worried that it would be a 'retreat', as he put it, and that the spur to writing it was financial rather than artistic: 'however if I can get 3000£ for my darters I mean 3000 *to put away* . . . I will go backwards or forwards or anyway'.

Together with Annie and Minnie he drifted eastwards via Nancy to Mannheim, looking for a quiet place where he could work and the girls enjoy themselves. By mid-July they were at Baden-Baden, with the journey proving a 'great success' – all down to the 'happiness of the girls, and their artless goodness and affection', he told the *bonnes soeurs*. Then it was on through Geneva, Lausanne, Vevey and Freiburg to Berne. Despite his early doubts, the themes of what was to become *The Newcomes* – in particular its assault on the early-Victorian marriage market – were already boiling away in his head. At the end of July in a letter to Sally he used a discussion of her own marriage prospects (he preferred her current American admirer to the highborn Mr Mildmay) as the preamble to a criticism of what he saw as the English preference for social position over love: 'They never feel love, but directly it's born, they throttle it and fling it under the sewer as poor girls do with their unlawful children – they make up money-marriages and are content. Then the father goes to the House of Commons or the Counting House, the mother to her balls and visits – the children lurk upstairs with their governess, and when their turn comes are bought and sold as respectable and heartless as their parents before them.'

From Vevey he wrote again to Mrs Elliot and Jane Perry, reporting two or three days of 'unwellness' and a sudden pang of displaced emotion that struck him on a coach trip. 'There was a corner of the carriage that of course I filled up with Somebody.' Despite illness and the spectre of Mrs Brookfield rising to disturb him, he decided that he had 'spent as pleasant a fortnight as ever I did in my life plenty of work play health money good children. What could man ask for more?' There was only one thing that he could not have, he concluded enigmatically, in what his readers would have known was a reference to the unfilled space in the carriage. But the usual worries oppressed him, and from vantage points around the Swiss lakes sped back letters in search of a governess or petitioning Bradbury & Evans for royalties owed on the six-shilling edition of *Vanity Fair*, published earlier in the year. They returned to London at the end of August, together with the first four numbers of *The Newcomes*, but the more ordered existence that Thackeray had anticipated was still some distance away. In their absence Young Street had been lent to his friend W.W.F. Synge and the latter's American wife, who remained on the premises for some time after their host's return. It was not an ideal arrangement. In any case Thackeray's seven-year lease would run out the following May, and he took the opportunity to buy a new property half a mile or so away at 36 Onslow Square. The cost – something over £2,000, payable over three years – added another weight to the family's exchequer. Tired and ill, he went down to Brighton to recuperate, his spirits further depressed by the news that his old friend Mrs Crowe was mortally ill. Happily one obligation had been shifted elsewhere. With the former *Punch* artist Richard Doyle engaged to produce *The Newcomes'* illustrations, he would not be forced to stay in England while he finished the book. 'I can go where I like now there are no pictures to do,' he told Proctor, sketching out another, extended continental jaunt that included two or three months in Paris and a longer stay in Rome. Its opening stretch complete – Bradbury & Evans intended to start publishing in October 1853 – the rest of *The Newcomes* lay invitingly before him.

Yet the prospect of compiling another quarter of a million words in the face of regular deadlines worried Thackeray deeply. It was not merely that he suspected that his creative powers were rusting; simultaneously he resented the compromises that he feared a novel like *The Newcomes* would exact. A letter to the *bonnes soeurs* from earlier in the summer carries some rueful speculations about the work in progress: 'not so high-toned or so carefully finished as Esmond', Thackeray suggested, adding darkly 'but that you see was a failure besides being immoral. We must take pains and write careful books when we have made 10000 for the young ladies.' Paradoxically, perhaps, the care that he took in planning and mapping out the novel's future course – it is one of his better-arranged books – is a mark of the exhaustion he felt in approaching it. Much of *Vanity Fair*'s sparkle had been attributable to its air of spontaneous improvisation. Seven years later Thackeray seems to have been slightly depressed at the prospect of what he imagined would be a long, twenty-month plod.

For all this *The Newcomes* is a highly personal and revealing novel, one of the most personal that he ever wrote. On the most basic level this is because it carries some obvious reworkings of his own experience. Clive Newcome, for example, is not a self-portrait, but his apprenticeship in the Soho art schools and his idling in continental ateliers reflects fairly accurately the kind of life Thackeray was leading as a young man in the 1830s. Colonel Newcome has his origins in Major Carmichael-Smyth, while Mrs Mackenzie is a savage projection of his own mother-in-law, Mrs Shawe. Life-into-art paradigms of this sort may not help our appreciation of *The Newcomes* as literature, but they do serve to locate it at the centre of concerns that mattered very much to Thackeray as a human being. The most obvious, perhaps, is the interest in art. The quickening of the literary pulse that takes place every time Clive begins to discuss painting techniques, for instance, owes everything to the novelist's part-time career as a caricaturist and illustrator of his own works. Most obvious of all, though, is the novel's relationship to Thackeray's deepening obsession with past time. As we have seen, even as an apprentice writer in the early 1840s, his perspective was almost invariably backward-looking: reading some of the evocations of childhood in his early sketches it is sometimes difficult to believe that they were written by a man in his early thirties. Now, ten years later, these attitudes were calcifying into an aching, effortless nostalgia. One of the most remarkable features of *The Newcomes*, for example, is the accuracy of its grounding in the early nineteenth century, the faithfulness of its incidental detail – something Thackeray seems to have picked up by a kind of osmosis – and, if nothing else, the novel is a series of vivid re-creations of long-dead worlds. The opening scene at the Cave of Harmony, for instance, with its evocations of Incledon, Professor Porson and Captain Hanger, takes us deep into the 1780s, and the sketch of the turn-of-the-century dissenting life practised by Sophia Hobson in the big house at Clapham, though it reflects some of the sternly Evangelical preoccupations of Mrs Carmichael-Smyth, shows his ability to bring bygone historical detail sharply to life.

Like nearly everything Thackeray wrote, *The Newcomes* has its roots in his own childhood and youth. But the book came at a significant time for him – plunged, as he saw it, into middle age, the great shifts and dissociations in his personal life complete. More than ever he seems to have wanted to look backwards, not forwards, to take solace in the re-creation of past time and, inevitably, to compare present uncertainties with the solidity of a bygone world. As well as being a hymn to the objects and environments of past life, the novel is also the most complete statement of his feelings about society and the processes of social change. From one angle *The Newcomes* is a study of social mobility, the tale of a family making its way into the upper reaches of Victorian society, rapidly shedding the hereditary baggage that might embarrass it, eager to contract the alliances that will sustain and enhance its position. Appropriately, the Newcome family is divided into three sub-groups: the two brothers who control the family banking business; a slightly less respectable group headed by the old colonel, son of the original Newcome by his first marriage; and the highly aristocratic clan into which Sir Brian Newcome has married. Against this background the question of Ethel Newcome's husband takes on a crucial importance. Marriage to Lord Kew will cement the Kew/Newcome alliance and create a powerful blend of aristocratic prestige and commercial acumen; marriage to Lord Farintosh – old Lady Kew's alternative plan – will ally both Newcomes and Kews to Farintosh money and éclat. The other option, marriage to her cousin Clive Newcome, would be a social disaster, reawakening ghosts from the family's former life that would be better left alone. In this way the work ceases to be a novel about a girl's choice of husband and becomes a no-holds-barred struggle for social advantage, conducted by an aristocratic class anxious to rejuvenate itself with infusions of middle-class money and an aspiring bourgeoisie keen to erase all trace of its former existence. Some of Thackeray's sharpest digs are reserved for the Newcomes' bogus pedigree and the Saxon Christian names bestowed on Sir Brian's children, while the constant invocation of the forebear who supposedly served as Edward the Confessor's barber-surgeon is a running joke on the folly of people who are ashamed of their ancestors.

Perhaps the clearest evidence of Thackeray's intentions comes in his subtitle: 'Memoirs of a most respectable family'. At bottom *The Newcomes* is a tremendous attack on early-Victorian notions of respectability, an assault on the type of society that sells its daughters off to the highest bidder and whose moral code turns a blind eye to dissipated young men (for a work written in the shadow of Mrs Grundy and the kind of prudery that Dickens was to satirise in *Our Mutual Friend*, the novel is reasonably candid about Lord Farintosh's carryings-on with actresses) while insisting on female purdah. As ever the moral point is usually a simple one – don't be selfish, don't cultivate unreasonable ambitions – barbed by an acknowledgment that hardly anyone can hope to live up to these exacting standards. It was G.H. Lewes who first pointed out the terrible impartiality of Thackeray's moral judgments, the disinterested way in which he doles out praise and blame. Selfishness – the chief human folly on display in *The Newcomes* – affects each of the principal characters like a sort of distemper. Ethel, Clive, Lady Kew, Mrs Mackenzie – each in their own way is guilty of an almost glacial self-absorption. Tellingly, the worst culprit turns out to be Colonel Newcome, the character whose disinterestedness has hitherto seemed one of the novel's fixed points, and Thackeray makes it perfectly clear that most of the major disasters in the book, from the collapse of the Bundelcund Bank to family acrimony, can be blamed, directly or indirectly, on old Newcome's ambitions for his son.

Inevitably, for a book concerned with hypocrisy and double standards, one of the main themes of *The Newcomes* is the position of women in early-Victorian society. Though one side of Thackeray's temperament lay eternally becalmed at the club-lounging, gourmandising end of Victorian life, he took a keen interest in what was even then coming to be known as 'the woman question'. The American critic Deborah A. Thomas has demonstrated how the long-running debate about female emancipation became linked in Thackeray's mind with the newer agitation over slavery that he had witnessed at first hand on his American trip, and the way in which this fusion contributed to the novel's symbolism. One of the more dramatic moments, for example, comes when Ethel steals a green 'sold' sticker in an art gallery and pins it to her frock. Thackeray's horror of the early-Victorian marriage market was undoubtedly sincere. At the same time many of his opinions on how women should live their lives are simply irresolute: characteristically, his response to the famous 'Address to Mrs Stowe', presented to the author of *Uncle Tom's Cabin* under the signatures of half a million Englishwomen, took the form of a pastiche 'Womanifesto', making clear that he found the whole exercise irretrievably futile and genteel. In the end, despite the good intentions, one returns to the question that had bedevilled Thackeray's marriage to Isabella: *what does he expect them to do with their lives?* If smiling head-nodders footling over the piano keys are merely laughable, while strong-minded bluestockings who take an interest in the topics of the day are sinister usurpers of male prerogatives, and the space between them is occupied by intolerable 'good' women like Laura Pendennis, then it seems as if a woman's only destiny is to be treated with an overweening patronage and condescension.

This kind of half-heartedness is symptomatic of the ambiguities of Thackeray's approach to social arrangements by the mid-1850s. The dilemmas of *The Newcomes* are the dilemmas of his own progress into the upper reaches of a world in which he enjoyed existing, certain of whose usages he disliked, and which he was paid gently to mock. In this way the novel has a curious double-life: on the one hand, a subversive deconstruction of early-Victorian orthodoxies about marriage; on the other, a repository for many of the patrician attitudes that the younger Thackeray would not have hesitated to attack. Even more so than Arthur Pendennis, Clive is a fine example of Thackeray's weakness for elegant young men of no particular distinction. Barnes Newcome, his spiritual opposite, may be a devious and calculating young hypocrite, one feels, but at least he goes to his office at nine o'clock every morning and doesn't sponge off his father, and his rare moments of animation generally come when Thackeray allows him to talk about his work. In dealing with the question of Clive's occupation, Thackeray shows the same reluctance to commit himself that colours his treatment of female employment. Compared to his industrious fellow artist Ridley, Clive is a dilettante, a failing that Thackeray, with his lifelong interest in art and his genuine respect for artists, never allows us to forget. But the relationship is complicated by our knowledge that Clive is – literally – Ridley's patron, an awareness that Clive Newcome is a fine young gentleman for whom 'art' is an agreeable hobby, while Ridley is the son of a domestic servant with a living to make. Thackeray is always scrupulously fair to Ridley, and admiring of his talent, especially in the early chapters, but there is a sense in which he fades away into the margins of the book, and the old colonel's reluctance to treat him as a social equal strikes a jarring note. Clive, too, seems more convincing as a journeyman artist, forced to work to support his wife and family, than a *jeune premier* with a sketching pad – one of those sharp transformations typical of Thackeray's work, in which a life of pleasant illusions is suddenly replaced by the grim reality of doctors' bills, sick wives and the dreadful feeling of there never being enough money. Significantly, perhaps, the occasions on which Clive comes nearest to assuming a life of his own are those in which Thackeray draws most clearly on his own memories of young manhood.

From Brighton in late September, recovered in health, he wrote a kindly letter to Brookfield, apologising for his inability to accept a dinner invitation and holding out an olive branch. 'God bless you now after 2 years asunder, when there are no more rages on my part,' he meekly enjoined. 'I pray you to forget savage words, as I do . . . forget all this if you can remember the friend of old days.' For all this outward humility, Thackeray's private feelings about the Brookfields were rather more complex. Husband and wife continued to turn up pseudonymously in his letters (mostly to the *bonnes soeurs*, but also to Mrs Baxter, whom he had taken into his confidence), Jane as '*l'autre*', William as 'The Inspector'. '*L'autre* and her lord & master are reconciled and I'm not in the least annoyed,' he had told Sally Baxter early in July. The references to Brookfield are characterised by sour grapes ('The poor inspector, who tries his best to smother his hatred for me'), those to Jane marked by a tendency to exaggerate the realities of her situation. This was particularly evident in his response to her friendship with the Catholic convert Aubrey de Vere. Thackeray delivered ominous warnings about the presence of de Vere in the Brookfield dining-room 'with his litanies, his rosaries & rubbish. If she meddles with that sort of people *she'll lose her children*.' But this portrait of a weak-willed female liable to slip into a confessional and come out converted almost by accident is a substantial misrepresentation. Jane, as recent events had shown, was well able to take care of herself.

In any case the Brookfields, too, were moving on to a new kind of life. Jane had her children. William, together with his fast friend Lord Ashburton, was at work on the 'Knowledge of Common Things', an ambitious scheme for working-class self-advancement, which created a minor sensation (and attracted a certain amount of sarcasm) on its unveiling later in the year. Somehow jokes about 'the poor inspector' seemed inappropriate. Thackeray saw them occasionally during the summer and autumn of 1853, but never got to talk to Jane on her own. He spent October and November shuttling back and forth between London and Paris, writing more of The Newcomes (frequently using Annie as an amanuensis) and dealing with the usual round of professional and social demands. The first number of the novel was generally approved, although public compliments probably meant less to Thackeray than a letter from Mrs Baxter assuring him that the family was 'greatly pleased' and making an immediate connection between Colonel Newcome and Major Carmichael-Smyth. Meanwhile he declined a request from Bentley to write a life of Walpole and spent the end of October 'stupefied by a horrid influenza; it has been all fog: bed: and blowing the nose'. The death of Mrs Crowe, which took place at this time in Paris, profoundly upset him, and not merely because he liked his friend's wife and worried about her children (Crowe was heavily in debt). There were pieces of himself caught up in the walk to the graveyard, and he recalled to Eyre Evans Crowe how fifteen years before the elder man would 'pay me 10 francs a day to do his work as a Newspaper Correspondent for him – and I very glad to get the job'. He was moved by the sight of the Crowes' daughter Amy 'in her black dress so sweet and kind looking' and wished that Eyre had taken up his offer of more secretarial work instead of resolving to concentrate on art. Thackeray feared he would fail, 'and then having refused my bread, where is he to get other?'

He was planning to take the girls to Italy at the end of November. In the meantime there was business to transact in London – arranging to send out the third number of The Newcomes by steamer to Harper Brothers in New York, writing to his old friend Cruikshank to turn down an invitation to contribute to the extremely short-lived George Cruikshank's Magazine (again the refusal hinted at Thackeray's own plans for editorship, and he noted that he had 'perhaps the project of launching some day a ship of my own, of wh. I shall be Owner and Captain'). Then it was back to Paris with Pearman to collect the girls and set out for Rome. Nearly forty years later Annie wrote a spirited memoir of this week-long journey via Marseilles and Genoa. Cosmopolitan Marseilles – 'the Jews, Turks, dwellers in Mesopotamia; chattering in gorgeous colours and strange languages; the quays, the crowded shipping, the amethyst water' – left an indelible impression on the mind of the sixteen-year-old girl. In particular, she remembered a barge piled high with great golden onions floating along one of the quays, guided by a woman in blue rags with a coloured handkerchief on her head, and Thackeray pausing to joke, 'There goes the Lady of Shallot!' On the voyage out the girls forgot to fasten the portholes of their cabin and woke drenched with sea spray, believing that the ship was sinking. At Genoa they went on a day's excursion to Pisa, but came back late and together with a group of fellow passengers were forced to hire a boat to take them out to the waiting steamer. As the ship began to send up rockets ahead of its imminent departure, the boatmen struck for an extra fifty francs. It was too much for Thackeray, who got to his feet in the stern of the boat and, with a fury that Annie had never seen in him before, shouted, 'Damn you, go on!' Meekly the rowers complied.

Subsequently they landed at Civitavecchia at around midday. There were rumours of brigands on the road, and Thackeray was anxious to press on to Rome. All that could be got in the way of a conveyance, however, was a 'mouldy post-chaise, with a gray ragged lining, and our luggage on the top'. Halfway across the flat horizon the vehicle stopped and Charles Pearman, stepping down to examine the impediment, reported that the traces were broken. On the instant the carriage was surrounded by people – 'satyrs, shepherds, strange bearded creatures with conical hats, and with pitchforks in their hands'. Happily they turned out to be representatives of the local peasantry, who, after some staring and a good deal of conversation with the postilion, went away. Dusk fell as the traces were being repaired, and Annie fell asleep to be roused by Thackeray's hand on her shoulder pointing out the dome of St Peter's, 'gray upon the dark-blue sky'. Driven to a hotel in the Via Condotti, they woke the next morning to the sound of church bells. They were comfortable quarters, Thackeray told his mother a day or so later, 'except for some animal that bit me furiously when I was asleep yesterday on a sofa'. Perhaps, he wondered, having heard the chambermaid's claim that she had never seen a flea in her life, the culprit was a scorpion?

Despite the scenery ('Gods what a flaming splendour it is,' Thackeray apostrophised the sunset over St Peter's), it was a difficult winter. He was ill at Rome, with two separate attacks of malaria – the first came on suddenly after a tea-party with the Brownings a week before Christmas – but insisted on working through his convalescence, getting to his desk at seven each morning and labouring until lunch-time. There were numerous petty irritations, not least the city authorities' attempt to stimulate the tourist trade by illuminating the Colosseum with pink and green fire ('as if the Sun wasn't good enough to light the place'). Amid an influx of visiting English people, it was hard to penetrate local society, and he complained that he did not enter a single Roman house. It was just as his friends had predicted, he complained in a letter to Mrs Proctor: the work could have been done just as well at Brompton. All this, though, was as nothing compared to his delight in Annie's and Minnie's frank enjoyment of their holiday. He thought them 'as happy as young women need be'. Several English society hostesses were at large in the city, including the Ladies Holland and Gainsborough, and Thackeray undoubtedly enjoyed the social junketings of Christmas and the New Year. He also met a number of visiting English artists, and Millais later remembered him commending 'a young fellow in Rome called Leighton . . .' and predicting – correctly as it turned out – that he would become president of the Royal Academy. Meanwhile a stream of favourable remarks on early numbers of *The Newcomes* continued to reach him. Though pleased by the large number of admirers, Thackeray was beginning to have doubts about the old colonel. 'He is a dear old boy but confess you think he is rather a twaddler?' he demanded of Mrs Proctor. He kept an eye on the literary news from home and admitted that his soul was 'full of envy' on learning that Dickens had addressed an audience of mill-operatives in Manchester. It was enough to make him think of coming home and reading *Yellowplush* in costume at an Islington music hall, he decided.

The routines of family life at Rome were painstakingly transcribed by Annie. The tumult of English tourists included several genuine friends – Robert and Elizabeth Browning, Mrs Sartoris, the banker Aeneas Macbean, who used to send the girls books. Directed by Browning, an old Italian hand, they changed their lodgings from the bug-ridden hotel to a large apartment over a pastrycook's in the Via Della Croce, lying at the top of an immense staircase girded by wrought-iron banisters, and presided over by a little old lady named Signora Ercola. This was a substantial residence: the drawing-room had seven windows, Annie recalled, and there was a Chinese museum and a library to add to the more usual requirements of dining-room, bedrooms, dressing-room and a 'cupboard' for Charles Pearman. Signora Ercola's offer of her sitting-room in addition to the rooms that Thackeray had engaged made Annie wonder what arrangements had been made for the landlady's own family: she retained a vague impression of her brood of daughters 'huddled away into some humble apartment . . .'

Although mindful of their father's illness and the sequestration of the study, Annie and Minnie were enraptured by their surroundings. At lunch-times they were sent to the pastrycook's downstairs to eat cream tarts and *petits fours*. Dinner was sent round on trays from a nearby trattoria. In the evening there were parties to attend, from which Pearman would come and fetch them, walking back through the moonlit streets 'past little shrines with burning lamps, by fountains plashing in the darkness' to climb the great echoing staircase. Too excited to sleep, they would sit up reading in their rooms long after Thackeray himself had come home and shut his bedroom door, and the only sound that remained was the tolling of the nearby convent bell.

Several people left accounts of the Thackerays' stay in Rome. Elizabeth Barrett Browning was wryly amused by Thackeray's complaining of dullness. He 'can't write in the morning without his good dinner and two parties overnight. From such a soil spring the Vanity Fairs!' she told her sister shortly before Christmas. She resumed this theme early in the New Year, apropos Thackeray's claim (he was recovering from his second bout of malaria) that Rome did not agree with him. Clearly it was a combination of Rome *and* dining out that did not agree with him, Mrs Browning deposed, so why not give up the dinners? But Thackeray had decided this was impossible. 'The inspiration dies without port,' she rather acidly concluded. John Gibson Lockhart, on the other hand, put Thackeray's bad health

'*Annie and Minnie in Italy*'

down to domestic cares. 'Those girls annoy him and tease him. If he wants to be well, he should get a governess, or an aunt, and dispose of the girls . . .' Lockhart's is an interesting view – not because he was at all intimate with the Thackerays, but for precisely the opposite reason: even as a casual observer he seems to have divined an air of tension beneath Thackeray's outwardly idyllic relationship with his daughters. Mrs Browning, too, was not the first person to note the mixed effects of 'going out into the world' on Thackeray's well-being. 'Society' was vital to his creative sense, and yet, patently, society wore him down and made him ill. In the last resort, what gave him his inspiration did him no good.

Simultaneously, though, amid the worldly criticism of the Brownings and the Lockharts (Elizabeth Barrett Browning thought him 'an amusing man-mountain enough and very courteous to us – but I never should get on with him much, I think'), what he did and said was being closely monitored by a much younger and more impressionable sensibility. Edith Story was the daughter of William Wetmore Story, an American lawyer with poetic leanings who had come to Rome with the aim of training to be a sculptor. Thackeray took to Story, and seems to have been impressed by his courage in the face of adversity: the family had been struck down by malaria, their small son had died and Edith herself was convalescent. On his visits to the family apartment, inspired by some drawings done for a Twelfth Night play, Thackeray began to write what became *The Rose and the Ring*, bringing the fairy tale of Prince Giglio, Princess Rosalba and the good offices of Fairy Blackstick chapter by chapter to the child's bedside. Edith, who eventually recorded her memories of these visits early in the next century, recalled a 'great benevolent giant' who sat on the edge of the bed or drew his chair close up to the coverlet. Having read his daily instalment he would announce, 'Now you must tell me a little story to amuse me.' As the little girl struggled gamely to invent something, he would sit at the bedside table and draw fanciful pen-and-ink sketches of characters such as 'Zachary Hubs and his foxtree teapot'. Thackeray kept up with the Storys. Later, when the family had an apartment on the Champs-Elysées, Edith remembered grave conversations about dolls. Once Thackeray was surprised by Mrs Story with a tiny sock in his hand, as the two examined a pile of baby clothes intended for a forthcoming arrival.

Early in February news came from Paris that his Aunt Ritchie was dead. Moved by the passing of a relative whose kindness to him in childhood he always remembered, Thackeray at first planned to return to France to pay his respects. At the last moment, however, he had a change of heart: '... lying awake, Thinking the girls were here that they mightnt see Italy again; that who knows what might happen to their father &c – I changed my mind and came South'. They left on 8 February ('Thackeray has left Rome,' Elizabeth Barrett Browning wrote in valediction, 'I like his two frank intelligent girls – and I like beside his own good nature and agreeableness') with the idea of visiting Naples and Florence. In the event, Naples remained their home for the next seven weeks, as Annie and Minnie both contracted scarletina. Fortunately neither was a serious attack, but Thackeray left his correspondents 'to fancy how pleasant our sojourn here has been'. Annie was the first to fall ill. Thackeray and Minnie shared the nursing duties between them, until Minnie too took to her bed and Thackeray was 'toppled over with a severe private attack of his own'. At this point they managed to secure the services of a professional nurse, 'otherwise with the three of us all on our backs in three adjoining rooms facing the Mediterranean Sea, shunned by waiters for fear of the infection, and constantly requiring our little arrowroots lemonades and draughts not so agreeable what would have happened to us all?' Local friends rallied round – the Hollands sent jellies and biscuits, and Thackeray seems to have had a small glimpse of Neapolitan society – but in most respects he had stepped out of life. 'What goes on I know no more than the folks who are buried at Pompei,' he told Kate Perry. Steering clear of the other guests, yet warned by the doctor not to explain their situation for fear that the landlord should turn them out of the hotel, 'I have to lie, therefore on many occasions, and prevent the ardour of people who want to come and be kind to my girls sit with them & what not.' Brooding over Annie and Minnie as they recovered resuscitated a bygone sadness. 'I was thinking of the girls convalescing,' the same letter continued, '... and of that day 15 years ago when their little sister died at sunrise.'

They returned to Paris in spring 1854 in leisurely fashion, Thackeray billeting the girls on their grandparents once again before going on to London, on the understanding that he would return for them once the removal to Onslow Square was complete. *The Newcomes* was by this stage four numbers ahead of publication – a luxurious state of affairs compared to the anxieties that had surrounded *Vanity Fair* – but Thackeray doubted his ability to maintain this pace. The business of leaving Young Street claimed more time than he could afford. A letter written to Lucy Baxter on 18 May, his first day at Onslow Square, gives a neat snapshot of the harassed householder vainly trying to work amid a tide of interruptions. Only two rooms were habitable, he grimly revealed, before breaking off to answer a ring at the door. The caller turned out to be a potential governess – once again the hunt was on for a companion for the girls – 'and there came in such a simpering ogling sighing sentimental spinster that at the end of $\frac{1}{2}$ an hour's silly conversation, I was glad to get rid of her ...' Desperately seeking to soften the blow of rejection, Thackeray told the woman she was too good-looking for a job that involved living under the same roof as a middle-aged man. Characteristically he then felt guilty about the governess's fruitless five-mile journey. Meanwhile, a stream of tradesmen followed in her wake. 'But O the upholsterers the carpenters and fenderers the looking glass people on coming into a new house!' he complained to Lucy, '– O their bills their bills.'

Presumably his return to London had brought another re-encounter with the Brookfields, as a letter to Kate Perry written two days after his arrival at Onslow Square indulges in some psychological speculation over Jane's attitude to her husband. The problem was that from the day she fell in love with the Inspector and 'fell a worshipping him' she had no companionship with him, he proposed. This was all very well while she continued to adore him, 'but now that he is no longer Divine in her eyes, only terrible and her Master, her loneliness is sad to think of'. Still, he was glad to hear of Jane's affection for her daughter, and hoped that her son Arthur would soon be another companion for 'a mother so sweet tender and unhappy'. Again, this looks very like Thackeray exaggerating a situation whose real elements – and emotions – lay substantially beyond him. One suspects, too, that by this stage the fragments of his relationship with the Brookfields had become a kind of game played out with the *bonnes soeurs* in which the principal object was to provide an outlet for his frustrations.

In the meantime, amid the gossip about Jane's flirtation with Roman Catholicism and the domestic arrangements at Onslow Square, 'business' of the kind he had complained about to Lucy Baxter pressed hard. Declining an invitation from Lady Tennent, on the official grounds that Annie had tumbled downstairs and strained her ankle, he complained of an amount of business and letters which would 'astonish anyone'. Doyle, engaged to supply two full-page illustrations for each monthly number of *The Newcomes* as well as a number of incidental engravings, was proving dilatory. Thackeray, who had already fired a warning shot about this laggardliness, now asked Bradbury & Evans to write an 'ultimatum' on his behalf. In the end Doyle was able to prove that the particular delay that had annoyed his patron was not wholly his fault, and matters were patched up, but the remaining work was executed in an atmosphere of some tension. Thackeray's next communication to his publishers was another request, this time for money: 'The carpet-man & the looking glass man are knocking at the gate. Their terms is ready money and they can't afford to wait.' Neither, apparently, could Thackeray. Given the state of his health, the air of exhaustion with which he approached *The Newcomes* and the difficulties that problems like Doyle's slowness lent to its production, the most sensible plan would have been to spend a quiet summer in out-of-season London, recruiting himself and getting on with his work. Instead he decided to leave for France again – on this occasion joining the girls at the Château de Brecquerecque, near Boulogne, which Major and Mrs Carmichael-Smyth had rented for the summer. He left London late in June, absenting himself from one of Mrs Gaskell's dinner parties to do so, and spent much of the next two and a half months at Boulogne, with occasional trips elsewhere in France, to Belgium and Germany. Letters of reassurance back to Bradbury & Evans were followed by messengers bearing copy (Mark Lemon volunteered to bring back the last part of the twelfth number and the thirteenth in mid-July). Six months before he had been four numbers in hand; now the monthly deadlines were beginning to irk him, and still the book would not be finished for nearly another year. Returning to London in mid-August, he gloomily informed Mrs Proctor that 'My house is desolate: my family at Boulogne: my number is as usual unwritten.' A further annoyance was the absence of some of the Thackeray family silver, mysteriously lost by the Carmichael-Smyth party *en route* for Brecquerecque.

His attempts to enliven a lonely week or two in Brompton – most of his friends were away and the grand houses were shut as their owners vacationed at continental spas – seemed doomed to failure. Rekindling the memory of his journeys around London while *Vanity Fair* boiled in his mind, he bought a new horse, promptly fell off it and was confined to bed for the best part of a week. Fortunately he had a new interest to occupy him. Worked up and fleshed out to marketable length, *The Rose and the Ring* was to be his Christmas book for 1854. As a reward for past support and a hint of things to come, it was given to George Smith to publish. A run of letters to Smith from late summer and early autumn as the book went into production shows the care that Thackeray was prepared to lavish on an idea that had caught his imagination. He was especially exercised by the illustrations. The book ought to have sixty or seventy at least, he told Smith. By late August there were more than a dozen woodblocks at Onslow Square waiting to be sent off to the engraver. By this point Thackeray had read his 'amusing piece of buffoonery' to Annie and Minnie, and was encouraged by their reaction: 'My girls say it is the best thing their papa has done.' A week later he left once more for Brecquerecque, fell ill again on arrival, but managed to communicate with Smith. He had seen the engraver Joseph Swain, he reported, who had agreed to produce seventy woodblocks for £100. This was a large number, but Thackeray was keen to stress how vital was the relationship between illustration and text: 'The story such as it is is written to the drawings wh. should be engraved before any of the letterpress is printed.' Throughout this period he was still trying to prepare the ground for Annie's and Minnie's return by hiring a governess, but the plan collapsed when the selected applicant – a Miss Smith – wrote to say that her father's illness compelled her to decline the offer. By a providential stroke, Miss Smith's letter arrived shortly after one from Amy Crowe asking if the position was still vacant. As with her brother Eyre two years before, Thackeray leaped at the chance to benefit the child of his old friends. '*Your company will be of the very greatest comfort & service to all of us,*' he enthused by return. 'I shall feel what I never felt for years that there's somebody with them whom we all like, who will look to me and them, who will be with them when I am away, and ease me of a part of the responsibility I feel about them.' In the event Amy stayed for eight years.

The letter to Amy Crowe was written from a sick-bed. Thackeray's correspondence from the autumn of 1854 is crammed with references to his ill health. He was at Brighton again early in October, writing to Mark Lemon that he had been 'dreadfully seedy & glum yesterday looking for another attack of my complaint this morning, but a walk by the sounding sea has done me good'. A plaintive note to the absent Mrs Proctor, written not long afterwards, suggests, 'I think I have been ill ever so many times since you went.' At forty-three, he was fast becoming chronically unwell. By this stage there were three aspects to Thackeray's 'seediness'. On the one hand, his stricture continued to bother him, often to the point where his urethra became inflamed. Quite apart from the pain, this meant that he had difficulty in urinating (the famous remark at a *Punch* dinner that he had met a Miss Peawell and felt like saying, 'My dear Miss Peawell, I wish I could' belongs to a slightly later date). There was little treatment available apart from rest and heat. Henry Thompson, a noted mid-Victorian urologist into whose hands he had fallen by this time, held out hope of a cure if Thackeray would submit to an operation, but the patient was reluctant. There were perhaps good reasons for this. The second and third aspects of his ill health had already begun the steady process of undermining what had never been a very strong constitution. For some time he had suffered from periodic vomiting fits, or 'spasms' as he called them. Undoubtedly these were exacerbated by his eating habits and the remorseless dining-out, but the once widely canvassed view that Thackeray was simply a glutton who ate himself to death has little basis in fact. The regularity of the attacks points to an organic cause, possibly even a condition such as Crohn's disease. Finally there was the malaria picked up in Rome during the winter, which quinine could mollify but not completely cure. The cumulative effect of these conditions was regular bouts of illness, often for three or four days a month, that left him worn out and listless. Standard Victorian painkillers such as laudanum and the calomel he used to treat his retching attacks also had a weakening effect, and he remained depressed and shy of company. As he put it to Mrs Proctor, 'I never hear any news or see anyone when in the dismals; like to avoid even my own angel girls and dine alone at a Club.'

There were many days of this kind in late 1854, spent at Brighton and London with a two-and-a-half-week break in Paris in November. But he was perpetually busy – in between labouring over the homeward stretch of *The Newcomes* and looking forward to publication of *The Rose and the Ring*, he composed a long essay for the *Quarterly Review* on his friend Leech's artistic career, little knowing what the consequences of his cavalier attitude to proof-reading would be, and set to work on a stage play, *The Wolves and the Lamb*, rejected by each of the managements that saw it. He was also manoeuvring himself closer to George Smith, using a letter of early December to suggest that they might make a success together of a new periodical, and even proposing a title: 'FAIR PLAY'. Christmas, though, found him in lowish water, with the girls in Paris and Christmas Day bringing only an 'invalid party' consisting of himself, Mrs Robert Wynne (the former Eugenie Crowe) and her sister. 'We 3 will dine on mutton broth by ourselves today,' he told W.W.F. Synge in declining the latter's invitation to dinner.

He escaped to Paris in the New Year, returning to find that the *Quarterly* article on Leech had brought down a volley of abuse on his head. Once again the row was symbolic, allowing old adversaries the chance to attack him on a front much wider than that opened up by what was theoretically at stake, and calling into question his whole relationship with the paper for which he had worked for so long. Thackeray's formal role at *Punch* had ended on his resignation, but he had continued to contribute occasional pieces and was on cordial terms with most of the staff – it was Mark Lemon, for instance, who brought back part of *The Newcomes* to Bradbury & Evans the previous summer. The *Quarterly* article, though, caused great offence. Discussing Leech's output in the context of the previous decade's periodical journalism, it asserted bluntly that the artist 'was *Punch*'. Thackeray may not have meant this remark to be taken literally, and as a *Punch* insider its inaccuracy can hardly have escaped him, but it was highly tactless. The reaction varied from public criticism (Jerrold, inevitably) to private remonstrations. Although Thackeray wrote at first to Mark Lemon defending himself, he soon came to realise that his position was indefensible, and a second letter, to Bradbury & Evans, was much more contrite. In it Thackeray admitted that Jerrold's attack was 'perfectly justifiable'. Recasting the incident in the light of his *Punch* career, he confessed that 'the man who sneered publicly at his old friends *was* a Snob; and I did; and I deserved what I got'. This did not mean that he forgave Jerrold, but the apology seems to have been genuinely meant. All the same it is an odd episode. How did Thackeray suppose that his friends would interpret the remark? Did he think that Leech, who relished the confraternity of the *Punch* table, would approve? His explanation, at any rate to Bradbury & Evans, was that he did not read the proofs properly, but this looks disingenuous. Writers know what they write, even when they fail to take the trouble to re-read it. Besides, this was an encomium to one of his oldest friends, and Thackeray would have taken pains with it. More than this, he would have wanted it to be known that he had done so. In some ways the *Quarterly* row resembles one or two of the faintly masochistic letters written to his mother in early manhood, in which stances seem to be struck in the near-certainty of rebuke. Did Thackeray want Jerrold to attack him in print? And did some tiny, concealed part of him want to be the cause of that attack? We shall never know, and yet bromides about unread proofs leave a larger story untold.

Undoubtedly the *Quarterly* episode, and Jerrold's response to it, preyed on his mind. As late as the end of March 1855 he was taking pains to insert complimentary references to his old colleagues in a lecture and writing to tell Whitwell Elwin, the *Quarterly's* editor, that 'All of them have quite forgiven me I think except Jerrold who would immediately if any misfortune happened to me but success is naturally odious to him and the conduct of a gentleman somehow puzzles him and other men who are not of that sort.' Angry that Jerrold appeared to be spreading falsehoods over the real reason for his severance from *Punch*, he went over the stages in his departure from the magazine's front-line: the long-term 'unease', the discovery that his rate of pay had been cut, the abuse of the Prince Consort and the Crystal Palace, the abuse of Palmerston, and finally the caricature of Louis Napoleon galloping towards hell with a blood-stained sword.

Much of his old life seemed to have detached itself. Fitz he scarcely saw from one year to the next. The tone of a letter from Mrs Carmichael-Smyth to Annie, recounting a chance meeting at church in Paris with John Allen, suggests that the archdeacon (as he now was) belonged to an older Thackerayan circle that had all but disintegrated. It was the same with Fitzgerald, now working on his translation of the *Rubáiyát*. Spring found him suffering what were by now customary complaints: want of money (another letter to Bradbury & Evans asked for funds to pay an exigent landlord); ill health; lack of time to finish his book. Gathering himself for a final spurt on *The Newcomes*, he seems to have thought that he could finish by the end of April (a letter to Thompson in March talks of three or four weeks' work before the writer can 'put myself under your hands again'). In fact several months of labour lay before him. The foreign trips, which he perhaps realised were a distraction, had temporarily ceased but he made occasional forays in England, going to Coventry, for example, in April (where he stayed with George Eliot's friends, the Brays) to deliver 'Charity and Humour'. Above all, there was little respite from the money spectre. A second American tour had ceased to be a rosy blur in his mind and had become hard and actual, set for October and requiring him to start thinking seriously about the set of lectures on the Hanoverian kings that he proposed to deliver. Something of his anxiety had begun to communicate itself to the girls. A letter from Annie from about this time to her friend Mrs Fanshawe tries to make a joke of paternal worry:

'Papa says in a few years we shall only have 200£ a year to live upon & as my favourite Miss Martineau says it is far nobler to earn than to save.' But it goes on to hint at a degree of frustration with her life in the house at Brompton Square. Annie thought she would like very much to earn money '& become celebrated like the aforesaid Harriet who is one of the only sensible women living beside thee & me & 2 or 3 more I know'.

Personal anxieties aside, he was also caught up in the general tide of anti-governmental hostility brought about by the Crimean War. Lord Aberdeen's coalition government of Whigs and Peelites, of which both Lord John Russell and Palmerston were members, had joined with the French to declare war on Russia in March 1854. The previous summer, this had seemed merely an opportunity for light humour – some of Thackeray's final communications to *Punch* were mock-communiqués from the battle-front entitled 'Important. From the Seat of War! By Our Own Bashi-Bozouk'. However the battles of autumn 1854 – the Charge of the Light Brigade took place on 25 October – and the exposures of inefficiency and mutiny brought back by, among other eye-witnesses, his friend the war correspondent William Howard Russell had profoundly shocked him. So, too, did the political fall-out. In late January 1855 Aberdeen's administration fell when the house backed the radical MP John Roebuck's call for a select committee to be formed to enquire into the condition of the army. Lord John Russell having failed to assemble a ministry, his replacement Palmerston calmly repopulated the Cabinet from the same exclusive group of peers. The 'pococurantism' of the Whigs was awful, Thackeray told his mother. 'It's an insult to the English honour . . . I can't bear it no longer and am turning horribly radical.' (This view was shared by Dickens, who lampooned Palmerston in *Household Words* as a 'jocular old gentleman throwing somersaults on stilts'.) In this spirit Thackeray was eager to become involved in a political ginger group called the Administrative Reform Association, set up by the MP Austen Layard and the industrialist Samuel Morley; he sat on its platform at a public meeting in June, and went so far as to draft a speech, which he planned to deliver at a later event. In the end the speech was never given, but the draft is interesting for the way in which Thackeray, just as in some of his private conversations with aristocratic friends, casts himself as the voice of reason steering an even course between governor and governed. 'Why gentlemen if we had hereditary seats in this theatre comfortably wadded stalls in *wh* we and our descendants might sit forever and see the opera for nothing we should be peevish I daresay and object to changes of a system *wh* worked very well and made us very comfortable.' The struggle between haves and have-nots, he concluded, 'makes what we call our glorious constitution'. Although the Association was soon dissolved, having accomplished little beyond a public meeting or two, Thackeray's involvement is a mark of his continuing political interests and points towards his decision to stand for Parliament a couple of years later.

In planning the final chapters of *The Newcomes*, Thackeray was gearing himself up for an especially demanding task: the death of Colonel Newcome. Victorian novelists approached the death-scenes of their favourite characters in a variety of ways. Dickens, famously, was reduced to near-prostration at the despatch of Little Nell and Paul Dombey. Trollope went home and killed Mrs Proudie in a fit of pique after overhearing some amateur literary criticism at his club. The pains that Thackeray was prepared to take in giving the old colonel a finale of Dickensian dimensions and pathos can be judged from the manuscript itself. Many of the preceding chapters are in Annie's handwriting, transcribed from her father's dictation. As the colonel's death approaches – the old man ends his days in near-destitution as a Charterhouse pensioner – Thackeray's own hand supervenes. At the same time the manuscript is full of interpolations, little polishes and improvements that heighten the tone, a spontaneous three-page improvisation that brings Madame de Florac, the colonel's old love, from her station outside the door to his bedside. Thackeray was proud of the result – his satisfaction was shared by most Victorian critics – which clearly exacted an emotional toll from him. James Russell Lowell, then in London, was marched into a coffee shop and read the relevant chapter from sheets brought out of Thackeray's coat pocket (the episode was repeated in the presence of a larger and somewhat less deferential audience in an upstairs room at the Cyder Cellar). Thackeray rarely read any of his work to anyone outside the family circle: the pre-publicity campaign lavished on Colonel Newcome's death shows something of the importance he attached to it.

There was still some concluding work to do on *The Newcomes*: the discovery of the will that restores Clive's finances and the deeply ambiguous 'happy ending'. (When he was staying in Coventry a deputation of admirers, led by George Eliot's friend Sarah Hennell, had begged that Clive be allowed to marry Ethel.) Thackeray took the manuscript to Paris, together with his daughters, where amid 'a pretty busy pleasant time', accompanied by too much to drink ('it's at those stupid dinners the claret is most dangerous', he complained to the *bonnes soeurs*), he wrote the last lines at seven o'clock on the evening of Thursday 28 June. The effect on him was such that he immediately fell to his knees and prayed. Despite the exhaustion of the past year and three-quarters, he was in two minds about the completion of his task, welcoming a temporary halt to his labours but 'quite sorry to part with a number of kind people with whom I have been living & talking these 20 months past, & to draw a line so——on a sheet of paper, beyond wh. their honest figures wouldn't pass'. The girls had gone to admire Signora Ristori, the celebrated Italian tragedienne, in *Mary Queen of Scots*. Thackeray dined alone and then proceeded to the pantomime, where he fell asleep.

With his novel complete, he allowed himself some brief diversions, went twice to the Fine Art Exhibition and to one of Lady Ashburton's parties. But the idea of a return trip to America was beginning to depress him – the thought of parting with the girls disgusted him, he told the *bonnes soeurs* – and the lectures were still unwritten. He made a brief trip to Germany before returning to London at the end of the summer, intent on several weeks' hard work, yet the omens were not good. Jane, meeting him by chance in Pall Mall early in September, received a budget of personal news. He said he had been very ill, she reported back to the Inspector; Annie and Minnie were staying on the Isle of Wight, where he intended to join them. 'I do not think that he looked well,' she concluded. Ill health notwithstanding, he pressed ahead with schemes of work, writing to George Hodder a couple of days later asking if he would like a stint as his secretary. Hodder, at this stage in his career perpetually on the look-out for commissions of this kind, was happy to accept. The work, he discovered, was far from arduous – mostly writing to Thackeray's dictation or making extracts from books, either at Onslow Square or the British Museum – and paid a far from negligible five to six pounds a week.

Thackeray's genial, avuncular side showed itself to advantage in his dealings with younger acolytes such as Hodder. He put them up for jobs (both W.W.F. Synge and George Augustus Sala, whose 'curious talent' Thackeray admired, were recommended to George Smith) and operated a much-recycled 'floating loan' for their benefit. Hodder himself had borrowed money from Thackeray earlier in the year after he had been sacked from a newspaper. 'When you are well to do again I know you will pay it back,' Thackeray confidently assured him, 'and I dare say somebody else will want the money, which is meanwhile most heartily at your service.' In his capacity as amanuensis and research assistant, working mostly in Thackeray's bedroom at Onslow Square, Hodder resisted the temptation to indulge in what he called 'Boswelling', but he was an observant man and the portrait he left is full of sharp little details. For the most part Thackeray dictated what became *The Four Georges* seated at a chair, rarely changing his position, and when he did so generally to one of maximum discomfort. If inspiration failed he would light a cigar and pace the bedroom carpet. Hodder was struck by his clear enunciation, and his ability to weigh his sentences, so that the man scribbling at his side rarely had to stop. Thackeray also took a knowing interest in the type of pen used and the quality of the paper beneath it, disliking smooth, satiny paper, he told Hodder, as it would not let the pen 'bite'. He was not energetic, Hodder thought, and when he made a joke never smiled.

This routine went on for several weeks. Thackeray's passage was booked on the *Africa*, sailing from Liverpool on Saturday 13 October. The preceding few days were a rush of work and regretful refusals of dinner invitations. Despite the late stage in the proceedings he was on the look-out for a secretary to accompany him to America. The original idea had been to take Maurice Marochetti, the son of his next-door neighbour, the Italian sculptor, but the scheme was aborted after the death of Maurice's brother (Thackeray was greatly upset by this, and Hodder found him in tears one morning a day or so before the child's death). Hodder was present at Onslow Square on Sunday 7 October when the subject came up. He volunteered, and was promised consideration. Next morning, however, Thackeray told him that he thought the state of his health probably required a valet rather than a secretary. 'I can ask a servant to hold a basin to me,' Thackeray explained, in a graphic illustration of his companion's probable duties, 'but I doubt I could so treat a secretary – at least he *might* object.' It was settled that Charles Pearman, whose loyalty and quick-wittedness Thackeray held in high regard, should go instead. In retrospect one regrets Hodder's absence from the trip – he was a shrewd man, and would probably have left a better account of Thackeray's travels than Eyre Crowe had done three years before. All the same, the time spent in Thackeray's company in the week before his departure provides some revealing glimpses of his employer's state of mind. That Sunday at Onslow Square he was in 'exceptionally high spirits', Hodder thought, but reflective, keen to talk about some of his literary experiences and the way in which his fortunes had improved in recent years. The *Quarterly* row clearly remained a sensitive spot, for he was eager to discuss the *Punch* contributors, and, as Hodder put it, 'was at some pains to show that he held the humorous brotherhood in high esteem'. And he had a plan for his return, he told Hodder, recasting once more the hints he had dropped to Cruikshank and George Smith: to start a magazine or journal of his own.

For some time there had been a plan to mark his departure with a farewell dinner at the Garrick. Originally conceived as a quiet evening in the company of a handful of friends, this had grown into a fully fledged commemoration, with invitations sent to sixty guests. Thackeray had watched this transformation with unease. Even at Onslow Square, he insisted, he wanted to avoid the symbolism of 'the last glass of wine – the last talk – the wistful faces of the girls'. Now he was nervous at the size of the gathering, and the prospect of speeches. In the end he rather enjoyed himself, appreciated the turn-out (Dickens took the chair, later succeeded by Jerrold, with whom some kind of *rapprochement* had been reached) and the whole-heartedness of the sentiment on display. It was typical of his current cast of mind that his own speech (in which, according to contemporary accounts, he 'outdid himself') should track backwards to the thirty-year-old world of his schooldays, and the feelings of 'the day before Dr Birch expected his young friends to re-assemble at his academy, Rodwell Regis'. Did his audience remember how the time was spent, Thackeray wondered, before going on to itemise the sensations of the last day at home in fanatical detail ('and how the gig came; and then, how you heard the whirl of mail-coach wheels, and the tooting of the guard's horn, as with an odious punctuality the mail and the four horses came galloping over the hill ...'). For a moment he had ceased to be a successful middle-aged man on the eve of an overseas trip, surrounded by his admiring friends, and become a schoolboy once more.

On the morning of his departure for Liverpool, Hodder arrived to find Thackeray in the study and Annie and Minnie in the dining-room, and the air of tension that habitually hung over family farewells at an unprecedented level. This was the moment he dreaded, Thackeray declared as soon as Hodder had stepped into the room. After disappearing into the dining-room to embrace his daughters, he asked Hodder to keep close behind him as he descended the steps to the waiting cab so that he could jump in unseen. The instant the door slammed shut he threw himself into the corner and buried his face in his hands. But the sight of Liverpool some hours later, with its forest of ships' masts and reminders of former travels, restored his spirits. On board the *Africa* he wrote his final letters: to Eyre Crowe, asking him to take the family plate along to Bradbury & Evans for safe-keeping, and to Whitwell Elwin. 'It's blowing jolly fresh,' he told Crowe from his vantage point above the Mersey. 'How you would enjoy it.' To Elwin he was more guarded: 'If I see my way into a pleasant letter from the States I'll send you one: and O how happy I'll be to come back and see you.' Given the anxieties that awaited him, it was a prophetic remark.

XVIII
The Public Eye

'Oh Ye Gods wont I be glad to come home leaving 500£ a year
behind in this country! Then grim death will not look so grim –
then the girls will have something to live upon or to bestow on
the objects of their young affections – then, when the house is
paid for, we may live and take things easily – then, when I have
written 2 more novels, for wh. I shall get 5000£ a piece – why
then, at 50, I shall be as I was at 21.'

> *Letter to his mother, 29 December 1855*

'It seems to me I am not near so much in love with the country
this time as before – doesn't it seem so to you?'

> *Letter to his daughters, 6 January 1856*

The voyage westward on the *Africa* took eleven
days. From the outset an air of grim resolution
prevailed. One of the last letters Thackeray
wrote on board ship before his departure was
to his mother. Here, writing at 6 a.m., with the
wind 'blowing most cheerily', he addressed the
reasons for the trip: 'I really think if I look out
now before very long we may pay the house
and have 5 or 6000£.' Almost immediately he was struck by a typical
shaft of foreboding. Was it right, he wondered, to be thinking of
material gain when all that lay between him and the ocean was a
wooden ship's hull? He consoled himself with the thought that he was
crossing the Atlantic 'for the dear young ones' sake ... We made a
famous party of it,' he apostrophised their leave-taking, 'and I was
relieved when it was over.' He did not enjoy the voyage, telling Annie
and Minnie a day before its end that the passage had been 'dreffly

stupid', and that there was scarcely a passenger aboard whom he would care to see again. To do Thackeray justice, he was conscious that advancing age lay at the heart of this indifference. Twenty years before he would have relished the foul weather and the company. But he was amused by the appetite of a teenaged girl whom he watched at breakfast one morning eating her way through a beefsteak and then a herring, after which she 'actually called for another bloater – the bloated little pig!' At this point Thackeray claimed that he was forced to leave the table in disgust: 'I couldn't see that darling child gobble up that second fish.' They reached Boston without incident on 24 October 1855.

What was Thackeray like as he approached his mid-forties? The question is not perhaps as idle as it sounds. Certainly it was one in which a great many people were interested. Eight years after *Vanity Fair* he was still very much in the public eye, the subject of newspaper comment, 'profiles' and simple gossip. To his friends, especially new acquaintances meeting him for the first time, most of this publicity seemed highly inaccurate – several of the people he encountered on his second American trip, for example, were struck by the disparity between the public image and the private man. The novelist John Esten Cooke, who interviewed him in Virginia early in 1856, puzzled over the 'malicious cartoons' he had read in imported English papers. Primed to expect a gloomy, cynical misanthropist, he was surprised to find a kindly, genial figure, 'a man of the world in the best sense of the phrase'. Bayard Taylor, whose acquaintance with Thackeray began at this time and lasted until the end of his life, had the same impression of a man whose opinions and demeanour had been almost wilfully misrepresented: 'his only manifestations of impatience . . . were when that which he had written with a sigh was interpreted as a sneer'. Both Cooke and Taylor left shrewd accounts of their dealings with Thackeray, whose value lies simply in the fact that their authors were not English. They noted his taste for good living – he told Cooke that he drank a bottle of Bordeaux at a sitting – and detected, almost from the outset, deep reservoirs of melancholy. The genial air came mixed with a barely concealed sadness: 'kind courteous and good-humoured, but not a hearty, cheery person', Cooke thought. Nor did he seem a man at all comfortable with his profession or the obligations that it exacted. He told Taylor, with evident sincerity, that he wrote only from necessity, and never took up his pen without an effort.

Without doubt Thackeray's reserve and his trade-mark aloofness sometimes disabled him publicly; his silences were often mistaken for disdain; and yet his private communications are shot through with boundless good nature and anxiety to please. Writing to an old family servant who proposed to pay him a visit, for instance, he could strike an unaffectedly warm-hearted note, profess himself 'glad to think that you are getting on well in the world' and convey Annie's and Minnie's pleasure that the man should remember his time with them. One of the best measures of Thackeray's humanity, in fact, was his ability to get on with and inspire loyalty in his servants. While the social protocols of the age sometimes interfered with these relationships – stranded in some godforsaken American hotel, he often wished that he could ask Charles Pearman to dine with him, but feared that it would be a step too far – his concern for the people he employed was transparently genuine. At one point in the American trip he asked Pearman what he did in the evenings. 'I read the paper, sir, and I lay on my bed,' Pearman replied. Guiltily comparing his servant's sequestration with his own eventful nightlife of dinners, parties and crowded lecture halls, Thackeray's eyes filled with tears.

For his own part, Thackeray was conscious of ageing. A letter to Mrs Elliot from early 1856 examined the drawbacks of growing old in some detail. 'We don't get amusinger as we get older, we grow prosy and repeat ourselves and talk about our complaints and selfish grievances.' If there was solace it lay in old friends and their conversation, 'and we don't care for making any new friends, and for young amusements or companions or conversations . . .' This is an exaggeration – Thackeray liked the company of younger men, especially those of a vaguely Bohemian cast, and continued to befriend them almost until his death – but the consciousness of a life that, at forty-four, was already beginning to wind down, remains. This awareness of waning powers and fading stamina underlies his second American trip and doubtless helped to make it more burdensome to him. Again, he spent half a year in America; again, the venture was a great success – he cleared £3,000 from his efforts, although the US railway shares in which much of the money was invested had to be sold at a loss in the early 1860s – but his initial enthusiasm at returning to the scene of his earlier triumphs was quickly dispelled. Almost certainly some of this disillusionment was a displaced psychological reaction to Sally Baxter, but a host of other factors combined to render his travels more fraught and less enlivening. He was nervous about the lectures, which were untried and barely complete; wary, too, of the likely hostility of

Anglophile listeners to his attacks on Hanoverian royalty. More generally, a tide of anti-British feeling was flowing through the country, propelled by the recruitment of US mercenaries to fight on the British side in the Crimea; the political élite kept away from touring Englishmen, and there were no more presidents among his audience. Confined to hotel parlours by a notably severe winter, and to hotel bedrooms by recurrent ill health, Thackeray found that the few glimpses he gained of street life were no longer to his taste. The free-and-easy manners he had praised three years before now looked like vulgarity; the routes to self-advancement that allowed millionaires to clamber their way out of the dirt were democracy gone mad. All this had an effect on his political sensibilities, and he later claimed that America had 'Whiggified him'. The net result was a change in his attitude to the task that lay before him: he was more calculating, less eager for social life; he went further afield, wrote more letters to the secretaries of local clubs and institutions that wanted his services. Lecturing had ceased to be an agreeable paying holiday and become a business. Amid non-stop travel, denied the gentlemanly conversation of Eyre Crowe, his temperament worsened. The letters written during his tour of the Deep South, where the audiences grew thin and the accommodation rudimentary, are faintly disturbing, full of humourless jokes about incipient insanity and strait-jackets, perpetual brooding about money and complaints about journeys that were 'stupefying beyond measure'.

Still, he was enthusiastic about his return to Boston and New York. The Baxters were there to welcome him, and 'a score more friends very glad to see me'. Installed once more at the Clarendon, he busied himself in preparing his lectures, which Pearman copied out 'in the most beautiful handwriting as clear as print'. There were compliments on all sides: the Arctic traveller Dr Kane reported that he had seen one of his sailors hunched for hours over a book that turned out to be *Pendennis*. As for the Baxters, Thackeray cast a discriminating eye over the two sisters who had so beguiled him on his previous trip. Lucy, he reported home, was 'just as nice & pretty'. Sally, however, seemed to have lost some of her bloom. 'She has been awfully flattered since I went away ...' Worse, Sally was engaged to be married to Frank Hampton, the son of a wealthy southern politician and plantation owner. An unaffianced Sally, one feels, would still have captivated him. As with Jane's pregnancy, it was the knowledge that a real woman lay beneath the fantasy figure which he had contrived for himself that irked. Though he approved of Sally's husband-to-be and his stately father, Thackeray's reaction was a by now characteristic raillery, which altogether failed to disguise the hurt he felt. He declined to attend the wedding.

He was booked to deliver the series of four lectures four times in New York before going to Boston early in December, and then to travel west. On the first night he discovered that he had written too much, and had to make running repairs. He sensed, too, that the audience was taken aback by the references to George I and his mistresses, and by the generally satirical treatment of 'that strange religion of king-worship' that distinguished *The Four Georges*. Writing back to the girls in mid-November ('one month over already!'), he decided that the lectures had gone 'pooty well', but complained of nerves. Already audience reaction was falling into set patterns: the 'pathetic business' of George III's descent into madness went down well; George I was less fervently received. Newspaper criticisms ranged between lavish encomia and wounding personal attacks: Thackeray claimed not to care. An appearance at Williamsburg, under the auspices of the local YMCA, was a flop ('the people no more understood what I was about than if I had been talking so much Algebra'), redeemed by an engagement in a brilliant lighted room in Brooklyn thronged to the ceiling with an audience that the lecturer put at 2,500. Despite mounting evidence of ill health, he decided that returning to America had galvanised him – 'There is some electric influence in the air & sun here wh. we dont experience on our side of the globe' – and eagerly estimated his likely receipts. He calculated that he would make £800 out of his first month on the podium, he told the *bonnes soeurs*: 'Isn't this worth crossing the water for and a comfort to be able to put away now that health is shaking and good folks are getting old?'

But the bustling New York routine was already beginning to weary him. There was no time for anything but work. He had been waiting for a day's quiet to send a letter, he told one correspondent, but there never *was* a day's quiet. The second series of lectures was finished, and both newspapers and public seemed better pleased. What the people liked was sentiment, he concluded. Already he was beginning to wonder whether his health would stand the strain of the western tour that had been proposed. Laid up at the Clarendon with 'a pretty little fever & ague yesterday', he told William Wetmore Story, who was involved in arranging his itinerary, that he thought he would have to stick to the familiar Philadelphia/Baltimore route. He had another attack – presumably malarial, as he dosed himself with quinine – after talking to the Press Club at Astor House. Writing to Annie and Minnie late in November he yearned to be sailing home on the next boat, but exhorted himself to have courage. Even 'these little illnesses & attacks ought to give it', he pronounced: 'They say my lad work during your brief period of strength & popularity. Try and replace some of that patrimony wasted.' The girls wrote cheerful letters back, but to be told, effectively, that their father was working himself into ill health on their behalf cannot have been a pleasant experience.

To make matters worse he had developed a bladder infection – no doubt connected to his stricture – which 'causes me great inconvenience, & is sometimes very awkward in ladys' society'. Offers of hospitality were declined, although he enjoyed a day spent in Yonkers in the company of Frederick Cozzens, a wine-merchant-cum-literary-man, 'the jolliest day I have had for a long time'. After talking to the Yonkers Library Association he went nine miles along the road to visit Washington Irving and his two nieces. Thackeray was charmed by Irving's house: 'a funny little in and out cottage . . . little bits of small parlors where we were served with cake and wine – with a little study not much bigger than my back room, with old dogs trotting about the premises with fleets of ducks sailing on the ponds – a very pleasant patriarchal life'.

Inspired by this vision of rural retirement, his health improved: fifteen days without a chill, he noted in Boston in early December. Predictably he fell ill again the very next day. The Baxter wedding loomed, and he wrote excusing himself on grounds of work, the nine-hour round trip and the fact that 'after four hours I am feverish anxious and obliged to lie down'. By this stage his presence in America had become widely known, and he complained that he could not sit for five minutes without a waiter arriving with a card that heralded a 'grinning stranger'. He was 'overworked, overdined, oversupped, overvisited' he told Mrs Proctor. In a queer psychosomatic reaction he had an attack of spasms on the day of the wedding – providentially, he assured the bride's mother, for 'how annoyed Baxter would have been that I should have lost 4 days and the proceeds thereof for the sake of a wedding which I would as soon see as see one of my children have a tooth out!' He did not intend to forgive the bride, he maintained: it was the highest compliment he could pay her. He spent the next two days recovering in bed, finding an ominous parallel between his shattered infatuation and a life of Goethe that lay to hand: 'that old rogue – he had an unhappy attachment at 75 and the young lady who shared it was *sent back to school*'.

It was time to be moving on. A week before Christmas he sketched out his short- and medium-term plans for Annie's benefit. He was due to lecture and then attend Edith Story's party where, he had been forewarned, the children would be dressed up as characters from *The Rose and the Ring*. Christmas at Troy would be followed by engagements in Buffalo, New York and Philadelphia before he moved south, working his way back up the Mississippi to St Louis in March, with the aim of returning to New York by April. Meanwhile, there were rumours of other unhappy attachments – in particular a hint from Mrs Carmichael-Smyth that Annie was disposed to look favourably on the attentions of a penniless young clergyman named Creyke. Thackeray wrote swiftly to lecture his 'dearest fat' on the insanity of this choice. 'You must marry a man that can keep you,' he declared, not unkindly, '– and you've just pitched precisely on the gentleman that can not.' He was later relieved to discover that the relationship existed largely in his mother's imagination. In the end Christmas Day found him in transit, heading north from Buffalo. Three days later he was driven by sleigh to the Niagara River before lecturing to 3,000 people. The snow, which prevented him from inspecting the Falls, came as rather a relief: he feared that the exertion would have been too great a day before a lecture. His takings in the two months since his arrival had now risen to £1,600, he noted, but the trip was proving expensive, and he calculated that he had already spent £200 on travel.

He was already pining to be home, bored by the train journeys, the effort of having to prepare himself to meet his audiences, the incidental annoyances of vulgar fellow travellers who used their fingers as handkerchiefs. He was conscious, too, that the fixations that worked their way into his letters were of scant interest to the people who read them. 'Aren't you bored by my perpetual talk about dollars?' he enquired of Kate Perry. Extra money was available across the border in Canada, but he feared the reaction of 'stout old loyalists' and instead turned back to Philadelphia. Here a snowstorm robbed him of listeners and he and Pearman were thrown onto their own resources for a couple of days. Again Thackeray was solicitous of the welfare of his manservant who, he told Annie, had not been out of the house all day, was too shy even to venture into the public areas of the hotel, and – unlike his employer – had no one to ask him out to dinners and suppers. Thackeray, on the other hand, decided that he had had 'too much of the dinners & suppers and would be very glad indeed to get a little quiet and his own way'. The bad weather followed him to Baltimore, where it was so cold that he scarcely went out and lay in his bed at the hotel most of the afternoon reading Macaulay. The snow was now beginning to disrupt his schedule and reduce his audiences – the Baltimore attendance was additionally depleted by the contending attraction of an opera company – but despite another storm he enjoyed a trip to Washington and a chance to dine with the English minister Crampton, whom he had met on his previous visit. The Washington dinner, above all, brought home to him the souring of his love affair with America. 'What a comfort it was to dine with an Englishman again!' he enthused to Annie and Minnie. 'To be treated civilly by servants, and hear the talk one has been accustomed to speak.'

From Washington he went south to Richmond, Virginia, and more dreadful weather. Bored as the *bonnes soeurs* may have been by the continual talk about money, he continued to itch away at his scheme to be worth £20,000 by the time he was fifty. 'And then we will be independent of all police magistrateships, government places & the like. And shall have made our means all out of our own brains.' John Esten Cooke, who met him on several occasions around this time, arrived at his hotel to find Thackeray lolling in a chair in the parlour and smoking one of the local 'Plantation' cigars taken from a bundle with which his visitor had previously presented him (Thackeray approved the brand but complained that his fellow novelist G.P.R. James, then English consul at Richmond, would keep coming over to sample them). Amid some routine questioning about his writing habits, Thackeray obligingly sketched out the plot of what was to become *The Virginians* and mused over his fondness for Becky Sharp. He had always liked her, he explained, and 'what are called Bohemians, and fellows of that sort'. Cooke listened admiringly for an hour or so, absorbed by 'the singular commingling of humour and sadness, of sarcasm and gentleness – the contrast between his reputation as the bitterest of cynics . . . and the real person with his cordial address . . .'

Pundits maintained that it was the worst winter for sixty years. On the way from Richmond to Charleston the engine broke down, compelling him to take refuge in a roadside hotel, or as he described it in the promised letter to Elwin, 'a tavern in a swamp in South

Carolina'. A letter from Charleston to his daughters shows just how equivocal his attitude to the slave question remained. 'How fond you would both be of the little blackies,' he told Annie and Minnie, 'they are the dearest little imps . . . I think I shall buy one and bring it home –.' And yet he was genuinely saddened by the thought of a 'pretty little child' who had held up a plate to him at dinner on his last visit, but who now, his owner having tired of Charleston and his establishment there, had presumably been sold along with the rest of his possessions. He took up the issue again after meeting Sally Baxter's husband Frank Hampton (at one point he stayed in the same hotel as the newly married couple, which must have been a painful experience). When cholera had struck the Hampton plantation the previous year, Hampton had 'staid and nursed his poor black people by whom he is adored'. What did this mean, Thackeray wondered? Hampton's sisters were effectively slaves too, 'up at all hours of the night to go see the sick working day & night for these thriftless folk . . .' He would like to set up an atelier, Thackeray concluded, and draw these 'niggahs', for

 they were 'endlessly funny'. What really irks about these attitudes – again, doubtless hardened by his exposure to a good deal of southern hospitality – is that Thackeray, rather in the way that he could unthinkingly patronise women and servants, did not mean to be unkind. Seeing the slave population as a kind of nigger minstrel show got up for his amusement, assuring himself that they were for the most part decently fed and clothed, he could not be got to recognise the greater constraint that mocked their incidental comforts and liberties.

Meanwhile, his sense of ennui grew stronger. He hoped to be back in June, he told the girls, leaving £5,000 in US investments and bringing £1,500 to settle the account on Onslow Square, but already there seems to have been some doubt as to whether he intended to stay the course. He was 'bored to extinction', he informed Eyre Crowe in mid-February 1856, setting out for Savannah, Georgia, to stay with a wealthy cotton-dealer named Andrew Low ('They are tremendous men these cotton merchants,' he told Kate Perry admiringly). Gratifyingly, one of Low's Negro houseboys remembered the quarter-dollar with which Thackeray had presented him three years before. Lecturing at nearby Augusta, 'a queer little rustic city', he came up against competition: a wild man speaking in the same hall. 'I tell you it is not a dignified *métier*, that which I pursue,' he lamented. Slavery continued to be 'nowhere repulsive', although he was honest enough to admit disquiet over the stories of escaping women who would kill their children rather than return to their plantations. The long journey from Macon to Montgomery and then down the Alabama River by steamer to Mobile bored him beyond measure: 'The dreariness of this country, *everywhere*, almost consumes me.' He was astounded by hearing people on the boat talking of their longing to be home, only for their destination to turn out to be a swampy sandflat with a hundred or so houses, a few churches, a hotel and a newspaper office, 'where they skipped out quite pleased to be back at this Elysium'. The bad weather kept up, reducing the take at Mobile to a bare three dollars.

There is a painful contrast between the letters Thackeray sent home from his second American trip and the despatches returned from his travels as a young man in Ireland and the Middle East. The enthusiasm for landscape and sensation has all but gone. Only occasionally was he inspired to something like excitement over scene. Or perhaps it was merely that he had lost the ability to reproduce the outlines of what he saw: 'Somehow I can't write a descriptive letter any more,' he complained to Mrs Elliot from New Orleans early in March. But the paddle-steamer's slow progress down the Alabama River to Mobile produced the odd vignette worthy of the *Irish Sketch Book* or *Cornhill to Cairo*:

> What an odd dirty scene it was – with dark troops of slaves landing here and there and marching up the dismal bank into the dingy wilderness beyond: with planters waiting to come on board with their cotton bales with starved ragged planters houses shuddering upon the steep river side with darkies bearing turkies for sales with ague stricken woodmen at whose wharves we stop and take in pinewood –

Mobile he thought pleasant, with a decent hotel, but the strain of this journey into the South was beginning to tell. A darkly ironic note to Mrs Proctor from New Orleans stirred ancient ghosts. As he felt himself advancing towards imbecility, Thackeray wrote, 'it is well that I should get a little money to keep me when I am in the Asylum. Proctor will come and see me there, I daresay I shall know him.' The trip along the Mississippi to St Louis brought an outpouring of disgust

to Whitwell Elwin: 'The journey, the incidents on it, the people I see along the road, the business I am on are all as disagreeable as can be.' Conscious, perhaps, of his inability to think the right thoughts about the tribe of black servants he met, he continued to fret over the slave question. The Negroes seemed to be happy, which did not make slavery right, 'but I can't mend it, and so leave it'. Again, he correctly foresaw the dismal consequences of slavery's end. American blacks would begin to suffer when a good Negro ceased to be worth $1,200 and had to contend with white labour in the cotton and sugar plantations. 'O it will be a terrible day, when 5 or 6 millions of these blacks will have to perish and give place to the white man wanting work.'

Here and there came twitches on the thread: 25 March was Jane's birthday – he prayed fervently that it might be happier than those of recent years. Cairo, near St Louis, was Dickens-haunted, supposedly the model for the gimcrack town of 'Eden' in *Martin Chuzzlewit*. There was a Dickensian air to some of his travelling companions, too: an on-board circus whose ornaments included a bearded lady, 'the Infant Esau' and a giantess eight feet tall. Thackeray consoled himself with three bottles of brandy and a dozen of claret sent up from New Orleans. In the end most of the claret remained undrunk, and he presented the remaining nine bottles to the ship's negro waiters. His tour of the South was nearing its close, and he prepared to return to New York. Tired of hotels, he arranged to stay with an acquaintance named William Duer Robinson, whose bachelor establishment at Houston Street he fancied would be to his taste. He was right, and spent an agreeable four weeks in an exclusively male society, eating his dinners and going to the theatre. The English actor Lester Wallack, who met him at this time, is another witness to the contrast between public and private man. Noting Thackeray's great height, his spectacles – these gave him a pedantic look – and his chin carried in the air, Wallack prepared to mark him down as 'the most pompous, supercilious person I had ever met'. In fact, an hour or two of

Thackeray's company persuaded him that he had made a grave misjudgment, and he became a fixture at Houston Street. Enraptured as ever by the smell of the greasepaint, Thackeray was happy to sit 'like a boy' listening to Wallack and Robinson talking into the small hours.

He had originally intended to stay in America until June, but the pattern of his previous trip was about to repeat itself. He was ill again, this time with a bout of his old urethral trouble, and had to be patched up by a local doctor recommended to him by Robinson. There was a plan for him to dust off his *English Humourists* lectures once more for the benefit of audiences in Philadelphia and possibly New York. Thackeray accepted the invitation, pocketed a cheque from the entrepreneur who had arranged the performances – a young man named William Bedford Reed – and set out for Philadelphia. Here the audiences were so poor that he seems to have decided there was no point in continuing. Having once again made a spontaneous decision to leave, he could not even bring himself to wait for a Cunard liner but booked a passage on the US mailship *Baltic* (Reed, who had had no word from him and only read the news of his departure in a newspaper, was pleasantly surprised when the post brought a warm letter and a banker's draft returning a quarter of the fee). Thackeray's last letters to American friends make clear how suddenly he had taken the decision: 'I little thought yesterday that I shd. go away without seeing – but never mind we must go sometime – it is such delicious weather – and O wont it be pleasant to see the girls again?'

The *Baltic* took only eight days to cross the Atlantic. Thackeray would probably have been better advised to opt for a more leisurely crossing, as he had a wretchedly uncomfortable trip – ill with spasms and an inflammation of the mouth. Finding shaving difficult, he grew a beard. 'Wine is ojus, cegars create loathing,' he reported to Robinson, adding that he had not been well for a single day. Fortunately the 'tinkering' of Robinson's medical friend had held up, and he proposed to 'set work straightway and get my water pipes cistern &c in complete order'. He arrived in Liverpool on 7 May, dined at the Adelphi and sped back to London, arriving just in time to attend the annual Shakespeare dinner at the Garrick, 'and didn't I make a Yankee speech, and Oh Lor Robinson haven't I got a headache this morning'. More than ever he relished the familiar sights of home: 'And so here's the old house, the old room the old teapot by the bedside, the old trees nodding in at the window.' It looked as if he had never been away, he reported, and the whole experience a dream that he had been spinning for six long months amid the dreary Alabama riverbanks and the teeming New York streets.

America had taken its toll. He was ill – his London doctors shook their heads over the effects on his system – and had to spend several weeks recovering. This included submitting himself to Thompson for a hydraulic overhaul. Financially the trip had been a success, although the £3,000 he amassed would have been greater still, had it not been for the heavy travelling expenses and some pricey farewell presents for his American friends bought at Tiffany's in New York. The social consequences were less promising. Word of *The Four Georges'* sardonic tone had got back to Thackeray's aristocratic friends: their disapproval brought a certain amount of mild social ostracism over the ensuing months. He told Bayard Taylor, who visited London later in the year, that Lord—— had dropped him from his dinner-party list for the past three months. Slowly his health began to improve. Writing to Mrs Baxter in the third week of June, he reported that he had given up business and pleasure 'and am doctoring and bettering myself every week I hope'. His chills and fevers had been gone for three weeks now, and he believed they would further diminish if he could be cured of his urethral problem. For all this, it was impossible to stir himself to activity. Bradbury & Evans had offered £6,000 for a new serial novel. He accepted with alacrity – again George Smith would have to wait – but could not bring himself to begin. He had been in London two and a half months, he told Mrs Hampton, to whom the former Sally Baxter's letters were now addressed, without doing the smallest bit of work. In a tone that foreshadows Evelyn Waugh's world-weary diaries from a century later, he explained that 'I am dead; go nowhere, do, think, write nothing.' If America had exhausted him physically and drained him creatively, it had left an indelible mark on his travelling companion. Charles Pearman, he noted with a mixture of amusement and annoyance, had been spoiled by his experiences, declined to wear his servant's livery, dressed in black and was 'much [the] greater man'.

At the end of July he made a brief attempt on *The Virginians* and then stopped, utterly without ideas and stamina. It was the holiday season, in any case, and he and the girls began on a round of visits. They started with Thackeray's distant cousin Frederick Thackeray and his wife Lady Elizabeth, who lived at Bagshot ('very kyind only it wasn't quite as good fun as the Coles', Annie reported judiciously to her grandmother) following this up with a trip to Windsor, where the service at St George's Chapel was enlivened by the sight of Edith Story running up to kiss them. They had planned to go on elsewhere, but another attack of the spasms sent Thackeray back to Onslow Square. Fortunately it lasted only a day, and within a week father and daughters set off on a continental tour, travelling via Calais, Ghent and Brussels to Spa, where they spent five days at the Hôtel des Pays Bas ('Papa is very well & says this agrees capitally with him') before moving on to Düsseldorf. Early September brought them to Paris, staying at Thackeray's old haunt, the Hôtel Bristol (the Carmichael-Smyths were away taking the water cure in Germany). Oddly, the girls later removed themselves to rue Godot to stay with what Annie described as 'a brown young lady from India'. There is no mention of this person in Thackeray's correspondence, and Annie's memoirs are silent, but it may very well have been the daughter of his half-sister Mrs Blechynden. The family went out dining, while back in his hotel room Thackeray mused elegiacally over the memory of bygone letters to Jane 'written in this very room at this table some 5 years since'. Amongst the news from home, he was shocked to hear of Gilbert à Beckett's death. Having returned to London the following month, he paid a warm private tribute in a letter to Charles Cavendish Gifford, secretary to the Prime Minister Palmerston, commending his friend's 'long & hard battle to fight with fortune' and the 'noble conduct' of Bradbury & Evans, who had written off an £800 debt. Typically Thackeray could not resist linking à Beckett's troubles to his own struggle to survive, and composed a prayer for literary persons: '. . . O Jove! When I die, may I die solvent; and may there be no need to send a hat round for my family! Amen . . '

Meanwhile, he was pursuing other routes to solvency. *The Four Georges* had been a hit with American audiences. Despite the disapproval of certain elements of the *beau monde*, there seemed no reason why it should not appeal to his British admirers, and accordingly much of the autumn was spent in making plans to go to Scotland and the North of England. Among other advantages the tour offered the chance to sample a great deal of friendly hospitality. Writing to Dr John Brown in Edinburgh, Thackeray revealed that no fewer than four people – including Lord Elgin and Brown himself – had offered to put him up. These preparations were interrupted by the sudden illness of Mrs Carmichael-Smyth, which summoned him to Paris in late October. Prostrate with a fever, the old lady assumed that she was on the point of death and seems to have sent for her son with the idea of saying goodbye. Arriving at the bedside, Thackeray, according to Minnie, 'cheered her up in no time', ordered grapes, previously forbidden by the medical attendant, '& she eat about a pound & thought them very nice & has been wonderfully well ever since . . .' He left Paris on 28 October to return to the London fogs, the girls remaining to nurse their grandmother, spent some time in bed with another spasmodic attack and then went north, intending to use Edinburgh as a base for a number of Scottish engagements. Settled in lodgings at Randolph Crescent, rather than billeting himself on one of his friends, he began his lectures on 4 November, addressing large audiences, being hissed for the poor opinion of Mary, Queen of Scots expressed in the lecture on George I, but rather enjoying the experience. It was famous fun, he told the girls, and made the lecture go all the pleasanter. Annie reported to Amy Crowe – then holding the fort at Onslow Square – that he was having a 'capital time'. Press comment was favourable, particularly a notice in an Edinburgh paper, which Annie thought was the best she had ever read. Roaming across central and lowland Scotland to Dumfries, Paisley and Glasgow, where he spoke to 2,000 people, his enthusiasm began to falter, and by mid-November he was looking forward to the tour's end, five weeks distant, and dosing himself with calomel 'for you see I am in a dreadful fright lest the spasms should come on'.

Though his health bore up, his weariness is evident in a letter of late November to Mrs Proctor. Full of gloomy forebodings about death – sparked off by the recent demise of Mrs Proctor's mother – it offers one of his most considered statements about the after-life and his religious beliefs in general. Heaven, he suggested, was a lonely place. To imagine it was to think of 'God Inscrutable Immeasurable, endless, beginningless, supreme, awfully solitary'. A child's death might tear the heart of its family, but it was difficult to lament the passing of the elderly. 'I go – to what I don't know – but to God's next world which is His and He made it.' He ended with another grim, solitary image: himself pacing up and down the shore looking towards the 'Unknown Ocean' and thinking of the traveller whose boat sailed yesterday. 'Those we love can but walk down to the pier with us – the voyage we must make alone –.'

Early December brought him to Hull, where he dined with a local worthy named Bright. 'What a bad dinner it was yesterday, and didnt the waiter spill a glass of port down my sleeve!' he told the girls, justifying his decision to decline Bright's offer of a bed in favour of 'a most splendid and comfortable hotel'. But he enjoyed the company of a tableful of Humberside merchants, the fat mayor of Hull resplendent in a blue coat and waistcoat with shiny brass buttons, and the presence of the brother of a boy he had known thirty years before at Charterhouse, now dead, 'one of whose songs I can sing at this minute'. The good reception by audiences and the press continued, although there were onlookers who detected a gap between the sardonic nature of what he had to say and the real temperament of the lecturer. Talking to a journalist named Charles Cooper who had covered his visit in the local paper, Thackeray asked him what he really thought. Cooper suggested that he used a great deal of cleverness to hide a kindly heart under the cover of cheap cynicism. Thackeray was taken aback, but not offended, even going so far as to wonder whether Cooper was right. In the middle of these triumphs, he invariably had one eye trained over his shoulder – noting, for example, that a parson he met received an annual stipend equivalent to what he was currently earning in a week, and worrying about his parents as they approached old age. His mother, he surmised, was worn down by years of gloom and solicitous watching over her husband, a man who really cared only for his fireside 'and her by it to read the paper'. He wanted to entice the couple to London, but the major disliked the idea and in any case Thackeray doubted whether the change would do his mother good. Another anxiety nagged away at him, too, the need to keep this atmosphere of 'doubt and trouble & gloom' from sixteen-year-old Minnie. Always worried about the likelihood of his younger daughter inheriting Isabella's condition, Thackeray watched her keenly for signs of nervous agitation, and tried to keep her away from situations that might depress her spirits. Juggling these obligations to older and younger generations sometimes needed a greater dexterity than he possessed. Aware that several more lecture tours awaited him, he suggested if that the Carmichael-Smyths did not like the idea of London, then the girls could return to them in France and come back during the early summer of 1857 when he would probably be lecturing in the capital. Afterwards, though, 'we must shut up our house in London, and arrange that Granny can have us near her for some time'.

At the end of the first week in December he moved on to Bradford, following this up with engagements in Derby, Manchester and Liverpool. He had hoped to stay with his friends the Stanleys at Alderley Park but was denied their hospitality by another attack, which forced him to rearrange the Oxford lectures. As the tour came to an end he grew reflective, pleased at his popularity, alarmed that the worsening state of his health might allow him only a short time to paw at this glistening honeypot. 'There is a deal more money to be made . . .' he reported to W.W.F. Synge. 'So much the better for my women who shall have 10000£ apiece if I live two years more.' The girls were due back in London on 18 December, either with or without their grandparents. In the end the Carmichael-Smyths balked at the journey. Thackeray wrote to his stepfather a day later from Liverpool, where he had attracted an audience of 1,200, with a detailed projection of his earnings. By May 1858, he proposed, he would be worth £20,000. Independence beckoned. He was going to look at a house at Bevis Hill near Southampton, he revealed. But then Annie and Minnie might marry, and it would be 'bad fun' to sit there alone. He was back in London a few days before Christmas to enjoy a festive season that included taking the girls to the 'Tavistock House Theatricals', a Christmas production of Wilkie Collins' *The Frozen Deep*, which Dickens staged in his own home.

The Christmas holiday was a brief interlude in what turned out to be seven months on the road. Early in the New Year he delivered the *Georges* four times in London, netting over £1,000. February and March found him back in Scotland and northern England. Undoubtedly these stints in the provinces did much to increase Thackeray's public reputation and popularity. Certainly as a public spectacle he was second only to Dickens: adding up the attendances for his Edinburgh lectures, at one point he calculated that 3 per cent of the city's population had come to hear him. Moreover, the memory of him that remained in the public imagination often derived from these performances. For provincial readers following the London charivari from afar, the lecture hall offered the only opportunity to see celebrities in the flesh. These sightings invariably left a strong, if not always favourable, impression. The Scots literary critic George Gilfillan, for example, who probably saw Thackeray when the tour reached Gilfillan's native Dundee, thought the lecturer 'dry as a demonstrator; imperious as a Lord; distant as a snowy mountain top'. Such was Thackeray's status on the lecture circuit that he was being courted by professional speculators. The provincial tour of spring 1857 was overseen by Cramer & Beale & Co. George Hodder, who was connected with the firm, left a revealing account of Thackeray's shrewdness in negotiation. When Beale proposed terms, Thackeray merely nodded, not letting on whether he thought the amount offered fair or otherwise. Later no one could remember whether the sum settled on per lecture was fifty pounds or fifty guineas. Hodder went back to check. 'Oh, guineas, decidedly guineas,' Thackeray assured him. When he met Hodder a day or so later the mask of professional diffidence slipped and he crowed over his good fortune, telling his younger friend that it was twice as much as he would have received for a *Fraser's* article a few years before. In fact, with the lecturer agreeing to defray his own expenses, the arrangement was less satisfactory than it seemed, but for the moment Thackeray was scarcely able to believe his luck.

With Hodder acting as manager, the three-week excursion began in late April, starting in the West Country before heading north to Birmingham, Oxford and Leamington Spa, with a final stint of four lectures on the other side of the country in Norwich. Turn-out varied. At Oxford, where the hall was thronged, Hodder had been warned of the care needed to control rowdy undergraduate audiences, whose members delighted in charging past the ticket-checkers and 'bonnet-ting' anyone who got in their way. Stationing himself and another of Cramer & Beale's employees inside the door, Hodder quelled the 'overwhelming rush of expectant youth', as he put it, by assuring them that Thackeray would be gravely offended by any bad behaviour. The stratagem worked; the crowd was notably sympathetic and informed; and the lecturer went so far as to admit a select band of undergraduates to his hotel room for a private audience. Leamington, in contrast, was a failure: Hodder ascribed the poor audiences to the town's population of genteel womenfolk not liking Thackeray's sardonic attitude to bygone royalty.

For a run-of-the-mill engagement in a provincial city, Thackeray's two days in Norwich in mid-May are surprisingly well documented. By conflating Hodder's reminiscences, the memories of Whitwell Elwin, who happened to be in the area at the time, and the punctilious reports of the local paper, one can construct a detailed account of Thackeray the lecturer in action. There had been a brief gap in the tour since the Leamington lecture, during which both parties had gone elsewhere, and Hodder and Thackeray arranged to meet on Ely station. One of the latter's first remarks, Hodder recalled, after asking if everything was settled for the evening, concerned Jerrold's election to the Reform Club. (Hodder always assumed that the supposed 'coldness' between the two was largely apocryphal, and certainly

Jerrold's death, barely a month later, touched all Thackeray's most human instincts. He was a pall-bearer at the funeral, together with Dickens, Forster, Mark Lemon and Okers, and later delivered the 'Charity and Humour' lecture for the fund got up to support Jerrold's family.) Lecturer and factotum then set off across the fens to Norwich, where Thackeray met up with the Elwins at an hotel (Hodder made a point of not pressing his company upon his employer, although they occasionally dined together). Attendances at St Andrew's Hall were good – 'very numerous and genteel', according to the local paper – and Thackeray was listened to 'attentively, if not always approvingly' from start to finish. Mrs Elwin remembered him leaving the dining-room of the hotel as the lecture hour drew near, coming into the room where she sat with her children and announcing in a 'grave, pathetic' voice, 'I am come to say goodnight.' He took each child's hand in his own, lingered for a moment, then stepped out onto the balcony and threw a shilling to a brass band that was playing beneath the windows. 'Now then for the sermon,' he declared, before going off to his own hotel to ready himself. Judging from the notes that Mrs Elwin made, he was unusually relaxed and talkative during the period of their stay, saying that he had thought of going to India the following year, and that 'twelve lectures would pay for it'. Together with Elwin he walked from Norwich to the village of Thorpe, a mile or two north of the city, and explored the cathedral cloisters and the castle. The latter was currently in use as the county gaol. Thackeray reported that 'the men in the zebra clothes' saddened him, and he 'panted to be out again'. Illness was looming and threatened to postpone his last lecture. Somehow he got through, but he had to spend a day or so laid up at his hotel, where Hodder found him 'suffering great pain'. Had he taken the best medical advice, Hodder asked anxiously when they next met back in London? Thackeray said that he had, but had ignored it. 'They tell me not to drink, and I *do* drink. They tell me not to eat, and I *do* eat. In short, I do everything that I am desired *not* to do, and therefore what am I to expect?'

With seven months of lecturing now at an end, a prudent man would perhaps have tried to lessen the pace of his life. Throughout the early months of 1857, though, Thackeray had been incubating another plan which, as the summer drew on, unexpectedly bore fruit: nothing less than to stand for election to Parliament. Most modern critics have tended to pooh-pooh his attempt on the constituency of Oxford (Catherine Peters, for example, calls it 'a faintly ludicrous episode, even for the middle of the nineteenth century'). While this kind of disparagement is understandable, it perhaps ignores Thackeray's continuing interest in contemporary political issues – most recently symbolised by his involvement in the Administrative Reform Association – and the range of contacts he had built up in the preceding ten years. This, after all, was a man who knew Palmerston, Prime Minister since early 1855, and Lord John, and who dined at Holland House – not bad attributes for anyone who fancied setting up as a prospective Liberal parliamentary candidate in the 1850s. Then again, it is sometimes easy to forget the enthusiasm with which Victorian literary men embroiled themselves in practical politics: Dickens had been a parliamentary reporter; Trollope stood at Beverley in 1868 (a jaundiced account of this disillusioning experience can be found in *Ralph the Heir*). John Morley, whose career on the *Saturday Review* began at around this time, ended up – in another century, admittedly – as secretary for India. Certainly the Whig faction that began the episode by approaching Thackeray to stand at Edinburgh in 1856 would have seen nothing ridiculous in the idea of having a novelist as their candidate. As it turned out, Thackeray declined this offer. It went unrepeated, largely because the sentiments of *The Four Georges* offended some of the senior aristocratic Liberals in whose gift many parliamentary seats still lay. But Thackeray was undeterred. He thought that his lecture tour had made him better known, to the point where he would have as good a chance of entering Parliament as an independent than as a Whig nominee. In any case he was still uneasy about the lack of principle that had brought Palmerston's administration into being. The General Election of March 1857 had passed without anything suitable offering itself, but by midsummer there was news of a vacancy at Oxford. Thackeray decided to stand.

For an aspiring parliamentarian from London, the Oxford constituency mixed advantages and drawbacks in about equal parts. It returned two members (James Langston, the senior MP, had sat since 1841) and was broadly Liberal in sympathy, although the Peelite reaction had returned a Tory, Donald Maclean, between 1835 and 1847. The electorate was small, barely extended by the Reform Act of 1832, and by the mid-1850s stood at under 3,000 voters. In these circumstances local connections were important, and most of the Oxford MPs of the period had significant links to the city. In the March General Election, a fight between four Liberals, Langston's seat was never in doubt, but suspicions of latent conservatism had led to the defeat of Edward

Cardwell, the other sitting member, by Thackeray's friend Charles Neate, fellow of Oriel. The subsequent by-election emerged out of Neate's removal, for what his aspiring successor described as 'two-pennyworth of bribery which he never committed'. The Whigs chose a somewhat languid Irish peer named Viscount Monck.

Thackeray's statement of his political beliefs for the benefit of the Oxford electors is of considerable interest: for one thing, it gives a public airing to opinions that in the previous quarter-century could in some cases only be inferred. He professed himself a 'radical', which even by the standards of the mid-nineteenth century had so many usages that, like 'Liberalism' itself, it defied exact definition. Yet this was largely in keeping with the sympathies put on semi-public display twenty years before. *The Constitutional*, for example, had been founded on a platform of moderate radicalism, and had the support of progressive Liberal parliamentarians. In his late twenties Thackeray had sympathised with Richard Cobden and contributed a drawing to the *Anti-Corn Law Circular*. 'I would like to see all men equal, & this bloated aristocracy blasted to the wings of all the world,' he had written in 1840. But Chartism had scared him, and he regarded any assault on the property rights of the well-to-do as robbery. Ten years later, particularly at the aristocratic houses to which he was invited, he saw it as his task to build bridges between a remote, paternalist Whiggery and the genuine grievances of the lower classes. His first public utterances, issued from the Mitre – though his campaign was also associated with St John's, where his old Charterhouse contemporary Stoddart had been a fellow until his death the year before – were strong on reform. In a 'Broadside' to the electorate of 9 July he promised, if elected, to use his best endeavours to broaden the constitution and 'popularise' the government of the country. 'With no feeling but that of good will towards those leading Aristocratic Families who are administering the chief offices of the State, I believe that it could be benefited by the skills and talents of persons less aristocratic . . .' An address given on 10 July at the town hall renewed this theme: 'The popular influence must be brought to bear on the present government of the country,' he declared; 'if they flinch remind them that the people is outside and wants more and more.'

Thackeray claimed that he found the experience of electioneering humiliating, and that he met only two people who knew who he was. He paid a particularly depressing call at a house where the maidservant enquired: 'Are you Mr Neate's friend? Master's h'out, but he said I was to say he would vote for yeow.' But his chances seemed sufficiently promising for the Whigs to draft in Cardwell once again in place of the ineffectual Monck. They also fastened on Sunday Observance as the issue most likely to undermine Thackeray's campaign (he had advocated the Sunday opening of museums and similar places, which was disliked by extreme Sabbatarians) and on 18 July he was forced to issue a pamphlet restating his preference for access to picture galleries and gardens but denying that he ever 'spoke of opening theatres on Sundays'. Polling day was 21 July. Assuming that he would lose, Thackeray nevertheless went down by a surprisingly narrow margin – a mere sixty-five votes out of the 2,075 polled. He made a well-received valedictory speech, invoking the memory of the prizefighters Gully and Gregson and Gregson's willingness to shake the hand of his victorious opponent. He retired, he told his listeners, to take his place with the pen and ink at his desk, 'and leave to Mr Cardwell a business which I am sure he understands better than I do' (Thackeray had described himself to Annie as a Cardwellite). Afterwards he declared that, even had he been elected, he would swiftly have been thrown out as a result of sharp practice on the part of his agents.* The parallels with Colonel Newcome's parliamentary ambitions should not be over-drawn. Thackeray knew what he was doing, and the kind of behaviour he would find; his motives, too, were hardly unsullied (a parliamentary seat offered another route to a public appointment); tellingly, he seems to have toyed with the idea of trying for another seat. If anything disappointed him it was how few of the enfranchised college servants – except at St John's – had taken his side. But the fortnight at Oxford had cost money he could ill afford. Some time later a letter from Annie to Mrs Stoddart noted that 'His Oxford bills have been coming in, over wh. I assure you he has been pulling very long faces. I can't tell you how disappointed we were he didn't get in,' Annie loyally asserted. 'We minded it a great deal more than he did, but I think the bills affect him a great deal more than us.' In the end the election cost

* In their defence, it should be pointed out that the constituency was notoriously corrupt. Langston was thought to spend £200–300 per contest in buying support. When Neate had been removed for 'Colourable employment' earlier in the year, it was noted that his opponent, Cardwell, had received between 400 and 500 applications for work as clerks and messengers. During the by-election the Thackeray-supporting historian J.R. Green was openly asked for money by an Oxford barge-master supposed to control many votes. The Royal Commission of 1881 concluded that one-sixth of the city's electorate might be affected by illegal inducements; it permanently disenfranchised 141 people (a sentence later reduced to disqualification for seven years) and reduced the number of seats to one.

him £895. After nine months in the spotlight, it was time for the public and private men to change places.

A
Word to the Wise.

BROTHER WORKMEN,

On Tuesday next, we the Working Men of this City shall decide whether Mr. Cardwell or Mr. Thackeray shall represent us in Parliament. The responsibility devolving on us is great, let us not be deluded by fair promises or false pretences. The battle is waging warm, the conflict is severe, the struggle is at hand, fellow workmen let us buckle on the armour; we can! We must! We will decide the conflict!!! Not Oxford alone, but England gazes on us with intense and feverish anxiety upon the Battle which it is our privilege to decide. Our Brothers, the Ballast Heavers of London, in their oppressed and fearful condition cried unto their Friend and he heard them, and now (with grateful hearts) they urge us to "*fight for the man who fought for the people.*" Many and grave reasons could I assign, why we the Working Men of Oxford, should support the "*Poor Man's Friend*," but in a few short words I must sum up the merits of the two.---

CARDWELL is a man of *Practice*.	**THACKERAY** a man of Promise.
Cardwell is a man of *Fact*.	*Thackeray* a man of Fiction.
Cardwell is a man of Political Renown.	*Thackeray* a man of *Novel* Greatness.
Cardwell helped to give the Poor Man Cheap Bread.	*Thackeray* gave him Vanity Fair.
Cardwell gave the Poor Ballast Heavers a fair day's pay for a fair day's work.	*Thackeray* has promised Concert Room Pleasures on the Sabbath Day.

Your Friend and Brother,

POOR RICHARD.

J. SALMON, PRINTER, 17½, CORN MARKET STREET, OXFORD.

Pro-Cardwell Election handbill.

XIX

The Garrick Club Affair

'I went away having got into trouble with a young fellow who told lies of me in a newspaper, wh. I was obliged to notice as we are acquaintances, and meet together at a little Club.'

Letter to Mrs Baxter, August 1858

'Anyone who thinks of journalism before Newnes and North-cliffe as uniformly dignified ought to keep a portrait of Yates near at hand.'

John Gross, The Rise and Fall of the Man of Letters

 y this stage in his life nearly any prolonged physical or mental effort had a bad effect on Thackeray's health. He had been ill in the run-up to the Oxford campaign, kept himself going throughout it by sheer high spirits, and now, with the votes counted and the bills continuing to arrive at Onslow Square, sank into torpor. He was anxious to start work on *The Virginians*, promised to Bradbury & Evans for the autumn, and worried that 'the muse has had to sit in the antechamber, all this while'. As ever he took himself off to Brighton to recuperate, following this up with visits to Paris (Major Carmichael-Smyth was also ill at this time) and a short continental tour, which took him as far as Hamburg. By the end of the second week in September he was back in London, with a hard winter's work before him.

Autumn 1857 found him edgy and indecisive. His election defeat still nagged. He would have won, he told Mrs Baxter, had it not been for Sabbatarianism: six months later, with a dissolution of Parliament in prospect, he was hankering for another try. Restlessness and foreboding about the task ahead bred depression, which he called 'fits of blue devils'. The early numbers of *The Virginians*, which began appearing in October, failed to inspire him. He thought he had worked at this story of the American Revolution, and believed that the research he had filed away during his two US visits would eventually bear fruit, but the early chapters seemed to drag. 'I don't think The Virginians is good yet though it has taken an immense deal of trouble,' he complained to Mrs Baxter, 'but I know it will be good in the end.' Would it? The thirty-five-year-old who had sat down eleven years before to write *Vanity Fair* had rushed through a quarter of a million words in twenty months, together with a mass of occasional journalism. The forty-six-year-old with nothing to do except write novels and attend to his health and social life was already conscious of fading stamina. As the autumn wore on, his physical condition improved – the intervals between his fevers and retching attacks seemed to be growing longer – but he knew that he remained 'silent and selfish', wrapped up in his own concerns, chary of new acquaintances and new ideas.

He was aware that the patterns of his life were changing. Annie and Minnie were growing older – old enough to be presiding over their own tea-parties (Thackeray called them 'drums' and monitored their progress with a certain amount of rueful interest) and organising their own social life. If they were to marry, where might that leave him, Thackeray wondered? He canvassed his friends' opinion of schemes to move house, perhaps to leave London altogether, until an awareness of the probable outcome (married daughters and a solitary, sequestered papa) made him see sense. On the other hand, he was slipping ever more irrevocably into routine. There is a sense in which the Thackeray of the late 1850s sometimes seems to fade away into the background of his own life, a crowded thoroughfare composed of *Punch* dinners, evenings at the Garrick and cosy socialising with old friends, but one in which the novelist himself is somehow less than central to the proceedings. More than ever, he was brooding about money, delighting in his earning powers but continually disparaging his profligacy. These anxieties were not misplaced. By early-Victorian standards, Thackeray was earning a great deal in the late 1850s – he calculated his annual earnings at this point at around £4,500 – but he contrived to spend nearly two-thirds of this figure. Worse, he knew that he was bad with money, and to a large extent the bills that exasperated him were his own fault: 'we are not good managers that's the fact'. But there was still not enough in the funds to subsidise either the lifestyle that he felt he owed himself or the annuities for his womenfolk in the event of his death: £680 a year and the value of the house was all that awaited him if he stopped writing, he calculated. Sulky, brooding about his work and his bank balance, he was ripe for small disagreements and petty mischief-making.

A hint of trouble in store came in a minor quarrel with his old adversary – their dislike of one another went back to early *Punch* days – Albert Smith. Smith, like Thackeray a member of the Garrick, had an old friend named Joe Robbins, whose theatrical ambitions had got the better of him: giving up his job for a career on the boards, he quickly ruined himself. Hearing a report that Smith had declined to contribute to a subscription got up on Robbins' behalf, Thackeray produced a cartoon of the parable of the Good Samaritan, with Robbins as the traveller who fell among thieves and Smith as the Pharisee passing by on the other side of the road. This was circulated around the Garrick. Subsequently, when Thackeray discovered the real facts of the case (in fact Smith had loyally supported his friend except in this particular instance) he was ashamed of himself. The damage was done, though, and the resulting semi-public tiff had important consequences for the conduct of the much more serious Garrick Club row in which Thackeray found himself embroiled six months later.

Meanwhile *The Virginians* had reached the news stands, and the struggle to keep up with publication dates was on. As usual social life beckoned him forward and drove him away. A part of him still believed that 'going into the world' was his 'vocation', as the letter of 1852 put it. But it robbed him of valuable time, while the incessant wining and dining, he had belatedly come to recognise, worsened his physical frailty. His traditional Christmas letter to his mother is a typical mixture of pleasure in hospitality received and worry at how his fourth number was to be finished in time. Father and daughters spent Christmas at the Walton-on-Thames home of Russell Sturgis, an American merchant who had become a partner in Barings in 1849, and whose lavish lifestyle (Thackeray rated him a 'Merchant Prince') was regarded with some suspicion by his senior colleagues. The highlight of the stay, as far as Thackeray was concerned, was the sight of Sturgis' two-year-old son 'trolling round the Xmas tree'. He went back to London on Boxing Day to preside over the annual dinner of a commercial travellers' association – then as now, celebrities were much in demand for events of this kind – before going off to stay with the Pollocks. But he was tired and spiritless. A letter written early in the New Year to William Duer Robinson notes the absence of anything 'very good, new or funny'. Increasingly his pronouncements about himself give the impression of a man who realises that his best days are behind him: his health would never be fully restored; his books would never scale the heights of a decade before. Thackeray seems to have accepted this, even in some ways to have been interested in the spectacle it offered. The letter to Robinson is a little catalogue of the series of diminuendos to which his life now seemed reduced. His stricture 'is never cured quite': the 'hydraulic engine' required Thompson's constant attention. Early sales of *The Virginians* were satisfactory, but only that. Having reckoned up the balance sheet, Thackeray decided to accept only £250 of the £300 per instalment to which he was contractually entitled. 'I like everyone who deals with me to make money by me so I cede those 50£ you see until better times.' Simultaneously 'an immoderate use of the fleshpots' was beginning to tell – Thackeray's way of explaining to Robinson that too much claret had brought on another spasmodic attack.

Although in the end he came to acknowledge that *The Virginians* was a 'horribly stupid story', Thackeray's mind became caught up in its detail in a way that recalls the pains he took over *Vanity Fair*. He consulted American friends over the exact colour of George Washington's uniform and the question of what historical verisimilitude would allow him to do with George Warrington at a crucial point in the novel's development. By the spring, at any rate, he thought the book was getting better. His family continued to offer its customary mixture of satisfaction and disquiet. In particular, Annie and Minnie were always there to solace him. As young women – Annie would be twenty-one in 1858, Minnie eighteen – their exploits greatly amused him. 'Their talk is capital,' he reported to his mother, 'it is delightful to hear the prattle, as they come home from their parties.' On Maundy Thursday, 1 April, he took them on a jaunt to King's Langley, near Watford. Thackeray was bored with the stately home and its accoutrements within half an hour, but the girls' enthusiasm made him judge the day well spent. At the same time the bills that their establishment managed to run up made him 'tremble'. Much of this over-expenditure, Thackeray acknowledged, grew out of sheer good nature. As he explained to Mrs Carmichael-Smyth, if he employed a reliable coachman during the season when he needed to be driven about, then he found it difficult to dismiss the man at the season's end when the need for his services diminished. In the case of Charles Pearman, who left Onslow Square in spring 1858 having impregnated the faithful Eliza, the situation's difficulties were compounded by genuine good feeling. Though he felt that Pearman had been 'spoiled' by the American trip, Thackeray had liked him and welcomed his accomplishments.

At the end of April Annie gave her first party, watched over by her benevolent papa. Other events in and around the family circle were not so kindly regarded. In particular, Thackeray was annoyed by Mary Carmichael. The circumstances of the row are unclear – although Thackeray had had a low opinion of his cousin for many years – but probably had something to do with rudeness that Thackeray decided had been offered to Annie, Minnie and himself. 'I don't respect her, or regard her, or forgive her,' he loftily informed his mother. The continued tension of his dealings with the Carmichaels – no doubt exacerbated by the news of Charles Carmichael's unwise business speculations – betrayed once more the hard, inflexible side to his character that occasionally declared itself when he thought his good nature was being abused, or a fixed idea rose up in his head, which no amount of contrition on the part of the offender could shake. All these characteristics were on show a month or so later in a much more serious quarrel, probably the most serious of his career, whose consequences were to hang over the rest of his life.

The origins of Thackeray's part in what became known as the Garrick Club Affair lie scattered throughout the previous two decades. By the late 1850s he had known Charles Dickens for over twenty years – ever since the day when, hearing of Seymour's suicide, he had rushed round to Dickens' chambers and proposed himself as the replacement illustrator for *Pickwick* – to the point where their lives, both as literary figures and men about town, were thoroughly intertwined. They sat together at the same dinners; they were members of the same clubs; they shared many of the same friends; Annie and Minnie had even named their cats after characters in Dickens' novels. Kept up over two decades, the acquaintance had never been intimate, but it had been cordial, involving visits to one another's houses and intermittent socialising. Literary diaries of the 1840s and 1850s are full of glimpses of this proximity. Jane Carlyle's account of Dickens' Christmas party of 1843, for example, contains a description of 'the gigantic Thackeray &c &c all capering like Maenades'. Annie's reminiscences contain evocative accounts of the Dickens family Christmas parties. If anything, this relationship had grown closer by the mid-1850s. The two families had seen a great deal of each other in the summer of 1854 when Dickens was staying in Boulogne hard at work on *Hard Times*: subsequently Annie and Minnie had struck up a friendship with Dickens' daughters, whom they discovered living on the other side of the Champs-Elysées when they were staying in the Carmichael-Smyths' apartment in the winter of 1855–6. Meanwhile, their fathers enjoyed a reputation as the two greatest novelists of the age, undertook joint good works (at Christmas 1857, for instance, both put their signatures to a letter inviting subscriptions from friends of the hard-up Lady Blessington) and appeared together at public banquets. In the context of mid-Victorian literary society, Dickens' chairmanship of the Garrick dinner prior to Thackeray's departure for America was wholly apposite.

To a certain extent, one expects this kind of relationship. The literary world is restricted enough now; 150 years ago it was even more turned in upon itself. Writers lived in each other's pockets, and the alliances formed at the beginning of their careers were rarely put aside. At the same time, there is a way in which Dickens' and Thackeray's careers shadow one another to a degree unusual even in the early-Victorian era, and from the morning on which they stood at Snow Hill watching Courvoisier step out to be hanged, their paths as writers seemed uncannily linked. Undoubtedly the awareness of this imbrication was all on Thackeray's side. To put it bluntly, from an early stage in his career he placed himself in a context which Dickens had in effect created. The journey that produced the *Irish Sketch Book* charts the beginning of this fixation, from the moment when, arriving in Liverpool, Thackeray learns that he has just missed Dickens' return from America, to the letter in which he assures Chapman and Hall that the *Sketch Book* will do well because it is conceived on the same lines as *American Notes*. In the end, as with his broodings about money, what had begun as a mild fixation turned into a kind of mania. John Cordy Jeaffreson noted that Thackeray had 'Dickens on the brain'. The evidence of this obsession piles up in nearly every corner of his adult life, and yet it was an odd form of mania: simultaneously admiring, emulative and envious, and capable of producing bizarre manifestations. Thackeray's correspondence is a monument to the thoroughness with which he studied Dickens' novels. The letters sent home from the second American trip are full of references to *Little Dorrit*, then publishing in monthly parts. Admiration for the books combined with an occasionally acute jealousy over Dickens' superior sales. There is, for example, a story of his marching into Chapman and Hall's offices, demanding to know the figure for such-and-such a book, and, on being told, turning white and muttering that he did not know it was so large. Simultaneously, he was a keen and – from his own point of view – rueful student of Dickens the man. George Hodder was struck by the occasion on which Thackeray was asked to chair the annual dinner of the General Theatrical Fund. From the outset he was convinced that Dickens – present in his capacity as the institution's president – would outshine him. Nobody knew how nervous he was, he told Hodder, "'and Dickens doesn't know the meaning of the word'". As the dinner proceeded, with president and chairman seated alongside each other, Thackeray's anxiety increased to such a point that when he came to speak, his speech – carefully prepared and spiced up with learned allusions – collapsed into commonplaces. Despite a kind rejoinder from Dickens, who followed him, he left as quickly as he could.

Stripping down this complex mixture of emotions to its essentials, one finds an absolute veneration of Dickens' work, and the elevation of his characters to almost iconic status (staying with the Elwins in Norwich, Thackeray proposed to travel the twenty miles further on to Yarmouth simply because of its association with the Peggottys), co-existing with a suspicion of Dickens' personality and behaviour that probably had its roots in upbringing. Certainly his occasional jibes at the Dickens family's 'vulgarity' – meeting them once on the pier at Ramsgate he described them as 'all looking embarrassingly coarse vulgar and happy' – owe something to a conception of gentlemanliness to which lower-middle-class bankrupts' sons could not hope to aspire. Moreover, he believed that Dickens' love of theatricality had infected his inner self: that he was always acting, and that genuine feelings lay concealed beneath a layer of spiritual greasepaint.

Given the weight of these obsessions, the relationship between Dickens and Thackeray was bound to be uneasy. It was made worse by the fact that Thackeray's fixation was not in the least reciprocated. Dickens took little interest in Thackeray's writings (his memorial notice in the *Cornhill* betrays this unfamiliarity) although he spoke kindly of them, and their author, when asked. Beyond the works, his comments to friends such as Forster reveal that he detected in Thackeray a public cynicism and an all-too-conspicuous worldliness that he did not much like. All this, the things both spoken and only thought, created an understandable reserve. The rows over Forster's incautious remark to Tom Taylor and the 'Dignity of Literature' contretemps had already demonstrated just how touchy both could be if they thought their motives were being called into question. Even at times of outward cordiality, onlookers noted the air of tension that enveloped some of their public appearances together. It was observed at the Garrick Club that if either entered a room where the other was talking or reading, the newcomer would look embarrassed, as if he were searching for something he had mislaid or someone he wanted to see, and then go out. This unease was reflected in several queer symbolic incidents that crop up in the 1850s. On one occasion, for example, Thackeray and Dickens were among a group of literary men invited to lunch at a country house in Hertfordshire. As the convoy prepared to set out, a message was brought from Dickens explaining that he was prevented from attending, and asking Thackeray to give his excuses to the hostess. When the message was delivered, the lady of the house could be heard loudly instructing the chef not to cook a certain dish as 'Mr Dickens isn't coming'. Clearly the episode lodged in Thackeray's mind, as he used a version of it many years later in *Philip*.

Whatever the personal antagonisms that may have underlain it, at bottom Thackeray's rivalry with Dickens was professional. Beginning as a simple belief that he was a better novelist than Dickens, it gradually developed into a conviction that their two styles of writing were aesthetically opposed. The seeds of this opposition dated back to early 1847, the appearance of the early numbers of *Vanity Fair*, and the claim, made in a letter to Mrs Carmichael-Smyth, that he was 'all but at the top of the tree – indeed there if the truth be known & having a great fight up there with Dickens'. Later in the same letter Thackeray pronounces of his rival that 'He doesn't like me – He knows that my books are a protest against his – that if one set are true, the other must be false.' The aesthetic divide between, on the one hand, Dickens' sentimentalism and, on the other, Thackeray's psychological realism is arguable, but the suggestion of animus is not. As Peter Ackroyd points out, it is merely Thackeray projecting his own feelings onto Dickens. From the vantage point of early 1847, the notion of two giants of the novel trading blows in search of supremacy is also misplaced. Commercially it would continue to be so. Dickens' sales always outstripped Thackeray's: even allowing for his longer life, the £93,000 he left on his death in 1870 was convincing proof of his greater popularity. Nevertheless, Thackeray had got it into his head as early as 1847 that he was the pretender to Dickens' throne. Almost certainly he was helped towards this position by sympathetic friends. Abraham Hayward, for example, after appraising the first eleven numbers of *Vanity Fair* for the *Edinburgh Review*, wrote to tell their author that he had 'completely beaten Dickens out of the inner circle altogether'. It was exactly what Thackeray wanted to hear, and he wrote an enthusiastic letter to Jane: 'how much richer truth is than fiction, and how great that phrase about "the inner circle" is'.

Other critics were quick to develop this comparison. To some – David Masson, for example, who produced an influential essay for the *North British Review* in 1851 juxtaposing *Pendennis* and *David Copperfield* – the resemblances and discrepancies of their writings and outlook simply made a useful starting point for objective critical enquiry. At a lower level, however, this degenerated into outright partisanship. The evidence of obscure satirical ephemerals of the late 1840s, such as *Pasquin* and *Puppet-Show* (both of which employed James Hannay), shows that the supposed oppositions between Thackeray and Dickens were being enthusiastically promoted at a very early stage in Thackeray's success. When *David Copperfield* began, for instance, *Puppet-Show* fabricated a letter from a cockney admirer 'to Charles Dickens Esquire' – Dickens could congratulate himself that he was losing his appeal to low-brow readers and becoming more like Thackeray, the paper thought. This kind of class antagonism masquerading as literary criticism recurs throughout the next decade, and the ultra-Tory *Saturday Review* barely troubled to disguise its conviction that Thackeray, as an educated gentleman, was preferable to the lower-middle-class upstart of the blacking factory.

Leaving aside the efforts of partisans, the polarity between Dickens and Thackeray – both as writers and human beings – struck many a more neutral observer in the 1850s. As the two most esteemed novelists of the day, their personalities, appearance and behaviour were taken out and examined on a regular basis by diarists and profile-writers. Mention of the one invariably produced mention of the other. Seeing Dickens in Covent Garden not long after Thackeray's death, the diarist Arthur Munby turned to what for him, and for any other mid-Victorian onlooker, would have been a natural point of reference. 'A man of middle height, of somewhat slight frame, of light step and jaunty air ... how unlike the tall massive form, the slow gentle ways, the grave sad self-absorbed look of Thackeray.' Victorian observers who conducted these exercises marked down what they considered some salient discrepancies: Dickens the more driven, business-like, conscious of his origins; Thackeray the more languid, unprofessional, 'gentlemanly'. The contradistinction that each offered in regard to their books struck more than one critic. The novelist Eliza Lynn Linton, whose memoirs later made themselves objectionable to both sets of descendants, was emphatic about this, diagnosing a divorce between intellect and character: 'Thackeray, who saw the faults & frailties of human nature so clearly, was the gentlest-hearted, most generous, most loving of men. Dickens, whose whole mind went to almost morbid tenderness and sympathy, was infinitely less plastic, less self-giving, less personally sympathetic.' Energetic to the point of neurosis, indomitably proud, as Mrs Lynn Linton puts it, this was not a man to be crossed.

The quarrel that rose up between them in early 1858 had a single immediate cause: Thackeray's role in the exposure of Dickens' private life. By the late spring Dickens had become estranged from Catherine, his wife of over twenty years, and taken up with a young actress named Ellen Ternan. Although supposedly secret, the affair was widely discussed in the literary, club-lounging circles that both men frequented. When news of the breakdown of Dickens' marriage reached Thackeray in early May, his sympathies were entirely with the deserted wife, whom he had always liked and rather pitied. 'To think of that poor matron after 22 years of marriage going away out of the house,' he lamented to his mother, adding rather cryptically that it was 'a fatal story for our trade'. As he admitted to Mrs Carmichael-Smyth, he was by this stage already caught up in the events that followed Dickens' decision to repudiate his wife. Told by a Garrick Club gossip that Dickens was involved in an intrigue with his sister-in-law Georgina Hogarth and trying, as he thought, to improve the situation Thackeray corrected the man: no, the affair was with an actress. Now, he told his mother, he feared that the remark had got back to Dickens 'and he fancies that I am going about abusing him'. In fact Thackeray seems to have been at pains not to take sides: a dinner at Greenwich where the guests were to have included Thompson and his wife and Charley Dickens was hastily rearranged as a men-only affair on the grounds that 'if he [Dickens junior] dines with my daughter, it will appear as if this house declared for Mrs Dickens, wh. we mustn't do'. Almost certainly, though, Dickens did believe that Thackeray had declared for his wife. By the early summer of 1858, harassed both by his marital difficulties and by the preparations for his forthcoming provincial reading tour, Dickens was in a highly volatile mental state. That some kind of intelligence network operated by Forster was busy relaying gossip back to him, and that the results of this exercise preyed on his mind, seems clear from his decision to publish an extraordinary 'public address' on the subject of his failed marriage, which both justified his own behaviour and denounced his repudiated wife. This appeared in *Household Words* on 12 June. Dickens had wanted it to double up in *Punch*, whose owners, Bradbury & Evans, were his publishers, but Mark Lemon refused, and was backed up by his proprietors, a decision that eventually led to Dickens taking his novels back to Chapman and Hall.

Curiously enough on the same day a profile of Thackeray appeared in the second number of an obscure periodical named *Town Talk*. The piece, which appeared above the signature of 'The Lounger at the Clubs', began with what was, according to current critical orthodoxies, a fairly accurate survey of Thackeray's career to date. *Vanity Fair* and *Pendennis* had established his reputation. *The Newcomes* ('perhaps the best of all') had, if anything, extended it. *The Virginians*, though well written, was thin on plot 'and proportionately unsuccessful'. All this was unexceptionable – the kind of thing that Thackeray might privately have agreed with, had it been suggested by someone whose opinions he respected. However, it was trailed by some defiantly personal observations tacked onto a discussion of *English Humourists*. 'The prices were extravagant, the lecturer's admiration of birth and position was extravagant, the success was extravagant,' the 'Lounger' informed his readers. 'No one succeeds better than Mr Thackeray in cutting his coat according to his cloth. Here he flattered the aristocracy, but when he crossed the Atlantic, George Washington became the idol of his worship, the "Four Georges" the object of his bitterest attack . . .' Moreover, the piece concluded, there was a want of heart in all he wrote, 'which is not to be balanced by the most brilliant sarcasm or the most perfect knowledge of the human heart'.

The author of this piece of mischief was a twenty-seven-year-old journalist and literary man of all work named Edmund Yates. To anyone not aware of the sometimes complex alliances and backstairs intrigues that characterised the world of early-Victorian journalism, Yates' eagerness to select Thackeray as the victim of his asperity looks odd. The two met frequently at the Garrick, and Thackeray, who had breathed many a youthful sigh over Yates' actress mother, had even sponsored his election to the club as a technically ineligible seventeen-year-old ten years previously. Yates' forte, then and in a career that peaked with the editorship of an enormously successful scandal sheet called *The World*, was society chit-chat, and 'The Lounger at the Clubs' marked what his autobiography describes, with only slight inaccuracy, as 'the commencement of that style of personal journalism which is so very much to be deprecated and so enormously popular'. In fact, malicious personal comment of the kind Yates espoused predates the 1850s, but if nothing else he deserves to be remembered as an early prototype of Paul Slickey. If, as one later commentator adjudges, Yates had not an ounce of earnestness in him, then he was capable of fierce loyalties. Ironically, at this point in his career, the object of this devotion was Thackeray himself. As his autobiography makes clear, like many another Victorian journalist the younger man had been inspired to pick up his pen by the pleasant vision of London literary life offered by *Pendennis*. This adulation continued throughout the 1850s, as Yates, who had a full-time job at the Post Office, tried to establish himself on the lower rungs of the magazine world. Only a few months before he had written to his mentor asking for an autograph. 'May every year increase your happiness,' Thackeray had replied, acknowledging the fact that Yates' wife had recently been delivered of twins, 'and good fortune attend your increase.'

Given this background of youthful deference and lofty approval, why should Yates suddenly turn on Thackeray, and in quite this way? In his memoirs he claimed that he was doing the magazine's late turn at the printer's, discovered that they were short of material and wrote the article on the spot, never thinking it would cause offence. This, though, is disingenuous, for the piece looks to have been carefully composed, and there is a deliberateness about the phrasing that seems incompatible with the idea of last-minute page-filler. And while the profile contained little that was not public knowledge – the accusation that Thackeray had toadied his aristocratic audiences had been made many times before – it was meant to injure, and Yates, already a scarred veteran of newspaper wars, must have known that his victim would take serious offence. Yates had various journalistic affiliations at this time – the literary man with whom he was most obviously connected was Albert Smith – but by the late spring of 1858 he had grown close enough to Dickens to perform what the latter enigmatically referred to as a 'manly service' in connection with Ellen Ternan.

The appearance of a hostile article on the same day as Dickens' defence of his conduct in *Household Words* may have been simply coincidence, but it seemed to Thackeray – almost certainly correctly – that Dickens was using Yates as a cat's-paw to punish him for taking sides in the dispute about his private life. If nothing else, this explains the virulence of his response and the unusual channels into which he steered it.

Yates could never keep quiet about his accomplishments, and the identity of the 'Lounger' was known to Thackeray within twenty-four hours of *Town Talk*'s appearance, when a friend showed him both the first two numbers. To make matters worse, the first contained a flattering portrait of Dickens and some inaccurate gossip about Thackeray's monthly cheque from Bradbury & Evans for *The Virginians*. The letter that Thackeray despatched to Yates on 14 June is worth quoting at length for the quite awesome frostiness of its tone. Its complaint was that in hypothesising about his personality and his private affairs, Yates had strayed beyond the bounds of objective criticism and into a sacrosanct area of his life, using information that he could only have picked up at the Garrick:

> As I understand your phrases you imply insincerity to me when I speak good-naturedly in private; assign dishonourable motives to me for sentiments wh. I have delivered in public, and charge me with advancing statements wh. I have never delivered at all.
>
> Had your remarks been written by a person unknown to me, I should have noticed them no more than other calumnies: but as we have shaken hands more than once, and met hitherto on friendly terms ... I am obliged to take notice of an article wh. I consider to be not offensive & unfriendly merely, but slanderous and untrue.
>
> We meet at a Club where, before you were born I believe, I & other gentlemen have been in the habit of talking, without any idea that our conversation would supply paragraphs for professional vendors of 'Literary Talk', and I don't remember that out of that Club I ever exchanged 6 words with you. Allow me to inform you that the talk wh. you may have heard there is not intended for newspaper remark, & to beg, as I have a right to do, that you will refrain from printing comments upon my private conversation, that you will forgo discussion however blundering on my private affairs; & that you will henceforth please to consider any question of my

personal truth & sincerity as quite out of the province of your criticism.

Many a young journalist would have quailed beneath the force of this kind of attack. Even the mature Yates, who amongst other exploits was briefly imprisoned for criminal libel, thought it 'severe to the point of cruelty'. He was shrewd enough to realise that, given the stature and the friends of his opponent, this was not a game that could be played on his own. Albert Smith would have been a natural source of guidance, but Yates worried that the trouble over Thackeray's cartoon of Joe Robbins might make this alliance prejudicial. Accordingly he consulted Dickens. Initially Yates had intended to send a fairly elaborate reply which, without stating the fact literally, would have accused Thackeray of hypocrisy. He had good grounds for this – several of the minor characters in *Pendennis* were based on literary figures of the period ('Captain Sumph', for example, with his Byronic reminiscences, was probably drawn from a Captain Medwin of the 24th Light Dragoons, author of *Conversations with Lord Byron*, while the engaging fantasist 'Archer' was based on an obscure hack named Tom Hills) and on Garrick *habitués* and incorporated details that could only have been picked up in smoking rooms; the younger Thackeray had represented himself to editors as a purveyor of clubland small-talk very much in the Yates mould. In the end Dickens persuaded him not to send this, and – according to Yates – dictated the terse reply that merely rejected the accusations: 'I cannot characterise your letter in any other terms than those in which you characterised the article which has given you so much offence.'

Disingenuousness was not confined to Yates. Thackeray claimed that he was not aware of Dickens' involvement until a much later stage, but this seems implausible: the gossip-mongers who had identified Yates as his assailant would soon have brought news of his counsellor. Moreover, the particular route by which Thackeray pursued Yates was carefully chosen with the aim of indirectly bringing down Dickens as well. As the offence had supposedly been committed at the Garrick, Thackeray would do his best to have Yates thrown out of the club. Dickens was on the Garrick's committee. Any step that the committee could be persuaded to take against Yates would be a simultaneous hit at his protector. It is difficult to imagine that Thackeray would have attacked Yates with quite the severity that he displayed had he not known of Dickens' involvement. Much later, when John Cordy Jeaffreson plucked up the courage to ask him why he had been so hard on Yates, he replied merely that he wanted to get at the man behind him.

Three days after receiving Yates' reply, Thackeray consequently referred the letter to the Garrick committee, asking them 'to decide whether the complaints I have against Mr Yates are not well founded, and whether the practice of publishing such articles as that which I enclose will not be fatal to the comfort of the Club, and is not intolerable in a society of gentlemen?' Yates, to whom news of this decision was communicated, wrote to the committee expressing surprise, and asking for time to consult his friends. In his letter of acknowledgment the club secretary advised him that a special committee meeting would be convened on the following Saturday (26 June) to consider the matter. Yates' reply to the committee, in which Dickens presumably had a hand, made what most neutral observers would have considered a reasonable point: Thackeray's grievance was not one that could be submitted to the club for judgment; the Garrick had not been mentioned in the piece; the committee, he respectfully pointed out, 'is not a committee of taste'. Strictly speaking Yates was correct, yet by this stage the row had ceased to be a disagreement between two club members and had taken on a much wider dimension. With Yates now consulting Dickens at every turn, Dickens' friends and supporters at the Garrick were lining up behind his protégé. A similar alliance, headed by Thackeray's friend Francis Fladgate, was assembling on the other side.

Broadly speaking, the Garrick divided along class lines. The older, aristocratic influence was, with certain exceptions, solid for Thackeray; the younger, more Bohemian, fringe for Dickens and Yates. The committee, however, with its six baronets, was – with the exception of Dickens himself – pro-Thackeray. On 26 June it decided that it was competent to adjudicate the matter, that Thackeray's complaint was well founded, and that Yates must either apologise or retire. Should he decline to do so, a general meeting of the club would be convened to examine the dispute. For all his bumptiousness, it is impossible not to feel some sympathy for Yates at this 'anxious time', if only because the evidence of his memoirs, with their talk of meetings with Dickens, Forster, Smith and W.H. Wills, Dickens' adjutant at *Household Words*, suggests that he was no longer a free agent in the affair, but had in fact been taken up by much more powerful forces who were using him as a front. His anxiety was compounded by the appearance of the July number of *The Virginians*, into which Thackeray had contrived to insert a last-minute and wholly gratuitous reference to '"Young Grubstreet", who corresponds with threepenny papers and describes the persons and conversation of gentlemen whom he meets at his "clubs"'. Whatever his private feelings may have been, Yates wrote back declining to apologise, asking for the general meeting to take place and appealing to it on two grounds. First, was it appropriate to submit the quarrel between Thackeray and himself to the Garrick at all? Second, did the club have a right to an apology from 'one whom he has so very arrogantly and coarsely addressed'?

Nearly 140 members of the Garrick assembled on Saturday, 10 July to vote on the question. Neither Thackeray nor Yates thought it prudent to attend, although Yates sent a letter offering to apologise to the club but not to Thackeray. This was deemed inadequate, and a six-point resolution was proposed by the journalist J.C. O'Dowd restating the committee's original position. In the debate that followed, Yates' advocates included Dickens, Wilkie Collins and – an indication of the feeling that the proposed punishment was excessive – Thackeray's friend Robert Bell. The result, though, was a foregone conclusion, and the club voted 70:46 in favour of Yates either apologising or being expelled. He declined to reply to the secretary's letter communicating this decision, and his name was taken off the books on 20 July.

Thackeray, by this time, was abroad on the Continent, where he was kept in touch with developments by Fladgate. Any hopes he may have had that the affair would die down were misplaced. A furious Dickens, who had resigned from the committee, urged Yates to take a legal opinion. Meanwhile the row was being eagerly discussed, and satirised, in the press, with partisans sniping from both sides. Yates, James Hannay told the readers of the *Dumfries Courier* early in August, was contemptible. 'What would your subscribers say to me if I photographed an eminent man of my acquaintance, or ... drew a gross sketch of him from having seen him in the smoking-room or coffee-room of a club?' Four weeks later he widened the attack to include Yates' satellites. He was one of a 'miscellaneous crew of writers of tales and farces, buffoons, hangers-on of theatres, jokers of jokes, fellows who never open a book more learned than a French novel ...' At the same time, comic writers quickly divined that the row offered ample scope for satire. The monthly paper *Quiz*, for example, soon furnished an elaborate spoof of the dispute, in which Thackeray featured as 'The Virginian' and Dickens as 'Carlo Pickwicki'. Some younger journalists who had previously been on good terms with Thackeray, but were allies of Yates, found themselves sympathising with the younger man on the grounds that he had been victimised. G.A. Sala, for instance, of whom Thackeray thought and continued to think highly, made several references to him in his book of London sketches *Twice Round the Clock* (1859) as 'Mr Polyphemus', hoping that readers would spot the nod to *The Kickleburys on the Rhine*, where Polyphemus is described as 'of cruel nature, and licentious appetite, and, to be sure, fond of eating men and women'.

Though the late summer brought a lull in the conflict – Dickens, too, was out of London – both sides were uneasily conscious that it had escaped their control, and would now be carried on at lower levels of the literary firmament whether they liked it or not. There was an embarrassing meeting late in August when Dickens bumped into Thackeray and Fladgate on the steps of the Reform Club. No reference was made to the row, although Dickens reported to Yates that Fladgate's eyebrows went up into the crown of his hat and he writhed with nervousness. Back on the Continent, this time in Paris, Thackeray was clearly perturbed by the hornet's nest he had stirred up. He had 'got into trouble', he explained to Mrs Baxter, 'with a young fellow who told lies of me in a newspaper, wh. I was obliged to notice as we are acquainted, & meet together at a little Club' – by no means the whole story, but an acknowledgment that the affair continued to worry him. Yates, meanwhile, was still exploring legal remedies. Staying at the Hôtel Bristol, and additionally anxious about his mother, who had been knocked over by a gang of street urchins and broken her hip, Thackeray was ready to take a more emollient line. He felt especially that he had been too hard on Yates, and was even capable of commenting disinterestedly on Dickens' affairs. A letter to Dr John Brown early in November moves from an account of his health – he had been ill again with spasms – to a hope that Dickens' lecturing 'will make a great bit of money for the 8 children'.

If Thackeray's hostility had begun to soften, then the indirect result of Yates' legal manoeuvring was to make things worse. Yates had engaged the services of Edwin James, a celebrated QC and fearsome courtroom adversary (Dickens later put him in *A Tale of Two Cities* as Mr Stryver, 'free from any drawbacks of delicacy'). James proposed a sensational court case in which Thackeray and several of his own former victims would be put into the witness box. He also declared that Dickens should be called upon to testify, at which point Yates' sponsor took fright. The upshot was a letter to Thackeray in late November in which Dickens suggested that it would be a good idea to seek 'some quiet accommodation of this deplorable matter' that would satisfy the feelings of all concerned. Once again reduced to fury by what seemed overwhelming evidence that Yates was merely Dickens' stooge, Thackeray wrote an immensely haughty – and again disingenuous – reply telling Dickens that ever since he submitted his case to the Garrick committee 'I have had, and can have, no part in the dispute. It is for them to judge if any reconciliation is possible with your friend.' Thirty years later Yates could still remember Dickens' rage when this letter arrived, and Forster's furious expostulation: 'He be damned with his "yours &c."' The newspaper guerrilla skirmishes were renewed. Yates contributed 'The Histrionic Baronet' to the *Illustrated Times* of 5 December, supposedly an unfavourable criticism of the theatrical talents of Sir William Don, then appearing at the Haymarket Theatre, but in fact an attack on the six Garrick Club committee baronets who had supported Thackeray. *Punch* joined the fray a week later with a piece advising the 'Lounger' that he would do much better if he remembered that a journalist should also be a gentleman – if Dickens ever discovered the identity of the author, he would have been more than usually pained, as the article was written by his eldest son. Other insults by Yates and his supporters culminated in a take-off of Thackeray's 'The Ballad of the Bouillabaisse', again in the *Illustrated Times*, which was so caustic that several staff members threatened to resign.

In the end money stayed the chief protagonist's hand. Having visited the Garrick in December for the purposes of being publicly denied admission, Yates discovered that his plan to bring an action (on the grounds that his ejection was illegal) was flawed. The Garrick committee pleaded that neither it nor its representatives who had denied Yates access could be sued as all the property was vested in the trustees. The Chancery suit that offered the only opportunity to continue the dispute was beyond Yates' means. By early 1859 he had given up the legal battle in favour of a pamphlet entitled *Mr Thackeray, Mr Yates, and the Garrick Club. The Correspondence and Facts.* Thackeray, by this stage, had long since tired of the irritation and the unwelcome publicity. The affair was 'only $\frac{1}{2}$ as exciting as it used to be', Annie reported to Amy Crowe towards the end of the year, and her father was 'getting disgusted'. In addition, his friends were 'bullying' him over his inflexibility. The letter is notable for the normally good-humoured Annie's sarcasm towards Dickens and the imputation that Yates was no more than a sneak: 'Can't you fancy him and his gusto over Manly Service (it was going off from the smoking room at the Garrick to tell all the stories Papa was telling of Mr Dickens).'

Nothing, perhaps, could be more trivial than the causes of the Garrick Club Affair – a few lines in an obscure weekly magazine – but its consequences lasted well beyond Thackeray's death. The partisanship endured: as late as 1868, when reports of Yates' bankruptcy appeared in *The Times*, Henry Silver could remark, 'How the shade of Thackeray must chuckle!' Thackeray himself remained sensitive to any mention of it, and once left a *Punch* dinner in a huff when one of his fellow diners was unwise enough to speak up on Yates' behalf. If the affair brought out Thackeray's worst side – he could not resist joining in the later stages of the newspaper stand-off, and there were further references in *The Virginians* to 'Bob Bowstreet' and 'Tom Garbage', both contributors to the 'Kennel Miscellany' – then Dickens, too, appears in a wholly disagreeable light. Significantly, when Yates' pamphlet appeared, Dickens made its author deny that he had ever received any financial assistance from him or that there had been any prior communication on the subject of the *Town Talk* article. Whatever the truth of these assertions, their shadow hung over the rest of Thackeray's life, a perpetual reminder of the antagonisms that continued to dominate his professional career.

XX

The Editorial Chair

'I am making and spending a deal of money have outlived my health, popularity and inventive faculties as I rather suspect – am building a fine house and wonder whether I shall ever be able to live in it . . .'

Letter to William Duer Robinson, 28 September 1860

lone in London – Annie and Minnie were still in Paris nursing their grandmother – Thackeray spent the Christmas season of 1858 brooding about the latter stages of the Garrick row. His mood fluctuated. To the girls he maintained that the affair 'stills roars on bravely. Three articles this week [the letter is dated 4 December]. Two against me and accusing me of persecuting Yates – private letter from Higgins to tell me that I am utterly in the wrong, that Yates' article *wasn't* malicious, and that I had best beware of Edwin James and the scarifying wh. I shall get in the witness box.' As the prospect of cross-examination receded, his hostility towards Yates began to soften. He did not mind his attacks, he told a friend, and indeed rather admired him for the determination of his animosity. He was not even angry with Dickens, he declared. 'He can't help hating me: and he can't help not being a . . . you know what I daresay?' – undoubtedly the missing word was 'gentleman'. At the same time Thackeray acknowledged that the strains of Dickens' private life had probably 'driven him frantic'. A letter to John Blackwood from mid-December shows both the detrimental effect of Dickens' olive branch of three weeks before and Thackeray's realisation that his own hauteur had been excessive. But Blackwood would see by his enclosure (in fact Dickens had asked Thackeray to burn his original note) the part that Dickens had played in setting up the conflict. 'O for shame, for shame! But what pent up animosities and long-cherished hatred doesn't one see in the business!'

The more Thackeray fancied he discerned of Dickens' role in the affair, the greater became his sympathy for Yates, a 'poor young man' who had simply thrust out his paw at his master's bidding. Long into the New Year, when the threat of a court case had wholly disappeared, he continued to brood over Dickens' antagonism. What pained him most, he told Charles Kingsley, was that Dickens should have been Yates' confidant, and that Yates, whom Thackeray believed to be 'hardly aware of the nature of his own offence', should have been so harshly punished (expulsion from a club ranked high on the list of Victorian improprieties, and Yates later referred to a 'shameful stigma' that he had borne for thirty years). Dickens' part had been as 'bad as bad can be', he finally concluded, and evidence of a 'fatal perversity'. Relieved that it was all over, Thackeray hoped that the hack-journalists who maligned him would one day understand that he was not the bad man they made him out to be.

It had been a gloomy autumn, made worse by illness and his daughters' absence. Ill health was always more difficult to endure when Annie was away. In fact his elder daughter's presence in the house seemed to have an almost prophylactic effect. When he was lying in bed, 'you know dreadfully ill with those spasms, and yet secretly quite easy', he told a friend he said to himself, 'Good God what a good girl that is.' Family troubles still pressed. In the light of the Carmichaels' current financial difficulties, he was conscious that the money lent to him so long ago towards Isabella's upkeep ought to be repaid. His parents' increasing frailty – the major had suffered a further stroke – made him wonder whether he ought not to rouse himself for another effort to persuade them to return to England. As for *The Virginians* which was now moving towards its close, he suspected that Yates' opinion of what even his admirers rated a shapeless work was probably correct. Increasingly he sought comfort in his daughters, an attentive audience for worries about his work and his finances, and an unflagging source of support. Annie, in particular, had reached the age where she was able to treat her father's problems with sympathetic matter-of-factness. 'If you know what it is to have a pianoforte played upon yr. nerves that is what papa is going thro',' she told a friend in 1862, when the critics seized on *Philip*. She was aware, too, of the pressures under which he laboured, working 'like mad ... wh. isn't very favourable to composition'. At twenty-one and eighteen respectively, the girls seemed – at any rate to the sharp and literary-minded Annie – very different from one another. A slightly patronising letter a couple of years later talks of Minnie being 'absurdly young for her age for she still likes playing with children and kittens'. She was clever, Annie allowed, although she 'does not do any thing in particular'. In fact Minnie's early letters are notably lively and intelligent, and one suspects that this is only an affectionate sisterly snub.

As ever, Thackeray was living his life simultaneously in several different compartments. The indulgent and much loved paterfamilias, gently scolding Annie for her unpunctuality at breakfast, was a world away from the bluff, claret-soaked veteran who appeared each week at the *Punch* dinner. Henry Silver's record of the *Punch* table talk, which begins at about this time – he had been introduced to Thackeray in October 1858 – portrays a convivial, genial figure of child-like humour, convulsed by bad puns and smutty jokes, keen to draw Silver and Leech into reminiscent talk about Charterhouse, occasionally sitting apart from the main body of diners to correct proofs. What planet did you see when you put your head between your legs, somebody once enquired. Hearing that the answer was 'Uranus', Thackeray 'laughed consumedly'. This fondness for gentlemanly bawdy and *double entendres* extended even to his own ailments. The Charterhouse talk – he revisited the school for the first time in thirty years in the late 1850s – found him ruefully nostalgic, and still absorbed by the question of beating. On his return trip, he told Silver, he had seen 'a little fellow' with his hands behind his back, in tears, and with two other boys supporting him 'and I knew what had happened and how they'd take him to the bog and make him show his cuts'.

As the *Punch* exchanges and Annie's letters reveal, his health was slowly declining. But there were bright spots amid the gloom. Apart from a brief attack on Christmas Day, the Christmas and New Year period seemed to bring an improvement. 'One doesn't like to boast about it yet, one can only hope and long for things to have taken a better turn,' Annie wrote cautiously to Dr John Brown late in January. By this stage both girls seem to have been aware that their father's health was the most important concern that the family faced, and that the worries about money and work were trivial by comparison. Annie admitted as much in a letter to a friend written during a subsequent bout of illness: 'These are very trifling troubles if he could get 3 days of wellness I shouldn't care . . .' Afflicted as ever by spasms and ague, Thackeray now discovered that his old urethral complaint was worsening, frequently to the point where he had great difficulty in urinating. His letters from early 1859 are crammed with accounts of his symptoms and their treatment. 'With the free canal the ugly symptoms disappear,' he told Brown in February. 'I pass an instrument every 3d. night and haven't heard of late of rigors &c.' The same month he reported to William Stirling that 'At present I am laid up with an instrument in my . . .' A graphic illustration of an inserted catheter followed. The chronic nature of the complaint demanded frequent trips to Thompson's surgery for periods of 'hospitalisation', and the benefit of Thompson's attempts to clear his urethral canal of obstruction could be short-lived. Giving his mother notice of 'a second bout of Thompson' in February, he noted that 'an accident rendered the first inefficacious, & left almost all the ground to be gone over again'. By now there was serious talk of surgery. Thackeray knew that the 'heroic remedy', as he put it, must come sooner or later, but now the stumbling block proved to be Thompson, who, although widely experienced in the field and the author of *Pathology and Treatment of the Stricture of the Urethra*, feared to operate on 'such a well-known public character'. The *ad-hoc* patching up with which he continued to treat his patient cannot have helped Thackeray's overall condition.

March seemed a better month altogether. The girls had returned from Paris, and now required to be escorted to balls and other social events ('as for Partners we had 22 each,' Annie remarked nonchalantly of one of these). His health had improved slightly – due to the effect of drinking lemonade instead of wine and spirits, Annie felt. Reunited at Onslow Square, the family seemed 'very jolly', she thought, 'that is as jolly as people are generally when they have everything they can wish for except Mr Yates' friendship'. With the Chancery suit given up, Yates' pamphlet was in the offing. The girls begged Thackeray not to read it, '& as he has taken to paying great attention to what we say I daresay perhaps he wont'. Inevitably he did. By this stage, however, having his suspicions about Dickens confirmed was perhaps less important than a new interest, which looked set to command his energies for some time ahead. By the late 1850s Thackeray had known the publisher George Smith for nearly ten years, ever since he had brought Charlotte Brontë to dinner at Young Street in 1849. Thackeray liked Smith, admired the enterprise and enthusiasm that had enabled him to take control of what had been his father's business at the tender age of twenty-one, and had kept up the association throughout the intervening period – sending Smith pieces of literary gossip and recommending bright young men and their wares (most recently Hannay, whose novel Thackeray was sure Smith would give a better price for than the first publisher to whom it had been shown). Over the years, too, Thackeray had allowed Smith to publish several of his books: *Esmond*, two Christmas books, *The Kickleburys on the Rhine* and *The Rose and the Ring*, and the printed version of *The English Humourists*. The really valuable property – full-length novels for serial publication – had always remained with Bradbury & Evans. By the late 1850s, as *The Virginians* drew to a close, it was clear that Thackeray intended to break with Bradbury & Evans. His letters to Smith from the middle years of the decade are full of tantalising hints about future schemes in which the publisher can expect to find himself involved, and it is possible to read them as a kind of advance marketing exercise: the novelist drumming up interest in his own work, flattering and enticing a potential sponsor. It was to Smith, too, that Thackeray had confided his long-held ambition to conduct his own literary magazine. Early in 1859 Smith, who was never frightened of offering large sums of money – some years later he gave George Eliot an unheard-of £7,000 for *Romola* – made a decisive bid for Thackeray's services: one or possibly two novels in twelve instalments at £350 a number. These were excellent terms, especially in the light of *The Virginians'* moderate sales, and Thackeray quickly accepted. In April Smith followed up his initial approach by offering him £1,000 a year to edit a monthly magazine.

In the context of the mid-Victorian magazine world, Smith's plans – and Thackeray's involvement in them – made perfect economic sense. This was the great age of periodical journalism, when small fortunes could be made by proprietors and editors who gambled successfully on public taste. It was also a time at which the links between the novel-buying public and the magazine readership were much closer than they subsequently became. A best-selling novelist whose constituency had been built up over a number of years could take his public with him into the world of periodicals. Dickens was the obvious example (*Household Words*, which ran from 1850 to 1859, was one of the success stories of the age), but the practice continued until well into the 1870s: the *St Paul's*, for instance, which began publishing in 1867, was nearly called *Anthony Trollope's Magazine* as a way of capitalising on the reputation of its founding editor. At the same time, leaving aside the scandal sheets published by Yates and his kind, the world of upper-periodical journalism had undergone substantial changes since Thackeray's arrival as a young editor/proprietor in the early 1830s, becoming at once more middle-class and less adventurous. *Fraser's Magazine* of the late 1850s, under John W. Parker, was a much more sober-minded proposition than the anarchic miscellany of spoofs, erudition and doggerel verse in which Thackeray had made his début. *Punch's* success had relied on its ability to reflect the sensibilities and aspirations of its middle-class and middle-brow readership. The tendency was to family-oriented publications, which carried serials by popular writers, took an interest in the issues of the day without being doggedly partisan and offered the mixture of edification, sentiment and popular science that found favour in the average Victorian drawing-room. From the outset this was what Smith – an astute operator who had done his market research – intended his new venture to be. His motive in securing Thackeray's services was straightforward. Much as Smith admired him as a writer, he did not imagine that he would be a good editor. As a figurehead, though, and a solicitor of high-grade contributions from distinguished friends, he would be well worth the £1,000 a year (later doubled) that Smith was prepared to pay.

This was exactly as it turned out. As plans for the new magazine were being formulated during the summer of 1859, Thackeray flung himself into the work with enthusiasm. His letters about the scheme – entreaties to potential contributors, endless notes passed back and forth between Brompton and Smith's office in the City – would make a volume in themselves. He spent a quiet summer, visiting Gravesend ('away with my books at a romantic village') and Folkestone and discussing the scope of the new enterprise with his publisher. In August the initial agreement for one or two novels at £350 per instalment was modified. Henceforth it was agreed that the magazine, as yet untitled, would include a short novel in six instalments – a device that would allow Thackeray to rework the material of *The Wolves and the Lamb* into what became *Lovel the Widower* – plus *The Four Georges* and a second novel in sixteen or twenty episodes. Subsequently Thackeray also undertook to provide a series of 'causeries' – a staple of Victorian journalism eventually given the title of *Roundabout Papers* – at twelve guineas a page. Annie provided a vividly impressionistic account of the Folkestone holiday for W.W.F. Synge: a brass band shrieking discordant polkas, an old gentleman with a yellow waistcoat and an umbrella under his arm walking across the street beneath the window, 'Papa wild in the next room Virginians brought to a sudden standstill'. The prospect of the new magazine and relief at finishing his novel (*The Virginians'* twenty-fourth and final instalment appeared in October) brought an improvement in Thackeray's health. Annie reported him in good spirits and 'jolly', recovered from his last attack of spasms and, she thought, 'really better of those'. From Folkestone he wrote to Smith with more suggestions. 'As I think of the editing business I like it. But the magazine must bear my *cachet* you see and be a Man of the World magazine, a little cut of Temple Bar, or Charles I on the outside?' This was very far from what Smith had in mind, but he was prepared to humour his celebrity editor. Simultaneously Thackeray began the search for high-grade contributors, writing a letter to Tennyson in which he recounted his rapturous brooding over *The Princess*.

At this point the enterprise still lacked a name. There was some initial enthusiasm for the *New Gentleman's Magazine*. Eventually, on a jaunt to Switzerland with his daughters early in the autumn, Thackeray visited Chur, the burial place of St Lucius, founder of the Church of St Peter, Cornhill, near the site of Smith's office. By early autumn they had settled on the *Cornhill*. Proceeding via Boulogne, Tours, Milan and Como, the continental trip was brought to halt when Annie went down with dysentery. It was not a severe attack, but the doctors counselled caution. Simultaneously Thackeray's hydraulics were giving 'rather serious cause for disquiet'. From Chur, on 1 October, Thackeray wrote one of his reckoning-up letters to his mother. He was struck by the cyclical patterns of his life. With Annie unwell, he had not the heart to work and yet he remembered trying to do so twenty years before, when she was suffering from the same complaint and money was needed for the doctor. If he could work for three more years, he calculated, it would 'have put back my patrimony and a bit more'. In the last thirty years he estimated that he had earned £32,000 – nearly £10,000 from the lectures, £6,000 from *The Virginians* and a modest £2,000 from *Vanity Fair*. But the task was by no means over. Three more years 'and the girls will then have the 8 or 10000 a piece that I want for them'. He refused to apologise for this overweening mercantilism: 'We mustn't say a word against filthy lucre, for I see the use and comfort of it every day more and more.'

Annie recovered slowly, subjecting the holiday to further delay. Thackeray amused himself with Jane Austen: 'I have been living at Bath for the last 10 days in Miss Austen's novels wh. have helped me to carry through a deal of dreary time,' he told his mother. By 4 October they had got as far as Zurich, where Annie was 'mending', although not up to rapid travel. After the boredom of the past fortnight Thackeray wanted to prolong his trip, provided Smith had no need of him in London, but a hint of anxiety about his own health was confirmed a day or so later when the spasms returned. By 10 October he was in Paris, again trying to realise his long-planned scheme of bringing the Carmichael-Smyths back to London. Conscious of their advanced age and increasing frailty, the old couple agreed, and Thackeray was able to tell Smith that 'please God I shall get the 3 generations safe across the water'.

The Carmichael-Smyths were eventually installed in a house in Brompton Crescent, where for all her advancing years Mrs Carmichael-Smyth remained a commanding presence. A friend of Annie's remembered being taken to see her as a child of five or six and revelling in the spectacle of 'a dainty beautiful stately vision – standing out clear and vivid from entirely hazy surroundings'. Meanwhile, the serious business of planning the *Cornhill's* launch was in hand. One vital step that needed to be taken was to commission the magazine's first full-length serial. Thackeray, who had admired *The Three Clerks*, was keen to secure Anthony Trollope, and in consultation with Smith devised a joint attack. 'I will write to Trollope saying how we want to have him – you on your side please write offering the cash.' Gratified by praise from a man he had long esteemed, Trollope offered what was to become *Framley Parsonage*. Thackeray wrote back welcoming him aboard and offering some well-intentioned but far from precise guidelines as to what the magazine looked for: 'Whatever a man knows about life and its doings, that let us hear about.' Inevitably the aftermath of the Garrick Club Affair cast a shadow over the list of potential contributors – a poem daringly sent in by Yates was smartly returned, although Sala pleaded with Thackeray to include it as a way of patching up the quarrel – but Thackeray seems to have cast his net reasonably wide. Prospective contributors ranged from dependable friends and promising young journalists like Sala (who supplied a series of articles on Hogarth) to professional men capable of offering a slant on the events of the day – Captain A.W. Young, for example, was signed up to write on the search for Sir John Franklin's vanished Arctic expedition – and celebrities such as the aged General Burgoyne, who was pressed, via his daughter, for an article on the Volunteer movement. Longfellow, to whom application was made for a poem

('Has Hiawatha a spare shaft in his quiver, wh. he can shoot across the Atlantic?'), declined.

Thackeray's essential mildness as an editor had already begun to declare itself by the time the *Cornhill* moved into its pre-publication phase. Smith had expressed reservations about two proposed contributions to the first number, one of which happened to be the work of Thackeray's friend Robert Bell. Thackeray could only temporise. 'My goodness! I *daren't* write to him & say it won't do – I wrote only yesterday to say I had sent to have it put into type – I can write to him *about* it, and keep it at all events out of no. 1.' In the end Bell's article 'Stranger than Fiction' appeared in August 1860. But to a certain extent both editor and proprietor were learning the business of magazine production as they went along (the lavishly framed *Cornhill*, it should be pointed out, was a much more complex proposition than the *National Standard* had been). From an early stage Smith seems to have possessed the power of veto – after Thackeray accepted some verses from Thomas Hood junior, he warned Smith that 'You must not refuse them or you will make a fool of me.' There was also the delicate question of whether to tell celebrity contributors in advance of changes made to their articles before they read them in print. Thackeray was particularly worried about Sir John Burgoyne's piece, and took advice on the subject from the *Edinburgh Review*. He concluded that it was best to assume responsibility for the changes, and to make up with the author afterwards. At the same time he was always open to suggestions for improving the look and processes of the magazine, and spent some time investigating an innovatory technique pioneered by the engraver William Linton.

As Christmas drew near his life became a frantic round of proof-correcting (or rather the supervision thereof – Thackeray tended to leave the editorial chores to underlings) and searching for mislaid contributions ('I am very sorry indeed that I can't lay my hand upon the verses,' he explained to Coventry Patmore). By 15 December he assumed that 'the No. was done and out of hand', only for a messenger to arrive with further corrections. 'The sight of the corrections in that last $\frac{1}{2}$ sheet made me half mad,' he told Smith. But by 20 December everything was complete, and advance copies awaited ahead of the official New Year's Day launch-date. Thackeray thought the inaugural issue, priced at a shilling, 'magnificent': the best thing in it, he thought, was Captain Young's account of the hunt for Franklin, a judgment that was shared by contributing friends. Monckton-Milnes wrote suggesting that the magazine was 'almost too good for the public it is written for and the money it has to earn'. Despite reports of snowstorms and blocked roads, Thackeray took himself off to Paris for a short, celebratory holiday. James Fields, who encountered him there, remembered having to restrain him from rushing into the jewellers' shops of the Palais Royal and filling his pockets with diamonds, such was his exultation at the launch. But amid the excitement he was mindful of older associations – taking pains, for example, to ensure that Catherine Dickens was sent a copy.

As Smith had hoped, the *Cornhill* was an immediate success. Although *Macmillan's Magazine*, a venture conceived on similar lines (and edited by Thackeray's friend David Masson) had appeared the previous autumn, Thackeray's first number sold nearly 120,000 copies. Sales subsequently fell back into the 80,000s, but by the standards of Victorian journalism this was a brilliant performance. Smith held a commemorative dinner, which Thackeray attended despite suffering from a spasmodic attack that restricted his small-talk (Trollope, eagerly anticipating a first meeting with his idol, was rebuffed with a curt 'How do?'). Looking at early numbers of the *Cornhill*, one is struck not only by their Thackerayan tone – largely achieved by the importation of many of his friends – but by the extent to which he and Smith managed to lash the enterprise to his reputation. The first number, for example, carried Father Prout's ode to the author of *Vanity Fair*, a theme revisited later in the year with Thackeray's own poem 'Vanitatis Vanitatum'. Although Thackeray used the magazine as a vehicle for pushing his friends' often slightly mundane work, he was also capable of imaginative strokes, such as commissioning Thompson's lively account of a surgical operation, 'Under Chloroform', which appeared in the April number. Throughout his editorship the prestige conferred by acceptance into the *Cornhill* contributors' circle was eagerly pursued by writers at the start of their careers. Frederick Locker-Lampson always remembered the 'first fine careless rapture' of receiving (via Annie) the proofs of his verses 'On a Human Skull'.

Although there was a certain amount of carping from the pro-Dickens lobby, critical reaction to the new paper was good. *Framley Parsonage* made Trollope's name. General Burgoyne's article on the volunteers carried sufficient weight to be mentioned in a *Times* leader. Writing to thank his venerable contributor, Thackeray supposed that he need not tell him 'the Magazine has been an immense success, such a sale has never been known in England before'. Pursuing a contribution from the Italian nationalist leader Garibaldi, he claimed a readership, as opposed to a circulation, of half a million. Gratified as he was by this success, Thackeray did not for a moment believe that he was a good editor. With his susceptibility to elegant lady contributors, his tendency to mislay copy and his reliance on Smith to fix up many of the 'grave articles', he was never more than the well-connected figurehead that the publisher had intended. It was Smith, too, who produced several of the magazine's early gems – robbing his Brontë archive to supply Emily's poem 'The Outcast Mother' in May 1860 and a set of Charlotte's verses entitled 'Waiting and Wishing' seven months later. Yet Thackeray very soon grasped the rationale of the magazine and in particular the moral constituency it aimed to address. This led to the odd spectacle of the former advocate of greater freedom of expression returning Trollope's short story 'Mrs General Tallboys' on the grounds of indelicacy. A poem by Elizabeth Barrett Browning went the same way.

In fact the Thackeray/Smith correspondence of early 1860 shows just how seriously and punctiliously he took his work. It has its amusing side, as when Smith was roped into a controversy surrounding Thackeray's use of the Greek word *aidoia* in a tribute to Macaulay that appeared in the February number. Thackeray, whose grasp of classical scholarship was not high, assumed that it could be used in the general sense of 'belonging to modesty' or merely 'private'. He was embarrassed to be told by the clerical editor of a Greek grammar that it had the exclusive meaning of 'private parts'. But he continued to make advances to political contacts among the Liberal leadership. Here a certain amount of caution was needed. Having interviewed one of the minions of the Foreign Secetary Lord John Russell, who was anxious to exploit the advantages of the *Cornhill*'s half-million readers,

'The angel'

Thackeray reported to Smith that the politician 'wanted to work them in a Whig sense'. Thackeray assured his contact that the magazine was Liberal in sympathy, 'but wanted no aggressive politics'. Aware of the need for objectivity, he was conscious that some topics would require a vigorous approach. How could you have an article about Italy without aggressive politics, Thackeray's man at the Foreign Office quite reasonably wondered? Thackeray agreed that such sympathies as they evinced should be on the Italian side. The *Cornhill*'s connection to the Whig government continued throughout the following months. March found Thackeray still pursuing a piece about the Italian situation, only to be told that Lord John did not wish recent correspondence to be made public, but that Thackeray's friend Joseph Crowe was welcome to write a previously suggested piece on Germany, France and the Savoy question. Significantly, Lord John got to see the proofs. The relationship was kept up, and Thackeray's engagement book records dining with the Russells in February of the following year.

The spring of 1860 brought constant hard work – as well as his editorial duties, Thackeray had *Lovel the Widower* to complete, plus a monthly *Roundabout* – and consequent ill health. In February he was again laid up with urethral trouble, writing detailed letters to Thompson about the appropriate size of catheter necessary to treat his blockages ('I went to bed with 3 & could easily do a 6 now'). His intimacy with Smith grew. He used his publisher as a banker and advised him on a suitable response to the accusation made by Samuel Lucas, the editor of Bradbury & Evans' *Once A Week*, that the *Cornhill* had been trying to poach his contributors (with the bitter lesson of the Yates affair behind him, Thackeray thought that Smith's initial response had been 'too angry'). There was another plan in the offing, too, to invest some of the money he had made from Smith in real estate. Though he had lived at Onslow Square for six years, Thackeray had never liked the place. Now he proposed to buy a dilapidated Queen Anne house on Kensington Palace Green, on which he had long had his eye. The news was conveyed to Smith early in March. In this new setting, Thackeray declared, 'the history of Queen Anne' (a continuation of Macaulay, which the two had occasionally discussed) 'will be written by yours truly'. There was, he realised, in one of his sudden bouts of high spirits, much to be thankful for. When Smith accepted Annie's 'Little Scholars', a descriptive piece about her visits to charity schools, which the editor had initially thought to send elsewhere, Thackeray was reduced to tears. A letter sent out to his old friend Sir Henry Davison, now Chief Justice in Madras, early in May consciously exults in this worldly success:

> We've got 2 hosses in our carriage now. The Magazine goes on increasing and how much do you think my next 12 months earnings & receipts will be if I work?
> 10,000£
> Cockadoodleoodoodloodle!

He was going to spend £4,000 on his new house, Thackeray declared. He had his health, he had returned his parents to England and the future looked bright. At least two of these claims were false. The house at Palace Green turned out to be in such a poor state that it had to be rebuilt, cost twice as much as Thackeray had proposed to spend on the refurbishment and would not be habitable for another two years. And his health was bad. May brought another spasmodic attack – 'a little fit . . . not bad', he told Thompson, although a week later he was forced to cry off the annual dinner of the Royal Literary Fund on the grounds that he was 'so weak that I could not face the chance of an after-dinner speech'. In the meantime he pressed ahead with plans for future numbers, renewing his acquaintance with Frederick Leighton, who illustrated Elizabeth Barrett Browning's poem 'A Musical Instrument' in the July number, and proposing a 'Stronghold of England' article on the need for a chain of coastal forts to defend the country from French invasion ('We ought to make a *great stir* with it . . . I will, if you like, write personally to every minister whom I know, beseeching his attention to the article').

But the Yates affair, in fact the whole question of his relationship with Dickens and his supporters, refused to die down. Publicly Thackeray remained unyielding. 'It is a quarrel, I wish it to be a quarrel, and it will always be a quarrel,' he pointedly told his friend Sir George Russell at around this time. It flared up again as the result of some gossip that Trollope somewhat naïvely communicated to Yates, and which Yates worked up into an article for the *New York Times*. Trollope, at this stage in his career not yet the circumspect literary operator he was to become, had made various observations about Smith, which Yates contrived to twist into a series of flagrant slurs ('his business has been to sell books, not to read them, and he knows little else'). At the same time Yates suggested that the *Cornhill*'s circulation had fallen to 40,000 (it was actually twice that) and that 'Little Scholars' had benefited from some discreet parental touching-up. The article's existence was brought to the attention of British readers by the *Saturday Review*, ostensibly as part of an attack on the scandalous usages of transatlantic journalism, in fact as a means of settling an earlier quarrel with the *Cornhill*.

There was little Thackeray could do, except complain to the (mostly) sympathetic audience of the *Punch* table. Summer came, bringing with it the end of the London season, and the family, together with the Carmichael-Smyths, departed for Tunbridge Wells. Here they rented Rock Villa, an old wooden house at the foot of Mount Ephraim with a view out over the common. The ancient associations that this evoked drove Thackeray to two of his most exalted flights of nostalgia. *The Roundabout Papers* 'Tunbridge Toys' and 'De Juventute' were written on the spot. From Rock Villa he addressed his old friend Mrs Gore late in August ('it rains sweetly . . . I am as glum as possible') joking at a critic's notion that he had based Colonel Newcome on a character in her novel *The Banker's Wife*, first published in 1843 but recently reissued. Half of Colonel Newcome (Major Carmichael-Smyth) was downstairs, he explained, the other half (the major's brother) was in London.

Thackeray remained a prolific correspondent. In the late 1850s he probably wrote between 1,500 and 2,000 letters a year. Many of these were merely brief notes on business, often connected to his lecturing engagements, and yet the volume of both business and personal letters diminished sharply towards the end of his life. He tried to account for this decline in a letter to William Duer Robinson written in the early autumn of 1860, which apologises for the delay in his reply to Robinson's last. He was lazy in writing letters, Thackeray explained, and irregular in sending them: if he did not write to his friends, surely they would remember what heaps of letters he had to write and forgive him? As it was, correspondence had to be slotted into the gaps of a strenuous routine, obligations both welcomed and resented. 'I have a Magazine once a month, a fever attack once a month, the charge of old folks and young folks whom I have to take to the country or arrange for at home – a great deal of business & bad health, and very little order.' There was a new challenge awaiting him in the autumn – the full-length novel that Smith wished to start publishing in January. But Thackeray managed to keep up with perhaps the best-loved of his American friends. Christmas Day 1860 found him ill and fatigued by a morning's work on *Philip*, yet anxious to hear news of the Baxters. Sally's situation particularly alarmed him in the light of recent US political developments: Lincoln had just been elected president and South Carolina, where Sally and her husband lived, had adopted an Ordinance of Secession. The Civil War was looming, and he feared for his old flame's safety. 'Aren't you in a fright at the separation?' he wondered. 'Is Sally going to be a country-woman of yours no longer, and will her children in arms fight Libby's?' It was a 'horrible thing' for him to read of, he confessed.

Palace Green would not be ready for another year. *Philip* began in the *Cornhill's* January number. No one was particularly enthusiastic about this attempt at a sequel to the twenty-year-old *Shabby Genteel Story*. The material seemed too thinly stretched and Philip himself too *farouche*. For all Smith's habitual deference, Thackeray was conscious of the depressing effect that a weak serial would have on the magazine's sales (sure enough, the circulation fell sharply when *Framley Parsonage* came to an end in April 1861). His initial delight in the *Cornhill* had waned, and he was already having doubts about the wisdom of carrying on. A draft letter along these lines to Smith remained unsent, however, and he resolved to persevere. In all kinds of ways he was drawing in on himself, giving up tasks he would formerly have taken on without complaint, settling down into what he acknowledged was a more sedate life. He found it difficult now to redraw the illustrations to *Philip* onto woodblocks and hired the young Frederick Walker to do the work in his place. Smith remembered Walker's engagement as an example of how Thackeray could put at their ease young men whom he liked and wished to help. Wanting to put the artist through his paces, Thackeray suggested that Walker draw his back while he shaved. Smith, who spent the time discreetly looking out of the window, divined that Walker was in a such a state of nervous trauma that he would have dropped the pen if asked to sketch his subject's face. Taken on to do the work, Walker eventually decided that redrawing was beneath him: characteristically Thackeray admired his spirit and eventually commissioned him to illustrate the book himself. Elsewhere, older associations were slipping away. Ill in bed, he had an odd, premonitory reverie in which he lay thinking of illness at Charterhouse and Mrs Boyes' face bending over him. When he got up, he decided, he would go and see her 'and shake a hand with the kind old times'. By the time he rose from his sick-bed, Mrs Boyes was dead.

His life was altogether quiet now, he told Synge. His chief friends were his Garrick cronies Bell and Fladgate, and their favourite amusement was to go and dine together at Greenwich or Blackheath. Such liveliness as he allowed himself was provided by his daughters – Annie's letters frequently mention the 'scrapes' from which Minnie was required to extricate her – and by the establishment at Onslow Square. A letter to Mrs Baxter from Annie offers a vivid picture of their domestic life at this time, supported by a dog named Perkins, a brace of puppies and a small cat 'passionately attached to Papa'. Annie's account of the domestic staff might have been drawn from one of her father's early sketches: 'a faithful but tearful & affectionate cook, a pretty little maid called Fanny who is literary and quotes the Cornhill Magazine; and a gawky housemaid; and also a faithful reckless youth who breaks the china & tumbles down stairs & is called the Butler'. Thackeray did not regret the lack of a liveried retainer to admit his guests and preside over his dinner table. They saw little grand company now and 'the swells have almost entirely left us off'.

'Self-caricature, 1861'

His feeling of detachment from the bustle of 'society' heightened his sensitivity to criticism. The newspapers continued to yield up wounding references, and this encouraged him to brood over his reputation. He thought sometimes that he was 'deservedly unpopular', he told Whitwell Elwin, deciding in a vintage bout of Thackerayan aloofness that 'in some cases I rather like it. Why should I wish to be liked by Jack and Tom?' He recounted an embarrassing incident at Drury Lane Theatre when, as he and Bell took their seats in the stalls, they discovered Dickens and Wilkie Collins in the next row. Thackeray and Dickens shook hands but said nothing. 'And if he read my feelings on my face as such a clever fellow would he knows that I have found him out.' This kind of public coolness was to be expected, but he was upset later in the year to be 'half-cut' by one of Dickens' daughters at a banquet. Fathers could hate each other as much as they wished, he told his friends at the *Punch* table, but why should their children quarrel?

He was a frequent visitor to the *Punch* suppers in the latter part of that year: nostalgic, eager to talk about Charterhouse with Leech and

Silver, occasionally in high spirits, sometimes depressed by illness ('had it 30 years' he explained of his urethral complaint, quitting a dinner in November 1861), rarely able to resist the temptation to air his prejudices in front of a sympathetic audience. When Disraeli made a speech in which he portrayed himself as a defender of the Church of England, Thackeray was 'indignant at this Jew's coming forward as a champion of the Christian Church'. Literary chat, if it did not touch on Dickens or some acknowledged enemy, invariably found him generous. Tennyson was the great man of the age, he assured his friends. Nonsense, someone interjected, *Vanity Fair* stood higher than anything by the author of 'Maud'. Would Thackeray change his reputation for the poet's? 'Yes.' But Charterhouse was rapidly becoming a fixation to rank with Dickens, his health and his bank balance: Charterhouse fights; Charterhouse floggings; Leech arriving as the youngest boy in the school at the tender age of six and a half. And inevitably the memories of his schooldays snagged themselves on the suspicion that he faced a fast-approaching death. Sending Boyes a book that they had read together thirty-five years before in Charterhouse Square, he pictured his life as an omnibus journey. 'And the carriage is going down the hill, isn't it? . . . The terminus cant be far off – a few years more or less. I wouldn't care to travel over the ground again: though I have had some pleasant days and dear companions.'

The precariousness of his hold on life was brought home to him by Major Carmichael-Smyth's death in late September while on a visit to Ayr, 'who had but a few hours illness, and was quite well and cheerful the night before he was sent for'. Annie, on holiday in Wales with Minnie and Amy Crowe, assumed that the telegraph boy stepping along the path was bringing bad news of her father, '& I could hardly open the paper'. Her subsequent account of the journey north makes clear her anxieties over Thackeray's health. 'It was a long long tiring journey & we were very sad & still very frightened about our father . . . Then we went to the inn still very frightened . . . & we said our name was Thackeray . . . The waiter said There is a gentleman of that name in bed upstairs . . . Then we rushed into Papas room and there he was.' Interestingly, Annie records that her step-grandfather's death, rather than the 'loss' of her mother, was 'the first break' to the family. Grandmother, son and granddaughters came sadly back to London, and the grieving wife was swiftly installed at Onslow Square.

News from beyond the family circle was just as disquieting. If Thackeray had a cause that autumn it was the conduct of the

American Civil War. Temperament, the pull of old friendships and his own experiences in America made Thackeray a natural supporter of the secessionist southern states. The incident in November 1861 when the two Confederate commissioners to Great Britain were taken off a British ship, the *Trent*, by a northern steamer moved him to fury. There was disquieting news of American friends: Andrew Low was a captive in Fort Warren (though he was later released); Sally Baxter stuck in South Carolina and suffering from tuberculosis. The bright, optimistic society that had charmed him less than a decade before was breaking up.

As he laboured on with *Philip* – at fifty, he complained, he was a tired old horse – and wondered about his relationship with Smith, Thackeray could at any rate console himself by overseeing the work at Palace Green. Here a lavishly constructed mansion had grown out of the rotted floorboards and crumbling stone. Part-coloured marble steps led up to a front hall, thence to a spectacular hall proper, with Corinthian pillars. The roomy cellar encouraged the new owner to consult his wine merchant. Ninety dozen bottles of claret and port were eventually laid down in its twenty-one bins. In early March 1862, as the date for the family's removal from Onslow Square loomed near, a disagreement with Smith finally pushed him to resign. The specific cause is uncertain, but it seems to have had something to do with Thackeray's inability to cope with day-to-day editorial duties. He told his *Punch* cronies that what he really needed was a co-editor: 'fact is, I don't do Editorial work – which is to read and to judge, not to write'. Smith, whose original aim in securing Thackeray's services had been abundantly fulfilled, accepted his resignation with good grace and perhaps some private relief. Their relationship did not suffer –

Thackeray contributed *Roundabout Papers* for the rest of his life and continued to esteem Smith as 'a noble fellow'. In a good-humoured circular to contributors and correspondents, he invoked the memory of a sea-captain met on one of his American trips, who was now a passenger on the vessel he had previously commanded. 'Let my successor command the *Cornhill*, giving me always a passage on board; and if the Printer's boy rings at my door of an early morning with a message that there are three pages wanting or four too much, I will send out my benedictions to that Printer's boy and take t'other half-hour's doze.' Dated 25 March, the circular coincided with the Palace Green housewarming, marked by a performance of *The Wolves and the Lamb*, with Minnie in the cast and Amy Crowe as property mistress. A week later Thackeray and his family moved in. He had just over twenty months to live.

XXI
Ending Up

'Think of the beginning of the story of the little Sister in the Shabby Genteel Story twenty years ago and the wife crazy and the Publisher refusing me 15£ who owes me £13.10 and the Times to which I apply for a little more than 5 guineas for a week's work, refusing to give me more and all that money difficulty ended, God be praised, and an old gentleman sitting in a fine house like the hero at the end of a story!'

Letter to his mother, 5 July 1862

 s he neared death his mind moved backwards. The novels and magazine articles he wrote in the last four years of his life are effortlessly elegiac, crammed with reminiscences of the books, the faces and the spectacle of long ago. To the elegist of the *Cornhill* the modern world was a great deal less real than Mrs Serle and her forty pupils or the Smithfield tart-women and their trays of hardbake. To do Thackeray justice, he was aware that this quest for his lost childhood was bound to disappoint. In one *Roundabout Paper* he confessed to visiting a pastrycook's during a trip to Charterhouse, only to find that the penny tarts were not as enticing as he remembered. Reading a review of a pantomime in *The Times*, he suspected that the description would interest him more than the performance itself: 'Perhaps reading is even better than seeing.' Or less unsatisfactory. As one who had relished the pleasures of his youth, Thackeray knew that re-creating them in print could never quite match up to the original experience. None the less, he made the attempt. Miss Porter's novels. Pierce Egan's *Life in London*. Christmases past. Tunbridge Wells in the 1820s. Somehow the regularity with which these talismans present themselves is never monotonous, for

one detects the vital part that they play in the elegist's sense of himself.

There are distinctions to be made, as well. *The Roundabout Papers* roam across the surface of this past life – its artefacts, scenes and passing sensations – but *Lovel the Widower* and *Philip* run beneath it, moving deep into the private compartments of this lost world. The best chapters in *Philip*, which even Thackeray admitted went sadly to pieces before the end, are those with some kind of autobiographical grounding: the scenes set in Madame Smolensk's raffish boarding house, or the accounts of Philip Firmin's Bohemian days in Paris. *Lovel the Widower*, too, is a deeply personal book, despite its origins as an unsuccessful stage-play – one of Thackeray's greatest late-period achievements. Set in a house at Putney, where the sedate and fogeyish narrator 'Mr Bachelor' is staying with his widowed friend Lovel, the story's tragicomic undercurrents pick up on a vein of feeling that had been absent from his work for several years. Lately relieved of a termagant wife, whose picture stares at dinner guests from the wall, Lovel and his children are being fought over by his mother and mother-in-law. The love interest is provided by Miss Prior, the governess, with whose down-at-heel family Bachelor used to lodge. In fact Bachelor is sweet on 'Elizabeth' himself, in which capacity he finds himself rivalled by Bedford, the diminutive butler, and the local apothecary. Unhappily Miss Prior has a guilty secret in the shape of a past career as an actress. When this is disclosed, to the horror of the resident duennas, Lovel ends the struggle for her hand at a stroke by proposing himself. 'Mr Bachelor' is not Thackeray, but there is a great deal of Thackeray in him, while the story, with its glimpses of undergraduate days, its glances below-stairs and, in Lady Baker, another of his venomous mothers-in-law, endlessly reproduces the themes of his major novels. Above all, the book is strewn with queer fragments of symbolism that give its essentially comic premises a glacial edge. Pride of place among the artefacts bequeathed by the late-lamented Cecilia and displayed in Lovel's dining-room is a harp. At one point a blackbird flies through the window and perches on it. Later, at the height of the dénouement, one of the strings snaps with an ominous twang.

Though he was sinking deeper and deeper into the past, he could not ignore the present, and in particular the changes to his life brought about by moving house. Life at Palace Green, which at least one friend thought should be called 'Vanity Fair' (Thackeray liked to refer to it as the 'Palazzo'), required new routines. Bigger than Onslow Square, it needed more servants and more upkeep. Six months after they moved in he was still being asked to settle an £800 decorators' bill. He felt better there, though, he declared, even if he suspected that 'the novel writing vein is used up through and through'. With *Philip* nearly complete, his editorial duties gone and only the monthly *Roundabout* for a regular assignment, he was ready to idle. For relaxation there were walks in Kensington Gardens, and the usual entertaining: Mary Senior, the daughter of his friend N.W. Senior, remembered Palace Green for its parties, most memorably a cooking party where the guests put on caps and aprons. As ever Thackeray's gaze roved anxiously over the house's other inhabitants. Mrs Carmichael-Smyth, inevitably, was sunk in gloom: 'Since her husband's death my poor old mother is wandering about happy nowhere,' he reported in a letter to the Baxters. Annie, meanwhile, was hard at work on what was to become her first novel, *The Story of Elizabeth*, which Smith would begin to serialise in the *Cornhill* later that year. Thackeray's comments on Annie's burgeoning career show his usual psychological acuteness in the realm of family relationships. Her style was 'admirable' he pronounced, and Smith, Elder were in raptures, but he was sure he would not love the author a bit better for her success. With both girls now of marriageable age, and all too aware that no suitors had yet stepped forward to claim them, a certain amount of tact was required on both sides. According to Annie, Thackeray once suggested that they ought to get married so that he could have grandchildren. On another occasion she demanded, 'Papa, you don't want us to marry, do you?' The reply, offered 'quite hastily' but with a turning away of the head, was an emphatic 'Certainly not.' Torn between the attractions of grandchildren and the fear that any marriage contracted by one or other of his daughters would substantially reduce his comfort, his attempts at neutrality were not always successful.

The spring brought a sad coda to his friendship with the Baxters in the shape of a melancholy letter from Sally – alone in Charleston, her husband away with the Confederate army, and incurably ill. Again the past had caught up with him, and Sally's current state mocked the memories of her that he continued to burnish: 'dying slowly of a disease which baffles all physic and all cure, I am far different from the gay girl you perhaps remember, years and years ago'. Thackeray's reply has not survived, but he was greatly upset by the story's final chapter. Travelling south late in the summer, as the Civil War raged around them, Lucy Baxter and her father were refused permission to cross the Confederate line. Sally died shortly afterwards on 10 September. 'That journey of Lucy and her father is the saddest thing I have read of for many a long day,' Thackeray told Mrs Baxter in a sorrowful letter written on Christmas Day 1862. 'What a bright creature! What a laugh, a life, a happiness!' The Baxters stayed in Thackeray's mind, and Annie kept up a correspondence with them for many years. Two years later she told Mrs Baxter about an odd incident once when they were dining out and a cross little American woman spoke unkindly of them ('She did not know you,' Annie explained, 'it was only some political madness'). Thackeray was so furious that he commanded his daughters not to talk to the American.

Late April took him to Paris, staying with the Ritchies (his cousin William, Jane and Charlotte's brother, had died in March). 'A fair passage,' he told the girls. 'Just enough not to be sick and to feel sick all the way in the train.' He was ill once more, came home and fell ill again, and was conscious of the effect that this kind of disturbance had on his writing. He forgot the sentences he put down on paper and grew 'awfully nervous', he told Smith. Nevertheless he came to the end of *Philip* in early July. Writing to his mother, he could not resist exulting over the change in his circumstances in the twenty years since he published *A Shabby Genteel Story*, which began the story of the 'Little Sister', Caroline Gann – his poverty now gone and 'an old gentleman sitting in a fine house like the hero at the end of a story!' Still only a fortnight away from his fifty-first birthday, he was aware of having passed a climacteric in his life, come to 'a little lull' after 'constant care and occupation'. Publicly he seemed a benign, rosy figurehead, decked about with the trappings of legend. Writing to Annie not long before her death, Lord Sandhurst remembered as a small child being propelled across the room by his uncle to 'a tall old gentleman who patted my head'. He could go to bed now, his uncle advised, 'and always remember that you've seen Mr Thackeray'.

His inefficient secretary Langley had little to do except answer letters (Thackeray resolved to sack him, wrote a courteous letter of explanation and then typically relented). Sedate pleasuring was the order of the day – a carriage ride to Twickenham, a trip to the opera with the girls ('where I had a most refreshing sleep in the back of the box)'. He celebrated the end of *Philip* by 'making a bad drawing'. The twenty-year-old Walker drew twice as well, he told his mother, 'and at twenty you know we all thought I was a genius at drawing. O the mistakes people make about themselves.'

His health continued to deteriorate. A doctor called in to examine him at Paris had diagnosed a fatal complaint. 'It turns out not to be true,' Thackeray explained to the Baxters, 'but, but, but . . .' Annie's accounts of life at Palace Green are full of foreboding, presentiments of doom. He looked thin and pale, friends thought. New acquaintances introduced for the first time marked him down straight away as an invalid. At the same time it was clear that the dietary regime he put himself through gave him no help. During the course of his adult life, he told John Cordy Jeaffreson, he had drunk enough to float a seventy-four-gun battleship. Even allowing for the exaggeration characteristic of these manly disclosures, the account of Thackeray's alcohol consumption given to Jeaffreson is staggering: two bottles of wine an evening on three days out of four, together with an extra two or three glasses at midday and various supplementary late-night grogs and punches. His eating habits varied. A few weeks before his death he was still unable to resist the tripe served up at the Reform Club. At other times, however, he drank brandy and soda first thing in the morning to give him an appetite for breakfast. Undoubtedly this kind of conspicuous consumption helped to weaken an already overloaded system, and there was an air of deliberation in the way that the later Thackeray went about overindulging himself (one remembers his remarks to Hodder in Norwich five years before). Many of his friends thought he could have prolonged his life had he taken the trouble. But it was increasingly obvious that a part of him did not want to make the effort.

The autumn passed without any fresh literary project presenting itself, although he knew that the state of his finances would soon oblige him to come up with something. He was a constant visitor to the *Punch* suppers, as ever abusing Yates ('base, ungentlemanly, mean') – Shirley Brooks defended him on the grounds that he was merely acting for Dickens – but acknowledging the irony of Yates' parentage, and his own love for the pretty actress of his boyhood. He was keen to discuss religious topics, Silver noted, claiming that when he was, as he suspected, on his death-bed in 1849 he was perfectly content and happy, that he was not deterred from wrong-doing by any fear of future retribution but by 'feelings of present disgrace and dishonour'. His perennial matter-of-factness about questions of religious belief emerged in a defence of the free-thinking Bishop Colenso, who had denied the historical accuracy of the creation story. Colenso was correct, Thackeray told his listeners: reason required one to view biblical accounts of the sun standing still as a fable. *The Story of Elizabeth*'s appearance moved him to a fervent tribute to Annie's talents: she had all his better parts, he maintained, 'and none of my worst'.

By early January 1863 he had an idea for a new book. *Denis Duval* would be a success, he thought: shorter, less weighed down by the ruminative moralising that had characterised *The Virginians* and *Philip* and, with its eighteenth-century setting and rapid pace, worthy to be ranked with Dumas. He remained enthusiastic about the novel – planned to run through eight numbers of the *Cornhill* – and wrote his usual letters to knowledgeable friends asking for historical detail. 'I went upon various smuggling expeditions,' he told Albany Fonblanque, assuming the persona of his hero, 'but as I don't know the difference between a marling spike and a binnacle, I must get information from somebody else.' Meanwhile another literary row, the last of the volcanic eruptions that had blighted the years of his success, was brewing. His opponents on this occasion were Yates' friend W. Hepworth Dixon, editor of the *Athenaeum* – Dixon had also been a close friend of Jerrold – and two of his staff: Jeaffreson, who until now had some claims to be regarded as a Thackeray ally, and his colleague Geraldine Jewsbury. As it happened the magazine's warning shot had been fired some time before in a review of *Lovel the Widower* – anonymous, but generally known to be by Jewsbury – which complained that the reader would be conscious of having suffered a 'moral deterioration' as a result of exposure to the 'engrained vulgarity of spirit' that typified the work. This might just have fallen into the category of objective criticism. A subsequent violently *ad-hominem* assault on *The Story of Elizabeth* patently did not. Again, the usual channels of Victorian literary gossip were opened. Shirley Brooks identified the reviewer as Jeaffreson (in his memoirs Jeaffreson blames Jewsbury, but says that etiquette forbade him to explain this to the injured party). Again, the venue for the ensuing conflict was a gentleman's club, on this occasion 'Our Club', of which Thackeray and Jeaffreson were both members. The quarrel went public late in April when Thackeray presided over the club's Shakespeare dinner at Clunn's Hotel. Jeaffreson, writing the event up years later, remembered Thackeray's appearance in morning dress and 'one of his high-collared white waistcoats', looking 'nervous and full of trouble'. His speech was unremarkable, except for a pointed word or two about the atmosphere of rivalry and contention in which Shakespeare had worked and the 'tattlers' who tried to disparage him. Thackeray then announced that owing to illness he would resign the chair to a worthier occupant. On his way out of the room he made Jeaffreson a perfunctory bow, while Shirley Brooks, following in the rear, flashed what Jeaffreson marked down as an 'exultant look'. Within a fortnight the usual sides had been taken and battle lines drawn up. Jeaffreson, still unprepared to unmask the author of the review, was ostracised by a swathe of literary society.

The *Athenaeum* row had some way to run. Ill and dispirited – at a *Punch* dinner some weeks before he had lamented 'that umbrella instrument', which he was compelled to insert in his urethra – Thackeray had little enthusiasm for the fight. Public accounts of him at this time reveal a streak of depression. Talking to the Earl of Aberdeen's son, Lord Stanley, at the Cosmopolitan Club, where the membership included leading literary men and politicians, he complained that the public had grown tired of him. The £7,000 that George Eliot had recently received from Smith for *Romola* clearly rankled. *Esmond* had brought him only £1,500, Stanley recorded. At Easter, three weeks in advance of the Shakespeare dinner, he and his daughters stayed with Richard Monckton Milnes, recently elevated to the peerage as Lord Houghton, at Fryston Hall before journeying on to Hampsthwaite near Harrogate in search of the family's birthplace. The guests at Fryston Hall included the Archbishop of York and the young Algernon Swinburne, whose after-dinner poetry reading on the Sunday evening of the week-long stay caused a sensation. According to Swinburne's biographer Edmund Gosse (who thought the choice 'injudicious'), Swinburne probably read 'The Leper' and definitely delivered himself of 'Les Noyades'. Shocked at the unorthodox sentiments being declaimed at him, the archbishop pulled such a disapproving face that Thackeray, who admired Swinburne, smiled at his host. Annie and Minnie, equally shocked, giggled aloud. Annie remembered the young poet arriving in the garden, hat in hand, the sunshine flooding his red-gold hair, and being so taken by his appearance that she burst into tears when he left.

Despite illness, Thackeray tried to get on with *Denis Duval*. Annie approved of the scheme ('not a long one & historical & *very* interesting') but noted that the excitement of writing it made him unwell. There was a sense, too, that he had begun to set his affairs in order. He discussed with Annie and Minnie the necessity of making a will: should he die intestate, he explained, Isabella would be legally entitled to one-third of the estate, which he thought excessive for her needs and unfair to the girls. Similarly, he was bent on a reconciliation with his greatest irritant. Some time in the late spring, meeting Kate Collins, the former Miss Dickens, at a social event, he told her that it was ridiculous that he and her father should continue to quarrel. Knowing that any olive branch would have to come from Thackeray – something he seems to have grasped himself – she agreed to act as intermediary. Some time in May the two men met in the hallway of the Athenaeum and, apparently at Thackeray's prompting, shook hands and spoke. Dickens later described his shock at how ill seemed the man who came uneasily across the marbled entrance hall towards him, hand extended in greeting.

The summer of 1863 wore on. His anxiety at the lack of progress on *Denis Duval* irked him – 'I have done nothing for a WHOLE YEAR and I MUST go to my horrible pens and paper,' he explained to one correspondent – but he grasped at the chance to go visiting, taking off in July, for example, to stay with Sir William and Lady Knighton at their house at Bletchworth. His gloom about his health and his inanition increased. Walking with Mary Senior in Kensington Gardens, he told her that his doctor had warned him to take great care or he would not live much longer. He was resigned to this, Thackeray added, for Annie and Minnie were old enough to look after themselves. His friend Samuel Hole, arriving at Palace Green at around this time with John Leech, found him sitting with his face turned to the back of his chair. Thackeray sighed, explaining that he was tired. Why not take a holiday, Hole asked, and go to the seaside with the girls? Thackeray said nothing, rose from his chair, stuck his hands in his pockets to their fullest extent, turned them out – they were empty – and sat down again.

Meanwhile the *Athenaeum* dispute was reinventing itself as a quarrel about the National Shakespeare Tercentenary Committee, formed to oversee the following year's celebration of the 300th anniversary of the poet's birth. Hepworth Dixon, in his capacity as general secretary, had manoeuvred Dickens, Tennyson and Bulwer aboard as vice-presidents, while apparently ignoring Thackeray. In his defence, Dixon maintained that he had sent Thackeray a letter, to which he had not troubled to reply. At this point Dixon decamped to the Middle East, leaving Jeaffreson to manage the committee's affairs in his absence. Jeaffreson, who seems genuinely to have wanted to conciliate a man he greatly admired, wrote a special letter of invitation to Thackeray. This too was ignored. As ever the situation was made worse by partisans, for whom the committee and the *Elizabeth* review were inextricably linked. One even told Jeaffreson that the committee should be wrecked in order to 'punish' it for its treatment of Annie and her father. Subsequently a meeting of the committee packed with Dixon's contributors voted overwhelmingly not to send a third invitation, but the battle continued in Our Club (from which Thackeray had resigned), whose officers voted to exclude Dixon if Thackeray could be persuaded to return. Remembering the consequences of Yates' expulsion from the Garrick five years before, Thackeray vetoed the plan.

Autumn came. He worked desultorily at his novel, fell ill, recovered and went about his clubs and his daily routine. As ever he tried to rouse himself to greater activity. He had done no work for a whole year, he grumbled again – this time to Dr John Brown – and must now sit down at his desk or there would be 'no beef and mutton'. He had spent too much money on Palace Green, he decided, and filled it up with gimcrack furniture, china, plate and the Devil knew what. To Annie, writing her memoirs in the years that followed, these months seemed full of significant moments, melancholy yet retrospectively satisfying glimpses of last things. One came when they were driving in the dusk by the Serpentine and passed Carlyle walking across the park. Thackeray leaned forward to wave: 'A great benevolent shower of salutations', Carlyle later remembered. Another was produced by an autumn Sunday when they attended Evensong at Temple Church, not far from the chambers where, thirty years before, Thackeray had idled away his hours as a tyro barrister. Coming out, Thackeray began to chant 'Rejoice' and commended the hymn – 'So simple and unaffected and so entirely to the purpose'. The sun had begun to set over the gardens and the nearby Thames, 'and everybody went away through the courts and archways, but we went and walked along the terrace and down some steps into the garden. It was all golden & shining when we came out of the lamp-lit church & the organ was booming ... and the sky was very bright & warm & red, but in the garden by degrees the twilight came and the lights faded out of the sky and the river.'

December drew on. On Saturday 12th he attended the Charterhouse Founder's Dinner, sitting opposite Leech, and was pressed to make a speech. Writing about the event years later, an onlooker could remember Thackeray 'very plainly now as he spoke, one hand thrust into his breeches pocket and the other held slightly forward, the fingers moving expressively as he made some quaint point, his head thrown a little forward with the chin somewhat projecting, after the manner of short-sighted people'. On the Sunday his urethra closed up and he was confined to bed. He lay there for thirty hours, he told Thompson, 'with no. 4 in me for the last 3', and would have stayed longer but for his desire to get on with *Denis Duval*. 'I shall keep myself open as well as I can meanwhile,' he decided, 'and wont put myself under discipline tomorrow that we talked of doing.' On Wednesday 16th he went to the *Punch* dinner and twitted Horace Mayhew, who had mischievously put him down on a subscription list as 'Arthur Pendennis' after he had particularly begged that his name should not appear. Now those 'd——d penny a liners' would be at him again, he feared. That night, after his return, Palace Green was broken into and a quantity of the girls' and Mrs Carmichael-Smyth's jewellery taken. Thackeray described the event in a letter to George Smith the next day, laid up once more 'with an instrument of torture in my urethra'. Yates had written something offensive in a newspaper, he told Smith, but Minnie had counselled him to remain silent. "'Don't say a word Papa. It will make them all the more angry'" (the *Athenaeum* row continued to burn on: Vizetelly's *Illustrated Times* of 12 December had carried a widely circulated article denouncing Dixon and his satellites). Curiously the weekend brought an unseen tribute that he would have welcomed, had he ever known about the future reputation of the man who wrote it. That Sunday the twenty-three-year-old Thomas Hardy wrote to his sister May:

> About Thackeray. You must read something of his. He is considered to be the greatest novelist of the day – looking at novel writing of the highest kind as a perfect and truthful representation of actual life – which is no doubt the proper view to take. Hence, because his novels stand so high as works of Art or Truth, they have anything but an elevating tendency, and on this account are unfitted for young people for their very truthfulness. People say that it is beyond Mr Thackeray to paint a perfect man or woman – a great fault if novels are intended to instruct, but just the opposite if they are considered merely as Pictures.

On the morning of Monday, 21 December Annie went into her

father's room early: 'he was so gentle that I felt a sort of *pang*'. His condition improved. He spent the day at the Athenaeum, at the funeral of his distant relative Lady Rodd at Kensal Green, and dined in one of his favourite corners at the Garrick – a niche dominated by a painting of a scene from *The Clandestine Marriage*. Coming home in the dark through Knightsbridge, Annie met their near-neighbours Charlie and Kate Collins, who reported that he had called earlier to show them something Yates had written in the *Star*. On the Tuesday he told Annie that he had composed an answer but decided not to send it. Later as she sat writing in her own room she heard his step overhead – a sign that illness had made him retreat to his bedroom. For the first time in her life, Annie believed, she waited before going to him. When she did, he had gone out in the carriage. He came back in the afternoon 'sad & cold & asking for something warm'. Fanny the maid brought him some brandy and water. He was ill the next morning, 'lay very still with large – large eyes', complained that he had not taken enough medicine the night before, but had upped the dose and would soon feel better. The doctor said he would be better in twenty-four hours. By the afternoon he was sufficiently recovered to sit in the mild winter sunshine of the Palace Green gardens with a book.

That night Annie had a curious dream. She and her father were climbing a high hill, 'higher and higher so that I had never seen anything like it before. And papa was pointing out something to me wh. I could not see & presently left me & I seemed to come down alone.' Some time in the early part of the night Mrs Carmichael-Smyth heard him retching. Annie had just finished dressing the next morning when there was a strange crying sound. Leaving her bedroom, she reached the landing and was met by Charles, the Palace Green manservant. 'He is dead, miss, he is dead,' Charles repeated. Mrs Carmichael-Smyth, too, emerged from behind her door. Summoned from his breakfast by the grieving women, Charlie Collins could 'never forget the day which we passed at the house . . . or the horror of seeing him lying there so dreadfully changed. It was apoplexy after all, and I don't think that what he had suffered from so long had much, if anything, to do with it.' The doctors were called, and the blinds drawn down. It was Christmas Eve.

'Mr Thackeray's passing'; George Eliot's journal, 30 December 1863 (lost entry)

A bright day of radiant sunshine, not the least inclemency. George, attending Mr Thackeray's funeral at Kensal Green, brought back with him Mr Martin, whom was I interested to meet. With his translations from the German I am of course familiar, yet was fascinated to learn his wife an *actress* ... In short a decidedly unusual representative of the literary species.

The talk inevitably of Mr Thackeray, his reputation, bearing, odd stories about his wife &c. I do not believe we met, unless it were in passing, though George and Mr Chapman used of course to talk of him. Indeed I recall George showing me the letter he received from him about Goethe, in which one might detect no very forcible powers either of recollection or reason. I remember, too, Mr Blackwood saying that he had shown him a copy of 'Amos Barton' and that he commented pleasantly on the few pages he had read ... I found myself considering the strong, if not singular, points of Mr Thackeray's character: the want of erudition (though erudition was a quality he distinctly esteemed), the bravery of a strong and truthful nature, the latter never disguising a certain frailty. George used to speak of his quarrels – the kind of quarrels perhaps that only men have – saying that they proceeded out of a heightened sensitivity, that his asperities were much exaggerated. I have a strong impression of a genial, sad man, noble and sympathetic in temperament, not insensible to prejudice, perhaps, but surmounting any defects of taste through a genuine and unforced goodness ...

Impossible, of course, to separate these thoughts – and at such a time – from the question of *belief*. I can remember a

good many years ago Mr Chapman – who had perhaps called
on him about some proposal – maintaining that he was at
heart perfectly 'free', that a vague spiritualism and
grandiloquence masked an altogether keener appreciation of
what was at stake. Yet I have met others who detected only
a simple piety, perfectly in harmony with his moral
excellence and intellectual capability. In any case these are
mysterious regions – twilit always – and I confess that I
should not care to have what I thought or supposed
examined by one whose slight knowledge ordained an
imperfect command of illustration. That he is gone into a
great unknown, mourned by those who knew him intimately
and those who regarded him from afar, is perhaps all that
can, or should, be said. George *sorrowful*. Said that Mr
Thackeray always friendly, encouraging to him, wanted him
to have the *Cornhill* after his resignation &c. Talk at the
funeral all of money, provision for the two girls, the crowd of
strange females, Mr Dickens's grief. All one would expect,
perhaps.

XXII

Afterwards

o his friends, the news of Thackeray's death came as a profound shock. They had known he was unwell, but few had expected him to die. John Cordy Jeaffreson compared reading the press reports to the letter from Missolonghi forty years before announcing that Byron was dead. It was the beginning of the festive season, and the story took longer than usual to travel: many of his close friends, consequently, only found out on Christmas Day. Dickens heard the news at Gadshill. Trollope, who had last seen him ten days before, declared himself 'stopped'. George Hodder, paying a Christmas morning call on Horace Mayhew in Old Bond Street, found his festive spirits instantly extinguished when Mayhew, his face ominously blank, asked, 'Haven't you heard?' David Masson, who a dozen years back had written the piece comparing *Pendennis* to *David Copperfield*, was urgently petitioned for a memorial article from the editor of the *Daily Telegraph*: his daughter remembered the printer's boy waiting throughout Christmas Day in the hall until her father finished. Thackeray would have been amused by this re-enactment of one of the recurring events of his own life. Simultaneously, the news penetrated into many a private corner of contemporary society, and the diary entries of several eminent, or relatively eminent, Victorians for Christmas Day 1863 reflect their sense of loss. 'Thackeray died yesterday morning in his bed, only fifty-two,' George Gilfillan wrote. 'He was a minor scourge of God, the Attila of fashionable life. He lashed flesh and bone alike to ribbons. His blows

447

were aimed at vital parts, the head and the heart.' He must be herding somewhere near Swift, Juvenal and Junius, Gilfillan poetically concluded. William Howard Russell recorded that 'My dear friend Thackeray died this morning. Oh, God, how soon and untimely!' In the evening he dined at his club, 'the talk all of Thackeray – of him alone'. Tennyson, writing to the Duchess of Argyll, touched on the eternal charge of cynicism: 'A man of most kindly nature, with a heart of true flesh and blood. It was only his outer husk that was cynical and that only in his books . . .' Brookfield's diary has only the stark entry 'Thackeray is dead.' A day or so later he and Jane called to commiserate with Mrs Carmichael-Smyth. Brookfield subsequently stood between Dickens and Sir James Colville at the graveside.

There were long and invariably affectionate obituaries. *The Times* produced two-thirds of a column, ranking him below Dickens – even in death the rivalry persisted – but stressing Thackeray's personal qualities. Dickens himself paid tribute in the *Cornhill* – warmly, but without displaying any great knowledge of or interest in the work, *Denis Duval*. There was an ominous complaint, too, about the deceased having 'feigned a want of earnestness'. Trollope followed suit, originally declining George Smith's offer of payment but then asking for a particular edition of *Esmond* for his wife Rose. Tom Taylor, on the door of whose law chambers Thackeray had optimistically nailed his name-plate in 1848, wrote a moving poem in *Punch*. The long round of tributes and memorials eventually culminated in a Royal Literary Fund dinner in May, addressed, consecutively, by the Prince of Wales, Lord Stanhope, Dickens and Lord John Russell.

In the days after the funeral Annie and Minnie went first to Freshwater on the Isle of Wight to stay in a cottage owned by their friend Julia Cameron. It was bitterly cold: Annie remembered Tennyson coming to visit wrapped in his cloak, and freezing nights spent dreaming of funeral processions passing endlessly over the downs. In the middle of January they went back to London to stay with Kate Collins. For the next eight months, while their father's estate was wound up, they lived a peripatetic existence: lodging with the Ritchies at Henley, back to Freshwater, at Putney Heath, with Mrs Sartoris at Warnford. For all Thackeray's long-expressed fears about his finances, his death realised a substantial capital sum. Palace Green was sold for £10,000 (nearly £3,000 more than it had cost to build), George Smith paid £5,000 for the copyrights – a bargain, seeing that they had earned nearly three times this sum for the author during the time Smith had published his books – while a sale of the furnishings and the contents of the wine cellar raised another £3,000: Trollope took the opportunity to buy himself a piece of his friend's plate. The money was used to buy annuities for the girls, provide for Isabella and buy a small but comfortable house at 16 Onslow Gardens.

The Palace Green establishment swiftly broke up. Annie reported that two of the old servants were staying '& we shall have a cook & Grannie to keep house besides at least that is the scheme we have made'. Thackeray had foreseen problems if Mrs Carmichael-Smyth and the girls were forced to live together without his own moderating presence, and for a short time at least he was proved right. There was a tense family holiday in Brittany in August, characterised by 'terrible religious discussions', whose lowering effect, Annie thought, was compounded by the girls' deep sense of isolation. They wanted to do their duty, she recorded, but seeing no one made their predicament so much worse. As it was, she felt herself 'torn & crazed between the two dear ones'. By early September she noted that 'I am crying, Minnie is crying, Grannie is crying and thinking of G.P. [the family's pet-name for Major Carmichael-Smyth]. How very miserable we are. What can we do?' Come Michaelmas they were installed in Onslow Gardens and being regularly visited by Mrs Brookfield. 'Did Papa ever tell you of Mrs Brookfield?' Annie enquired of Mrs Baxter. 'She has taken us under her kind wing she is coming to live close by only to be near us. All this terrible year she has been so good to us all three that I do not know how we could have dragged through without her.' The three were shortly to be reduced to two. Mrs Carmichael-Smyth, who joined them in November, was visibly fading, grown unexpectedly emollient and confiding, prone to reminisce about her early life, her youth in India, Richmond Thackeray on his white horse coming to court her. On the evening of 18 December she kissed her granddaughters goodnight, left the room for bed, but died before she reached the staircase. She was buried next to her son at Kensal Green on Christmas Eve, a year to the day after his own death.

Thackeray had died comparatively young. Various of his friends and acquaintances, particularly the younger literary element, survived him for many years. As a result he maintained a constant presence in the tide of late-nineteenth-century literary autobiographies and memoirs. Eyre Crowe and Sala, who wrote two of these, were still going strong in the 1890s. Thackeray's protégé Hannay died an alcoholic at his consular desk in Barcelona in 1870. Fitzgerald survived until 1883.

Yates prospered as a society scandalmonger, wrote a highly self-regarding autobiography and ended up editing the *World*, where among other accomplishments he was an early patron of George Bernard Shaw.

Thackeray's nearest and dearest were equally long-lived. Isabella survived until 1894 – she died within a week of her husband's old friend Vizetelly – living at various addresses in the south of England, at first with the Bakewells and their allies, later with the family of her husband's old doctor, Henry Thompson. She never regained her reason, but enjoyed the company of her daughters and – eventually – her grandchildren, and made occasional appearances in Annie's vast correspondence. In 1877, for example, Annie recorded that 'Mama is now at Wimbledon & I go to see her when I can, she has got the most charming little house there . . .' Although Annie's journals are matter-of-fact about her mother being 'mad' and 'raving', her letters to the old lady, of which a few survive, are determinedly chatty and conventional. Summoned by telegram to Isabella's final residence at Leigh-on-Sea in Essex early in January 1894, Annie was deeply moved by the experience of watching her mother die: 'her dear face lighted into serene and unspeakable wisdom and knowledge. It seemed to me that the room was full of light.' Returning to London, she was strangely affected by the sight of the newspaper placards announcing 'Death of Mrs Thackeray'. 'Dear Mama, so silent, so undemanding, so loving, so contented,' Annie later wrote to a friend. 'I have no words to tell you how great she seemed to me.' Isabella's death released a torrent of memories of early life, and Annie's *Chapters from Some Memoirs* – probably the book for which the late twentieth century best remembers her – was in the press by the year-end.

The Brookfields' fortunes waxed and waned. Jane began her literary career in 1866 with *Only George*, which went through three editions. Later novels such as *Influence* (1871) and *Not a Heroine* (1873) were less successful. Brookfield's *annus mirabilis*, professionally speaking, came in 1868, when he dined with the queen at Windsor and was subsequently appointed her honorary chaplain. He died in 1874. Not perhaps as amply provided for as she would have wished – the Elton money was somewhat dispersed by now – Jane seems to have been induced to publish her heavily edited selections from the Thackeray/Brookfield correspondence for financial reasons. She survived almost to the end of the Victorian era, keeping up with former admirers and old friends such as Tennyson, Spedding, Kinglake and Venables, and eventually dying in 1896. Her style in these later years is best captured by the descendant who wrote that 'she dressed becomingly and appropriately, with feeling and good taste, and her stately picturesque figure was for many years one of the most pleasing sights of the West End of London' – which makes her sound rather like an equestrian statue, but such tributes were habitually framed in these terms. Her son Arthur, Tory MP and diplomat, wrote one of the most politically incorrect novels of the late-Victorian period, a fable called *Simiocracy* (1884), in which the Liberal party extends the franchise to orang-utans and then imports millions of them to keep itself perpetually in power.

Thackeray's greatest anxiety had been what would happen to his daughters after his death. 'It will be a very dismal life for you when I am gone,' he once told Annie. In fact his fears were misplaced, and though Minnie died young, both made happy marriages and, in so far as one can make these assumptions about any human being, lived rewarding lives. Early in 1866 the Miss Thackerays were invited to a luncheon party at Portman Square and introduced to the son of the house. Leslie Stephen was at this point an ex-Cambridge don who had resigned his fellowship on the grounds of agnosticism and set up as a literary freelance. Following a return picnic, a meeting on holiday at Zermatt in the summer and a certain amount of prevarication on Leslie's part, he and Minnie became engaged at the end of the year. An initial arrangement by which the three of them kept house together was not a success, largely because Leslie both admired his sister-in-law and was unable to stop himself from scolding her. Minnie's daughter Laura was born in 1870, three months prematurely, said 'Papa' at six months, but by the age of three was being described as 'very backward in her little intellects'. She spent a long, twilit and mostly undocumented existence in the hands of governesses and private asylums (a letter from Leslie following a visit to one of these in 1897 notes that she was 'unable to recognise any of us clearly') before dying of cancer as late as 1945. A cousin remembered a tall, striking woman known as 'Aunt Laura' being brought to family parties in the 1930s. By this time her mother had been dead for over sixty years, of pre-eclampsia shortly before the birth of what would have been her second child. Leslie consoled himself with the beautiful widow Julia Duckworth, continued to pursue a distinguished literary career (he was already editor of his father-in-law's old magazine), and became founding editor of the *Dictionary of National Biography* and the father of Virginia Woolf.

Annie's own literary career continued to flourish, with a series of well-received novels, including *The Village on the Cliff* (1867), *Old Kensington* (1873) and *Miss Angel* (1875), each published serially in the *Cornhill*. Nearly forty at the time of her sister's death, she surprised everyone – not least Leslie Stephen, who found the couple canoodling on the sofa – by getting engaged to Richmond Ritchie, the son of Thackeray's favourite cousin William Ritchie. Seventeen years younger than the bride-to-be, and still at Cambridge, Richmond abandoned his studies for a junior clerkship at the India Office. They were married in 1877, prompting George Eliot to note that 'This is one of several instances that I know of lately, showing that young men of even brilliant advantages will often choose as their life's companion a woman whose attractions are wholly of the spiritual order.' Despite the difference in years, and Richmond's intermittently roving eye (Annie wrote enigmatically that she loved him 'not well enough to refuse him'), the marriage was a success and produced two children, Hester and Billy. Richmond's career at the India Office flourished, and he ended it with a KCB and a permanent under-secretaryship before dying prematurely of pneumonia. His widow, meanwhile, survived into an old age of extraordinary esteem. She was the friend of Henry James; Robert Louis Stevenson had written her a poem; George Eliot had declared that, with the partial exception of Trollope, she was the only modern novelist that she cared to read. Annie's portrait by John Singer Sargent, to which a troop of admirers subscribed, shows a serene and grey-haired old lady with distinct traces of her father's physiognomy. At eighty, in the midst of the First World War (her house in Chelsea had its windows blown in by an enemy bomb), she wrote wistfully: 'I wish, how I wish, I could cut up into four entire young women of twenty to come and go. I should like wings to fly with, and intelligence to know what would be of use.'

Annie died in 1919. Some of the most vivid recollections of her were produced by her stepniece Virginia Woolf. The former Miss Stephen sincerely admired her father's sister-in-law, read her books on 'a liberal scale' and wrote her obituary in the *Times Literary Supplement*. Elsewhere she noted Annie's habitual reserve on the appearance of young people, 'as if we'd gone far off and recalled unhappiness, which she preferred not to dwell on'. Annie was transparently the model for

Mrs Hilbery in *Night and Day*, the daughter of a famous Victorian writer engaged on his biography:

> She was a remarkable-looking woman, well advanced in her sixties, but owing to the lightness of her frame and the brightness of her eyes she seemed to have been wafted over the surface of the years without taking much harm in the passing. Her face was shrunken and aquiline, but any kind of sharpness was dispelled by the large blue eyes, at once sagacious and innocent, which seemed to regard the world with an enormous desire that it should behave itself nobly, and an entire confidence that it could do so . . . Certain lines on the broad forehead and about the lips might be taken to suggest that she had known moments of some difficulty and perplexity in the course of her career, but these had not destroyed her trustfulness . . . She bore a great resemblance to her father.

Woolf also captured Annie's odd style of literary composition – pacing the room until the right phrase presented itself and then scribbling furiously until the impulse burned itself out. Inevitably the long, but not unfriendly, Bloomsbury shadows hanging over much of the second- and third-generation Thackeray life provide all kind of unexpected connections: an ancient photograph of Minnie, for example, with Woolf's pencilled identification on the reverse, or the division of Laura's surprisingly large estate – she left £7,000 – between Adrian Stephen and Vanessa Bell.

Thackeray's death had a lasting impact on his friends. Several of them – for instance his Garrick Club crony Robert Bell – left instructions in their wills to be buried at Kensal Green, in order that their association with him might be posthumously strengthened. Trollope, in particular, provides a fine example of the way in which Thackeray's memory could be perpetuated by someone who had known him well. Trollope had received many kindnesses from his friend. As an editor, Thackeray had virtually made Trollope's name by taking *Framley Parsonage* for the *Cornhill*. As a clubman, he and Bell had inducted the younger writer into the Garrick (in a neat stroke of continuity, Trollope was invited to fill the vacant committee place left by Thackeray's death). Trollope survived his friend for nearly twenty years, but Thackeray remained a constant, ghostly presence in his life. His picture took pride of place in the gallery of literary portraits that decorated the study at Waltham House, together with a small silver statuette showing the novelist in a characteristic pose – standing with his hands stuffed in his trouser pockets. Years later, when the talk at a London dinner party turned metaphysical, Trollope suddenly announced to his fellow guests, 'If I thought I should never see dear old Thackeray again, I should be a very unhappy man.'

But of all the people that Thackeray left behind him, it was Annie who felt the keenest hurt and tried the hardest to re-create the time she had spent with him. The circumstances of his death stayed in her mind for years, and took on an immediacy that could sometimes crowd out contemporary realities. As late as 1875 she could write to Mrs Baxter in America, 'I think I am writing to tell you that Papa is dead. It always seems to be that come back, not anything new.' In Annie's later years this sense of filial duty assumed a practical focus – writing the series of biographical introductions to one of the several collected editions of Thackeray's work, taking part in the 1911 centenary celebrations when 2,000 guests congregated on the lawns of the Middle Temple. Even in her seventies she could be found exchanging letters with Dickens' daughter Kate Perugini, as Kate Collins subsequently became, on what their fathers had said to one another half a century before, and the urge to assemble odd scraps of Thackerayana stayed with her until her death.

And yet the most intense expression of her feelings for her father emerges in a pair of private journals. The first was begun a few weeks after he died. The second, written in 1878, was officially intended for a grown-up Laura Stephen (who would never be able to read it), but is actually a kind of love letter to the little girl's dead mother and grandfather. The 1864 journal, in particular, is a catalogue of raw and quite unmediated emotion, underpinned by Annie's feelings of guilt and self-reproach at having survived when someone so much worthier than she was gone. Occasionally this strikes an oddly masochistic note. An entry from late January, for example, recasts a scene from six months before when Thackeray scolded her for coming down late to breakfast, adding that when he was dead she would remember, but by then it would be too late. 'God knows I at least cannot be more unworthy of [his love] than I was then,' Annie noted wretchedly. Elsewhere she reflects that 'Papa always liked every thing we did, & we never liked anything until we knew he approved.' Inevitably this kind of assertion can work both ways: an indulgent papa, perhaps, but one whose daughters were so carefully attuned to his sensibilities that they worked almost subconsciously to harmonise their opinions with his own.

Another indication of the intense emotion that these memories stirred comes in Annie's attempt to refashion part of his declining months with the help of his diary and by means of a kind of mental embroidery. Thackeray's entry for 9 June 1863, for instance – Annie's birthday – is a laconic 'Dined with the girls at Star & Garter'. Annie's version is full of detail, twilight hues and grave forebodings. Later this desire to re-create her father's past life prompted her to seek out some of its venues and settings. Towards the end of 1864 she and Minnie visited Cambridge: 'It was like feeling nearer to Papa to go & see his youth with our own eyes – It was like living then & when we came back it seemed as if we had travelled from one century into another almost ...' They turned up a friendly clergyman to act as tour guide, who remembered Thackeray in Fitzgerald's rooms, and scribbling sketches at a party on the river.

Such is the fervour of Annie's descriptions of her father, and the terrible sense of loss that underlies them, that the prose frequently loses its moorings and sweeps off into the present tense to hit a pitch of emotion that is practically sexual in its intensity:

> Papa has beautiful white hands with pink knuckles and long nails ... His eyes are so soft and large ... his voice is low & gentle ... he holds down his cheek to kiss & he presses our foreheads.

> I can see him passing his hand through his hair laughing at the children pouring out his tea ...

> I can see him swinging his arms as he walks. I can see him looking out over the ship side & placing his spectacles that are always slipping.

But if one wanted a stopping-off point for this long and intricate journey through the teeming early-Victorian world, and its lost, dead faces – Isabella, Jane and Mrs Carmichael-Smyth, Dickens at the graveside, Maginn in the fourpenny brothel, Courvoisier swinging from the block – it might be Annie's birthday dinner at Richmond. Such a bad dinner, Annie remembered Thackeray saying, 'but we liked it so much, all three of us'. When the entertainment was over, 'Papa called a little open carriage & we drove home past the river through clouds & clouds of mists, & coming through Birnes [sic] & over the bridge. And all the people were out in the street at Kensington & we got home in the calm summer eveg.' It is a captivating image, for some reason perhaps the most captivating of all in Thackeray's life: white-haired papa, doting daughters, the carriage rolling on through the twilight into the city's dark yet welcoming heart. But, to borrow another image from perhaps the greatest novel of the whole Victorian age, it is time to put the puppets back into the box, for our game is all played out.

Appendix: A Thackeray Scrapbook

This volume came to light some years ago when it was bought at auction. Neither vendor nor purchaser have discovered its actual provenance. In fact Thackeray's ownership of the book – a large, brown-paper ledger embellished with the single word 'Scraps' – was not even suspected when the item changed hands.

The book carries a book-plate with the arms of the Collett family, whose connection with Thackeray, if any, remains obscure. Although the earliest item in it (a tiny watercolour on the theme of 'Lochinvar') is on paper watermarked in 1827, while the latest (a preliminary design for the *Irish Sketch Book*) dates from 1842, the bulk of the material belongs to the 1830s. It is extremely various, including cuttings from periodicals – notably Cruikshank's *Comic Almanack* from 1838 and 1839 – and prints of places with Thackerayan associations (for example, West Country scenes and Addiscombe, where Major Carmichael-Smyth was employed as superintendant of the military school). However, the bulk of the book consists of over 150 pencil sketches, drawings in pen-and-ink and small watercolours. The nature of the subject matter – copies of Old Masters, Parisian 'views', portraits of popular actors – suggests a tentative date of 1833–5, when Thackeray was making serious efforts to train himself as an artist. In many cases items have been stuck on top of one another, or in some cases removed altogether. For example, an intriguing note, in Thackeray's handwriting, refers to a portrait of Schiller, shown to Goethe, which the latter approved. Unfortunately, this likeness was removed at some point in the past. It seems reasonable to suppose that Thackeray kept the book up during the 1830s, adding and subtracting material from time to time.

Several of the illustrations have a direct biographical significance. A watercolour of a young man, looking not unlike Thackeray, smoking a large meerschaum pipe, is captioned '15 Jermyn Street, 13 November 1831.' A drawing of a convict sentenced to death was made during Thackeray's passage through Rouen the following summer, while a sketch of the church of Saint-Germain-des-Prés is dated '24 February 1835'. Most fascinating of all, perhaps, is a pencil drawing of the interior of the church at Chaillot, which occurs on the same page as the portrait of a young woman in a bonnet bearing a distinct resemblance to Isabella.

Other items prefigure, or are variations on, known Thackeray illustrations containing awful visual puns. Among them are a gleeful, necrophagous imp chewing human flesh taken from an open grave whose tombstone reads 'WT OB 1802', and a watercolour of Thackeray and an imaginary family composed of a short, fat wife and a brood of children and domestics. Juxtaposed caricatures of a seedy looking Frenchman and a stout John Bull each accepting refreshment, one a glass of wine, the other ale, reflect some of the national stereotyping of a piece such as 'Memorials of Gourmandizing'. There are also several try-outs for the *Paris Sketch Book*, *Irish Sketch Book* and other early works. Though currently uncatalogued and unknown to scholars, it seems clear that this material will eventually play a significant part in re-shaping our appreciation of Thackeray's artistic interests and development in the 1830s.

Notes and Further Reading

Two of the principal sources for this biography are Gordon N. Ray's four-volume edition of Thackeray's letters and private papers and Edgar F. Harden's two-volume supplement. To have noted each reference from Ray and Harden individually would be to enlarge the book's extent beyond manageable proportions. Consequently I have tried to indicate within the text when and to whom relevant letters were sent.

Some works of reference are mentioned so frequently that I have identified them simply by author or abbreviated title. These abbreviations are listed below. Unless otherwise stated, the place of publication is London.

Ashburton Papers Letters of Thackeray to Lord and Lady Ashburton, National Library of Scotland, Mss Acc. 11388. These are reproduced almost entirely – slight cuts marked – in K.J. Fielding's 'Letters of Thackeray to the Ashburtons', *Dickens Studies Annual*, vol. 27, 1999

Mrs Brookfield Charles and Frances Brookfield, *Mrs Brookfield and Her Circle*, single-volume edition, 1906

Chapters Anne Thackeray Ritchie, *Chapters from Some Memoirs*, 1894

Checklist Edgar F. Harden, *A Checklist of Contributions by William Makepeace Thackeray to Newspapers, Periodicals, Books, and Serial Part Issues, 1828–1864*, Victoria, British Columbia, University of Victoria UP, 1996

DNB Dictionary of National Biography

Interviews Philip Collins, ed., *Thackeray, Interviews and Recollections*, 2 vols, 1983

LPP Gordon N. Ray, ed., *The Letters and Private Papers of William Makepeace Thackeray*, 4 vols, Oxford, 1945–6

Ritchie Papers Unpublished correspondence, notebooks, manuscripts and typescripts belonging to Anne Thackeray Ritchie, held in the University of London Library, Ms 907. As the process of cataloguing this mass of fragmentary materials is incomplete, I have referred to the number of the box in which the relevant item is stored.

RP Thackeray's *Roundabout Papers*

Shankman Lilian F. Shankman (Abigail Burnham Bloom and John Maynard, eds), *Anne Thackeray Ritchie Journals and Letters*, Columbus, Ohio State UP, 1994

Silver Diary Constance Smith, ed., *The Henry Silver Diary: An Annotated Edition*, facsimile of Saint Louis University doctoral dissertation, 1987

Supplement Edgar F. Harden, ed., *The Letters and Private Papers of William Makepeace Thackeray: A Supplement to Gordon N. Ray, The Letters and Private Papers of William Makepeace Thackeray*, 2 vols, New York, 1994

Two Thackerays Introductions written by Lady Ritchie (Anne Thackeray) for the thirteen-volume 1899 Biographical Edition, subsequently expanded for the twenty-six-volume 1910 Century Edition, and reprinted as *The Two Thackerays*, 2 vols, New York, AMS, 1988

There is no complete modern edition of Thackeray's works, although one is in hand under the expert supervision of Professor Peter Shillingsburg. Saintsbury's seventeen-volume Oxford edition of 1908 is the most reliable of the existing editions, but difficult to get hold of outside academic libraries. However imperfect from the point of view of modern scholarship, my chief resource has been the twenty-four-volume edition (subsequently expanded to twenty-six volumes) published by Smith, Elder in 1878–9, easily and cheaply procurable in second-hand bookshops.

I The Road to Kensal Green

For George Hodder's remarks on Thackeray as a biographical subject, see his *Memories of My Time*, 1870, 238. The excerpt from John Blackwood's letter of rejection to an aspiring memorialist is taken from Mrs Gerald Porter, *Annals of a Publishing House: John Blackwood*, 1898, 99. Both are reprinted in Philip Collins' introduction to *Interviews*, I: xiii–xiv. Sir William Fraser's comment is taken from *Hic et Ubique*, 1893, part of several pages of reminiscence reprinted in *Interviews*, I: 140. For the letter by Kate Perugini, the former Kate Dickens, to Annie complaining about Mrs Lynn Linton's memoirs, dated 13 February 1905, see *Ritchie Papers*, box 7. For Thackeray's comment about remembering only the impression he got of the author when reading, see *LPP*, III:19.

Noel Annan's comment to Leonard Woolf about the unreliability of letters and diaries is quoted in Regina Marler, *Bloomsbury Pie*, 1997, 86.

For some comments on Thackeray's reputation in the years immediately after his death, see G.A. Sala, *Things I Have Done and People I Have Known*, 2 vols, 1894, I: 39; and Frederick Locker-Lampson, *My Confidences*, 1896, 330. For some late-Victorian critical views, see Andrew Lang, 'Thackeray', in

Essays in Little, 1891; W.E. Henley, 'Thackeray', in *Views and Reviews*, 1892; and George Saintsbury, 'Thackeray', in *Corrected Impressions: Essays on Victorian Writers*, 1895. Desmond MacCarthy's comments on Thackeray's declining popularity in the inter-war years are quoted in Winifred Gerin, *Anne Thackeray Ritchie*, Oxford, 1981, 268. For 'Gunning-Forbes" comments, see John Wain, *Hurry On Down* (Penguin edition), 1960, 68.

For Orwell's essay 'Oysters and Brown Stout', which originally appeared in *Tribune*, 22 December 1944, see Peter Davison, ed., *George Orwell: The Complete Works*, vol. 16, *I Have Tried to Tell the Truth*, 1998, 498–501. Thackeray's influence on Orwell was considerable. Asked to name the writers Orwell most admired, a friend suggested 'Dickens of course . . . Swift . . . He quite liked some of Thackeray's work but felt he was a bit pedantic I think.' (Audrey Coppard and Bernard Crick, eds, *Orwell Remembered*, 1984, 105.) A deliberate example of Orwell's cross-referencing comes in one of Flory's ruminations in *Burmese Days*, on the subject of British rule in India and the destiny of its servants. 'Ah, those poor prosing old wrecks in Bath and Cheltenham! Those tomb-like boarding houses with Anglo-Indians littered about in all stages of decomposition, all talking and talking about what happened in Boggleywalah [*sic*] in '88!' (Davison, op. cit., vol. 2, 72). Boggleywallah was where Jos Sedley held his collectorship.

There are accounts of Thackeray's funeral in Hodder, op. cit., 310–12, and John Black Atkins, *The Life of Sir William Howard Russell*, 1911, reprinted in *Interviews*, I: 155. For Millais' recollections, see the same, 153. Contemporary newspaper accounts are quoted in Lucinda Lambton, 'Kensal Green', in *Lucinda Lambton's A–Z of Britain*, 1996. Lambton also prints a useful list of Victorian celebrities buried there. For Dickens' behaviour at the graveside, see Peter Ackroyd, *Dickens*, 1990, 937–8. Annie's memories of the funeral are in *Shankman*, 126. For Lewes' meeting with Theodore Martin, see Rosemary Ashton, *George Eliot: A Life*, 1996, 277.

II Eastern Child

The account of Thackeray's antecedents and early childhood is drawn largely from Mrs Richard Pryme and Mrs William Baynes, *Memorials of the Thackeray Family*, privately printed, 1879; Sir William Wilson Hunter, *The Thackerays in India: and Some Calcutta Graves*, 1897 – bearing in mind Gordon N. Ray's comments on the accuracy of its detail expressed in *Thackeray: The Uses of Adversity*, Oxford, 1955, 24, n.5–; and Leslie Stephen's *DNB* article.

James Hannay's comments on Thackeray's Saxon descent are quoted in George J. Worth, *James Hannay: His Life and Work*, Lawrence, Kansas UP, 1964, 82. For John Cordy Jeaffreson's account of conversations with

Thackeray on the subject of gentlemanliness, see his *A Book of Recollections*, 2 vols, 1894, I: 250–1.

Thackeray's admission that he was never able to bear the sight of people parting from their children occurs in 'On Two Children in Black', *RP*. For a discussion of Anglo-Indian history as reflected in *The Newcomes*, see R.D. McMaster, *Thackeray's Cultural Frame of Reference: Allusion in The Newcomes*, 1991, ch. 4. For Thackeray's use of Anglo-Indian slang, see K.C. Phillipps, *The Language of Thackeray*, 1978, 145–7.

The memory of 'that first night at school' is in 'On Two Children in Black', and Thackeray's recollection of wishing that he might dream of his mother comes in 'On Letts's Diary', *RP*. The description of Chiswick in the immediately post-Regency period is taken from Warwick Draper, *Chiswick*, 1923.

For Annie's description of her grandmother, see *Chapters*, 15. Thackeray's memory of his mother telling him Old Testament stories is in *LPP*, III: 217. For Henriette Corkran's opinion of Mrs Carmichael-Smyth, see her *Celebrities and I*, 1902, 28. For Annie's account of Dr Turner, see *Two Thackerays*, I: 17.

Thackeray's evocations of childhood are taken from 'Tunbridge Toys', 'On a Peal of Bells' and 'De Juventute', *RP*.

III The 370th Boy

On Charterhouse under Russell, see William Haig Brown, *Charterhouse Past and Present*, Godalming, 1879. For Tupper's recollections of the school in the early 1820s, see his *My Life as an Author*, 1886, ch. II. Details of Thackeray's Charterhouse contemporaries can be found in W.D. Parish, *List of Carthusians 1800–1879*, Lewes, 1879. Annie's introduction to *Pendennis* (*Two Thackerays*, I) contains much useful information.

For a first-hand account of Thackeray's relationship with his schoolfriends, see J.F. Boyes, 'A Memorial of Thackeray's Schooldays', *Cornhill Magazine XI*, 1865. There is a good description of Bartholomew Fair in William Hone's 'A Day in the Life of Bartholomew Fair', reprinted in John Wardroper, ed., *The World of William Hone*, 1997, 35–55. Liddell's memories, taken from Henry L. Thompson, *Henry George Liddell, DD: A Memoir*, 1899, are reprinted in *Interviews*, I: 17–18. Again, the atmosphere of Larkbeare is reproduced in Annie's introduction to *Pendennis* (*Two Thackerays*, I: 56–61).

For Thackeray's later feelings about Charterhouse, and their emergence in his fiction, see John Carey, *Thackeray: Prodigal Genius*, 1977, 26–8. For a selection of his later reminiscences, see *Silver Diary* entries for 21 October 1858, 4 December 1861, 11 December 1861 and 8 January 1862. The address to 'Morality' occurs in 'On Some Late Great Victorians', *RP*. The conversation with his fellow guest in the New York hotel appears in 'On Screens in Dining-Rooms', *RP*.

For a discussion of Thackeray's contributions to *Flindell's Western Luminary and Family Newspaper*, see H.S. Gulliver, *Thackeray's Literary Apprenticeship*, privately printed, Valdosto, Georgia, 1934, ch. I. Gulliver attributes the five 'Dorothea' letters to Thackeray, but they are absent from Harden's *Checklist*.

IV Alma Mater

For Cambridge in the nineteenth century, see Michael Sanderson, ed., *The Universities in the Nineteenth Century*, 1975, ch. 1. 'Struggles of a Poor Student Through Cambridge' by 'Senior Wrangler' appeared in the *London Magazine*, April 1825.

For Trinity in Thackeray's time, see W.W. Rouse Ball, *Trinity College Cambridge*, 1911, ch. VI, and his *Cambridge Papers*, 1918. The details of Thackeray's admission are recorded in Rouse Ball and J.A. Venn, *Admissions to Trinity College, Cambridge IV, 1801–1850*, London, 1911.

Thackeray mentions Swift's continuous correspondence with Stella in 'De Finibus', *RP*. For Cousin Jasper's advice to Charles Ryder, see Evelyn Waugh, *Brideshead Revisited*, revised edition 1960, 35. On Thackeray's contributions to undergraduate magazines, see Gulliver, op. cit.; Harden, *Checklist*; and Charles Whibley, *William Makepeace Thackeray*, 1903, 8–9.

William Hepworth Thompson's memories of Thackeray at Cambridge are in Pryme and Baynes, op. cit., 347–8. Extracts from Allen's diary for 1830–1 are printed in *LPP*, I: 493–8. Thackeray recorded the details of his illicit French trip in 'Desseins', *RP*. He recast his re-encounter with Mlle Pauline in 'Shrove Tuesday in Paris', one of a series of 'Loose Sketches. By Mr Michael Angelo Titmarsh', *Britannia*, 5 July 1841, 363. Fitzgerald's letters and diary entries are reproduced in Alfred Mckinley Terhune and Annabelle Burdick Terhune, eds, *The Letters of Edward Fitzgerald*, 4 vols, Princeton, N.J., 1980, I: 1830–50.

The identification of Whewell with 'Crump' is made by Whibley, op. cit., 7. For more sympathetic accounts of Whewell and details of his academic career, see *DNB*, vol. 60, and 'Half a Century of Cambridge Life' in *Church Quarterly Review*, vol. XIV, April 1882. The latter, while celebrating Whewell's accomplishments, admits that the value placed on his copyrights after his death was precisely nil.

V Weimar Days

The discussion of novelists' upbringings in the nineteenth century draws on

David Newsome, *The Victorian World Picture*, 1997, especially I: V, 62–76. Thackeray remembered asking Sloman to dine with him at the *Punch* table, 15 February 1860 (*Silver Diary*).

On Weimar in the early 1830s, see S.S. Prawer's magisterial *Breeches and Metaphysics: Thackeray's German Discourse*, Oxford, 1997, by far the most comprehensive study of Thackeray's German influences. For a contemporary account of a visit to the principality (sometimes attributed to Thackeray by early biographers), see 'Recollections of Germany, III: Dresden, Weissenfeld, and Weimar', *Fraser's Magazine*, XXI, January 1840, 64–70. There is no real evidence to suggest that Thackeray wrote this piece. The style is anonymous and the writer's letter seeking an audience with Goethe makes it clear that he was still a student.

The Weimar sketchbook is in the Berg Collection, New York Public Library. See Catherine Peters, *Thackeray's Universe: Shifting Worlds of Imagination and Reality*, 1987, 41–3. For Thackeray's contribution to *Chaos*, and his literary occupations in Weimar, see Gulliver, op. cit., ch. III.

Prawer discusses 'German' references in Thackeray's work at length in *Breeches and Metaphysics*. For German allusions in *The Newcomes*, see McMaster, op. cit. For Thackeray's mature opinion of Goethe, expressed in a letter to G.H. Lewes, see *LPP*, III: 442–5.

VI London and Paris 1831–5

For an informed account of the smart London world of the early 1830s, see Captain Gronow's *Reminiscences and Recollections*, abridged and introduced by John Raymond, 1964, 44–5, 56–7. Fitzgerald's side of his correspondence with Thackeray, and his letters to mutual friends, are reproduced in Terhune, op. cit., I: 103–11.

There are several sources of information on Maginn. Annie's introduction to *Pendennis* (*Two Thackerays*, I: 80–2) supplies interesting details, but quickly descends into euphemism, with approving references to 'brilliant gifts' balanced by intimations of 'fatal instincts'. Considering her father's diaries from the period, she concludes, 'At first there are constant mentions of Dr Maginn, of his scholarship and kindness, and brilliant talk, then come others far less to the Doctor's credit. The reverse of the medal appears: it is not the king's head any more that we see, but the dragon's, with its claws and ugly forked tongue, and alas! no St George to the rescue.' For other accounts of Maginn, see *DNB*, XXXV, and Logan Pearsall Smith's essay 'Captain Shandon' in *Re-perusals and Re-Collections*, 1936.

On the early history of *Fraser's*, see John Gross, *The Rise and Fall of the Man of Letters*, 1969, 16–18. Henry Vizetelly's *Glances Back Through Seventy*

Years, 2 vols, 1893, I, provides an entertaining, if not always accurate, near-contemporary account (Vizetelly was born in 1820) of the 1830s' literary scene.

For an eye-witness account of the realities of the 1832 election campaign, see Gronow, op. cit. 212–13. Asked to stand for Grimsby in the Whig interest by Lord Yarborough, Gronow and his companion Hobhouse accepted on condition that there was to be no bribery. They subsequently came bottom of the poll.

The question of how Thackeray lost his patrimony is dealt with by Ray, *Adversity*, 162–3, and in Ann Monsarrat, *Thackeray: Uneasy Victorian*, 1980, 62–3. A previously unknown letter to Robert Langslow of 9 February 1838, complaining about six years' unpaid dividends, is in Harden's *Supplement*, I: 29. Fitzgerald's letter to Allen of 7 December 1832 is printed in Terhune, op. cit., 126–8.

On the background to bill-discounting in the early 1830s, see David Kynaston, *The City of London, volume I: A World of Its Own 1815–1890*, 1994, 88. David Deady Keane's account of his dealings with 'Bill Crackaway' ('Illustrations of Discount', *Fraser's Magazine*, XXVII, April 1843, 398–409) is reprinted in *Interviews*, I: 72–3. Thackeray's account book for 1833 is in *LPP*, I: 504–5.

The best account of the short history of the *National Standard* and of Thackeray's involvement with it is Donald Hawes, 'Thackeray and the *National Standard*', *Review of English Studies*, new series XXII, no. 89, 1972. Gulliver, op. cit. ch. IV, discusses Thackeray's contributions and makes several attributions, not all of them accepted by Harden's *Checklist*, 14–15. The verse attack on Lord Rothschild and the wider question of Thackeray's anti-semitism is discussed in S.S. Prawer's comprehensive study *Israel at Vanity Fair: Jews and Judaism in the Writings of W.M. Thackeray*, Leiden, 1992, see in particular 17–20. For Gronow's comment on the Jew as businessman, see the Raymond edition previously cited, 110–11.

Vizetelly's account of the 'romantic stories' concerning Thackeray's loss of his fortune is in *Glances Back*, I: 128. For the Fitzgerald letters of late 1834, see Terhune, op. cit., I: 148–54. The account of Thackeray returning the set of engravings to a print-seller is taken from R.H. Barham, *The Garrick Club: Notices of One Hundred and Thirty-five of its Former Members*, privately printed, 1895, IV: 'Thackeray'. Henry Reeve's letters to his mother describing meetings with Thackeray in Paris in early 1835 can be found in John Knox Laughton, ed., *Memoirs of the Life and Correspondence of Henry Reeve*, 2 vols, 1898, I: 35 and 47. The first extract is reprinted in *Interviews*, I: 24.

For Thackeray's accident at Mrs Trollope's picnic, see Pamela Neville-Sington, *Fanny Trollope: The Life and Adventures of a Clever Woman*, 1997,

227. Thomas Trollope's account is given in T.A. Trollope, *What I Remember*, 2 vols, 1887, I: 88–9.

VII 'The Gal of my Art'

Henry Reeve's letter about Isabella appears in *Memoirs of the Life and Correspondence of Henry Reeve*, I: 59, and is reprinted in *Interviews*, I: 24–5. Fitzgerald's letter to Allen of 31 October 1835 is printed in Terhune, op. cit., I: 175–7.

On the political background to the *Constitutional*, see Robert Blake, *The Conservative Party from Peel to Churchill*, paperback edition, 1972, chs I and II. Thackeray's and Isabella's courtship is largely reconstructed from their letters. For the only surviving information on their honeymoon, see *LPP*, I: 318n.

A complete run of the 249 issues of the *Constitutional [and Public Ledger]* exists in the Huntingdon Library, callmark 152182. I am grateful to Professor Michael Slater for providing me with a synopsis of some of the early numbers, a copy of the subscribers' list and copies of the opening and closing editorials.

Harden prints two previously unknown letters from Isabella to Mrs Carmichael-Smyth in the *Supplement*, I: 20, 22–3. For Thackeray's account of Annie's birth, see *Shankman*, 124.

VIII The Drowning Woman

Fitzgerald's letter of 1 September 1837 is printed in Terhune, op. cit., I. Thackeray remembered turning down the chance to rent a house in Brunswick Square at a *Punch* dinner of 5 July 1862 (*Silver Diary*).

On the London literary scene when Thackeray began his career as a freelance writer, see Gross, op. cit., ch. 2: i and ii, and Whibley, op. cit., 23–7. On Thackeray's career as a freelance 1837–40, see Gulliver, op. cit., chs VII and VIII.

Thackeray's early association with Charles Dickens is covered in Edgar Johnson, *Charles Dickens: His Tragedy and Triumph*, revised edition 1977, 100, 139. On his friendship with Tennyson, see Donald Hawes, '"Better and Worse Voices": Tennyson and Thackeray', *The Tennyson Research Bulletin*, vol. 6, no. 3, November 1994. As Hawes points out, Tennyson held Thackeray in high personal regard throughout his life ('A man of most kindly nature, with a heart of true flesh and blood'), while maintaining private reservations about the degree of cynicism he thought manifested in the books. Fitzgerald suspected that, like Dickens, Tennyson was not particularly familiar with Thackeray's work. Having been persuaded by a friend to read *The Newcomes*, however, he noted, 'I do not wonder that there is no youth among the young if this is the food on which they feed.'

Thackeray's friendship and literary association with Cruikshank is chronicled in Robert L. Patten, *George Cruikshank's Life, Times and Art, Volume 2: 1835–1878*, Cambridge, Lutterworth Press, 1996. For his possible collaboration with Dickens – albeit at different times – on *More Hints on Etiquette*, see the same, 74. Cruikshank's observation that to be an artist was to 'burrow along like a mole', made to the American abolitionist pastor Moncure Daniel Conway at Thackeray's funeral, is quoted by Patten, op. cit., 420. For the collaboration on *Stubbs's Calendar, or The Fatal Boots*, see 193–4.

Vizetelly mentions the *Punch* try-out, which he dates to late 1838, in *Glances Back*, I: 166–7. For Annie's memories of Great Coram Street, see her introduction to *The Great Hoggarty Diamond* (*Two Thackerays*, I: 154–6).

On N.P. Willis, see Henry A. Beers, *Nathaniel Parker Willis*, Boston, 1885. Thackeray's review of Willis' *Dashes at Life with a Free Pencil* appeared in the *Edinburgh Review*, no. 82, October 1845, 470–80, his only contribution to that journal.

For Thackeray's role in the 'Newgate' controversy, see Patten, op. cit., 125–7. For an account of Courvoisier's trial, which excited tremendous public interest, see the appendix to the *Annual Register 1840*, 229–45. There is a report of the execution in *The Times* of 7 July 1840. For Dickens' presence at Snow Hill, see Ackroyd, op. cit., 313–15.

Annie's memory of Isabella's attempt to drown her ('She held me by the hand & once pulled me in a little way, & then her love struggled with her madness & so we came back safe . . .') is recorded in her journal of 1864, *Shankman*, 132. For her recollections of Minnie as a baby in Ireland, which appear in the journal of 1878, see the same, 197.

The journey from Cork to Paris, culminating in a forty-hour coach trip across France, remained one of Annie's most traumatic memories, and she returned to it several times in her published and unpublished writings. The journal of 1864 (*Shankman*, 130) remembers Thackeray 'in the stagecoach after Mamma went out of her mind. He was very grave & when I kicked & talked he told me I must be still or I should wake baby, & when I still went on he said he must put out the light if I was not quiet, & then still I was not quiet & the light suddenly went out.' The journal of 1878 (*Shankman*, 197) has 'I can remember being in the dark in a diligence & the baby was crying & I began to cry & my father struck a light to cheer me up. There was a sick man in the corner moaning & then the dawn came . . .' This account is taken from the biographical introduction to *The Great Hoggarty Diamond* (*Two Thackerays*, I, 168–9).

IX The Uncleared Table

There is a description of the Carmichael-Smyths' Paris apartment building in *Chapters*, 33. For Annie's memory of Isabella 'raving' in the room next door, see *Shankman*, 130.

On Esquirol's early career and methods, see the extract from Alexis Jean-Baptiste Parent-Duchatelet, *De la Prostitution dans la ville de Paris, considerée sous le rapport de l'hygiène publique, de la morale et de l'administration*, 2 vols, Paris, 1836, quoted in *The London Journal of Flora Tristran*, 1982, 103–4.

The account of Laura Stephen's condition is based on records of her admission and treatment kept by the Asylum for Idiots, Earlswood, Redhill, Surrey, currently at the Surrey County History Centre, Woking (refs 392/11/1/1 and 392/11/4/4 respectively). The twenty-two-year-old Laura was admitted in July 1893 on the authority of her stepmother, Julia Stephen, and discharged in January 1897 at her father's request. On her admission she was described as 'quiet', 'shortsighted', able to eat with a knife and fork, able to read, write, work, paint and make straw baskets. Like her grandmother, she was fond of music and singing.

For the letter to Chapman and Hall (15 March 1842) enquiring about the editorship of the *Foreign Quarterly Review*, see Harden's *Supplement*, I: 117. Annie's recollections of Napoleon's reinterment are in *Chapters*, 29–30. For her memories of visits to Thackeray's lodgings, see *Shankman*, 129.

For Thackeray's stay with Bowes (25 June–13 July 1841) and the background to *Barry Lyndon*, see Ralph Arnold, *The Unhappy Countess*, 1957, 181–9. The diary of 27 July–11 August is reproduced in *LPP*, II: 30–3.

Thackeray's review of E.D. Lane's *Life at the Water Cure* appeared in the *Morning Chronicle*, 1 September 1846.

X A Cockney in Ireland

On early-Victorian Ireland, see R.F. Foster, *Modern Ireland 1600–1972*, 1988, XIII.

For the later letter to Lever (15 October 1860), see Harden, *Supplement*, II: 996. For Lever's conversations with Thackeray, and Major Dwyer's recollections, see W.J. Fitzpatrick, *Life of Charles Lever*, 1879, vol. II, 396–7 and 405–20, reprinted in *Interviews*, I: 64–71. On early-Victorian Romanticism and the reaction against it, see Jerome Hamilton Buckley, *The Victorian Temper*, Cambridge, Mass., Harvard UP, revised edition 1969, 14–27. The latter quotes Macaulay's review of the *Prelude*, 17.

For the remarks made to Thackeray by Trollope's Irish groom Barney, see Richard Mullen, *Anthony Trollope: A Victorian in His World*, 1990, 446.

XI The Vagrant Heart

On the early history of *Punch*, see M.H. Spielmann, *A History of 'Punch'* 1895; R.G.G. Price, *A History of 'Punch'*, 1957; and, pre-eminently, Richard D. Altick's monumental *Punch: The Lively Youth of a British Institution*, Columbus, Ohio UP, 1997. There are also interesting details in an anonymously written booklet, *Mr Punch: His Origins and Career*, 1870, published to mark the magazine's thirtieth anniversary and the recent death of Mark Lemon. The comment about *Punch* not being born in a tavern parlour is taken from this source.

For Thackeray's dealings with *Punch* and his relationship with the magazine's staff, see numerous references in Altick, op. cit., and Peters, *Thackeray's Universe*, ch. 6. On Jerrold's connection with *Punch*, again see Altick. Thackeray reviewed *Mrs Caudle's Curtain Lectures* in the *Morning Chronicle* of 26 December 1845, observing of Mrs Caudle that 'a foreigner, or a student in the twentieth century, may get out of her lectures an accurate picture of London life as we can get out of the pictures of Hogarth'. For Thackeray's later comment on Jerrold's election to the Reform Club, see Hodder, op. cit., 302. For Vizetelly's account of Jerrold in his dealings with Thackeray, see *Glances Back*, I: 290–3. The anecdote about Jerrold's reaction to Thackeray's presence at the christening was contributed by J.B. Groves to *The Farmer's Advocate*, 23 December 1915.

Fitzgerald's letters from Great Coram Street are printed in Terhune, op. cit., I: 385–9. The *Tablet* review of the *Irish Sketch Book* appeared on 13 May 1843. See also Lever's review in the *Dublin University Magazine*, which he edited, CXXVI, June 1843, 647–56. Vizetelly's visit to Thackeray's rooms in Jermyn Street is recorded in *Glances Back*, I: 249–51, and reprinted in *Interviews*, I: 43–4. On Thackeray's connection with the *Morning Chronicle*, see Gordon N. Ray, ed., *William Makepeace Thackeray: Contributions to the Morning Chronicle*, Urban, University of Illinois, 1955.

Annie's memories of the summer holiday of 1844 are in *Two Thackerays*. Fitzgerald's comments on the 'Academy Exhibition' spoof occur in a letter to Frederick Tennyson of 24 May 1844, Terhune, op. cit., I: 385–9. The account of the Near Eastern tour is largely based on Thackeray's letters. For Catherine Peters' comparison of the *Punch* despatches with *Cornhill to Cairo*, see Peters, op. cit., 123. For Annie's account of his return, see *Shankman*, 199.

XII Duty Kept

For a discussion of Cruikshank's possible influence on *Vanity Fair*, see Patten, op. cit., 96–7. On Henry Colburn, see John Sutherland, *The Longman Companion to Victorian Fiction*, Harlow, 1988, 136–7.

On the Brookfields' early life, see *Mrs Brookfield*, chs I and II. The remark about Brookfield finding himself in 'grand company' is taken from a memoir by Lord Lyttleton included in Jane's edition of *Sermons by the late Rev. W. H. Brookfield*, 1875, xxxiii. For Brookfield's diary entries of 1845, see the same, 145.

Annie's recollections of her life in Paris in the 1840s are in *Chapters*, 18–20. For her account of the visit to London in summer 1845, see *Shankman*, 199. For Brookfield's diary entry of 5 August, Jane's letter to him of 17 August and Brookfield's account of dining with Thackeray on the night of Isabella's installation at Camberwell, see *Mrs Brookfield*, 155, 172 and 179. Harden's *Supplement* prints the letter to 'Mr Sterling', II: 1302.

For John Sutherland's essay 'Dickens, Reade, *Hard Cash* and Maniac Wives', see his *Victorian Fiction: Writers, Publishers, Readers*, 1995, 55–86. For information on late-nineteenth-century lodging-house charges, see George Gissing, *The Odd Women*, 1893, ch. I. For Cruikshank's comment on Thackeray's devotion to his wife, see Patten, op. cit., 420.

Vizetelly's account of Thackeray's dealings with Bradbury & Evans is in *Glances Back*, I: 283–5, and reprinted in *Interviews*, I: 45. Dwyer's recollection of Thackeray's offer to use his influence with Palmerston is in Fitzgerald's life of Lever, op. cit. On the political background to the late 1840s, see Blake, *Conservative Party*, chs II and III. The review of Mrs Gore's *Sketches of English Character* appeared in the *Morning Chronicle* of 4 May 1846.

For Brookfield's account of his first visit to Young Street (15 July 1846) see *Mrs Brookfield*, 187. Annie's description of the arrival at Young Street is in *Shankman*, 133.

XIII 'All but at the Top of the Tree'

For 'Mr Punch's Fancy Ball', see Altick, op. cit., 50. Altick helpfully identifies the contemporary personalities caricatured in the foreground. For an authoritative discussion of the composition and publication of *Vanity Fair*, see John Sutherland's introduction to the Oxford World's Classics edition, 1983, xxxi–xli, and Peter Shillingsburg, *Pegasus in Harness: Victorian Publishing and W.M. Thackeray*, Duke, Virginia UP, 1992, especially 28–9. On the novel's compositional style and the 'Interpolations', see Sutherland, *Thackeray at Work*, 1974, ch. I.

For Thackeray's 'misremembering' of pieces of minor detail, and what John Sutherland calls his 'psychological need ... to leave unmended pot-holes in his work', see the latter's 'Thackeray's Errors', *Victorian Fiction*, 1–27, and 'How Many Pianos Has Amelia Sedley?', in *Can Jane Eyre Be Happy? More Puzzles in Classic Fiction*, Oxford, 1997, 81–7. On Thackeray's excursions of

1847–8 and the topography of *Vanity Fair*, see Joan Stevens, 'A Roundabout Ride', *Victorian Studies XIII*, no. 1, September 1969, 53–7.

Thackeray's review of *Coningsby* appeared in the *Morning Chronicle* of 13 May 1844. For Thackeray's relationship with Disraeli, see Stanley Weintraub, *Disraeli: A Biography*, 1993, 221–3, 396. For his comments to Hodder about *Dombey and Son*, see Hodder, op. cit., 277.

Annie's memories of life at Young Street can be found throughout Hester Fuller and Violet Hammersley, *Thackeray and His Daughter: Some Recollections of Anne Thackeray*, 1951, and in *Chapters, passim.*

For a discussion of the illustrations to *Vanity Fair*, see Peters, op. cit., ch. 7. On the processes of early-Victorian wood-engraving, see Amanda-Jane Doran, 'The Development of the Full-Page Wood Engraving in *Punch*', *Journal of Newspaper and Periodical History*, vol. 7, no. 2 (1991).

The correspondence arising out of Forster's 'false as hell' allegation is printed in *LPP*, II: 294–304. For Annie's letter speculating on the contents of the August 1847 number of *Vanity Fair*, see *Shankman*, 24. Brookfield's letter describing Thackeray at work on his August number, dated 26 August 1847, is given in *Mrs Brookfield*, 242. For Jane's letter to Harry Hallam about her supposed connection with Amelia and Lady Jane Sheepshanks, see the same, 247–8.

On the Kembles, see the biographical memoranda that introduce *LPP*, I (cxliii–iv). For James Hannay, see Worth, op. cit. Annie's identification of Hannay as the model for Arthur Pendennis occurs in *Shankman*, 131. For the Garrick Club in the late 1840s and early 1850s, see Barham, *Garrick Club Notices*, and John Timbs, *Clubs and Club Life in London*, 1872, 218. The description of Arcedeckne comes from John Cordy Jeaffreson's *Recollections*, 330.

Frederick Goldsmith's account of Thackeray's visit to Addiscombe, which originally appeared in .the *Athenaeum*, is quoted by Ray, *LPP*, II: 360. On *Vanity Fair's* sales figures, see Shillingsburg, op. cit., 11.

For Torrens McCullagh's conversation with Thackeray about the ending of *Vanity Fair*, see Eyre Crowe, *Thackeray's Haunts and Homes*, 1897, 56, reprinted in *Interviews*, I: 135. McCullagh (1813–94), who later changed his surname to Torrens, was MP for Dundalk 1847–54, and subsequently for English constituencies.

XIV The Angel at the Hearth

For Trollope's comments on Thackeray's campaign to be appointed assistant secretary at the Post Office, see Anthony Trollope, *Thackeray*, 1879, 34.

Lewes' remarks on the disinterestedness of Thackeray's moral judgments, taken from an essay on 'Thackeray's Early Work', *Morning Chronicle*, 6 March

1848, are reprinted in Rosemary Ashton, ed., *Versatile Victorian: Selected Writings of George Henry Lewes*, 1992, 108–12. There is a selection of Charlotte Brontë's views on Thackeray in *Interviews*, I: 106–11. R.S. Rintoul's review of *Vanity Fair* appeared in *The Spectator*, 22 July 1848.

For Mrs Sartoris' visit to sing to Mrs Brookfield, see *Mrs Brookfield*, 267–8. Brookfield's letter of 10 August ('a much overrated person') and Jane's remonstrance of 17 January 1849 are quoted in Monsarrat, op. cit., 209–10. The *Punch* Authors book entry of 12 August 1848 is quoted by Altick, op. cit., 48.

Ray prints and discusses the authenticity of 'What Might Have Been' ('which in any event one would willingly believe not to be by Thackeray') in *LPP*, II: 477–8. For Thackeray's and Brookfield's visit to Cambridge of March 1849, see *Mrs Brookfield*, 273–5. For Jane's letter to Harry Hallam of April 1849 and the family's response to Thackeray's illness, see the same. Annie gives an account of the Carmichael-Smyths' return to London in *Shankman*, 205.

XV Edged Tools

The identification of Thackeray as the anonymous reviewer of Carlyle's *Life of John Sterling* is made by K.J. Fielding in 'Thackeray and "The Great Master of Craigenputtoch": A new review of The Life of John Sterling – and a new understanding', in a forthcoming number of *Victorian Literature and Culture*. John Chapman's remarks are taken from Gordon S. Haight, *George Eliot and John Chapman*, New Haven, Conn., 1940, 178–9, reprinted in *Interviews*, I: 138. The conversation with Bray, recorded by an unknown female onlooker during a visit to Coventry in 1855, appears in *Two Thackerays* I, 383–6, and is also reprinted in *Interviews*, I: 139.

For the letter in which Thackeray proposes to write a book 'containing not the portraits of my friends, but the results of experience . . .', which K.J. Fielding dates to early summer 1850, see *Ashburton Papers*. The Brookfields' movements at this period are described in *Mrs Brookfield*, chs IX and X.

For Annie's memories of Thackeray's lectures of 1851, see *Chapters*, 123–7. For reactions to Thackeray's performance, see Monsarrat, op. cit., 250. Jane's letter of 31 May 1851 is quoted in *Mrs Brookfield*, 353. Annie describes the incident of the ribbons in *Chapters*, 205.

For Dr John Brown's assessment of Thackeray in late 1851, see Alexander Peddie, *Recollections of Dr John Brown*, 1893, 51.

Eyre Crowe's *With Thackeray in America*, 1893, has a good account of the lecture series in Manchester and Liverpool that preceded Thackeray's American tour of autumn 1852 and gives dates for his twelve appearances. The letter to the *Liverpool Mercury* of 1 October 1852, and Thackeray's memories of Savile Morton, are taken from this source. On Hannay's engagement to supply notes to the printed version of *English Humourists*, see Worth, op. cit., 96–8.

XVI Stepping Westward

Many of the details of Thackeray's US visit of 1852–3 are taken from Crowe, op. cit. Field's memories of the tour can be found in James T. Fields, *Yesterdays with Authors*, 1872. Henry James Sr's *Tribune*, is quoted in Crowe, op. cit., 43–4.

Annie's letter to Laetitia Cole (2 December 1852) is printed in *Shankman*, 37–8. For Minnie's letter to Thackeray, see the same, 38–9. The *Spectator's* review of *Esmond* (by George Brimley) appeared on 6 November 1852. For the letter analysing New York's 'Upper Ten', dated 14 December 1852, see *Ashburton Papers*.

XVII *The Newcomes*

The comments on Thackeray the 'friendly, genial man', are quoted in Monsarrat, op. cit. 322. On sales figures for *The Newcomes* and *The Virginians*, see Shillingsburg, op. cit., 11 and 123.

Deborah A. Thomas discusses Thackeray's views on female emancipation, and the link with his observations on slavery in the southern states, in *Thackeray and Slavery*, Athens, Ohio UP, 1993, ch. 6. On the Brookfields' life together in the mid-1850s, see *Mrs Brookfield*, ch. XI. Millais' memory of Thackeray's enthusiasm for Leighton is quoted in *Frederic Leighton 1830–1896*, Royal Academy of Art, 1996, 14.

Annie's recollections of the trip to Rome in late 1853 and their subsequent stay in the city are taken from *Chapters*, 174–93. Elizabeth Barrett Browning's and John Gibson Lockhart's comments are reproduced in *Interviews*, I: 104–5. For Edith Story's memories, see La Marchesa Peruzzi de' Medici, 'Thackeray, My Childhood's Friend', *Cornhill Magazine XXXI*, 1911, 178–81. For the letter in which Thackeray states that he has 'to lie, therefore on many occasions . . .', dated 8 March 1854, see *Ashburton Papers*.

The (unpublished) letter to Lady Tennent declining an invitation, dated 11 June 1854, is owned by Eton College.

Thackeray's anecdote about his meeting with a 'Miss Peawell' was delivered to a *Punch* dinner of 2 March 1859 (*Silver Diary*). Mrs Carmichael-Smyth's letter recording a meeting with John Allen in Paris (6 March 1855) is in *Shankman*, 41. For Annie's letter to Mrs Fanshawe, see the same, 43.

For valuable background material for the political crisis of early 1855, see

Michael Slater, ed., *The Dent Uniform Edition of Dickens' Journalism, volume III, 'Gone Astray' and other papers from Household Words, 1851–59*, 1998, 283–91. This reprints the attack on Palmerston, 'Gone to the Dogs'.

Lowell's account of meeting Thackeray in the street, shortly after he had written Colonel Newcome's death scene, is recorded in *Interviews*, II: 216. Jane's letter describing the chance meeting in Pall Mall in September 1855 is quoted in *Mrs Brookfield*, 418. Most of the details of Thackeray's last few weeks in England in the autumn of 1855, and the text of his speech at the farewell dinner, are taken from Hodder, op. cit., 256–68.

XVIII The Public Eye

The account of Thackeray's second American tour is largely put together from the letters in *LPP*, III, and Harden's *Supplement*. The reminiscences of Bayard Taylor and John Esten Cooke are taken from, respectively, 'William Makepeace Thackeray, by One who Knew Him', *Atlantic Monthly*, XIII, 1864, 371–6, and 'An Hour with Thackeray', *Appleton's Journal*, XXII, 1879, 249–54, both reprinted in *Interviews*, II: 256–73. Wallack's memories of Thackeray are drawn from his *Memories of Fifty Years*, New York, 1889.

For Annie's letter to Mrs Carmichael-Smyth describing the trip to Bagshot and Windsor of August 1856, see *Shankman*, 44–6. For the letter to Amy Crowe recounting the subsequent continental holiday, see the same, 46–9.

The summary of the (unpublished) letter to Charles Cavendish Gifford of 14 October 1856 is taken from a sale catalogue issued in 1998 by the firm of Roy Davids. For Minnie's description of Mrs Carmichael-Smyth's illness of October 1856 (the second half of a letter to Amy Crowe of 26 October), see *Shankman*, 49. Annie's account of Thackeray's trip to Scotland in November is taken from the same source, 59.

Charles Cooper's conversation with Thackeray during the visit to Hull appears in James Samuelson, *Recollections*, 1907, 116–20, reprinted in *Interviews*, I: 129–30. Gilfillan's description of Thackeray lecturing is taken from *Sketches Literary and Theological*, Edinburgh, 1881, 82. For an account of the provincial lecture tour of spring 1857, see Hodder, op. cit., 268–74. The description of Thackeray's two days in Norwich is taken from the same source, 302–6, from Whitwell Elwin's memoir, reprinted in *LPP*, IV: 371–80, and from the summary of 'Mr Thackeray's Lecture' given in the *Norfolk Chronicle and Gazette* of 16 May 1857.

On the Oxford by-election of July 1857, see *LPP*, IV: 381–9 (this reproduces the 'Broadside', three public addresses and a pamphlet outlining Thackeray's views on the 'Sabbath Question'). A general account of Oxford politics during the early-Victorian period can be found in Alan Crossley, ed., *A History of the County of Oxford, volume IV: The City of Oxford* (Victorian

History of the Counties of England), Oxford, 1979, 250–7. For Annie's letter to Mrs Stoddart of late summer 1857, see *Shankman*, 54–5.

XIX The Garrick Club Affair

On Russell Sturgis, see Kynaston, op. cit., I: 184.

For contemporary accounts of Thackeray's and Dickens' attitudes towards one another, see Jeaffreson, op. cit., and Hodder, op. cit., *passim*. A balanced modern analysis of the relationship appears in Ackroyd, op. cit., 540–2. For an account of the country-house visit, see Atkins, op. cit., reprinted in *Interviews*, I: 154. The role of *Pasquin* and *Puppet-Show* in inflaming the rivalry between Dickens and Thackeray is discussed in Worth, op. cit., 35–6. For the comparisons drawn by Arthur Munby and Mrs Lynn Linton, see Ackroyd, op. cit., 946 and 540–1.

The account of the Garrick Club controversy draws on the following sources: *LPP*, IV, *passim*, which includes a facsimile of Yates' *Town Talk* article; Yates' pamphlet *Mr Thackeray, Mr Yates and the Garrick Club*, privately printed, 1859; and *Edmund Yates, His Recollections and Experiences*, 1884, vol. II. For the personal alliances that supported the quarrel, see P.D. Edwards, *Dickens's 'Young Men': George Augustus Sala, Edmund Yates and the World of Victorian Journalism*, Aldershot, 1997, ch. 2. On Yates' subsequent career, see Edwards, op. cit., *passim*, and Gross, op. cit., 94–6.

For Hannay's role in the Garrick Club Affair, see Worth, op. cit., 81. On *Quiz*'s spoof, see Barham, op. cit. For George Sala and 'Mr Polyphemus', see Edwards, op. cit., 66. Ray prints 'The Histrionic Baronet' in *LPP*, IV: 119–20.

Annie's letter to Amy Crowe of late December 1858 is in *Shankman*, 56–8. For Henry Silver's comments on Yates' bankruptcy, see *Silver Diary*, 1 July 1868.

XX The Editorial Chair

For Yates' sense of 'social degradation', see Edwards, op. cit., 67. Annie's comment on Thackeray's reaction to criticism of *Philip* is in *Shankman*, 84. The letter that describes Minnie as being 'absurdly young for her age' is in *LPP*, IV: 230.

For Thackeray's conversation at *Punch* dinners at this period, see especially Silver's entries for 21 October 1858, 26 January 1859 and 2 March 1859. For Annie's accounts of Thackeray's ill health, to Dr John Brown and Amy Crowe respectively, see *LPP*, IV: 127, and *Shankman*, 84. Annie's account of the Mount Felix ball and the remark about Yates' pamphlet occur in a letter of 6 March 1859 to W.W.F. Synge, *Shankman*, 73.

On George Smith and the firm of Smith, Elder, see the *Longman Companion to Victorian Fiction*, 590–1. The account of Thackeray's professional relations with Smith 1859–62 is based largely on the mass of letters printed in Harden's *Supplement*, vol. II. For the magazine world of the 1850s and 1860s, see Gross, op. cit., *passim*. Annie's letter to Synge describing the family holiday to Folkestone, dated 27 August 1859, is in *Shankman*, 75–6.

For the description of Mrs Carmichael-Smyth in later years, taken from a letter to Annie from Mrs A.F. Yule dated 15 January 1904, see *Ritchie Papers*, box 7.

For Fields' memory of meeting Thackeray in Paris at New Year 1861, see *Yesterdays with Authors*, 30–1. Locker-Lampson records his delight in receiving the proofs of his *Cornhill* contribution in *My Confidences*, 175.

For Yates' *New York Times* article, see *LPP*, IV: 189–90. Annie's letter to Mrs Baxter, dated 25 April 1861, is printed in the same, 229–31. For the *Punch* table talk of 1861–2, see *Silver Diary*, *passim*. Annie's memories of the death of Major Carmichael-Smyth are quoted in *Shankman*, 196. Ray prints Thackeray's inventory of the furnishings of 2 Palace Green as an appendix to *LPP*, IV: 405–7. Fitting out the study alone cost £340. The remark to his *Punch* friends about not doing editorial work, which includes the description of Smith as a 'noble fellow', was made at the dinner of 12 March 1862 (*Silver Diary*).

XXI Ending Up

Details in the opening paragraphs are taken from 'De Juventute' and 'Tunbridge Toys' (*RP*). Thackeray complained of the Palace Green decorating bill at the *Punch* dinner of 18 September 1862 (*Silver Diary*).

For Mary Senior's reminiscences of Thackeray at Palace Green, see M.C.M. Simpson, *Many Memories of Many People*, 1898, ch. VI. Annie's recollections of the conversation on marriage is in *Shankman*, 135. Annie's letter to Mrs Baxter about the hostile dinner guest, dated 30 April 1864, is in *LPP*, IV: 298–300. For Lord Sandhurst's memory of being introduced to Thackeray as a small boy, recalled in a letter to Annie dated 23 October 1918, see *Ritchie Papers*, box 7.

For John Cordy Jeaffreson's account of Thackeray's eating and drinking habits, see *Recollections*, 301. For Thackeray's attendance at the *Punch* suppers during autumn 1862, see *Silver Diary*, especially the entries of 8 October and 29 October. Jeaffreson has a lengthy account of the quarrel that arose out of the *Athenaeum* reviews of *Lovel the Widower* and *The Story of Elizabeth* (op. cit., 305–16). For the conversation with Lord Stanley, see Mullen, op. cit., 442.

On the visit to Fryston Hall and the encounter with Swinburne, see *LPP*,

IV: 285–6. Annie's comments on *Denis Duval*, included in a letter of 19 July 1863 to W.W.F. Synge, are in *Shankman*, 92. For Mary Senior's account of the conversation about Thackeray's worsening ill health, see Simpson, op. cit., VI. Hole's recollections of his meeting with Thackeray at Palace Green are recorded in *The Memories of Dean Hole*, 1892, 85. On the Shakespeare Tercentenary Committee, see Jeaffreson, op. cit., 316–22.

Annie's account of the autumn of 1863 is in *Shankman*, 122–3. For Thackeray's attendance at the Charterhouse Founder's Dinner, see G.S. Davies, 'Thackeray as Carthusian', *Greyfriar*, II (1890–5), 65–7, reprinted in *Interviews*, I: 17. The Hardy letter of 19 December 1863 is quoted in Martin Seymour-Smith, *Hardy*, 1994, 65.

The description of Thackeray's last days is substantially drawn from Annie's journal of 1864, *Shankman*, 124–6. For Charles Collins' letter describing the events of 24 December 1863, see *LPP*, IV: 296.

XXII Afterwards

For reactions to Thackeray's death, see Jeaffreson, op. cit., 326; Mullen, op. cit., 433; Flora Masson, 'The Two Novelists', *Cornhill Magazine*, XXX, 1911, 795–9; Robert A. Watson and Elizabeth S. Watson, *George Gilfillan: Letters and Journals with Memoir*, 1892, 347–8; Atkins, *William Howard Russell*, diary entry for 24 December, reprinted in *Interviews*, I: 155. For Tennyson's letter to the Duchess of Argyll, see Cecil Y. Lang and Edgar F. Shannon, eds, *The Letters of Alfred Lord Tennyson*, 3 vols, Oxford, 1981–90, II: 346–7. For obituaries, see *The Times*, 31 December 1863, and *Cornhill Magazine*, IX, 129–32 (Dickens) and 134–7 (Trollope).

For Annie's account of the immediate aftermath of Thackeray's death, see *Shankman*, 141–50. On George Smith's purchase of Thackeray's copyrights, see Shillingsburg, op. cit., 141–3. For Annie's description of visiting her mother at Wimbledon, given in a letter to Henrietta Synge, see *Shankman*, 186. Her account of Isabella's death is given in Gerin, op. cit., 230.

On the Brookfields' later careers, see *Mrs Brookfield*, *passim*. For Minnie's marriage to Leslie Stephen and Annie's relationship with her brother-in-law, see John W. Bicknell, ed., *Selected Letters of Leslie Stephen*, 2 vols, 1996, *passim*. The memory of 'Aunt Laura' attending family parties in the 1930s was communicated privately to the author by Mrs Belinda Norman-Butler.

For Annie's literary career, see Gerin, op. cit. George Eliot's comment on her marriage to Richmond Ritchie is quoted in *Shankman*, 171. The eighty-year-old Annie's remark about wishing to cut up into four twenty-year-olds is quoted by Gerin, op. cit., 274. For the 'Bloomsbury shadows', see Regina Marler, *Bloomsbury Pie*, *passim*. For Trollope's posthumous veneration, see Mullen, op. cit., *passim*. Annie's letter to Mrs Baxter of December 1875 is in

Shankman, 183. For full versions of Annie's journals of 1864 and 1878, see the same, 119–40 and 197–212. The descriptions of Thackeray's appearance are taken from the former (130–1), as is the account of the dinner at the Star and Garter, Richmond (127).

Supplementary Bibliography

John Buchanan-Brown, *The Illustrations of William Makepeace Thackeray*, Newton Abbot, 1979.

Margaret Forster, *William Makepeace Thackeray: Memoirs of a Victorian Gentleman*, London, 1978.

Victoria Glendinning, *Anthony Trollope*, London, 1992.

Edgar F. Harden, *Thackeray's* English Humourists *and* Four Georges, New Jersey, Associated University Presses, 1985.

Barbara Hardy, *The Punishment of Luxury: Radical Themes in Thackeray*, London, 1972.

Douglas Jerrold, *Mrs Caudle's Curtain Lectures*. New edition, Edinburgh, 1950.

Walter Jerrold, *Douglas Jerrold: Dramatist and Wit*, 2 vols, London, 1918.

Isadore Gilbert Mudge and Earl M. Sears, *A Thackeray Dictionary*, London, 1910.

John R. Reed, *Dickens and Thackeray: Punishment and Forgiveness*, Athens, Ohio U.P. 1995.

Andrew St George, *The Descent of Manners: Etiquette, Rules and the Victorians*, London, 1993.

Andrew Sanders, ed., *William Thackeray: Barry Lyndon*, Oxford, World's Classics edition, 1984.

Joanne Shattock, ed., *Dickens and Other Victorians*, Basingstoke, 1988.

Robert Tener and Malcolm Woodfield, eds, *A Victorian Spectator: Uncollected Writings of R.H. Hutton*, Bristol, 1989.

Index